'This is a wonderfully [...] [Alexandria's] history, written with vim and vigour'

Dominic Sandbrook, Books of the Year, *Sunday Times*

'I was charmed by Islam Issa's *Alexandria*, which recovers elegantly and poignantly the long history of rich interactions among the many communities of the city'

David Abulafia, Books of the Year, *Times Literary Supplement*

'A fascinating and important book, telling the story of Alexandria from antiquity to modernity with great erudition worn lightly'

Natalie Haynes, author of *Stone Blind*

'Alexandria comes to life . . . this book is a fitting tribute to a city that has survived, changed and grown for so many centuries'

Francesca Peacock, *Daily Telegraph*

'Issa, an Alexandrian himself, is an assured narrator with an easy, undemonstrative manner, who unearths myths and stories that give vivid life to his more sober account of Alexandria's travails and triumphs'

Michael Prodger, *New Statesman*

'Lively and engrossing . . . Issa combines love for the city with nostalgia for its vanished past'

Literary Review

'Fabulous . . . a work of brilliant and informed scholarship, as well as being a labour of love. It is as if Islam Issa was born to write this book'

Paul Strathern, author of *The Medici*

Professor Islam Issa is an award-winning British-Egyptian author, broadcaster and curator, named by the BBC as 'one of the UK's most significant new thinkers'. He is Professor of Literature and History at Birmingham City University, has written several academic books and curated internationally renowned exhibitions. As well as contributing to the *Guardian*, *New Statesman* and *Times Literary Supplement*, he has presented and featured in television and radio documentaries on the BBC and Netflix.

ALEXANDRIA

The City that Changed the World

ISLAM ISSA

Sceptre

First published in Great Britain in 2023 by Sceptre
An imprint of Hodder & Stoughton Limited
An Hachette UK company

This paperback edition published in 2024

1

Copyright © Islam Issa 2023

Maps © Mike Parson / Barking Dog Art 2023

The right of Islam Issa to be identified as the Author of the Work has been asserted
by him in accordance with the Copyright, Designs and Patents Act 1988.

A CIP catalogue record for this title is available from the British Library

Paperback ISBN 9781529377620
ebook ISBN 9781529377606

Typeset in Dante MT by Hewer Text UK Ltd, Edinburgh
Printed and bound in Great Britain by Clays Ltd, Elcograf S.p.A.

Hodder & Stoughton policy is to use papers that are natural, renewable
and recyclable products and made from wood grown in sustainable
forests. The logging and manufacturing processes are expected to
conform to the environmental regulations of the country of origin.

Hodder & Stoughton Limited
Carmelite House
50 Victoria Embankment
London EC4Y 0DZ

www.sceptrebooks.co.uk

For Alaa . . .

Contents

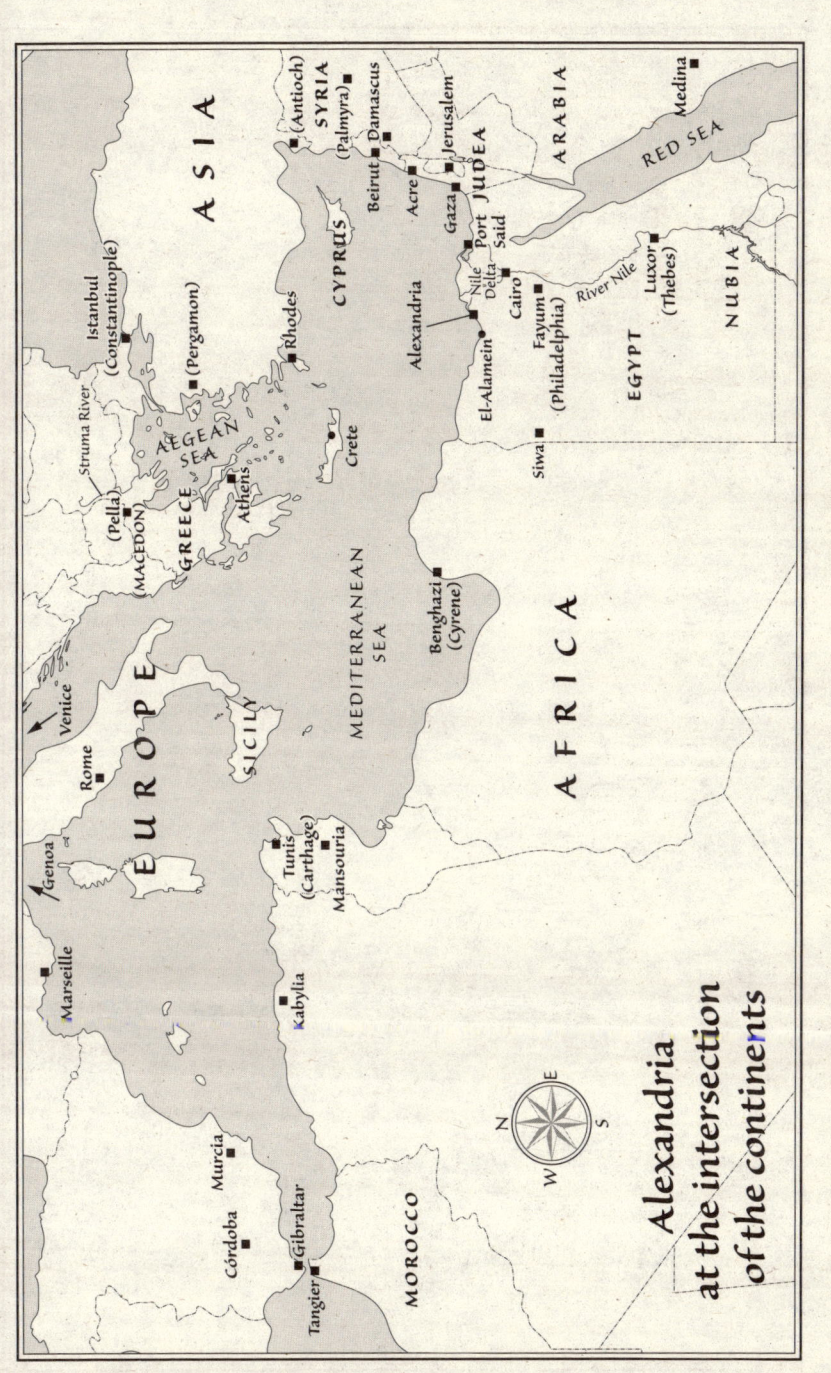

Alexandria
at the intersection
of the continents

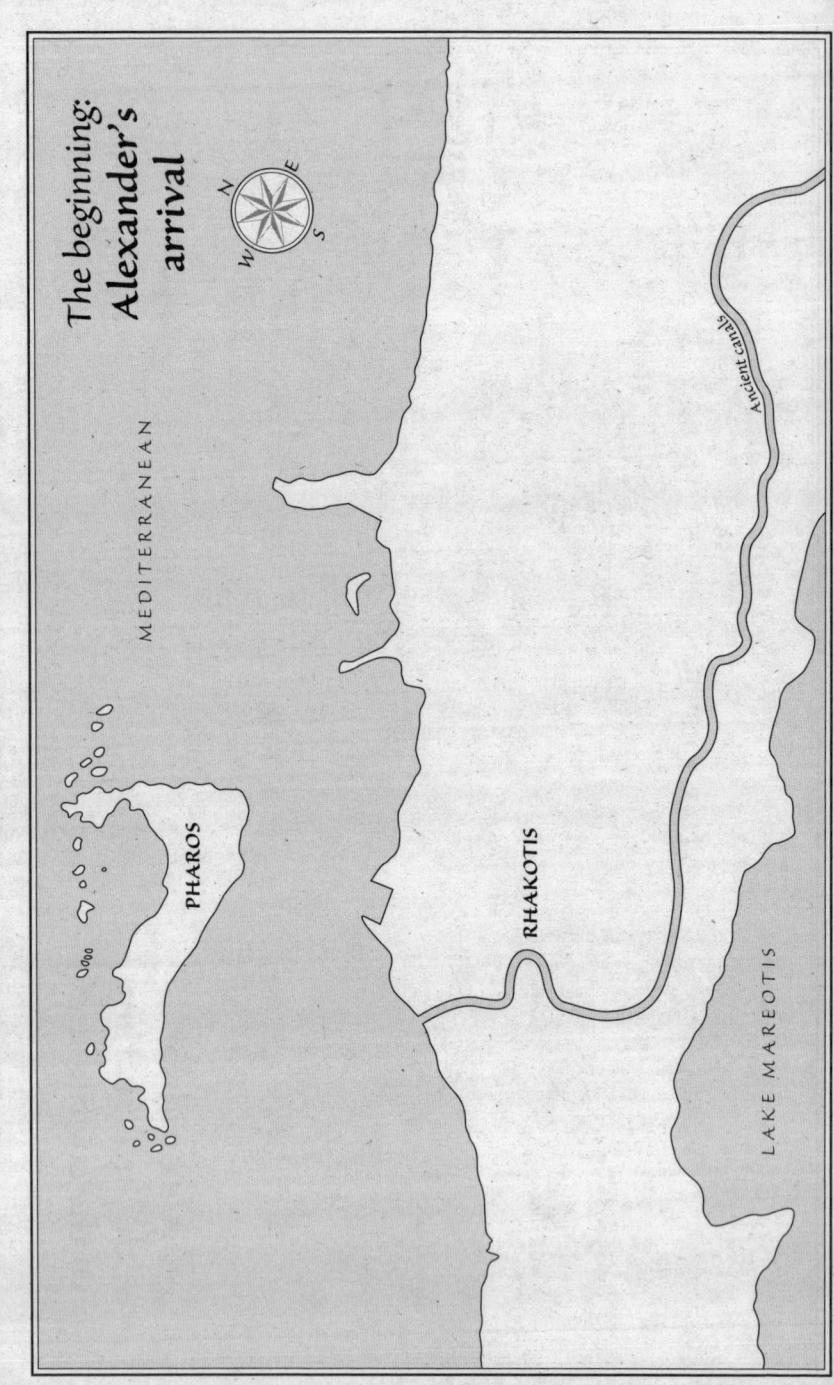

The beginning:
Alexander's arrival

MEDITERRANEAN

PHAROS

RHAKOTIS

LAKE MAREOTIS

Ancient canals

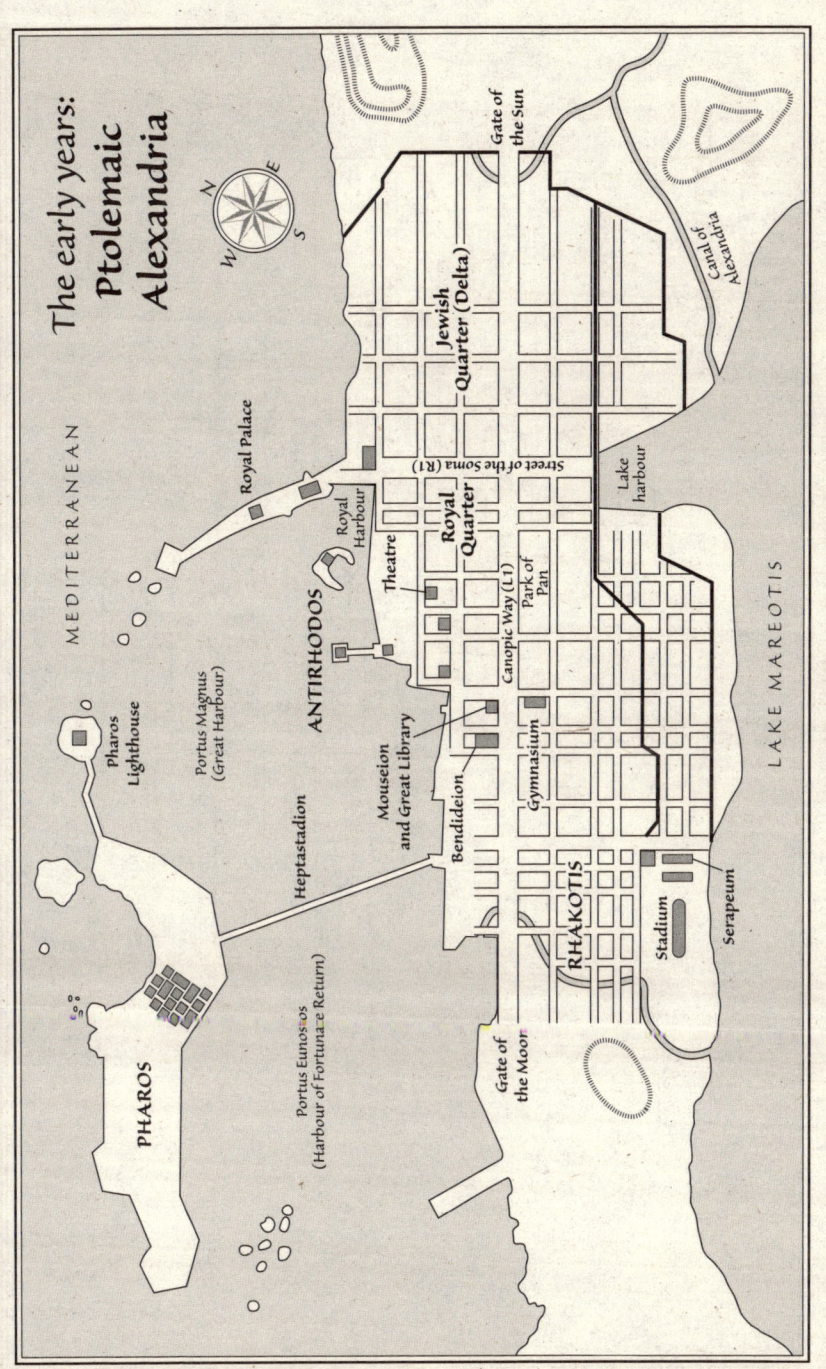

The early years:
Ptolemaic
Alexandria

MEDITERRANEAN

Pharos
Lighthouse

PHAROS

Portus Eunostos
(Harbour of Fortunae Return)

Heptastadion

Portus Magnus
(Great Harbour)

ANTIRHODOS

Royal Palace

Royal Harbour

Theatre

Mouseion
and Great Library

Bendideion

Canopic Way (L1)

Park of Pan

Gymnasium

Street of the Soma (R1)

Royal
Quarter

Jewish
Quarter (Delta)

Gate of
the Sun

Canal of
Alexandria

RHAKOTIS

Gate of
the Moon

Stadium

Serapeum

Lake harbour

LAKE MAREOTIS

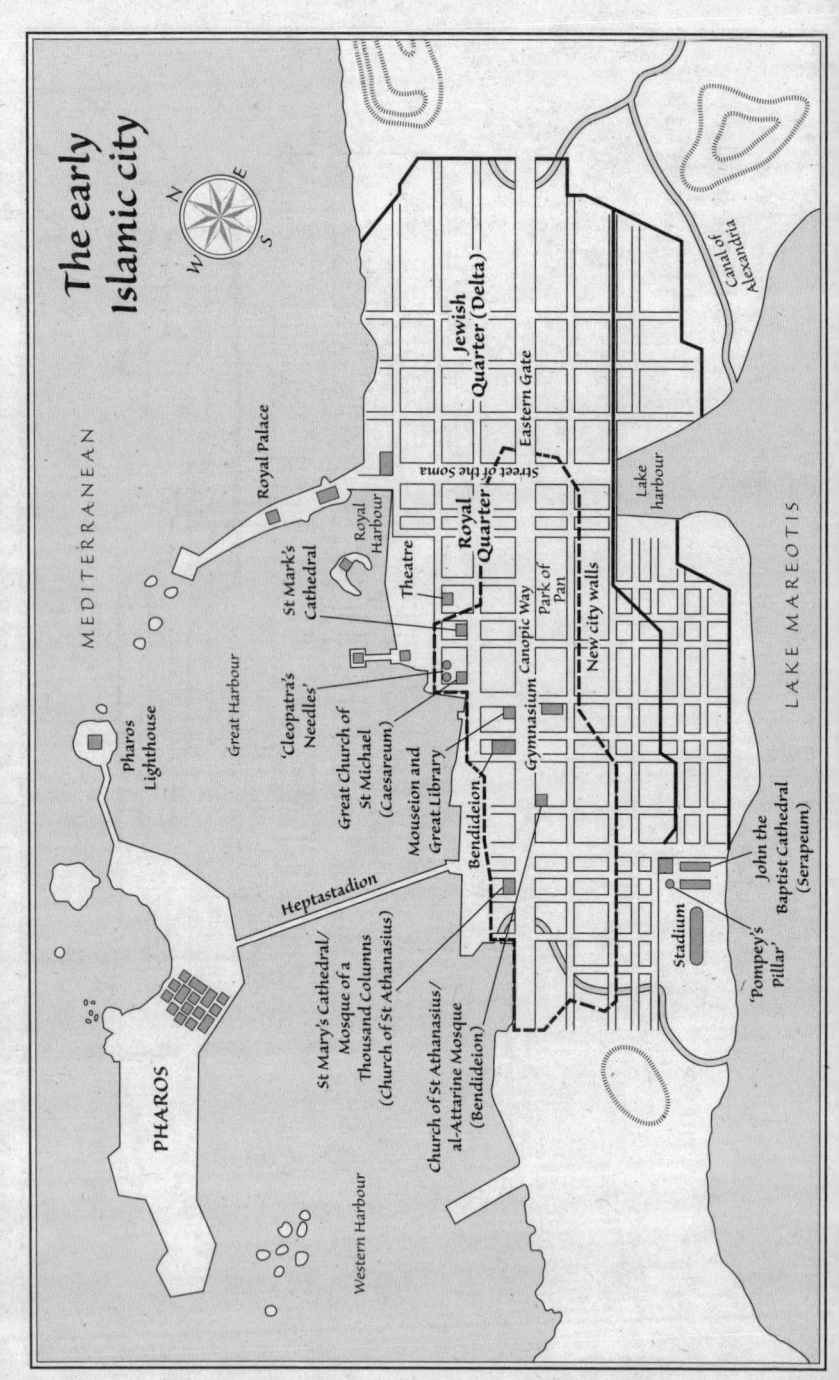

The early Islamic city

MEDITERRANEAN

PHAROS

Pharos Lighthouse

Western Harbour

Great Harbour

Heptastadion

Royal Palace

Royal Harbour

St Mark's Cathedral

'Cleopatra's Needles'

Great Church of St Michael (Caesareum)

Mouseion and Great Library

Theatre

St Mary's Cathedral/ Mosque of a Thousand Columns (Church of St Athanasius)

Church of St Athanasius/ al-Attarine Mosque (Bendideion)

Bendideion

Gymnasium

Canopic Way

Park of Pan

Royal Quarter

Street of the Soma

Eastern Gate

Jewish Quarter (Delta)

New city walls

Lake harbour

Canal of Alexandria

Stadium

'Pompey's Pillar'

John the Baptist Cathedral (Serapeum)

LAKE MAREOTIS

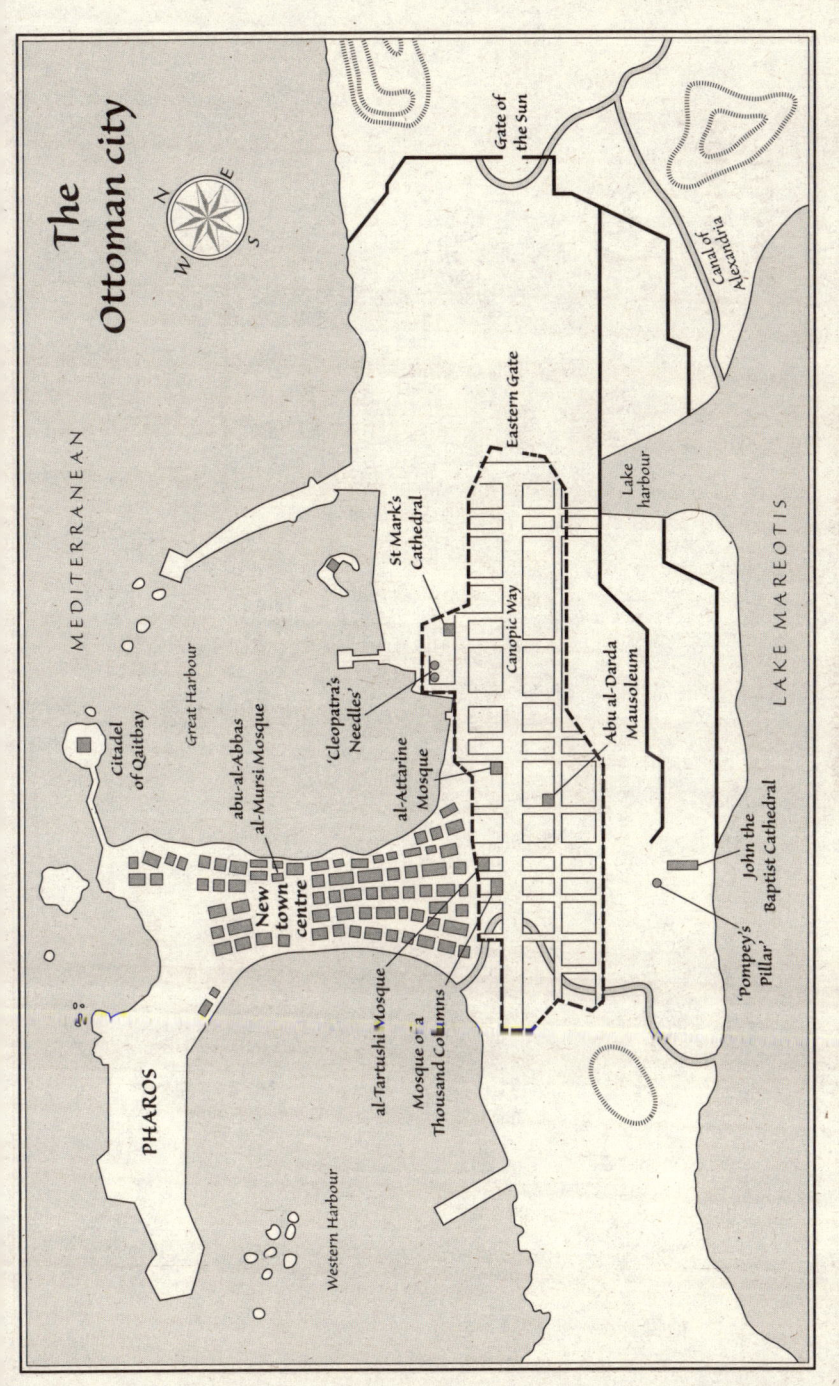

The
Ottoman city

MEDITERRANEAN

Citadel
of Qaitbay

Great Harbour

abu-al-Abbas
al-Mursi Mosque

New
town
centre

PHAROS

Western Harbour

al-Tartushi Mosque

Mosque of a
Thousand Columns

al-Attarine
Mosque

'Cleopatra's
Needles'

St Mark's
Cathedral

Canopic Way

Eastern Gate

Gate of
the Sun

Canal of
Alexandria

Lake
harbour

Abu al-Darda
Mausoleum

'Pompey's
Pillar'

John the
Baptist Cathedral

LAKE MAREOTIS

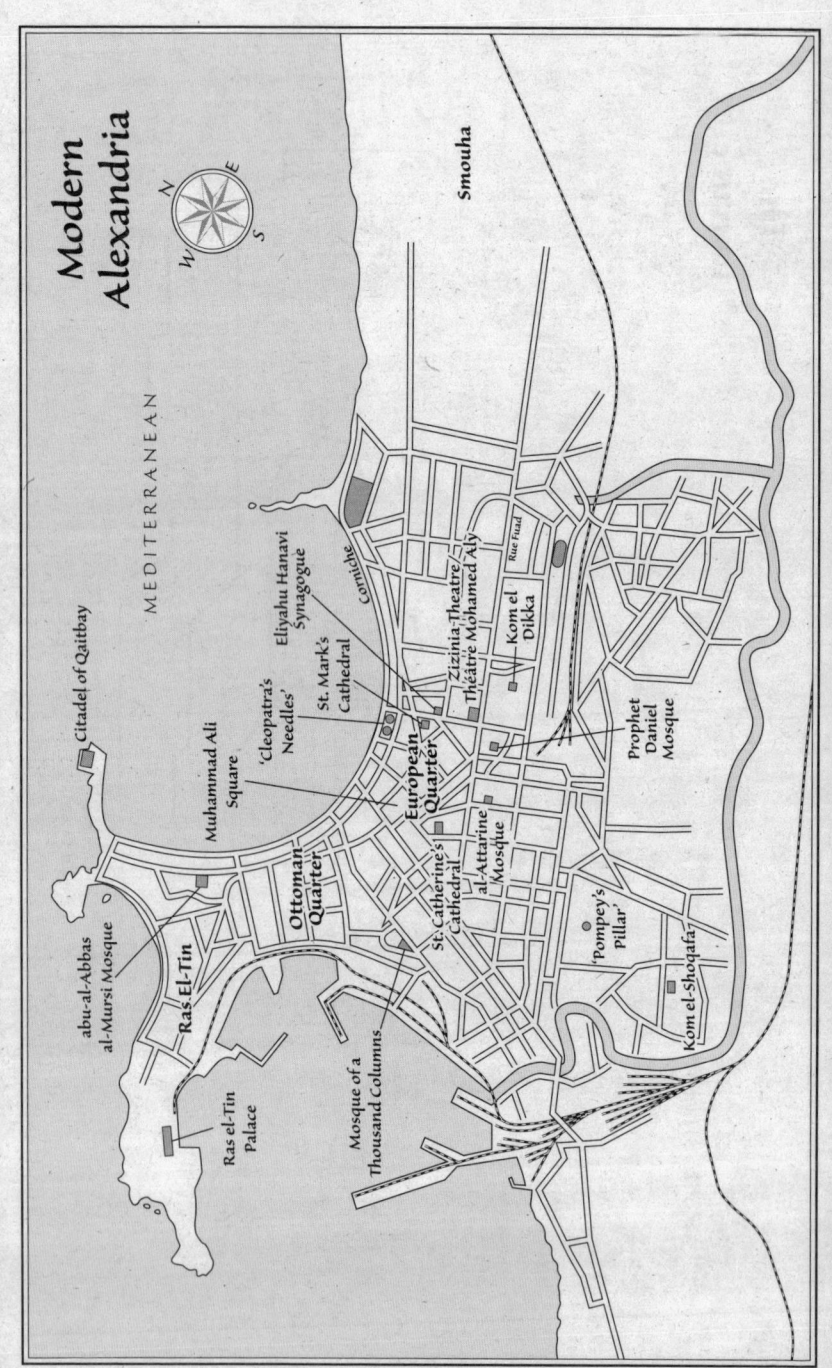

Modern Alexandria

MEDITERRANEAN

Citadel of Qaitbay

abu-al-Abbas
al-Mursi Mosque

Ras-El-Tin

Ras el-Tin Palace

Muhammad Ali Square

Ottoman Quarter

Mosque of a Thousand Columns

St. Catherine's Cathedral

al-Attarine Mosque

'Cleopatra's Needles'

St. Mark's Cathedral

Eliyahu Hanavi Synagogue

Corniche

European Quarter

Zizinia-Theatre
Théatre Mohamed Aly

Kom el Dikka

Rue fuad

Prophet Daniel Mosque

'Pompey's Pillar'

Kom el-Shoqafa

Smouha

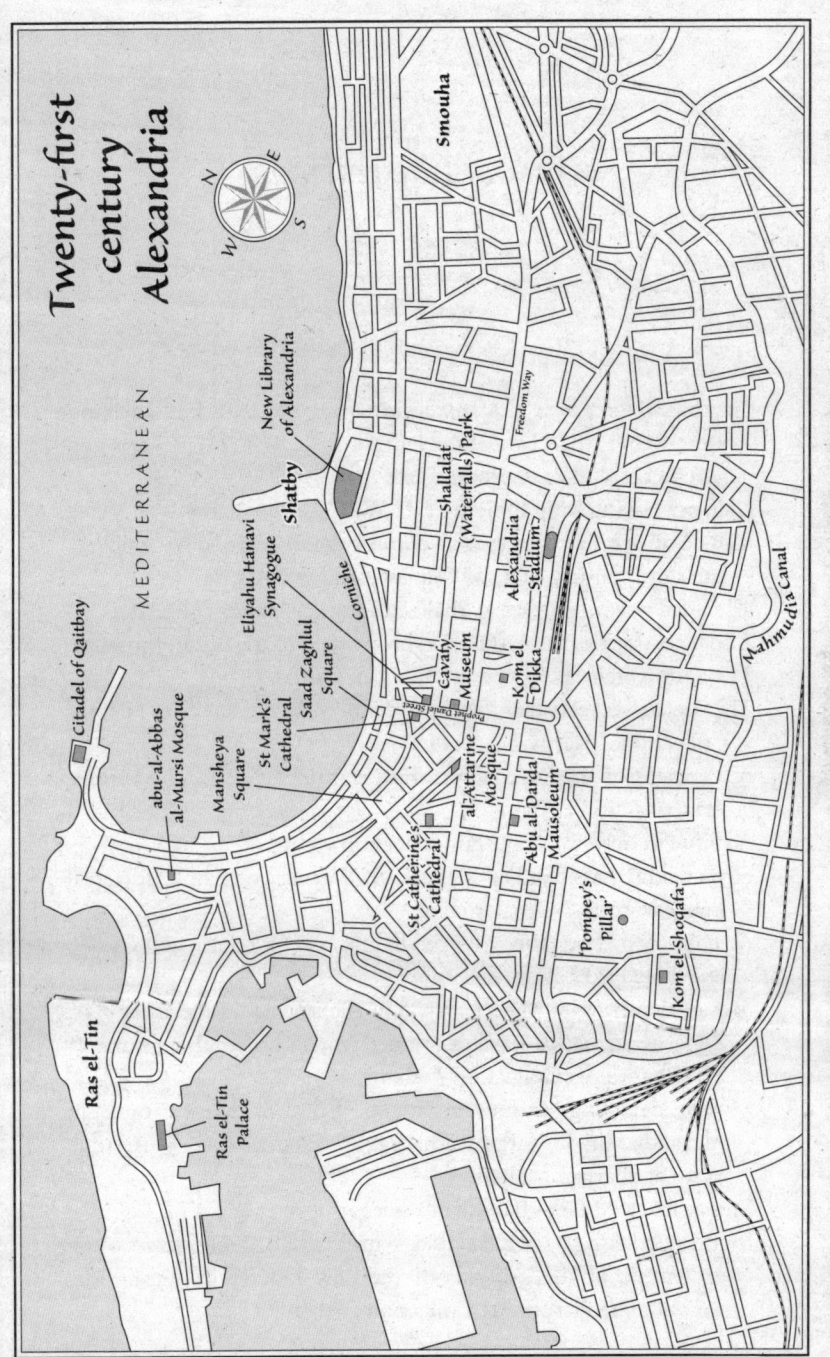

Twenty-first century Alexandria

MEDITERRANEAN

N E W S

Citadel of Qaitbay

abu-al-Abbas
al-Mursi Mosque

Mansheya
Square

Ras el-Tin

Ras el-Tin
Palace

St Mark's
Cathedral

Saad Zaghlul
Square

Eliyahu Hanavi
Synagogue

Shatby

New Library
of Alexandria

Corniche

Cavafy
Museum

Prophet Daniel Street

Kom el
Dikka

St Catherine's
Cathedral

al-Attarine
Mosque

Abu al-Darda
Mausoleum

'Pompey's
Pillar'

Kom el-Shoqafa

Shallalat
(Waterfalls) Park

Alexandria
Stadium

Freedom Way

Smouha

Mahmudia Canal

List of Illustrations

Statue of Ptolemy II, outside the Library of Alexandria. © Ahmed Sherif / Wikimedia/ CC BY-SA 4.0

Map of Alexandria from Al-Idrisi's *Tabula Rogerian*, 1154. © Library of Congress, Geography and Map Division

Fragment of *Alexandrian World Chronicle* depicting Pope Theophilus, 392. © The Picture Art Collection / Alamy

The ancient theatre in Kom el-Dikka. © Author collection

Interior View of the Catacombs at Alexandria, by Luigi Mayer, 1804. © Heritage Images / Getty Images

Entry of General Bonaparte into Alexandria, by Guillaume-François Colson, 1812. © Icom Images / Alamy

School of Athens, by Raphael, 1511. © PAINTING / Alamy

School of Alexandria, by Mohamed Nagy, 1939. © Mohamed Nagy Museum. With permission of the Ministry of Culture – Sector of Fine Arts

At the Ballroom, Mahmoud Said, 1949. © Mahmoud Said Museum. With permission of the Ministry of Culture – Sector of Fine Arts

Fish Market in Alexandria, by Khaled Hanno, 2019. © Khaled Hanno.

Muhammad Ali Square, circa 1890. © Pump Park Vintage Photography / Alamy

Cleopatra's Needle at Thames Embankment, London, 1890. © Chronicle / Alamy

Plaque commemorating Cleopatra's Needle's arrival, London. © Author collection

A diver and ancient sphinx, Alexandria, 1995. © Stéphane Compoint

Transporting an early Ptolemy statue, Alexandria, 1995. © Stéphane Compoint

Portrait of Muhammad Ali, by Nan Qadria, 1993. © Author collection

The erroneously named Pompey's Pillar. © Author collection

Au Pavillion de Florelle on Fuad Street. © Author collection

The abu-al-Abbas al-Mursi Mosque. © Holgs / E+ / Getty Images

The Corniche. © Peter Adams / Stone / Getty Images

Protesters filling the Corniche. © Associated Press / Alamy

The Qaitbay Citadel. © Ahmed ElKabbani / istock / Getty Images

Statue of Alexander the Great, by Constantinos Baliou Loghos, 2002. © Hemis / Alamy

A Note on Style

For clarity, throughout the book all dates before the common era are followed by BCE, and dates from the common era are followed by CE only up to the year 100.

I have used endnotes to cite direct quotations and when a source is quoted for the first time.

I have modernised spellings and the translations from Arabic, French and Latin are my own.

Preface

The space surrounding the Qaitbay Citadel is always buzzing: families enjoying bright mango ice cream, kids on dangerously large bikes or rhythmically plodding horses, and street stalls competing to sell every imaginable size of conch shell. It might be a weekday, but this is a festive weekend atmosphere – and in the shadow of grand surroundings. As the evening draws to a close, the sounds suddenly begin to mellow. The manic rattle of horses' hooves against the hard concrete ground slows down like a recovering heartbeat. People walk away chattering, the adults nibbling on charred corn cobs while the children, the quietest they've been all day, lag behind clasping oversized shells to their ears in wonder. Like a well-rehearsed scene change, young, enamoured couples now begin to pepper themselves across the tip of this eastern harbour. They curl up on the large rocks. For hours on end, they stare longingly into one another's eyes, into the night's glittery sky and into the dark, noisy ocean.

The waterfront promenade known as the Corniche, facing north-west into the Mediterranean Sea, connects the entire city of Alexandria from its peripheries: around thirteen miles from one end to the other. I sit on a ledge on the far side of the promenade, looking back towards the city library. The Great Library of Alexandria, one of human history's most magnificent centres of knowledge, was conceived in the third century BCE but has long since vanished. Over two millennia after its establishment, a new library was constructed in close proximity to where the ancient one may have stood. I look at the library with wonder, not because its glass roof tilts towards the sea like a sundial, but because its very symbolism is transporting me to a different time. I gaze back at the unfailingly bustling promenade, then into the distance, momentarily forgetting the present and reflecting on the past. My father had always told me stories about our city's glory days, often as I lay in bed, and at this moment all those tales come rushing back. If you breathe deeply enough, history is in the air.

Alexandria is living proof of the kaleidoscopic relationship between history and cultural mythology. Around the world, many places have a founding myth, a story about origin that serves to create identity. In Alexandria's case, there are many such myths and no straightforward identity. Partly because of the absence of hard history of the ancient city – physical and architectural evidence – underneath the modern metropolis and in the depths of the surrounding sea. Partly because its founder, Alexander the Great, is himself one of the most legend-steeped figures of all time. In Alexandria, myth plays a role in both the founding and advancement of the city, its landscape and its people.

Here, the factual and mythological stories of Alexandria's history, like the ones my ancestors passed on to each other and the ones I'm about to tell you, are sure to combine. They mix together like colours on an artist's palette. Each stroke of the paintbrush adds an individual, an event, an era, to the eternal canvas of this everchanging city.

The Egyptian city of Alexandria was founded almost two and a half millennia ago, and the land around it has been inhabited by fishing communities for even longer. A city like no other, only Alexandria can boast direct influence on its design by Alexander, the renowned polymath Aristotle and the eminent architect Deinocrates.

It is a city whose origins stem from the power of vision: an apparition in Alexander the Great's sleep that urged him to venture there, and an ambitious plan that was realised by its early rulers, the Ptolemies. The dreams and decisions of Alexandria's originators represent a radical perspective on how cities can be created and sustained. They gambled on two outrageous hypotheses: that gathering a diverse set of people to live and work together would make the strategically located spot a world trading centre; and that collecting and generating knowledge would render it a global power. By enacting these beliefs, they redefined the very idea of a city, transforming traditional notions of where and how to build a space and the ways to attract people to it. They also grasped the fact that there are multiple routes to achieving political supremacy, one of which was the wide-reaching influence that came with being the guardians of knowledge.

Far from a mere book-collecting project, the Great Library of Alexandria's collation, dissemination and instruction all became reliable sources of soft power, and the Ptolemies went to great lengths to ensure that nothing came in the way of the project's success. Within decades of Alexandria's establishment, the city became a centre of learning where the greatest minds of each generation gathered to philosophise, debate, research and innovate. Its early scholars proved that the earth isn't flat and that it revolves around the sun. Without them, there would be no steam engines, windmills, vending machines, musical keyboards, leap years, geometry or punctuation. Through its founders and intellectuals, in addition to its varied residents and subsequent conquerors, Alexandria changed and transformed the philosophies, technologies, politics, theologies and geographies of the world.

By virtue of its location at the intersection of three continents, its busy harbour welcoming visitors from around the globe, and a fast-developing Alexandrian Dream that compelled migration to its shores, the city became a meeting point of cultures, enacting in its early days a previously inconceivable diversity, from Egyptians and Greeks, to Jews and Buddhists. It became a place where East and West could meet, one that took something of Africa, Europe and Asia, and where great civilisations – not least Egyptian, Greek and Roman – could amalgamate. Its story is therefore one that transcends the bounds of the city to encompass the most conceptual ideas about place. Generations of different people – with their rituals, races, faiths, skills and values – arrived in Alexandria, each making a mark on its traditions, architecture and levels of tolerance. Interwoven into its history are questions about what a city can be and what two millennia of cultural exchange can do.

A century after its founding, it was a highly coveted centre of commerce and knowledge, larger than Carthage, eclipsing Athens and the biggest challenger to Rome, whose livelihood depended on grain from Alexandria. As well as signifying the perils of speedy expansion and the temporality of life, it came to serve as a representative illustration of some of history's most consequential empires, including the Ptolemies, Romans, Arabs, Ottomans, French and British.

Alexandria is a megalopolis without which Judaism, Christianity and Islam would be unrecognisable. Its founder finds his way into all three traditions and the city's name appears in the Talmud and the Bible. Every group that found its way to Alexandria took something of the city's philosophies. At times a place of pilgrimage for emperors visiting Alexander's mausoleum and neoclassicists reliving his vision, Alexandria also became a haven for misfits and pioneers alike. It attracted Jews seeking safety or a different way of life from those in the Holy Land, Christians with nonconformist views and Muslim mystics looking for a simple life. And over the various golden ages of discovery, East and West, scholars have been inspired by the writings of Alexandria, a city that also serves as a setting for such literary works as the popular Renaissance dramas of William Shakespeare and George Chapman, and the Nobel Prize-winning novels of Anatole France and Naguib Mahfouz.

In Alexandria, the protagonist is the ocean. With its perpetual presence, vivid colours and noisy waves, it is inescapable and interminable. But the heroes who followed the sea, and whom you'll meet in this book, are plentiful. Aside from its eponymous founder, this is the story of Helen of Troy, Homer, Aristotle, Julius Caesar, Cleopatra, St Mark the Evangelist, Prophet Muhammad, ibn-Battuta, Napoleon Bonaparte, Admiral Nelson, E. M. Forster, Gamal abdel-Nasser – and many more intriguing characters, men and women, famous and lesser known, including members of my own family. The various times that these figures lived through also confirm Alexandria's prominence as a hub for architecture and art, fashion and theatre, nonconformist dissent and satire, sexual epiphanies and early suffragettes.

This is also a place that has witnessed destructions and fires, natural disasters and plagues, crusades and ethnic cleansing, mass murders and suicides, as well as smuggling, lynching, decapitation and even cannibalism. Its story highlights the double-edged swords of ambition and modernity, and the successes and failures of a place brimming with contradictions. In the words of the fourteenth-century explorer ibn-Battuta, Alexandria alone is a place 'uniting in herself' what is otherwise 'shared out by other cities'.[1] But Alexandria captivatingly blurs more lines than it connects: East and West, tradition and renovation, rationality and superstition, religion and science, peace and conflict, tolerance and tension, myth and reality, preservation and destruction, and ultimately, past and present.

Yet despite its classical renown and enduring impact, Alexandria is neglected in comparison to other centres of antiquity. Not only do tourists flock to Egypt and the Mediterranean without passing through, but it is largely overlooked in contemporary conversations. This is, in fact, starkly ironic, since so many of the urgent questions being asked today – about our values, relationships and politics – concern the very connections and dichotomies this city has always explored. Alexandria is a lens through which people, civilisations and ideas came and went – and yet the city still stands.

Today, off its coast you will find a densely populated and animated urban landscape, and an assorted mix of sights and smells and sounds. The vast majority of its six million-plus residents go about their everyday lives unconscious of their position in the ongoing history of the space. Like me, Alexandrians today represent the one-hundredth generation who can call themselves by that demonym, a fact made all the more striking when my father's ancestry test revealed a staggering 97.5 per cent next to the word 'Alexandria'. To me, Alexandria is a pleasant feeling in my core, a little root that sprouts no matter where I might be. It's warm days and breezy nights. It's loud waves and quiet sunsets. Ancient artefacts, art deco theatres, palm trees, street florists and green shutters. It's people-watching from the balcony and cats roaming around my feet. It's the sound of a classical melody in the moonlit café.

This book is a roughly chronological history and examination of a place close to my heart. It is based on a vast array of sources, including manuscripts, reports, letters, images, maps and objects found in the archives of Alexandria and beyond; visits to sites, museums and galleries; classical accounts, biographies, anthologies and mythologies; recorded histories from times old and new; modern research in fields ranging from archaeology to zoology; religious scriptures; folk tales; oral histories; family stories; conversations with friendly strangers and eccentric vagabonds; and my experiences as a *flâneur* wandering Alexandria's streets.

Together, they uncover the rich and gripping story of a city that changed the world.

The Ancient Era

Since the beginning of human existence, our ancestors have gravitated towards water. It's for this reason that the one hundred million inhabitants of Egypt, one of Africa's most populous nations, live on just 5 to 7 per cent of the country's one million square kilometres, neglecting the vast deserts and congregating around the River Nile, Red Sea, Mediterranean Sea and a handful of oases to survive and flourish. It's a phenomenon I recognised most clearly when flying south over the continent at night, my cheek wedged against the aeroplane window in amazement. The lights – representing urban development, or, more simply, life – form a T-like shape in the abyss as the Mediterranean coast and the perfectly defined Nile glow radiantly in the dark.

The western edge of the Nile Delta – where the north-flowing river spreads out into the Mediterranean Sea – begins precisely at the site of Alexandria's citadel. Many centuries ago, this location was but a small island that the ancient Greeks knew as Pharos.

Pharos is a rather insignificant limestone outcrop. Though its soil doesn't confirm early settlements on the island, the masonry in the surrounding waters does suggest that at some stage a few millennia ago a harbour was created nearby. Recent scientific research around the harbour has discovered lead contamination from as early as the twenty-seventh century BCE, timing backed up by radiocarbon dating of seashell fragments in the area. This means that the coast opposite Pharos, now the winding Alexandria promenade, has been occupied for a staggering five thousand years – and maybe even more.

Excavations revealing organic remains and human-made objects further confirm that settlements certainly existed by 1300 BCE and probably much earlier. This spread of seaside land was so brilliantly positioned for fishing that dozens of families eventually assembled their homes, created from a mixture of sundried mud and papyrus, along its shoreline.

For Egypt, the Bronze Age was a time of prosperity and, vitally, unification. For centuries, the top and bottom halves of Egypt were separate states: Lower Egypt to the north and Upper Egypt to the south, thus called because, until the sixteenth century, most maps showed the south at the top. Lower Egypt had water: its bustling capital, Memphis, was right on the mouth of the Nile Delta, where the river split into seven branches while canals zigzagged across the region. Upper Egypt was more prosperous: its economic centres, the lost capital Thinis, and Thebes, were trading with the north and further afield with Mesopotamia.

Around 3150 BCE, the historic unification of Egypt took place. Conventionally, this has been regarded as the birth of ancient Egypt as we know it today, or more accurately, its move from predynastic to dynastic Egypt, from what has often been curiously termed prehistory (the time before written records) to history (the times we have at least some written records about). It has long been thought that a king named Narmer unified Upper and Lower Egypt, making him the first pharaoh. The Narmer Palette, a ceremonial engraving shaped like a chevron shield, shows Narmer heroically uniting the tribes of the country with the gods in full approval. Significant as one of the earliest hieroglyphics ever found, the engraving depicts Narmer as a warrior brandishing a weapon, suggesting that he might have invaded Upper Egypt prior to any unification. Or, perhaps, this was a gradual and inevitable process as traders moved northwards and the water continued to attract people. Either way, the unification was a considerable moment that would push the country, then known as *Kemet* – meaning Black Land, in reference to the colour of its fertile soil – into a new era.

In hindsight, Alexandria's rise wouldn't have been possible without this unification. The land on which that small fishing village stood would eventually become the heart of a key power, resulting in the decline of cities like Memphis, Thinis and Thebes. The founding of Alexandria in the fourth century BCE, by a Macedonian, would also come to represent the end of native Egyptian pharaonic rule.

Though the unification was a drastic change, some things in Egypt stayed the same. As it had for thousands of years, life remained focused on the Nile Valley more than the Mediterranean. The Nile was the source of all life and something with which the gods were intimately involved: they initiated its annual flooding, turning sand into soil so that crops could grow. But the fishing village on the Mediterranean had a special asset. A few miles south, a vast lake provided freshwater for drinking and farming that attracted yet more people to the area. At some stage, heavy currents and waves had deposited elongated mounds of sand, closing the gulf and creating a significant lake. As a result, several neighbouring villages, including one called Marea, grew along the land between the ocean and the lake. The lake, soon known as Mareotis, covered a huge area. Now called Lake Mariout, it is around fifty square kilometres, but in the ancient era was at least ten times larger. Finally, a few miles north-east of the fishing villages, three more settlements were also built nearby, right at the edge of the delta: Pikuat (later Canopus), Thonis (later Heracleion) and Menouthis.

The land around the main village was swampy. It became shrubbier as it neared the lake, where there were marshlands that were considered to be impenetrable from the south. For those who were here, though, this was an ideal place for agricultural development and stock rearing. The land suited goats, whose population surged. A variety of birds also flourished so that chirps and peeps formed an acoustic backdrop to these villages. The residents occupied themselves with fishing and farming and lived alongside a variety of creatures. Egyptians were obsessed with domesticating animals and had varying levels of success. They had a hard time trying to capture and domesticate hyenas, but dogs had already been tamed and were able both to provide company and to splash around the shallow waters gathering fish. The activity of fishing wasn't yet commercialised as it would be in later centuries, and local fishing boats were rather small, accommodating no more than five men. Different methods were used to catch fish including nets, spears and hooks. The different varieties of seafood – including shark, cuttlefish, red mullet and squid – were either roasted on an open fire, boiled with herbs and berries, or dried, salted and preserved. By the fourth century BCE, locals would begin to realise that landlocked countries without access to fresh fish were prepared to pay good money for salted treats.

From as far back as the fourth millennium BCE, Egypt boasted copious papyrus plants; their vivid green stalks stood five metres high and were regarded as a precious gift from the Nile. Papyrus – from which the word 'paper' originates – would become a key practical component of Alexandria's rise as a centre of knowledge and handicraft, but it was also used as much more than a writing surface. As well as construction, the plant was utilised for making important day-to-day objects: from amulets to shields to reed boats, in addition to boxes and baskets, sails and sandals, mattresses and medicines, rugs and ropes, toys and tables, cords and cloths.

Papyrus stalks were even a staple food, cut into small pieces and baked in clay ovens before consumption. Egyptians here had two main meals a day. In the morning, thick emmer wheat bread, cloudy barley-based beer and fragrant onions. In the evening, more bread and beer, plus vegetables like the papyrus stalks, or garlic, spring onions, celery, gourds and melons. Meat was a little less important, but still consumed regularly: waterfowl and geese were popular, as were goat and oxen. The smaller birds, like quail, were salted and eaten uncooked. Red meat usually came from bigger animals so needed to be preserved, which was done by keeping it in brine, honey or beer. The Egyptians also stuffed food into their live geese and calves to fatten them as early as 2500 BCE. This would continue until Alexandria's founding centuries later, when the livers of geese were enlarged by feeding them dried figs. From Alexandria, this would spread to the Romans, for whom it became a luxury that eventually inspired the French speciality *foie gras*.

Some animals were off limits as food. Pigs were quite useful as they rooted through the soil so it could be planted, but swineherds were nonetheless a despised class and were not even permitted into the temples. The ancient Greek historian Herodotus writes that in Egypt the animal was considered so unclean 'that if a man in passing accidentally touches a pig, he instantly hurries to the river and plunges in with all his clothes on'.[1] While pigs weren't eaten because they were frowned upon, some animals were spared because they were held in high regard. The bull had a significant cult and one in particular, named Apis, was seen as a direct incarnation of the creator god Ptah. Apis was probably the luckiest, most spoiled animal on earth: he lived a life of absolute luxury and veneration in a special temple. When the bull died, in addition to being mummified like royalty, the search for a newborn calf would begin until a new Apis was conferred amid country-wide celebrations. Then there were crocodiles, which grew to six metres in length and posed such a threat to humans that they were given divine status in the hope that they would show their appreciation by being less inclined to attack them. At times, they were still hunted in order to be mummified for worship. Perhaps crocodiles weren't eaten because they were just too dangerous; after all, hippopotami were also associated with the gods but were still hunted. But the crocodile and hippopotamus, despite having divine links, just couldn't compete with one particular animal.

The Egyptian word for cat was delightful in its simplicity: a feline friend was a *miw*. History tells us that the power and popularity of cats today is nothing new. Cats had long been domesticated companions in Egypt but were also seen as protectors of the pharaoh. The *miw* was loved and revered. Not only did it keep rodents away, it was observed to have god-like qualities: at once gentle and aggressive, graceful and dangerous. A tomb from the thirteenth century BCE even depicts one cat wearing a silver earring: a gift from its owner at a time when silver was rarer and more valuable than gold. Taking a cat's life was inexcusable – and punishable by death. Today, slightly smaller than their cousins in Europe and North America, local cats of all shades and patterns hang around Alexandria's streets in abundance. They enter people's homes during teatime to demand leftovers and invite themselves into closets during labour and rearing. They go where humans aren't allowed to venture: under the legs of unsuspecting diners at the outdoor fish restaurants near the sea and atop the city's towering citadel. In fact, it's hard to imagine them resisting a climb up the great Lighthouse of Alexandria when it stood on that spot, too.

The coastline where Alexandria would be founded was more than a piece of land: it was a location of mythological significance. To get a sense of this, we must cross the Mediterranean to late eighth-century BCE Greece, where two epic pieces of writing are being composed that will become some of the most influential poems in Western culture. To the Greeks of this time, the enigmatic author of *The Iliad* and *The Odyssey* came to be known as Homer. Clearly composed by a master poet or poets, these pieces amalgamated reality and fiction and were the culmination of centuries of oral tradition. They would go on to inform Greek education and culture for centuries. In the absence of an established clergy or sacred scripture, they also spelt out the most important aspects of Greek theology, including how people were expected to perceive their gods. We still don't know who Homer was exactly, or whether this person even existed: this enigma creates a compelling poetic narrator who unashamedly boasts divine inspiration and universal authority.

Helen of Troy is likely to have been known in tales predating Homer. The daughter of the most powerful god, Zeus, and the Spartan queen, Leda, Helen is famously described as the most attractive woman in the world. Known more simply in Greek mythology as 'beautiful Helen', she was not only that, she was also the most charming. The *History of the Fall of Troy*, a supposedly first-hand account, fixates on her striking legs, stunning lips and a memorable beauty spot resting between her eyebrows. Meanwhile, the son of the Trojan king and queen was a handsome and intelligent man called Paris. But he was also known by another name: Alexandros, meaning 'the defender of the people'. In later years, this Greek name would be pronounced in Eastern languages as Iskandar, and in Western languages beginning with Latin, as Alexander.

Although Helen was married to King Menelaus of Sparta, the lovelorn Paris stormed into her home one night, intent on taking her away. Some ancient authors suggest that Paris abducted Helen; others that they had fallen in love and eloped. This single event, which has been portrayed in paintings thousands of times, would lead to Spartan attempts to retrieve Helen from Troy, thus sparking the colossal Trojan War. But in Troy, Helen was nowhere to be found. According to several narrations, Paris and Helen had ventured to Egypt, perhaps forced to do so by strong winds at sea. Legend has it that they arrived at an island off the Nile Delta – this was Pharos, where Alexandria's citadel now stands. When she landed, however, the young Helen was wholly underwhelmed. She moaned about having only seals for company. A few centuries after Homer, Herodotus wrote a lesser-known account of the island's King Proteus being so appalled by Paris' actions that he refused to let him continue towards Troy with Helen, sparing him death as he was a visitor but banishing him from the island and keeping Helen safe in Egypt for the entire decade of the Trojan War.

Helen would eventually find herself on the island once again. This time, thought to be around twenty years later, she was in the company of her husband, Menelaus. Blown off course and entirely by chance, the pair found themselves on the very same spot of land. Now, though, humans had joined the seals. As they stepped off their wooden boat, Menelaus signalled to and stopped the first person he saw. It was an elderly man. Menelaus enquired as to their whereabouts: what is this island? The man replied with an explanation of its ownership, using the old Egyptian word 'Prouti's', meaning the 'Pharoah's'. Menelaus understood this either as 'Pharos' or as a reference to the sea deity 'Proteus'. Clearly not too sure, Menelaus would take both terms back with him: the island would be known as Pharos and its patron deity would be Proteus. And to add to the imprecisions, when the couple narrated the story back in Greece, the seals were purposely turned into nymphs.

In Homer's *Odyssey*, which has the earliest mention of Pharos, Menelaus remained stuck there for twenty long days and was desperate to escape. It's then that he bumped into a beautiful human-like creature named Eidotheë. She explained to Menelaus that the island was ruled by her father: 'This place is the haunt of the truth-telling Old Man of the Sea, immortal Proteus, an Egyptian, who knows the deep places of the entire sea.'[2] Seeing his distressed state, Eidotheë took pity on Menelaus, helping him to overcome her father and depart the island.

We do not know what the island was called before this. Alexandria's third-century BCE librarian, Callimachus, called it Helen's Island. Beyond these legends, one suggestion is that it may have been named after the seals that lived on it or the sound they make; how locals referred to seals is unknown and it's arguable whether the word Pharos sounds like a seal's bark. The etymology of the island's name was further popularised after Homer by ancient

Greek authors including Euripides and Herodotus, who writes that he visited Egypt to speak with locals.

As a result of these stories, the deities that came to be associated with the island of Pharos are Proteus, the formidable water-god, and Eidotheë, the gracious sea-goddess. Folklore has often presented Eidotheë as a nymph, but nymphs are personifications of nature with long lives, whereas she was a goddess with immortal life. That she plunges in and out of the sea suggests that she is a mermaid-like entity. Nowadays, one of Alexandria's names is the Bride of the Mediterranean Sea. In Arabic, the phrase 'bride of the sea' means 'mermaid', making Alexandria the Mermaid of the Mediterranean: beautiful, magical, fleeting, mythical. The edge of the large rocks that now surround Alexandria's citadel – where sweethearts huddle together every night – is the very spot where mythical Eidotheë appeared from the ocean to Menelaus before she enchantingly 'plunged beneath the surging sea' once more, never to be seen again.

The living mythology of this region extends to the figure who informed our knowledge of these characters and events: Homer. If this renowned bard did in fact exist, he may well have travelled around the Mediterranean and near the island, perhaps around the eighth century BCE. And according to some legends, an intellectual Egyptian woman named Phantasia helped him write with confidence about these locations. Phantasia, a poet and daughter of a prominent philosopher in the ancient capital of Memphis, is said to have written accounts of the Trojan War and its hero, Odysseus, that were deposited in a nearby temple before Homer acquired them as his main source. It's even been claimed that Homer stole Phantasia's work when visiting Memphis and passed it off as his own, a version of events that became quite popular among nineteenth-century European classicists. Others go as far as claiming that Homer and Phantasia – meaning 'imagination' – are one and the same. And the Byzantine scholar and bishop Eustathius suggested that Homer was Egyptian or at the very least studied in Egypt: a notion that the city to be built around Pharos would embrace in years to come.

Myths aside, what we do know is that in ancient Greece a rhapsode was a full-time professional reciter of the epic poems. Dressed in a long cloak and holding a staff, the rhapsode moved from town to town, stopping in public places to read the literature aloud, both to entertain and to inform. While the Homeric poems were transmitted orally at first, they were eventually recorded in writing: sometime between the eighth and sixth centuries BCE, the rhapsodes, many of whom were illiterate, dictated the poems to scribes. The earliest surviving manuscript is from the third century BCE, when Alexandrian scholars working in the city's Great Library produced the text on papyrus paper. These papyri were then used by scribes to produce further copies around the world. This fact also leads scholars to believe that the first time that *The Odyssey* and *The Iliad* were ordered and divided – into 24 rhapsodes, or books, the division that we still know and use today – this took place in Alexandria. The editors who originated a canonical version of Homer's epics include three of the Library of Alexandria's early librarians. Zenodotus was the mastermind behind dividing the poems into books. He also produced the first critical edition of Homer, revising the text and deleting doubtful lines, as well as penning a useful glossary of Homeric terms. Aristophanes produced another early edition of the poems and Aristarchus followed this up by editing what would become the most influential versions, adding an accent system to the text, ensuring the poetic metre was accurate and writing critical pamphlets about the works. Before these editors completed these tasks in Alexandria, no authoritative version of the Homeric epics existed.

We shall return to these three librarians when looking at how Alexandria swiftly developed into the knowledge capital of the world. But at this stage, during the ancient era, it's safe to say that this area of Egypt was steady, but hardly ambitious. Here remained a series of fishing villages and marshlands on the Mediterranean coastline and further south around Lake Mareotis. Despite its legendary status, the small nearby island of Pharos appeared lifeless.

Sitting in the frenzy of the city's citadel today – at least five millennia after this area was first inhabited – one could be forgiven for overlooking Alexandria's humble beginnings. But the little villages and empty island that once occupied this land were meant for greatness. The forces of reality and myth were destined to combine in mysterious and unpredictable ways. They were going to create a city that would change the world.

Alexander's Dream

Half a millennium after Homer, in the mid-fourth century BCE, a teenage boy with noticeably slim legs, narrow eyes and immaculate hair ventured to the ancient city of Athens in order to enrol in the Platonic Academy, where he would be taught by the celebrated polymath Plato, who was himself a student of the first known moral philosopher, Socrates.[1] The youngster, whose name was Aristotle, came from a well-respected family. His father was court physician to King Amyntas III, ruler of Macedon and son of former King Alexander I. Amyntas had three sons who would all become kings, one after the other: Alexander, Perdiccas and Philip, who was born around the same time as Aristotle. The king also had a daughter, Eurynoe, who might only be mentioned in a single historical source – by the Roman historian Justin – but has a dramatic story to tell: she saved her father's life by informing him of an assassination attempt instigated by her mother and her mother's lover.

Aristotle attended the Platonic Academy for two decades, only departing in 348 BCE when Plato died in his eighties. The loss of his mentor, with whom he'd been associated for his entire adult life, is likely to have hit Aristotle hard. But it also helped him make the tough decision to leave Athens, crossing the Aegean Sea to resettle in Aterneus (today in western Turkey). He may have felt inclined to make the move when Plato's nephew, Speusippus, became head of the Academy, while Aristotle, still regarded as an alien non-Athenian, was neglected. With the expanding power of the Macedon kingdom, tensions had been building between the Greeks and Macedonians, who despite having much in common regarded themselves as distinctly separate. Athens was becoming a hotspot for anti-Macedonian sentiment and it was commonly known that

Aristotle's family had links with the latest public enemy. Aristotle continued to establish close connections with the Macedonians to the extent that, by his thirties, he was spying for them. Having further proved his loyalty, he received an invitation to move to Macedon from an old acquaintance, Philip, who was now on the throne as King Philip II.

Philip was keen to have his twelve-year-old son tutored privately and was only willing to consider the greatest minds of the time for this vital role. A rigorous and competitive search for the coveted academic post was well underway. Philip thought about Isocrates, the celebrity speechwriter who charged phenomenal prices in his selective school of rhetoric but was now in his nineties. He considered Plato's nephew, Speusippus, who upon hearing of this potential royal interest, hurriedly offered to resign from his leadership of the Academy to take on the role. But there would only be one winner.

Aristotle was born in Stagira on the hilly Greek–Macedonian border and in the same year that Plato died King Philip had invaded and ransacked the city. Aristotle made it clear that in return for tutoring the prince, Philip was required to rebuild Stagira and free its people. Philip was so adamant that his son should receive a special education that he not only freed the enslaved citizens, but also rebuilt the city complete with a state-of-the-art water system. The next step was to find a place for the school. Philip settled on the town of Mieza, arranging classrooms and bedrooms at the Temple of the Nymphs. This temple utilised two natural caves, between which a rectangular space was cut out from the rock. It had colourful pillars and façades adorning its walls. The selective boarding school was far away from distraction and ready to welcome the sons of Macedon's most noble families. The young students included names that will become familiar: Ptolemy, Hephaestion, Cassander, Cleitus, Lysimachus, and of course Philip's son, named after the king's brother and grandfather. He was Alexander.

Alexander was born in 356 BCE, in the Macedon capital of Pella, to Philip and Olympias. Philip had fallen deeply in love with Olympias on the Greek island of Samothrace (equidistant between the mainlands of modern Greece and Turkey). Since she was from Epirus (west of Macedon), Olympias was regarded as a foreigner and more specifically as a barbarian, a term used for anyone who didn't speak Greek. But her noble family actually claimed to be descendants of the great Greek warrior Achilles. Philip's family, meanwhile, boasted as their flattering ancestor a most important Greek hero turned deity: Heracles (or Hercules). With both Achilles and Heracles regarded as having divine ancestry, Philip and Olympias were a match made in mythical heaven.

The story of Alexander's conception is filled with remarkable legends befitting of an ancient hero. The night before his parents wed, his mother had the strangest dream: that her body was struck by a thunderbolt that created a blazing fire. Philip had a dream that he placed a papyrus seal displaying a lion onto his wife's body. The sages interpreted the lion as confirmation that the couple would have a courageous son. The papyrus plant only grew in the lands of Egypt, so this linked the newborn to the chief Egyptian deity, Amun-Re, known and often worshipped in Greece as Zeus Ammon, recognisable for the two ram's horns on his head. In another legend, the last pharaoh, Nectanebo II, disguises himself as Amun-Re and impregnates Olympias. As for the thunderbolt, Philip was advised to give sacrifice to Zeus Ammon, the god of sky and thunder. Later in Alexander's adult life, when his mother told this story, the thunderbolt was regarded as potential evidence that Olympias was impregnated by the thunder-god himself, making Zeus the father of Alexander. Philip is likely to have given Olympias, his fourth wife, a special status compared to his other wives (he married seven women in total), in large part because she bore him Alexander. As a boy, he was cherished by his father, for whom these omens surrounding the birth created high hopes. On the day Alexander was born, Philip's army won a battle and his racehorse won at the Olympic Games, cementing the belief that his son would be unstoppable.

Before joining the new school, Alexander had already been raised as royalty. He learnt to read and hunt at an early age. He also played the lyre, a string instrument not too dissimilar to a harp, thought to make boys more cultured and better behaved. The instrument was also used to provide music to accompany poetic recitations, not least the Homeric epics. In *The Iliad*, the hero Achilles himself plays the lyre while singing about the actions of heroic men.

Much of what we know about Alexander is from the Alexander romances, largely fictional biographies that used historical events as their bases. Legends about Alexander's exploits began to be written in Alexandria shortly after his death. The most important of Alexander's mythical biographies is the *Alexander Romance,* which served as both a compilation of what had already been written, and had stories added to it in different languages over the centuries to the extent that multiple versions existed. The *Romance* in its current form has long been thought to date from the third century CE, but there is much to suggest that the original text was begun shortly after Alexander's death in the third century BCE.

The *Romance* claims that one day, fifteen-year-old Alexander heard the high-pitched neighing of a locked-up horse. He was informed that the horse, which had human corpses scattered around it, was 'a man-eater'. When Alexander approached it, the horse's demeanour changed and he began to nuzzle the prince affectionately. Alexander forced his way into the enclosure and mounted the demonic horse that everyone so feared. The *Romance* adds mythical prowess to the horse, noting that the Oracle of Delphi had prophesied to Philip that whoever managed to ride this horse would 'rule the whole world'. When Philip heard what his son had done, he embraced him and declared: 'Hail, Alexander, ruler of the world!'[2] The early second-century historian Plutarch provides a different version of events, writing that when Philip was offered an expensive horse that refused to be mounted, ten-year-old Alexander challenged his father that he could solve the issue or otherwise pay the horse's full price. Alexander had noticed that the horse – a large black colt with blue eyes and a distinctive white star on the forehead – was confused by the movement of his own shadow. Alexander 'turned' the horse 'directly towards the sun' so that the animal could calm down, before 'stroking him gently' and mounting him. As Alexander sped away on the horse, the king and his men, who'd moments earlier sniggered at Alexander's confidence, were left astonished. As he turned back towards them, they burst into applause, his father 'shedding tears' of joy and ecstasy. Philip 'kissed him as he came down from his horse' before urging him to aim high: 'O my son, look thee out a kingdom equal to and worthy of thyself, for Macedonia is too little for thee.'[3] In both versions, Alexander is rewarded by taking this horse as his very own, naming it Bucephalus, or ox-head, either because of its stubbornness or because it had an ox-head mark on the haunch. Legends aside, we can be sure that Alexander was taught how to ride horses and play polo, and that he did have a loyal horse called Bucephalus who would go on to become one of the most famous horses in history.

At the boarding school, Alexander received an intensive education as Aristotle, now in his early forties, spent hours standing at the blackboard scribbling with his chalk. The key value instilled in Alexander was known as *arete*: the pursuit of excellence, a term also used to describe the Homeric heroes. Alexander observed his teacher's own striving for excellence through intense contemplation: Aristotle sat reflecting for long periods on the stone seats, and in the breaks strolled slowly around the shady green surroundings. In fact, decades later, those who followed Aristotle's schools of thought became known as the Peripatetics: an homage to Aristotle's habit of striding around as he thought and taught.

Alexander had grown up around many languages and was at least bilingual in standard Greek and his nurse's Macedonian, and quite possibly in his mother's Epirote dialect. Aristotle apparently taught the students to write in four languages: Greek, Babylonian, Hebrew and Latin. He taught them a wide range of subjects, including astronomy, ethics, geography, logic, medicine, metaphysics, politics, rhetoric and, of course, literature. He discussed the nature of the world – the sea, the winds and the stars. He shared with them his views about life and morality. Some of his maxims appear to have stayed with Alexander: that 'all men by nature desire to know', that 'man is by nature a political animal', and the striking assertion that 'poetry is finer and more philosophical than history, for poetry expresses the universal and history only the particular'. Later, Aristotle would reflect on how 'the young' were powerless against their desires but full of passion, ambition and hope. In a curious memo, he recollected:

They are passionate, hot-tempered, and carried away by impulse, and unable to control their passion . . . They are ambitious of honour, but more so of victory . . . And their desire for both these is greater than their desire for money, to which they attach only the slightest value, because they have never yet experienced want . . . [They are] full of hope . . .[4]

Plutarch writes that Alexander loved Aristotle just as much as he loved his own father. The affection appears to have been mutual: in later legends, Aristotle is said to have told Alexander that he was destined to 'be the greatest king'. Perhaps Aristotle was trying to encourage the prince or, as is more likely, these stories came about later as Alexander's power and Aristotle's renown grew. Aristotle probably cared deeply about his key student, who was in turn deeply interested in learning. But young Alexander was clearly no philosopher: he was rash and excitable. 'They think they know everything, and confidently affirm it', Aristotle noted about his students: not the most flattering report. But when the subject was poetics, things were very different. Alexander could recite significant passages of the tragedies by heart. In fact, Aristotle had never seen a teenage student take such a remarkably keen interest in the Homeric epics as Alexander, who in his captivation is said to have devoured *The Iliad* in a single sitting. So passionate was Alexander that Aristotle was compelled to present the youngster with his own personal and carefully annotated version of Homer's poetry.

By this stage, Alexander was no ordinary teenager or even prince: he was becoming part of an astounding educational tree consisting of the most respected scholars of each era who had all but founded Western knowledge and philosophy. Socrates taught Plato. Plato taught Aristotle. Now, Aristotle was teaching Alexander.

As an adult, Alexander stood at around five feet, not much shorter than the average Macedonian man at the time. His military training likely made him a stocky, well-built figure, and Alexander really cared about how he looked. It was commonly known that only one sculptor, the finest of the time, was permitted to portray Alexander. It is thanks to Lysippus – essentially his official portraitist since boyhood – that we have a relatively good idea of what Alexander looked like. Similar to photographs today, sculptures and paintings of Alexander obviously served political purposes by presenting him in a certain way. But there are many features that appear often enough in depictions of Alexander to merit attention.

The most important portrayal is a bust known as the Hermes Azara, a Roman copy of one of Lysippus' works that was sculpted from life and probably at Alexander's request. Today it sits in the Louvre in Paris after being gifted in the early 1800s to Napoleon Bonaparte by the Spanish, who'd discovered it during an excavation in Italy. Like most sculptures and paintings, it presents Alexander with voluptuous curls waving down his head and neck, a well-aligned nose and a short, wide jaw. He is clean-shaven, perhaps by choice or perhaps because his beard grew too scantly. Both the abundant hair on his head and the lack of hair on his face were highly unusual for royalty, soldiers and athletes of this period. Like the line of kings that came before Alexander, including his father, he was expected to sport a close-cropped haircut and suitably bushy beard. Alexander's long hair, with its parting near the centre, would have signalled moral laxity, and a shaven face was seen as weak and effeminate. Alexander clearly liked this look, though, and kept it defiantly. It would gradually gain popularity until it became a commonplace look among his successors. Alexander looked young to those around him even well into adulthood.

The bust shows deep, intense eyes, though we are unable to confirm their colour. In an attempt to give him enchanting qualities, legends make the improbable claim that he had one dark and one light eye. Copies of contemporary paintings show brown eyes and brown streaky hair, and the romances describe hair like a lion's mane, which does less to confirm a colour than it does to symbolise valour. Plutarch writes that 'he was fair' with some 'ruddiness', but adds that Apelles, Alexander's court artist, portrayed his 'complexion browner and darker', perhaps indicating exposure to the sun. Apelles' actual paintings have unfortunately not survived, though subsequent artists have been inclined to paint scenes of him painting Alexander.

Unlike Aristotle, Alexander had a brisk walk. He spoke quickly, too. He was fond of bathing, even plunging into freezing water after battle to the astonishment of his troops. In Pella, public bath-tubs were common, but men were expected to bathe only in cold water; hot baths were for women, especially during pregnancy.

Alexander's cleanliness led to accounts of his pleasant odour. Sweet spices could be used to make ointments and Alexander would show great interest in perfumes when he ventured to Persia, rushing to King Darius III's perfumery as soon as he defeated him.

Only 'sleep and the sexual delight' reminded Alexander of his mortality, Plutarch wrote.[5] Sleep and sexual climax represent momentary unconsciousness and weakness: mini deaths, like the French expression *la petite mort* that eventually came to signify orgasm. Sexually active from a young age, Alexander would end up having three wives and at least four mistresses. He also took his pick of concubines on a nightly basis and slept with a eunuch. On his campaigns, Alexander's men enjoyed the company of *hetairai*, whose stimulating and witty conversation was as important as sex. Unlike the common sex workers, the *pornai*, who were owned by pimps and worked from streets and brothels in red-light districts, the *hetairai* were the highest rank of sex workers at the time. These sophisticated women were highly educated in art and music, able to maintain refined composure and wit. Such was their power that they made their way into the most influential symposia to dine and converse with the mightiest men in the empire.

It's thought that Alexander's first sexual encounter was with the famously beautiful Campaspe, who would fast become his most cherished mistress. In fact, Alexander managed to combine his love of sensuality and art: according to the Roman historian Pliny the Elder, Alexander asked Apelles to paint Campaspe. While undertaking the task, Apelles fell in love with his attractive subject. Alexander admired Apelles' work so much that he gave his mistress to the artist – but made sure to keep the painting.

When Alexander met a Persian woman called Barsine, it was her knowledge of Greek literature that captivated him. Around that time, a group known as the Amazons was notoriously difficult to infiltrate. Formed of female warriors and hunters, they were led by a queen who could outpower even the strongest of men. They moved around Greece, West Asia, and reached Egypt. Their only interactions with men were brief sexual encounters. If this resulted in a son, the baby would be given to the father or killed in order to maintain a female-only society. According to legend, their queen Thalestric planned to bear a mighty heiress, so she sought out

Alexander to impregnate her. They proceeded to have sex for thirteen energetic days and nights. This was a particularly useful story for Alexander and his successors to spread: it showed the vigour of Alexander's pedigree and sexuality. That the Amazons are mentioned in *The Iliad* is further indication of Alexander's obsession with mimicking aspects of the epic.

A moderate level of polygamy was quite normal at the time – or in the case of royalty, a not so moderate level. When Alexander was told that his only sister, named Cleopatra of Macedon, was having an affair, he simply exclaimed that she was entitled to enjoyment. At the time and especially among the Macedonian nobility, combining heterosexual marriage with occasional homosexuality was also unsurprising, though not necessarily discussed in the open. While more popular among younger men, a gay relationship could also involve an older man with a younger one. It's therefore possible that Alexander had such relationships. Alexander was particularly close to his classmate Hephaestion. In the past, historians assumed Hephaestion was older than Alexander, paralleling the relationship of the Homeric hero Achilles with the older Patroclus, but Alexander and Hephaestion were around the same age. The pair certainly shared a mutual love and continued to have a strong relationship until the latter's death. We know for sure that they were at least the very closest of friends.

Alexander had just turned sixteen when his father entrusted him to take charge of Macedon. Philip, who wore a patch over his right eye after an arrow had penetrated it, ventured eastward to lay siege to Byzantium, so he needed both a regent to take charge in his absence and an heir in case he didn't make it back. As the favourite son, Alexander was given the nod ahead of his older half-brother, Philip Arrhidaeus, whom sources indicate had learning difficulties. For the first time, the crown prince had the king's seal at his disposal. Alexander immediately took an active approach to his new role. He might even have been excited to learn that the Thracian Maedi tribe – who resided a few hundred miles north-east of the capital – were preparing to rebel against Macedonian rule. Alexander swiftly took an army to confront them, driving the tribe out of their town and settling Macedonians in their place. A couple of years earlier, his father Philip had renamed a town Philippopolis. So, Alexander decided to mark his first success by eagerly renaming this town after himself. It became the first city of Alexander: Alexandropolis. It didn't, however, share in the success of its eponym: the town was all but abandoned soon after it was renamed and faded into insignificance. Today, we don't even know where exactly Alexandropolis stood, though we can deduce that it was in south-west Bulgaria along the banks of the Struma River.

Despite the success of his attack on the Maedi, it wasn't all plain sailing for Alexander and his life took a sudden and tumultuous turn. Alexander's father claimed to have fallen in love with a young woman named Cleopatra Eurydice, the adopted niece of his army general Attalus. Alexander's mother had held a special status and Alexander was the obvious heir, but none of Philip's six wives had been Macedonian. This was about to change as he married Cleopatra Eurydice: not only was she Macedonian and by far the youngest of the wives, but she also had an influential uncle in whom Philip confided. Olympias was fuming – and Alexander was well aware of his mother's distress.

At the wedding, the nobles of Macedon gathered around bottomless drinks to celebrate this popular union. They drank wine, at the time differentiated as white or black and mixed with varying quantities of water for strength. Eighteen-year-old Alexander watched on despondently. Attalus had obviously had a lot to drink and, as he got up to give his toast, he swayed from side to side, hardly able to stop the wine from dripping out of his golden goblet. Plutarch records Attalus raising his hands and beginning to pray: may his niece gift Macedon 'a lawful successor'. Immediately and unexpectedly, a cup soared towards his head. It came from Alexander, who was now screaming: 'You villain, what, am I then a bastard?' As guests rushed to check on Attalus, an enraged Philip got up to berate his son. He reached for his sword and in that moment his eyes suggested that he might even kill the prince. But as Philip stood up, in his anger and drunkenness, he took a loud, dramatic tumble and fell to the floor. As he sat on his backside, Alexander walked over to him and asked how he wanted to 'pass out of Europe into Asia' when he was incapable of 'passing from one seat to another'. With that, Alexander stormed out of the wedding and prepared to leave the court. He took his mother to her homeland and continued to Illyria on the Balkan peninsula. Suddenly, after years of education and training and a brief but thrilling stint at the helm, he was unsure whether he was still the heir to the throne and whether he was even welcome in his father's kingdom. But when he shouted at the wedding, Alexander had managed to summarise a tactic for world domination: the ability to navigate between the continents of Europe and Asia, something that would soon place the location of Alexandria at the centre of imperial ambitions for centuries to come.

It took months of mediation for Alexander to make the prodigal return to his father. In this time, Alexander had become closer to his mother and had also developed a support network that consisted of his best friends, including Ptolemy and Hephaestion. But it didn't take long for more problems to start brewing. This time, Philip arranged the marriage of Alexander's half-brother Philip Arrhidaeus to a Persian governor's daughter. Alexander discussed this eagerly with his mother and friends, becoming convinced that this tactical betrothal was a sign that his brother was being groomed as heir. In response, he decided to offer himself as husband instead, but how was he to get this message to Persia? Alexander enjoyed the company of Thessalus, a famous tragic actor who was known for his fine performances. Thinking outside the box, Alexander asked Thessalus to go to the Persian governor and use his acting skills to convince them to change their mind. There, the actor delivered to them news about the original groom: that he was an illegitimate son and an unstable fool. The governor was both shocked at the news and pleased that his daughter could instead marry Alexander. But word of this plot had already reached King Philip, who cancelled the plans and berated Alexander, claiming that there had been another plan to pair him with a more befitting bride. The actor Thessalus ended up in chains while Alexander's best friends, including Ptolemy, were exiled for their roles in the scheme. The incident had shown both Alexander's desire to control his own destiny and his belief in the power of the arts. But the network Alexander had built now vanished: like his mother, his friends were no longer nearby.

In summer 336 BCE, shortly after Alexander's twentieth birthday, fate took yet another wild turn. It was at another Cleopatra's wedding, this time his sister's, that things would get horribly out of control. The marriage of the princess was a state occasion and Philip wanted to make full use of it. He instructed his seven body-guards to let him walk into the theatre alone so that the guests of honour and common citizens could see how approachable and unafraid he was. It did not go well. Within minutes, one of the bodyguards lunged towards Philip and stuck a dagger into the king's ribs. Gore and chaos devastated the wedding as the father of the bride breathed his last. The murderer made a rapid exit towards a horse strategically positioned for the escape, but as they galloped away, a wild vine caught the horse in mid-stride and threw the rider. Seconds later, the killer, now identifiable as Pausanias, was also lying in his own blood.

Alexander's fortunes were changed by the death of his father. It's unlikely that Alexander or his mother planned the king's murder; it would make more sense for it to be a Persian plot instigated by that empire's new king, Darius III. But according to three sources, includ-ing Aristotle, Pausanias also had his own issues with the king, and in particular with the king's friend Attalus. As a young pageboy, Pausanias had boasted good looks, and Philip is thought to have had an affair with him. One evening, Attalus invited Pausanias to dinner, but there was an ulterior motive. Attalus poured Pausanias copious amounts of unmixed wine, waited for his chance and proceeded to rape the helpless boy. Not stopping there, he even handed him to friends for their own sport. The traumatised Pausanias pleaded with the king to punish the perpetrator. But Attalus was Philip's general and since the king had married Cleopatra Eurydice, Attalus had become a kind of father-in-law. To Pausanias' dismay, the king refused to punish Attalus. Instead, he tried to appease Pausanias with a promotion to personal bodyguard: quite literally a deadly mistake.

These events ended up changing the fate of Alexander in ways nobody could have predicted. First, the toast at Philip's wedding led Alexander to a world beyond the court, as well as showing him the consequences of acting rashly and the value of having close friends. Second, Philip's death cut short any plans he may have had to name an alternative successor. Alexander had already been entrusted to deputise in the past so was best positioned to take charge, meaning that Pausanias' assassination of Philip prematurely ended any doubt about who would be the next king. In hindsight, without this series of unsavoury and despicable actions by Attalus and the subsequent responses of Philip and Pausanias, Alexander may never have become king.

Now sitting firmly on the Macedonian kingdom's throne, twenty-year-old Alexander III was determined to cement his power so that he could be free to make a mark on the world. He immediately ordered the execution of Attalus, whom he predicted would defect to Athens. Alexander's mother is said to have arranged for Cleopatra Eurydice and her baby daughter, Alexander's half-sister, to be taken onto a vessel that was then set alight. The newly crowned Alexander tried to establish his authority on the region. In the city state of Thebes, which for the last century was the independently governed capital of its region, there was some rebellion against Macedonian rule. In response, Alexander took his army to Thebes, where the locals refused to surrender and Alexander set an example by destroying the city, executing all its men, enslaving its women and children and burning it to the ground. Alexander ordered only one house to be spared: that of a lyric poet he admired named Pindar. Alexander's destruction of Thebes was a key event: it led him to the realisation that a major city could be toppled and that a new one could be founded instead, on his own terms, and, better yet, one whose location could complement his goal of attacking the ancient world's first superpower, the Persian Empire.

Initially presenting himself as a ruler for all Greeks, Alexander ruthlessly conquered Anatolia and the Levant before heading westwards to Egypt. Here was an established, wealthy country boasting countless natural treasures, including gold and grain. It had access to resources and slaves from Asia to its east and the rest of Africa to its south. If conquered, all these resources would help support Alexander's empire and military, and if he could maintain and elevate its trade, he could also make profits. Egypt was accessible via sea and river and boasted a pharaonic canal system that could provide access towards the Indian Ocean from which Alexander could continue to expand his empire. Then there was the knowledge that stemmed from Egypt, where the economic reliance on nature, especially the Nile, meant that scholars were skilled in astronomy, alchemy and medicine. Economically and practically, Egypt was key to Alexander's larger plan: world domination.

Egypt had been coveted by the Persians for centuries. In 525 BCE they managed to conquer and rule it as part of the Achaemenid Empire. Around 404 BCE, the Egyptians successfully rebelled and gained independence, but the Persians reconquered the country in 343 BCE. Just a decade before Alexander set foot in Egypt, the Egyptians tried to rebel once again but they were brutally quashed. To show them who was in control, the Persians destroyed Egyptian temples. Also around this time, the Persians supposedly held an outrageous and deliberately provocative barbeque in which they roasted Apis, the holy bull. Even if this didn't occur, it confirms the negative contemporary Egyptian narrative about the Persian colonisers. As such, though Alexander's army met resistance in Gaza, he marched with ease into Egypt, forcing the Persian governor's resignation. After centuries of self-governance, Egyptians couldn't have been happy with yet another foreign power ruling over them. But the timing of Alexander's arrival worked in his favour, as most Egyptians welcomed him as a liberator.

His first action was a calculated stunt: he offered a sacrifice to Apis, showing Egyptians that he respected their traditions and helping endear him, at least comparatively, to the Egyptian people. He also arranged for a festival of sporting and literary games in which both Greeks and Egyptians were invited to perform, showing the Egyptians that he was not going to treat them as barbarians. Alexander was now ruling a celebrated land and etching his name in its long and illustrious history. The *Romance* is alone in its claim that the Egyptian priests crowned Alexander as the new pharaoh, but the title does appear alongside his name in later temple inscriptions.

Alexander's childhood enthusiasm for literature had matured into an adult passion. He'd always disliked competitive sports like athletics and boxing, unlike his father, who'd felt strongly about fielding horses in every Olympic Games, and great grandfather, Alexander I, who had personally taken part in the Olympics' most important event, the stadion (a 180-metre sprint), as well as the pentathlon. Instead, wherever he happened to be, Alexander was keen to engage with the best rhapsodes, musicians and dramatists, for whom he created several awards. The value he placed on art continued to inform his perceptions and even his decisions. After all, Aristotle had used literature to instruct the students about life. For example, Homer's stories of the Trojan War had been used to teach leadership. Aristotelian philosophy utilised epics and tragedies to present examples of the link between politics and ethics, emphasising how every person, let alone leader, must first develop excellence of character. In *The Iliad*, courage is a political rather than individualistic trait, emphasising the significance of ambition and teamwork. Alexander admired how the rulers in the poem were strong both in character and in battle. And it's important to remember that for Alexander and everyone around him, these Homeric tales weren't mere fictions – they were valuable histories. With his newfound authority, Alexander could imitate his heroes yet more. During his lifetime, Lysippus had sculpted Alexander naked, with his weight on one leg and an arm extended holding a spear. Variants of this original statue have lost the spear, but they still emphasise a heroic stance. Alexander wanted to style himself on the heroes he had grown up reading about, especially Achilles, and over time the tables would be turned so that sculptures of Alexander began to inform perceptions of how Achilles looked.

When Alexander's army looted the riches of Persia, he was given a rare golden casket. For some time he wondered what he should use it for and even deliberated with friends. Alexander greatly cherished that special copy of Homer's poetry, the edition presented to him by Aristotle, and carried it with him wherever he went. And so, by day, during his campaigns, he kept it in the solid gold casket. By night, wherever he happened to be sleeping, he would lift his pillow and carefully place the treasured book beneath it – alongside his dagger. Plutarch writes that one night, as he tossed and turned, Alexander appeared to recall Menelaus' words in Homer's *Odyssey*:

There is there an island, set in the ever-surging deep,
off the coast of Egypt, and men call it Pharos; it is as
far out to sea as a hollow ship can run in a full day,
if a shrill stern wind is blowing it along. There is on it
a harbour, well-sheltered, where men can draw dark water
and launch their trim ships again on to the open sea.

As Alexander slept, he dreamed that an old and venerable grey-haired man appeared before him. Standing right in front of Alexander, the man spoke with brevity and accomplishment: 'An island lies, where loud the billows roar, / Pharos they call it, on the Egyptian shore.' Plutarch records that the startled Alexander 'immediately rose up', and without any delay he began his voyage to Pharos.

Alexander's Dream City

In 331 BCE, halfway in the timeline between us and the great Pyramids of Giza, which had already been standing for some 2,200 years, Alexander made the hopeful journey to the island of Pharos.

Armed with his copy of Homer and with long locks styled in the image of his hero Achilles, the twenty-five-year-old boarded a barge from Memphis northward on the Nile. Aristotle had taught him that 'knowledge of the fact differs from knowledge of the reason for the fact'. Alexander had no doubt that he needed to understand his vision of this unfamiliar island.

Aristotle was still part of Alexander's support network and they corresponded no matter the distance between them. Aristotle, who also continued to spy for Alexander, had returned to Athens but introduced the king to his favourite nephew. Callisthenes, a few years older than Alexander, was a budding historian who had written a ten-volume history of Greece and was now tasked with recording Alexander's story as and when it happened so that the king could earn an enthusiastic following. Auspiciously titled the *Deeds of Alexander*, much of Alexander's history today is based on this lost text, the original source for later biographies. Alexander was also supported by his schoolfriends – Ptolemy, Hephaestion, Cassander, Cleitus and Lysimachus – each given a considerable role as commander or general. And he had his trusted black horse, Bucephalus, whom he'd saved a decade and a half earlier. Bucephalus was still healthy despite possibly being as old as twenty-five and Alexander can be forgiven for starting to believe Achilles' opinion that some horses were immortal.

By this time, Pharos was presumed to be the home of the sea-god Proteus. Alexander arrived at its uncertain shore, and the *Romance* narrates that he 'saw a great open space, stretching into the infinite distance, and occupied by twelve villages'. In reality, the place might easily have been a complete anticlimax. There wasn't a soul on the island. Across the water, scattered villages punctuated an otherwise vacant space along the coast. The largest of these ran primarily on fishing, though some pirates, skilled at navigating the winter waves of the ocean, had also settled here.

But this was love at first sight. Within a matter of seconds, Alexander noticed the immense potential of this rocky spit of land. The distance between the island and the coast was relatively short: if he were to connect the island to the mainland via a narrow strip of land, this could be turned into one of the most strategically located harbour-towns in the world.

There were many immediate and prospective advantages to this location. If anything, the geographical position was even better than he'd have initially realised. Here was a place that was as close as possible to the Nile without any danger of being affected by the river's regular flooding. There was a freshwater supply from Lake Mareotis further inland and the Nile Delta was nearby. Though some had been purposely drained or filled in, pharaonic canals linked the river to the lake and the lake to the sea. Soon, another canal would connect the location to the westernmost mouth of the Nile Delta, the Canopic branch of the Nile, just east of this spot, where the river channels into the Mediterranean Sea. These even provided access, via the Arabian Sea, to the Red Sea and then the Indian Ocean. In other words, it was a spot at the intersection of the three continents of Europe, Africa and Asia. Strategically, or perhaps ideologically, creating a base at this precise location could do even more than support geographic dominance: it could bring the Hellenistic world closer to the great Egyptian civilisation. That Greeks were already familiar with Pharos through Homer's *Odyssey* could only be an advantage.

Alexander wasted no time. Straightaway, a temporary connection was developed between Pharos and the coast. Next, he ordered a larger link to be constructed across the sea to connect the island with the mainland. This causeway measured 1,300 metres in length, or in the Greek unit of 'stadium', seven stadia, thus earning the name *Heptastadion*.

Such was his excitement for this new venture, the idealistic Alexander was itching to draw a design of this dream city. He looked around for a piece of chalk. He expectantly demanded one from his men, including the respected architect Deinocrates of Rhodes. Then, Alexander reached for some grains of barley and to everyone's surprise, got down onto his knees. Rushing with exhilaration, he began to use the barley and his fingers to sketch a messy map out onto the sandy floor. It would be a city right between the lake and the ocean. There would be streets angled to welcome the sea breeze and enable eight lanes of horses and chariots to move efficiently. There would be a market square and temples serving both the Greek and Egyptian gods. And there would be a library dedicated to the Muses.

Plutarch writes that as Alexander finished his design on the ground, a flock of birds appeared from the horizon and descended onto the grain, all but devouring it. Alexander was startled and confused, but was quickly assured by those around him. This was a sign that the city would 'be the nurse and feeder of many nations'.

Another version of the founding story indicates that it is the city's perimeter that was marked using barley flour. Alexander wanted to get a sense of just how large the new city could be, so asked for the perimeter to be drawn out. Hundreds of his men were tasked with creating a kind of blueprint on the floor. The soldiers kept rations in their personal mess tins, so a builder went round collecting barley from every one of them and awaited Alexander's orders. According to the Roman historian Curtius, the perimeter ended up measuring eighty stadia, almost ten miles. The very idea of Alexander using barley is hugely symbolic: this was to be a rich and booming land. It indicated, as the Greek historian Arrian notes, 'that the city would prosper, and there would be particular prosperity from the produce of the earth'.[1] The *Romance* adds that when the birds consumed the barley, Alexander was told that the city 'will feed the whole inhabited world, and those who are born in it will reach all parts of the world; just as the birds fly over the whole earth'.

When the plan was finished, Alexander put the idea to the test by offering a sacrifice to the gods, which the priests announced as having been accepted. On that twenty-fifth day of the ancient

Egyptian month of Tobi, in the year 331 BCE, the foundations of the city were laid.[2]

And it was to be named Alexandria.

The new city's name was Alexandria *by* Egypt – not Alexandria *in* Egypt. This might indicate its founder's perception that it was too far from what was traditionally regarded as Egypt. It also suggests that Alexander was still uncertain about whether he really was in charge of such an expansive land as Egypt. More simply, it demonstrates how Alexandria was to be its own capital: a city like no other that did things on its own terms. And it flourished almost immediately.

Egyptians had generally welcomed Alexander and his plans here intrigued the locals. It may have been at this stage that they began to call the main village Raqote – Egyptian for 'that which is built up' or 'building site' – and Rhakotis in Greek. Classical Greek and Roman sources suggest that the settlement bore this name before Alexander's arrival, but it is unknown precisely when the village was named, and it is possible that this term was only used to describe it after the construction of Alexandria began. What we do know is that sometime before the space was named Alexandria, locals called this area Raqote. Its Egyptian residents, and those of the nearby villages, refused to accept a new name that could erase their heritage and signify a shift in power and ownership. Until a new generation was born and until more non-Egyptians arrived, locals continued to refer to the area as Rhakotis.

As a teenager, the first mission Alexander led had resulted in Alexandropolis. And the majority of the cities he founded from that date were called Alexandria. Historians have long tried to confirm how many he founded and even the most conservative estimates name six cities. At least three of the cities assumed to have been founded by Alexander were named after his death, but this still shows his continued legacy. Nonetheless, there is reason to believe that he also founded Alexandria in Aeria, Alexandria in Arachosia, Alexandria Ariana, Alexandria Asiana, Alexandria Bucephalus, Alexandria Carmania, Alexandria in the Caucasus, Alexandria Eschate, Alexandria on the Hyphasis, Alexandria on the Indus, Alexandria by Issus, Alexandria by the Latmus, Alexandria in

Margiana, Alexandria in Opiania, Alexandria in Orietai, Alexandria on the Oxus, Alexandria Prophthasia, Alexandria in Susiana and Alexandria in Troas!

On today's map, they span a large area that indicates the extent of his ventures, covering Bulgaria, Turkey, Iraq, Iran, Turkmenistan, Tajikistan, Afghanistan, Pakistan and India. Alexandria in Aeria is modern-day Afghanistan's second city of Herat; Alexandria in Arachosia forms the foundation of modern-day Old Kandahar in Afghanistan's third city. Alexandria Eschate, literally Alexandria the Furthest, is Tajikistan's second city of Khujand, one of the oldest in Central Asia with its own fascinating history until the Soviet Union renamed it Leninabad. Alexandria by Issus has become the Turkish port town of Alexandretta, or little Alexandria. And the eagle-eyed reader of this list of Alexandrias will have noticed Alexandria Bucephalus. Alexander did indeed name this town in memory of his beloved horse. In 326 BCE, around five years after the founding of Alexandria by Egypt, the horse who'd carried Alexander as far as India died; according to Plutarch, Bucephalus was thirty. So Alexander named the very next town he founded, located on the Jhelum River in the Jammu–Kashmir region, after both himself and his horse, though over time it became known as Bucephala.

Most Alexandrias haven't survived. Even those that did survive don't have Alexander's personal or ideological stamp on them. Some were simply conquered and renamed. Both in his day and to this day, none compare to Alexandria by Egypt. This wasn't a city that came about from a war, or from a geographical split. It certainly didn't come about organically either. This was a city that he had created from scratch, that Alexander envisaged, that was born from one man's ego.

The *Romance* records that as soon as the foundations had been laid, Alexander inscribed, from the top downwards, the first five letters of the Greek alphabet, ABGDE (alpha, beta, gamma, delta, epsilon). Influenced by the riddles of the Greek storyteller Aesop, each represented a word:

(A)lexandros
(B)asileus
(G)enos
(D)ios
(E)ktisen

'Alexander, king, descendant of Zeus, built the city.' The riddle confirmed both Alexander's divinity and his role in the creation of Alexandria. It was to feature five different quarters, each named after one of these letters. Since the 1990s, excavations of the city and its surrounding waters have found references from as early as the third century BCE that confirm the five quarters, each named after the first five letters of the Greek alphabet.

The conception of Alexandria was idealistic. It was ambitiously intended as a global capital, a cultural melting pot, a state-of-the-art metropolis. Rather than create an empire that imposed its own beliefs (in this case, Alexander might have been expected to Hellenise the local population), Alexandria was a *polis* founded on the notion that it is possible to *harmonise* different cultures and people. Having been a relatively conservative and obedient child, Alexander was becoming more fervent and eccentric as the years passed and the ideas behind this city were living evidence of his outrageous nature, going against tradition and proving extraordinary ambition.

In fact, excitable Alexander didn't even wait around to see his new city being built.

In typical fashion, ever hungry for his next challenge, he left as soon as it was founded. Before a single building had been completed. He probably looked back at it over his shoulder as he left, but only briefly. According to both Arrian and Plutarch, after giving orders on its design, he ventured south-west to the isolated Siwa Oasis. This magical settlement, built around hundreds of sparkling springs, lofty olive trees, and palm trees heavy with dates – all in the middle of an endlessly barren desert – feels like something of a miracle. Its abundance led to the oasis's name during Alexander's time: the Field of Trees. It may also have been known as Ammonium: some centuries earlier, Siwa's principal temple had been dedicated to Amun-Re, the god adopted in Greece as Zeus Ammon. Alexander already had the idea that he might be related to Zeus Ammon: his mother told him as much and his development of Pharos linked him to Zeus' daughter, Helen of Troy. Despite being Egyptian, the oracle in Siwa had become an important Greek shrine, too, as Athens had recently dedicated a temple to Ammon. Alexandria was some 300 miles north-east of Siwa, and with almost perfect symmetry the coastal Greek city of Cyrene (today not too far from Libya's

Benghazi) lay north-west of Siwa. The oracle had become especially important to Cyrene, where Ammon had revered cult status. By going to Siwa, Alexander could impress the Egyptians, as well as the Greek cities of Cyrene and Athens. Alexander also went to the shrine to ask questions, a common thing to do with the gods: perhaps about his next move or what he should do with his newly founded city. Alexander could also have been emulating his ancestor Heracles, who was thought to have visited the shrine. Whatever the reason, ancient historians are certain that this was a journey of major personal meaning to Alexander: he was desperate to understand – or perhaps manufacture – his ancestry.

During Alexander's travels, Aristotle's nephew Callisthenes was living up to his uncle's conviction that he'd become a fitting aide to the king. Alexander had begun to send him on exploratory missions. Now, he was ordered to accompany Alexander to Siwa Oasis. Despite travelling with camels and carrying copious quantities of water in animal skin bottles, the strong south winds were even harsher than expected. Any markers they planned to use for directions were wiped away and they were left in a sea of sand. For four long days, Alexander and his group were hopelessly lost. Then, all of a sudden, according to Aristobulus, one of Alexander's contemporary chroniclers, they spotted two crows hovering above them. Delighted to see another lifeform, the group followed the birds in the faint hope that they'd be searching for water – and indeed they were. Arrian calls Aristobulus' account the main version of events, but Alexander's friend Ptolemy later writes of two snakes appearing and leading Alexander to the oracle. That both sources note such an occurrence means that in all likelihood Callisthenes himself recorded some sort of divine intervention. This kind of detail means that none of Alexander's contemporary biographers, even his primary historian Callisthenes, can really be trusted. This is because the myth-making around Alexander was intentional, spear-headed by the leader himself and those closest to him. He even attempted to manufacture his own humility. On one boat journey, the historian Aristobulus is said to have read out a hagiographic account of one of Alexander's duels. Alexander was so incensed about being overpraised that he hurled the book overboard, telling the author to count himself lucky not to have been thrown with it.[3] Alexandria is certainly an extension of such active myth-making: its founding story, like its founder, is inevitably full of legends, beginning at Alexander and expanding over time, forcing us to compete with doubts and contradictions.

Alone in the oracle at Siwa, Alexander asked the priest three vital questions. One concerned past events: whether everyone involved in his father's murder had been caught. The answer was that while Philip's murderers had been eliminated, his real father was immortal. Another spoke to his endless ambition: whether he was destined to rule the world. The answer, unsurprisingly, was a profound yes. And the most important question was about his ancestry. But much as the name of Pharos island was based on a combination of an elderly man's pronunciation and erroneous listening on Menelaus' part, Alexander's unflinching claim to divinity was about to be built on a mix-up. Plutarch writes that in Siwa the polite presiding priest attempted to speak to Alexander in Greek. But instead of 'O paidion' (O, my son), the priest uttered 'O pai Dios' (O, son of Zeus). Alexander didn't need to be told twice. In other ancient sources, though there's no mix-up, Alexander is addressed directly as a son of God. After this visit, he announced himself son of Zeus Ammon, giving him unprecedented authority and filling him with confidence before his advance towards Persia. As the first Western king to be deified, the trip to the oracle would most importantly go on to cement his pharaonic status among the people of Egypt: they very much expected their rulers to possess divine roots. Such integration on the ruler's part hadn't occurred with the Persians beforehand, so this was refreshing for the Egyptians. Alexander was now becoming less Hellenistic and more cosmopolitan, as the new city he'd just founded would also become.

The fact it's steeped in myriad myths and legends makes Alexandria's creation all the more special. The *Romance*, in particular, details supernatural occurrences as the foundations were being laid. One story describes how, as the city gate was erected, a large, ancient stone tablet fell out of it, followed by an army of friendly snakes which dispersed into the newly built houses. After the city was established, Alexander made a sacrifice on an altar that was instantly swooped upon by a huge eagle and the carcass dropped onto another altar, the god of which then appeared to Alexander in his sleep. Alexander asked the god: 'Tell me if the city of Alexandria that I have founded in my name will remain, or if my name will be changed into that of another king?' The god refused to answer straight away, instead leading Alexander to a grand mountain. There, he looked towards Alexander and asked a single question: 'Can you move this mountain to another place?' Impossible, answered Alexander. And so the god prophesied that, unlike the other cities sharing the same founder, this one's name – Alexandria – would remain intact: 'Even so your name cannot be changed into that of another king.'

Alexander went on to enquire about the future, specifically his death. The god's response explained the magnitude of Alexandria:

This city that you found will be the apple of the world's eye.
As the years and the ages go by, it will grow
In greatness, and it will be adorned
With numerous temples, magnificent sanctuaries,
Exceeding all in their beauty, size and number.
Everyone who comes to dwell in it
Will forget the land that bore him.

The god also revealed something about Alexander's immortal relationship with the city:

You shall live in it (Alexandria)
For all time, dead and yet not dead.
The city you have built shall be your tomb.

This god, so concerned with the new city, turned out to be Serapis: an amalgam of two Egyptian deities, Osiris and Apis. Serapis would become the most important deity in Alexandria and its divine protector. This legend proved true in more ways than one. Unlike other places established by Alexander, this city does keep its name. It will grow and grow, becoming the only imperial metropolis he founded. It will boast temples of many different faiths. And many of those who move to it will end up staying.

* * *

As Alexander left his new city, he handed a confidant named Cleomenes of Naucratis the job of developing Alexandria and the well-known architect Deinocrates of Rhodes the task of designing it.

As the Roman engineer Vitruvius narrates in his architectural encyclopaedia, Deinocrates boasted 'good looks and imposing presence'.[4] He set out to meet Alexander, who was stationed with soldiers in the Levant. Deinocrates armed himself with written references from several high-standing members of his home island of Rhodes. Alexander's noblemen told him that he'd eventually meet the king, but nothing happened for days. So Deinocrates came up with a slick plan – literally. Walking outdoors, the royal entourage all turned around to look at something, so Alexander did, too. It was a tall, well-built man walking in their direction. In a nod to Heracles, he'd stripped and oiled his entire body, placed a poplar wreath on his head, flung a lion skin across his left shoulder and carried a big wooden club in his right hand. Curious, Alexander allowed him to approach, asking who he was. 'A Macedonian architect,' the slippery man announced, 'who brings thee ideas and designs worthy of thy renown.'

Deinocrates immediately made a first suggestion with which he hoped to win the favour of the king: turning Mount Athos 'into the statue of a man, in whose left hand I have represented a very spacious, fortified city, and in his right, a bowl to receive the water of all the streams'. Deinocrates wanted to create for Alexander something grander than the Americans did for their presidents, over two millennia later, at Mount Rushmore (in fact, it's thought that Deinocrates' ambitious plan served as inspiration for the Rushmore sculptor Gutzon Borglum). Initially intrigued by the idea, Alexander asked his aides whether such a city, under the statue's hand, would have access to abundant supplies of food. When they explained the difficulty, Alexander rejected the offer because the site was unsuitable. But he asked Deinocrates to stay: 'I would have you stay with me, because I mean to make use of your services.' Perhaps Alexander wasn't quite as much of a megalomaniac as he might seem, though this is probably a better indication of his clear vision for establishing cities as functional places with ample supplies of food and water. And no city he founded had such ample supplies as Alexandria. Deinocrates swapped his lion skin for a cloak to become Alexander's architect, and he was soon entrusted with the task of designing the king's most prosperous city.

Alexandria was intended to exist on a gigantic scale that would impress the entire world. A megalopolis that would send a message of power about its founder and his empire. A super-city that would rival Athens and Carthage. And a crossroads that would link Alexander's Hellenistic world with the treasures of Persia.

Deinocrates used the grid system championed by the Greek architect Hippodamus of Miletus the previous century. The father of urban planning, Hippodamus' ideas were held in high regard, not least by Aristotle. They contended that cities should look like grids: big, straight streets that cut one another at right angles. And in his writing, Aristotle devised what he perceived to be an ideal city. One of its principles was to angle the roads in order to profit from the sea breeze and to shelter citizens from strong winds, something Deinocrates chose to do. The coast at Alexandria was rather low-lying, so by linking Pharos and the mainland to create two large ports, this also helped to shelter the city from the winds.

The streets were more spacious than anything seen before. The two main roads, thirty metres wide, had the equivalent of eight lanes each, with the rest of the roads about half this width. Traffic was expected, so the roads were designed to accommodate horse-riding and chariot-driving. The central street, Via Canopica (Canopic Way), was forty stadia long, around five miles, and is described by first-century BCE historian Diodorus as being 'of unbelievable size and beauty' and dividing the city in two.[5] There would be one main square, the *agora*, and a main market, the *emporium*, near the new docklands and harbour.

Lying between sea and lake, Alexandria was easy enough to secure from the two land entrances, where high walls were constructed. The city's shape was like an oblong, or, as ancient writers described it, a chlamys or military cloak. Hippodamus valued uninhabited space so the central area was left unbuilt so that it might evolve as the city and population grew. The city is likely to have been split according to Hippodamus' categories: sacred, public and private. Alexander wanted a grand palace and temples serving both the Greek and Egyptian gods. From its very founding, Alexandria was intended to promote religious tolerance, integrating two cultures more seamlessly than both its residents and onlookers expected. Egypt wasn't used to this and as a city within a country that had its own rich heritage, Alexandria was sure to raise eyebrows before its powerful hybrid culture filtered to other parts of Egypt.

Since the Egyptians had already built canals stemming from the Nile, just a little adjustment meant that the city also had a constant supply of clean water. A new canal was also built to link the city to the Canopic branch of the Nile, spreading more freshwater and bringing a supply of grain, stone and labourers. Irrigation was left to Alexander's hydraulic engineer, Crates of Olynthus, who established its sewer system. The new canal was used to replenish underground cisterns for washing and cleaning. In a clever move, these cisterns were filled annually, around the end of the summer, when the Nile flood neared Alexandria, turning something historically problematic into something beneficial. The canal became central to Alexandria and would require constant cleaning, maintenance and widening. Within a few years, more canals were opened and celebrated in city-wide festivals.

Within six centuries of the city's founding, the cisterns consisted of thousands of underground chambers, all built of stone, and Alexandria would be referred to as 'the city of one thousand cisterns'. In the early fifteenth century, when Henry V of England sent ambassador Guillebert de Lannoy to Alexandria, he reported:

> The city is all hollow underneath the streets and houses. There, it leads to conduits roofed with arches, through which the wells of the city are watered from the River Nile once a year. And if it were not so, they would not have fresh water in the city, because there is little to no rain, and there are no natural springs in the city ... Every year, at the end of August or throughout the month of September, the River Nile, which rises abundantly at that time, flows to fill all the wells of the city for a year, and the wells outside, whose gardens are watered.[6]

In the late eighteenth century, Napoleon's scholars noted that every house had an underground chamber with a cistern for freshwater.

That the irrigation and sewage systems were established so soon after the founding, and so competently, indicates a location intended and ready to house a significant population. They remained in use until water storage evolved in the nineteenth century. From day one, the cisterns of Alexandria signalled the founding of a magnificent city vying to surpass its contemporaries.

Toilet waste might have been dealt with, but it didn't take long for other messes to surface. Cleomenes, the man Alexander entrusted to develop the city in his absence, swiftly became a hugely unpopular figure.

Alexandria still lacked one of the most important assets required by a city of this size: people. Aside from the original villagers, there were only some construction workers, soldiers and sailors here. Attempting to solve this, Cleomenes travelled to the nearby port town of Canopus, the location of a big bazaar particularly famous for its ointments. The plan was simply to force its residents to relocate to the new city. The Canopus officials didn't appreciate being given such a notice of eviction, but were aware of their new neighbour's power. They solved the issue by offering Cleomenes money in return for staying. This cash would come in useful as Alexandria was being built, though there's every chance that he put a large chunk of it in his own pocket. As the months passed, it was clear that the population of the new city still needed addressing, so Cleomenes tried the same thing again. On this occasion, though, Canopus' officials couldn't afford to make another offer and gave in. Hundreds of disgruntled families relocated their homes westwards to Alexandria.

Cleomenes made no friends with this move and was quickly becoming known for widespread corruption, using every opportunity to make or save money for the city administration and, more importantly, for himself. He decided that he no longer wanted to fund the Egyptian priests, explaining to them that the religious establishment was costing the state too much money. They gave him their 'sacred treasure' so that he would leave them alone. This was probably an empty threat in order to extort money. On another occasion, as one of his servant boys sailed by the river, he was purportedly killed by a crocodile. Cleomenes ordered crocodiles to be wiped out entirely. But the crocodile had long been one of Egypt's most sacred animals – as the deity that protects people and land from the dangers of the unpredictable Nile, the Egyptians believed the crocodile to be vital for their survival – and the extermination plan was going to cause serious upset. The priests of Alexandria met to discuss the potential disaster and came up with the only plan they thought might work: they collected all the gold from their temples and offered it to Cleomenes in exchange for the safety of the sacred creatures. The crocodiles were spared.[7]

Hundreds of miles away, Alexander continued to receive regular updates about Alexandria. News of Cleomenes' corruption was arriving regularly, but Alexander appeared to be turning a blind eye. After all, the city was taking shape. There were tall outer walls, wide central streets, public grounds, royal palaces, temples and private houses. Furthermore, the harbour was attracting ships from across the Mediterranean. This trade was bolstering the economy as taxes were put in place and significant quantities of corn were being exported. The shrubbery around the lakes had also been transformed into vineyards and the lakeside ports accessing the Nile were even busier than those on the coast.

Meanwhile, Alexander was sending Aristotle any books found during his travels. He also sent Aristotle reports and specimens of plants and animals so that his teacher was able to research them and to open the first recorded zoo and botanical garden in the world. Plants included cotton, pepper, cinnamon, myrrh and frankincense. Aristotle's library and school in Athens, the Lyceum, began to attract scholars from around the region, and Alexander was probably its greatest donor. But in 327 BCE, four years after Alexandria's founding, something once inconceivable occurred: Alexander and Aristotle fell out.

Aristotle's nephew, Callisthenes, had been chronicling Alexander's expeditions, but he would become the reason for the irreconcilable breakup of the longstanding relationship between the king and his mentor. The controversy started when Alexander, who had recently conquered Persia, decided that adopting local traditions would earn the respect of his new subjects. While there, Alexander started to wear the local clothes – a purple and white tunic and diadem – and introduced *proskynesis*, the name Greeks gave to Eastern greeting rituals. Depending on one's rank, when someone met Alexander they were to bow, kneel or prostrate themselves before him. Arrian narrates that Callisthenes was outraged by the implementation of what he deemed a 'barbarian' practice, and he voiced his concerns to the court. Alexander was unimpressed and their relationship crumbled from this point. Not much later, a page named Hermolaus, who worked as a valet (for horses, that is), conspired to assassinate Alexander. The plot was foiled but the conspirator's tutor happened to be Callisthenes, and – rightly or wrongly – he was also implicated. Some accounts report that Callisthenes was put in chains until he died, others that he was tortured on the rack, with his wrists and ankles tied up, then crucified. Callisthenes' final breaths signalled the end of Alexander's relationship with Aristotle. Neither could bear to speak to the other.

Alexander must have been sad to lose such a father figure as Aristotle. Three years later, he was even more greatly affected by the death of his childhood friend, confidant and general, Hephaestion. The loss began a sharp downward spiral for Alexander. Arrian reports that 'Alexander spent most of the day prostrate over the body of his friend and would not leave it until he was dragged away'. In similar vein to how the ancient Egyptians respected the Nile, ancient Greek men offered locks of their hair to their local river as a way of thanking it. When in *The Iliad* Patroclus dies, Achilles mourns the death of his closest companion by cutting a lock of his own hair and placing it onto the corpse. It is no surprise that Alexander is thought to have done the same with Hephaestion. 'Alexander was a long time in mourning' and 'for two full days . . . took no food or attended to any other physical need, but lay there on his bed consumed by grief, sometimes expressed in open lamentation, sometimes kept silent within him'. He refused to appoint a replacement commander for his friend's cavalry, renaming it Hephaestion's Regiment, and ordered the execution of Hephaestion's doctor for failing to save his life. After two weeks of ignoring everyone, Alexander finally signed off a lavish funeral for his friend and insisted on driving the funeral carriage himself. He also ordered the sacred flames in the Persian temple to be extinguished, something reserved for the death of the king himself.

Though it occurred hundreds of miles away, Hephaestion's death certainly affected Alexandria. Alexander sent messengers to the oracle in Siwa to check whether Hephaestion could also be worshipped as a god. When the answer came that Hephaestion was not a deity but a divine hero, Alexander decided to honour his friend by building monuments inscribed with dedications to 'the hero Hephaestion'. He ordered Cleomenes to build two such monuments in Alexandria, one on Pharos and one in the city itself. If the task was fulfilled pleasingly, Alexander would turn a blind eye to Cleomenes' corruption. The death also concluded the architect Deinocrates' work in Alexandria, as he was now required to design a magnificent 600-foot tomb for Hephaestion in Babylon. It has long been believed that the most local memorial to Hephaestion is the Stone Lion in the Iranian city of Hamadan, where, long after it was built, local women still smear the lion's nose with jam in the hope that it will bless them with fertility.

By this stage, especially after seizing the Persian palaces, Alexander was by far the richest king and probably the richest person in the world. At his own death, he's said to have still had 50,000 talents (a weight of silver), making him, in today's money, a billionaire in cash alone. It's particularly impressive for someone who never once tried to save money, but, rather, spent it lavishly. Seemingly at the top of the world, here was a wealthy, powerful man for whom an overwhelming sense of loss made him hit rock bottom. Hephaestion was, in many ways, the only certainty in Alexander's life as a ruler and celebrity surrounded by inauthentic interactions: he was someone Alexander could trust and their relationship was unconditional. Losing Hephaestion so suddenly couldn't be compensated. Achievement and wealth could not quench Alexander's despairing grief. Hephaestion's death served as a negative omen. From that day, Alexander's drinking became heavier, first in engrossing desolation and then in distracting imprudence. Less than a year later he would suffer the consequences.

Alexander, who'd also been wounded at least eight times in battle, including a serious chest injury in the Punjab, spent his nights in heavy drinking and wild orgies, before coming down with a fever, possibly typhoid or malaria. Hippocrates, known as the father of medicine, had earlier that century written about wine as medicine: a small amount was a useful cooling agent for fevers, and it could be used to dress wounds, help urine flow, nourish the body and purge sadness. Over the next three centuries, these ideas about wine would be advanced by several physicians in Alexandria including Erasistratus, Apollonius and Cleophantus. But for now, Alexander took Hippocrates' word for it with the caveat that if a little wine was good for fever, then a lot of wine must be even better. He treated his fever with excessive drinking at consecutive parties.

The third-century Greek grammarian Athenaeus cites a now lost note by someone who attended the second party, in which it's reported that Alexander read an extract of the tragedian Euripides' now lost play, *Andromeda*, from memory.[8] The tragedy was part of a trilogy that included *Helen*, the plot of which dramatises Helen and Menelaus' time in Pharos. Diodorus reports that Alexander then downed a final, large cup of unmixed wine in honour of Heracles. Much as literature had inspired Alexander's growth and ambition, it also helped to bring about his end. After this drink, Alexander collapsed.

He was apparently unable to speak in his final days. Several historians contend that he passed his signet ring, with which he would literally stamp his authority, to one of his generals, Perdiccas. Some legends, however, note that when he was asked by the power-hungry men at his side to name a successor, he managed to whisper a single word: *kratistos*. It's a term he'd learnt reading epic literature, one that described his heroes: 'the best and most powerful.'

As the sun set on a June day in 323 BCE, Alexander died in Babylon, aged only thirty-two. It had been eight years since he had laid the foundations of Alexandria by Egypt. Astoundingly, he was never to see the city that bore his name.

Given the risk of endangering his empire, Alexander's death was deemed classified information. But reports soon began to spread. Given his young age and the secrecy surrounding the announcement of his death, it's no surprise that rumours began to surface. His widow, Roxana, was pregnant, so it seemed odd that Alexander died just as he was finally getting an heir (if the child was male). Fingers were pointed at the guests at the final party who were accused of poisoning the wine, at different members of his family and staff, and even at Aristotle. The teacher outlived his student, though his relationship with Alexander continued to haunt him many years later when the political leadership of Athens changed and Aristotle's ties with Macedon forced him to escape the city and leave his Lyceum behind. The theories of conspiracy and assassination related to Alexander's death might never be truly quashed.

What are we to make of Alexander? This is naturally a tough question to answer, but as far as the city of Alexandria is concerned, when he founded it as a young man his personality was a concoction of the ambitious and the tactical, the idealistic and the rash. He followed his gut instinct and his mythical heroes, and in turn attempted to create his own myth. He knew the power of making locals work with him, not against him, and of embracing their cultures and faiths to the extent that he presented himself as something of a cosmopolitan. Rather than force people to worship him, he felt that his success – military, economic and personal – would lead to deserved reverence. In hindsight, Aristotle's note on the nature of his young students is probably the finest summary of the man Alexander would turn out to be: passionate and impulsive, striving for honour and victory, hopeful and impatient.

To some extent, Alexandria was an exception to other settlements Alexander conquered or founded in that he put his own stamp on its governance. Such places were often allowed, on agreed terms, to govern themselves, but Alexandria was governed by his confidants. Alexandria had no substantial history, so his ambitious vision for it could easily outstrip whatever character the place had beforehand. Put simply, other places he conquered, Alexandria he conceived.

When Alexander died, it became evident that the empire was of his own making, almost single-handedly, and that his ultimate power had allowed him to improvise and work things out as he went along. The creation of Alexandria – travelling to Pharos before conceiving and founding it so speedily – is an example of this spontaneity. That he never saw a single building rise in Alexandria attests to his impatience. That he believed that it would be possible to rule the world from the perfect location, and that he could harmonise rather than Hellenise that world, attests to his idealism.

Alexandria was the junction for his biggest geographic and societal ambitions. Diodorus reports that Alexander left detailed plans for his ideal world: a unified and expanded empire; roads and ports that connected the Mediterranean and the Atlantic. Moreover, 'there were cities to be founded and populations to be transferred from Asia to Europe, and also the other way around, from Europe to Asia, the intention being to use intermarriage and the creation of family ties to bring the two largest continents into concord'. He saw migration and multiculturalism as new and effective types of power, making him well ahead of his times and perhaps even ours. If Alexander died with this worldview, then Alexandria – located at the heart of three continents and with its vast cultural makeup – was his ideal when he founded it. As we shall see, Alexandria has variously lived up to *and* resisted its founder's dreams over its long history.

After his passing, with no heir apparent and with an expansive kingdom, there followed an expectedly colossal rush for power that included a race to claim the new city of Alexandria. Even after his death, Alexander would remain the centre of attention as different groups fought over his body, leading to one of the most fascinating mysteries related to Alexandria: just where is its founder resting today?

Alexander's legacy has lived on in literature, art and the scriptures of the Abrahamic faiths. Though he probably wouldn't have predicted it, Alexandria remains his greatest physical legacy. Many well-known cities are named after individuals, including Chennai, Ho Chi Minh City, São Paulo, Sydney, Washington DC and Vancouver. But Alexandria, as the deity Serapis promised Alexander, remains the most striking and enduring example of such a city even today.

Ptolemy the Saviour

A colossal escort was trooping through the inconsistently sandy, hilly and shrubby terrain. The procession had voyaged from Babylon and was heading towards Macedon. At the heart of this substantial convoy was a distinctly special carriage that had taken two years to build. Eighteen feet long and twelve feet wide, this magnificent mini temple was being pulled by 64 mules in rows of four. Its arched golden roof was studded with diamonds, under which stood long beams of gold. The beams had horned rams carved on their tops and were supported by a series of perfectly aligned golden columns. Between the two front columns, a pair of perfectly symmetrical golden lions faced forwards, spears clutched in their sharp-edged teeth. In the very centre of the carriage's roof was an oculus embellished with a miniature palm tree: its branch, along with an olive wreath, cast zigzagged shadows that evoked lightning. Beneath this, the casket, too, was solid gold, but draped with a bright and precious purple cloth embroidered with yet more golden patterns. At the front of the escort, engineers and roadmenders worked hastily to ensure that the carriage had an impeccable ride so that the casket didn't rock. It caught the attention of every village it passed: the ends of the central carriage's beams were decked with bells that, with any movement, made a loud and striking sound that could be heard miles away, while the mules were each adorned with bells that created a constant high-pitched chiming.

The carriage was now travelling westwards through Syria in the direction of the Mediterranean. But rather than continue to edge towards its final destination in Macedon, its commanding officer – a former general of Alexander's named Arrhidaeus – looked apprehensively around him one last time before raising his hand to bring the procession to a sudden halt. He shouted orders for a most unexpected diversion. The escort would now be heading south towards Egypt.

This change of course was nothing short of an elaborately planned hijack that had taken months to devise. Its target? The prize possession lying in the wide casket in the centre of that most stunning carriage: the corpse of Alexander.

The plan was conjured by a boyhood friend of Alexander who had served him in every single campaign. He was known as Ptolemy. If Hephaestion was Alexander's closest friend, Ptolemy was his closest ally. Ptolemy had always accepted living in Alexander's shadows: not only was he loyal, he also chronicled Alexander's life. It had been around two years since Alexander died in Babylon and his corpse, now dressed in a purple cloak, had been embalmed and anointed with honeyed perfumes and placed into a golden coffin lined with scented herbs. Finally, it was to be moved to the traditional royal burial grounds in Macedon under the instruction of Perdiccas, who'd risen to become the commander of the weakened imperial army after Alexander's death. Despite Perdiccas' position as the most powerful person in the Macedonian Empire, Ptolemy was unwilling to accept his authority. Perdiccas ordered the corpse to be brought to Anatolia, where he was stationed, so that he could enter Macedon with it: an entrance that would make him popular and legitimise his imperial rule. But as soon as Ptolemy heard that the corpse was finally going to make a move, he made his own cunning plan. He colluded with Arrhidaeus, who had been in charge of Alexander's body and the hearse's construction over the previous two years. In secret, Arrhidaeus was riskily keeping Ptolemy informed about the status of the corpse and Perdiccas' plans. It's likely that Ptolemy paid the two men and the personnel in charge of the escort a handsome sum, or bribe, in order to take his side.

It didn't take long for news of the hijack to reach Perdiccas, who swiftly sent an army in pursuit. Given the size of the escort and the design of the special carriage, it was moving at a painstaking pace. The carriage had poor suspension on the uneven roads, and there would have been nothing imaginably worse than the corpse falling off. The soldiers, on their galloping horses, managed to catch up in no time. Ptolemy, however, was one step ahead. He'd predicted this exact scenario and was already waiting near Damascus with his very own army. Diodorus writes that Ptolemy was simply waiting to welcome and see Alexander's corpse, but in reality this sizeable army must have been there to ensure the success of the hijack. Ptolemy's army reinforced the escort by surrounding it – Perdiccas' men, who'd been sent with only light weapons for speed, then realised that they had no choice but to retreat empty-handed.[1]

After Alexander's death, complex negotiations had ensued and it was agreed that his generals would support the deceased leader's intellectually challenged half-brother, Philip Arrhidaeus, who would rule alongside Alexander's son. The added complication, though, was that Alexander's child was still a foetus: Alexander's wife had yet to give birth and a baby girl would complicate the plan by not providing a clear successor. This led to a critical and highly anticipated gender reveal. Whether the generals were relieved that it was a boy – Alexander IV – or whether they were only pretending to be happy, is another matter. The truth is that neither Alexander's half-brother nor son were ever really going to rule. Each of the generals was already busy conceiving his own plan for dominance. In no time, the imperial army split into several factions. And within a year of Alexander's death, the regiments were fighting one another. Alexander, who wanted 'the best and most powerful' to rule, would have been disappointed that his successors immediately failed to continue his vision of a harmonised world.

Ptolemy had noticed that the other generals were keen to claim as much of Alexander's empire as possible. So, he had decided to focus on a single slice of the cake, albeit a very enticing one: Egypt. In the immediate aftermath of Alexander's death, his generals reached a compromise, distributing the territories between them. Ptolemy became governor of Egypt.

Two years later, the hijacking of Alexander's body was a significant turning point. This was no ordinary corpse: across his empire, Alexander had succeeded in creating a myth about his supreme power. To most he was a symbol of stability because, despite taking the political autonomy of those he had conquered, he'd respected their cultures and ways of life. To others, he was a saviour from crueller captors. And to some, he was superhuman, even a demi-god. There was no doubt that his tomb would be venerated for ever. Its possession shifted legitimacy to Ptolemy, reducing Perdiccas' own imperial ambitions and allowing Ptolemy's soon-to-be capital, Alexandria, to rise. Had he not made the gamble to snatch the corpse, Ptolemy would have been forgotten, and Perdiccas would have built an empire centred on a different city. Instead and in hindsight, it was thanks to a heist on a cortège and one dead man's body that Alexandria could boast authority so soon after its founding.

Rather than being buried beside his biological father in Macedon, Alexander had requested that he be buried beside his mythical father at the oracle of Ammon in Siwa. Ptolemy had actually accompanied Alexander on that life-changing trip to the oracle and knew how much this place had meant to his deceased friend. Ptolemy could easily claim that the other successors were disrespectfully neglecting Alexander's own desires. Ptolemy's initial plan was to cross the desert and honour his late companion's wish. But he began by taking the body towards Egypt's capital, Memphis, to use it as a way of trying to assert himself as a pharaoh. He passed Palestine and avoided Alexandria, which at this stage in 321 BCE was largely a building site.

But Perdiccas was also bringing his army to Memphis. The lure of Alexander's corpse continued to accelerate the imminent war between his ex-generals. Alexander had captured many elephants for battle but never got to see them in action and, now, his successors were using them to fight one another. The attack on Egypt was complicated by the Nile, which separated the two armies. Perdiccas' infantry and cavalry struggled to cross the river. The elephants were large enough to wade through the water, but their movement was too slow. About halfway into the river, Perdiccas' army was met by Ptolemy's. Suddenly, an arrow bulged from the lead elephant's eye – apparently released by Ptolemy himself – and an onslaught against Perdiccas' troops ensued. The imperial army struggled, drowned and died in their thousands. Witnessing the assault of their friends, Perdiccas' disgruntled men slew their leader. Ptolemy had come out on top and his reputation was strengthening: not only had he shown himself effective on the front line, but he ordered the gathering of all dead bodies from the shore so they could be cremated and the ashes delivered to their families. Like Alexander, he made sure that such deeds were recorded so that his new subjects could perceive their ruler as a man of honour.

At this stage, a seemingly obvious idea hit Ptolemy: Alexander belonged in Alexandria. Ptolemy knew that keeping the corpse in Egypt would further legitimise his rule of the land. He had kept the capital in Memphis, possibly out of respect for the Egyptians, but also because Alexandria was susceptible to naval attack. He had to create allies around the Mediterranean in order to keep Alexandria safe. Once his alliance with Cyprus was secure, Alexander's tomb could create a vital religious cult around Alexandria, helping Ptolemy shift the capital to his desired city. This would allow him to keep the vital corpse in close proximity and to bring some Hellenistic character to Egypt. His friend's wish of being buried in Siwa was no longer convenient.

Alexander was laid to rest in Memphis while a most splendid tomb was prepared in Alexandria. Modern historians suggest that it's from this moment, when Ptolemy presented the stolen corpse to the people of Egypt, that Alexander received the title that has withstood the test of time. He was now *Megalexandros*, or Alexander the Great.

Ptolemy was bringing back to the city that most prized object, the body of its founder. In doing so, he would fulfil a prophecy that the god Serapis had given to Alexandria's creator:

> You shall live in it
> For all time, dead and yet not dead.
> The city you have built shall be your tomb.

We do not know precisely where Alexander was laid to rest. The tomb's exact location remains one of the most prominent and unresolved mysteries of all time.

Alexander wanted to conquer the entire world. Ptolemy, on the other hand, was keen on ruling smaller though significant areas effectively. According to the first-century Roman historian Curtius Rufus, despite being 'a first-rate soldier, Ptolemy was even more talented at, and better known for, the civilian rather than military skills'.[2] And his rule of Egypt was certainly effective.

He began by immediately sacking Cleomenes, the corrupt governor of Alexandria – and, it transpired, a secret agent for Perdiccas. Ptolemy put Cleomenes to death and announced that he'd taken the fortune Cleomenes had amassed and put it towards the city's construction costs. Both moves won support for Ptolemy in Alexandria.

Ptolemy was an ambitious but pragmatic ruler. His experiences gave him confidence and in some ways he took the best of Alexander and avoided the worst. He placed value on economic power and on knowledge and scholarship, and he believed in the effectiveness of cultural hybridity, in his case, Greco-Egyptian. One of his most famous busts, currently in the British Museum, is unusual in that it shows a leader sporting a huge smile. Even his profile on the silver coins of his period have the hint of a smile. Curtius Rufus writes that Ptolemy's 'manner was modest and unassuming', but to me he looks quietly confident.

Alexandria was being built with Alexander's tomb as its centrepiece. Ptolemy also knew that to become the capital, it would need a religious cult of its own. Serapis, whom it was believed had prophesied Alexander's eternal return to Alexandria, was the perfect Greco-Egyptian deity for this task. Serapis was an amalgam of two key Egyptian gods: the green-skinned Osiris and the bull-shaped Apis. While Egyptian deities were often animals, the Greeks were used to human-like, anthropomorphic gods. Ptolemy's sculptor, Bryaxis, gave Serapis a stern face, curly locks and a beard reminiscent of Zeus'. Ptolemy pushed Serapis as a unifying deity that was both Greek and Egyptian, establishing Alexandria as the god's dwelling, and in turn the god as the divine protector of the city.

Ptolemy ordered the construction of a magnificent sparkling temple to honour Serapis. The Serapeum complex was to be built on the highest hill of the not very hilly terrain, the south-western district still referred to as Rhakotis, where a village had long existed. Finally completed in the reign of Ptolemy's grandson, Ptolemy III, the Serapeum ended up housing the largest and most magnificent temple in Alexandria, accessible via over 100 steps of marble, and boasting excesses of gold, silver and bronze. To confirm the Egyptian link, two giant sphinxes were placed on the doorway of the temple. Porticoes ran around its circumference both inside and outside. In the centre stood a vast statue of Serapis made of wood and covered in shining ivory and gold, lit by perfectly positioned windows so that it glowed divinely. In the complex, a staircase led down to a nilometer, a device that measured the Nile's clarity and level during the flood season, fed by an underground channel from the Canal of Alexandria; by placing it in the temple, the gods would protect the Nile's waters from drying up or overflowing. With its own deity in an appropriately grand temple and with the Alexander cult established, Alexandria was now positioned to become a key city.

In 311 BCE – two decades after Alexander first laid its foundations and a decade after his corpse was snatched – Alexandria became the new capital of Egypt, the new capital of the Ptolemaic Empire. Little did people know that this was the start of the city's millennium-long period as the country's seat of government.

That year, the name 'Alexandria' made its first recorded appearance in the Egyptian language on the Stela of the Satrap, a large inscribed tablet. The appearance of 'Alexandria' in Egyptian form signifies the official adoption of its new name and an imposition on the locals, who would still refuse to call it Alexandria for some years to come. The Stela of the Satrap is the most significant object related to Ptolemy today, outlining his role and policies. It confirms Alexandria as the capital as well as the city's direct link to Alexander. The large inscribed tablet marks the heart-breaking end of native Egyptian rule, confirming the forced acceptance of a foreign power. But it also marks the beginning of a new dynasty, the beginning of Ptolemaic Egypt. Under a winged sun and images depicting a king in two sacrificial scenes, the tablet's words note the following about Ptolemy:

> He made as his residence the Fortress of the King of Upper and Lower Egypt, 'Beloved of the spiritual double of Amun, Chosen by Re, Son of Re: Alexandros' – a priestly epithet for the city of Alexandria, on the shore of the great green sea of the Aegeans; Rhakotis its former name.[3]

It remains unclear whether Alexander's tomb was built at this time or later. What we do know is that Ptolemy was chronicling and recording Alexander's adventures, including, perhaps, compiling the mythical *Alexander Romance*. This would make sense since it is the *Romance* that gives Serapis such a key role in Alexander's life and even has the god prophesy Alexander's eternal dwelling in the city: both very useful details for Ptolemy. These stories increased the importance of Alexander yet more and helped to confirm Ptolemy as his rightful heir. Ptolemy even started a rumour that he was Alexander's illegitimate half-brother: all the more effective given the luckless fate of Alexander's relatives.

In 317 BCE, Alexander's mother Olympias led an army to invade Macedon, where some of the troops refused to fight against their former leader's mother. She swiftly arranged the murder of her stepson, the Macedonian king Philip Arrhidaeus. Cassander, one of Alexander's childhood friends and generals, who aspired to rule Macedon, felt that Alexander's relatives stood in the way of his authority, so he had Alexander's mother stoned to death. Around 309 BCE, he went on to kill Alexander's Persian mistress, Barsine, and their illegitimate son, Heracles, as well as poisoning Alexander's widow, Roxana, and their now thirteen-year-old son, Alexander IV. Alexander's last living relative was his only full sibling, Cleopatra of Macedon. After Alexander's death, she was approached for marriage by her brother's generals, including Perdiccas, but, conscious that she was a pawn in a big power game, she went into hiding. Soon after Alexandria was announced as Ptolemy's capital, she began writing to the new Egyptian governor, who ended up paying her a visit. Having grown up with Ptolemy and now aware of his power, she decided to marry him. However, her journey to Alexandria was interrupted as she was kidnapped and taken to a group of women who carried out instructions to kill her. Having now disposed of Alexander's family, Cassander named himself King of Macedon and ruled from Pella, Alexander's capital in Macedon. Alexander's empire had truly broken down and there was no longer a clear centre of power. But only one ruler, Ptolemy, and one city, Alexandria, could now claim a direct tie to Alexander the Great.

The Alexandria we know today might have been founded by Alexander, but it was Ptolemy who created the city. Curiously, the city's origin myth, steeped in the story of Alexander and his exploits, was purposely amplified during Ptolemy's time to increase its fame and status. The citizens walking around the new city bumped into something that referred to its founder at every other corner. Marble sculptures and statues of Alexander were erected, in addition to busts of stone and clay and ivory.

Ptolemy brought together Egyptian and Greek engineers and sculptors to further develop Alexandria. They laid their plans out on big sheets of papyrus. Giant blocks of stone would be used for construction, as well as wood from the forests of Cyprus and the coveted cedars of Coele-Syria, around today's majestic Beqaa Valley. Stepping into Alexandria was like stepping into the future: it was immaculately planned, abnormally spacious, and, under the blue and sunny Mediterranean skies, everything looked slick and sparkling. The city now housed many dazzling temples and palaces, in addition to wide streets and green public parks. To the far east, it was guarded by the Gate of the Sun. To the far west was the Gate of the Moon. The two were connected by the main boulevard: a street known as the Canopic Way. Alexandrians walking along the Canopic Way would enjoy a torch-lined road, marble colonnades, arcaded squares and polished façades. They would be surrounded by soldiers protecting the nearby palace quarters, carriages pulled by horses and wagons drawn by mules and oxen. They may have found some shoppers here, too, women carrying sacks of spices and baskets containing various vegetables home for the evening meal. Colourful villas were built here over the next decades. There was also a space known as the Park of Pan: a pleasure garden in which people lazed around and enjoyed a marble-seated amphitheatre and public bath, all in close proximity to the city's landmark mausoleum.

Alexandria was already a rich city. Not only had Ptolemy seized Cleomenes' monies, he also poured much of Egypt's wealth into the new capital. Ruling Alexandria by itself wouldn't have been sufficient. In Nubia, to the very south of Egypt, vast quantities of gold had been discovered. One of Ptolemy's daughters from a *hetaira* (an educated sex worker) named Thaïs had married the King of Cyprus, so Ptolemy had secured influence on the island, where silver was in abundance. Ptolemy utilised the valuable metals through a royal mint in Alexandria, turning them into coins that bore his smiling face. The silver was used to pay his army, architects and engineers, and, most importantly, the gold helped bankroll the construction of the grand city.

Ptolemy went on to treat Egypt more as an autonomous kingdom than the centre of an empire. Now in his fifties, having won the goodwill of the population, he was being referred to as Soter Ptolemy: Ptolemy the Saviour.

Now that he was establishing a dynasty, Ptolemy needed an heir. He already had three children from Thaïs. Quite the character, Diodorus writes that when Alexander's army rallied to victory in Persia, Thaïs interrupted the celebrations by rallying Alexander to set on fire the palace in Persepolis, including the royal library that held the most important Zoroastrian texts. Alexander is said to have agreed in a 'triumphal revel'. Ptolemy eventually married Eurydice, daughter of one of Alexander's regents, making her the first Ptolemaic queen of Egypt. Ptolemy continued to see other women, including the queen's lady-in-waiting, twenty-three-year-old Berenice, who had accompanied her to Egypt. Within a few years, he married Berenice, who was less than half his age. Berenice became the second Ptolemaic queen of Egypt – but the first queen in Alexandria. She gave birth to his next three children: two daughters named Arsinoe and Philotera, and a son, Ptolemy, who, as Ptolemy II, would be responsible for continuing his father's vision for the city.

Alexandria's centrepiece was Alexander's tomb, known as Soma, or 'the body'. It must have been placed in or around the royal palace quarters. Ptolemy's successors ended up adding their own palaces to this complex, so it grew in size and perhaps in secrecy. Ptolemy had spent at least fifteen years preparing the memorial and it became one of the most famous monuments in antiquity. For centuries, it made Alexandria a pilgrimage destination, a revered place of inspiration, visited by Julius Caesar, Mark Antony and many Roman leaders over the next six centuries, including Octavian (Augustus), Vespasian, Hadrian, Septimius Severus, Caracalla (Antoninus) and Aurelian.

The most baffling question, then, is how this mausoleum could have disappeared.

With so many legends surrounding Alexander, his tomb represents our search for a real and tangible version of the city's founder.

It would help us understand the way he was viewed around the time of his death, the extent to which his folklore was formulated straight after his passing and the way in which his legacy was hijacked by those who followed him. It would also help us comprehend and appraise much of the mythical history surrounding Alexandria's early years.

We can assume that the Street of the Soma was so named because it housed the tomb. Today, this is Prophet Daniel Street, which cuts right through downtown Alexandria, from the centre of the east harbour all the way south to the main railway station. About a mile away, part of the eastern gate remains intact at the Shallalat (Waterfalls) Park, which has a tiny lake, empty footpaths dotted with palm trees and groups of stray dogs enjoying the sun under the ancient wall's ruins. In 2019, archaeologists discovered a marble statue of Alexander in the park, prompting speculation that this could be his burial place. Given his relation to the sun-god, Amun-Re, burial at the Gate of the Sun isn't a far-fetched thought.

According to a second-century text by Achilles Tatius, one of five surviving ancient Greek romance novels, Alexander's tomb stood on the corner of two main streets, at the time known as R1 and L1. Street R1, or Prophet Daniel Street, led from the palace down to the royal port on Lake Mareotis, while L1, or Fuad Street (officially Freedom Way), was the Canopic Way, the ancient city's main boulevard. Today, in the commotion of downtown Alexandria, it certainly doesn't feel like Alexander the Great is resting here. Prophet Daniel Street is full of high street stores and honking cars, not to mention worshippers flocking to one of its three adjacent places of worship: the Eliyahu Hanavi Synagogue, St Mark's Cathedral and the Prophet Daniel Mosque. Fuad Street is packed with besuited men and women coming and going from its many banks, endless queues of people waiting to try the latest iPhone at the telephone network shops and groups walking out of the various chains, some clutching Papa John's pizza boxes and others carrying Costa Coffee takeaway cups. The modern city might follow the exact pattern of the ancient streets, but in all likelihood the ancient city is lying *underneath* the modern one. The family sharing that pizza on the bench and the teenagers nonchalantly sucking at frappuccinos as they lean on the wall might be loitering on the very top of the lost mausoleum. Most Alexandrians do believe that Alexander's tomb is at the intersection of those two streets.

After I walked past the rows of hotels and shops, I had to trek uphill – ten metres above sea level – towards the steeper, winding and narrow roads of the historically affluent but now more modest central area called Kom el-Dikka, meaning the Hill of Rubble. Here, a series of worn-out houses remain colourful, in keeping with a two-millennia-old tradition that the residents refuse to end. In this area, a concentration of unique wall paintings and multicoloured mosaics has been found, including a bust portraying Alexander, discovered in the 1960s and dating from as early as the second century BCE. The discovery has led to the common local assumption that Alexander's resting place is nearby.

Why don't we know the location of Alexander's tomb? For one, it's possible that no one needed to record the spot of such a famous and central landmark. Around 30 BCE, the historian and geographer Strabo visited Alexandria, and much of what we know about the ancient city comes from his writing. He observes that 'a part belonging to the palaces consists of that called Soma, an enclosure, which contained the tombs of the kings and that of Alexander'.[4] It's possible, then, that Alexander was buried in one place initially and moved to a bigger tomb soon afterwards so that Ptolemy and his successors could lie beside him. We might also have the years wrong if the body was brought to Alexandria later than expected; for instance, not by the first but by the second Ptolemy, in order to have a joint funeral for Alexander and Ptolemy I in 282 BCE, thus giving the ruling family further legitimacy. Though unlikely, Alexander might even have been cremated, as Hephaestion was – in which case we would be looking for a monument to his ashes. The tomb may also have been stolen or destroyed in later years as different factions vied for authority over the city. Such possibilities complicate the search for Alexander. Bafflingly, after excursions to the tomb by Roman leaders through the third century, records of such visits all but disappear. Hundreds of attempts to discover the tomb have led hardly anywhere and I have spent hours listening to one theory after another, one of which elaborately places him at the promontory that was once Pharos island.

As I walk around Alexandria's highly urbanised downtown, it's easy to forget that somewhere right here – almost certainly between the western and eastern gates of the Ptolemaic period – and deep under the ground, Alexander is probably resting in a remarkable sepulchre. One of history's most famous humans and one of the world's most sought-after landmarks. It could be anywhere, possibly where we least expect. Maybe under my foot right now, maybe under that couple's bed, that man's kitchen, that woman's herb garden. This entire mystery adds to the aura of the city and its present link with such a monumental past. The infatuating search for Alexander's tomb also confirms the founder's strange immortality. If we do ever find the tomb, though, we might be forced to remember his very mortality.

The Ptolemies

During their life, an Egyptian pharaoh was believed to serve as an intermediary to the gods. Upon death, they become an embodiment of the gods. By passing their sacred earthly powers to a successor, the deceased pharaoh was incarnated as Osiris, god of the underworld. Six years after Ptolemy announced Alexandria as his capital, the Egyptian priests finally accepted him as a pharaoh.[1] So when he died in the winter of 282 BCE, aged eighty-four, it was time for him to be deified.

Ptolemy had successfully transformed Alexandria in several ways that would characterise the city for the next three centuries. When Alexander died, Ptolemy had proposed that the empire should be split into loosely united states, each with a leading governor and with an accompanying council for bigger decisions. Such a radical idea wasn't welcomed by the rest of Alexander's generals. Ptolemy nonetheless managed to position Alexandria as a friend and ally to its neighbours on the one hand, on the other as a city that was politically independent and prioritised its own economic prosperity. Ptolemy was often able to stay neutral while his neighbours scuffled, something rarely heard of at the time. Not only did he give Egypt autonomy within his empire – which reached Libya, Cyprus and Coele-Syria – but Alexandria appeared to have its own added sovereignty within the Ptolemaic dynasty.

When it came to the economy, in a continuation of his unification policies Ptolemy introduced a single currency. The circulation of any other currency in Ptolemaic lands was illegal. This meant that his dynasty was able to monopolise Egypt's vital and valuable grain, which they were shipping into Alexandria via the canals. The city was also minting its own precious currency. The royal mint gave the coins an Alexandrian personality. For centuries, many coins included a portrait of Serapis; those that had the ruler's portrait on them would, on the reverse, have images of such deities as Apis or Zeus, or Alexander the Great with Ammon's two ram's horns on his head, or animals like the eagle or crocodile. By minting the Egyptian drachma – literally meaning a 'handful' – the Ptolemies also controlled a state-run currency exchange system. In modern terms, this was similar to the power of the dollar as the international currency of banking and petroleum. Naturally, the rewards were felt in the state capital, the new centre of world trade, Alexandria. Ptolemy's was a planned economy: the first conscious mercantile economic policy, built around maximising exports, minimising imports and increasing tariffs. As the main harbour with transport links in every direction of the compass via its sea, river, lake and canals, Alexandria's role was vital. In fact, from Alexandria Ptolemy created an intriguing thalassocracy: an empire that ruled the waters, in this case, of the Mediterranean. Focusing on Alexandria made it possible to develop a sea-based empire, and both literal and figurative routes to prosperity for the empire and its increasingly cosmopolitan population.

On top of this, Ptolemy commissioned the most important monuments that defined the ancient city: Alexander's tomb, the Pharos Lighthouse, the Library and adjacent research centre known as the *Mouseion*, as well as the many temples and public gardens. Among these is the oldest surviving garden in the world. Constructed in the late fourth or early third century BCE, it was named Eleusis, meaning Advent, and is now Nouzha Park in the centre of the modern city.

Ptolemy was succeeded by his son of the same name. Ptolemy I made his final marriage in his fifties and Ptolemy II was his youngest child, so although the king lived into his eighties, his successor was still only in his mid-twenties. But as the pharaoh's closest son, young Ptolemy had worked intimately with his father from childhood and had even been elevated to co-regent during the king's final two years in power. Ptolemy junior and his sisters were also educated by one of the most respected intellectuals of the period, a frail poet named Philitas of Cos, who'd been invited to move from his Aegean island to Alexandria.

Meanwhile, Lysimachus, one of Alexander's officers, was now ruling Macedon, and at around the age of sixty he married Ptolemy II's fifteen-year-old sister, Arsinoe. Lysimachus offered his own daughter (also called Arsinoe) to Ptolemy II as a way of confirming support for the new pharaoh, who went on to have three children with her, including another creatively named Ptolemy.

When her husband Lysimachus died in battle, Ptolemy II's sister Arsinoe was forced to flee for her life. She ended up seeking sanctuary with her half-brother Ceraunus, who was himself keen to control Macedon and eventually Egypt. But Ceraunus had plans beyond sanctuary: he offered to marry his half-sister so she could be consort. She agreed under the condition that he protect her children. Instead, he killed both her sons. It was an unsurprisingly sour relationship and they're unlikely to have consummated this political marriage. Before long, Arsinoe was fleeing to her full brother, the new pharaoh Ptolemy II. Far from a heroic homecoming, this was the last resort for Arsinoe, returning to Alexandria crushed, lonely and empty-handed. As she arrived around 276 BCE, her childhood town was unrecognisable. When she had departed as a teenager over two decades earlier, it was still a developing space with several building sites. Now, thanks to her father, it boasted numerous wide roads and towering buildings. Her parents were no longer alive and her little brother, eight years her junior, was a mighty king. But like many individuals in the centuries to follow, it turns out that in Alexandria she could reinvent herself. She convinced Ptolemy II that his wife was conspiring against him. It's at this stage that her brother made a controversial move that would come to represent a peculiar aspect of Alexandrian rule for the remainder of the Ptolemaic dynasty: he decided to marry his full sister. Around 273 or 272 BCE, she became Queen Arsinoe for a third time.

Egyptians often called their spouses 'brother' or 'sister', but suggestions that the royal siblings misunderstood this habit are unlikely. In reality, this kind of union was anything but normal. To the Egyptians and Greeks alike, it was both unconventional and abhorrent. It raised eyebrows.

Mortals weren't supposed to marry their siblings, although the immortals did it all the time. So at the siblings' wedding in Alexandria, a rhapsode was wise enough to read carefully selected lines from

The Iliad: 'Then Zeus addressed Hera, his wife and sister' (18.356). But Sotades, an infamous poet described as being possessed by demons, was championing obscene verse and clever lines of poetry that read the same forwards and backwards as palindromes – now known as Sotadic verse – such as 'llewd I did live, evil did I dwell'. When he found out that the pharaoh was marrying his sister, he decided it would be funny to write about it. One line about the king and queen copulating might have gone just a little too far: 'He pierced forbidden fruit with deadly sting.'[2]

Satirical poetry was rife in Alexandria, but on this occasion Ptolemy II was less than impressed. Plutarch notes that Sotades was arrested and left to die in prison. But the poet Athenaeus, who may have lived in second-century Alexandria, records that Sotades eventually managed to make a run for it. Somehow, probably by bribing the guards, he was able to escape. He hurried straight to the harbour, taking the first boat out of Alexandria. Its destination was the island of Kaudos (just south of its bigger neighbour, Crete). As he arrived, he breathed a sigh of relief: Ptolemy II would be satisfied with his exile and there was no chance they'd send anyone to chase him. This issue hardly required formal extradition either; such requests from foreign governments always came with something in return.

One day around 267 BCE, five years or so after the fateful marriage, Ptolemy II's navy arrived on the island. Its leader, Patroclus, is likely to have heard about an exiled poet when he landed. He found and arrested Sotades. What was he to do with the outspoken poet? He decided to take things into his own hands. Sotades found himself being grabbed and shoved into a heavy metal chest. As it slammed shut into pitch black, he knew he was now paying the ultimate price for what he'd written. The ship sailed back towards Alexandria and, en route, the chest was thrown into the sea. Sotades' demise was Patroclus' rise: the admiral was promoted to fleet commander of the Ptolemaic navy, which boasted 336 ships. And the people of Alexandria now knew better than to mock the incestuous marriage.[3]

The king and queen became known as Ptolemy Philadelphus and Arsinoe Philadelphus – 'the sibling lovers'. Ptolemy would soon rename the city of Fayoum to Arsinoe in her honour, as well as creating a new town on its borders called Philadelphia, or 'sibling love'. A couple of millennia later, the Quakers would name their new city on the east coast of the Americas by the same name, unaware of its incestuous connotations and assuming that it meant 'brotherly love'.

We will probably never know why Ptolemy and Arsinoe married. In truth, if they had wanted to sleep with each other, they could have done so without tying the knot. While we can't dismiss sexual attraction, it does seem likely that this was a political marriage. It indicates divinity since both Greeks and Egyptians knew that gods married their siblings, like Zeus and Hera, and Osiris and Isis. It also suggests a tight hold on the dynasty and clarity in succession (Arsinoe now adopted Ptolemy II's children from his previous marriage). While he could have made her queen without marrying her, the polygamous relationships of the king meant that he had to be clear about ranks: that none of the other women could claim authority. Ptolemy II also seems to have believed in the power of pairs, eventually creating the cult of *theoi soteres* (the saviour gods) for his parents and the cult of *theoi adelphoi* (the sibling gods) for himself and his sister queen.

The marriage also began something that would further define Alexandria: a tradition of strong female rule. Arsinoe was an active and influential queen. Female pharaohs had existed in previous Egyptian dynasties; Sobeknferu ruled from 1806 BCE and there is some evidence that a queen named Merneith ruled as early as 3200 BCE. Influenced by Alexander, though, the Ptolemaic hierarchy initially, almost unconsciously, remained male-oriented. Women during the period had long exercised power but without the public's knowledge. Often, these stints of power were for the sake of their children's futures, after which they took more of a back seat. Arsinoe's new role – exercising serious political and economic influence from a fully public platform – affected Alexandria's future under the Ptolemies by legitimising the potential for women to rule from the very top, something that would endure and prove inspirational right up to the famous Cleopatra VII. The king and queen began to appear alongside one another at public events, but Arsinoe became in her own right a religious and literary patron. She won three Olympic events as a chariot driver and may even have joined in battle. Importantly, she developed a religious cult – a set of temples and a system of rituals devoted to her – which the Egyptians expected of their ruler. She also appeared on coins, sometimes alongside the king, sometimes alone. A temple was built in her honour; a giant Egyptian obelisk was transported 150 miles north from Heliopolis (near modern-day Cairo) to signal the importance of the new temple. Arsinoe also had an historic red crown made especially for her: with ram's and cow's horns, bird's feathers, a sun disk symbol and a small emblem of the sacred cobra in its upright form, it is a crown that Cleopatra VII later cherished. Above all, Arsinoe had an official monarchical title, thus giving Alexandria its first female ruler.

The new king and queen were different from any previous rulers in the sense that Alexandria was their home. Their father, Ptolemy I, had moved his residence from Memphis to Alexandria, so both Ptolemy II and Arsinoe were raised in the young city. As children then as rulers, they resided in the palace complex, which, according to Strabo, spanned a whole quarter of the city. Its buildings, which included living quarters, banquet halls and temples, were surrounded by vast green gardens that were also used for outdoor audiences and feasts. The gardens included little streams and direct, private access to the harbour. There was also an area that Ptolemy II kept as a game reserve for recreational hunting and fishing, as well as another area that was his personal zoo. Outside the palace complex, to accompany the sculptures of Alexander, new statues were erected, including large figures of the king and queen at Alexandria's harbour, to symbolise a united dynasty.

Ptolemy I had waged fewer wars than Alexander. Now, Ptolemy II was even less concerned with expanding his empire but more with ensuring that Alexandria was an effective capital. The empire's finances were being controlled from Alexandria, purposely establishing it as the administrative and economic centre of the region through its port, mint and record-keeping. As a result, the coastal city began to swim in a seemingly endless sea of bureaucracy. This is clear from the Zenon Papyri, a stash of ancient documents compiled by a man named Zenon of Kaunos, who was an employee at the treasury before becoming private secretary to Ptolemy II's financial minister in Philadelphia. The three decades of papyri provide the earliest available glimpses into Ptolemaic rule: administration (including land ownership), economy (including agricultural production), taxation, and even one detailed memorandum to Zenon that reports two Greek men for abusing and selling women as sex slaves.

The bureaucratic system included a royal secretary for diplomatic affairs, a chief secretary, a drafter of royal edicts and military leaders. Civil administration was largely concerned with finances: this was headed by the *dioiketes*, a chancellor or chief financial minister with headquarters in Alexandria, with local *dioiketai* around the country reporting to him centrally. When Alexander died, he'd left Egyptian nomarchs, or governors, in charge of the country's 36 nomes, or provinces. Ptolemy II increased this number to 42. Each nomarch had his own administration consisting of toparchs, who oversaw agricultural production, and *oikonomoi*, who oversaw finances. The royal and local scribes were in charge of administrating land and estates. The nomarchs, toparchs and scribes tended to be Egyptians, but Greeks took the most important positions in the civil service. Ptolemy II also appointed a troop commander, or *strategos*, directly to each nome. By the time of his successor, Ptolemy III, these *strategoi* had become more powerful than the *dioiketai*. The bureaucratic system was being extended to the foreign territories and, as the years passed, the capital began to send officials away as *strategoi* to ensure that the most powerful people in Libya, Cyprus and Coele-Syria were from Alexandria. The *oikonomoi* who oversaw the finances of these territories were all under the direct control of Alexandria and the *dioiketai* of these areas were answerable to the chief *dioiketes* in Alexandria.

During Ptolemy II's reign, a serious war ensued between the rising Republic of Rome, which had overthrown their monarchy a couple of centuries earlier, and the most dominant force in the western Mediterranean, Carthage. Initially, the two states were contesting the isles of Sicily and the battles were fought ferociously at sea. Here was a naval war right on the Mediterranean that Alexandria tried its best to ignore. The First Punic War continued from 264 to 241 BCE, though the conflicts carried on for another century. The devastating war, which second-century BCE Greek historian Polybius dubbed the 'longest, most continuous, and most severely contested war', benefitted Alexandria in a number of ways.[4] It continued Ptolemy I's vision of Alexandria's autonomy and his insistent prioritising of the city's interests. The war also weakened Rome and Carthage materially, economically and militarily. Rome ultimately won and ordered Carthage to pay reparations, and it was only then that Alexandria made its decision to create positive relations with the up-and-coming city through the establishment of an embassy for the Roman Republic. Meanwhile, Carthage pleaded with Alexandria for a loan of 2,000 talents (today around £40 million): a perfect indication of the decline of one power and the rise of another. Keen to confirm its loyalty to Rome, Alexandria responded with a resounding no.

Alexandria's foreign policy was flexible and adaptable, and now a small number of Romans began to move to the city. Some even joined the Ptolemaic army, and by the time of Ptolemy IV (known as Ptolemy the Father-Lover) a couple of decades later, a Roman was occupying a high military rank. The army in Alexandria was initially a mix of Greeks and Macedonians who'd fought in Alexander's already diverse army before the city's founding, and it was strengthened with Egyptians. Multi-ethnic armies were considered hard to manage effectively, but the Ptolemaic army proved otherwise.

The diverse makeup of the city was becoming a unique and recognisable feature. It was now home to tens of thousands and, by the first century BCE, hundreds of thousands. The historian Diodorus, who visited Alexandria then, writes that its census reported 300,000 free residents – but the population itself could have been double that. The city attracted thousands of immigrants from around the Mediterranean and beyond. They were following the Alexandrian Dream. As for the city, it was created from scratch and always had trade in mind, so welcoming rather than othering people was an economically sound plan. In Alexandria, economic prosperity and societal tolerance were inextricably linked.

Shortly after Alexandria's founding, Greeks became the most significant and influential minority. Thousands crossed the Mediterranean from Thrace (modern-day Bulgaria, Greece and Turkey), from the Aegean islands, from Sicily, as well as from mainland Macedonia, Asia Minor (west Turkey) and Syria. Alexandria also became home to Jews (especially Judeans, from Palestine), Libyans, Midianites (nomads from north-west Saudi Arabia), Minaeans (Yemen), Nabateans (northern Arabia and the southern Levant, today around Jordan and north Saudi Arabia) and Phoenicians (from the Mediterranean side of the Levant, today around Lebanon and Syria). From the third century BCE, they would be joined by Bactrians (Central Asia, around Afghanistan), Cilicians (the Turkish–Syrian border), Ethiopians and Romans, and over time, by Judhams (from the deserts of southern Levant, today south Jordan and west Saudi Arabia), Lakhmids (Yemen), Scythians (nomads of Iranian origin who were scattered as far north as Ukraine and Russia) and Indians.

Buddhist missionaries came to Alexandria as early as the mid-third century BCE. In South Asia, inscribed edicts from the time of the Indian emperor Ashoka, who ruled from 268 to 232 BCE, confirm that he sent emissaries and medicinal plants to the Mediterranean, naming Ptolemy II as the recipient. It is likely that those emissaries developed a religious community and even started families in Alexandria, becoming a part of the city's early makeup.

And, of course, there were the Egyptians: not just the few who were living in the region already, but those who had heard about the new city and migrated northwards from as far south as Nubia. Alexandria was becoming famous as a wholly different kind of Egyptian city, one where work was readily available and it was possible to prosper.

Alexandria didn't develop a vast slavery system like Athens and Rome because employees, especially the peasants from the Nile villages, were very cheap to hire. Instead of slavery, the Ptolemaic system was one of fiscal exploitation. When their military took captives, however, a slave market developed that included Levantines, among them some Jews.

During the reign of Ptolemy II, Egyptians still formed the majority of the population – though within a few decades the Greeks became the majority. Egyptians worked predominantly in agriculture and construction, and there were also opportunities in the city for trade, commerce and official positions. Alongside the tax system that funded the army, Egyptian employment, especially in farming, was vital to economic stability. Egyptians were also needed elsewhere within the system as translators and administrators who could help spread the government's messages to the population. And there remained a small but important elite of priests who preserved the indigenous culture. The Ptolemies wanted to remain popular among the native population and were wary of overtaxing the Egyptians or trampling on their cultural habits and beliefs.

The strong Greek hierarchy, in addition to the existing geographical division of the city into five quarters, made Alexandria susceptible to segregation. Just because someone lived in Alexandria, it did not necessarily make them an Alexandrian. In fact, the benefits of being a 'free citizen' of Alexandria were substantial and closely guarded. This was the case in Athens beforehand, where citizenship, reserved for males, was a way of ensuring differentiation between mainland Greeks and 'barbarians'. Following Aristotle's notion that a citizen isn't just someone who administers the law and rules, but can also be someone who upholds the law and submits to rule, the Ptolemies allowed both men and women to be citizens. Alexandrian citizens paid less tax, were better protected and treated by the judicial system, sometimes received monetary gifts from the government and had the right to participate in the Olympic Games. To become a citizen, rather than a resident, there were strict prerequisites. For one, both your mother and father had to be Alexandrian citizens, meaning that the citizen population increased gradually over time. When a child reached adolescence, their application for citizenship would be scrutinised. On specific days of the year, teenage boys and girls would crowd around with their parents at a wall in the great gymnasium, where the list of accepted citizens was put on display. Documents and inscriptions suggest that if you made it to the list, you would be assigned to a specific suburb of the city. Citizens were also guaranteed a school place in one of the many new gymnasia offering a high-quality education.

Both boys and girls could receive a primary education. The wealthier chose private home-schooling, and some tutors opened businesses. Young Alexandrians studied the Greek tragedies and epics, including Homer. A second-century terracotta lamp depicts a scene from an Alexandrian gymnasium. Set in grand surroundings under colonnades, it shows three scenes of school life: a schoolmaster disciplines a student on the left; in the middle a pupil cleans himself with strigil (an instrument with a curved blade that scrapes off dirt and sweat before bathing); and on the right a boy is sprinting while holding a torch. Terracotta figures from the Ptolemaic period also show girls wearing cloaks, suggesting that they were educated outside the home: one holds a diptych (a tablet used like an exercise book) in her lap; another is playing the lyre; and one is dancing, which girls studied instead of athletics. That said, some girls studied only until they could read and write, and those without citizenship remained illiterate.

The thousands of Greeks who had moved to Alexandria formed the second group in the hierarchy: respected residents but not yet citizens. Below these were two important groups that were generally excluded from the key privileges: the Egyptians, whom we've already mentioned, and the Jews. The majority of Alexandria's Jews had arrived from the Holy Land immediately after the city's founding, under the rule of the first two Ptolemies, who'd decided to create a separate area of the city for the Jews. This would allow them to observe their own laws and customs without affecting or being affected by other Alexandrians. The Jewish quarter occupied the eastern part of the city, on the shore, but without a harbour. Beyond this area, some Jews lived among the general population and, over time, synagogues were built all around the city.

This was a far cry from Alexander's vision: a harmonised *polis* in which free citizens enjoyed equal status. Instead, this was a highly stratified society, an example of absolutist and divine rule and one that was about to get even more geographically demarcated.

When it came to language and religion, however, Alexandrians were able to find common ground. They communicated using a new language, or, more precisely, a new Alexandrian dialect of Greek that came to be known as Koine (Common) Greek. The dialect appears to have begun in Alexander's armies but took shape as different Egyptian and Hebrew speakers tried to communicate in the new official language, and as second- and third-generation citizens changed and often simplified the Greek. Eventually, Koine Greek would become the language of the Bible and spread beyond Alexandria to the Greek mainland in the post-classical period, when scholars like Plutarch used it. As for religion, Alexandria had a number of popular gods. Poseidon, the god of the sea, was especially important in the harbour area. And the city was relatively united thanks to the cult of Serapis. It also had a new, albeit less important deity in Agathos Daimon, the Noble Spirit: this god took the form of a serpent, a reminder of the city's founding legend when snakes spread into the new homes as its gates were being raised. Many Alexandrian families had little figurines of this deity in their homes and offered him wine after evening meals to show gratitude and seek good fortune. Agathos Daimon became a much-loved deity and constituted a key part of the city's anniversary celebrations every year. Such public events began to play a major role in Alexandria's calendar. Most notably, Ptolemy II began an extravagant four-yearly celebration in honour of his father.

People gathered in their thousands around the city's main stadium, part of the expansive royal quarters, where the grand procession was about to begin. Throughout the city's main streets, many more lined up, ready to enjoy the festival. The pharaoh had promised them something more spectacular than they could possibly imagine: giant mechanical floats.

We have a first-hand account of one of these grand processions. Callixenus of Rhodes – about whom we know little apart from the fact that he probably lived in Alexandria during Ptolemy II's reign – wrote a book that has never been found, *Peri Alexandreias*, or *About Alexandria*. That work would have explained so many unknowns about the city at the time. However, the author Athenaeus, who lived near Alexandria in the early third century, included some of Callixenus' work in his own writing, so we have access to four fragments today.[9] Without full context, the material doesn't make complete sense, but it does give us an idea of the festival's fascinating themes and sheer extravagance. This was a show of power and wealth from the Ptolemies that also served to deter any potential invaders. It gave Alexandrians the first taste of their own independent cultural identity: they became a festival-loving society famed for indulgence and frivolity. Trade also increased during this time, as southern Arabian tradesmen (from Yemen) made their way to Alexandria for the festivals.

The event had many different phases. To kick things off, men dressed as horses ran out of the stadium to huge cheers; they approached the crowd directly, both as part of the entertainment and to act as a guard for the procession. These men were *sileni*: in Greek mythology, drunken followers of Dionysus, also known as Bacchus, the god of wine, festivity and theatre. Next came the absurd and hilarious satyrs, drinking and cavorting, carrying gilded torches made from ivy leaves and costumed in silly ears, pug noses, tails and even the odd giant penis. As the roar of the crowd grew and the procession moved towards the main boulevard, the *nikai* ran around with enormous incense burners – almost three metres high – adorned with gilded ivy leaves. The *nikai* represent Nike, the goddess of victory, who has golden wings and is always barefoot (ironic, given the famous usage of the deity's name today). As the trumpets grew louder, two dramatic heroes entered: a man and woman wearing tragic costume and carrying palm branches. Many women followed carrying fruits and berries, vines and ivies, and even snakes and daggers.

Eventually, the floats appeared to the waiting crowds – and they were worth the wait. The first was almost six metres long by four metres wide, pulled by 180 men. On it was a statue that fed into the city's developing fascination with the arts: decorated with little crowns, drums and dramatic masks, it represented the three theatrical genres of satire, comedy and tragedy. Alexandrians then looked on in awe as the next float displayed an incredible four-metre-high mechanical statue that stood up and sat down over and over again. Even more astoundingly, when it stood it revealed a golden vessel that poured out milk for the masses. As though milk wasn't enough, the next float, pulled by 300 men, carried a gigantic wine press measuring eleven by seven metres that spread the local wine into the streets. Sixty men dressed as satyrs jumped up and down on the heaps of local grapes to the sound of flutes. Several floats later, an array of animals, some from the royal zoo and others brought especially for the ceremony, showed how far the Ptolemies were travelling. They included leopards, cheetahs and caracals, as well as animals the locals had never seen before like rhinoceros, a giraffe and a 'large white bear'. Men also carried branches from trees, wild birds hanging from them, as well as cages that housed noisy parrots and multicoloured peacocks. After the animals came the direct propaganda: small statues of the city's founders – Alexander and Ptolemy I – golden crowns of ivy on their heads. But the pair also had their own larger sections of the procession, when a bigger, golden statue of Alexander was carried on a chariot pulled by elephants and Ptolemy I's shiny crown was displayed on his huge throne. Finally, the rowdy entertainment ended with a display not only of power but organisation as the uniformed infantry and cavalry marched impeccably in their thousands through the city. The status of Ptolemaic Alexandria was crystal clear: the festival was intended to put this advanced, cultured city on a par with Athens and its Olympic Games.

The first two Ptolemies well and truly established Alexandria as a powerhouse in every sense. Ptolemy II enhanced what his father built, adding columns and marble to the streets and scented perfume to the temples and courts using rare ingredients his father and Alexander had found in the Persian perfumeries, all shows of luxury and wealth. With the most important civic sites constructed, Ptolemy III focused on building places of worship; the Ptolemies paid special attention to Egyptian temples in order to confirm their pharaonic status. The city had established deities and iconic figures, too, to help promote its reputation and prowess. Alexander the Great and Ptolemy the Saviour remained symbols of its power, and after his death Ptolemy II joined them as Ptolemy the Great. The Ptolemaic period remains one of the most important in Alexandria's history. It is not only the time when the city was built but when it began to develop and consolidate its own cultural character, different from both its Egyptian and Hellenistic neighbours. The Ptolemaic treatment of Alexandria as a regional state capital and world trade centre resulted in economic growth and sparked a new era of Egyptian – and particularly Alexandrian – architecture, art, culture and intellectual achievement, best epitomised by two new light-emanating landmarks that were about to set the city apart from the rest: a majestic lighthouse and a great library.

Wonder of the World

I've just stopped at a street vendor to purchase some *termes* – bright yellow lupini beans. They're soaked in warm water for days before being showered with salt and lemon juice. You put the circular bean between your middle teeth and pop the seed directly into your mouth, keeping the skin in your fingers. One of my favourite seaside snacks, there's evidence that lupini beans existed thousands of years ago in Egypt, as early as the twenty-second century BCE. At this particular, panoramic spot of the Corniche, one small thing has long captivated me in the distance: a bright light that flashes leisurely in the mist. I have no idea how far away it actually is. As a child, the flashing lighthouse often made me visualise being at sea by night; rather than appreciating its light, it emphasised that limitless feel of the ocean in the pitch black.

It also served as a reminder of the fact that, for centuries, Alexandria boasted one of the tallest man-made structures on earth. The last of the ancient Seven Wonders of the World.[1]

When Alexander arrived, he built a causeway that connected the island of Pharos to the coast in order to found the city. Alexandria's great lighthouse – the first in recorded history – was placed right there on the island and came to be known as Pharos.

Visitors from other seaside locations are often surprised by the sheer vigour of the waves on the Alexandrian sea: they are high, noisy, incessant. The blue colour of the water, unlike the lighter turquoise of other Mediterranean locations, makes the bright white waves obvious even from a distance. Onshore winds cause waves to break earlier and further out to sea, with white foam falling into the water. These are those lethargic waves that look excited at first but suddenly get too lazy to come all the way over to greet you. Offshore winds cause waves to break later in the shallow water, much closer to land. These aren't the foamy ones, but the ones that jump vertically at the last second as if they're trying to surprise you. They make a thunderous noise; 'loud the billows roar', as Homer somehow knew about this location. Alexandria gets both types of wind and both types of wave.

The Heptastadion causeway did more than connect the mainland with the island: it created a peninsula that provided the opportunity to have not one but two major harbours, one on either side of it. A choice of two harbours was useful due to the heavy winds and waves. Soon after being built, it was cleverly cut down the middle to create two channels with bridges above them so ships and carriages could get from one harbour to another without going all the way around. This meant that ships were protected from wave disturbance because they could move depending on the type of wind and wave hitting the shore. Making the unpredictable harbour safe meant that Alexandria could import and export at leisure.

The geographer Strabo describes the two harbours as 'beautifully enclosed both by the embankment and by nature' and so 'close to the shore that the largest ship can be moored at the steps'. To the west, between Pharos and where Rhakotis existed, was Portus Eunostos, also known as the Harbour of Fortunate Return. To the east, the larger Portus Magnus, or the Great Harbour. Just off it, there was a tiny island called Antirhodos, and to the far east was the royal section of the harbour. On the far south of the western harbour was a mini harbour called Kibotox, or 'the box'. This led to a canal that connected Alexandria to the rest of Egypt, southwards through the western suburbs of the city, then either into Lake Mareotis, or eastwards across the southern wall of the city on the Canal of Alexandria, which led to the Nile. Ptolemy II developed a trading town, Taposiris, on the waterway of Lake Mareotis, and just west of it, the lakeside village of Marea was also built up so that Mareotis had its own port and additional canals leading to the Nile, and in turn to the Red Sea.

Uniquely, then, the city was connected with Africa via the Nile, the Levant and Europe via the Mediterranean, and Arabia and India via the Red Sea. Alexandria became the only link between Europe, Africa and Asia, allowing trade, movement of people and cultural exchange. Its series of interconnected harbours linked the lake, the river and the oceans – and they connected Alexandria with the world.

Ships of all sizes and colours would spread around the harbours. Exports were varied and in demand: glass, lamps, pottery, silverware and bronzeware, in addition to textiles and papyrus. As well as monopolising the Egyptian oil market, Alexandria grew abundant quantities of wheat, olives and vines on the shores of the lake. Enormous amounts of wheat were being sold to an ever-increasing population in Rome. Delivered via barges on the River Nile and Lake Mareotis to southern Alexandria, the grain was inspected for quality, packed and transported via canal to the Great Harbour, where it would either be stored in docks or loaded onto ships heading for Rome. There were three further items produced in Alexandria that brought particularly valuable returns: olive oil, beer and wine. Recently discovered wine amphorae – wine bottles with two small looped handles – from as early as the first century BCE prove the export of local wine from the Mareotis area around the lake. Fascinatingly, such traces have been found on the Strait of Sicily and further away at the Gulf de Fos in France, near Marseilles, proving that Alexandrian wine was in demand. In the first century BCE, both Virgil and Horace praise Mareotis wine in their writings, describing it as white, sweet and aromatic.

Alexandrians also made the most of their location to travel. In the second century BCE, the Ptolemies learnt how to use the monsoon winds to sail directly from the Red Sea to the Indian coast, thus taking complete control of the Red Sea ports. Strabo records fleets of more than 120 ships setting sail towards India. According to a cargo list on a papyrus discovered in the late twentieth century, a huge ship named *Hermapollon* crossed the Indian Ocean and its crew returned to Alexandria with some 140 tonnes of pepper, 80 boxes of muskroot plants and 167 elephant tusks weighing 3.3 tonnes. On other occasions, they would return with sparkling gemstones and pearls, in addition to fine silks. They also brought back malabathrum (a cinnamon-like plant) and spikenard (a honeysuckle plant) whose leaves were pressed to make essential oils for perfume and medicine.

A disproportionately high number of wealthy individuals began to roam the city: rich beyond what most people at the time had imagined possible. The import and export potential in Alexandria meant that landowners and merchants, mainly Greek, became wealthy very quickly: by today's calculations, they were becoming millionaires. Money came coupled with power. For instance, Ptolemy II's chancellor Apollonius rose to power after making a fortune from land and international trade, and he eventually owned properties in Philadelphia further south and Galilee in Palestine. The rich also employed thousands of locals on low wages. The harbours were at the epicentre of all this activity.

At night-time, navigating towards the harbours was a challenge even for the best sailors. The shores of the Egyptian coast have very few contours and, before the advances in navigational technology, mariners relied heavily on assessing sea level. The country's coastline was also broad and featureless; once on shore, you could find yourself in a desert. It's for that reason that Homer had described Pharos in *The Odyssey* as the solitary harbour in the 'long and wearisome journey . . . over the misty deep to Egypt' (4.483–82). What's more, some sources suggest that near Pharos were several wreckers, who purposely brought about shipwrecks so they could steal from the wreckage. These factors meant that one simple but vital addition – light – could propel Alexandria into an even more prosperous future. It would not only help navigation from a distance and increase the number of ships arriving, but it would also serve as reassurance for their safe entry into the harbour. And so, towards the end of Ptolemy I's reign, variously thought to be between 300 and 282 BCE, construction began on something that would adorn the city's harbours: a wondrous lighthouse.

Fourteen years after construction had begun, the lighthouse stood taller than anything the locals or visitors had ever seen before. A product of the first two Ptolemies, it was devised by Ptolemy I and inaugurated by Ptolemy II shortly after his father's death.

The Pharos rose majestically into the sky and overlooked the shore. At least one hundred metres tall, the most detailed estimates place it at either 117 or 135 metres. The Arab travellers who saw it between the tenth and fourteenth centuries consistently reported its height being between 103 and 118 metres. It might even have been closer to 160 metres, or, in the less realistic accounts of Epiphanes, 306 fathoms (560 metres). The Pharos was visible from a distance, probably more than thirty miles away, or in one account, as far as 300 miles.

In the thirteenth century, the Andalusian traveller ibn-Jubayr reports of the city:

> Among the greatest of its wonders that we have seen is the lighthouse that God Almighty has placed via the hands of whoever created this 'sign for those who discern' (Quran 15.75) and a guide for travellers without which they would not be guided from the sea to the land of Alexandria. It can be seen from more than seventy miles and its build is extremely lofty and reliable, in length and width, competing with the skies in height. Description falls short of it and the eyes fail to comprehend it, relating it [in words] is inadequate, and the spectacle is vast.[2]

The lighthouse was built of white limestone that reflected light and seemed to glow. It was formed of three tiers that got smaller as they rose into the air, and it rested on a ten-metre cylindrical base. The lowest and biggest tier was rectangular and formed almost half of the structure. The middle tier, about half the size of one beneath it, was octagonal, and the top tier, housing a mirror and a furnace, was a hollow cylinder with pillars around its circumference. A long, arched ramp provided access to the lowest tier, from which stairs led to around seventy rooms, including one that led underground to the sea.

Standing loftily at the very top of the lighthouse was a sculpture of the god of sky and thunder, Zeus, holding a flame-like thunderbolt in his hand. The city's links to Zeus were already plentiful due to his relation to the Pharos island in Homer and his supposed fathering of the city's founder. On the seaward side of the tower, a large Greek inscription dedicated the Pharos to Zeus. Al-Masudi, the tenth-century Arab historian, writes that he saw an inscription in large letters of lead, each one a cubit (about half a metre) in size, making the dedication easily visible to everyone arriving.

As the bright rays of the sun shone during the day, they reflected on the mirrors that were placed at the very top of the lighthouse. At night-time, as the Byzantine poet John Tzetzes celebrated, it was 'a beacon for salvation'.[3] Light emanated from the fiery furnace like a candle in pitch black, enhanced by the mirrors.

There are tales of tired donkeys trekking up the building with firewood and fuel on their backs. Given the short supply of timber in Egypt, the momentous lighthouse might have been running on animal dung, though it's also possible that the fire was oil-fed. Ancient mariners preferred to sail during the day anyway, so the bright limestone and the mirror, made from polished metal and burnished bronze, may have been sufficient. On top of this, the lighthouse was a landmark in and of itself.

Replicas began to be built around the region, including one that still exists today: the Pharos of Abusir by Lake Mariout. Constructed at around the same time, it tells us something about how the main lighthouse might have looked. But at only a fifth of the original Pharos' probable height, it may have been a non-functional commemorative ode to the Ancient Wonder.

Much of what we know about the original lighthouse has come from the Arab historians who travelled to Alexandria over a millennium after it was constructed, and there are just three reliable sources from ancient times: geographer Strabo and historian Diodorus in the first century BCE, and author Pliny from the first century. In 2001, for the first time in thousands of years, a contemporary account of the lighthouse finally became available. It was discovered by luck in 1903, when tomb raiders disturbed an anonymous corpse around two millennia after it had been laid to rest. They'd found exactly what they were looking for: a tomb housing a mummy. They opened the sarcophagus to see what lay beneath the lid, unfurling the linen to examine the person inside. To their surprise, they unravelled a roll of papyrus from the chest cavity. Composed in the third century BCE, this papyrus had been preserved for over two thousand years. When mummies were prepared, it was a long, strenuous and expensive process. The organs were removed and dried, the body rinsed with wine and spices and the corpse covered with salt. At around the fortieth day, the corpse was stuffed: the cavity filled with linen, sand, sawdust or leaves. On the seventieth day, the mummy was wrapped with hundreds of yards of linen before being placed in a sarcophagus. So, in the second century BCE, a mummy maker, or embalmer, was busy preparing a corpse in his workshop when he must have run out of materials with which to stuff the body. He used scrolls of discarded papyrus that nobody needed, including a piece five feet long and a foot wide, which he placed in the chest cavity.

It's not known where the papyrus ended up for the next several decades after the raid, but in 1992 it appeared on the European grey market – not illegal like the black market, but unofficial and unlinked to the original supplier or creator – where it was purchased by the University of Milan. It turns out that the papyrus was inscribed in Ptolemaic Alexandria. It has writing on both sides: one side contains over 100 poems totalling 600 lines of poetry, the other contains mythological materials. Its length makes it among the earliest surviving examples of a full poetry book. Since two of the poems were already known to be written by a man named Posidippus, the rest were attributed to him.

Posidippus lived in Alexandria and was a member of the courts of Ptolemy I and Ptolemy II. Before the discovery of this papyrus, he was thought only to have written poetry about love and wine. But it turns out that he'd written dozens of poems about a range of topics including the Pharos, probably around the time of its completion. The rarity and value of this source can't be exaggerated: it's the earliest and only piece of writing on the lighthouse from the very period of its installation.

And so this tower cutting through the breadth and depth
    of heaven beacons to the farthest distances
by day, and all night long the sailors borne on the waves
    will see the great flame blazing from its top—[4]

Our only contemporary source on the lighthouse starts the poem by thanking someone called Sostratus of Cnidus: 'The Greeks' saviour god – O mighty Proteus – shines from Pharos / thanks to Sostratus of Cnidos, son of Dexiphanes.' Before this papyrus was discovered, Sostratus had been mentioned elsewhere, though this poem might be the source used by early historians before it was lost. There is a record, in the 270s BCE, of an ambassador for Ptolemy II by that name, who's likely to have been a wealthy diplomat and perhaps a member of the monarchical court. We also know that in the 330s BCE an engineer named Sostratus helped Alexander's then-general Ptolemy capture Memphis by devising a plan to divert the Nile's waters. When it comes to the lighthouse, Strabo claims that 'a friend of kings' named Sostratus is the one who gifted this landmark to the mariners. But Pliny notes that 'King Ptolemy, in a spirit of generosity, allowed the name of the architect, Sostratus of Cnidus, to be inscribed on the building itself'.[5] In the second century, Lucian of Samosata makes the claim that Sostratus 'wrote his name on the masonry inside, covered it with gypsum, and having hidden it inscribed the name of the reigning king', knowing that before long 'the letters would fall away with the plaster and there would be revealed: 'Sostratus of Cnidos, the son of Dexiphanes, to the Divine Saviours, for the sake of them that sail at sea.'[6] Changing the dedication from the sovereigns to the sailors is as heartening a sentiment as it is a challenge to authority. So, how should we treat these suggestions that Ptolemy I might not have financed the lighthouse, or that his architect made a secret dedication? There should be no doubt that the Ptolemies did pioneer the lighthouse, but we cannot be sure who designed it.

If the lighthouse were funded by Ptolemy I, wouldn't there be more noise about that and a clearer inscription praising the king? The obvious answer might be yes, but the more accurate answer is that *everything* of note in Alexandria was funded by the rulers, so they didn't need to inscribe their names. Instead, there was probably a big state-sponsored festival when the lighthouse was completed. Sostratus might be behind the construction – in other words, the design – and, over time, the notion of what it means to create something could have diverged. However, architects didn't usually sign their names on their work. Lucian and Pliny suggest that the architect did so deceptively without anyone knowing, or that the king kindly allowed him to do so, which isn't entirely out of character for either Ptolemy. After all, 'the Divine Saviours' in the inscription could refer to the king and queen, not just Zeus and Proteus. But even Sostratus' role as architect is open to debate. Recently, classics scholar Peter Bing made a convincing case that Posidippus' poem was actually dedicated to the statue of Zeus at the top of the lighthouse, not to the lighthouse itself.[7] The poem starts with 'The Greeks' saviour god . . . shines from Pharos / thanks to Sostratus' and ends as the 'sailors . . . find Zeus the Saviour'. Sostratus either designed that sculpture of Zeus, or the most likely conclusion is that he was a wealthy courtier or merchant who donated the statue of Zeus specifically, which could have been a later addition to the lighthouse.

Indeed, the cost of constructing the lighthouse suggests that it would be difficult for one person to fund it: even if the statue at the top was donated, the lighthouse itself was certainly a state endeavour. According to Pliny, the lighthouse cost 800 talents, which in today's money comes to no less than £16 million – a tenth of Ptolemy I's treasury. That the Ptolemies were not necessarily concerned with having their names on the lighthouse suggests that they commissioned many more lavish buildings that we don't know about.

Alexandria's lighthouse was only partly built for practical purposes. It was also a symbol of power intended to impress. Its imposing grandeur demonstrated to the world the strength and supremacy of the Ptolemies. It also came to represent the fact that the light of knowledge was being spread far and wide from these shores. Alexandria became defined by its most famous building. As a rich capital undergoing constant renovation, residents of all walks, from courtiers to poets, were engaging with Alexandria's developing character, and the Pharos in particular became a part of everyday life and people's perceptions of their own city. As they walked through Alexandria by day, they could see the Pharos shooting into the sky, and by night it created a bright, starry glow. As Alexandrians in the first and second centuries purchased their own yellow lupini beans from the street vendors, they would bring out one of a variety of coins that bore a little imprint of the city's iconic lighthouse. It marked a grand entrance that left travellers in no doubt that they were arriving at the world's foremost city. The imposing lighthouse gave them their first impressions of the megalopolis. This was a 'New World' that was as dazzling as it was futuristic. For those who dared to dream and make the move to the city, there was an anticipation that their lives could be transformed for the better: Alexandria was something of a New York, the Pharos Lighthouse its Lady Liberty.

The lighthouse set a trend that reverberated around the world. As the first architecturally developed lighthouse in existence, it became a model in its design. Its name, Pharos, swiftly became the term for lighthouses further afield, first in Greek and now in an array of European languages from Albanian to French to Italian. In the early Middle Ages, a good millennium after its construction, as ships sailed at sea, flashes reflected from the lighthouse sent them messages in translatable code: an early version of the heliography that would become common in the nineteenth century and be developed into Morse code.

The Pharos Lighthouse is a key piece of Ptolemaic architecture. Unfortunately, not one Ptolemaic building stands in modern-day Alexandria. The remaining fragments of the buildings do, however, indicate the significant influence of Ptolemaic architecture. The city's architects combined Greek and Egyptian styles to create a unique Alexandrian style. Even the Egyptian temples developed their own style during the Ptolemaic period, differentiating them from the rest of the country's temples. Such structures included, for instance, distinctive capitals (the tops of columns), rock-cut decorations and wall paintings. Alexandria's early architecture formed the origins of the Roman Baroque movement and went on to influence Islamic and Christian architecture in the centuries to follow. To get a sense of early Alexandrian architecture, one is better off going to Jerusalem or Rome. To give two examples, the first-century doors to the Temple in Jerusalem were made in Alexandria using gilded bronze, and the Roman emperor Hadrian, who visited Alexander's tomb in the second century, is thought to have modelled the Castel Sant'Angelo in a similar style.

In 1962, when a young fisherman who'd dived into the sea spotted enormous rocks on the seabed, he reported his find. A further archaeological dive concluded that one of the pieces, more than six metres long, was a fragment of the Zeus statue that once stood at the pinnacle of the lighthouse. Since then, attempts to recover the remains of the lighthouse have yielded exciting but disparate results. These include historic dives around the area in the mid-1990s, led by

French scholar Jean-Yves Empereur. After a long wait in front of an anticipating crowd, the first item to be fished out of the sea was a torso: neck, shoulders, and then, a gasp was heard as the glistening, rounded breasts of an unidentifiable goddess – rather than a god – emerged from the water. The divers also found thousands of small items, around thirty of which related directly to the lighthouse, like broken blocks of its granite and one huge block from its doorpost.

The Pharos Lighthouse remained intact for seven centuries and survived in an increasingly damaged form for seventeen. It withstood earthquakes, floods and conflicts. Over time, its incremental demise saw its stones fall, one by one, into the deep sea. Christian and Muslim rulers would add their own touches to the building until its destruction in the fourteenth century and the eventual reuse of its rubbly remains to build the city's citadel. Today, though vanished, the lighthouse holds a prominent place on the city's emblem and is the central item on the flag of both the Alexandria governorate and city.

All the Books in the World

In the ancient Athenian port town of Phaleron, an unpretentious man by the name of Phonostratus watched his two sons grow up to become public orators. During the bitter years of rivalry between Greece and Macedon, the sons took different sides. Himeraeus supported the popular, notoriously anti-Macedonian party. Demetrius, meanwhile, had been educated in Aristotle's Peripatetic school by Aristotle's successor Theophrastus and possibly Aristotle himself. So Demetrius' allegiance was to the pro-Macedonian party. In 317 BCE, one of Alexander's successors, Cassander, who was now leading the Macedon kingdom, managed to invade Athens. Keen to appoint an Athenian ally as governor, Cassander picked Demetrius, who was still in his early thirties. The appointment polarised Athens and there were many, especially among the lower classes, who saw Demetrius as nothing more than a Macedonian puppet promoted to limit democratic freedoms. It's said that he had 360 sculptures of himself placed around Athens, no doubt an exaggeration but still indicative of the power he wielded. Rumours were also spreading about Demetrius' excessive spending on women and parties. When Athens changed hands in 307 BCE, the sculptures were demolished, some even turned into urinals. Demetrius was on the verge of being executed. He had to escape.

And here begins the unlikely story of the Great Library of Alexandria. The politician turned fugitive first went to Thebes, where he's said to have occupied his days by rereading and analysing Homer's poetry. Eventually, when it became clear that returning to Athens wasn't going to happen and he needed a place to settle, he sought refuge with Ptolemy I. Aside from their shared loyalties to Macedon and Aristotle, Alexandria's ruler, by this stage nearing his

seventies, saw this as a golden opportunity. He needed a tutor for his
son. And in Athens, Demetrius had penned extensive legal reforms
and successfully arranged a census; Ptolemy needed someone to do
the same for Alexandria. In addition, Demetrius could offer good
counsel: he provided Ptolemy I with a list of books the king should
read about sovereignty and leadership, advising him that while royal
aides might hide some of what they're really thinking, books won't
hide anything from him.

A couple of decades earlier, when Alexander had sunk to his
knees to design the city on the sandy ground, he had included a
library dedicated to the Muses. Ptolemy, himself a student of
Aristotle, had now established the city's physical foundations. The
time had come to set the city's intellectual foundations. He gave
Demetrius the task of creating a major library for the city. As with
the lighthouse, this project is likely to have been initiated by
Ptolemy I before being completed by Ptolemy II in the early third
century BCE. Ptolemy III would then play a major role in enhancing it further.

The earliest written reference we have to the Library is from the
second-century BCE Letter of Aristeas, thought to be written by a
Jewish scholar who worked there. It notes the project's extraordinary ambition and audacity: 'Demetrius . . . was furnished with
much money in order to collect, if possible, all the books in the
world.'[1] Unlike previous libraries that served their local or regional
area, the Library of Alexandria was intended to be a global hub: as
universal as the city it stood in. It was to show off a city ahead of its
time. And by gathering every book, the Ptolemies could prescribe
themselves as caretakers of the world's knowledge. If they managed
this, they reckoned, they could garner ultimate power.

Alexandria's new and prized complex was named the *Mouseion* –
the shrine of Muses. Built in the royal quarter of the city, it consisted
of two buildings. There was the *Biblion* building – the shrine of
Books – where the texts were held. The task at hand wasn't only to
acquire and retain books, but also to translate and analyse them, so
adjacent to the Library stood the *Mouseion* building itself, a hub
where knowledge was learnt and exchanged. Both of these were
state institutions with royal bounty funds at their disposal. It might
be that they were founded around the same time: the concept of

two interlinked but separate institutions appears to have been present from the very start. But it is more likely that Ptolemy I built the Library before Ptolemy II added the research centre, or that both constructions were initiated by Ptolemy I and completed under Ptolemy II.

This *Mouseion* – a place at once dedicated to the Muses and inspired by them – where research would lead to preservation of knowledge, led to the Latin word we now know as 'museum'. The Muses, the nine inspiring goddesses of literature, science and art, are daughters to Zeus and Mnemosyne, the goddess of memory. Since Alexander championed himself as the son of Zeus, the Muses share a common ancestor with the city's founder. And their father continued to watch over the city from the top of the Pharos Lighthouse. They are Calliope, the muse of eloquence and epic poetry who taught Alexander's hero Achilles how to sing, and who usually holds a writing tablet. Clio, the muse of history, who also invented the guitar, holds a scroll. Erato is the muse of lyrics and love poetry; Euterpe, the muse of music and flutes; Melpomene, the muse of tragedy; Polyhymnia, the muse of sacred poetry; Terpsichore, the muse of dance; Thalia, the muse of comedy and pastoral poetry; and Urania, the muse of astronomy. Together, these goddesses epitomise the power of literature and the arts, as well as Alexander's interests and the areas of knowledge that the Library would come to prioritise. They would come to be loved by the Egyptians, too. And the presence of the Muses in the founding of Alexandrian culture would foreshadow the vital role that women would come to play in the history of the city.

The ancient sources give us limited information about how the Library looked. It's likely to have been a grand design: large columns both inside and out, sculptures dotted at every corner. The books were housed in its main halls, known as the *bibliothekai*, where papyrus scrolls bulged from the rectangular shelves of the ceiling-high wooden cabinets. At the time, all books were rolls; folded books as we know them today (codex) only appeared centuries later. The rolls were stacked on top of one another like logs, so that tens of piled circles were visible in each shelf and one could be pulled out without much trouble. The scrolls were organised by subject and labels of clay attached to them so they could be identified without being unrolled. Above the shelves, an inscription read: 'the place of the cure of the soul'.

To acquire 'all the books' meant having a copy of every single piece of writing that existed in the known world. The quest to do so meant that the Library ended up housing a colossal collection. Some estimates have the number of books at 700,000 by the first century BCE, others at over one million. In Ptolemy I's reign, Demetrius is said to have collected 200,000 scrolls, of which a quarter were originals and the rest were copied by scribes. Some longer works might have been abridged, writings on similar topics were often combined, and there were also duplicates of some titles. The most direct report, by Byzantine scholar John Tzetzes and apparently citing Alexandria's second librarian, notes that in Ptolemy II's time the Library housed around half a million scrolls, 400,000 of which contained multiple works, with 120,000 of these amassing the entire corpus of Greek literature.

Ptolemy I paid regular visits to Demetrius in the Library to check on progress. Demetrius also reported regularly to his superior about the collection and restoration of books.[2] Demetrius played a key role in the first decade or so of the Library's existence, making decisions about the way it would be run, what it would stock and what its wider intellectual aims would be. These aims were in line with the cosmopolitan, tolerant city being developed around it. For instance, he suggested to Ptolemy I that the Library should acquire the books of Jewish law and that translators should be hired from different parts of the world.

However, in 284 BCE, when Ptolemy I was preparing to share his throne with his successor for the last couple of years, Demetrius made the deadly mistake of supporting the wrong prince. This was received with fury and Demetrius was exiled southwards to a remote village. A year later, he was found dead. Had Ptolemy II, now yielding power, ordered an assassination? Physicians couldn't determine whether this was suicide, murder, or simply an accident. Demetrius was going about his day as normal when he felt a sudden and unusual stabbing in his right wrist. A venomous snake had bitten the de facto creator of the world's greatest library, whose body was found motionless among his books.

*   *   *

What started as an ambition to collect every book in the world became something of an obsession. It also came to signal Alexandria's unique nature and how the Ptolemies would stop at nothing to make it the knowledge capital of the world.

Demetrius used his knowledge and contacts as a member of the Peripatetic school to locate some of the first major acquisitions, which included several works by Aristotle and Theophrastus.

The Ptolemies also sought the support of other leaders. The fourth-century writer Epiphanius records that after Ptolemy I was told that there were valuable books in east Africa, Babylon, India, the Levant, Mesopotamia and Persia, he contacted 'every king and prince on earth', asking them in his letter to send books 'by poets and prose writers and orators and philosophers and physicians and professors of medicine and historians and books by any others'.[3] Many such books would have been picked up during international trade trips, too. When it came to the Library and learning, there was no space for prejudice about where the knowledge came from.

Borrowing books from elsewhere and copying them proved the easiest method of collection. Instead of returning them, though, the Alexandrians decided simply to keep the books. Word got round that the Library of Alexandria was not to be trusted.

But the Ptolemies were rich and powerful, so cities still wanted to maintain ties with them. Other leaders began to introduce deposits for borrowing their books. Surely Alexandria wouldn't pay such huge amounts to keep those books – or so they thought. For Alexandria, it wasn't just about the quantity of books: the Library wanted to acquire works that were known to be precious. Homer was central to the very concept of Alexandria. It's no surprise, then, that there was a particular fixation on procuring his works and the Library ended up with dozens of manuscripts of Homeric poetry. Ptolemy III also managed to obtain the original papyrus works of the three famous Greek tragedians, Aeschylus, Sophocles and Euripides. Stored as national treasures in Athens, Ptolemy persuaded Athenian governors to lend them to Alexandria for copying, paying a huge deposit of fifteen talents (then 450 kilograms of gold or silver; today more than £300,000). Once the Library had its hands on these jewels, they weren't going back. Instead, and in act of nonchalant defiance, they stunned the Athens governors by returning copies of the works. Ptolemy III didn't mind losing the significant pledge he had deposited as insurance.

But he quickly became dissatisfied with the main book markets of Athens and Rhodes, and followed his grandfather's initial suit of writing letters to other leaders. Letters from Egypt's mighty pharaoh sought their cooperation – not in a war, not in trade, but, rather, requesting to borrow the most important books in their possession. The decision of whether to copy or to keep the original now depended on how the book's value weighed up against that specific diplomatic relationship. Like his predecessors, Ptolemy III also sent agents far and wide on the search for books. With a substantial budget at their disposal, their initial task was simply to bring back any books by any author. As time went on, they were to pay special attention to the most reputable classics, to purchase them or, if that wasn't possible, to borrow them for copying. They began to show special interest in older versions since they were less likely to be copies or forgeries and might therefore be truer to the original text.

Tactics were one thing, policies another. New laws were put in place so that the Library could make use of both the city's global visitors and the nearby harbour. Anyone who entered Alexandria had to hand their books over for inspection. As soon as a ship docked, it was subject to an official search – not for contraband, but for books. If a book was found, it would be rushed instantly to the Library where an immediate decision had to be made about whether to return it or seize it. In all likelihood, the owner would never see their book again. While there wasn't much choice about the confiscation, the officials would return to the ship later to hand the owner a copy of the book that had been made on the spot as well as some monetary compensation. Such books were then designated in the Library stock as being 'from the ship'. And the simplest new law was that no book was allowed to leave the city without inspection. Like precious stones, like papyrus, oil and wheat, for the first time in human history books had now become a valuable commodity.

The great book rush wasn't without its troubles. Some people, especially those who were themselves well read, realised that if they wrote anything, they were pretty much guaranteed to earn money from the Library. After all, acquiring every book was the opposite of being selective. The scamming began. The most common was to claim that you'd been taught by a famous scholar or that you'd heard them speak, before writing a book that supposedly relayed their ideas. Understandably, the number of anonymous books increased. Sometimes they weren't anonymised, like Cratippus, who pretended that he was a confidant of the Athenian historian Thucydides and penned a book titled *Everything Thucydides Left Unsaid*, which became so important that Plutarch used it a few centuries later. This tactic was subsequently emulated and was especially common in Renaissance Europe.

Unauthorised content was floating around, but forgeries posed an even greater threat. As Alexandrian agents searched for books around the world, it became clear that not every book was as precious as its seller was claiming. To complicate matters further, the local economy began to respond to the wild book chase. Corruption in Alexandria itself was making book acquisition all the more challenging. Scribes and failed authors had spotted a lucrative opportunity. They produced strikingly precise forgeries of respected books, sometimes patching together various works and sometimes creating them from scratch. They then teamed up with well-known booksellers, who were also in on the trick. These booksellers then sold the texts as originals. More often than not, their unwitting customer was an official charged with stocking the city's Library, though if the stockists were paid depending on the number of books they secured, they may have been fully aware.

More visibly, the city's merchant quarter began to change. Stalls that once sold vegetables, bottled oils and woven baskets began to be replaced with those stacking rolls and rolls of books. These were copies of varying qualities, never originals, being sold to both locals and foreign visitors, who after having them inspected as they departed, could return home happy having purchased the best possible souvenir from the famous library city. The booksellers were also fast developing their own notorious habits. They bribed officials from the Library to discreetly take scrolls out of the collections to be copied. As a result, the occasional book went missing from the Library, unauthorised publications were rife and piracy became an unsolvable problem.

The fact that books had rapidly become such a precious commodity was leading to relentless underground activity: the multiple layers of this black market meant that control was slipping out of the authority's hands. More than ever, trusted experts were needed to make decisions about book acquisitions and values.

On the plus side, the global quest for books ensured that the contents of the Library were surprisingly diverse and inclusive. The Library was intended to be a Greek-language institution, but the books originated from every known culture and were written in every known language. The staff included many translators and *charakitai* – or scribblers – so called because they wrote on *charta* (papyrus). And Egypt was already a country that valued the written word, which was considered to be divine. In fact, in Egyptian, 'writing', or *medu netjer*, meant 'god's words'. The Ptolemaic translation of the term was 'hieroglyphics', which means 'holy carvings'. The Ptolemies ordered the Egyptian priests to write and deposit their works in the Library, so Greek and Egyptian books were plentiful. These were garnished with polytheist, Buddhist, Hindu, Jewish and Zoroastrian writings, making the Library something of a religious site, though a place of no official religion. For example, an Egyptian priest named Manetho penned a history of Egypt – based on Egyptian sources but written in Greek – and dedicated it to Ptolemy II. Another priest, Horapollo, wrote a book explaining hieroglyphics. The varied content of the Library became, besides the city's geographical location, the first tangible example of Alexandria benefitting from its hybrid culture at the intersection of East and West. Its collections were internationalising knowledge.

But this universalisation also became an act of monopolisation. As the decades passed, Alexandria's was no longer intended to be the world's premier library – rather, the world's *only* library. The city had an immense advantage that helped towards this goal: control over Egypt's papyrus plant. Papyrus was perfect for scrolls and the single most common material for writing around the world. The *librarius* (scribe) would copy the author's manuscript onto another papyrus. In an attempt to ensure everything was legible, scribes weren't only paid for the number of lines they wrote (every 100 lines), but for the quality of their writing, too. The *librariolus* (copyist) would then add titles and decorations. The *bibliopegus* (bookbinder) ensured that the first sheet was blank and that the sheets all aligned. The sheets were also wrapped around the *umbilicus*, a wooden rod with knobs at either end. This bound the sheets together, protected them and allowed the scroll to be unfurled for reading. Not content with the fact that Alexandria had such ready access to the plant, in 190 BCE Egypt decided to put an embargo on its papyrus trade to give the Library an unparalleled advantage over all other libraries.

The library in the Greek city of Pergamon (in modern-day Turkey) held a significant but hardly competitive 200,000 books. Its existence was a particular nuisance. For one, Alexandrian agents ended up buying more forgeries because they couldn't risk something being snapped up by their rivals. The Pergamon school was also attracting intellectuals from Athens and even some from Alexandria. The papyrus embargo was intended to hurt other libraries, especially Pergamon. There, they began to write on animal hides, or *pergamenos*, the origin of the word 'parchment', which would only replace papyrus as the main writing surface some five centuries later.

Eventually, the Library of Alexandria began to overflow with books. By 295 BCE, it had far more books than space to store them. Ptolemy III established a daughter library in the Serapeum, the opulent temple to the god Serapis. This offshoot collection alone comprised over 42,000 books that couldn't fit into the Library; recent excavations found nineteen such rooms. As the years passed, like papyrus plants emerging from the soil numerous smaller libraries began to spring up all around the city. Alexandria's royal quarter became something of an academic district, similar perhaps to Paris' Latin Quarter or European university towns like Bologna and Oxford.

Today, not too far from where the original Library may have been, Prophet Daniel Street in Alexandria's historic district is famous for its second-hand bookstalls. Thousands of worn paperbacks are stacked on top of one another. The atmosphere is filled with the oddly satisfying scent of dusty books that overpowers even the smells of the sea and the petrol fumes of the taxis, motorbikes and trams whizzing by. Sellers navigate their heaped, spiralling stocks effortlessly like experienced mariners in a familiar ocean. They proudly speak of how their families have sold books here for four generations. They are continuing the city's bookselling tradition two and a half millennia after it began.

*   *   *

When Ptolemy I needed a tutor for his children – two of whom would go on to become the royal couple – he hired Philitas of Cos, who arrived to discover an ambitious library under construction. In Alexandria, Philitas founded the Hellenistic School of Poetry that would go on to influence the Roman poet Ovid a few centuries later. Philitas is likely to have been asked to help with the Library, not least to start arranging the books that were being acquired. By the time the Library was holding thousands of scrolls, it became clear that somebody was required to take responsibility for the collections. The man entrusted with this task in 284 BCE, Philitas' student Zenodotus of Ephesus, is the first librarian in recorded history.

We can assume that the Library staff included clerks, copyists, couriers, sorters, repairers and cleaners. As soon as a book was acquired, it was sent to a warehouse to be checked and sorted into one of two big piles: literary or scientific. Each scroll then had a label affixed to it indicating the author's name and geographic origin (there were no surnames and many names were repeated) before being stored in a jacket of leather or linen. Further labels were used to differentiate multiple copies of the same work or to add details about acquisition. Zenodotus then assigned the categories to different rooms of the Library, where the books would be stacked thematically and the authors ordered alphabetically. Homer was again given a special status, partly due to his prominent position and partly because there were so many of his books here. Each copy of Homer's poems had a special tag indicating the city from which that particular copy had been obtained. As a scholar, Zenodotus wrote a *Life of Homer* and is thought to have divided the Homeric epics into 24 books.

Zenodotus' assistant and successor was a man famous for his encyclopaedic knowledge, Callimachus of Cyrene. Though the scrolls were labelled and organised into general subjects, the number of books was increasing into the hundreds of thousands. Finding a specific stack of scrolls was painstakingly time-consuming, and it was impossible to know what titles were actually stocked. Callimachus decided to take on the mammoth task of creating the first ever subject catalogue, or, as he called it, the *Pinakes* (meaning tablets or tables). The ambitious bibliography was without precedent and took months to compile. Once completed, the revolutionary reference tool allowed users to find the right room and stack seamlessly. Callimachus decided to separate the authors into nine categories: doctors, historians, legislators, philosophers, rhetoricians, comic poets, epic poets, tragic poets, and miscellaneous writers. He then listed every important text in the Library, grouping the books into eleven different branches. History, law, mathematics, medicine, natural science and rhetoric were separated. As for the literature, there was so much of it – the catalogue recorded 120,000 literary scrolls – that he spread it across four subcategories: comedy, epic, lyric poetry and tragedy. That left just one category of book that was simply labelled miscellaneous (the place to go to find cookbooks). Under each entry, a brief biography included the author's father, hometown and education. Callimachus' work, *Tables of Persons Eminent in Every Branch of Learning together with a List of Their Writings*, comprises 120 scrolls by itself. He also compiled a *Catalogue of Dramatic Writers Arranged Chronologically from the Earliest Times*.

The influence of Zenodotus and Callimachus cannot be underestimated. Over the subsequent centuries, their practice became a model in Europe and the Arab world. Arranging the books on each shelf in alphabetical order might sound ordinary, but the first librarians actually did something ground-breaking. In fact, the Library's first major contribution to the world is alphabetisation. It marked a shift in the use of the alphabet as a tool for organisation. Rather than being something that was merely learnt, it was now going to be used. Given the expanse of the library, Callimachus also expanded the possibilities of alphabetisation so that for the first time, books – not just authors – were arranged alphabetically rather than thematically. This remained single-letter alphabetisation (for example, Homer could come before Herodotus) until the second century when fuller alphabetisation using more than the first letter began. Furthermore, through his bibliography, Callimachus introduced the concept and proved the potential of detailed cataloguing, which also generated the idea of what we now know as the index.

The first librarians were celebrities: a papyrus fragment from Egypt, released by archaeologists in 1914, shows a school exercise where students had to list the names of the first six librarians. In fact, for the first two centuries, the position of chief librarian came to represent high office. The director of the Library could only be named by the pharaoh and they maintained a direct line of communication. The librarian received special royal protection, partly because of the important role but also because much of the Alexandrian population was unhappy with the scale of public investment in the Library; the director's status and salary outraged thousands of residents. Such substantial remunerations and incentives were not only meant to honour him, but to curtail any chance of his bribery by book dealers or other libraries. He also doubled as a royal tutor, living in the royal palace grounds where he was obliged to tutor the king's children. The head of the Library also had to be a member of the *tiasos*, or the priesthood, at least notionally. To all the people of Egypt, he was presented as the Priest of the Muses. After all, tradition dictated that books belonged in temples and the Library was one of the city's shrines.

While special agents were on the hunt for books, library staff buried themselves in piles of scrolls that needed sorting. As the books increased, diligent translators were working equally hard to render the most important texts into Greek. The translators were enlisted from different parts of the world and the texts were allocated for them. According to the first-century Roman author Pliny, the Persian writings of Zoroaster – over two million lines of verse – were translated in Alexandria. Ptolemy II was especially convinced that translation could serve many purposes for the city. He decided that it was time to translate into Greek one of the most influential books around. Translating the Hebrew Bible might have been an act of democratisation, but it was also a powerful comment on integration. Some Jews had moved to Alexandria immediately after its founding and the Jewish community was constantly on the rise. Many occupied the lower classes but the majority were now second- or third-generation Alexandrians, meaning that a large proportion could only speak Greek. On the one hand, then, translating the Hebrew Bible meant that they could finally understand their scripture. On the other, the Jews couldn't now make excuses not to become integrated Hellenists – and in turn, Alexandrians – especially as they were already studying Homer and Aristotle in school.

According to the Letter of Aristeas, Ptolemy II contacted Jerusalem's High Priest Eleazer in order to summon 72 Jewish scholars (70 in most sources) to Alexandria to translate the Hebrew Bible, or at least the Torah, its first five books. According to the first-century Jewish philosopher Philo of Alexandria, this group consisted of six scholars from each of the twelve tribes of Israel. The first-century Jewish historian Josephus claims that they arrived with parchments containing 'the Laws written in gold letters', suggesting that they, or at least Josephus' Jewish contemporaries, perceived Ptolemaic Alexandria to be a lavish place where precious metals were used unsparingly.[4] Aristeas, the most contemporary source to the event, records that Ptolemy II greeted them on their arrival and arranged a lavish, week-long banquet in the royal palace. The scholars were then told what to expect. They would be taken to Pharos, right next to the newly erected lighthouse. There, they were to live in a secluded house away from the bustle of the city until they completed the translation.

Later versions of the story are more miraculous, including the one in the Talmud, which for much of the Common Era remained the central text in Jewish life. Here, Ptolemy II doesn't explain anything to the 72 elders, but gathers them on Pharos before locking each of them into a separate chamber and assigning them the task one by one. That way, not only would there be no distractions, but they would be forced to translate independently. The Talmud adds that the results were remarkably similar and proved the divinely inspired nature of the translation: God moved each of them to come up with an identical translation, and a curse was placed on whoever might alter it in future. Aristeas states that the 72 scholars agreed on the translation of the Hebrew Bible and Apocrypha after 72 days. It's most likely that the scholars worked collaboratively and that the translation was transcribed by Museum officials as it progressed.

Eventually, the Jews of Alexandria assembled excitedly in their numbers to hear their holy book being recited in Greek. They were captivated: men and women who had grown up hearing their scripture in a foreign language were moved to tears as they listened to it in their mother tongue for the very first time. The translation was also read to Ptolemy II, who was apparently fascinated by its content. The scholars had succeeded in their task. As they boarded their ship back to Jerusalem, they carried with them precious local gifts of bronzeware, glassware and fabrics, endowed to them as payment by the city of Alexandria. The scripture was named *The Translation of the Seventy*. In Latin, this became shortened over time to just *Seventy*, or as it's known today: the Septuagint.

The original Septuagint, soon referred to as the Greek Old Testament, would become one of the most influential translations in history, in large part because it was used in the composition of the New Testament and adopted by the Church. The translation, though, wasn't error-free. Ancient rabbinic sources, including the Talmud, claim that the list of unclean animals included the rabbit, but was translated as piglet, leading to the Jewish prohibition on eating pork. At first, this looks like Egyptian influence since pigs were considered unclean in Alexandria. But the translation of hare, *lagos*, sounded exactly the same as Lagos of Eordaia, the name of Ptolemy I's father and Ptolemy II's grandfather, rumoured to have been named so because of his big ears. An accurate translation might suggest the king's grandad was unclean. Although modern scholars of Judaism regard this as a fabrication, it nonetheless highlights the difficult job of the translators and the potentially political nature of the endeavour. A second example is more easily proved: God's name, Yahweh, which appears thousands of times, was translated as *Kyrios*. This word was used in everyday life, referring to the head of household, for instance, and it meant Lord, as in Master, not God. This alternative term, Lord, would soon become cemented in the New Testament as the most common name for the Christian deity.

To some extent, Alexandria did get carried away. Twentieth-century Argentinian author Jorge Luis Borges once said that 'the fancy or the imagination or the utopia of the Total Library has certain characteristics that are easily confused with virtues'.[5] The concept of *complete knowledge* – let alone a deadly serious and unflinching aspiration to amass and achieve it – is something that has repeated itself at key moments since the Library's foundation. In Europe, for instance, it defined aspects of the Renaissance, the Age of Discovery and the Enlightenment. We assume it today in our perceptions of what digital advancement can accomplish, not least in our relationship with the limitless repository that is the World Wide Web. In a way, all of these subsequent attempts and landmarks build on Alexandria's idealistic vision, beginning with Alexander's ability to envisage garnering absolute power, the Ptolemaic idea that absolute knowledge is a means of achieving that absolute power, and the willingness to tangibly action such a concept.

It is fitting that the city founded and developed by two students of Aristotle housed a prominent library. Aristotle himself had collected books, beginning when he was just a child and continuing until his death, developing and maintaining what was regarded for centuries in Europe as the first substantial private library. Strabo popularised this claim and extended its influence to the Library of Alexandria, writing that Aristotle is 'the first man, so far as I know, to have collected books and to have taught the kings in Egypt how to arrange a library'. Aristotle's personal collection developed into the library at his school, the Lyceum, to which Alexander had often donated. It housed Aristotle's own works, as well as research by his followers, including his successor, Theophrastus (who taught the Library's founder Demetrius). By the time of Theophrastus' death, there were almost 400 works written by either Aristotle or Theophrastus on more than 1,000 rolls of papyrus. When Theophrastus died, it was revealed that his will included a strange clause that bequeathed the entire library to a single student, Neleus of Scepsis. This ended up being a costly mistake. For one, the governors of the Lyceum didn't like Neleus and decided to make Strato of Lampsacus, who had the advantage of having tutored Ptolemy II, the third director of the Lyceum. Neleus, probably the only person still alive who'd actually been taught by Aristotle, retaliated by packing his bags and taking all the 10,000-plus scrolls with him. The only complete living record of the Aristotelean school found itself in Neleus' family home in the small town of Scepsis (modern-day Turkey).

There had been some unease in Alexandria about the relative lack of books by Aristotle, so Ptolemy II was relieved that one of his tutors, Strato, who'd previously resided in the Alexandrian court, was heading the Lyceum. Their decades-long personal relationship made it very likely that Alexandria could now acquire a sizeable chunk of the Aristotelian library. If only it were that straightforward. Strato was forced to have an awkward conversation with the monarch in which he explained that the books had vanished into thin air, and that, thanks to an obscure will, Neleus was their rightful owner. Ptolemy II had no choice but to send representatives to Neleus in the hope that sacks of money would be enough to persuade him to hand the scrolls over. They returned to Alexandria with hundreds of scrolls, recorded in the Library as 'the books of Aristotle and Theophrastus, from Neleus of Scepsis'. Before too long, it became clear that Neleus had daringly duped the royal ambassadors, selling them the least important books in his possession: common works by Theophrastus and books that Aristotle owned rather than wrote. As far as Neleus was concerned, he hadn't lied; they were still from 'Aristotle's library'.

When Neleus died, his confused heirs were unsure what to do with the books and it's unclear whether they thought them precious or worthless. Either way, they dug a huge hole under their house, stashing the scrolls deep below the ground. A couple of centuries later, they sold the surviving books to a wealthy Greek man, who copied and returned them to the Lyceum. When the Roman Republic invaded Athens in 87 BCE, they took these books with them so that the extant works of Aristotle and his students ultimately ended up distributed between Rome and Alexandria. Theophrastus' will and Neleus' stunt, though, probably cost the world at least a fifth of what Aristotle wrote: texts and ideas that have been lost for ever.

There is a case to be made for Aristotle as the godfather of Alexandria, or, more precisely, as its intellectual father. His teachings on ambition and knowledge, on the importance of spaces for learning and reflection, and even the hoarding of books, greatly impacted Alexander and Ptolemy I, one of whom dreamed up the idea of a city that included a grand library dedicated to the Muses before the other began to turn that dream into a reality.

But with intellectual activity at the adjacent Museum in full flow, many of Aristotle's theories were about to be put to the test.

Shrine of Knowledge

The Library of Alexandria was becoming a global sensation. Next door, Alexandria's Museum was also attracting attention, and before too long it had cemented its position as the finest research institute on the planet.

Within a couple of decades of its founding in the early third century BCE, the Museum had gathered thinkers and specialists from almost every field and specialism imaginable. The spark for these developments came from the very top. Alexandria's early royal family had been raised in a consciously intellectual environment in which they had respect for scholars. Members of the royal family sent out personal invitations to the Museum. Some scholars travelled to Alexandria to use the Library's resources, and many were invited to stay. Scholarship in Alexandria was clearly an attractive offer. Resident scholars would be in close proximity to the Library, the most tangible and significant home of written knowledge in existence. They could use the books as they pleased as long as they didn't take them out of the vicinity; they would also be careful not to take their own books into the Library lest they were confiscated. As they read in the Library, some wrote marginal comments on the scrolls, adding their own ideas to the texts and instigating discursive conversations on the pages. They were given tenured contracts so they could feel settled. And as though the stipend they were paid wasn't enough, they were also exempted from tax. The greatest minds of the world began packing their bags and making tracks for Alexandria. One didn't even have to be invited in order to make use of the facilities: anyone doing serious research could access the books, was served free food and given free accommodation.

For 700 years, until the fourth century, scholars continued to come to Alexandria in great numbers. They made monumental discoveries, proved important theories and interrogated assumed knowledge. A full book dedicated to Alexandrian scholarship would still feel like a summary. Over the centuries, Alexandria's scholars pioneered and advanced multiple fields including agriculture, astronomy, biology, geography, mathematics and philosophy. They gave extraordinary thought to literary craftsmanship and criticism. Among other things, they developed geometry (Euclid of Alexandria), proved that the earth isn't flat (Eratosthenes of Cyrene) and invented the steam engine (Heron of Alexandria). Over several centuries, Alexandrian scholarship collated and emended the classics, attempted to invent new technologies that could transform civilisation into the next age of modernity and, most importantly, asked and sought to answer humanity's grandest questions about life. In doing so, it served as a precursor to the daring movements of the future, including the Islamic Golden Age, Europe's Renaissance and Age of Enlightenment and the industrial revolutions.

To reach the Museum, the scholars walked into a portico, a grand, colonnaded porch reminiscent of the Greek temples. This led to a series of covered walkways with large, spaced columns supporting the roofs and connecting the complex's various buildings. Inside were a series of gleaming structures surrounded by verdant gardens. Scholars could listen to one another in a lavishly decorated lecture hall or study quietly in private rooms. There were seating areas and a banquet room where they could share ideas as they ate the fish, vegetables and bread prepared especially for them. For conversation, they gathered in an exedra, an outdoor seating space with a semi-circular arrangement of stone benches. There were also interior patios, one of which included shelving and private cabinets. The complex had some small theatres for performances, too, which the scholars could enjoy before strolling back to their lodgings.

All this sounds idyllic, which makes it understandable that Alexandria's citizens weren't very fond of the Museum. That scholars weren't obliged to pay tax caused particular irritation. Alexandria already felt like a different place from the rest of Egypt. And the scholars living in Alexandria were in their own little world. The sceptical poet Timon of Phlius captured this public sentiment when he derided how, in Alexandria, 'they breed a race of bookish scrib-blers who are fed as they argue their lives away in the cage of the Muses.'[1] The Library and Museum weren't viewed as objective establishments, but, rather, as somewhere the Ptolemies could enclose scholars, breeding them to advance a set of appropriate ideologies. In the longer run, allowing foreigners to live a more privileged life than the citizens became a source of recurrent trou-ble in the city.

If the work produced is anything to go by, the scholars were given relative academic freedom and followed whatever school they pleased. In Athens, for instance, the democratic system meant that philosophers and scientists could vote to exile one of their peers on grounds of impiety, but in Alexandria a lack of organised democ-racy was actually liberating for the scholars, who were surprisingly free to speculate, experiment and challenge long-held beliefs and rituals. The intention here was actually rather radical: to challenge the philosophy, science and culture of both Greece (as represented by Athens) and of Egypt in order to confirm Alexandria's unique-ness and power. The city's centre of knowledge was now going to create and propagate a new school: neither Greek nor Egyptian, but Alexandrian.

It may have had a global impact, but Alexandrian knowledge was also intended to serve Alexandria directly. As a city whose economy was driven by the harbours and sailing, constantly affected by the winds and tides, it's no surprise that early research was concerned with geography, astronomy and mathematics.

In the early third century BCE, Timocharis of Alexandria and his pupil Aristyllus made discoveries about the movements of the stars. Timocharis is the first astronomer to mention the planet Mercury, while Aristyllus compiled a catalogue of stars. It's the reason one of the moon's craters, whose latitude is similar to Alexandria's, now bears the name of the astronomer Aristyllus.

Plato and Aristotle's writings described a geocentric universe, with the sun moving around the earth. This conclusion made sense because, from the earth, the sun appears to be revolving around us and we can't feel the ground moving. But in the third century BCE, the Alexandrian astronomer Aristarchus of Samos proposed a different theory that the universe is a lot bigger than previously thought, and the sun is especially larger than the earth. The sun, then, is at the centre and the stars are other suns further away. And the earth not only revolves around the sun but rotates about its own axis once a day. With this hypothesis, Aristarchus was the first to advocate heliocentrism: that the sun is at the centre of the universe. He set out to research the sizes of the sun and moon and their distances from the earth. His work in Alexandria drew serious attention – and caused a stir. For one, there was an attempt from Greece to indict him on grounds of impiety. For centuries, philosophers rejected his outlandish theory, in particular because the mathematician Claudius Ptolemy, also from Alexandria, went on to champion the geocentric model in the second century. Remarkably, it wasn't until 1,800 years later that the Renaissance mathematician Nicolaus Copernicus made a similar discovery that revived and established Aristarchus' heliocentric theory. That being said, Copernicus was clearly troubled by the fact that his discovery had already been made in ancient Alexandria. In his old age, as he prepared to publish his groundbreaking book, he went back and removed references to Aristarchus before sending it to print. A century later, during the scientific revolution of the 1600s, astronomers like Johannes Kepler, Galileo Galilei and Isaac Newton devoted huge efforts to proving that two millennia before them Aristarchus had been right all along.

One of those who rejected Aristarchus' theory was Hipparchus of Nicaea, nevertheless regarded as one of antiquity's greatest astronomers. Hipparchus was an early weather forecaster who compiled records of the weather throughout the year to create a calendar that predicted the onset of winds and storms. He also managed to calculate the first and last days of every season for each year. In doing so, he discovered that certain stars had moved a couple of degrees compared to the sunlight, so he hypothesised that stars were slowly moving planets, before making the correct conclusion that stars move gradually eastwards. By spotting the movement of equinoxes (days when the sun is directly above the equator), he also discovered axial precession: while the earth's axis appears stable, it actually wobbles like a spinning top. To add to these ground-breaking discoveries, Hipparchus is also credited as the founder of trigonometry.

When it came to mathematics, Euclid of Alexandria had arrived in the city within a decade of its founding and was already a respected mathematician when the Museum opened. He went on to write a book outlining the basics of geometry. The thirteen-volume *Elements* would end up being used as a key textbook up until the early twentieth century. Ptolemy I was fascinated by Euclid's concepts but when he tried to understand them, they were too complex. He summoned Euclid to the palace and surprised him by asking whether it was possible to learn geometry without studying the *Elements*. Euclid replied frankly: 'There is no royal road to geometry.'[2]

Maths continued its advancement in Alexandria through the likes of Conon of Samos, whom Ptolemy III had invited from Sicily. Conon was an expert on cones, the favoured shape for the army's bronze helmets. Selected as court astronomer, he knew how to make royalty happy and how to raise Alexandria's profile, proving that the Museum's scientific enquiry was a useful political tool. Excavations tell us that paintings and statuettes of Aphrodite, the goddess of love and lust, adorned Alexandrian homes; a recently discovered statue portrays her birth as she rises from the water, wet drapery clinging to her smooth, curvaceous body. Legend has it that Aphrodite fell in love with Adonis, a mere mortal whom she was destined to lose to death, but whom she continued to love evermore. The women of Alexandria commemorated the story in an annual festival, gathering at the seashore to mourn the death of Aphrodite's sweetheart. Ptolemy III went to battle for five years in 246 BCE, and back in Alexandria, Berenice II, his apprehensive queen, prayed for his safe return by visiting Aphrodite's temple, where she dedicated locks of her hair as an offering. News soon reached her that the hair had disappeared – a mystery that became the talk of the town until Conon informed the palace that he had located the lock among the stars. Conon named the constellation 'Coma Berenices' (Berenice's Hair), today one of the 88 recognised constellations in the sky. In doing so, Conon immortalised the Ptolemaic queen and her curls to this very day.

Many mathematicians travelled to Alexandria especially to attend Conon's lectures, including Archimedes of Syracuse. Despite returning to his native Sicily, Archimedes kept in touch with Conon about his theories, and built weapons of war for the Romans, including catapults and large cranes that clasped ships out of the water. Apollonius of Perga, who studied then settled in Alexandria, was known as 'the Great Geometer'. He ended up inventing a hand-held analogue calculator for making astronomical observations and modelling the universe; it was named the astrolabe, meaning literally the taker of the stars. Astrolabes can calculate the time of day, latitude and altitude, the height of a mountain and the width of rivers. His *Conics*, spread over eight books, contained almost 400 propositions that inspired the advancement of geometry in the medieval Islamic world, and when translated in sixteenth-century Europe, alongside Euclid, provided the key mathematical concepts for the Renaissance's scientific revolution.

Over the following centuries, Alexandria produced many more leading mathematicians, including the fourth-century women Pandrosion of Alexandria and Hypatia of Alexandria.[3] But none were quite as influential as the polymath Claudius Ptolemy, born in 100 CE, whose mathematical, geographical and astrological discoveries went on to inform scientific research for more than a millennium and a half.

Known in his day as the Great Astronomer, Claudius Ptolemy's eight-book *Geography* was a guide to map-drawing and served as an atlas, complete with attached maps that placed cities, rivers and mountains with remarkable accuracy, and his conventions continue to be followed by mapmakers. On his spherical earth, Europe, North Africa and the Middle East look similar to today's map, though Africa and East Asia seem to extend endlessly. His objective descriptions of the earth and sky, without mentioning the supernatural, went on to inspire scientific researchers. Later translations into Arabic and Latin in the ninth and fifteen centuries made the *Geography* especially influential in the Islamic Golden Age and the Age of Discovery. His book *Harmonica* argued that in the same way that mathematical laws influence the cosmos, so too do they influence musical systems. He introduced new scales and divisions to musical theory, adding that these musical notes correspond to the movements of the planets. This extended his argument that mathematics is superior to theology and metaphysics because it is factually certain. Such an idea was unpopular and counter to Platonic and Aristotelian traditions, in which theology and metaphysics were always superior. But Claudius Ptolemy didn't argue that science and religion go against one another; rather, that they can work together. So he was popular over the centuries because he served both sides of the debate: on one hand, theologians were attracted to the idea that the earth was at the centre of the universe because it meant God had given humans a special status, while secularists could claim that this was anthropocentric, proving humankind as the most important element of existence.

When Claudius Ptolemy looked at Alexandria's starry sky, he felt himself being transported: 'I know that I am mortal and ephemeral, but when I scan the multitudinous circling spirals of the stars, no longer do I touch earth with my feet, but sit with Zeus himself, and take my fill of the ambrosial food of the gods.'[4] By his own admission, he would not have wanted to live anywhere but Alexandria, where he was inspired to thrive.

Alexandria's mathematicians were essentially engineers using their theoretical acumen to invent practical objects. The Pharos Lighthouse's mirror, made from metal and bronze, was already a sign of pioneering innovation. And it was a mirror that began the creative journey of one of the Museum's earliest inventors, Ctesibius of Alexandria. Young Ctesibius spent time at his father's barbershop, where he met different people and learnt the family trade. A haircut in third-century BCE Alexandria involved an ivory bodkin, a razor and an instrument halfway between scissors (not yet invented) and hair curlers. Each client saw the result in a hand-held mirror; a highly polished, sun-shaped disc of bronze or copper with a decorated handle made from papyrus stem. When Ctesibius started cutting hair, he realised that having a mirror in front of the patron throughout would be a good idea. He attached one to a cord that he installed on the ceiling, then enclosed the cord in a tube and placed a lead ball on the end as a counterweight. Now, he had an adjustable mirror with a concealed mechanism, which he could pull up and down depending on the customer's height.

Every time Ctesibius pulled the cord, he heard a pleasant whistling noise and wondered what it could be. On closer inspection, he noticed that the air compressed by the lead ball was making a sound as it escaped through the tube's narrow hole. Ctesibius began to experiment with air and sound until he invented the first keyboard instrument. The hydraulis, as it was called, was a musical organ that required a light touch of the keys to drive pressurised air out of a water cistern and through the pipes to make a sound. It would become a popular instrument in Alexandria and the Roman Empire for centuries before being developed into the pipe organ found in churches all over the world.

Ctesibius used his understanding of air, water and sound to create items used in everyday Alexandrian life. He produced singing statues for festivals, one of which depicted Arsinoe as the goddess Aphrodite with its music activated by the outflow of wine. His most acclaimed contribution was enhancing the water clock, or *klepsydra* (literally, the water thief), which was used as a timer. Simply a jar with a hole in the bottom, when the water ran out it signalled that time was up. It was used in political circles to time orators' speeches, in courts to give defendants time to make their cases and in brothels so that clients didn't overstay their welcome. Ctesibius realised that since the volume of the water was changing, the water clock wasn't fully accurate, so he created an indicator system using a float that held a pointer which would rise as the water dripped. This became the most precise timer and remained so for two millennia, when water was replaced with weights in the seventeenth-century pendulum clock. Ctesibius became known as the father of pneumatics (gases) and, before too long, the former barber was heading the Museum. Technological advances continued to spread in the city's daily life as Alexandria's reputation became as iconic as Silicon Valley's today.

Around the first century, an Alexandrian Jew named Maria the Jewess developed the field of alchemy, to the extent that she is now regarded as the first alchemist of the Hellenistic and therefore Western world. Alchemy was rooted in both chemical science and philosophy and had grand aims such as turning metals into gold, finding a universal cure and ultimately a route to immortality. Maria is not as well-known as she might have been had any of her complete works survived. We only know about her from a fourth-century Egyptian alchemy encyclopaedia and some later Arabic translations, though her influence on Alexandria's alchemists continued for centuries. Variously referred to as Miriam the Prophetess, the Sister of Moses and the Daughter of Plato, Maria theorised about the nature of colour and was able to make purple pigment. She also hypothesised about the sexuality of metals, which she believed had genders that had to be paired effectively. Maria also invented laboratory equipment such as a distiller and a furnace, developing versions of which are still used in chemical labs now. Most notably, she invented a double boiler, also known as a water bath, which allows substances to be heated at different paces; its name in French, *bain-marie* (Mary's bath), commemorates its creator.

The early first century also saw Heron of Alexandria make huge advances in mechanics. Visitors gasped as they saw Alexandrian children playing with elaborately moving toy birds that could sing and puppets that danced of their own accord. They even saw robots on the streets: Heron invented a self-powered cart propelled by a falling weight and strings wrapped around the drive axle. When they went to the theatre, audiences witnessed special effects not seen anywhere else: Heron introduced a system of ropes, knots and cogs that transformed possibilities on the stage, as well as realistic sound effects during performances, like thunder, which he produced with a machine that dropped metal balls onto a hidden drum. Visitors also walked past Alexandria's stand-alone fountains (still named after Heron) and couldn't believe how normal it was for Alexandrians to purchase holy water from coin-operated devices: the world's first vending machines. When you deposited the bronze coin in the machine, it fell on a pan attached to a lever, which in turn opened the valve and let water out. The pan tilted with the weight of the coin and when the coin fell off, a counterweight snapped the lever up and closed the valve. Heron was also the first to use wind power by inventing a wind-driven wheel that provided power to a machine, essentially the world's first windmill. He also created self-trimming oil lamps, syringes, fire engines that used force pumps, and some credit him with inventing the thermometer. But Heron's most famous invention was the *aeolipile*, better known as the first steam engine. He mounted a sphere on a boiler that, using nozzles, produced a rotary motion as the steam escaped. Two millennia later the idea became paramount to the success of Europe's Industrial Revolution.

Following Zenodotus and Callimachus, for four decades the Library's director was a polymath named Eratosthenes. Taking charge from 245 BCE, he brought something different to Alexandria: a Stoic philosophy. Having been taught in Athens by the very founders of Stoicism, Eratosthenes was something of a Cynic, a philosophy related to Stoicism that summarised life's purpose as aspiring for virtue while being at one with the natural world. Like his teachers, Eratosthenes believed that people shouldn't be emotional about either pleasure or pain, but should seek knowledge, live in harmony with nature and appreciate the universe's divinity. He introduced new theories about musical tuning and argued that perfect musical scales can cure the soul (Claudius Ptolemy later writes that Eratosthenes invented the 'semitone', the smallest musical interval commonly used in Western music). All of these things – knowledge, nature, spirituality, music – were abundant in Alexandria.

When thirty-year-old Eratosthenes arrived to head the Library, the ageing astronomer Aristarchus was still promoting heliocentrism in Alexandria, and Eratosthenes appears to have been convinced. The new librarian set himself the task of studying the earth in more detail than anyone had previously attempted, combining geography, astronomy and geometry. Some of his discoveries were significant to Alexandrian trade, such as how the oceans are all connected. Two of his further findings were even more important.

By calculating the earth's orbit around the sun, Eratosthenes devised a new calendar that accurately represented the days of the year. He determined that each year has 365 days, but that every fourth year should have 366. Ptolemy III was persuaded and ordered an immediate reform of the calendar. But the Egyptian priests and population weren't ready to accept the replacement of their own longstanding calendar. Realising this could cause unnecessary tension, the king conceded and Eratosthenes' calendar was put aside. A couple of centuries later, though, the Romans took up his idea. The Roman dictator Julius Caesar adopted what was by then known as the Alexandrian calendar from 45 BCE, naming it the Julian calendar, before the emperor Octavian imposed it on Egypt twenty years later. Minor modifications then resulted in the Gregorian calendar of today.[5]

By the time of Alexandria's founding, scholars had observed how ships disappeared over the horizon but their masts remained visible, so the earth might not be flat. Eratosthenes proposed that the earth was perfectly round. He even worked out its circumference, with Alexandria at the centre of his calculation. Eratosthenes erected a pole in Alexandria. Then, on the sunniest day of the year (the solstice), he looked for a shadow. The shadow proved that the sun wasn't directly above Alexandria, but a little to the south, or 7.12 degrees to be precise. Eratosthenes then compared this to a famous well in the Egyptian city of Syene (today's Aswan), where at noon on that day every year, the sun's rays shone straight into the well like an arrow. By dividing 360 degrees (the earth's circumference) by 7.12, and then multiplying it by the distance between Alexandria and Syene (5,000 stadia), Eratosthenes was able to calculate the circumference of the earth with remarkable accuracy. Based on this circumference, he also calculated the earth's diameter which we now know was just fifty miles shy of the exact figure: one of the earliest proofs that scientific calculation works.

Eratosthenes' contributions also included a new map of the world with latitudinal and longitudinal lines that split it into sections: two freezing zones (the poles), two temperate zones and the central equator. He listed and described hundreds of regions of the world, but in doing so made a controversial statement about the geographic inaccuracy of Homer's epic landscape. Coupled with rejecting some of Aristotle's social ideas – such as his separation of the world population into Greeks and barbarians, and opposition to interracial marriage – Eratosthenes ended up becoming surprisingly unpopular. Seen as being interested in too many fields, he was cruelly dubbed Beta (number 2) by Museum colleagues, for whom such multiplicity stopped him from being exceptional in any one field. But Eratosthenes' breakthrough feats in geography were nothing short of Alpha: it's no wonder he became known as the first modern geographer, as the father of geography. In the process, Alexandria became the intermediary between the earth and the cosmos. When

Eratosthenes erected that pole into Alexandria's soil, he had essentially engaged the city as the symbolic centre of the earth – and of the universe. Shortly after he turned eighty, Eratosthenes lost his sight and with it his wellbeing. Being unable to read in the Library or observe the nature of the Mediterranean surroundings appears to have been too much: he refused to eat until he starved to death.

It only took twenty years from the city's founding for the Alexandria School of Medicine to be born. Alexandrian doctors were expected to wear plain clothing and avoid perfumes. Leading physicians spent time in their *iatreion* (physician's office) just outside the Museum, where they saw patients and trained apprentices. Though both paid them, they received the bulk of their earnings from the state.

Egypt already had a good reputation in medicine. The earliest medical document in existence is an Egyptian papyrus on trauma surgery from 1600 BCE based on material from as early as 3000 BCE. Treatments included stitching and bandaging, as well as placing honey on infections and raw meat on bleeding areas. Meanwhile, Hellenistic medicine followed the teachings of Hippocrates, though since his death in 375 BCE it hadn't really evolved. Much of his work, collected in the Library, relied dangerously on generalisation and speculation – as in the case of Alexander's remedial drinking before his death. Influenced by both the Greek and Egyptian schools of medicine, but unashamed about critiquing them, Alexandria was once again suitably positioned to lead a transformation. Soon after its founding in 311 BCE, the School of Medicine swiftly became the most respected institution of its kind in the world, through both its innovative ideas and its position as a place of learning that educated physicians from the wider region. For example, the second-century Roman physician Galen of Pergamon picked up theories and techniques from a variety of schools, which he wouldn't have done at a narrower institution. Galen's teachings, which he developed upon returning to Rome, would go on to influence medieval Arab medicine and form the basis of modern medical practices championed during the European Renaissance. He is particularly important because, unfortunately, not a single original work of Alexandrian medicine has survived. Thorough medical writing jumps from

Hippocrates straight to Galen, who bridges this historical gap by telling us what he learnt in Alexandria.

The school's mantra was as simple as it was transformative: that ideas about the human body should stem from direct observations, not from hypothetical hunches. This meant that the Alexandrian school rejected the Hippocratic belief that an imbalance of humours (bile, phlegm and blood) could cause death. It also rejected the idea that diseases had occult or supernatural causes, a controversial move away from what the majority of people believed.

The first key figure in Alexandrian medicine was Praxagoras of Cos, who followed in the footsteps of his father and grandfather to become a physician. Praxagoras studied Aristotle's anatomical theories in detail and enhanced them by making, for the first time, the important differentiation between arteries and veins, as well as explaining the importance of the pulse. But Praxagoras made his greatest contribution as a teacher, for it was his student Herophilus of Chalcedon who was fundamental to the founding of an Alexandrian medical school.

The heart was long regarded as the unrivalled key to human life; Aristotle called the heart the seat of the mind and, for him, the brain's function was to keep it cool. The Egyptians preserved important organs during mummification, but not the brain. In a process called excerebration, they would drill a hole near the nose before inserting a seven-inch hook into the skull, slowly scooping out bits of brain before rinsing the skull clean. In Alexandria, however, the brain began to take centre stage. Herophilus identified it as the body's controlling organ and introduced four forces: thought (brain), heat (heart), perception (nerves) and nourishment (liver). Aside from describing the brain accurately and linking it to the spine and nerves, Herophilus found a net-like membrane in the eye (the retina), and discovered oval-shaped glands on either side of the female uterus (the ovaries), which he compared with the male testicles.

Next time you're getting a check-up, the doctor will probably get their stethoscope out. You might then remember that it was Herophilus who pioneered the practice of beginning a diagnosis with pulse. Remarkably, he utilised Alexandria's music and poetry scene to relate dilation and contraction of the artery to upbeats and downbeats (the last and first beats of a musical bar) and to the arsis and thesis (the stronger and weaker part of a musical measure or poetic foot). From this, he made a list of expected pulses based on age and health. Next, he invented a method of measurement: by putting the right amount of water in a water clock, he could compare the patient's pulse with what it should be. So, on his home visits around Alexandria, when he walked into a room and placed his bag on the table he would pull a portable water clock out of it.

At Alexandria's medical school, women were welcomed. From that came the legend of Agnodice, regarded for centuries as the first female physician but today presumed to be fictitious. The young woman, said to have lived in the fourth century BCE, fled Athens, where the law prohibited women from studying medicine, evidence of Alexandria's less prejudiced educational culture. After being educated by Herophilus and graduating in Alexandria, she returned to Athens where she was forced to disguise herself as a man in order to practise.

Herophilus was succeeded by his colleague Erasistratus of Ceos, who founded the Alexandrian school of anatomy and became known as the father of physiology. Rather than the pulse, Erasistratus championed body temperature as the first point of diagnosis. He worked out how air enters the body and reaches the heart via the lungs. There, it is transformed into a 'vital spirit' that gets pumped around the body via the arteries.

Erasistratus shot to fame when he cured the prince of the Seleucid Empire east of Alexandria, around the Levant and Mesopotamia. Before becoming king, Seleucus I was one of Alexander's generals and Ptolemy I had helped him take Babylon. When Seleucus' only successor, Antiochus, fell terribly ill, doctors were at a loss. Erasistratus was summoned to the palace and, recognising that it might be a lengthy assignment, took his wife with him. The prince, twenty-seven years old, was barely moving. Erasistratus concluded that there could only be one ailment: love. He decided to observe in particular the prince's reaction to any young woman who made her way into his chamber. But there was nothing. Until, that is, his step-mother walked in. Six years earlier, the king had married the beautiful Stratonice, around forty years younger than him. Plutarch notes that when twenty-three-year-old Stratonice entered the room,

Antiochus' 'voice faltered, his face flushed up, his eyes glanced stealthily, a sudden sweat broke out on his skin, the beatings of his heart were irregular and violent, and . . . he would sink into a state of faintness, prostration, and pallor'. Erasistratus realised the severity of the situation: had it been any other woman, the prince wouldn't have kept it in. The malady was love, he informed the king, but there was no cure. Erasistratus then decided to say that the prince was in love with his own wife, rather than with the queen. The king asked Erasistratus to give his wife up and save the only heir, to which the doctor replied: 'You, who are his father, would not do so if he were in love with Stratonice.' Now in tears, the king answered that he would 'part not only with Stratonice, but with my empire, to save Antiochus'. The doctor took the king by the hand and told him the truth. Antiochus and Stratonice were wedded; she remained his only wife until his death more than thirty years later. Erasistratus, who was gifted 100 talents (around £2 million) for saving the prince, had done something vital: he had linked sexual desire with mental deterioration and more strikingly shown that both of these can result in discernible symptoms in physical health.

Much of the research being carried out by these two early Alexandrian physicians relied on opening up the human body and exploring it, to find out its functions and to better understand pain and disease. Herophilus and Erasistratus were the first to carry out systematic dissections on humans, opening corpses up from the large ventral cavity to explore the various organs, including the heart, liver and intestines. Egyptians had long honoured their dead through elaborate funerary practices, while Greeks regarded cutting skin to be sacrilegious and, more vitally, thought corpses impure and polluted until cremated or buried. Aside from very exceptional surgical cases, cutting up a human – living or deceased – was simply unacceptable. But Herophilus and Erasistratus were not going to stop there. They wanted to see what the body was doing when still functioning. They wondered what the organs should look and sound like as well as how they were linked to one another.

As its population rose, crime in Alexandria was on the increase. Papyri show reports of such crimes as theft, breaking and entering, destruction of property, extortion, illegal habitation, assault and in fact wrongful arrest. The main square, or *agora*, was used for some public punishments; records show this was the case for those who committed crimes while drunk. According to research by John Bauschatz, Ptolemaic police had relative autonomy and were rapid responders.[6] The police chiefs (*archiphylakitai*) received surprisingly polite written petitions from citizens who wanted to report crimes. The lower ranked police (*phylakitai*) were responsible for patrolling, responding to emergencies and hunting criminals. There's also evidence that police were required for crowd control. Police treated criminals harshly, though this was often welcomed by the victims. Herophilus presented the royal palace with an idea: he could conduct his research on criminals. Ptolemy I gave his blessing and in another first, dissections were carried out on living humans. Convicted criminals must have been shaken to the core as they were called out of their prison cells, since these human vivisections took place regularly. The philosopher Celsus, who lived in second-century Alexandria, writes:

> And while breath still remained in these criminals, they inspected those parts which nature previously had concealed, also their position, color, shape, size, arrangement, hardness, softness, smoothness, connection, and the projections and depressions of each, and whether anything is inserted into another thing or receives a part of another into itself. For, they say, when pain occurs internally, it is impossible for one who has not learned in which part each internal organ or intestine lies, to know what hurts the patient. Nor can that part which is ill be treated by one who does not know what it is.

Celsus casually dismissed the fact that this was torture, maintaining that it couldn't be cruel 'that remedies for innocent people of all times should be sought in the sacrifice of people guilty of crimes'.[7]

Aristotle wrote about 35 animals in such detail that he certainly dissected them; most of them would presumably have been dead. But Aristotle never dissected a human – and he would never have imagined the existence of such a liberal city that would allow this. Nonetheless, he unknowingly played his part by arguing that the body and soul are united and cannot exist without one another. This cast doubt on the soul's immortality, in turn reducing the importance of the lifeless body. It therefore made sense for dissections to take flight in Alexandria, where scholars were influenced by Aristotle and where the ruler himself was raised among those ideas. In a short time, the advances made during the living dissections were astounding and continue to influence anatomical understanding and practice. As time went on, however, physicians who wanted to dissect even deceased humans couldn't do that: when word got out, dissection caused too much upset and even protests in the city, which for the Ptolemies was a step too far. Herophilus and Erasistratus were the first and last to dissect living humans and dissection of deceased humans wasn't practised again systematically until the European Renaissance centuries later.

Herophilus' disciples were labelled as Herophilian physicians. But some of his students turned their backs on his practice. Philinus of Cos dubbed Herophilus and Erasistratus as *logikoi* (rationalists) and self-styled himself in a new school of *empeirikoi* (empiricists). This school didn't need dissection, instead focusing on experience. For them, predecessors were too concerned with, for instance, how we breathe rather than how to relieve shortness of breath; it was much more important to cure an illness than to understand it. This could be done by observing patients and collating successful remedies. A long line of empirical researchers followed, including Serapion of Alexandria. Their practical approach would become fundamental to Greek and Roman medicine in the centuries to come.

Herophilus had already pioneered treatments for a variety of illnesses using minerals, plants and animals – and Alexandria had access to an array thanks to Alexander's expeditions in the past. Herophilus called the drugs *munera divina*, 'the hands of the gods'. Poisons had long been used by the Greeks for capital punishment, most famously at the start of the fourth century BCE when Socrates was found guilty of impiety and sentenced to death by drinking hemlock. While this wasn't as much of a concern for the first Ptolemies, fear of assassination began to surface from Ptolemy IV's reign and it became important to find antidotes. The surgeon Zopyrus of Alexandria invented an antidote to poison, but wanted to be sure that it worked. Following Herophilus' example, he asked to test it on criminals.

In the centuries that followed, many more physicians, including Leonidas of Alexandria, developed ground-breaking techniques. The second- or third-century surgeon wrote about how to recognise breast cancer and revolutionised its treatment. While Galen would remove breast tumours with a wide incision then bleed out what he called black bile, Leonidas excised tumours with a precise incision after which he cauterised the tissue with hot irons, or, if necessary, carried out a mastectomy. Precise incision followed by cauterisation would be used for the next millennium and a half, another example of the lasting importance of the Alexandria School of Medicine, an institute that progressed the fields of orthopaedics, gynaecology, pharmacology and toxicology.

While the third librarian, Eratosthenes, was a polymath primarily interested in geography and astrology, the fourth librarian, at the turn of the second century BCE, was a playwright and grammarian. Aristophanes of Byzantium, who took over in his sixties, made a name for himself during the city's prestigious poetry competition when he accused a contestant of passing verses off as his own. Aristophanes ran to the Library, somehow recalled the exact location of the scroll in which he'd read these lines, and returned brandishing the evidence. Aristophanes had already introduced accents into the Greek language in order to aid pronunciation. This helped cement the importance of Greek literature because even schoolchildren could learn to read it. With the Ptolemies advancing Greek as the lingua franca of the region and city, Egyptians and non-Greeks could learn the language more easily. Around 200 BCE, Aristophanes also invented one of the earliest forms of punctuation, single dots that separated verses of poetry so readers and orators knew to pause depending on the position of the dot, which could be at the top, middle, or bottom. The shortest of these was the *komma*, the intermediate one a *kolon*, and the longest pause, with the dot at the top, was the *periodos* (today's full stop is at the bottom). With the arrival of the Romans, the punctuation system was immediately abandoned, the argument being that pauses should come naturally depending on the rhythm. But Aristophanes' idea had already made its mark; his system evolved and, though they look different, the comma, colon and period have exactly the same functions today.

In addition to new ideas, the linguists also worked on compiling words. Aristophanes wrote down all the unusual and archaic words he could think of so that they didn't become obsolete. Lexicography would continue for centuries, as evidenced by the work of Hesychius of Alexandria in the fifth or sixth century, when he wrote an early Greek dictionary named the *Alphabetical Collection of All Words* that contains the earliest reference to many enduring words, including 'amazon'. Aristophanes' students included Aristarchus of Samothrace, who applied his teacher's accent system to Homer's poetry to produce the most influential version of the epics.

Agallis, a female philosopher and grammarian, whom we hear about through the third-century Greek grammarian Athenaeus, also wrote about Homer. In her analyses, she emphasised the role of women, namely Nausicaa from *The Odyssey*, who after washing her clothes in the river and hanging them to dry, enjoys a game of ball with her handmaidens that wakes Ulysses from his sleep in a nearby bush. Agallis argued that Nausicaa was the inventor of ball games, something which over the centuries inspired artists to paint this scene from the epic. Historians have claimed that Agallis must have been a *hetaira*, an educated sex worker, but such unprovable suggestions undermine Agallis's importance: she shows that women were educated under chief librarians and joined the Museum as scholars.

Alexandrian scholars advanced the study of Homer in a different way from their Greek counterparts. In Pergamon, readings of Homer were based on hidden meanings and allegories. The Alexandrian school, however, was interested in close reading, line-by-line, word-by-word, pausing for analysis at every moment. Everything had to be explained. In fact, the first librarian, Zenodotus, believed that the famous description of Achilles' shield in *The Iliad* couldn't be about the shield since it was too different from the rest of the poem, so it must be a description of the celestial spheres. The last recorded librarian, Aristarchus of Samothrace, appointed around 153 BCE, not only continued literary criticism but prioritised it to such an extent that the Museum began to be seen as a literary hub. Aristarchus read Homer so closely that his period is regarded as the birth of detailed critical reading, and the term 'aristarch' came to denote a severe critic.

By gathering all literature and then marshalling it to create a hierarchy of texts, Alexandria essentially invented the idea of a literary canon, or classical texts, a heritage that continues to this day. Alexandria's scholars developed the Canon of Ten: the ten Attic orators of the fourth and fifth centuries BCE who were to be studied and emulated. They also created a selective literary canon of ancient Greek poets worth studying and pairing to music, which they called the list of Nine Lyric Poets.

But Homer still took centre stage. In fact, despite the vibrant literary critical tradition, doubting Homer's greatness remained controversial. The Roman writer Vitruvius claims that when the Greek critic Zoilus came to Alexandria in the fourth century BCE, his attacks on Homer were so contemptible that Ptolemy II had him crucified. Homer's status only grew: towards the end of the third century BCE, Ptolemy IV built a shrine dedicated to the great poet, known as the Homereion, possibly the first deity-like veneration of a Western poet. According to the third-century Roman author Aelian, the centre of the temple boasted a magnificent statue of Homer in a seated position. The statue was placed within a semi-circular arc that included an inscription of each city that claimed Homer as its own. There was also a painting by an artist named Galaton that, rather strangely, depicted Homer vomiting, other poets gathering his bile from the ground. It's not clear what this painting means: it might have been ridiculing the Alexandrian epic poets, or more simply showing how all poets have been inspired by Homer. It might also represent how Alexandria had successfully gathered all of Homer's scattered words and ideas. Of course, Alexandria was founded too late to be Homer's birthplace. But the city subverts the relationship between poet and birthplace: rather than a poet who originates from a place (such as Shakespeare's relationship with Stratford-upon-Avon), Alexandria is a place that originates from a poet (since Homer's poetry inspired Alexander to found it). By boasting such a unique relationship with a hero, as it had done when Alexander's mausoleum was built, Alexandria was able to claim further social and political weight. An Alexandrian poem from the time imagined Homer repeatedly being asked where he's from, with the bard's refusal to answer confirming the message of the Homereoin temple: that it doesn't matter where he was born. The Homereoin was meant to represent a universal Homer so that while other cities fought over their claim to him, Alexandria was presenting itself as the universalising capital of the greatest writer.

Given the Museum's interest in collecting and discussing poetry, Alexandria soon began its own poetic tradition. Ptolemy II's court employed a group of seven leading tragedians known as the Alexandrian Pleiad (a reference to a cluster of seven stars). They were tasked with writing, compiling and researching poetry.

Greek poetry was long and serious: it was concerned with heroic deeds and existentiality. Alexandrian poetry saw a startling shift towards themes of love, eroticism, peace and optimism. Alexandria's poets were light-hearted, witty and experimental. Alexandria's unique poetic scene spoke to its identity. Though it did have a founding myth, Alexandria didn't have a local heritage to continue like the rest of Egypt and Greece. Instead, it was a rapidly growing city trying to make its mark, so its poetry was consciously about Alexandria and for Alexandria. Moreover, its writers came from different ethnicities and tried to appeal to a diverse audience. The Greek tradition of performing poetry aloud was also being combined with the obsessive creation of written scrolls for the Library, where the challenge of categorising the literature also got the poets thinking about different types of poetry. Sadly, the vast majority of early Alexandrian verse has now been lost; we know about it through later Greek and Roman writing.

The early poets include Lycophron, who's said to have written a poem in which Alexander the Great unites the world. There was Theocritus, who wrote idylls, or 'little poems', in contrast to the heroic epic that could go on for dozens of books. Theocritus is credited as the inventor of pastoral poetry as his poems were set in nature, their heroes shepherds, shepherdesses and nymphs. The librarian Callimachus, who catalogued the Library's holdings, was also a prolific poet. He wrote *The Lock of Berenice*, which commemorated the queen's hair being found in the stars. In one of his poems, the god of poetry Apollo tells him to 'keep the Muse slender', or in other words not to write long poetry.[8] Callimachus felt that the epic genre was saturated and that poets weren't very good at it, so he championed the epigram, a short poem that has since been adapted into many languages, such as Latin in the first century and English from the Renaissance period. The fact that epigrams were supposed to be inscribed makes them brief and informative, suitable as decoration for tombstones and monuments like the lighthouse. As scholars copied epigrams onto papyrus for the Library, the epigram developed into a transcribed and therefore literary poetic form.

The Ptolemaic development of Alexandria, particularly its libraries and lighthouse, were obvious forms of soft power, but it's fascinating that even something as abstract as a type of poetry was also used in this way. Some Alexandrian epigrams have survived, and they make clear that the city's sites, like its harbours and lighthouse, played an important role as a backdrop to the literary and more importantly romantic life of Alexandrians. In one epigram, Callimachus laments separation as the poetic speaker sees the love of his life fading into the distance. In another, by the early third-century BCE poet Asclepiades of Samos, the erotic nature of the Alexandrian epigram is clear, and in turn, the liberal nature of the city:

> You protect your virginity? For what purpose?
> When you go to Hades you will find none to love you there.
> The joys of Love are in the land of the living,
> . . . dear virgin, we shall lie in dust and ashes.[9]

But in a sign of how fragile Alexandria's makeup could still be, most poetry excluded Egyptians, and when it did include them they were often depicted as barbaric 'muggers'. Moreover, the fact that the city had its own poetic school meant that feuds were common. In particular, Callimachus had a rift with his student and fellow poet Apollonius of Rhodes. When Apollonius recited part of an epic he was writing, Callimachus attacked the genre, which he likened to a crowded street: 'I hate the epic poem, nor do I take pleasure in the road which carries many to and fro.'[10] Apollonius, of course, replied, and a back and forth ensued in which they slammed poetic insults at one another. Alexandria's literati were forced to side either with Callimachus, the librarian and inventive court poet, or with

Apollonius, the young champion of traditionalism. In the end, the establishment's support for Callimachus meant that Apollonius was forced to leave Alexandria. He headed for Rhodes, where he finished his epic and basked in its success. When Callimachus died, Apollonius returned to Alexandria and became its third librarian. And when Apollonius in turn died, he was buried next to his great poetic rival.

It wasn't just poetry that had forged an Alexandrian distinctiveness, but drama, music and visual art did, too. Ptolemy II enjoyed plays, so ordered a theatre to be built in the royal gardens, which he dedicated to Bacchus, most famous as the god of wine, but also the god of theatre. Inside and outside the royal grounds, theatres played both classic and contemporary tragedies and comedies to packed crowds. One long-running play was about King Candaules, who, in the most anticipated scene, hides his minister in the chamber to watch the beautiful queen undressing as the audience cheered. There were also mimes, parodies and satires, with musicals becoming just as popular as serious tragedy and audiences varying from the pristine to the rowdy. Dancing was taught in some schools and was an important part of the city's festivals. Many preferred to travel during holidays, taking the canal to the neighbouring town of Canopus, which the Ptolemies had redeveloped with a temple dedicated to Serapis. Surrounded by fields of flowers, Strabo writes in the first century BCE, Alexandrians would sing and dance the nights away 'without restraint, and with the utmost licentiousness'. In Alexandria, cabaret-like venues were packed with dancing women and the patrons often joined in. When it came to music, the advances in musical tuning by Eratosthenes and Claudius Ptolemy came in handy. With its impressive music scene, Alexandria became particularly famous as the flute capital. The leading flautists, both male and female, became adored celebrities. The second-century BCE historian Polybius writes about two famous flute players, women named Mnesis and Pothine, who both enjoyed the company of the king himself, Ptolemy II. And one of his descendants, Ptolemy XIII (father of the famous Cleopatra), who reigned in the first century BCE, was known to Alexandrians as Auletes, or the flautist. A more serious pastime was to watch rhetoricians debating. In Athens, debating was political, but in easy-going Alexandria, with an autocratic government, it was a form of entertainment. Some of the more famous rhetoricians garnered celebrity-like followings. In the first century, when the Romans began to stamp more of their identity on the city, gladiator shows and horse racing became popular.

When it came to visual art, sculpting was common in Alexandria. Small statuettes of terracotta, silver and bronze were displayed in homes and shops; larger statues of Alexander and the first two Ptolemies watched over the streets and squares. What differentiated sculpting in Alexandria was its content: caricature-like depictions of everyday or comic occurrences with commoners and peasants of all ages, as well as animals, as the subjects. Like poetry and debating, Alexandrian sculpture was much less serious than its Athenian counterpart; it was for everyone's enjoyment. Hundreds of terracotta statuettes have been excavated over the decades, suggesting that they were commonly used as decoration in homes across all the classes.

Alexandrian art, as demonstrated through poetry and sculpture, was small in size. Nothing highlights this more than a key Alexandrian invention: the art of the mosaic. The mosaic makers produced medallions, known as *emblemata*, using tiny pieces of coloured glass, stone and clay to produce detailed mosaics. The glass *emblemata* that survive today – from the first century BCE and just an inch in size – prove how these bright colours were used to create ornaments that celebrated both Greek and Egyptian cultures. The first-century scholar Pliny writes about these ornaments being exported to Rome, and excavations show that mosaics were an Alexandrian speciality well into the second century. Digs have also revealed many larger mosaics made of tiny pebbles and tesserae tiles, which adorned the floors and walls of streets, palaces and homes across the city. In 1993, when the new library's foundations were being dug, fabulous floor mosaics were found that demonstrated the variety of shades used to create realistic art. One floor mosaic depicts a domesticated dog and dates as far back as the first half of the second century BCE. Despite or maybe because Alexandrian creations were so commonly available, they were regarded as *art* across the region, making the city an important artistic centre for centuries.

Cleopatras

What's in a name? The ancient Greek words *kleos* and *patér* – glory and father – combine to form *Cleopatra*. Each Cleopatra had a Ptolemy for a father. But each wielded authority in her own right. That being said, never has one person overshadowed her namesakes as Cleopatra VII has to so many previous queens. Every one of the Cleopatras, though, has her own unique story. Convoluted in incestuous communions that led to serious family disputes, the Cleopatras all had one thing in common: power.

Under the first three Ptolemies, Alexandria had been imagined, assembled and transformed. It had become the capital of Egypt and the Ptolemaic Empire, developed a strong army, attracted residents from around the region and staked everything on the idea that ultimate knowledge yields ultimate power.

During the reign of Ptolemy IV, the city was in trouble for the first time since its founding. Ptolemy IV, who took the throne around 222 BCE, was heavily influenced by two prominent aristocrats: the first was Sosibius and the second was Agathocles, brother of the king's cherished Egyptian mistress, Agathoclea. They convinced him to eliminate any family member who posed a risk, including his mother, who was poisoned, and his brother, who was scalded to death while bathing. Ptolemy IV married his sister Arsinoe III, and they became the first of the siblings to reproduce. Their reputation was best symbolised by a giant ship, the *tessarakonteres* (forty-rowed), which, according to Plutarch, was 128 metres in length and required 4,000 rowers. Always moored in the harbour, this pleasure boat, equivalent to today's superyachts but more reminiscent of an aircraft carrier, served as a symbol of the monarchy's new state: decadent and out of touch. Ptolemy IV also enjoyed Nile cruises on the *thalamegos*, a 115-metre, two-storey yacht. Its main dining hall had columns of ivory and gold and twenty couches under its decorated ceiling. On the upper deck, another dining room was designed in Egyptian style, with black and white columns, and a third dining area boasted columns of Indian stone and marble statues of the royals opposite a circular shrine to Aphrodite. This lavish personal spending came at the same time as a decline in the living standards of the rising population, in part due to increased taxation to fund the Syrian War against the Seleucids, in which Arsinoe III served as an infantry commander, and in which conscripted Egyptians were forced to fight.

When in 204 BCE Ptolemy IV died in mysterious circumstances, Ptolemy V – officially the first Ptolemy born of a sibling marriage, but also rumoured to be Agathoclea's son – was named king despite being only five years old. Agathocles was the de facto ruler and immediately ordered the killing of Ptolemy IV's wife and sister Arsinoe III. A single announcement informed Alexandrians that both their king and queen were dead. That is when Alexandria saw its first serious protest, one that expanded to become the first of many Alexandrian revolutions. From hereon, Alexandria would develop a reputation for the power of its demonstrators and mobs.

Agathocles was concerned with the rising power of Tlepolemus, a man of Persian origin in charge of the nearby region of Pelusium just east of Alexandria (near modern-day Port Said). Agathocles arrested and publicly shamed Tlepolemus' mother-in-law: something that the Alexandrian population found unsavoury. When Agathocles gathered the military, including the palace guard, to a briefing in advance of the royal coronation, the troops hurled insults at him; sensing danger, he escaped the event. Next, Agathocles accused royal bodyguards of having ties with Tlepolemus; one of these, Moeragenes, was stripped and tortured, but managed to escape. Feeling wronged, he convinced the rest of the army to turn against Agathocles. Meanwhile, the local women turned against his sister Agathoclea, the deceased king's mistress, attacking her and her mother when they spotted them in the temple of Demeter. This was an irredeemable situation as the revolt now involved regular citizens, both men and women, as well as the army. The local population surrounded the royal palace in their thousands and at dawn the army forced its way in. Agathocles surrendered and days later, both he and his sister were dragged into the stadium and killed. Their mother sought refuge in the temple but was also dragged out, stripped, and led to the stadium where she suffered the same fate. The stadium now took on a new purpose that it would maintain for millennia: a place of public rule where dissatisfactions were bluntly expressed.

Ptolemy V was barely six years old, so the army presented him on horseback to the crowds in the stadium. The military may have joined the popular revolution against the courtiers, but they still managed to protect Ptolemaic rule. Even though Agathocles had been defeated, his fellow courtier Sosibius maintained authority and continued to govern as Ptolemy V matured. But Alexandrian residents had begun to take things into their own hands and chasing their leaders out of the city – or killing them before they could get out – became a common occurrence in the decades to come.

The Alexandrian revolt was one thing, but the Egyptian revolt was another. For the next twenty years, the whole of Upper Egypt rejected Ptolemaic authority as increasingly popular movements tried to revert the country to native rule. By 185 BCE, the uprising was successful with the Ptolemies losing the majority of southern and parts of northern Egypt. As the pharaohs and therefore the high priests of the gods, the Ptolemies appeared on temples throughout Egypt, usually engravings of them making offerings to the gods. Now, images of Ptolemy IV and Ptolemy V were being removed from walls up and down the country – for Alexandria, this meant that Egyptians were now beginning to perceive the city as an even more separate state.

Such troubles meant that, rather than venturing to Alexandria, for the first time since its founding, people began to leave it. By the second century BCE, Greek and Egyptian identities had begun to merge as mixed marriages became normalised in Alexandrian culture. The monarchy had given reserve troops land allotments on the outskirts and budding entrepreneurs were moving into the countryside to benefit from its more spacious land and riches; these two groups in particular began marrying Egyptian women. But the new hybrid Alexandrian identity that the first Ptolemies had worked hard to create was falling apart. The Ptolemaic dynasty was losing

its prestige, the city felt unsafe, and having the wrong political affili-
ations was now dangerous. When Ptolemy V became a teenager, he
made the drastic decision to move the royal court out of Alexandria.
On his thirteenth birthday in 196 BCE, a council of priests gathered
to crown the young king at a temple in Memphis. The event involved
them passing a decree that was inscribed on a slab of black basalt to
be displayed on a plinth in the temple courtyard. Two millennia
later, this slab would be found just east of Alexandria in the town of
Rosetta. The document we now known as the Rosetta Stone was
carved in both Egyptian and Greek, its contents confirming and
celebrating Ptolemy V as king. In reality, the decree's terms signal
the increased power of the native priests, who agreed with the
Ptolemies to revert some of Alexandria's powers, as symbolised by
the transfer of the royal court to Memphis.[1]

In 169 BCE, Ptolemy VI was succeeded by his brother, Ptolemy
Eurgetes, or the Benefactor (in later records Ptolemy VIII since
Ptolemy VI's son took the numeral VII). By this time, Alexandria
had all but lost its identity. With revolts around Egypt, the first half
of the second century BCE was a time when the Ptolemies feared
that the Egyptians could stop supporting them altogether, even in
Alexandria, where they were regularly the object of ridicule. Their
answer was to work harder at Egyptianising the city; more Egyptian
priests were included in the political decisions and the scholars were
ordered to update Greek ideas to make them more universal. But
rather than merging Greek and Egyptian identity, Alexandria had
unknowingly become both anti-Greek, on the part of the establishment, and anti-Egyptian, on the part of its intellectual elite. The
atmosphere in the Museum was changing: rather than supporting
the rulers, the scholars were becoming critical of them. So, under
Ptolemy VIII – whom people were now calling Physcon (the
Sausage, or the Potbelly) – many of the remaining intellectuals,
already fewer in number than before, were evicted from the city.
Neglecting the prestige of the office, the king appointed one of his
palace guards as chief librarian. This spearman, named Kydas, probably knew next to nothing about the Library and Museum. Ptolemy
IX – derided as Lathyros (the Chickpea) – didn't do much better,
giving the position to one of his political allies. The decline of the
Mouseion was well and truly underway.

It is in such a context of rising unrest that the women of the palace had to take charge of the political affairs of Alexandria. This is the backdrop against which the first Ptolemaic queen to rule alone, without a king, rose to power. Her name was Cleopatra I.

Queens had long existed in Egypt, usually the pharaoh's mother or consort (principal wife). In Greek society, though, women generally didn't play an active political role. Alexander's father, Philip II, gave the women around him some level of authority, but in Alexandria the queen's role was cemented when Arsinoe married her brother Ptolemy II to become a respected ruler, goddess and role model for the royal women who followed.

Throughout the Ptolemaic period, even non-royal women experienced relative freedom in Alexandria compared to their counterparts in the Hellenistic world. There was a high proportion of formally educated women in Alexandria. Ancient records confirm that first-century BCE Alexandrian women were buying, leasing and inheriting land. There is textual evidence of non-royal Greek women owning property, vineyards and horses, and Egyptian women owning and working farmland. They were also allowed to petition for divorce – if there was no good reason for this, they had to return the wedding dowry, but if the husband was at fault the woman kept it and took a share of his assets. Women could go out unaccompanied in public and did their own shopping in the market. For these reasons, Alexandria developed a reputation as a place where women had a significant influence on public and social life. Writing in the first century, the philosopher Philo of Alexandria described how, if a woman disagreed with a man, she would not hesitate to grab his 'genital parts'.[2] And the embittered fourth-century poet Palladas complained in verse about husbands being beaten with sandals and the number of unfaithful wives in the city.

Both the men and women of Alexandria were open about their sexual urges, especially as they'd long had access to aphrodisiacs and birth control, though neither was entirely effective. In Greek mythology, when Aphrodite, the popular goddess of love and lust, emerges from the sea, she is lying on an oyster shell, before giving birth to the god of sex, Eros. This was enough evidence for most

Alexandrians to treat oysters as aphrodisiacs. When it came to contraception, Egyptian women had long placed honey or acacia leaves in the vagina to block semen. The heart-shaped silphium plant that grew in Cyrene was also in huge demand; Roman poems note that it was worth its weight in silver. Women swallowed a chickpea-sized pill made from the plant monthly to avoid pregnancy, while men would take one as an aphrodisiac. Silphium was available in Alexandria since Cyrene was part of the Ptolemaic Empire. By the second century BCE, demand had become so great that the plant became extinct.

Cleopatra I is important as the first Ptolemaic queen to rule alone and to mint herself on coins. Her father, the Seleucid king Antiochus III, ruled from Antioch (today in the southernmost part of Turkey, a province also claimed by Syria). Antiochus III invaded Ptolemaic territories in Asia Minor and the Romans tried to resolve the conflict on behalf of the Ptolemies in 195 BCE. In response, rather than returning the territories to the Ptolemies, Antiochus III tried to prove his goodwill by announcing that his ten-year-old daughter would marry Egypt's sixteen-year-old king. The following year, instead of marrying in Alexandria or Syria, which would have suggested one king's power over the other, they wed at the halfway point on the Gaza Strip. Papyrus from 191 BCE describes Cleopatra I, who had no blood relation to Ptolemy V, as 'his sister and his wife', confirming that sibling marriage was now a tradition among the Ptolemaic royalty. In Alexandria, Cleopatra I was colloquially referred to as 'the Syrian'. In the 1970s, a gold coin from the period showed up in the antiques market and was purchased by the British Museum. It's the only certain portrait we have of any of the first three Cleopatras: it depicts Cleopatra I with a long, straight nose, plump lips and a rounded chin. Compared to previous Ptolemaic women, at least, we might deduce that Cleopatra I was attractive, bringing welcome genes to the Ptolemaic line.

Ptolemy V was keen to get revenge on the Seleucids, whom the Ptolemies had fought in numerous Syrian Wars since Ptolemy II's reign, and who had now taken several Ptolemaic territories. When Ptolemy V died suddenly in 180 BCE, it appeared, according to the historian Diodorus, that he was poisoned by his courtiers who'd heard that he was about to seize their assets to fund the campaign against the Seleucids. Cleopatra I's husband had died just as he was waging war against her dynasty of origin – so the twenty-six-year-old unapologetically abandoned his plans as soon as she took sole control. Since their oldest son was only six, she immediately declared herself regent; in reality, she had become the sole ruler. Papyrus from the time displays dates that begin with the year, followed by reference to the monarch: on these, Cleopatra I takes the title Thea (Goddess) and precedes her son's name. The local coins displayed her portrait on one side and her son's on the other. In truth, an attack on the Seleucids may have weakened the Ptolemies further. That Cleopatra I took charge was something of a saving grace: she was able to restart diplomatic ties with the Seleucids, especially as her brother was now leading them. Cleopatra I died before she was thirty. It's no coincidence that her first son, Ptolemy VI, became Ptolemy Philometer (Mother-Lover). She had also given birth to another Ptolemy (VIII) and another Cleopatra (II).

On her deathbed, Cleopatra I surprised everyone by picking two regents to take care of her children's empire: a eunuch named Eulaeus, who'd tutored her late husband, and Lenaeus, a Syrian slave who'd accompanied her to Alexandria two decades earlier. In 175 BCE, a couple of years after their mother's death, despite not yet reaching their teens, Ptolemy VI and Cleopatra II were married. But Alexandria was about to face another challenge as Seleucus IV, their maternal uncle who had ruled the Seleucids for the last decade, was assassinated. His brother Antiochus IV secured power and had different plans, beginning a relentless advance into Egypt. Without Cleopatra I, there was no reasoning with the Seleucids.

In 170 BCE, the regents decided that the best course of action was for the three siblings to show a united front. The Ptolemaic army tried to steer the Seleucids away from Alexandria by confronting them in Sinai, a plan that ultimately failed. Amid the chaos, two generals, Comanus and Cineas, seized the opportunity to complete a military coup and take control of Alexandria. Finding himself in a tricky position, seventeen-year-old Ptolemy VI began plans to sneak Alexandria's currency and gold out of the city. He also took the risk of departing to meet Antiochus IV. They struck a deal: the Seleucids would spare Alexandria but Ptolemy VI would now be working for them. News of this deal and the treasury's ransacking dispersed around the city – and riots ensued. Citizens went out in their thousands, protesting and looting. Seizing the opportunity for a second time, the generals Comanus and Cineas appeased the crowds by rejecting the treaty with the Seleucids and replacing Ptolemy VI with his younger brother, Ptolemy VIII. Intriguingly, their sister, Cleopatra II, would remain in power, though this meant a second marriage to a second brother. The Seleucids weren't giving up: their army surrounded Alexandria and placed its entire population under siege. For several months, Alexandrians suffered, but as time passed Antiochus IV realised that entering the city posed the risk of weakening his army and attempting to rule it would mean being subject to constant uprises. He therefore retreated, making Ptolemy VI puppet leader in Memphis, but leaving Ptolemy VIII in control of Alexandria.

Within just a couple of months, the three siblings tried triple-rule again, bringing Ptolemy VI back. Angry with these developments, in 168 BCE Antiochus IV returned, occupying Memphis and declaring himself King of Egypt. As he advanced to Alexandria, the siblings did something that changed Alexandria's fate and shifted the global balance of power: they appealed to Rome for support. According to the first-century BCE historian Livy, the Romans, led by ambassador Gaius Popillius Laenas, met the Seleucids just 'four miles from Alexandria'. As Antiochus IV reached out to shake Popillius' hand, Popillius handed him the tablets confirming the Roman Senate's position. In similar fashion to Alexander's design of the city, Popillius then used a stick to draw a circle in the sand around Antiochus IV, adding that the king could not step out before he replied to the Senate. Shocked but shaken, Antiochus IV agreed not to advance, Popillius shook him by the hand, and after six bursts of conflict that had spanned over a century the Syrian Wars were now over. For the Alexandrians, the gods had saved them. The truth was that Alexandria was now indebted to Rome.

The internal rifts, however, refused to subside: in 164 BCE, Ptolemy VI was ousted by his brother and spent several months at the home of an artist friend in a shabby part of Rome. Meanwhile, the Alexandrians rose against Ptolemy VIII's hard-handed rule and overpowered his bodyguards, forcing him to flee to Cyprus. Ptolemy VI returned and with Cleopatra II had at least four children, including two more Cleopatras and their heir Ptolemy Memphites (later Ptolemy VII). Their elder daughter, Cleopatra Thea, was married to the Seleucid prince Alexander Balas, who would soon become king, but who complicated things further when he elected to attack his father-in-law's army near Antioch. The Ptolemies stood firm during battle, but Ptolemy VI was unlucky, falling from his horse and into a coma. Experienced surgeons worked tirelessly and, to their delight, the pharaoh awoke briefly on the fifth day – just in time for him to be presented with a plate bearing the severed head of his treacherous son-in-law.

The deceased pharaoh's brother, Ptolemy VIII, swiftly returned to Alexandria with his army and remarried his sister. According to the Roman historian Justin, during the wedding celebrations, as the bride was holding her young heir, the groom surprised everyone by murdering his nephew. Justin goes on to describe a short and obese Ptolemy VIII advancing on his grieving sister on the wedding night still 'stained with the blood of her child'. Dressed in a transparent robe that emphasised his grotesque features, he proceeded to rape Cleopatra II.

Ptolemy VIII didn't stop there: Justin adds that he went on to rape his virgin niece, Cleopatra III. Even if, as others suggest, Cleopatra III consented, he had added insult to injury by developing this relationship with his sister-wife's daughter. When Cleopatra III bore her uncle a child around 141 BCE, he married her, making him the first polygamous Ptolemy. Once again, there were three rulers, though this time two of them were women, referred to by Alexandrians as 'the sister' and 'the wife'. Though she had another boy with him, Cleopatra II clearly disliked her brother and married him to maintain power – but having killed her son and married her daughter, the palace's internal feuds were, to put it mildly, becoming more personal than ever.[3]

The public had become used to the ongoing incestuous madness of their overlords and remained fearful about criticising it. But Ptolemy VIII's respectively non-consensual and adulterous relationships with his sister and niece didn't go unnoticed. He was despised for his excessive fornication and feasting, and became notoriously tyrannical, leading many Alexandrians to pack up and leave. He carried out indiscriminate murders, persecuted local Jews and expelled scholars. Alexandria lived in a climate of fear, not least the upper classes on whom he kept tabs. On one occasion, perhaps assuming that certain young men had gathered to plot against him, he ordered troops to surround the gymnasium, slay everyone inside and set it alight. Despite persecuting Cleopatra II's supporters and trying to replace her with Cleopatra III, Ptolemy VIII must have realised that killing his sister would be a step too far – she was simply too popular. Rome had also sent ambassadors to Alexandria ordering Ptolemy VIII to maintain the peace so that their vital grain supply from Egypt – 150,000 tonnes of wheat per year – wouldn't be affected. So, instead, in 132 BCE, with the support of the local population and the army, it was Cleopatra II who made a move. The Alexandrians attacked the palace and exiled her brother and daughter from the city. Cleopatra II was now following her mother's suit by becoming sole ruler of Egypt. Diodorus and Justin write that the couple, who fled to Cyprus, responded by sending a gift to Cleopatra II on her birthday. To her horror, in the middle of the celebrations she opened it to find the dismembered head, hands and feet of her teenage son and heir. Cleopatra II responded to this brutality with her own shocking act of political theatre: rather than honouring her son's remains, she placed the body parts on public display so that everyone could see the kind of people Ptolemy VIII and Cleopatra III really were. The locals tore down the remaining statues of Ptolemy VIII, though when he returned two years later, despite resistance from Cleopatra II's army on the city's borders, he defeated them and regained power.

Alexandria and Egypt were now in a state of constant civil unrest that occasionally tipped into civil war: people variously supported Cleopatra II, Ptolemy VIII, native Egyptian rule, and Roman interests. In 116 BCE, Cleopatra III found herself in a predicament when her uncle-husband died, leaving instructions for her to rule alongside one of her sons, Ptolemy IX or Ptolemy X. With her mother, Cleopatra II, still alive, she also had a powerful enemy. In a sign of how the power dynamic of the city had shifted so that the people had the final say, Alexandrians protested against Cleopatra III's decision to pick her younger son, Ptolemy X. She retracted it and ruled with Ptolemy IX, sending Ptolemy X to Cyprus.

Cleopatra III managed to appease the population by assimilating Greek and Egyptian tradition, introducing herself not as a priestess to the gods, but as the goddess Isis, who by this time was worshipped by both Greeks and Egyptians. But her troubles were only too human, revolving around her children's intermarriages and power struggles. Her oldest daughter, Tryphania, married the Seleucid king Antiochus VIII. Her second daughter, Cleopatra IV, married her son Ptolemy IX. Either Cleopatra IV had a dispute with her mother, or Ptolemy IX preferred Cleopatra Selene, his other sister. Either way, Ptolemy IX left Cleopatra IV for their sister. This would prove to be one of the most dramatic divorces in history. When she learnt of the divorce, Cleopatra IV crossed to Cyprus with the intention of preparing an entire army to fight her ex-husband. To do so, she offered her hand to the powerful Seleucid prince, Antiochus Cyzicenus, in order to support her operation. To strengthen their army, though, they decided to overthrow Antiochus Cyzicenus' bitter rival, his brother and her brother-in-law, King Antiochus VIII. The two Antiochuses fought a bitter war which Antiochus Cyzicenus won to become Antiochus IX. Cleopatra IV was gaining power in Antioch, where she was in charge of the royal palace and was readying the army to return to Alexandria. But in 114 BCE, in her husband's absence, Antiochus VIII took the opportunity to reinvade Antioch. Cleopatra IV went into hiding and when she was found her sister Tryphania ordered her punishment: with Cleopatra IV's hands attached to a holy altar, both were chopped off. Shortly later, she was executed – just before she could carry out the master plan against her former husband.

Back in Alexandria, Cleopatra III was still determined to rule with Ptolemy X, the son she'd originally picked. So she ordered some of her own guards to be beaten, then in a public square announced that they had saved her from Ptolemy IX, whom she claimed was trying to kill her. The Alexandrian residents chased Ptolemy IX out of the city. Cleopatra III divorced her final daughter Cleopatra Selene from Ptolemy X and married her to Ptolemy IX. A few years later, in 102 BCE, she divorced her again and offered her to

Antiochus VIII in order to make peace with the Seleucids. But Cleopatra III's grip on power irritated even those closest to her. Ancient sources note that the following year, Ptolemy X reached the end of his tether and ordered the killing of his controlling mother. Cleopatra III had made a mark by getting people across Egypt to revere her as Isis, but she died having failed to unite the Ptolemies.

After his mother's death and sister's departure, Ptolemy X needed a queen, so he married his niece, Berenice III. To continue the family's naming traditions, she became Cleopatra Berenice. Without his mother, however, Ptolemy X was a weak ruler. His obesity and reputation for decadence didn't look good in light of Alexandria's diminishing food supplies and failing economy. In 88 BCE, protests once again deposed the king and his exiled brother Ptolemy IX returned to Alexandria. Cleopatra Berenice remained popular, so was kept as queen. When Ptolemy IX died in 81 BCE, she had enough local support to rule alone.

Three key developments occurred at this time. The first is that when Ptolemy X was expelled from Alexandria he sought further support from Rome. In return, and we can only speculate on the exact circumstances, his will specified that in the event of dying without an heir he would bequeath Egypt to Rome. This may have been collateral signalling the extent of the loans he was taking. Though Rome didn't act on this will, it became a bargaining tool that essentially gave them power to intervene in Egypt. That power is visible in the second development: the Romans – who remained the only force stopping a Seleucid advance on Alexandria – made it clear that they weren't prepared to accept that Egypt could be ruled solely by a woman. Six months into Cleopatra Berenice's reign, they ordered her to find a man. Ptolemy X's son, her nephew from an unknown mother, married her to become Ptolemy XI. It seems that he had been previously exiled from Alexandria for having 'plundered', to use historian Strabo's term, the gold sarcophagus of Alexander, although it's just as likely that the gold of Alexander's tomb was removed and melted down to pay off debts. Nineteen days after taking the throne, in an attempt to rule alone, Ptolemy XI murdered the queen. The local population were already referring to him as Ptolemy Pareisactus, meaning the Usurper or the Illegitimate, and Ptolemy Cocces, literally meaning the Scarlet, but actually a slang term that made him Ptolemy the Cunt. The local mob swiftly rioted against the new king, forcefully dragging him out of the palace and lynching him in the stadium. The third development is that, despite staggering efforts to intermarry in order to keep the bloodline royal, the brothers Ptolemy IX and Ptolemy X now introduced illegitimate children into the mix. Next on the throne was one of Ptolemy IX's sons, Ptolemy XII, whose mother was also unknown and whose nickname in Alexandria, Nothos (the Bastard), emphasised the point.

As he took the throne around 80 BCE, it was clear that a major change had crept up on Alexandria. The city was essentially under Roman jurisdiction.

Ptolemy XII was a noted womaniser who became known as Auletes, or the flute player. He married his sister, Tryphania, who became Cleopatra V. Mentioned on only a few papyri and etched on only a few walls, the scarcity of sources suggests that Cleopatra V might have been the illegitimate daughter of one of Ptolemy IX's mistresses, who was possibly Egyptian. The siblings had at least one child, Berenice IV, though Ptolemy XII also fathered four children whose mothers can't be confirmed, namely Arsinoe, Ptolemy XIII, Ptolemy XIV, and a girl who would go on to become the most famous Cleopatra of all.

In Rome, the elections of 59 BCE saw bitter rivalries and corruption as well as the rise of an army general turned governor in his early forties named Gaius Julius Caesar. A man who'd read Alexander's biographies, he harboured significant ambitions and held himself in such high regard that, in his twenties, when kidnapped by pirates a few hundred miles off the coast of Alexandria, they were amused by his arrogance and astonished when he objected that the ransom they were demanding for him was too low. Successfully elected as consul, Caesar made the argument that since Ptolemy XII was illegitimate, Rome could claim its contractual right to Egypt. Rome started by invading Cyprus, where Ptolemy XII's brother, Ptolemy of Cyprus, was king. As he was about to be captured, Ptolemy of Cyprus decided to kill himself. Alarmed, Ptolemy XII instigated conversations with the Roman politicians, including Caesar. He offered financial incentives in return for their support. In particular, he won the backing of a leading general named Pompey, whom he sent a golden crown and 8,000 cavalrymen, and whose own life would impact Alexandria greatly in the next decades. These bribes signified a huge expense for Alexandria and that meant Rome was now even more powerful. Ptolemy XII was, ironically, borrowing money from Roman creditors in order to fund bribes to Roman politicians. The cost was felt on the ground: papyrus from the time shows Alexandrian soldiers being ordered to fight for Rome, strikes by farmers working on royal land, and most significantly, taxes reaching an all-time high. Plus, Alexandrians were shocked that the pharaoh had lost traditionally Ptolemaic land, was grovelling to the people responsible for his brother's death and was succumbing to Rome in this way. Five years earlier, they'd received news of Syria becoming a Roman province and they feared the same fate. For weeks, Alexandria was embroiled in protests and civil unrest as Ptolemy XII's reign hung by a thread. In an atmosphere that was more tense and more anti-Roman than ever before, mobs roamed the city and boasted more power than the government. Diodorus writes how he witnessed a mob chasing a Roman who'd killed a cat and surrounding his house. Despite pleas from the king's officials, the man was lynched. While in Alexandria, Diodorus advises, if you happen to walk past a cat's corpse, make sure to shout 'it was already dead'.

In response to the carnage in Alexandria, Ptolemy XII travelled to Rome to seek military support. His eleven-year-old daughter hopped onto the boat with him. He was no doubt training her to become queen, though surely not anticipating that she would one day become the most famous queen of them all. Meanwhile, Alexandria's citizens were one step ahead: in his absence, they declared his deposition, nominating his daughter Berenice IV instead. Now restyled as Cleopatra Berenice IV, she ruled with her mother – and for the first time, two queens, two Cleopatras were in power.

Just months later, in 57 BCE, Cleopatra V died and her daughter Cleopatra Berenice IV was ruling alone. She looked for a husband to rule with her but refused to settle for just anyone: when a Syrian prince came to Alexandria, she was unimpressed by his character and ordered for him to be strangled, before then marrying an Anatolian prince.

Meanwhile, Ptolemy XII was being hosted by his ally Pompey in Rome. Pompey had formed a coalition with Caesar and Rome's richest man, Marcus Crassus. The exiled pharaoh continued to try convincing Rome to facilitate his return to Alexandria, and with mounting pressure from the creditors who wanted him back in power in order to get their returns, the Senate decided to help Ptolemy XII. But they still didn't believe that invasion was worth the potential losses. As news of Rome's stance spread, Alexandria prepared its response. According to the Roman historian Cassius, an envoy of 100 Alexandrians, led by a respected philosopher named Dio of Alexandria, was sent to Rome to explain that Egypt didn't want Ptolemy XII back. On hearing this, Ptolemy XII arranged for Dio to be poisoned and sent men to kill the group on the outskirts of Rome.

Finally, in 55 BCE, Ptolemy XII managed to convince a Roman general named Aulus Gabinius to invade Alexandria for him. The price? Ten thousand talents (more than £200 million today). To put this into perspective, Ptolemy I's early treasury totalled around 8,000 talents. The wondrous lighthouse had cost 800 talents to build. That this much money was borrowed signified the beginning of the end for Ptolemaic Alexandria. Within a century of its founding, Alexandria had become larger than Carthage and the biggest challenger to Rome. Now, two and a half centuries after its founding, there was no doubt that Rome was on top.

From the outskirts of Alexandria, the Roman army attacked the city's defence lines and marched straight into the palace. Ptolemy XII immediately ordered the execution of his daughter, Cleopatra Berenice IV, and all who supported her. To maintain power, he introduced disastrous measures that further signalled an imminent Roman takeover. First, Roman soldiers and mercenaries of Germanic and Gallic origin – known as *Gabiniani* – manned the streets of Alexandria to put a stop to the idea that the people could overthrow the government. The 2,000 infantrymen and 500 cavalrymen initially maintained strict order, but within a few months, it became clear they were above the law as they threatened and terrorised citizens. Over the next few years, it became hard to imagine the streets without the *Gabiniani*, a staple of Alexandria's setup who would eventually settle and raise families in the city. Second, with the creditors seeking repayment, Ptolemy XII needed to raise taxes. Knowing that this would be a fatal mistake, he appointed his main Roman creditor, Rabirius, as the *dioiketes*, or chancellor, so that he could take the blame for the tax rises instead. Rabirius had free rein over Egypt's treasury and took swathes of land for himself. Third, Ptolemy lowered the value of Alexandrian coins in an attempt to pay the loan back quickly. This meant mixing less valuable metals with the gold and silver coins so that they still weighed the same and appeared to have equal value, whereas in reality their intrinsic value had been diminished.

The Roman cavalry that stormed Alexandria in 55 BCE was led by a commoner in his late twenties named Mark Antony. During the expedition, he had caught a glimpse of Ptolemy XII's fourteen-year-old daughter, Princess Cleopatra. In May 52 BCE, realising that his health was deteriorating, Ptolemy XII announced this daughter, now seventeen, as co-regent, and a year later he died. It was now time for the most famous Ptolemy of all, for the most famous queen in history. Cleopatra VII took power.

Ageless Cleopatra

'Age cannot wither her' – the most pertinent description of Cleopatra VII in Shakespeare's tragedy *Antony and Cleopatra* stands true even today. While it alludes to Cleopatra's beauty and status, it also points to her ageless prevalence as an historical icon. Cleopatra's character continues to intrigue and defy the tests of time. Her story involves an enigmatic heritage, sibling rivalry, power grabbing and love affairs.

With the exception of those three years in Rome between the ages of eleven and fourteen, Cleopatra was raised in Alexandria. Tutored privately in the palace by a scholar named Philostratos, she learnt philosophy and oration. Frequenting the nearby Museum and Library, she took an interest in medicine and would have been able to read about the powerful queens of ancient Egypt. Images engraved on stone slabs suggest that she may have dressed as a man in order to attend some subjects, such as rhetoric and philosophy. She also developed her language learning, enabling her to communicate in at least eleven languages and perhaps more. In addition to Greek and Latin, Plutarch notes that she didn't need an interpreter among the 'Ethiopians, Troglodytes, Hebrews, Arabians, Syrians, Medes, Parthians, and many others'. Her linguistic acumen suggests an international vision for her empire, beginning with its capital. That she preserved Macedonian, a Hellenistic language abandoned by her predecessors in favour of the Alexandrian dialect of Greek, shows her nostalgia for the earliest Ptolemaic ideals, the ones that came with the founding of Alexandria. That she became the first Ptolemaic ruler to speak, read and write Egyptian confirms her hybrid Alexandrian identity and would become evident in her choice of clothes, too, a mix of Hellenistic and Egyptian. It also signalled her respect for the Egyptian population and priesthood, and above all the desire to be a popular queen.

Although her father died in March 51 BCE, the Roman Senate only learnt of this some three or four months later. This suppression of information is the first indication of Cleopatra's ambition to rule without bowing to Rome, an ambition that would quickly become impossible. Despite her father's will specifying co-regency, official documents from the time indicate Cleopatra as sole ruler, proving that she was able to shun her brother Ptolemy XIII; after all, he was only eleven.

Spring had now run its course and the Egyptian sycamores around Alexandria were laden with figs when Cleopatra became queen. It had been 280 years since Alexander had founded the city and 260 years since her forefather, Ptolemy I, had established it as the capital. Now, Alexandria and its fortunes would have been unrecognisable to both founders. For one, the population was in the hundreds of thousands – maybe even becoming the first city to reach a million inhabitants. More drastically, many of its citizens were struggling. Taxes had been raised because, thanks to her father's ineptitude, Cleopatra inherited a hefty 17.5 million drachmae debt to Rome (approximately £550 million). Nature wasn't cooperating either: Egypt was experiencing a drought and the annual Nile flooding came at a lower level than usual, so food supplies were falling short. Ironically, the *Gabiniani* who'd been sent to Alexandria to maintain order had finished their tenures and were now wreaking havoc, disobeying the law in every way imaginable. Though they'd kept her father in power, Cleopatra immediately wanted rid of them. When the governor of Roman Syria sent his two sons to Alexandria to recruit the unemployed *Gabiniani* to his army, the *Gabiniani* tortured and murdered the guests. Cleopatra used the opportunity to exile them to Syria to be tried for murder. In a sign of what was to come, she was stunned to find the *Gabiniani* sent back to Alexandria with a message that she should not interfere in Roman affairs. When young Cleopatra had accompanied her father to Rome, they were hosted by the general Pompey, who had since fallen out with Julius Caesar in a bitter civil war. In 49 BCE, Pompey's son arrived in Alexandria to request military support on behalf of his father, so Cleopatra used the opportunity to send him some *Gabiniani*, as well as 60 ships and 500 troops that counted towards the debt repayment.

Ptolemy XIII's tutors had their own plans, and with the help of Pompey announced Cleopatra's brother as sole ruler, forcing her to leave Alexandria and travel to Syria, the home of her younger sister, where she could rally troops for a return. When Cleopatra attempted to come back, however, her brother's army was waiting, strengthened by the remaining *Gabiniani*; she was unable to enter Alexandria and forced to camp near the Nile Delta. Meanwhile, Caesar had defeated Pompey, who now sought asylum in Egypt, certain that Ptolemy XIII would honour his late father's friend. As Pompey's ship docked in September 48 BCE, he was immediately ambushed and stabbed to death, his head severed and his body thrown into the sea. With this act, Ptolemy XIII's advisers had hoped to win Caesar as an ally, so when Caesar arrived three days later in pursuit of Pompey, he was presented with his enemy's head. Plutarch writes that Caesar 'turned away from him with abhorrence' and 'burst into tears'. Plutarch may have sought to present an honourable Roman, but Caesar had arrived in Alexandria with an army, immediately demanded the owed money, and swiftly made himself at home in the royal palace. The first-century Roman poet Lucan writes that frightened Caesar 'distrusted the city's walls and defended himself by closing the gates of the palace' like a 'beast, penned in a narrow case, [who] roars and bites the bars'.[1]

Cleopatra and Ptolemy XIII were barred from their own palace and their city. At this stage, Cleopatra decided to form an allegiance with Caesar. Known for his sexual excess – 'every woman's man and every man's woman', according to the first-century Roman historian Suetonius – Cleopatra went to meet him.[2] The historian Cassius Dio writes that she dressed attractively and charmed him with her wit and knowledge. Plutarch adds:

> For her actual beauty, it is said, was not in itself so remarkable that none could be compared with her, or that no one could see her without being struck by it, but the contact of her presence, if you lived with her, was irresistible; the attraction of her person, joining with the charm of her conversation, and

the character that attended all she said or did, was something
bewitching.

Plutarch narrates that Cleopatra took a small boat to the palace at
dusk. In order to gain entry, she was wrapped in a rolled-up bedcover
and smuggled into Caesar's chamber. In a remarkable moment
repeatedly portrayed in Hollywood, the cover (soon depicted as a
Persian rug) was unfurled before Caesar to reveal the young queen.
Plutarch adds that 'captivated' Caesar developed a 'passion for
Cleopatra', who at twenty-one, was more than thirty years his
junior. The details of the story are probably an embellishment, but
that the world's most powerful man was infatuated with Cleopatra
is not.

Ptolemy XIII was livid to discover that his sister was residing with
Caesar in the palace. So he resorted to a powerful Alexandrian tool:
the local population. But before any riot got into full swing, Ptolemy
XIII was arrested and Caesar stood in front of the protesters to calm
them using persuasive oratory. Under the ongoing influence of
Rome, Alexandria now had an Assembly that passed legislation, so
Caesar gathered the siblings there to reveal their father's will for
them to govern together, adding that their other siblings, the teenagers Arsinoe IV and Ptolemy XIV, should rule Cyprus.

To Ptolemy XIII and Arsinoe IV, this setup unfairly favoured
Cleopatra, and they assumed that their army of 20,000, plus the
Gabiniani, could defeat Caesar's 4,000 troops with ease. In August
48 BCE, the Siege of Alexandria began. The Roman army was
besieged at the harbour, the palace surrounded and attacked – with
Caesar and Cleopatra inside. Blocked on both land and sea, Caesar
and Cleopatra remained in the palace for months.

Without warning, an immense and devastating fire began to
spread from the harbour towards the city. Caesar had deduced that
his only chance of repelling the enemy was to burn their ships, but
the fire spread rapidly to the docks, nearby houses and into the city.
Every summer, Etesian winds from the Aegean Sea hit Alexandria
from the north, providing a much-loved Mediterranean breeze.
This time these winds were pushing the fire into the city. Plutarch
describes not only fire but 'carnage'. After visiting Alexandria, the
historian confirms that this was no accident, adding that Caesar's

fire 'spread from the dockyards and destroyed the Great Library'. Caesar even boasts about this decision in his written *Commentaries* on the war, in which he refers to himself solely in the third person:

> the enemy endeavored to seize with a strong party the ships of war . . . They were all of either three or five banks of oars, well equipped . . . Besides these, there were twenty-two vessels with decks, which were usually kept at Alexandria, to guard the port. If they made themselves masters of these, Caesar being deprived of his fleet, they would have the command of the port and whole sea, and could prevent him from procuring provisions and auxiliaries . . . But Caesar gained the day, and set fire to all those ships, and to others which were in the docks.[3]

The extent of the conflagration's damage is unclear, but the Great Library was one victim of this great fire. Rumours that Caesar ordered the Library's burning were inevitable. After all, it was the shining beacon of the Ptolemies and Alexandria. We may never know the extent to which the Library was damaged, but we can pinpoint this moment, when smoke hit the Library, as the beginning of its decline. We can also deduce that some of the sister libraries closer to the harbour and storerooms near the dockyard are unlikely to have survived. As Cassius Dio notes, the fire destroyed storerooms full of grain and books that were 'great in number and of the finest' quality. The philosopher Seneca writes that 'forty thousand books were burned at Alexandria' and the historian Ammianus Marcellinus, writing in the late fourth century, puts the number at '700,000 volumes'.[4] So rather than the Library structure, which did survive in some form, the biggest loss is the writing that was destroyed: tens or maybe hundreds of thousands of scrolls collated and written by nine generations of scholars. These works may have illuminated our understanding of numerous discoveries, including the source texts used by some of the greatest philosophers, and of course they could have helped us to build a clearer image of the ancient world and Alexandria. Despite being a serious self-chronicler, Caesar remained silent on the fact that his fire may have caused the loss of some of the world's greatest books. The fire made him an increasingly unpopular figure, and Alexandrians are said to have glimpsed him on a ship and stormed on board, only for Caesar to strip his armour off and plunge into the water, hand raised high to save some documents from the waves. If the story is true, there is an irony to Caesar's insistence on saving these papers as smoke was still emanating from the Library.

What was going through Cleopatra's mind as she watched her city and its famous Library in flames? It seems she had no choice but to stick with Caesar – whose child she was now carrying – in the hope that her choices would pay off. Cleopatra was playing a longer game, using Caesar and his army to install herself as sole ruler of Egypt. Objectively, this was a war between the Roman and the Alexandrian army, which had recruited citizen militias, so Cleopatra's traitorous allegiance to Caesar represented a huge risk. They watched from the palace as thousands of Alexandrian soldiers and residents lined up ready for battle. Roman military rule was clearly not welcome. And to the people, Cleopatra was nothing more than a Roman puppet.

When her sister Arsinoe IV was declared queen by the Alexandrian army, new tactics were deployed, again at the city's expense. Arsinoe IV's tutor, the eunuch Ganymedes, was familiar with the city. He knew that since Deinocrates designed Alexandria, the drinking water available near the harbour, including the royal quarters, relied on river water flowing into the canals and through the cisterns. So in an early form of chemical warfare, he split the canal into two and added water pipes to pump seawater into the royal quarters. For days, panic hit the palace. Cleopatra, knowing that Alexandria was built on limestone, responded by digging freshwater wells.

Caesar had long marvelled at the Pharos Lighthouse. He even provides us with one of the only surviving first-hand descriptions: it was of a 'prodigious height', he wrote, 'built with amazing works'. He knew that the key to capturing Alexandria was the harbour. Although he sent for reinforcements, the winds made their landing in Alexandria more difficult. As they approached, Arsinoe IV's navy attacked and a battle ensued just north of Pharos. Before long, every Alexandrian battleship, even those that needed maintenance, had arrived to assist. The Romans, much more used to close sea combat, managed to prevail. Caesar ordered an attack on the Alexandrians stationed on Pharos so that he could control the harbour, before placing defence lines around the Heptastadion. The causeway had a channel under its bricks through which ships could pass from one port to the other; fearing that Alexandrian ships could do just that, the Romans began blocking this arch with stones. But on land, the Alexandrian army hadn't given up: heavily armed troops sneaked behind the Romans at the causeway and attacked them. Though the Romans controlled Pharos, they didn't yet control its surrounding area. The Siege of Alexandria was essentially a stalemate. But the expansive nature of Rome's army and allies across the region meant that there was only ever going to be one winner. In early 47 BCE, a year and a half after the siege began, major Roman reinforcements arrived. The Alexandrian army escaped towards the Nile; Caesar chased them for a while before returning to Alexandria to declare victory. Cleopatra's brother, Ptolemy XIII, was drowned in the river as he tried to escape. On the streets of Rome, her sister Arsinoe IV was captured and paraded in chains alongside a burning effigy of the Pharos lighthouse – so humiliating was the display that the crowds, used only to seeing grown men in this context, sympathised with the weeping girl and chanted for her life to be spared.

And Cleopatra, who had stayed in the luxury of the palace all along, was now carrying Caesarion – 'little Caesar'.

In his early thirties Caesar had wept at a statue of Alexander the Great, lamenting how much Alexandria's founder had achieved at that age compared to him. Two decades later, Cleopatra was taking him on a tour of the city that Alexander established. They visited the founder's mausoleum. The sarcophagus' gold had been stolen, but the less impressive glass tomb didn't diminish Caesar's excitement. A long line of Roman leaders would follow suit by visiting the mausoleum. Cleopatra and Caesar then cruised the Nile. Far from the usual depiction of a romantic trip on a slender barge, this was an indulgent journey on the colossal *thalamegos*, the two-storey pleasure cruiser built for Ptolemy IV.

After their expedition, Caesar departed, leaving three Roman legions to protect – or keep an eye on – the queen. Since she was a woman, he also placed her brother, Ptolemy XIV, not yet a teenager, as nominal co-ruler. As the Roman historian Orosius explains, 'Caesar, now victorious, obtained control over Alexandria, by far the richest and greatest of all cities.' But the conquest led to unprecedented inflation: 'Its riches so enhanced Rome's wealth that the abundance of money raised the value of property and other sellable goods to double what they had been up to this time.'[5]

Another reason for the quick departure was that Caesar's illegitimate son with Cleopatra now posed a risk to his reputation. Alexandrians had accepted the reality of Roman control, but they also realised that Alexandria could yield some influence on Rome. They referred to Cleopatra's son as little Caesar, while his name was inscribed in temples as Pharaoh Caesar. Though Caesar denied fathering him, Cleopatra made no secret of it, including her son's parentage on official declarations and building for the baby a grand temple on the harbour. Meanwhile, in Rome, Caesar erected a bronze statue of Cleopatra as a goddess, something the Romans condemned since their tradition reserved divinity for those who've left the world, not those still living in it. Cleopatra, in turn, began constructing the Caesareum of Alexandria, a temple in Caesar's honour.

Cleopatra was now commuting between Alexandria and Rome. In 46 BCE, one of her guests in Caesar's suburban park villa was the republican senator Cicero, whose request for Cleopatra to bring him books indicates the reputation that Alexandria still retained. Cicero was disappointed to learn that Cleopatra's aides hadn't brought the requested books, leading to a letter in which he admits that he 'hate[s] the queen' and her 'insolence'. Alexandria was still a centre of knowledge and Rome wanted to make use of that. Cleopatra's party included the astronomer Sosigenes of Alexandria, who helped Caesar adopt a new calendar. The Roman calendar's twelve months totalled only 355 days. Alexandrian scholars had two centuries earlier worked out that, based on the sun, each year should have 365 days, with an extra day every fourth year. With Sosigenes' help, Caesar introduced a new calendar that remains in use today. To celebrate this new Julian calendar, Caesar's birth month, Quintilis, was renamed Julius, or July.

But it is another month that would become most identified with Caesar. Roman historians report that in 44 BCE a soothsayer warned

Caesar to beware the Ides of March: the fifteenth day of the month, associated with misfortune and debt repayment. Caesar must have suspected that certain senators wanted to curtail his increased powers, yet still went to meet them on that day. More than sixty politicians had conspired against him and when he arrived at the Roman Senate, he was stabbed 23 times.

Caesar seemed to have left Rome heirless; his only daughter had died and he hadn't had a child with his fourth wife Calpurnia. The stage looked set for Cleopatra's son, but the Romans disputed his legitimacy. Either way, Cleopatra now waited in Rome to see whether this was Caesarion's moment. It wasn't: Caesar had actually left a will naming his grand-nephew, Octavian, as successor. Within a month of Caesar's death, Cleopatra was back in Alexandria.

At this time, she may even have been pregnant with a second child by Caesar. A letter from Cicero written just weeks after Caesar's assassination refers to a miscarriage suffered by the general Cassius' wife, adding: 'I am hoping that it is true about the queen and about that Caesar.' To the relief of the Romans, Cleopatra appears to have miscarried.[6] But her plan to yield power through her son wasn't lost. Since mothers could co-rule with their sons, that summer she elevated Caesarion to co-ruler as Ptolemy XV Caesar. It's probably not a coincidence that her fifteen-year-old brother Ptolemy XIV died at this time, though the only record that Cleopatra killed him is in biased Roman accounts. This signalled a new and important chapter for Cleopatra, who was self-styling herself – like Cleopatra III but with considerably greater success – as the much-adored Egyptian goddess Isis.

Isis is the wife of one of Alexandria's most significant gods, Osiris, whose resurrection was the most important tale in ancient Egyptian belief. In the story, Set embarks on murdering his elder sibling Osiris in order to usurp the pharaonic throne. To prevent any possibility of Osiris coming back to life, Set dismembers his brother's body and hides it. Osiris' sister-wife, Isis, goes in search of her husband's corpse. Once found, she mummifies him and manages to reassemble the disjointed body parts. Osiris is magically revived and impregnates Isis with their child, Horus, the future god distinctively born of a resurrected father and the rightful heir to the throne, whom Isis raises as a perfect single mother. Isis' epithet summarised her venerated role, 'mother of the gods' (a variation of which would soon describe a woman born a couple of decades later, Mary, mother of Jesus). By presenting herself as Isis, Cleopatra was able to win the Egyptian people over and add legitimacy to Caesarion as her divine son.

Alexandria was facing many challenges: a reduced harvest meant more hunger and civil unrest still permeated the city following the events of the previous decade. Worst of all, prices were consistently rising. People looked to Cleopatra, the incarnated spouse of the god of agriculture, to solve the reduced harvest. She responded by ordering Alexandria's mint to reduce the silver and bronze content in the coins, while increasing production of bronze coins. The coins were also inscribed with their values so that, for the first time in the city, money had a nominal rather than tangible value that everyone would have to accept. Where her ancestors tended to put their faces on Alexandria's silver coins, used by the wealthy, Cleopatra put her face on everything, for everyone, including the low-value bronze used by the public for everyday purchases.

But Alexandria's destiny was still linked to Rome. There, alongside Mark Antony – who had met a young Cleopatra a decade earlier – Octavian was attempting to capture the ringleaders behind Caesar's assassination, Brutus and Cassius. Both Caesar's successors and assassins turned to Cleopatra for military support in return for recognising Caesarion as co-ruler of Egypt. Cleopatra tried to delay the decision: either her union with Caesar was more tactical than heartfelt, or her political ambitions outweighed any prior affection. Forced to choose an allegiance, she opted for Caesar's heir, claiming to Cassius that she couldn't take risks because Alexandria was suffering from famine. It was probably in her best interest that a mighty storm hit the Mediterranean as she went to support Octavian. Her damaged fleet returned to Alexandria, where news shortly arrived that Brutus and Cassius had committed suicide.

With Octavian ruling in Rome, Antony was in Tarsus (modern-day Turkey), where he summoned Cleopatra, accusing her of supporting Cassius – this was untrue and probably an attempt to extort money as appeasement. Cleopatra left Alexandria on the *thalamegos* and the people gathered to watch her arrival. The boat's silver oars and bright purple silk sail shone in the sunlight as

Cleopatra reclined under a golden canopy dressed in the most colourful robe. A wonderful scent emanated from the boat, where incense had been lit, as flutes, lutes and pipes created a magnificent musical backdrop and young boys dressed as Cupid raced around its deck. Cleopatra's awesome entry was part of a plan, which she continued by declining Antony's invitation to dine, asking him instead to her own banquet on the boat. Pliny's accounts indicate that Cleopatra was viewed as an enchanting, eccentric and excessive woman. She allegedly wagered with Antony that she could host the most lavish meal in history. Alexandrian coins from Cleopatra's time show the queen wearing pearl necklaces, both long and short, and she wore pearl-embroidered dresses. Cleopatra surprised Antony by taking off one of her pearl earrings – purported to be worth ten million sesterces (over £25 million) and dropping the pearl into a cup of wine vinegar before drinking it. She was interested in alchemy, so she may have added enough acid to ensure the pearl melted, or she may have crushed the pearl, or even swallowed it whole. Legend has it that the Romans screamed at Cleopatra not to melt the second pearl and later cut it into two and placed it inside Venus' ears in Rome's Pantheon.

Antony had promised his fighters huge rewards but could not afford them, while Alexandria was under threat from Pompey's son who was controlling a fleet of pirate ships around Sicily. Cleopatra wanted Antony to execute her sister Arsinoe, whom Caesar had spared in Rome and who remained a threat so long as she was alive. And so it came to be that Cleopatra and Antony needed one another: Antony needed money and Cleopatra needed protection. By the end of the visit, she was financing his campaigns, he was protecting her rule of Egypt – and they were in love. Within a few weeks, by winter of 41 BCE, Cleopatra and Antony were in Alexandria.

Antony swapped his Roman tunic for a Greek cloak and began to embrace life in Alexandria, a city famous for its many clubs and associations that citizens joined to create a community, usually in the form of drinking or debating. Rome perceived Alexandria, and in turn Cleopatra, as an overly extravagant, wasteful city. The word Alexandria didn't only conjure thoughts about a capital of knowledge, as it had done for the last couple of centuries, but also alluded to a party capital, a foodie capital. Its residents were most concerned with the next festival and the upcoming play. The stereotype was that Alexandrians of all classes loved to display their wealth through their clothes and overly decorated homes, and that they cared about nothing as much as the culinary arts. Cleopatra and Antony formed their own exclusive club, the Inimitable Livers. Plutarch writes that there was 'an extravagance of expenditure beyond measure of belief' as the group enjoyed lavish feasts, played games and drank into the night. According to a student at the School of Medicine who knew one of the royal cooks, a dinner for twelve included eight roast boars. At night, Cleopatra and Antony disguised themselves as servants and walked the streets of Alexandria 'to disturb and torment people at their doors and windows'. As irritating as these pranks sound, Plutarch writes that 'the Alexandrians in general liked it all well enough, and joined good-humouredly and kindly in his frolic and play'. On another day, when they went fishing for perch on the Nile, Antony was embarrassingly bad, so he ordered fishermen to dive under the water and place fish they'd caught onto his hook. Cleopatra pretended to be impressed and invited friends to see Antony's skills the next day. But she was playing her own trick, having ordered a fisherman to place a big saltwater fish not found in Egypt but in the Black Sea (probably a tuna) onto Antony's hook. As everyone fell about laughing, Cleopatra told him to leave fishing to Alexandrians, to the 'sovereigns of Pharos'. Amid all the fun, the couple had twins, imaginatively named Cleopatra and Alexander, before Antony left Alexandria.

Sometime before 40 BCE, Alexandria welcomed an unexpected guest: this was Herod, a Judean prince in his early thirties. His father had recently been executed, so he feared for his life and that of his new wife Mariamne, who had Alexandrian heritage. After a windy voyage, his ship docked into Alexandria, a city he hoped would provide a haven. Cleopatra gave Herod a royal welcome and offered him a permanent stay, including control of an army. But Herod had a change of heart, braving a storm towards Rome where he was promised confirmation as the new King of Judea, one of the former Ptolemaic territories Cleopatra wanted to regain. Thus ensued a permanently bumpy relationship between Cleopatra and Herod. Soon, Herod would restyle himself Herod the Great, and, according to Matthew's Gospel, he would infamously instigate the

Massacre of the Innocents, executing every baby in Bethlehem at the time of Jesus' birth.

In the meantime, Octavian had garnered enough support to defeat any potential rivals, including Antony's politically active wife whose death opened the way for Antony to marry Cleopatra. Instead, just a few weeks after his twins were born to Cleopatra in Alexandria, he made the diplomatic decision to marry Octavian's half-sister Octavia. Antony insolently disappeared from Cleopatra's life for the next three years. During this time, while raising the children of two mighty Romans, Cleopatra ruled Egypt alone – and she did a fine job. One document used to wrap a mummy in the first century – discovered in 1904 but stored in a German museum basement until 2000 – reveals the extent of Cleopatra's involvement in day-to-day affairs. A papyrus granting a tax exemption is dated 23 February 33 BCE and signed γινέσθωι – *ginestho*, or 'let it be' – in Cleopatra's own hand. That she makes a basic error (it should be γινέσθω) is puzzling; it could suggest a busy schedule rather than a queen with bad spelling. Either way, Cleopatra was becoming a uniting figure through her embodiment of Alexandria's hybridity. Her mix of Greek and Egyptian attire, her proficiency in Egyptian and perhaps most importantly her position as the goddess Isis incarnate all meant that for the first time in decades Egypt enjoyed relative stability. She raised taxes and prioritised foreign trade, which rose to a value of 12,000 talents (£240 million) annually. Within a decade of becoming ruler, Cleopatra had managed to change Egypt's fortunes, from debt to wealth, from owing the Romans money to lending them money. What's more, scholars had been leaving the city for several decades but were now attracted back, with many philosophers departing a tense Athens to settle in Alexandria.

Octavian was now controlling the western Roman territories, while Antony held the east, near the old Iranian empire known as Parthia, which was a real threat. When Antony invited Cleopatra to visit him in Antioch in 37 BCE, he met his three-year-old twins for the first time. The power dynamic was clearer than ever: Cleopatra was on top. She had become Antony's financier, agreeing to lend him money and providing military support against the threats from the east. In turn, she requested control of Ptolemaic land from

Alexandria's early years, namely Ptolemy II's period, including Cyprus and Crete. This meeting appears to have rekindled their passion and they may even have married. Antony reportedly presented Cleopatra with new books for the Library of Alexandria. Plutarch notes that Antony bestowed on 'her the library of Pergamus, containing two hundred thousand distinct volumes', with the original wording suggesting that the books each contained a single author. This present was even more worthwhile since Caesar's fire had damaged many of Alexandria's books a few years earlier. Whether they married or not, this period resulted in another pregnancy. In 36 BCE, Cleopatra named her baby Ptolemy Philadelphus, alluding to the glory days of Ptolemy II.

After defeating the Parthians, the couple celebrated in Alexandria. The locals did love a festival, but this one in 34 BCE, known as the Donations of Alexandria, had grave consequences. Dressed respectively as Isis and Bacchus, whom Antony now regarded as his divine protector, the pair paraded through the city on golden thrones as the captured king was flaunted in golden chains. They arrived at the gymnasium, where Cleopatra was declared Queen of Kings, Caesarion King of Kings, and territories were distributed between her children. But the Roman Senate hadn't approved this distribution and the parade was an emulation of Roman triumphs, reserved especially for the most important victories. Rome interpreted these celebrations as a declaration of hostility. It's at this moment that Octavian's propaganda machine launched into full swing. Antony, it was claimed, wanted to move the imperial capital to Alexandria. And Cleopatra was depicted as a drunken, sexually excessive temptress who was able to trick two of Rome's greats through sorcery and witchcraft. It is these very sources that have affected our perception of her for millennia.

Cleopatra and Alexandria were forced to face Octavian. With a combined force of 100,000 soldiers and around 800 battleships, the pair led their respective troops towards Actium, western Greece, to fight Octavian. The battle commenced in 31 BCE, exactly three centuries after Alexander had founded Alexandria. At first, Octavian appeared to be on top, but the presence of Cleopatra's troops at the back stopped his army from finishing Antony's off. By evening, however, Antony couldn't find Cleopatra's fleet behind him. It had disappeared: Cleopatra had made the controversial decision to retreat before combat, returning to protect Alexandria from civil unrest. By then, Antony is said to have been horribly depressed, even suicidal, but he soon followed Cleopatra to Alexandria. There, he lived alone and began to build a palace on the eastern harbour, the foundations of which have recently been located. He called it the Timonium, a tribute to Timon of Athens, who was famous for his reclusive existence – a reflection of Antony's mental state. By this stage, Cleopatra was pragmatic enough to know that the end was near: she sent gold to Octavian and offered to abdicate in favour of her sons, probably looking to exile herself towards India. Octavian agreed under one condition: Antony must die. Cleopatra had to choose between her own life, her children's lives, her family dynasty and the safety of her country – or Antony. He may have been the love of her life, but Cleopatra's choice was clear enough.

Meanwhile, Octavian was advancing towards Egypt with the biggest invading army in Roman history. But the city wasn't going to fall easily, and on 1 July 30 BCE the Battle of Alexandria began. From the outer walls, 34,000 soldiers attacked Octavian's 44,000 exhausted legionaries, with initial success. For a month, Octavian's troops attacked Alexandria from its peripheries, until 30 July when Octavian launched a hard offensive and fighting spread deep into the city. Finally, on 1 August, Octavian surrounded the city from both east and west, storming to victory.

In the meantime, Cleopatra had been building a mausoleum, two storeys above and one underground, brimming with precious treasures. These could come in handy whether she lived or in the afterlife. It's at this stage that she may have sent a note to Antony, suggesting her imminent suicide; as though waiting for such a signal, troubled Antony stabbed himself. While taking his last breaths, Antony was dragged to Cleopatra's mausoleum so that he might die in his lover's arms. As Octavian entered the city, he wanted Cleopatra alive so that he could secure her treasures. With his men coming for her, Cleopatra stabbed herself, but not fatally.

When Octavian reached Cleopatra's palace, they met for the first time. There are two very different versions of what happened next. Plutarch claimed that she was a dishevelled mess who begged Octavian for mercy, while Cassius Dio wrote that she lay seductively on a couch to entice Octavian. Probably neither is true. But with a spy network still operating, Cleopatra knew that Octavian's real plan was to capture and parade her humiliatingly around Rome. After Octavian left, Cleopatra sent him a note asking to be buried next to Antony. When the note was received, his men hurried desperately to the palace to stop her from killing herself. But Cleopatra was already bathing and dressing in her best clothes.

Although her personal physician, quoted by Plutarch, does not mention the cause of death, Roman historians suggest that Cleopatra poisoned herself. Having arranged for poison to be delivered to her, she placed the toxic ointment onto a needle or hairpin and dug it sharply into her arm. Strabo, however, the earliest extant source, writes that Cleopatra received a fig basket, inside of which was an asp; *aspis* was the Greek word for the deadly Egyptian cobra prevalent in North Africa, including Alexandria. She lifted the venomous reptile and placed it on her arm, before suffering the lethal bite.

Egypt's queen breathed her last. But quite how she died we do not know. She most likely took her own life, though she may have been murdered. Poisons had long been researched in Alexandria and Cleopatra may have had some knowledge about them. The snakebite remains debatable, but may have been a rumour of her own making, since the cobra was the sacred servant of the sun-god and royal protector, thus signifying a royal death. Later popular culture, not least Shakespeare, has popularised the snakebite version and rewritten it to create the more sexually charged image of the asp biting her nipple.

According to Roman sources, Octavian tried to show his graciousness by holding a royal funeral for Cleopatra and Antony, agreeing to Cleopatra's request to bury them together. But he may also have feared that the couple would be venerated, so it's possible that he considered laying them to rest a little further away from the city or anonymised their tomb or even cremated them. Like Alexander's, the location of Cleopatra and Antony's tomb is one of the world's greatest mysteries. It's most likely to be somewhere in or around modern-day Alexandria. Under the city, perhaps. Or under the surrounding waters.

After five centuries as the Roman Republic, Octavian's successful capture of Egypt essentially marked the birth of the Roman Empire.

As Rome celebrated, Octavian, the first Roman emperor, was given the honorific name Augustus, or the venerated. He had conquered Alexandria on the first day of the month of Sextilis. To commemorate entering Alexandria, he renamed the month with his own name, Augustus.

Victorious Octavian entered the city's gymnasium alongside his Alexandrian teacher, Arius Didymus. It is this Stoic philosopher who advised Octavian to eliminate Cleopatra's son, Caesarion. Fearing that group gatherings might spark political opposition, Octavian then banned associations in Alexandria with immediate effect; this largely affected local drinking clubs. He also ordered the burning of thousands of unapproved books. One of the first things Octavian did was visit Alexander's tomb, where he ordered the sarcophagus to be opened and placed a golden crown and flowers on Alexander. According to Cassius Dio, Octavian ran his hands over the mummified body, but as he did so he broke Alexander's nose – a symbol, perhaps of how Roman rule would break whatever unity remained in the city. Octavian also went on to complete the harbourside Caesareum conceived by Cleopatra in Caesar's honour, an indication that Alexandria was to be a Roman city. Facing the harbour, the Caesareum was

> huge and conspicuous, fitted on a scale not found elsewhere . . . around it a girdle of pictures and statues in silver and gold, forming a precinct of vast breadth, embellished with porticoes, libraries, chambers, groves, gateways and wide open courts and everything which lavish expenditure could produce to beautify it.[7]

In 13 CE, towards the end of his reign, Octavian would transfer two huge fifteenth-century BCE obelisks from the temple of the sun-god Re in Heliopolis to Alexandria where they were re-erected in front of the Caesareum. In the eighteenth century, the French decided to call them 'Les aiguilles de Cléopâtre', or Cleopatra's Needles, despite their having nothing to do with her. Today, they stand on London's Victoria Embankment and in New York's Central Park.

As for Cleopatra's passing in August 30 BCE, it signalled a major political event: the end of the Ptolemaic kingdom. Alexandria was entering its third phase. Gone were the Hellenistic and Ptolemaic days. Gone, too, were the days of Roman jurisdiction. It was now under Rome's direct imperial rule.

Cleopatra was survived by her children, who were paraded in Rome; only one of them was spared, her daughter from Antony, Cleopatra Selene II. The only living Ptolemaic royal, she married King Juba II of Mauretania. Over 2,000 miles away in the north-west of Africa, she built a small Pharos lighthouse in honour of her hometown. Two decades after her mother had died, Cleopatra Selene gave birth to a son, whom she named Ptolemy. As king, Ptolemy of Mauretania travelled to Alexandria to see the city of his ancestors. He ruled until 40 CE when the emperor Gaius, better known as Caligula, seized Mauretania for the Romans.

Little physical evidence survives from Cleopatra's time. Most notable, perhaps, are the coins she had minted – a reflection of how she wanted to be portrayed. With braided hair that has curly ringlets at its front, a prominent nose and a long chin, she isn't quite the stereotypical beauty we might assume, at least not according to current ideals. Knowing her story, we begin to sense a different type of beauty: one based on charisma, wit and intelligence. It also becomes clear that Cleopatra has effectively served as a conduit for people's own contemporary agendas. In Western art, for instance, during the Middle Ages she is blonde; during the neoclassical craze, she is a stereotypically Hellenic woman; during colonialism, she becomes passive, lying down, needing a European to save or even conquer her; during the slave trade, she is painted as a servant being examined by Caesar. Then there's the hyper-sexualised view of Cleopatra as the great seductress, championed by writers from Geoffrey Chaucer right up to twentieth-century Hollywood (where in 1963 the queen was played by the world's highest paid movie star, the emerald-loving Elizabeth Taylor). But it is Octavian's writing straight after the conflict – which Plutarch then used as his source – that led to her reputation as an opportunistic and wanton woman. Cleopatra was, after all, a foreigner at the heart of a Roman civil war. Biased Roman sources had to present a worthy enemy as well as justify how a woman was able to divert two of their most prominent men – and men who were heroes. Cleopatra was given the superpower of seduction.

For Alexandrians, it is a very different story. I grew up hearing celebratory tales about Cleopatra. She was a source of pride who, I would learn, was an intellectual who debated powerful men. She was multilingual, had a significant personal library and was well read in philosophy and astronomy. She was also a writer, producing a pharmaceutical book about maintaining physical appearance. She did indeed wear kohl makeup around her eyes, which had medical benefits. Cleopatra also wore many jewels; Egyptians had recently discovered emerald mines in the mountain valleys. Mining would continue for the next half-millennium, with exports leaving through Alexandria. She was also famed for her perfume, perhaps even owning a perfume factory near the harbour. She was serious about fashion, introducing new trends that combined Greek and Egyptian attire, as well as mixing both simple and highly elaborate designs.

Medieval Arabic sources, often overlooked in Western Egyptology, portray Cleopatra respectfully, without referencing physical appearance. The tenth-century explorer al-Masudi writes that 'she was wise and philosophical, close to the scholars (mighty to the rulers), and she has [written] assorted books on medicine, treatment, and other wisdom, translated in her name, attributed to her, known among professional people of medicine'.[8] Historians from her time might also have told such tales. One such example is Timagenes of Alexandria, variously described as a self-made man who began life as a cook, or as an educated son of a royal money exchanger. Whatever the case, he was the most respected historian of Cleopatra's period and knew her personally. The author of the no longer extant *Universal History* that went all the way to Cleopatra's defeat, Timagenes was arrested by the Romans and had his writings burnt, or, as legend has it, burnt them himself. Texts like his may have given a different version of events.

Today, as xenophobic and sexist portrayals of Cleopatra begin to be acknowledged, questions about how she looked are constantly being asked. It's impossible to know for sure, especially as coins and engravings from her time served political goals to portray her as a respectively Hellenistic and Egyptian leader. We can deduce that, starting from Ptolemy IV's relationship with an Egyptian woman, who may have given birth to Ptolemy V, the Ptolemaic family line ceased to be fully Macedonian or noble. Cleopatra's great-uncle and grandfather both had Egyptian mistresses, and both had illegitimate children. One of these was Cleopatra's own father, Ptolemy XII, commonly known as the Bastard. He married Cleopatra V, about whom we know very little, suggesting that she may have been an illegitimate sister, half-sister, or cousin. It's possible that Cleopatra V died in 69 BCE, because her name disappears from all monuments and papyri, even those on which you'd expect it to appear. Since this is the same year as Cleopatra VII's birth, it's conceivable that she was not her mother and that Cleopatra VII was illegitimately born to an Egyptian mother. The enigmatic nature of both Cleopatra's grandmothers, as well as her own mother (whether Cleopatra V or otherwise), suggests that Cleopatra may have had Egyptian heritage.

If she did, it's worth noting that DNA samples recovered from Egypt, spanning around 1,300 years from the New Kingdom to the Roman period, reveal that Egyptians had southern European and Near Eastern (such as Levantine) ancestry, and that sub-Saharan African ancestry in the samples ranged from 6 to 15 per cent in the ancient times, compared to 14 to 21 per cent in modern-day Egypt.[9] As for Alexandria, since its inception, there has been no homogenous Alexandrian ethnicity – to use today's terms, many Alexandrians were and remain neither Black nor White. As there was no normative race, with the exception of Jews, ethnicity wasn't always recorded. Alexandrian genetic makeup is varied. Names, nuptials and burial practices over the centuries have pointed to a convergence of traditions, and it is safe to assume that this happened with genetic mixing, too.

In the 1950s, the Alexandria-born Egyptian president Gamal abdel-Nasser made a point of insisting the country become more self-sufficient, establishing for instance a national car manufacturer, Nasr. With the whole country seemingly reliant on imported cigarettes, in 1961 he ordered that Egypt produce its own cigarettes as a symbol of self-determination. The brand had to indicate power, independence and a challenge to the West. Cleopatra Cigarettes were born – and they remain one of the ten best-selling cigarette brands in the world. In Alexandria today, it's impossible to miss the queen's presence. Aside from inevitable passive smoking, you'll encounter her name on the tram, passing Cleopatra Station on one line, and on another (my dad's daily commute as a teenager) both the Little Cleopatra Station and the Cleopatra Baths Station. The change you pick up when buying Cleopatra Cigarettes or getting a ticket at Cleopatra Station will include a fifty-piastre coin, or as the locals call it with distinctively Alexandrian pronunciation, *noss-geny* (half a pound). Cleopatra's face on this copper coin long made her the only woman on modern Egyptian currency. In 2023, she appeared on the new twenty Egyptian Pound polymer banknote, becoming the only figure on two different denominations. The iconic queen and her tomb may have disappeared, but no matter the age, around the world and particularly in her own city, she remains inescapably, unwitheringly present.

Jewish Hub

I am in Alexandria on New Year's Eve. *'Kol sana wento ttayebeen'*, people scream from their cars as the new year beckons. The greeting translates literally as 'every year and you are well' and the new year itself is *rās el-sana*, the head of the year. Today's Alexandrians celebrate in different ways. Groups of women are walking down the street in elaborate gowns and sporting intricate hairstyles, ready for a ballroom soirée in one of the stylish seaside hotels. There are queues at concert venues as pop stars get ready for the new year's eve gigs. Groups of friends gather around malls and cinemas. Couples hold hands on the beach. Thousands of people are overlooking the water from the city's Stanley Bridge, built in Islamic architectural style, ready to count down and party in one of the most popular street carnivals in Egypt. A constant hum of impatient and celebratory car horns resounds. Fireworks go off in the distance from various venues and beaches on the coast. And some families are gathered at home with their neighbours, eating and drinking joyously.

All of this seems normal enough. But as the countdown reaches its finale and the new year beckons, something very different can be heard. At exactly midnight, the sound of glass breaking begins to spread around Alexandria and often lasts for a whole hour. A city tradition, those celebrating at home throw a piece of glass or pottery from their balconies onto the ground below. As the material shatters, so too does any bad luck for the upcoming year. Breaking the glass symbolises the last of anything negative from the last twelve months and the welcoming of a new and better time. It is a tradition that adults and children can enjoy, regardless of their class or faith. And it is a tradition that Alexandria owes to its early Jewish population. The Greeks of Alexandria and elsewhere continued breaking glass at special occasions, but the first reference to the ritual is in the Jewish Talmud, the record of rabbinic teachings and debates from the second through to the fifth century. In the Talmud, the third-century rabbi Mar son of Ravina smashes glass at his son's wedding, not for good luck, but to remind the celebrating guests of their mortality.

As the new year gets underway, the sounds of the cheering, fireworks, car horns, music – and breaking glass – combine with the vibrant colours of the decorations, clothes, skyline and the flashing lights filling Alexandria's night sky.

Legend has it that as Alexander arrived at the gates of Jerusalem over two millennia earlier, the High Priest of the Jews, dressed in white garments, stood in his way. To everyone's surprise, Alexander prostrated himself before the Priest and they entered the city hand in hand. Alexander was using Palestine as a corridor to Egypt and during his passage the Jewish leaders asked him, as they had previous kings, to be allowed to live in peace according to the laws of their forefathers. So when Alexander occupied Palestine, he allowed the Jewish people to continue their own customs. And it is Alexander himself who is said to have allocated a district for Jews in his new city of Alexandria from its very first design.

Alexander's alleged visit to Jerusalem and his subsequent piety were popularised by the first-century Jewish historian Josephus in his *Antiquities of the Jews*. Jerusalem-born Josephus, who married a Jewish woman from Alexandria, confirms that the city's founder became a part of Alexandrian Jewish identity. In fact, around that time, the *Alexander Romance* began to include a fascinating addition, claiming that when Alexander laid eyes on the rabbis of Judea, he exclaimed: 'How divine is your appearance! Tell me, I pray, what god do you worship?' They replied: 'We serve one God who created heaven and earth and all things in them. But no man is able to tell His name.' And, just like that, Alexander swiftly converted to monotheism: 'As servants of the true God go in peace, go. For your God shall be my God.'[1] This interpolation to the legendary biography must have been added by an Alexandrian Jew, possibly around the time of Roman persecution in the first century, in order to show that the city's founder wasn't only sympathetic to Judaism, but was a believer.

There is no sure evidence that Alexander visited Jerusalem. And in the story of Judea, the rabbis present him with the Book of Daniel, which wasn't written until the 160s BCE, some 170 years after Alexander marched through the Holy Land. But what we can deduce is that in 332 BCE he did go to Tyre (modern-day Lebanon) and Gaza, and by the next year he had moved on to found Alexandria. During those two years, in an attempt to win them over, he created a tax exemption for the Jewish populations. This popular policy led to migration in the direction of his new city. Some Jews were already in Egypt before Alexandria's founding: the Hebrew Bible notes that a large number took refuge in Egypt after the destruction of the Kingdom of Judah in 597 BCE, and some of these would have heard about the new city to the north. What's more, after Alexander's death, the Ptolemies ruled Palestine – apparently entering Jerusalem on the Sabbath when there was minimal resistance. The third century BCE was a period of relative peace for the Jews in the Holy Land, but like the residents of other Ptolemaic cities, thousands ended up moving to the new capital. Josephus writes that some Jews moved to Alexandria during the city's early years, 'invited by the goodness of the soil, and by the liberality of Ptolemy'.[2] The first two Ptolemies, in particular, played a key role in bringing Jews to Alexandria. Ptolemy II freed thousands of Jewish prisoners who'd been captured when his father went to Syria. This initiative made Ptolemy II especially popular among Jewish leaders – the High Priest of Jerusalem called him a 'sincere friend' – and gave the Ptolemies an opportunity to boost their army with Jewish soldiers. Though Jerusalem remained important to the Jewish diaspora in Alexandria, by the first century BCE Alexandria was home to the largest Jewish community in the ancient world. From that time, they formed one-fifth of Alexandria's population.

From the third century BCE to the first century BCE, Alexandria was one of the most populated cities on earth, if not *the* most populated. It has been speculated that between the first centuries BCE and CE, Alexandria may have become the first city in history to reach a population of one million. We know that Alexandria was home to at least 300,000 free citizens in the first century BCE, and that by the first century the population was at least half a million. Rome did reach a million around then, but Alexandria still formed a significant proportion of the Greco-Roman world's urban population, which was somewhere between seven and nine million. Compared to other cities, Alexandria also occupied a considerable area, though it was also a very dense city, second only to Rome. In *The Wars of the Jews*, Josephus records a speech by a king named Herod Agrippa II in 66 CE in which we find a hidden description of Alexandria as being thirty by ten furlongs, in other words six kilometres by two kilometres, totalling twelve square kilometres. This remains the most contemporary note about its size, but recent calculations by archaeologists place the ancient city at around ten square kilometres with a population that reached 670,000 by the Roman times.

So there were tens of thousands of Jews in Alexandria. According to Josephus, they resided close to the royal palace, and the local grammarian and Homeric scholar Apion confirms that they lived without a harbour. As such, the Jewish district appears to have been just east of the royal quarter, something that disgruntled Apion, who complains that the Jews are able to live in one of the finest areas in town. Initially, this separation was supposed to allow Jews to follow their own customs and protect them from the polytheistic population. As the first-century Jewish philosopher Philo tells us, not only did the Jews begin to spread around all areas of the city, they became the majority residents of two areas, so the one Jewish district very soon became two, the second probably on the eastern harbour.

The main Jewish quarter was known as Delta, almost as large as the Greek quarter and with its own local governor, council and laws. Synagogues were dotted around the city, but Delta housed an especially large one. Though they lived in separate quarters, the Jews of Alexandria were involved in everyday life, could travel around the city freely and welcome non-Jews into their shops and homes. For the first 369 years of Alexandria's existence, there was no ghettoisation.

The Jewish districts coincided with three trade quarters – the linen workers' quarter, the leather workers' quarter and the portico of perfumers – that indicate some of the industries in which

Alexandria's Jews may have worked. The majority were artisans, silversmiths and carpenters, though there were also merchants, moneylenders and those who worked in shipping and sailing in the harbour. The elite Jews were just as wealthy as their Greek counterparts and just as removed from ordinary society. Since they spanned the entire social ladder, synagogue seating in Alexandria was grouped by occupation. Jewish priests were clear that their faith forbad them from erecting statues or making sacrifices in the synagogues, so non-Jews in Alexandria would no doubt have been curious, even suspicious, about what went on in these seemingly secretive spaces. When accusations did spread, they could be extreme: in the first century, Apion spread the conspiracy that Jews fattened and then sacrificed helpless Greek victims every year in the synagogues before consuming their flesh.

It's often claimed, and assumed, that Alexandria's Jews were not given citizenship, but this is not true. Philo writes that the Jews enjoyed the same civil rights as the Alexandrians, including education. Becoming an Alexandrian citizen was only possible if both your mother and father were born there, so, over time, more Jews were able to become citizens if they swore an oath of civil and military loyalty, probably in the civic square when they became adults. Josephus notes that 'at Alexandria', the city's very founder 'gave them equal privileges of citizens with the Macedonians themselves' and in exchange 'required of them to take their oaths that they would keep their fidelity'. Josephus adds: 'nor any one that came after him, thought of diminishing the honours which Alexander had bestowed on the Jews.'[3] But the fact that some new rulers, like Cleopatra VII and Julius Caesar, had to declare the Jews as citizens, suggests that they were not always guaranteed this right or that it needed confirmation. Even in the best scenarios, it appears that Jewish citizenship could be partial, in doubt, or periodic. As Roman rule tightened, things became further complicated: until the third century, Alexandrians were the only group in Egypt entitled to Roman citizenship, which made Jewish Alexandrian citizenship problematic for the Romans.

In theory, however, for the first four centuries after Alexandria's founding, it made complete sense for Jews to move to such a liberal and diverse city where they could enjoy relative freedom. As the third century BCE got underway, Alexandrian Jews had become distinct from the more conservative Jerusalemites: far more open to relations with gentiles and more interested in philosophy and art. They accepted, as Alexandrians did, the views of Plato and Aristotle, and the educated class of Jews produced fascinating writings that were added to the Library.

As the second and third generations only spoke in the local tongue, language became a controversial subject. Some believed that it only made sense for Greek to be used in synagogues, others that Hebrew had to be maintained. Over time, worship in Greek became normalised especially after Ptolemy II commissioned the Septuagint, which rendered the Hebrew Bible into Greek. For the Ptolemies, this translation could make the capital's Jews independent of Jerusalem – and it coincided with their creation of a Jewish High Priest role specifically for Alexandria. The Jews ended up Hellenising at a faster pace than the Egyptians, some of whom disliked the way the Jews were integrating. Ironically, many Greeks still accused both the Jews and Egyptians of remaining isolated from the largely Hellenised Alexandrian society. In truth, Alexandria's Jews were hardly isolated, but they did sometimes have to underplay their Jewishness. Some rose to high ranks in the Library of Alexandria, and the second-century BCE account by the Jewish official Aristeas mentions his own brother Philocrates' role in influencing decisions at the Library, possibly including the idea to translate the Hebrew scriptures. Aristeas also claims that he was among those sent by Ptolemy II to find translators in Jerusalem for this task.

Nonetheless, the Jews lived in a society whose values could be very different. Philo described the Alexandrian population to be 'like pigs and goats in quest of enjoyment' and wrote with disapproval about how couples are 'pleasure-lovers when they mate', reminding fellow Jews that sex was intended for married couples, in order 'to procreate children and perpetuate the race'.[4] Less racy Alexandrian pastimes included watching plays, so Jewish theatres were created as early as the fourth century BCE and enjoyed on the Sabbath when the community closed their businesses. Residents may have felt that the Jews were excluding themselves from regular society as Jewish theatres played, for instance, the tragedies of

Ezekiel, an Alexandrian-Jewish playwright who managed to merge Hellenistic tragedy with biblical stories. Ezekiel's only partly surviving play is about the Exodus from Egypt, with Moses as its protagonist. The alterations of the holy text, the profanity on the stage and the fact this was all in Greek caused discomfort for some Jewish residents, who wanted the plays banned, especially since synagogue sermons were telling them how to avoid getting caught up in sinful Alexandrian society. When it came to the plays, the overriding opinion was that exclusive theatre was the best way of having Jewish entertainment that fitted the identity and arts scene of the city. Intriguingly, when non-Jewish playwrights attempted to cash in on the genre, they were unsuccessful. The poet Theodectes of Phaselis wrote one such play: a dramatic failure so unpopular that in the *Antiquities of the Jews*, Josephus claims that because Theodectes dared to mention Jewish law in one of his poems, God punished him by taking his sight.

By the second century BCE, parts of Palestine had fallen to the Seleucids and the Jews of Palestine were split between the Hellenisers and the traditionalist Maccabees. By Ptolemy V's reign, Alexandria housed a magnificent basilica-like, colonnaded synagogue. 'One who did not see the great synagogue of Alexandria', said the second-century rabbinic sage Judah ha-Nasi, 'never saw the glory of Israel.'[5] Alexandria was also influencing Jerusalem, where a gymnasium was built to host athletics competitions. More Jews, either those who opposed the Syrian rule or those keen not to compromise their Hellenistic lifestyle, ended up travelling to Alexandria. One of these was Onias IV, whose father had served as High Priest of Israel for over a decade and who'd fallen out with the new High Priest. Onias fled to Alexandria where he was welcomed by Ptolemy VI and Cleopatra II, who took his counsel on Jewish affairs and allowed him to build a temple near Memphis – modelled on Jerusalem's – in a town called Leontopolis that is now known as Tell el-Yehudiye, or the Jewish Mound, and would shortly become a Jewish colony. For the newly arrived Jews, this was a haven: the scriptural story of Jacob had taken place near this location, they could escape the oppressions of the Seleucids and it even provided some respite from

lexander's incredibly lavish funeral procession, as imagined by Andrew Bauchant, 1940.

Ptolemy I was known as Soter, meaning the Saviour. The Ptolemies enforced a single-currency policy across their empire, confiscating other monies.

Alexandria was famed for its intricate mosaics. Signed by an artist named Sophilos in the late third century BCE, this mosaic personifies Berenice II as Alexandria and emphasises the city's naval power.

Alexandria was guarded by the Gate of the Moon to the far west and the Gate of the Sun to the far east until the Muslims built new city walls. At Shallalat Park parts of a Ptolemaic fort and the Eastern Gate remain intact.

Cleopatra I, whom locals called the Syrian, was the first Ptolemaic queen to rule alone and the first to mint coins of herself.

This large, inscribed tablet from 311 BCE, the Satrap Stela, boasts the first recorded appearance of the term 'Alexandria' in the Egyptian language. It marks the official adoption of the city's name, as well as confirming its status as capital and its direct link to Alexander, who had laid the foundations two decades earlier.

ΑΡΙϹΤΕΑϹ   ΦΙΛΟΚΡΑΤϹΙ

ae second-century BCE Letter of Aristeas,
ought to have been written by a Jewish
holar, contains the earliest written reference
the Great Library of Alexandria.

The third-century BCE Septuagint, or *The Translation of
the Seventy*, rendered the Hebrew Bible into Koine Greek.
The Alexandrian work would become one of the most
influential translations in history.

Greco-Egyptian god Serapis was the popular
divine protector of Alexandria, pushed by
the earliest Ptolemies as a unifying deity. A
magnificent temple housed a huge statue of
Serapis, and it was believed that the god had
prophesied Alexander's eternal return
to Alexandria.

Ornamental glass miniatures were an
Alexandrian speciality. Artisans melted
rods of glass to create intricate images,
many of which were no larger than one
or two square inches. This one portrays
the head of a Maenad, a female
follower of the god Bacchus.

Currency minted in Alexandria depicted many symbols of the city, such as the celebrated Pharos Lighthouse on this second-century coin.

AGIOALEXADRIARADITCALIAM TVRVPTSUTOIPOCU
RAVITMANS SACSMARCSANAV

An early thirteenth-century mosaic depicting St Mark's arrival in Alexandria, from the Chapel of Zeno at St Mark's Basilica in Venice. Ahmad ibn-Tulun added a dome to the Pharos Lighthouse in the ninth century, but this mosaic erroneously includes it during St Mark's arrival more than 800 years earlier.

The mosaics at St Mark's Cathedral in Alexandria depict various moments from his time in Alexandria. They date from 1968, shortly after the cathedral's renovation and exactly 1,900 years after Mark's death.

Three aptly named seventeenth-century mosaics, *Stealing the Body of St Mark*, 1660, can be seen in an arch above one of the doors of St Mark's Basilica in Venice. In this central lunette, the Muslims at Alexandria's port turn away from the pork-filled container, unaware that St Mark's body is inside.

A mosaic of a friendly dog that adorned the floor of someone's house in ancient Alexandria. Made with small and closely set tesserae, it dates to the second century BCE, and was found in 1993 as the grounds of the new Library of Alexandria were being excavated.

An ancient statue of Ptolemy II – who pioneered many of the ancient library's activities – stands outside the current incarnation of the Library of Alexandria.

Al-Idrisi, a respected Moroccan geographer who visited Alexandria, went on to publish a ground-breaking atlas in 1154. In his *Tabula Rogerian*, he follows Claudius Ptolemy's conventions and labels Alexandria clearly by drawing a lighthouse.

The *Alexandrian World Chronicle*, an anonymous history published in Alexandria in 392, included miniatures of important events. Here, a haloed Pope Theophilus holds the gospel in one hand and a piece of the mutilated Alexandrian god Serapis in the other, as he stands on top of the destroyed Serapeum temple.

The ancient theatre in Kom el-Dikka. An engraved figure of a monk wearing a cross can be seen clearly on a pillar at the entrance.

In the nineteenth century, European artists like the Italian Luigi Mayer painted many scenes of Alexandrian life. This one, from 1804, depicts the inside of Alexandria's famous catacombs.

Napoleon was a key subject of French art. In *Napoleon's Entry into Alexandria*, 1812, Guillaume-François Colson commemorates Napoleon's arrival at the city's gates in 17. The artist falls short of portraying an accurate Alexandrian setting, instead focusing on Napoleon, who takes centre stage, entering the city as a hero and saviour.

Alexandria's diversity. For the Ptolemies, this was a chance to make Egypt home to a second Jerusalem, a plan which could win them the loyalty of a significant population. True enough, thousands of Jews joined the Ptolemaic military. When they were younger, the king and queen had witnessed the Seleucids marching through Egypt, so placing Jewish refugees turned soldiers who detested the Seleucids in this location, guarding the route between Alexandria and Memphis, was a great tactic. By the time Ptolemy VI died, the Jews had their own branch of the army, one which supported his wife's right to rule and would take sides in Alexandria's civil wars. Onias IV's role as adviser to the royal family elevated the status of Jews in Alexandria, and his sons would serve as generals for Cleopatra III and support her when she fought Ptolemy IX.

Taking sides, however, came at a price. When the Alexandrian Jews supported Cleopatra II against Ptolemy VIII, the latter retaliated by erecting a pillar in the royal quarter with an anti-Semitic inscription and then rounding up Jewish people, stripping them naked and chaining them to be trampled to death by elephants. According to legend, the elephants, which he had intoxicated, refused and instead turned on his own men. While this event, mentioned in the Third Book of Maccabees, is likely to be exaggerated, it nonetheless became an important story for the Jews of Alexandria, who celebrated it in an annual festival.

The rising number and status of Alexandrian Jews meant that the city continued to influence the Holy Land. Some of the strongest Jewish families there maintained ties with Alexandria, including Herod the Great, whose wife Mariamne's father and grandfather were Alexandria-born Jewish priests. Josephus writes that Mariamne 'was esteemed the most beautiful woman of that time' and that when Herod saw her 'he was smitten with her beauty'.[6] But that didn't stop him from executing her twelve years into their marriage.

In Alexandria, an important Ptolemaic policy was to build and maintain temples, both Egyptian and Jewish, and there is evidence that this was carried out for centuries. An inscribed marble plaque from the time of the famous Cleopatra VII indicates that 'the queen and king' – her and her son Caesarion – commissioned the renewal of a *proseuche*, or Jewish place of worship. This rare evidence is important because Josephus writes that when Cleopatra fed a previously starved Alexandria around 41 BCE, she 'refused to distribute necessary grains to the Jews'. This claim is probably false, since Josephus was a profoundly pro-Roman historian writing after Cleopatra's death. It is unlikely that Cleopatra would be so different from her predecessors, and the Jews of Alexandria supported her during the Alexandrian wars.

After Cleopatra fell and the Romans took over, we have no evidence of further decrees for synagogues to be built, restored, or dedicated to the rulers. In the first century, Philo writes about the destruction of the synagogues under Roman rule, stating that nothing of the sort had ever happened under the Ptolemies. Initially, Egypt's Jews did support the Romans financially and militarily. But ironically, with the Roman rise in Alexandria, the Jewish population began to suffer more systematically – eventually leading to Jewish rebellion against Rome and wars that would result in the historic destruction of Jerusalem in 70 CE, and in Egypt the closing of their grandest temple.

By the first century BCE, the alabarch of Alexandria had become a traditionally Jewish role. The alabarch was in charge of the harbour's taxation and customs, making him the most powerful Jewish man in Alexandria. The alabarch Alexander Lysimachus, born in 15 BCE, became one of the richest people in the world. His influence extended beyond Alexandria and he funded silver and gold renovations in the Second Temple of Jerusalem. His brother, Philo Judaeus, took a very different route, studying among the elites and going on to write influential works that championed allegory and philosophised rhetoric. His readings of Jewish scripture, which he combined with Greek and Alexandrian philosophy, were innovative and influential. Later known as Alexander the Alabarch and Philo of Alexandria, these brothers prove how the Jewish community was able to influence Alexandrian society, particularly when they had money and adopted Hellenistic names and ideas.

For many Alexandrians, however, the Jews were betraying the city by supporting the Roman occupiers. The common perception was that ordinary Jews were actually being favoured by the Romans, since they were still a citizens' council while the rest of Alexandria's population, both Greek and Egyptian, was forced to succumb to Roman policy; Alexandrian Greeks who had opposed Octavian even lost their senate and with it hopes of a devolved leadership. With the exception of Jews, Alexandrians were forced to take part in the cult of the Roman emperor, placing Roman statues in their temples. Moreover, when the Romans banned Alexandrian clubs from gathering, they made an exemption for Jewish worship, or the 'association of the synagogue'. The Greeks were no doubt livid to be controlled by their great rivals, while the polytheistic Egyptians knew all too well that the Romans looked down on their traditions.

With the majority of Alexandria resistant to their authority, the Romans spotted an opportunity: *divide et impera*, divide and rule (a phrase variously attributed to Alexander's father Philip II and to Julius Caesar). This was nothing particularly new to Rome, especially in their dealings with Jews: as Josephus writes, the Roman consul Aulus Gabinius (who invaded Alexandria on Ptolemy XII's behalf in 55 BCE) divided the Jewish nation into five categories with the intention that they fight among themselves. And Alexandrians began to turn on one another, particularly on the Jewish population.

After Octavian defeated Cleopatra, he was succeeded by Tiberius in 14 CE. Tiberius wasn't fond of Alexandrians: they had warmly welcomed the Roman general Germanicus – famed for his dashing looks and military prowess – with street celebrations when he visited. Tiberius was unhappy that a general could be so popular and saw this a challenge to his authority. He subsequently picked Avillius Flaccus as Roman governor of Egypt, a man who would go on to upset the dynamic of Alexandria. The troubles began in the reign of the next Roman emperor, Caligula, who took power in 37 CE and whose policies signalled a key change in Alexandria's ethnic relations. Tax categories were altered so that different ethnicities paid different amounts, with Romans paying the least and Egyptians and Jews suffering a newly introduced higher personal tax. This move no doubt increased tensions between the different groups. Under the Romans, taxes had become an even more stressful aspect of Alexandrian life; Philo records an occasion when a tax evader's family, including women and children, were arrested and tortured in the public square until the man paid his dues.

Keen to keep his position as Egypt's governor, Flaccus sought to appease both Caligula and the non-Jewish Alexandrian population, receiving counsel from three Greek nationalists that targeting the Jews would make him popular. So Flaccus began introducing policies that violated the civil and property rights of the Jews. He neglected to forward the Jewish delegation's letter of congratulations to the new emperor, before banning meetings in synagogues and confining Jews to just one of the city's five districts. Having occupied two areas for decades, this decision caused severe overcrowding and poor conditions in the Jewish quarter. The Jewish leaders reached out for support from Herod the Great's grandson, Herod Agrippa, who had political and military weight but had previously relied on Alexander the Alabarch for finances. When he went to Alexandria on a diplomatic visit, the Jews gave him a hero's welcome, something that irritated the Greeks and Egyptians.

Herod Agrippa's popularity also aggravated the power-mad emperor Caligula. Many sources portray Caligula as sadistic and sexually perverted. According to Cassius Dio, when Caligula became bored watching gladiators fight lions and bears, he ordered his guards to throw a section of the audience to the wild beasts for his entertainment during the intermission. He emulated Alexander, too, dressing in Alexander's armour after ordering his officials to loot the breastplate from Alexander's tomb. He also planned to make his beloved horse a consul. More importantly, he pushed citizens to worship him like a god, specifically Zeus. Statues of Caligula began to appear around Alexandria, an influential city that he was particularly keen to control. Philo writes of Caligula:

> For he was possessed by an extraordinary and passionate love for Alexandria . . . For he thought the city was unique in that it had both given birth to and would foster the idea of godship which occupied his dreams, and that its vast size and the worldwide value of its admirable situation had made it a pattern to other cities of the worship due to him.[7]

The existence of the statues angered all non-Romans in Alexandria, but especially the Jews, when the sculptures were forced into their synagogues. As the synagogues rejected these, the rest of Alexandria felt that there was one rule for them and one for their Jewish neighbours.

Both the Egyptians and Greeks turned on the Jews. Apion, who studied in Alexandria at the time of the unrest, writes that the Egyptians and Jews shared good relations, but it was the Greeks and Jews who were enemies. Apion's version is different from Philo's, which is unsurprising since one was a Hellenised Egyptian and the other a Hellenised Jew. Since the city was founded, though, both Egyptians and Jews had certainly been treated less favourably than the Greeks, so they did have shared experiences. They both took their religious identities more seriously than the Greeks. Neither of them ate pork and both groups circumcised their boys. The Greek Alexandrians were more likely to look down on the Jews than the Egyptians were, but at this particular juncture it appears that everyone in Alexandria jumped on the anti-Semitic bandwagon.

Anti-Semitic clubs may have been initiated around this time. Gathering in the gymnasium, the mobs laid down their own plans. They started to cause havoc in synagogues, looting them and placing statues of the emperor inside. They even transported an old statue of a charioteer into the grand synagogue, knowing that placing something of human likeness in the temple would insult the Jews. But these sporadic quarrels with other citizens were about to become more state-endorsed and sinister. For over three and a half centuries, the different inhabitants of Alexandria had lived in relative stability. Now, in 38 CE, the first recorded pogrom took place, known as the Alexandrian Riots.

Philo writes that the governor Flaccus used the unrest to announce the Jews 'as foreigners and aliens'. With this declaration, the mob had the power to do as it pleased. They forced every last Jew out of the four other districts of the city, ghettoising the Jewish quarter. Flaccus carried out a search for arms in all Jewish homes, before Jewish-owned houses and boats were looted, some burnt and destroyed. Alexandrian Jews, previously traders, neighbours and friends, were now being attacked in the markets: some stabbed, some stoned, others dragged from one street to another. Jewish women were arrested and paraded into the gymnasium where they were tortured and forced to eat pork. A city-wide boycott of Jewish businesses and customers caused some Jews to starve. Previously,

Jews enjoyed their own theatres; now, they were being used for horrific on-stage entertainment, hung up on walls and bound to spinning wheels. Jews who'd been travelling were in for a shock as they stepped off the harbour and were hit about the head with branches. The elite Jews, previously among the wealthiest people in the city, had their land seized and were treated no less severely than the poorest ones. Flaccus forced the more secluded higher-class women and girls out of their homes and onto the streets, where they were publicly mocked. Their leaders were also made to suffer as Flaccus ordered the arrest of 38 members of the Jewish senate in the gymnasium. They were flogged, a particularly demeaning punishment ordinarily reserved for lower-class Egyptians; some died, others were then crucified.

As news of the physical and economic destruction reached Rome, the emperor Caligula sent a centurion to Alexandria to arrest Flaccus, who would be punished by banishment for initiating such severe civil unrest. Finally, as the summer sun shone brightly over a darkened Alexandria, calm settled over the torn city. Thousands of Jews had been killed and imprisoned – and those who remained had fallen into a state of mistrust, despair and mourning.

With the same Roman policies still in place, the next year Alexandria sent two delegations to Rome to meet the emperor. Two reputable scholars led the way: Philo represented the Jews and Apion acted for the wider population, especially the Greeks. Philo's task was to reinstate the Jewish right to Alexandrian citizenship, as well as the city's Jewish senate. But Caligula left the delegation waiting for months, possibly irritated that plans to place a statue of himself as Zeus in Jerusalem's grand temple were cancelled due to fears of rebellion. When the delegations finally met the emperor, he refused to give them his full attention and nothing significant transpired. But Caligula was thought to be planning a permanent move to Alexandria, where he felt the Egyptians were more likely to worship a living god than the Romans. Ironically, the possibility of his leaving Rome was the last straw for many of the leading Romans, who'd simply had enough of the damage he had done to the empire. In January 41 CE, Caligula suffered the same fate as Julius Caesar: he was stabbed tens of times in an underground passage only recently unearthed by archaeologists. News of the emperor's assassination spread to Alexandria, where the Jewish population assumed that this moment of chaos meant that a revolt was achievable. They took up arms and civil unrest began once again, this time instigated by the Jews.

Meanwhile, Caligula was succeeded by his uncle, Claudius, whose Jewish friend Herod Agrippa made a case for reinstating some freedoms for the Jews. Having not yet heard of the most recent unrest in Alexandria, Claudius made a statement condemning 'the great folly and madness' of his predecessor, adding that both 'Alexandrians' and 'Jews' should have the 'rights and privileges, which they formerly enjoyed . . . and that they may continue in their own customs'.[8]

Alexandria's latest civil disorder continued for months and a new delegation made its way to Rome, among them Greek nationalists and two different Jewish factions. What happened next remained unknown for centuries, until the 1920s when a papyrus was discovered in village records near Fayum, where the ancient city of Philadelphia stood. The *Letter of Claudius*, made public in November 41 CE, outlines the recently instated emperor's response, addressed to the city of Alexandria. He indicates that he does not wish to be worshipped and refuses Alexandria's request for its own senate. And he orders the Jews and non-Jews to get along – but in doing so names only the non-Jews as 'Alexandrians'. To them he says:

> Wherefore I conjure you yet once again that, on the one side, the Alexandrians show themselves forbearing and kindly towards the Jews who for many years have dwelt in the same city, and offer no outrage to them in the exercise of their traditional worship but permit them to observe their customs.

And to the Jewish population:

> I bid the Jews not to busy themselves about anything beyond what they have held hitherto, and not henceforth, as if you and they lived in two cities . . . but to profit by what they possess, and enjoy in a city not their own an abundance of all good things; and not to introduce or invite Jews who sail down to Alexandria from Syria or Egypt, thus compelling me to

conceive the greater suspicion; otherwise I will by all means take vengeance on them as fomenting a general plague for the whole world.[9]

From this moment we can pinpoint a switch in the narrative: this significant portion of the population were no longer *Alexandrian Jews*, but Jews *dwelling in Alexandria*. Claudius did try to solve the issues of that particular moment, but in doing so he further confirmed that Roman rule was a turning point for Alexandria's Jews. They might be able to live in peace but were clearly second-class citizens. In fact, the Roman impact on Jews is reflective of their pompous view towards Alexandria. In the early first century, the Roman historian Livy wrote that the Macedonians had 'degenerated into Egyptians', confirming that the Roman elites perceived Alexandrian Greeks as inferior to Athenian Greeks, and, more tellingly, that the Romans looked down on all three groups of Alexandrians: Greeks, Egyptians, Jews.

Many Jews outside Alexandria actually fared better under the Romans. Alexandria's Jews were a more unique group who'd come to expect freedoms and privileges, and whom the imperial capital knew to keep an eye on. From now on, it was thought, they were bound to be more loyal to the Holy Land, or the temple-city as they might have called it, than to their home city. So when the people of Judea revolted against Rome in 66 CE, Alexandrian Jews did the same and it took the two Roman legions in the city, plus 5,000 more soldiers, to stop them. According to Josephus, 50,000 people were killed in the uprising. Just four years later, in 70 CE, during this Jewish-Roman War, a weak Jerusalem that relied heavily on Alexandrian corn was destroyed by the Romans, its grand temple razed. Josephus suggests that over a million civilians died and that many of them were Alexandrians who had travelled to Jerusalem to celebrate Passover, only to find themselves under attack.

Then, in 115, a bigger Jewish uprising against the Roman Empire began. The Jews, predominantly from Judea, formed an army in the hundreds of thousands and sought revenge on the Greeks, too, killing them across the Holy Land and leading to further Greek emigration to Alexandria. The next year, the rebel army made its way into Alexandria, where they set fire to the city. Now, it was the non-Alexandrian Jews causing havoc in Alexandria, destroying the Egyptian temples and damaging the magnificent Serapeum. Local Jews are thought to have assisted their fellow believers, but they might well have been caught in the middle. With help from the Greek and Egyptian population, the Romans quashed the rebellion violently the next year, significantly reducing the city's Jewish population.

Still, it was the ethnic cleansing in the first pogrom of 38 CE that most changed life for Jews in Alexandria and beyond, foreshadowing much of the persecution that would follow. In his *Legatio*, Philo writes that when he ventured to Rome, he wanted to clarify, on behalf of all Jews in the city, 'that we are Alexandrians'. Instead, for the first time, Claudius' resolution made a clear differentiation between 'the Alexandrians' and 'the Jews' – residents of Alexandria who from that moment were bluntly informed that they are living 'in a city not their own'.

St Mark the Evangelist

In the mid-first century, a local cobbler, Anianus, sat cross-legged feeling the warmth of the sun and the breeze off the nearby sea. As usual, he was people-watching as he waited patiently for his next customer. For many years, Anianus had set up shop near the harbour, with a small wooden stool to sit on and a rectangular wooden box that contained his tools. The location meant that he had met numerous travellers from every corner of the Mediterranean. Like many of Alexandria's citizens, he had become acquainted with the monotheistic beliefs and traditions of Judaism. But he believed in the Egyptian gods, not least the green-skinned Osiris and the bull-shaped Apis, and their amalgam, the Greco-Egyptian god Serapis, Protector of Alexandria, pushed by the earliest Ptolemies as a unifying deity. As he worked, Anianus had a good view of the stunning, sparkling temple that housed Serapis: the Serapeum was the first building those arriving in Alexandria would see as their ships approached the city and its bustling streets. He could also see the huge Caesareum of Alexandria, conceived by Cleopatra in honour of Caesar.

From a distance, a bearded man could be seen approaching Anianus at a leisurely pace. As he drew nearer, it became clear that this man's sandal strap was loose, which made him hobble awkwardly. The man explained how he had just set foot in Alexandria that very day. The moment he stepped off the boat, as is the way of things, the sandal strap had become loose. It was clearly an over-worked pair, Anianus thought, as he began to mend the defective one. After all, his customer had already travelled from Jerusalem to Cyprus in this footwear. Anianus began to bang the sandal repeatedly and consistently with his awl. Suddenly, and strangely, the awl slipped – right into the centre of his palm, piercing his hand. In his excruciating pain, he screamed something no Egyptian should utter: 'God is one!'

To Anianus' confusion, the painful moment was made all the more awkward when, without warning, the sandal's owner took hold of his hand. A crowd had now gathered and onlookers began to wonder what this visitor was about to do. Within minutes, the wound began to disappear and the pain to subside.

This, according to Coptic Christian tradition, was St Mark the Evangelist's first miracle in Alexandria before he went on to found the regional Church. Anianus the cobbler was not only his first Alexandrian convert, but would very soon become the city's first bishop.

Before arriving in Alexandria, Mark – to whom the second Gospel was traditionally ascribed – is said to have been present for some important biblical events, from the wedding in which Jesus of Nazareth is reported to have turned water to wine, to hosting the resurrected Jesus in his Jerusalem home. While historical sources are scarce, it does appear that a few years after Jesus lived, Mark made his way to Alexandria. The Greek historian Eusebius places Mark's arrival around 41–44 CE (most scholars estimate the crucifixion year to be 30 or 33 CE). A thirteenth-century Italian mosaic depicts Mark on a small boat approaching the unmistakable Lighthouse of Alexandria. Soon after entering the city from its eastern gate – accounts of this miracle have suggested that it occurred the day he arrived – Mark preached the gospel to the masses. He also created an education centre, thought to have developed into the pioneering Didascalia, also known as the Catechetical School of Alexandria. If this is all true, it means that Mark founded Christianity in Alexandria and, in doing so, Christianity in the whole of Africa. The newly formed Church of Alexandria was an important step in the global spread of the faith. Today, it is the Coptic Orthodox Church and continues to be a key Christian hub, while Murqus (Mark) is unsurprisingly the most popular name among Christians in Egypt.

When Mark arrived in Alexandria, he would certainly have considered the fact that Jesus himself had been to Egypt. According to Matthew's Gospel, when Jesus was still an infant, the Holy Family travelled to Egypt to escape Herod's persecution and what became known as the Slaughter of the Innocents:

> And when they were departed, behold,
> the angel of the Lord appeareth to
> Joseph in a dream, saying, Arise, and
> take the young child and his mother,
> and flee into Egypt, and be thou there
> until I bring thee word: for Herod will
> seek the young child to destroy him.[1]

This story also exists in the Gospel of Thomas, the main section of which was found in Egypt in 1945 and is included in the New Testament Apocrypha. The early Church Fathers didn't approve of these texts: in the third century Origen of Alexandria deemed the writings heretical and in the fourth Athanasius of Alexandria banned non-canonical gospels. These texts are therefore likely to have been hidden in the fourth century – perhaps after being smuggled out of Alexandria – though parts may have been composed as early as the mid-first century. The Infancy Gospel of Thomas presents a very similar narrative to Matthew but is even more detailed, adding three versions of how the family left Egypt. All of the gospels were composed for specific purposes and may be liberal with facts. But the authorised gospels in fact contain fewer details than the Apocrypha. Although historically considered to be obscure and therefore less credible, modern biblical scholars now believe that versions written independently of the canonical gospels may provide a potentially more accurate version of Jesus' life. This is especially true in cases of multiple attestation: when an account exists in both the canonical and non-canonical gospels, it's less likely to be a fable, which further legitimises the possibility of the Flight into Egypt having occurred.

Alexandria would also have been a natural place for the persecuted family to go for several reasons. It was the famous capital city, and likely to provide easy employment opportunities especially for a craftsman like Joseph. It was a vibrant centre of Judaism, one which had a religious history but also welcomed alternative opinions. It was also known as a safe haven for refugees and travellers.

Another important fact is that Herod the Great was hated in Alexandria, where Cleopatra had fallen out with him towards the beginning of his reign a few decades earlier when he took Rome's side and became King of Judea, one of the former Ptolemaic territories Cleopatra wanted to regain. Herod also executed his Alexandrian wife Mariamne. According to Josephus, Mariamne had insisted that Herod place her teenage brother Aristobulus as High Priest. When Aristobulus drowned within months of his appointment, Mariamne's mother blamed Herod and wrote to Cleopatra in Alexandria asking her, one mother to another, to avenge his death. Cleopatra gave Antony the task: Herod was summoned by Antony but released shortly thereafter, and in the end both Mariamne and her mother were executed.

In the Infancy Gospel of Thomas, Jesus arrives in Egypt at the age of two and stays there for at least a year. Jesus is thought to have been born in either 6 or 4 BCE, and Herod traditionally thought to have died in 1 BCE, though others place his death a couple of years later. Either way, if the family only returned after Herod's death, Jesus may have remained in Egypt for several years. The text notes: 'As they went, Joseph said that as it was hot they might go by the sea coast', before they eventually set eyes on a city, not a town or village. At that time, two roads serviced the Middle East region: they were trade routes, frequented by anyone who wanted to travel, covering the whole region and connecting Palestine with Egypt. One of these was called Via Maris, which went along the Mediterranean shoreline. It would make sense for the family to have travelled to somewhere nearer coastal Palestine, in other words northern Egypt, and to have stayed near the sea rather than travel through the desert. When he was three, the Infancy account adds that Jesus brought 'a dried fish' back to life; the very mention of reviving a fish suggests a place near the water, and since ancient Egyptian times the traditionally dried fish was mullet, from the sea not the river.[2]

The key sources, including the New Testament, make no mention of Jesus setting foot in Alexandria, and as an adult not even Egypt. But there are some signs that he may have done so. For instance, Jesus is thought to have been able to communicate in Koine Greek, the Alexandrian dialect, despite the fact it wasn't of much use where he lived in Judea or Galilee. He wouldn't have picked it up when he returned to Nazareth as this was a small hamlet, but he may have done so in Egypt during childhood. Moreover, Matthew the Apostle is said to have based his writing on St Mark, who was born in the year 12 CE, so would have been only eighteen at the time of crucifixion, meaning that he would have had to become Jesus' follower aged around fourteen or fifteen. This doesn't sound very probable, especially given that he was born in Cyrene in Libya. It's unlikely he would have travelled all the way to Jerusalem at such a tender age, but perhaps he met Jesus somewhere else, like Alexandria, the only major city right between Cyrene and Jerusalem.

It should not be forgotten that the Holy Books cover a mere three years of Jesus' ministry, from 28 to 30 CE, beginning when he was around thirty. This points to a huge gap in what is known about Jesus' life, especially the lost years before his fame. It wouldn't be surprising for him to have travelled to the foremost city of his age, a place that was, as we have seen, also a knowledge capital. The New Testament indicates that Jesus was literate, so may have been interested in the Library's holdings. Even the three years for which there are records indicate that he was extremely mobile. Most of the recorded locations, other than the final sojourn in Jerusalem, are sites where he performed miracles, so must have been deemed worth preserving for posterity. There may have been many more that weren't recorded because they weren't considered important, or there may have been fewer witnesses to miracles in his earlier life.

I have here raised a question that has been oddly absent over the centuries: did Jesus travel to Alexandria? It's impossible to know. It is also worth asking, however, whether he *may* have done so. That is a definitive yes. To Alexandrians, Jesus lived a little over 200 miles away, as the crow flies. The distance between the two lands is far from insurmountable: the journey from Jerusalem to Alexandria, by foot or on a donkey, would have taken twenty days. So it is certainly possible that – while nobody recorded it – Jesus was taken to Alexandria as a baby, and that he chose to travel there as an adult.

Fast-forward all the way to 1900, near the city's harbour markets. Men and women of all ages walked through this area, often with their freshly acquired fruit and vegetables, sometimes dragging their donkeys and mules, and generally circumventing the large neighbouring cemetery as they went about their business. One September afternoon, a donkey trotting innocently through the same area suddenly disappeared, as if it had stepped through a trap-door. The donkey had plummeted twelve metres, and this ill-fated accident revealed the main passage to a sizeable burial ground. At this stage, the locations of six of the Seven Wonders of the Medieval Mind were already known: the Great Wall of China, Nanjing's Porcelain Tower, Istanbul's Hagia Sofia, Rome's Colosseum, the Leaning Tower of Pisa and Wiltshire's Stonehenge – but one remained at large. Now, a grand archaeological discovery had been achieved by a wandering donkey. The missing wonder of the Middle Ages had been revealed: Alexandria's Catacombs.

The grimy passage into the underground cemetery led to a six-pillared central shaft and three whole floors (the lowest now under the water) that had all been cut with great purpose through solid rock. In the middle, a spiral staircase wound down and around the tomb of the Main Catacomb. The dead bodies were once lowered by rope down the shaft in the middle of the staircase. Inside, tombs were housed in enclosures, dozens of adjoining, rectangular, rock-cut niches in which the bodies could be placed. The bodies lay near a purpose-built banqueting hall for visitors, a large, square chamber with benches cut into the rock known as the triclinium. On discovery, this area housed huge heaps of broken pottery and glass. Many centuries earlier, visitors to the Catacombs would stock up on food and wine for their visits to deceased relatives and, rather than cart everything home, would smash the empty jars and bottles and leave the pieces behind. For this reason the Catacombs, and in fact this whole area of Alexandria, are now known as Kom el-Shoqafa, or the mound of shards.

The discovery of the Catacombs of Kom el-Shoqafa, first constructed and used in the first century, shed new light on the beliefs of Alexandrians just before the arrival of Christianity and helps to explain why the new faith would become popular in a short space of time. In particular, on a wall just above two sarcophaguses, two paintings remain unblemished. One depicts the Egyptian myth of Osiris and specifically the scene of his mummification. Osiris was an important Egyptian god, competing for number one deity in

Alexandria. After all, he was the god of agriculture and vegetation in a city that was both self-sustaining and a major trading power, and the god of fertility and life in a city that boasted a huge population.

The elaborate story of Osiris' fraternal murder, vital to ancient Egyptian belief, mixes mythology and tragedy and has since resonated in different forms, from the Bible and Quran (Cain and Abel) to Shakespeare (Claudius and Hamlet) to Walt Disney (Scar and Mufasa). Osiris' jealous brother, Set, embarks on murdering his elder sibling in order to usurp the pharaonic throne. Osiris' sister-wife, Isis, insists on finding her husband's corpse before managing to puzzle his body parts together so that he can temporarily return to life, after which he impregnates her with the god Horus.

The second painting in the Catacombs shows not an Egyptian but a Greek myth: that of Persephone and Hades. Persephone was the daughter of Zeus – to whom the inscription on the Alexandria Lighthouse was dedicated and whom Alexander regarded as his father – also making her the sister of Helen of Troy, who had apparently visited Pharos in the ancient era. In the legend, described in detail in the Homeric Hymns, the beautiful Persephone is abducted as she innocently gathers flowers in a field. She is taken by Hades, god of the underworld, and her mother Demeter, goddess of harvest and agriculture, begins an intense search for her. With Demeter distracted by her search, the earth fails to produce its vital riches. Pressed by the cries of the hungry mortals, Zeus orders Hades to return his daughter. Before doing so, in a serpentine move, Hades tricks Persephone into eating the seeds of a pomegranate, forcing her, since she has tasted the fruit of the underworld, to spend a third of each year there for all time: symbolic of the harsher wintery months in which the harvests struggle. This story – which also presented a type of resurrection – was important to Alexandrians. In fact, a fragment from fourth-century saint Epiphanius notes that there was a temple dedicated especially to Persephone in the city.

The Osiris story, in particular, was the most important and influential of all myths in ancient Egypt: with the restoring of his body, Osiris essentially becomes the first mummy. This forms the basis for the famous Egyptian embalming practice intended to prevent the departed body from decaying and offers the deceased a prospect of eternal life. Like the harsh winters imposed by Hades' temptation of Persephone, the annual flooding of the Nile was thought to represent the flow of Isis' mourning tears and the shedding of Osiris' blood.

The paintings in the Catacombs also reveal how Alexandria had become a meeting point for Egyptian, Greek and Roman traditions. They present beliefs, stories and artistic depictions that point towards Greek and Roman influences on the pharaonic funeral cult. There are Egyptian statues with lifelike Greek carving styles and unmistakably Roman dress. There are carved demons on either side of the entrance to the inner tomb: snakes wearing Egyptian crowns, and carrying Greek wands and Roman staffs. Significantly, they also show the prominent position of the afterlife in the belief systems of Alexandrians. In addition, whether from Egyptian or Greek sources, the notion and prominence of resurrection could hardly be clearer.

These resurrection stories and their emphases on eternal life may have influenced their biblical counterparts. In fact, the common funerary sketches of Isis protecting Osiris would soon be echoed in the early Christian icons of Mary protecting Jesus. Even the Christian Eucharist is similar to the Egyptian beliefs in Osiris: the deity was remembered via effigies composed of grain that would be watered until harvest so that the new grain represented Osiris' flesh. One passage in the funerary Pyramids Texts reads that 'Osiris appears . . . The Lord of wine in flood', while Plutarch writes that for the Egyptians, 'Not only the Nile, but every form of moisture they call simply the effusion of Osiris; and in their holy rites the water jar in honour of the god heads the procession'. And like Persephone, Eve, innocently dwelling in a garden, is tempted into eating fruit, with devastating consequences.

But the impact went both ways and would also serve the missionary goals of the early evangelists. The double resurrection story of Jesus – the first, three days after crucifixion, and which Mark claimed to have witnessed; the second, in the promise of a Second Coming at the end of time – could certainly strike a chord with the Alexandrians. Here were significant parallels with the stories of their own gods, not only in terms of resurrection and afterlife, but also accounts of Jesus' Passion, which like the legend of Isis and Osiris, combined suffering, tears and blood.

What is more, despite some troubles, many of Alexandria's citizens had become close to the city's Hellenised Jews. The exclusivity of Judaism meant that conversion was never an option but, now, there was a new but proselytising monotheistic religion – and for many, this was attractive. Conversions to Christianity commenced in Alexandria.

As Christianity gained a foothold in the city, Mark, who had founded a small chapel, decided to depart, but not before ordaining the former cobbler Anianus as his bishop. Anianus was to be supported by three priests and seven deacons while Mark continued his travels towards Rome, where he would reunite with fellow apostles Peter and Paul.

Mark didn't go back to Alexandria until 65 CE when he paid a brief visit before travelling to Pentopolis in northern Italy for two years. After that, then in his sixties, he finally returned to Alexandria, where a new church had been built in the suburb of Baucalis next to the sea, according to the fourth-century Alexandrian text the Acts of St Mark, and allegedly upon the site of an earlier shrine to Serapis. While the exact location is unknown, the church is thought to have been located where a private school called the Collège Saint-Marc currently sits in the seaside Shatby area near the new library.

With their long-established religious traditions, not all Alexandrians were happy with this new faith. According to Coptic lore, it was in 68 CE – when the feast of Serapis fell on the very same day as Easter – that Alexandria saw one of its most infamous murders. Angry at his anti-idolatrous preaching, a local group seized Mark from his church in Baucalis and imprisoned him. Here, the account continues, Jesus briefly appeared to him in a vision. The following morning, the mob tied a thick rope around Mark's neck and dragged him humiliatingly through the streets of Alexandria until he was dead. Though some histories record that Mark's body was then burnt, it is thought that his followers managed to get a hold of it before the mob was able to cremate it. The Christians then arranged a secret burial under the altar of the Baucalis church.

This horrific story doesn't emerge until the fourth century. With Alexandria's rising prominence in the Christian world, having a local and distinguishable martyr was essential. In fact, Mark's influence on Alexandria might even have been intentionally inflated. But if the accounts are untrue or exaggerated – perhaps Mark was not so successful but his disciples were – the least we can take from them is that the early church leaders of Alexandria had both the inclination and the confidence to associate the city with such a key biblical apostle and companion of their Lord.

This confidence foreshadows the rise of Christianity in the region. Originally seen as a more obscure religion followed by poorer inhabitants around Palestine, Alexandria gave Christianity a significant boost. Being a popular faith in such an influential capital served to make it more fashionable. Its rise in the undisputed centre of the world's knowledge meant that it also became more authoritative. Over time, Christianity would become a more philosophically disposed faith and Alexandria would generate some of its finest early scholars, most notably the two Church Fathers, Clement of Alexandria and his student Origen of Alexandria. The Alexandrian School would enhance biblical interpretation in the early Church to incorporate Platonic and Neoplatonic beliefs, as well as establishing the prominent position of allegory in the Christian scriptures. But such a rapid rise also served as a catalyst for the zealous entitlement some Christian leaders would show towards the polytheistic population in the decades to come.

To this day, Alexandrians commemorate the man who brought Christianity to their shores. They do so at St Mark's Cathedral, built near the site at which he founded the first chapel, the foundations of which are probably underwater. Rebuilt in the 1950s after it was ruined in the thirteenth and eighteenth centuries – during the Crusades and French invasion respectively – it is essentially a reincarnation of the oldest church in Africa.

On Palm Sunday in 2017, a suicide bomber killed seventeen worshippers at the cathedral's entrance. A few years later, with memories of this tragedy still heavy in the air, I pass regrettably tight security and surrender my passport at the gate. A surprisingly large cathedral with six marble pillars emerges. Inside, I am struck by a bright mosaic of St Mark sitting on Alexandria's Corniche with the Pharos Lighthouse emerging from the blue water behind him. A vestibule with a bright red Persian rug displays on its curved wall intricate mosaics depicting the various events of Mark's life: healing the cobbler Anianus, being dragged through the streets by the mob (Alexandria's yet-to-be-built citadel seemingly in the background), and his followers carrying the corpse to safety. Down the stairs, a small window in the hallway provides a glimpse of some of the saint's relics. This cathedral is the historical seat of the Coptic pope, the Patriarch of Alexandria – a title inaugurated by none other than Mark and passed on to Anianus, the cobbler who never finished mending his sandal.

Horror

The luckless donkey's plunge into the vaults of Kom el-Shoqafa set off a series of discoveries deep under the ground. It quickly transpired that there was, in fact, a breach in the rock of the Catacombs, leading to another set of tombs. The Nebengrab burial hall, inside which nobody had set foot for centuries, contained both human bones, and for a reason we don't yet know, the remains of many horses. It has since been referred to as the Hall of Caracalla, because many believe that it was used to house the bodies of hundreds of young men killed by the Roman emperor Marcus Aurelius Antoninus, better known as Caracalla, who ruled for two decades from 198. Although there is no way of proving who was in these tombs, the story of Caracalla and what he did to Alexandria and its people is historically true.

The emperor got his unofficial name, of which he never approved, because he always wore a *caracallus*, a long-hooded tunic, made in the fashion of the Gauls. Caracalla was Alexander-mad. Much as Alexander had emulated Achilles, so Caracalla emulated Alexander. He even carried some of Alexander's personal items around with him, such as weapons and cups. He filled Rome with statues and paintings of his hero, and statues and paintings that presented him as the new Alexander. On coins, the image of Caracalla held a shield bearing Alexander's face. This mania didn't always serve him well. When going into battle, he arranged a 16,000-strong unit of his army in the phalanx style used by Alexander: soldiers advanced as a group huddled together with their spears facing out, a tactic that was entirely outdated. Some aspects of his obsession were more sinister. Caracalla heard an inaccurate legend that it was Aristotle who had poisoned Alexander, so he persecuted the Aristotelian philosophers and burnt their books.

When his father Septimius Severus died, despite bequeathing a dual leadership, Caracalla then quarrelled with his brother Geta, just as they'd done from a young age. The brothers agreed to split the empire, only for their mother to intervene by ordering a reconciliation meeting. As Geta entered the gathering, guards loyal to Caracalla surrounded and murdered him. Geta died in his mother's arms as Caracalla ran off, blood on his clothes, claiming that he was escaping an ambush intended to kill them both. Caracalla went on to allege that he killed his brother in self-defence. Few believed him, especially as he persecuted Geta's supporters and their families, killing 20,000 people altogether. Now, as sole ruler, he saw himself as the new Alexander. En route to attacking Persia, Caracalla couldn't resist seeing the city his hero had founded. Caracalla openly disliked his wife and, before venturing to Alexandria, he had executed her father for treason and had her banished and then murdered.

By the third century, given the Alexandrian mob's successes in changing the political and social makeup of the city over the decades, the people of Alexandria thought it only natural to ridicule the higher authorities. Their insistence on challenging authority – in part because they had no power to change Roman rule – was combined with a love of witty comedy. This paved the way for satire, which became a key aspect of Alexandrian identity. Caracalla was a godsend for the satirists: he provided exquisite material. Here was a man who couldn't cope with his wife, who killed his brother and made a ridiculous claim that it was self-defence, who really believed himself to be the new Alexander, and who, to top it all, was famously tiny of stature. He became a prime target of these satires, which also referred to his mother, a Syrian Arab, as Jocasta – for the woman who sleeps with her son Oedipus in Greek mythology – in response to rumours that may have started in Alexandria, that she and Caracalla were in an incestuous relationship.

In 215, after a series of strikes and riots, particularly by weavers, Caracalla passed an edict expelling Egyptians from Alexandria in an attempt to quash the city's working class. Egyptians who'd moved to the city at this time, largely from rural areas, were not regarded as Alexandrians. The fragmented papyri of the edict notes that they are 'easily recognisable . . . by their different dialect, appearance, and dress', in addition to 'their way of living and their customs'.[1] As well as confirming the separation between the Egyptian city folk of Alexandria and those who'd more recently moved there, Caracalla's law signalled that even natives were under threat of expulsion, something that was never the case under the Ptolemies.

Soon after, as he entered Alexandria in December 215, the city's leaders made their way to welcome the twenty-seven-year-old emperor, something they did for any high-profile guest. Writing in Greek a few years later, the Roman civil servant Herodian gives one version of events. He describes how the people of Alexandria 'prepared a superlative reception for the emperor', adding:

> Everywhere bands were performing on all kinds of musical instruments and playing a variety of melodies. Billows of perfume and the smoke of incense spread sweet aromas throughout the city. The emperor was honored with torch-light parades and showers of floral bouquets.[2]

Caracalla appeared to enjoy the festivities and went to visit (and perhaps loot some of) his hero's tomb. After the visit, he claimed that Alexander's spirit had entered his body.

But Caracalla's pleasure was a pretence. The 'endless jokes about him' had reached Rome – and the Alexandrians were not going to get away with mocking him. A large crowd had congregated, so Caracalla ordered all the Alexandrian men to organise a phalanx in honour of Alexander, and, as the men huddled together, the emperor left with his bodyguards. The unarmed Alexandrians found themselves surrounded by his soldiers, who began 'butchering them in every conceivable fashion'. While some soldiers killed the men, the others dug trenches into which they dragged bodies and piled mud onto them – some were already dead, others were buried alive. Herodian notes: 'So great was the slaughter that the wide mouths of the Nile and the entire shore around the city were stained red by the streams of blood flowing through the plain.'

In another version of events, seemingly more likely, Caracalla doesn't even wait to enter the city. According to the Roman historian Cassius Dio, who also records the events a few years later, Caracalla slaughters the leaders who await him at Alexandria's gates, before advancing into the city. As the news of his advance spread, riots began on every street, to which Caracalla responded by unleashing his army, who blocked the city's entrances and exits before gathering every young man and woman they could find onto the Rhakotis hill, massacring all 25,000 people and throwing them in a fire whose smoke and stench hovered over the city for weeks.

The Massacre of the Satirists was yet more proof of the ever-complicated relationship between Rome and Alexandrians. Since the start of Roman Alexandria, there was never really a time when the vast majority of the city didn't harbour anti-Roman sentiments. The particular events of 215 remained in the Alexandrian conscious-ness long after the bloodied water regained its usual clarity and the smoke disappeared into the atmosphere. The 'fury of Caracalla' would go on to influence the city for decades to come. The Romans, despite their enthusiasm for Alexandria's founder, were clearly not to be trusted. Religious beliefs were being indiscriminately tram-pled on: Caracalla was happy to kill Alexandrians because they were followers of the Egyptian gods, and monotheistic Jews and Christians were even more vulnerable. And Caracalla may have attacked Alexandria's books as well as its people. Even before he went to Alexandria, Caracalla was persecuting the followers of Aristotle, burning their books and closing their communal dining room. He may have destroyed that section of the Library and Museum. The loss of life and workforce during the massacre also changed the priorities of a city needing to recover and maintain its trade activity. And scholars might now think twice about moving to a place so at the mercy of the Romans. A year and a half later, while emulating Alexander by taking an expedition eastwards, Caracalla stopped on the side of a road to relieve himself. As he did so, one of his own guards, angry at being overlooked for promotion, stabbed Caracalla to death. The news of Caracalla's humiliating demise trig-gered celebrations in Alexandria, and the anniversary of his death became an annual city-wide celebration.

The Romans had continued to expand eastwards and southwards in the immediate aftermath of the Ptolemaic downfall. Egypt was not a priority for investment or protection. Alexandria may have remained prosperous and boasted the second highest urban

population after Rome, but its fortunes and rulers kept changing as
the shape of the Roman Empire shifted.

The Palmyrene Empire was one of the breakaway states: a
Semitic population of Arameans and Arabs who separated from
Rome and made Palmyra (modern-day Homs in Syria) their capital. Led by the ambitious Queen Zenobia, the Palmyrenes quickly
captured the Levant area before moving towards Egypt in 270.
Meanwhile, pirates from a Germanic people known as the Goths
were causing havoc in the Mediterranean, so as the Roman prefect
of Egypt went out to deal with them, Zenobia's army advanced
by land. By now, the majority of Alexandrians had negative feelings towards the Romans, so a new queen who defied the imperial
establishment was an attractive proposition. The sixth-century
Greek historian Zosimus writes that, with the support of many
locals, an army of 70,000 Palmyrenes entered Egypt's eastern
frontier, defeating 50,000 Romans on the way to Alexandria.
There, the Palmyrenes left only 5,000 soldiers: a bad decision that
made it relatively easy for the Roman prefect returning by sea to
reclaim the city. But the Palmyrenes didn't give up, recalling their
army to Alexandria and forcing their way back into the city. Now,
they annexed Egypt from the Roman Empire and declared Zenobia
the Queen of Egypt. For centuries, Rome had needed Egypt for its
grain supply, and that remained the case. In fact, every last grain in
the city of Rome, which now had a population of over a million,
was imported from elsewhere. The emperor Aurelian, who was
born during Caracalla's reign, maintained ties with Zenobia for
that very reason, to ensure that there was enough bread for his
imperial capital.

In 272, Zenobia decided to cut these trade supplies, triggering
Aurelian's decision to go to war. That spring, the Roman army
recaptured Egypt. Zenobia, fearing that her empire would fall apart
without Syria, pulled back much of her army eastwards to her capital. Still, Aurelian was too strong. Zenobia was captured and paraded
humiliatingly around Rome as free bread was distributed to the
celebrating masses. The Palmyrene Empire, founded just a couple
of years earlier, was extremely short-lived.

Despite its demise, the Palmyrene influence on Alexandria wasn't
quite over. A man named Firmus wanted to restore Palmyrene rule

in Alexandria, inciting local protests. In a biography of Roman emperors, the *Historia Augusta*, it is claimed that Firmus declared himself king, but this source adds other contentious details, emphasising Firmus' weight (for dinner he apparently ate a whole ostrich) and excessive drinking. In any case, even if Firmus is a mythical character, it remains true that Alexandrians protested Roman rule that summer, leading to a harsh response from the emperor. Hearing of the trouble, Aurelian left Palmyra for Alexandria where he ruthlessly quashed the protests. In the process, the royal quarter was burnt to the ground. Since this district held the Museum complex that included the Great Library, this may have been a key moment in the Library's physical demise. As for Alexander's tomb, after being consistently visited by Roman emperors, no such trips to the tomb are recorded after the third century CE. It is a real possibility that Alexander's mausoleum may have been destroyed in the attacks and riots of this time.

Seizing Egypt via Alexandria was becoming more common. In 297, two Romans named Domitius Domitianus and Aurelius Achilleus usurped Alexandria from the emperor Diocletian, making use of an unpopular new tax policy to garner local support and declare Domitius ruler of Egypt. Though the Romans were quick to take back much of Egypt, Alexandria had an organised army led by Aurelius that resisted the Romans for around four months. In the end, the rebels only governed for a total of eight months before defeat. This was nonetheless a longer time than the Romans would have anticipated – and long enough for Domitius to put his face on the coins created at the Alexandria mint that year. As the city returned to imperial Roman rule, it was punished by losing its power to mint money independently, something it had done since the time of Ptolemy I.

In Rome, bread remained the most important commodity; as the Roman poet Juvenal had jibed, all Roman citizens wanted was bread and games. This demand for bread made Alexandria integral to Rome's wellbeing, which was why the emperor Diocletian returned to Alexandria at the turn of the fourth century, creating and enforcing a system in which the grain supply was fully run by his government. He also ordered the persecution of Alexandria's alchemists and the suppression of their work, triggering the decline of alchemy.

It is likely that during this imperial visit in 302, one of Alexandria's historical landmarks was born: Pompey's Pillar.

The vast monument is one of the largest monolithic columns in history, standing at almost twenty-seven metres. Originally, it held a statue of an armour-clad Diocletian at its topmost point. Built from magnificent rose granite, with a grey granite capital and a sparkling porphyry statue, this was a triumphal pillar celebrating the emperor's military and economic success. But it was also a show of Roman power: to the horror of the locals, it was built on the land of the Serapeum right next to the temple, the highest spot in the city. Today, not far from the main railway station and on a conspicuously ordinary road with rundown apartment blocks and yellow and black tuk-tuks playing loud music and darting about, the monumental pillar still stands tall, sphinxes on either side of it.

There is no longer a statue at the top. In the eighteenth century, a large 1.6-metre fragment of Diocletian's thigh was discovered at the foot of the column, which indicated that the statue would have been around seven metres high. This and other fragments were smuggled into Europe and have since gone missing.

The Pillar, it was believed, was dedicated to Pompey the Great, the man killed by Cleopatra's brother in 48 BCE, and some thought that his head or ashes were at the top. This assumption was made by Crusaders who, on arriving in Alexandria in the twelfth century, incorrectly interpreted the inscription on the Pillar's pedestal: 'Publius, governor of Egypt, set this up to the most revered emperor, the guardian-god of Alexandria, Diocletian the invincible.' By misreading the Greek letters for Publius (ΠΟΥΠΛΙΟΣ) as Pompey (ΠΟΜΠΗΙΟΣ), this bizarrely erroneous name has lasted until today. In Arabic, no such issue exists: the Arab travellers thought it looked similar to the spars of their ships so named it *Amud al-Sawari*, the Pillar of Masts.

Marble pillars, rocks and tunnels scattered in the Pillar's vicinity serve as a reminder that the sparkling Serapeum once stood here, too. When I last visited, a guard excitedly walked me down into an underground tunnel to show me what was left of the Serapeum. With his machine gun – tourist spots are heavily guarded – he casually pointed at the cubic niches carved into the walls, no doubt to hold books, since this was where the daughter library once was.

Then, shallow stairs led to a long corridor, at the end of which the statue of an Apis bull stood firmly in position, as though refusing to budge.

As the fourth century got underway, Alexandria's landscape was changing. Since Roman rule, there was a new amphitheatre and imperial baths. Temples were built in honour of the emperors, especially as Egyptian temples had stopped being built from the second century. The five Greek letters used to name each of the quarters were no longer in use, and the *agora* had become more of a market than a civic square. Most tellingly, as Alexandria ceased to mint its coins, and as the new Roman pillar rose out of the deteriorating Serapeum, it became clear that although Alexandria was on the face of it becoming more Roman, the gap between Alexandrians and Rome was only growing wider.

A Syriac notitia (an official public register document) from this time gives important and rare details about the city:

> the total number of temples is 2,393; of courts, 8,102; of houses, 47,790; of baths, 1,561; of taverns, 935; of porticoes, 456 . . . Alexandria is the greatest of the cities of the inhabited world.[3]

Alexandria, it is clear, was still bustling and had recovered from the mid-third-century plague. As the few surviving domestic buildings in the Kom el-Dikka area reveal, houses had Egyptian-style light shafts in the courtyards and mosaic-floored Greek-style dining rooms. Roman architectural styles were also becoming more common as large houses were rebuilt, with some including small annexed shops. Porticoes and ambitious redbrick bathhouses indicated prosperity and leisure time, as did the wealth of some sex workers. One account details how a prostitute at this time regularly purchased fish dinners and as much wine as she desired. Bathhouses enabled people to socialise in steam baths, hot plunge pools and shaded cold pools.

One summer morning in 365, as the sun was rising and the darkness of the night fading, the earth shook for a few moments, a harsh thunderstorm broke out then subsided and the sea on the coast of Alexandria began to recede. As it did so, the dozens of boats anchored in the harbour were upturned. The ships were now resting on the sand and fish of all shapes and sizes dotted the seafloor. Locals ran out exuberantly to collect the fish and to look inside the ships. As they did so, without warning, an enormous wave swept onto the shore, so high that it threw these ships three miles into the city and covered the tallest buildings. In the city, which was well-built, the tsunami damaged most of the homes and destroyed thousands of others. Around 5,000 people were immediately drowned. Ships were perched on the roofs and corpses lay strewn in every direction. Neighbouring villages fared even worse and were simply wiped off the map. Contemporary Roman historian Ammianus Marcellinus, to whom we owe this detailed description, refers to it as 'the mad conflict of the elements', adding that 'the whole face of the earth was changed'.[4]

It is now estimated that there were two successive earthquakes, reaching a magnitude of 8.6 on the Richter scale, making this one of the most intense seismic events in history. Alexandria would feel the devastation of the undersea earthquakes and subsequent tsunami for decades to come. The shoreline was permanently changed, the tiny island of Antirhodos, just off the western harbour, was swallowed, and the saltwater rendered the surrounding farmland all but useless.

Parts of Antirhodos now lie five metres underwater, very close to the seashore. Divers searching for remains have discovered unexpected items. The artefacts, which lived in seawater for centuries, are essentially pickled and preserved. Upon removal from the water, though, the salt becomes corrosive, so the artefacts are placed in freshwater tanks to dissolve it, and they slowly regain their features in the process. In 1998, a thirty-metre shipwreck was found, thought to have been rammed by another ship sometime between the first century BCE and first century CE. Over the years, divers have also found floors and obelisks from Cleopatra's royal quarters. A stone head of her son and a sphinx of her father that sat on the seabed for centuries like a cat relaxing on a window ledge. They have found gold, coins and jewellery, as well as jars, mirrors, spoons and ladles. Such everyday objects are a reminder of the real people who lived on these shores and who were shaken to the core by the devastation of the natural disasters. An anonymous epigram from the time commemorates their experience and the changed relationship with their hometown:

> The dead used to leave the city alive behind them,
> but we living now carry the city to her grave.[5]

The horrific occurrence became a part of popular culture for years and an important event in the writings of late antiquity. Alexandrians solemnly commemorated the tsunami's anniversary for centuries, fittingly naming it the Day of Horror.

Roman emperors and natural disasters had wreaked shocking devastation on Alexandria with long-lasting ramifications. And with the continued rise of Christianity, the city was destined for yet more change.

Early Christianity

For centuries, Alexandria was known as a comparatively open-minded and progressive place. It made sense for the early followers of Jesus – already treated with suspicion and hostility – to gravitate towards such a free-thinking capital. And, for centuries, Christians and polytheists did live in relative peace in Alexandria, a city that would end up changing the course of the new faith.

When St Mark was killed at Easter 68 CE, Christian converts in Alexandria, mainly from the lower classes, as was the case with Anianus the cobbler, were keeping a low profile. But it didn't take long for their numbers – and influence – to increase.

The first Alexandrian popes – Alexandria's was the first bishopry to use the term 'pope', deriving from the Greek for 'father' in the third century – most of whom had been baptised by Mark himself, focused on spreading Christianity outside the metropolis, heading westwards and southwards to modern-day Libya and Sudan. By the time of the fourth pope, Kedron of Alexandria, the Romans were intensifying their persecution of Christians. In 106, Kedron was arrested and executed after a rift with a Roman governor who had proposed that Christians continue to worship their god, only along-side the Roman gods.

Since the first century, Alexandria's Christian scholars had been affected by the city's mixed makeup, incorporating aspects of Egyptian mysticism, Greek thought and Jewish tradition – as well as some Babylonian, Buddhist and Hindu ideas that had arrived by sea – to create new philosophies. Indeed, we know that by this stage Alexandria was also home to the Therapeutae, a group often associated with the descendants of the Buddhist missionaries. Philo of Alexandria describes the Therapeutae as existing in every quarter of

Alexandria, especially towards Lake Mareotis, where they lived a simple and spiritual life of 'perfect goodness'.[1]

A clear end product of these influences on Christianity was Gnosticism, a term Plato had first used to describe knowledge (*gnosis*) sought from considered thought rather than practical discovery. Gnostic thinking was a result of real-life challenges: after the Roman invasion and the subsequent maltreatment that spanned the social strata, Alexandrians began to think about their position in the grander cosmos and within the human race, and about the extent of divine wisdom. Influenced by their tough experiences and polytheistic neighbours, an influential section of Alexandria's Jews became Gnostics interested in the esoteric and mystical. And some of Alexandria's Christians followed suit, contemplating Gnostic beliefs, thinking about how God can be reached through *gnosis* rather than faith, or, in other terms, mystically rather than ritually. To them, seeking enlightenment was more important than repentance. Gnostic instructors included Basilides in the early second century, whose teachings helped attract many Alexandrians to this new branch of Christianity, especially women, who began to take a more active role in the faith's development as a result. Alexandria, then, was the birthplace of Gnosticism because its rising Christian population was heavily affected by its Greek and Jewish counterparts, and because such mysticism could attract all strands of society. Gnosticism permanently boosted the role of allegory in scriptural interpretation, something that started in first-century Alexandria with Jewish scholars like Philo. However, most church leaders rejected Gnosticism, temporarily creating two sects of Christianity in Alexandria: Gnostic and Orthodox.

Importantly, such a pattern of travel – from Egyptian and Greek philosophy, to Judaism, to Christianity – became a standard trajectory for both sets of Alexandrian Christians. Greek philosophy remained most influential. Aristotle's teacher, Plato, was resurgently popular, as was Stoicism. Among those who studied and taught these ideas in the second century was Pantaenus the Philosopher, who, upon converting to Christianity, tried to make his Greek philosophical beliefs reconcile with his newfound faith. Together with other converts, Pantaenus began to teach at a new school, the Didascalia, or the Catechetical School of Alexandria, the first institution of theological learning in Christian antiquity. Alexandria became home to the world's only centre for Christian theologians, which following the example of the Museum, gathered scholars who could reflect upon and revamp their faith and philosophy. The school began with an intention of increasing conversions, but as the religion became established it developed into both a teaching and research institution. The Didascalia hosted important Christian scholars from outside Alexandria and its students and researchers were not interested in theology alone; they also studied philosophy, literature and the arts. This meant that a range of new biblical interpretations – some regarded as deviant or heretical – would stem from the Alexandrian Church. By the end of the second century, Alexandrian theologians were spreading their beliefs elsewhere, like Valentinus, who left for Rome where he founded a Gnostic school. And by the third century, swathes of Alexandrians were converting to the increasingly popular young religion.

Among Pantaenus' students was Clement of Alexandria, whose dismay at a morally corrupt society led to his conversion to Christianity and a journey of self-discovery around the region. Returning to Alexandria at the age of thirty to be taught at its Christian school, he soon began to record his beliefs, all of which were shaped by the city's philosophical schools. Clement took the philosophies that existed as templates and placed Christianity within them. He divided life into three elements: character, actions and passions, showing that Jesus teaches all three. When he preached, crowds turned up, many not yet Christians. To explain Christianity, he referred extensively to Stoic philosophy and to literature, citing Homer over and over again. Clement indicated that the Christian vision for Alexandria was very different from what preceded it: there was no room for idolatry or hagiography. 'Alexander', he wrote, 'wished to be thought the son of Ammon, and to be depicted with horns by the sculptors, so eager was he', but instead, time 'proved him mortal'.[2] Responding directly to Alexandria's way of life, Clement contended that people shouldn't overeat, and that alcohol, music and perfume were only permissible in moderation. He stated that promiscuity was wrong, but so was sexual abstinence; he prohibited prostitution; he suggested that angels had sex with humans. He ordered men to act and look masculine and women to be feminine, hinting that he opposed same-sex relationships among both genders. But he also added that both men and women could lead the church since God was both male and female, Christ neither male nor female and salvation was open to both. This was, however, at odds with his strong condemnation of abortion, something that was carried out in Alexandria either physically with the use of copper spikes invented by the city's early physicians, or medicinally using herbs, like Galen's potion for abortion that could either be consumed or inserted into the vagina. For centuries, abortion was morally acceptable in Alexandria since Aristotle believed that the foetus only developed a soul at forty days (male) or ninety days (female), and the Stoics regarded a human as such only when born and breathing air; the Romans, influenced by the Stoics, generally allowed abortion. Clement's anti-abortion views propelled Christianity as the key force that changed attitudes towards the practice, in Alexandria and further afield. With increased Roman persecution, Clement eventually left Alexandria, dying in Jerusalem in 215 as his hometown was being ravaged by the emperor Caracalla.

Clement was a Christian convert, but some of the up-and-coming theologians were born Christian. Ammonius Saccas was born in 175 into a poor family and educated at a Christian school before working at the harbour, hefting sacks to and from the docked ships to earn the name Saccas (or sack carrier). There, he met a variety of people from different cultures, who spoke different languages and used different spices. As his curiosity increased, he began to attend philosophical lectures after work, and before too long became known as *theodidactor*, the god-taught. As a self-made philosopher, Ammonius didn't write anything, but instead began the Platonic School of Alexandria, where he taught his theories: that there exists an absolute deity, that humans are mortal but have a soul, and that anyone is capable of experiencing divinity. As he became more famous, students from around the region came to learn from him. Those who were enrolled would be sworn to secrecy but ironically issued with conspicuous cloaks that had to be worn at all times. It soon became clear that Ammonius' vision could speak to those who championed Plato and Aristotle, as well as those with Jewish and Christian beliefs. For Christians, it made sense that there was a God, that humans could experience death and the afterlife, that anyone could experience spiritual heights and that a man (Christ) could be divine.

Among Ammonius' students, an unlikely friendship blossomed between two young men named Origen Adamantius and Plotinus. Origen was raised in a strict, almost fanatical Christian environment. As a teenager, he witnessed the Roman persecution of his community: his father was beheaded and his family's property seized. The eldest of nine, he needed to provide for his family, so when a wealthy Christian woman agreed to sponsor his private education, Origen seized the chance with the ambition of becoming a teacher, at that time a highly respected job. Plotinus, on the other hand, was a polytheist who had enjoyed a classical education and a comfortable upbringing. In many ways, they couldn't have been more different.[3]

Plotinus went on to establish the first Neoplatonic school. Plotinus' Neoplatonism theorised that there is an absolute deity, the One, who created and transcended the universe, generated all that is good, and to whom humans strive to return. Plotinus described how the One floods humans with intellectual capacity and conscience to make their own decisions. The One supports the three other principles: the Intellect, the Soul and Nature. These three formed a trinity. He described this trinity as *hypostasis*, meaning the underlying state that supports everything else. Plotinus' school attracted huge numbers of men and women, as well as boys and girls sent by their parents to learn about the universe. After eleven years, Plotinus decided it was time to travel; the cheapest way to do this was to join the Roman expedition to Persia, so he left, ending up in Rome where he started an academy. He had already made a clear mark on Alexandria, where horoscope readers and soothsayers now risked going out of business: the rise of Neoplatonism shifted people away from fatalism to the belief that they could now affect their own fortunes.

The two friends, Plotinus and Origen, used to take long walks during which they discussed their beliefs about Plato and Christ. It is no coincidence that Origen, too, ended up advocating the idea of trinity as *hypostasis*, advancing the relatively new concept of the Holy Trinity. Similarly to his friend Plotinus' theory about the One, he described Logos – literally 'the Word', but in the opening of John's Gospel, 'the Word was God' – as a principle that permeates the universe, presides over all and transcends everything. As the One supports the Intellect, Soul and Nature, Logos, too, supports a trinity. Logos, Origen explained, is the Hypostasis of the Father, the Hypostasis of the Son and the Hypostasis of the Holy Spirit. Each of these three is limited: the Father by his justness and goodness, the Son by his human nature and the Holy Spirit by the extent to which humans can receive it. As a trinity, though, these limitations are solved. Through these concepts, Origen made an important contribution to explanations of the Holy Trinity, especially by naming the Holy Spirit as an explicit member of the godhead.

Origen's only surviving writings consist of two letters. But from his students and subsequent writing about him, we know that he perceived Christ as both human and divine, the world as being full of symbolism, meaning that the scriptures were surely allegorical; even the violence and gore of the Old Testament couldn't be real, he argued, but, rather, metaphoric. Fire represents inner anguish, Origen claimed, and Christianity is a non-violent faith to the extent that if it were embraced, no empire would require an army. Origen's detailed and comparative commentaries on the Bible essentially made him the founder of biblical studies. They led to his title, the father of theology, and cemented his reputation as the most influential Christian theologian until St Augustine over a century later. Neoplatonism had become a key influence on the development of Christianity. The godhead and his immateriality became identified with the One, and Origen was championing allegory and peace, two emphases that remained prevalent in Christianity.

Ammonius went from carrying sacks on the harbour to teaching two students – Plotinus and Origen – who would affect the world in unexpected ways. Neoplatonism transformed Greek philosophy to become the dominant school of thought in Europe for the next millennium. It would go on to influence Jewish enquiry into the nature of God, and Muslim philosophers applied its logic to create a new and vital speculative theology called the science of discourse. The European Renaissance, too, adopted metaphysics and symbolism in its scholarly and creative endeavours, seeking to understand and explain what it means to be human.

In fourth-century Carthage, though, a different Christianity was developing; later known as the Latin Church, it opposed the Alexandrian views as heresies. Nonetheless, the Catechetical School was celebrated beyond Egypt because it was the first of its kind, merging philosophy and theology. Its early leaders all established key foundations of Christianity and are therefore among the Church Fathers. They are Clement of Alexandria, Origen of Alexandria and Athanasius of Alexandria.

Athanasius, who was influenced by Origen, became pope at thirty in 328 and remained in the role until he died in his late seventies. He increased conversions by using the Coptic language, which had developed from Egyptian over the previous century and which had taken flight alongside the faith. During his term, Athanasius was exiled five times by the Romans, only to return each time to cheering crowds.

Alexandria's leading theologian for the second half of the fourth century was Origen's student, Didymus the Blind. Didymus was something of a polymath, concerned with philosophy, poetry and astronomy, among other subjects. As a toddler, he had lost his sight. Following in the footsteps of the Museum's founders, his innovation differentiates him from the rest of the church leaders. Didymus believed that he could use his other senses to understand the world, so he listened and memorised, before coming up with the idea of using touch to read. Wood surfaces were engraved with letters so that he could first learn the letters, then to read and write. Christians from around the region came to hear Didymus speak – and to witness what they perceived to be a miracle when he read. At this time, eye diseases were common in the region, so the Catechetical School, and in turn Christianity, was uniquely able to accommodate the visually impaired.

Two of Didymus' students became even more influential than him, helping to propel Christianity into the Latin-speaking world. The original scriptural languages didn't include Latin, but were limited to biblical Hebrew, Jesus' native Aramaic and Alexandria's Koine Greek. The Church Fathers of Alexandria were using the Greek Old Testament, already translated in Alexandria. Then, all of the books that were to form the New Testament were first written in Alexandria's very own dialect of Greek, before their translation into Latin and other languages. The first of Didymus' students was Tyrannius Rufinus who translated the Christian texts of Alexandria, including Origen's, from Greek to Latin. This was remarkably important, because it spread Christian ideas from Alexandria across the Roman Empire and beyond. The second student was St Jerome, most famous for translating the Bible from Greek, Hebrew and Aramaic into Latin, a version of the Bible that became known as the Vulgate. At the turn of the fifth century, Alexandria's Christian scholars went on to combine the Old Testament and New Testament into a single manuscript now known as the Codex Alexandrinus. Still deemed the most authoritative text, the Alexandrian text-type is the basis for most modern translations of the New Testament.

Alexandria was a Roman city and the Romans were polytheists. A new religion taking their cities by storm – especially Judea and Alexandria – was perceived to be a dangerous development. Though there were just a few hundred global followers of Christ in the first century, by the middle of the second century there were an estimated 40,000, by the end of the second century as many as 200,000, and by the middle of the third century over a million.

Until the emperor Constantine began his reign and declared freedom of worship in 313, Christians suffered regular persecution. In 64 CE, a great fire hit Rome: the emperor Nero accused the Christians of starting it and persecuted them. In Alexandria, many Christian scholars and students were killed around 202, as noted by the Christian historian Eusebius, who studied in Alexandria the following century. Eusebius describes how locals joined the persecution imposed by the Roman emperor Septimius Severus. The men were tortured and beheaded. The women were scorched, with one story telling of the fate of Potamiæna, who was lowered into a searing cauldron, 'boiling pitch being poured slowly and little by little over different parts of her body from head to toe'.[4] Potamiæna, whose body was said to be 'in the full bloom of its youthful beauty', became a celebrated martyr for Alexandrian Christians who remembered her through song for decades to follow.

The most significant Roman persecution of Christians came in the third century. Eusebius records street fighting in 249 with

Christians being attacked and killed by local mobs. The spark appears to have been a deadly plague that hit cities across the Roman Empire, which the new emperor Decius blamed on the sacrilegious Christians. Clashes with Christians continued into the new year, when the emperor issued a staggering decree that every inhabitant of the empire – Jews excepted – was to make a sacrifice in front of Roman officials to prove loyalty to the Roman gods. As the officials arrived at their homes, Christians were faced with a choice. Some elected to sacrifice animals or light incense to the Roman gods to spare themselves, receiving a certificate to prove that they'd done so. Around fifty of the certificates from that year survive today. Some scribes scrambled to produce forgeries for those Christians who could afford to buy them. For those who couldn't bring themselves to do either, there were two options. One was to flee, the other was to refuse to toe the line. Those who refused were promptly arrested and led to torture, execution, or both. The Roman edict also empowered local polytheists to abuse their Christian neighbours. The Christians who had lived in peace in Alexandria were suddenly in mortal danger. The local Roman governors also used the chance to attack the bishops. Origen of Alexandria was imprisoned and tortured, eventually dying as a result. Didymus the Blind was hunted by assassins and went into hiding, then fled westwards into the desert, where he remained for months until the persecution ceased. The edict also caused issues in the Church as some believed that the Christians who had feigned allegiance to the Roman gods could remain Christians. But the official line, in both Alexandria and Rome, was that these people should be refused because true Christians would remain so even when faced with death.

The deadly pandemic that instigated these events in 249 was the Plague of Cyprian. It ravaged Alexandria's population. The outbreak of the illness – the symptoms of which variously included severe diarrhoea, fever, throat ulcers, limb pain and loss of hearing and sight – shook the region. The plague was a mystery as people reported it being spread 'by sight', as a tenth-century fragment notes, meaning that it was probably an airborne virus that didn't require contact. Alexandria's location, for so long a huge advantage, suddenly became a liability as the plague spread around the

city through the travellers who came and went. Probably coming
from further south, it arrived in Alexandria in 249 before spreading
to Carthage and Rome by 251. In Alexandria, Eusebius describes
how 'wailings resound throughout the city because of the number
of dead'; 'not a house' managed to escape the plague.[5] At the height
of the pandemic, thousands were dying each day and it got the
better of two Roman emperors (Hostilian and Gothicus). The
stench of death spread across Alexandria as the dead were dumped
in huge, uncovered pits. As recently as 2014, Italian archaeologists
discovered bodies in Luxor (then called Thebes) that dated to the
plague and revealed how some of the dead were covered with
quicklime and cremated in order to stop the disease from spreading to the living. Lasting at least fifteen years, the plague must have
killed tens of thousands in Alexandria. The pope at the time,
Dionysius, gives a stark but detailed indication of the numbers,
describing how 'this immense city no longer contains as big a
number of inhabitants'. In his letter, he claims that the population
of Alexandria dropped by more than 60 per cent, from 500,000 to
190,000.[6] The numbers may be exaggerated, but they aren't out of
line with other reports about the daily death tolls or population
estimates based on the public grain records. Some of these
Alexandrians died, no doubt, but many would also have fled the
domains of the heavily populated city.

Ironically, the Christians who were blamed for the pandemic
were the only faction to benefit from it in the long run. They
proclaimed their dead as martyrs and preached about their rewards
in the afterlife. They argued that even two mighty polytheistic
emperors had been powerless against God's plans. Perhaps most
importantly, though, they provided care for the sick and helped with
burials; in Alexandria, Dionysius led this charitable activity. These
actions were appreciated by the population who once again began
to embrace Christianity in numbers.

This charity marked the start of an Alexandrian group called the
parabalani – the reckless ones. This was the group of Christian men
who brazenly risked their lives by carrying the diseased on stretch-
ers and hurling the dead into the pits. An illiterate class from the
bottom of society, they steadily displayed blind devotion to their
bishops and were persuaded to complete such acts for the sake of

God. Over time, their willingness to sacrifice themselves, coupled with a tendency towards violence, would make them much feared in Alexandria.

In the late third century, the Roman emperor Diocletian created a Tetrarchy – the empire was to be ruled by four people, two senior emperors and two juniors. As if the earlier persecutions weren't bad enough, the turn of the century witnessed episodes of violence, instigated by the four emperors, that spread across the empire to become known as the Great Persecution. Hundreds of Alexandria's Christians were killed. Many were forced to flee, including a popular physician known as Father Cyrus and even the pope, Peter of Alexandria. In his absence, different factions began to emerge, threatening harmony within the Christian community itself. By 311, however, some of the edicts were nullified and, importantly, the emperor Constantine was edging towards Christianity. Later known as Constantine the Great, he was the first emperor to convert to Christianity, though it's thought that he was only baptised on his deathbed. Still, his sympathy with – and legalisation of – Christianity legitimised the faith further and would have a huge effect on the religious landscape. The religion, and especially its leaders, began to garner legal and political power.

At this time, a priest who was born during the mid-third-century Plague of Cyprian was about to create the biggest factional controversy in early Christianity. His name was Arius. In a rare account, Arius is described by Epiphanius as tall and lean, as a man whose good manners were hugely attractive to women. In 311, after a dispute in which he contended that lapsed Christians were being welcomed back too easily, Arius was excommunicated from Alexandria by Pope Peter. He returned a couple of years later, but responded to a sermon by the new pope, Alexander of Alexandria, about the similarity of the Father and the Son by stating that since the Father begat the Son, the Father must be unique and unbegotten, while the Son, who at one stage didn't even exist, must derive his subservient divinity from the Father. Although Origen had expressed somewhat similar views, this was a much clearer indication that the Father is superior to the Son.

Arius' views distressed the local priests, who in 321 met and decided that he would be exiled from Alexandria once more. Arius immediately wrote to his Beirut-based friend, the bishop Eusebius of Nicomedia, who was distantly related to Constantine and would eventually baptise the emperor. In Alexandria, Arius' views were popular. According to Athanasius, who was writing against him, Arius attracted people by putting his ideas into rhyming songs set to catchy melodies, popular with his supporters, who preached to men and women in the markets and docks. Arianism garnered support in part *because* it was quashed by the Romans and the Church, and was thus firmly anti-establishment. All Alexandrian Christianity was regarded as a populist threat by Rome: it had long challenged Roman authority by refusing the divinity of the emperor and translating the holy scripture so anyone could access it. It was no wonder that the Romans purged or at least tried to control the Alexandrian Christians. Arius had also garnered the support of some local bishops, who began to protest the hostile treatment he received. And with Arius' writing spreading further afield, it was becoming clear that the godhead debate couldn't be resolved in Alexandria. It needed a major intervention.

So significant was Arius' impact that in 325 the emperor called for a council of Christian bishops to gather in the city of Nicaea (north-west Turkey) in order to settle the issue. The Arian sympathisers were led by Eusebius of Nicomedia and the anti-Arians by Alexander of Alexandria. According to Athanasius of Alexandria, who was present, 318 bishops attended. Athanasius himself was still a twenty-seven-year-old deacon, probably an assistant to Pope Alexander on the trip since each church leader brought five colleagues with him, making the number of travellers for this event pass a thousand. One of the decisions made at the Council was that the date of Easter should be more accurate and unified, and because Alexandria was renowned for its astronomy the responsibility to make the announcement would hereon fall on the city's bishop, who would do so by writing an annual 'Easter Letter'. These festal letters would soon be used for political purposes. When it came to the main matter at hand, Arianism was ultimately denounced, even by Arius' friend Eusebius, who said that his hand signed, not his heart. The end product of the Council of Nicaea was the Nicene Creed,

Christianity's most influential, unifying statement of belief in the nature of God. It attests to the belief in God the Father, the Son who is made of the same substance as the Father, and the Holy Ghost. And it ends with a surprising anti-Arian addendum: 'But those who say: "There was a time when he was not"; and "He was not before he was made"; and "He was made out of nothing", or "He is of another substance" or "essence", or "The Son of God is created", or "changeable", or "alterable" – they are condemned . . .'

The controversy that started in Alexandria was finally settled, at least in theory. But uniformity also marked a change in Christianity. The essence of Judaism was debate and Christianity was indebted to that tradition: Alexandria was a place where early Christianity prospered because of the multiple opinions and ideas in its Catechetical School and churches. Such open-minded days were already coming to an end. The emperor ordered the burning of all of Arius' works; Arian ideas are known to us only through the writings that denounced them.

In Alexandria, Athanasius replaced Alexander as pope just three years after the Nicene Creed and vowed to oppose 'Arian heresy', a policy now supported by the majority of the city's Christians. Athanasius' harsh dealings with the Arians were among the reasons the Romans – fearful that civil unrest could have economic consequences – kept banishing him. When Athanasius was exiled in 338, his Arian replacement was rejected by the city's Christians, who began to protest. To counter the Christian population's mobilisation, the Roman governor paid a mob of polytheists and Jews to intimidate them by breaking into churches, where they kidnapped monks and nuns. With the insistence of the bishops, Athanasius returned in 346, only to be exiled again in 356. The bishop who took his seat was deemed a Roman puppet and Alexandria's Christian mob lynched him: a message to Rome that if the Alexandrians opposed someone, they would get rid of him. A few years later, when an anti-Nicene bishop arrived at Alexandria from Antioch, the Christian mob was already waiting for him, so imperial guards escorted him straight out of the city.

While Alexandria was getting embroiled in these religious disputes, the emperor Constantine was busy building a new city of his own. Constantinople (modern-day Istanbul) was founded in 330 and immediately became the capital of the imperial East – the Byzantine Empire – and a new force to rival Alexandria.

Despite the rise of Christianity, Alexandria continued to be seen as a place of excess, as a Las Vegas of its time. For the last few centuries, the city was famous for its brothels, which became especially numerous to meet the demand of travelling tradesmen and pilgrims passing through the city. Women arrived from different parts of the region to find work as prostitutes, and men ventured to Alexandria from faraway towns to satisfy their urges. Even monks from the nearby desert travelled to the city for sex. To discourage this, early fifth-century monks recorded how one of them, whose urges were on 'fire', returned from Alexandria suffering from syphilis: 'a carbuncle developed on his private parts, and for six months he was so ill that the parts rotted away and fell off'.[7]

For Christianity, Alexandria's reputation was another reason why saints could be made here: temptations were everywhere in this sex capital, so repentance was all the more impressive. The majority of Alexandria's Christian stories about penitence from sexual immorality involved women. St Thaïs, for instance, was a poor fourth-century orphan who parleyed her incredible beauty into riches. Denounced as a sinner for selling her body, she converted to Christianity and imprisoned herself in a convent cell for three years until her death. There's St Mary of Egypt, who escaped her family to Alexandria so that she could enjoy a life of casual, uninhibited sex that lasted seventeen years, before undertaking a sacrilegious journey to see how many pilgrims she could seduce. Despite her success in this endeavour, an invisible force stopped Mary's entrance into Jerusalem's Church of the Holy Sepulchre, so she repented and became a hermit.

Alexandria's most famous female saint is also depicted as a beautiful woman: in a frequently painted mythical scene in Christian art, she kneels down in pure white, about to marry an infant Jesus being held up by his mother. This curious wedding ceremony, depicted repeatedly in the medieval and early modern periods, is known as the Mystic Marriage of St Catherine. So, who was this woman? Legend has it that Catherine of Alexandria was born in 287 during the reign of Maximinus Daza, a superstitious Roman emperor who blamed Christians for natural disasters. Catherine came from a wealthy, noble family; her father was Constus, the governor of Alexandria. A vision of Jesus and Mary changed her life as a teenager and led to her controversial conversion to Christianity. Four years later, when she was eighteen, the emperor began the persecution of Christians and her father presumably intended to carry out his orders in Alexandria. Given her family's position, Catherine was able to meet the emperor and challenge him on his beliefs. According to *The Catholic Encylopedia*, the emperor was 'astounded at the young girl's audacity' and summoned scholars to change her allegiances. But Catherine was able to debate the scholars to the extent that, 'conquered by her eloquence', they became Christians and were immediately executed.[8] Catherine was imprisoned in a dungeon, where she was tortured, but where according to legend she was fed by a dove from heaven and her wounds tended by angels. Intrigued, the emperor's wife visited her and became one of many whom Catherine converted to Christianity. With torture failing, the emperor offered to marry Catherine, but she refused, stating that she was already married to Christ. Sentenced to die on a spiked execution wheel that agonisingly mutilated the body before death, it's said that when her body touched the wheel the instrument shattered. Instead, she was beheaded, and milk, not blood, poured from her neck, before the angels carried her away to Mount Sinai.

These events are mythical, as appears to be Catherine's name. In his *Ecclesiastical History*, Eusebius notes that Alexandria's Christian women 'yielded up their souls to death rather than their bodies to seduction'. He then writes about one particular 'Christian lady' who was wealthy, educated and propositioned by the emperor:

> A certain Christian lady, for example, most famous and distinguished among those at Alexandria, alone of those whom the tyrant ravished, conquered the lustful and licentious soul of Maximin by her brave spirit. Renowned though she was for wealth, birth and education, she had put everything second to modest behaviour. Many a time he importuned her, yet was unable to put her to death though willing to die, for his lust overmastered his anger; but punishing her with exile he possessed himself of all her property.[9]

There is a case to be made for Catherine being this 'Christian lady' of Alexandria. Indeed, St Catherine is said to have died at the beginning of the fourth century during the reign of Maximinus Daza, and Eusebius would have been a contemporary of both. Yet, his *Church History*, although featuring many named martyrs, makes no mention of a Catherine. She may have had a different name: St Dorothea of Alexandria's story is remarkably similar and is mentioned by name by other Alexandrian writers in the fourth century. As a historian, Eusebius did embellish, but his work was fundamentally factual, and as a contemporary of the martyred woman if he'd known her name he would have used it. We can deduce a constant factor in his narrative and those that followed: that there was a young, educated Alexandrian woman who was executed for her Christian beliefs, and that it's highly unlikely her name was Catherine. The Greek origin of the name (*katharos*) means 'pure', suggesting that this woman is meant to symbolise chastity. Over time, the legend of this anonymous woman grew to include miraculous details that took precedence over the facts until she became Catherine: an amalgam of many Christian women who had come before her and were to come after her.

St Catherine is just one of Alexandria's saints and the Mystic Marriage is just one example of her influence on Christian mythology over the ages. The Catherine cult was particularly strong in France and England as early as the ninth century, when news spread that her body was supposedly discovered in Sinai (although ancient pilgrims in the five centuries before don't mention anything related to her when they travel there). On his pilgrimage, the eleventh-century king Edward the Confessor claimed to bring back oil from her body, which was placed in the cathedrals of Canterbury and Westminster. The cult became more prominent when the fifteenth-century French heroine Joan of Arc saw visions of Catherine, who inspired her to support the French king Charles VII in his battles against the English. Across Europe, shrines, altars, cathedrals, colleges and murals have since been dedicated to her, and she has had a particularly large female following. In France, unmarried young women were called 'Catherinettes', and on St Catherine's Day they sent postcards to one another, wore colourful hats and prayed for the right man to come along. Today, Alexandria's St

Catherine's Cathedral – on a street named after her – is a neo-Baroque basilica with two storeys of pillars on either side of its entrance and though invisible from outside due to the Baroque façade, a dome that surprises anyone who enters. Wooden carvings depict Jesus visiting Catherine in her captivity, and a large painting of Catherine dominates the central area behind the pulpit. Constructed in the mid-nineteenth century, it is the primary Catholic building in Alexandria today. It was built and frequented by Franciscans, European pilgrims who arrived in the seventeenth century en route to the Holy Land, but decided to settle in Alexandria instead.

On the ceiling of St Catherine's Cathedral we see the portraits of some of the city's saints. One is St Athanasius, who led the Church for almost half of the fourth century. Another is St Cyril, a controversial figure whom we'll meet in the next chapter. And then there is St Anthony, notable as the founder of Christian monasticism.

Anthony of Egypt is the original monk. Born around 251, his life changed at around the age of twenty when his wealthy parents died.[10] Taking Jesus' advice to the wealthy man in Matthew's Gospel literally, he sold his earthly possessions in return for heavenly treasures, giving the money to the poor. As the Christians escaped persecution, many had fled to the undeveloped outskirts of Alexandria, where the desert forced them to live ascetic lifestyles that would spread across the Christian world. The ascetics lived with their families in huts where they would spend hours praying and fasting. But Anthony took things a step further, living in a cemetery for fifteen years, then in an old fort for even longer. He would fast for half the week, although bread was conveniently thrown over the walls for him every day. Many aspiring monks travelled to meet him – but he stubbornly refused to leave his abode. As the number of visitors increased, they built huts around his fort, ultimately establishing a community of monks, inspired by an enigmatic man who declined to meet them. Some twenty years after he'd entered his fort, Anthony finally emerged, ready to spend a few years sharing what he'd learnt before returning to the solitude of a new monastery. Anthony lived until the age of 105; his fasting and strict diet of bread, salt and water seems to have granted him longevity.

The Life of Saint Anthony, a biography written by Athanasius, details how, after his long retreat, Anthony began taking trips to Alexandria, some sixty miles away, and was tempted by demons en route. He also took a group of monks to the city during the persecution of the early fourth century, wearing bright white so that he could easily be spotted and martyred. He went to the prison, packed with Christians, in order to preach. He also attended the trials and interrogations of some Christians, where he encouraged them not to lose faith, and accompanied to their executions those sentenced to death. After returning to his monastery, he heard about the Arian controversy, so left for Alexandria again in order to publicly denounce Arianism, also using the opportunity to debate with the Neoplatonists.

When Athanasius visited Rome in 341, he introduced Egyptian monasticism to the West. But many of those affected by monasticism were ordinary Alexandrians. For instance, Macarius had a small confectionary shop in Alexandria until the age of forty, when he chose to be baptised before venturing into the desert. He ended up founding one of three major monastic sites just south of the city. One of these is in the Nitrian Desert, around thirty miles away (visible from the desert motorway today if one drives from Alexandria to Cairo). Nitria became a favoured spot for monks; when St Jerome visited Nitria in 386, he recorded that over 5,000 monks were residing there.

When St Anthony's grave was discovered in the mid-sixth century, he was immediately transferred to Alexandria's Church of John the Baptist, the former site of the Serapeum. The following century, it was moved to Constantinople, then, in the eleventh century, to the Rhône-Alpes region of France, where it lies today. This relation to France explains his second ongoing link to Alexandria: that St Anthony, with a long beard and a black monk's habit covering his head, is often depicted in art alongside St Catherine. They weren't in Alexandria at the same time, but the imagined connection links both figures to martyrdom.[11]

Today, the main monastery in Alexandria is dedicated to a saint called Mina. Initially a soldier in the Roman army, Mina resigned in light of the persecutions against Christians, retiring to a life of ascet-icism. In 309, when he professed his faith publicly, Mina was executed. Keen for him to be buried near Alexandria, his sister is said to have bribed soldiers to bring his body home. According to Coptic legend, his body was being carried by a camel, which, upon approaching Lake Mareotis, suddenly refused to move. Mina was buried at this spot. For centuries, pilgrims have gathered at a well nearby in order to be healed, and many little two-handed flasks (ampullae) from the fifth to seventh centuries have been discovered there, engraved with an image of St Mina and the camel. Today, the Monastery of St Mina stands in close proximity to the city's airport and major football stadium.

In 68 CE, St Mark was murdered on the streets of Alexandria. But despite numerous challenges, in a relatively short period Christianity had managed to take Alexandria and its surrounding areas by storm, cementing the city as a pioneering Christian centre.

Destruction

Fourth-century Alexandria remained diverse and each faith group had continued to transform its religious beliefs and practices. The downside of such variety was that, like striking a match, the city could turn into a fiery battleground in an instant. As a melting pot of different groups, its centuries of multicultural stability had been punctuated by brutal persecutions, with Egyptians, Jews and Christians all suffering. But the rise of Christianity led to a particularly aggressive attack on the city's polytheistic beliefs. As the Roman Empire became Christian, the Alexandrian Koine Greek language began to be associated with polytheism – even if Jesus himself spoke it. The polytheists were referred to as *Hellenes*, literally meaning the Greeks. From this time, up until the European Renaissance, referring to someone as a Hellene went from a form of praise to clear derogation. From the fourth century, Christians also began to refer to polytheists using the Latin term 'pagan'.[1]

Faiths had always developed new characters in Alexandria, and Christianity had been no exception, first through its amalgamation of Greek, Egyptian and Jewish philosophies, then when different Christian factions formed, through harsh intellectual and martial opposition to one another. Christians regularly rioted and fought, but now their indignation concerned such ongoing controversies as the nature of Christ and his relation to God the Father. They also rejected non-Alexandrian bishops sent by the emperor. As a result, Alexandria became more divided from Constantinople and Rome during the fourth century, initiating the imperial neglect of Alexandria that would eventually pave the way for an easy Arab invasion. But before that, the Christian leaders and citizens were about to turn on their non-Christian neighbours, the polytheists and the Jews.

The rise of the bishops was changing the social stratification of Alexandria. Previously, the most influential group were the civic elite, those who enjoyed Alexandrian old money and continued to receive a classical Greek education. By the fourth century, the Christian leaders were becoming just as influential, maintaining political ties with the governors and administrators, and able to sway public opinion. But the bishops often came from humble social backgrounds and had moved to Alexandria rather than been born into multi-generational Alexandrian families. These were two reasons why some Christian leaders played a significant role in reducing what tolerance remained in Alexandria, undermining the non-Christian cultures that characterised the city and maintaining a de facto army in case troubles necessitated fighting with another faction. The lower-class Christians who'd selflessly cared for people during the third-century plague, the *parabalani*, were now effectively the pope's bodyguards and the Church's private militia, numbering around 800 men in the fourth century. Perceived as being above the law, the locals didn't dare question them.

Legend has it that in the 350s an orphan named Theophilus and his younger sister were living in Memphis, left in the care of an Ethiopian slave woman. She took them to pray in the temple one morning. In the chamber they jumped to their feet as the two gods in front of them, moments earlier standing majestically, crashed to the ground and shattered into pieces. This, their alarmed carer concluded, was a sign that they must travel north to Alexandria, where they could learn about the popular Christian faith. As they arrived in the church, God had revealed their story to Pope Athanasius, who baptised all three. The girl was taken to be raised in a nunnery – but around 378 she gave birth to a baby, Cyril. The boy, Theophilus, was taken to a Christian school where he became an exceptional student before being recommended for the priesthood. In 385, as he turned forty, he was ordained as pope. His nephew, Cyril, would follow him as pope in 412. Through their hostility to non-Christians, both Theophilus and Cyril would go on to change the history and identity of Alexandria.

Unlike the rest of Egypt, Alexandria's civic and spatial centre wasn't an Egyptian temple; the Serapeum was its greatest building but it stood on a hill to the far west of the city. It appears that, by now, the city's centrepiece wasn't the tomb of Alexander either; when the archbishop, St John Chrysostom, visited Alexandria in 400, he reported that 'his tomb even his own people know not'.[2] But there remained multiple temples from different periods and devoted to different gods (Egyptian, Greek, Roman, Jewish and now Christian). Alexandria's buildings became even more mixed: while some aspects of the city started to look more like the Roman East, original buildings were also maintained, so there was now a combination of Egyptian, Greek and Roman architectural styles. By the time of Theophilus' papacy, with followers of Christ exceeding 100,000, Alexandria had become majority Christian. The Church was further empowered by the fact that the Roman emperor Theodosius was a devout Christian. We know of at least a dozen parish churches in Alexandria at this time, though these probably didn't accommodate the rising number of worshippers. There were also three larger churches from the third century, including the Church of Theonas and St Mary's Cathedral, both of which served as papal bases until the mid-fourth century when, under Athanasius, the Caesareum – a temple to the Roman imperial cult – was turned into the episcopal Great Church of St Michael.

Before that, around 324, the Temple of Kronos and Thoth was turned into the Church of St Michael: as the first major conversion of a temple into a church, this was a turning point for Alexandria. It also indicated the clear intentions of the Church. By cutting the statues of Kronos and Thoth into pieces and carving crosses on them, these gods were not entirely erased, instead serving as a reminder to people that they were inferior to the Christian god. Thoth was the Egyptian god who judged the dead, something with which St Michael was also linked, confirming Christianity as a direct replacement for the Alexandrian religions.

On the western side of the city, Alexandria had boasted one of the world's greatest religious buildings: the Serapeum. Dedicated to Serapis – the Greco-Egyptian god promoted by Ptolemy I as the divine protector of Alexandria – the opulent temple had remained the city's largest and most stunning since its completion by Ptolemy

III in the third century BCE. Despite being damaged during the early second-century Jewish rebellion, it was swiftly refurbished by the emperor Hadrian. Its shining marble, gold and silver, as well as its majestic height, made the Serapeum the first building that travellers saw as they arrived by sea, though for the last century or so it was visible alongside the colossal statue of the emperor Diocletian on top of the giant column we now know as Pompey's Pillar. Ammianus Marcellinus, writing in the late fourth century, notes how Alexandria still had 'many temples with lofty roofs, chief among them the Temple of Serapis', which housed 'two priceless libraries'. He goes on to praise the grandeur of the Serapeum:

Its splendour is such that mere words can only do it an injustice, but its great halls of columns and its wealth of lifelike statues and other works of art make it, next to the Capitol, which is the symbol of the eternity of immemorial Rome, the most magnificent building in the whole world.[3]

Ammianus wrote this just years, maybe even months, before the emperor granted all the temple grounds of Alexandria to the Church. This forced worshippers to barricade themselves inside the Serapeum to protect it from a takeover. Coupled with Christians mocking polytheistic traditions and gods in the public square, street fighting ensued and there were deaths on both sides. From Constantinople, the emperor ordered the destruction of all idols, 'so that once these were done away with, the reason for the conflict might also disappear'. The much-loved Serapis went from deity to demon: he began to disappear from Alexandria as statues were torn down, figurines smashed and pictures scratched off walls. The fourth-century Christian historian Rufinus writes that

in Alexandria: the busts of Serapis, which had been in every house in the walls, the entrances, the doorposts, and even the windows, were so cut and filed away that not even a trace or mention of him or any demon remained anywhere. In their place everyone painted the sign of the Lord's cross on doorposts, entrances, windows, walls, and columns.[4]

The unrest culminated one morning in 391, a moment when Christianity confirmed its dominance in Egypt. Alexandrians watched as Pope Theophilus led a large, boisterous crowd of Christians into the Serapeum, the city's greatest religious symbol. As they entered the complex, they demolished the nilometer that measured the Nile's water and was thought to link the river with the gods. After they had mounted the marble steps to the courtyard, they began to tear down the artworks, knock over the statues and cut through the temple walls. A polytheist historian from the time, Eunapius, writes that the Christian mob 'fought so strenuously against the statues and votive offerings that they not only conquered but stole them as well . . . Only the floor of the temple of Serapis they did not take, simply because of the weight of the stones which were not easy to move from their place.'[5]

In the centre of the temple they arrived at the holy Serapis statue. Rufinus writes of their reluctance to attack, for it was common knowledge in Alexandria that touching the god would cause the sky to fall in. A soldier took the risk and struck Serapis' ivory face repeatedly with an axe. The sky stayed put and roars emanated around the temple. Serapis was knocked over, ropes wrapped around him and pulled in different directions. Unlike previous gods they had carved crosses on, Serapis had to be annihilated. The deity was promptly decapitated, his feet and hands axed off – and then, like the Great Library before it, the Alexandrian god was set on fire alongside a final stock of books that had no place in the Christian world.

Indeed, as Christianity became more established, book censorship increased. The bishops of Alexandria were writing the annual Easter Letter confirming the date of the festival. The thirty-ninth such letter, dated 367 and written on the bishops' behalf by Athanasius, is notable for containing the first complete reference to the 27 books of the New Testament. It also specifies the canonical books that should be read alongside scripture, before adding that other writing should be rejected as heretical, a statement that confirmed Alexandria's changing relationship with the written word. In the fourth century, beginning in Constantine's reign, possession of allegedly heretical books became a criminal offence and any such writings were burnt and destroyed – a far cry from the city's former goal of gathering every book in the world. At least one person at this time, probably a monk, hid his books for future generations. In 1945, in the sandy cemetery of a town called Nag Hammad not too far from Luxor, a young farmer by the name of Mohammed al-Samman discovered an old sealed jar. Inside it were thirteen leather-bound papyrus books – containing over fifty Gnostic treatises and the now apocryphal Gospel of Thomas – that had survived for at least 1,600 years. A few years after the discovery, the Dutch historian Gilles Quispel secured one of the papyrus books for psychoanalyst Carl Jung as a birthday gift.

Other gods and their temples in and around Alexandria suffered similar fates to Serapis. Idolatrous images and statues were destroyed, both those in private homes and the ones in public buildings, baths and squares, where they were burnt amid celebrations and chanting. The temples that were destroyed were usually repurposed as churches. As temples remained state property, this was a systematic attempt both to quash the polytheistic traditions and to Christianise. As well as being a show of power, it is the case in crowded cities that prime locations for places of worship are already taken, so religious sites are instead changed, in this case from temples to churches (and soon, from churches to mosques). As for the numerous synagogues, within a year or so of the Serapeum's destruction a law was passed to 'restrain with proper severity the excesses of those persons who, in the name of the Christian religion, presume to commit certain unlawful acts and attempt to destroy and to despoil the synagogues'.[6] The wording suggests that synagogues had begun to suffer the same fate as the temples. In Alexandria, no fewer than fifty churches emerged in this period, at least nine founded by Theophilus, the grandest of these apparently plated in gold. As for the Serapeum, a cathedral dedicated to John the Baptist was built on the site as Christianity began to be imposed on the population.

Within months of the Serapeum's destruction, the emperor Theodosius banned entry into polytheistic temples and the practice of public sacrifices, effectively outlawing the religion of a significant proportion of Alexandria and the Roman Empire (in which at least 80 per cent of people weren't yet Christians). The outlawing of 'paganism' in 392 signalled a new page in history: in some ways the start of a world more familiar to the one we know today. With such a drastic decision, the look of Alexandria was bound to change, too. One key emblem spread everywhere: the cross. Examples that survive today include a sculpture of the Roman general Germanicus, who was celebrated when he visited the city in 18 CE and commemorated with a statue. In the fourth century, a cross was stamped right onto the polytheist's forehead. Another key example is in the Kom el-Dikka area, where a small, pleasingly intact theatre survives, made from marble blocks with a horseshoe-shaped auditorium. Some of the pedestals and seats include engravings, like graffiti, of chariot race winners. But the very first pedestal at the entrance of the theatre has big crosses engraved on its sides.

Theophilus became a polarising figure who didn't accept dissidence. One such example involved four men who were known as the Tall Brothers. The four siblings chose an ascetic life in the Nitrian Desert, but when they subscribed to Origen's philosophical view of God as non-anthropomorphic, they were hunted down by Theophilus. In fact, Theophilus armed the monks of Nitria against them, forcing the Tall Brothers to flee to Constantinople. Ironically, the ascetic monks became some of the most prone to violence. In light of such events, the ruling class felt that Theophilus was causing instability, while the Christian elites criticised his dictatorial style; in one letter, a prominent contemporary Christian refers to him as an 'Egyptian pharaoh'. But he remained hugely popular and respected among the majority of Alexandria's Christians.

In Coptic tradition, he remains a hero, the pope who built churches and fought for Christianity against the evils of his time. The most important portrait of Theophilus is included in the *Alexandrian World Chronicle*, an anonymous volume published in Alexandria in 392 that covers the history of the world from creation until the year of its publication. Although lost, fragments of a fifth-century reproduction survive, complete with miniatures illustrating various political and biblical events. Among the miniatures is a fading picture of a haloed Theophilus, the gospel in one hand and a piece of the severed Alexandrian god in the other as he stands triumphantly on top of the Serapeum temple, once 'the most magnificent building in the whole world'.

* * *

Cyril was around seven when his uncle Theophilus became pope in 385. Cyril had a classical education, although later in life he would remark that 'Hellenic learning is vain and pointless'.[7] Even as Alexandria became Christian, it maintained some of its classical heritage, especially when it came to education. Egyptian, Greek and Neoplatonist traditions remained popular among the educated. Commoners, too, didn't know a world without festivals, so continued to celebrate some non-Christian holidays until the Church introduced new ones. The city in which Cyril grew up did not, despite the pressures, give in to uniformity. As always, a mix of people inhabited its homes and walked its streets. Even Christians, despite crackdowns on dissidents, were far from monolithic. For a start, their relationship with the faith varied: depending on whether one believes the Christian or non-Christian contemporary historians, conversions either occurred because Alexandrians realised the value of the teachings or because they were downright terrified.

When Theophilus died, Cyril took the top job within a couple of days. Some of the elites didn't want to see a second Theophilus, so advocated archdeacon Timothy for the role, and a crowd gathered to protest against Cyril. According to fifth-century church historian Socrates Scholasticus, Christian supporters of the two candidates brawled in the streets for days, the *parabalani* fighting for Cyril. As the dead began to stack up, Egypt's military commander intervened with an army of soldiers.

Cyril of Alexandria became pope, but the chaos that occurred in his first week of office demonstrated that he had no qualms about resorting to violence. The *parabalani* now served as his private militia, and, following his uncle's lead, Cyril made sure to arm the monks in the mountains south of the city. In his first public statement, he distanced himself from his uncle, calling for unity among the Christians and emphasising the importance of the monks to the community.

While the fourth century saw attacks on polytheists, attention was now returning to the Jews. Read today, some of Athanasius' Easter Letters are clearly anti-Semitic. But according to Socrates, Alexandria's Jews were now a fun-loving group, more interested in the theatre than the Torah.

Alexandria was essentially ruled by the governor of Egypt, appointed by the Romans. At this time, a Christian aristocrat called Orestes occupied the role. Since Alexandria's Jews now gathered at public theatres more than private synagogues, Orestes viewed them as potential locations for civil unrest. So he created a new law regulating the mime shows being performed. Keen to find out more, Cyril sent one of his men – a primary school master – to the Jewish theatre. That teacher was well-known for initiating the loud applause during Cyril's speeches, so when the Jews spotted him they assumed that Cyril's hype man must be on a spying mission. The Jews became angry at the provocation, and, interpreting Cyril's actions as an incitement of trouble, Orestes had the spy arrested and brutally interrogated. He seems to have been understandably anxious about the ever-increasing power of the Church and its attempted involvement in civil matters like this. And Cyril was probably right to interpret Orestes' actions as a blatant show of authority. This trouble had begun at the Jewish theatre, so the governor also summoned the Jewish leaders, telling them in no uncertain terms that, if they caused more trouble, he was prepared to drive them out of the city.

Shortly after this, Socrates reports that in the middle of the night some Jews started screaming that the Church of St Athanasius was on fire. As their Christian neighbours ran out of their homes towards the church, they were surrounded by the Jews and attacked; several died. The next morning, with the help of the *parabalani*, Cyril launched a direct offensive on the synagogues, forcing his way in and converting them to churches, and in the process plainly breaking the law. He went as far as ordering Jewish homes to be looted and driving out Jews from the city's boundaries into the desert. Socrates writes that during this event of 415, every last Jew was expelled from Alexandria. In reality, it was probably a significant chunk of the Jewish population; the Jewish elites are likely to have stayed. For Orestes, who had to report to the emperor, this was bad news: not only was the civil unrest getting out of control, but many Jews worked in jobs vital to the city's economy, not least its ongoing supply of grain to Rome and Constantinople.

From outside the city, pressure mounted on Cyril and Orestes to come to a reconciliation. After mediation, they agreed to meet.

Cyril 'extended toward him the book of the Gospels'.[8] But Orestes didn't kiss it: doing so would look like submission to the Church, and, worse still, to Cyril. The relationship between the two most powerful men in Alexandria – the imperial governor and the pope – had well and truly come to a head. Their troubles wouldn't stop there. They were soon to involve one of the greatest minds in Alexandria, arguably the greatest female scholar of the classical age. A woman by the name of Hypatia was about to be dragged, and not just figuratively, into their merciless chaos.

Hypatia

Born into a respected polytheistic family in the mid-fourth century, Hypatia's father was an esteemed mathematician and philosopher named Theon of Alexandria. From his records, we know of two eclipses in 376 Alexandria, one solar and one lunar, when his daughter was no older than eleven. Theon lectured and wrote on two famous Alexandrian predecessors, Euclid of Alexandria and Claudius Ptolemy, editing new editions of their work with the assistance of his daughter, whom he took under his wing by training her as a scholar.

In general, Alexandrian women were highly literate: even the lower classes were trained to understand the alphabet. The daughters of Alexandria's elites received as complete an education as their brothers, with supplementary time spent learning how they should conduct themselves. Hypatia's early education would have differentiated her from the common Alexandrian by emphasising the language, grammar and oration of classical Greek – different from the Alexandrian dialect. Hypatia is also likely to have been inspired by the slightly earlier female mathematician Pandrosion of Alexandria, none of whose writings remain, but who was mentioned by her rival Pappos of Alexandria as having developed a method for doubling the cube.

When she was around thirty, Hypatia's father passed the baton on to her and she became the new tutor at his university-like school. The sixth-century Neoplatonist Damascius, who was educated and taught in Alexandria, writes that 'she had greater genius than her father, she was not satisfied with his instruction in mathematical subjects; she also devoted herself diligently to all of philosophy'. Alexandria's philosophical scene was dwindling in comparison to its mathematical one, so Hypatia reignited the teachings of Plato and Aristotle. Students came from far and wide to learn from her. Hundreds of men and women were attracted to Hypatia's talks on philosophy: her style and content were accessible and outdoor crowds gathered attentively as she spoke. Damascius reports that she 'used to put on her philosopher's cloak and walk through the middle of town and publicly interpret Plato, Aristotle, or the works of any other philosopher'.[1]

Hypatia published commentaries and textbooks on legendary Alexandrians including the mathematician Diophantus of Alexandria, 'the Great Astronomer' Claudius Ptolemy and 'the Great Geometer' Apollonius of Perga, who'd invented her favourite device, the astrolabe. She also developed instruments for distilling water, for measuring water level and a hydroscope for determining the gravity of a liquid. Hypatia also taught a more exclusive group of students, among them two wealthy Christian brothers, one called Synesius, whose letters survive. One letter explains how Hypatia taught him to make an astrolabe. Synesius also seeks Hypatia's opinion and approval regarding his literary style, as well as his books about the interpretation of dreams and how to breed dogs. The letters also speak of the love that these students had for one another and for their intellectual 'mother' Hypatia. This adulation, based on Plato's *Symposium*, is grounded on a love of knowledge and spirituality, a love of soul rather than body. It is from Plato's idea that we now use the term 'platonic love', and this is what Hypatia's students shared.

The historian Socrates, a contemporary of Hypatia, describes her as having 'extraordinary dignity and virtue', but Damascius goes a step further, indicating that she died a virgin. Such an image fits neatly with her popularity among some Christian elites, like Synesius, for whom virginity was related to the monastic tradition and Mary, mother of Jesus. It also aligns with her philosophical views: Plato is one of many philosophers thought to have made a choice not to marry. Apart from Damascius' note, there is nothing to confirm that Hypatia was celibate, but we can deduce that she was at least regarded as such during and immediately after her life. We might also deduce that she had bigger, more time-consuming priorities than romantic love.

'She was so beautiful and shapely', writes Damascius. Hypatia's looks, especially her alleged curvaceousness, make any emphasis on her chastity even more curious. They also serve as a reminder that Hypatia, as a young woman, was operating in a male-dominated world. It is hardly surprising that one of her students became infatuated with her. When he declared his love, Hypatia is said to have tried to help him using music as a method to calm his passions. But Damascius claims that Hypatia responded to the man in another way: she threw her equivalent of a used sanitary towel at him. The story teaches the superiority of perfect spiritual love over imperfect bodily love. 'This is what you love, young man', Hypatia said, as she showed him the white rag stained with her menstruation blood, 'and it isn't beautiful!'

By the 380s, Alexandria had two competing Neoplatonic schools. Plotinus' Neoplatonism theorised that there is an absolute deity, the One which floods humans with their capacities. His student, Porphyry, who engaged critically with Christianity, added that the human soul could ascend into higher realms of existence and salvation through strife and virtue. And his student, the Syrian Iamblichus, believed that salvation could only be achieved via awakening the soul to its own divinity, through symbolism and ritual. Hypatia adhered to Porphyry's idea, that intellectual enquiry and learning could spark virtue – something which brought Alexandria's Christian elites to her school – while Alexandria's polytheists sought to revive their own beliefs in the power of symbols and rituals by teaching Iamblichus' arguments in the Serapeum before its sacking in 391.[2] Ironically, Hypatia's so-called 'pagan' beliefs didn't clash with Christian ones. But in her mid-thirties, as she saw her faith being outlawed, temples like the Serapeum being destroyed, and artistic masterpieces, like the statue of Serapis, being defiled and even melted down for gold, she must have been saddened and troubled. Many other polytheistic scholars were alarmed enough to move away from the city. But Hypatia chose to stay. In fact, her Neoplatonic teachings appeared to be bridging the different faiths, her school offering an increasingly rare space for debate. As an elite member of Alexandrian society and on good terms with its civil leaders, she expected her freedoms to be unaffected whether in her established school or in her home space, likely to have been a sizeable house with a garden.

Pope Cyril passed the house one day and 'saw a great crowd of people and horses' gathered there. 'Some were arriving, some departing, and others standing around.' He enquired 'what all the fuss was about' and was informed that this is 'the house of Hypatia'. There, she also welcomed visitors and new residents of the city who had arrived with letters of recommendation from her friends. Such examples indicate that Hypatia was not philosophising in solitude, but actively trying to put her theories into action in a city that had begun to see its religious leaders having an adverse effect on its harmony. By staying in Alexandria, Hypatia cemented herself as the city's leading public intellectual. According to Damascius, 'the whole city rightly loved her and worshipped her in a remarkable way'. So respected was Hypatia that when guests came to Alexandria, the aristocratic Christian governor, Orestes, would take them to visit her. But her frequent sightings with him were not going unnoticed.

In 415, after the governor Orestes arrested one of Pope Cyril's men at a Jewish theatre and tortured him, Cyril reacted by ransacking the synagogues of Alexandria and expelling as many Jews as he could. Efforts to reconcile the governor and the pope didn't work, leaving Alexandrians to wonder why Orestes, a Christian, was refusing to make amends with Cyril.

Far from reconciling, things were about to get a whole lot worse. Cyril had already armed hundreds of monks in the surrounding mountains of Nitria, and one night he summoned 500 of them into the city. In a planned operation, they watched Orestes from the top of a nearby hill. Then, like a herd, they sprinted down to surround the governor's chariot. They dubbed him an idolator and in the commotion he tried to assure them that he was a baptised man. The ultimate intention of the monks isn't entirely clear; perhaps it was to intimidate him, to let him know that he should not underestimate Cyril's power. But amid the furore, one of the monks threw a rock straight at Orestes' head. Even as blood gushed from his face, the imperial guards ran for their lives, and, instead, Alexandrians came to the governor's rescue.

Orestes survived the incident, but he made sure to find the monk who had thrown the rock. He was caught and subsequently tortured to death. Seeking to keep the monks loyal, Cyril didn't condemn their actions. Instead, he held a church funeral for the dead monk, proclaiming him a martyr and saint – something many of Alexandria's Christians opposed. Orestes wrote to the emperor about what had happened, but so too did Cyril. To Constantinople, it could easily look like Orestes wasn't in real control of Alexandria. So, with things heating up even more, the city's aristocrats and philosophers, including Hypatia, offered their unequivocal support to Orestes. Along with other respected Alexandrians, Hypatia may have been approached by Orestes for advice on stabilising the situation, or even acted as some sort of mediator.

Rumours had already been spreading that Orestes was spending so much time with Hypatia that she must have been affecting his decisions. Socrates writes that 'it was calumniously reported among the Christian populace, that it was she who prevented Orestes from being reconciled to the bishop'.[3] Given her status, and the expected public intellectual role that philosophers had long played in Alexandria, it is likely that Hypatia was offering private advice to leading figures, and that in turn some public personalities would want to be seen with her in order to raise their profiles. But as both a woman and a non-Christian, Hypatia was becoming an easy scapegoat. Not only was she seen to be influencing the governor, but the narrative developed that she was carrying out the work of the devil. Rumours that Hypatia was using her knowledge to supernatural, demonic ends were spreading fast. The Christian governor had 'ceased attending the Church', and there could only be one explanation: 'she had beguiled him through her magic.'[4] What kind of sorcery was this? Some Alexandrian Christians believed, as the seventh-century Egyptian bishop John of Nikiu does in his *Chronicle*, that 'she was devoted at all times to magic, astrolabes and instruments of music, and she beguiled many people through Satanic wiles'.

In March 415, as Hypatia was riding in her chariot and approaching her house, she suddenly found herself blocked from every angle. Ordered to step down onto the wide road, she was immediately seized and dragged through the city amid shouts of 'to the church'.

Inside the church, formerly the Caesareum, her abductors carried out one of the most significant and brutal murders in Alexandria's history. Using broken pottery, roof tiles and even oyster shells, the mob ripped through Hypatia's clothes (oysters were regarded as impure by Egyptians, so may have been used to add insult to injury). Now that Hypatia was naked, the mob took things even further: they began to skin her. As though this wasn't enough, they proceeded to gouge out her eyes. Covered in blood and with her limbs broken and dislocated, Hypatia's battered body was then dragged through the streets of Alexandria once again before being thrown into a fire.

Hypatia's vicious slaughter marked the end of the major conflict between Christianity and polytheism in Alexandria: 'paganism' had been defeated. The city's leading scholar and thinker of the last 35 years, someone born and raised in Alexandria and who, out of choice, never once left its shores, was now gone, slain by fellow Alexandrians. She would now serve different but opposing purposes as a simultaneous reminder of the city's esteem as well as its decline.

As the roars of celebration subsided, the pitiless assassination sent shock waves across the city. Alexandria had long been famed for new knowledge and relative tolerance. Hypatia represented both of these – as well as a previous era. With her death came confirmation of changing times.

Understandably, Alexandria's frightened scholars began to leave for Athens. For the first time since the founding of the Museum, the city could no longer call itself a knowledge capital. Platonic philosophy would only survive another century or so before the emperor Justinian shut its schools down. The Library, too, was going from bad to worse. The Roman historian Orosius visited Alexandria within five years of Hypatia's death and was baffled by the Library's empty shelves. The books had steadily been decreasing in number, but the events of that year may have involved mobs destroying some books, or the departing scholars taking books with them.

When it came to faith relations, there was now something irreconcilable between Christians and polytheists. Each group's philosophers, historians and even citizens began to create a stronger sense of identity, not so much built on what they were, but what they were not. A negative identity politics had well and truly arrived in Alexandria.

Damascius blamed Cyril for Hypatia's murder, adding that he was much loved for it since 'he had destroyed the last remains of idolatry in the city'. But there is no evidence of Cyril's involvement. He may have incited hatred towards Hypatia, but it is unlikely that he ordered her murder, which would have been risky and undiplomatic. Socrates writes that her murder resulted in serious criticisms and resentment of the Alexandrian Church and its leadership, and Cyril had to stop his followers from causing any more trouble. In a way, like the tsunami exactly 50 years earlier, there was now going to be some calm after the storm.

The imperial response to Cyril's various troubles with the Jews, the governor and Hypatia appears to have targeted the *parabalani*, the group who'd transformed from selfless heroes to religious fanatics to death squads. A law passed just months later, in 416, stated that new rules were being introduced 'because of the terror of those who are called attendants of the sick'. Its first band limited their powers by ruling that they 'shall not be more than five hundred' and ensuring that 'their names have been submitted' in advance to the governor. Its second band ended their 'liberty to attend any public spectacle whatever or to enter the meeting place of a municipal council or a courtroom', effectively banning them from any gathering, such as the theatre.[5] Alexandrians were relieved to see this violent group regulated. But rather than banishing them as might have ordinarily been the case, the law actually stopped them from leaving Alexandria in order to protect the rest of the empire. The *parabalani* would remain Alexandria's problem – and in future, though they ceased to be involved in secular issues, they continued to be involved in ecclesiastical ones (such as intimidating bishops during synods). Furthermore, the Alexandrian Church didn't go unaffected, but was treated warily by other churches. Shortly after Cyril's death, a major split occurred at a synod, when his successor Pope Dioscorus refused the majority opinion that Christ's divine and human qualities are separate. The Alexandrian School, still wary of previous issues with Arianism, believed Christ combined these two qualities. Dioscorus was sacked and, going forward, the Byzantines became keen for Alexandria to have a bishop whom they'd appoint themselves. As a result, there were now two factions. First, the original Coptic Orthodox Church; at this stage, Coptic, or *kubti*, simply meant a native Egyptian, but would soon denote the Christians of Egypt because their language was Coptic. Second, the smaller Eastern Orthodox Church of Greek-speaking Romans.

As for Hypatia, her murder was remembered vividly by Alexandrians over the following decades, and it became a regular point of reference. The Alexandrian epigrams by the fourth-century poet Palladas indicate how Hypatia was revered, particularly among the polytheistic population. Palladas, who presented himself as a polytheistic schoolteacher trapped in both a Christian city, and worse yet, an unhappy marriage, wrote:

> I look on you and kneel in reverence,
> And on your writings, when I see the sign
> Of Virgo entering her starry House:
> For your work touches heaven, HYPATIA,
> You sacred ornament to literature,
> Pure shining star of teaching that is wise.[6]

To Palladas, Hypatia is a saintly martyr whose work had divine qualities. She is now with Virgo, who according to Greek mythology is also a virgin and as classicist Gideon Nisbet explains, 'walked among men telling them unwelcome truths, but eventually gave up on them to assume her place among the stars'.[7]

Hypatia has since been used to symbolise many different ideas. By the twentieth century, she was adopted, though not universally, by the women's rights movement. Before that, during the European Renaissance, Hypatia of Alexandria was conflated with St Catherine of Alexandria to create an amalgamated Alexandrian superwoman who was both learned and pious. During the French Enlightenment, Hypatia was presented as an areligious scientist who could make a case for secular enquiry. Voltaire praised her as a rational woman who didn't give in to dogma. But by quipping that 'when one strips beautiful women naked, it is not to massacre them', Voltaire remained unable to look beyond her femininity, a reminder of how gender affected and continues to affect perceptions of her life. During attempts to revive classical ideas in Europe, Hypatia was again a point of interest as an idealised, Hellenised figure. In nine-teenth-century sculptures, she is completely naked. The Victorians especially read her as a symbol of femininity by depicting her as a heavenly nude. The Pre-Raphaelite artist Charles William Mitchell's most famous piece presents an attractively naked Hypatia sugges-tively leaning backwards towards a stone altar, her ginger hair reach-ing her knees and covering her genitalia but only one of her breasts. Hypatia would be disappointed to know of this continued sexualisa-tion a millennium and a half after she lived. She would also be disap-pointed to know that her major works are lost, that she is most famous for the manner of her death, and that Alexandria would for ever struggle to revive the tolerance of its early days.

Mitchell's painting is in stark contrast with Raphael's early sixteenth-century *School of Athens*, which adorns a wall of the Vatican Palace. In this large fresco, the painter gathers the greatest scholars of antiquity under one roof. Some stand, some sit, others write and converse. Plato and his student Aristotle, the godfather of Alexandria, take a central position. On the far right, other figures from Alexandria's history are present, like Claudius Ptolemy and Plotinus. Among all of the men stands one woman, the lone female in the scene. She wears a crisp white robe. And she is doing some-thing no other figure dares to do: she is gazing straight out of the painting, making eye contact with me, with you, with whoever is looking.

Islamic Conquest

Seventh-century Alexandria would have been unrecognisable to the likes of Ptolemy I, Cleopatra VII and even Hypatia. A major plague had broken out in 541. Known as the Justinian Plague (and recently as the Old World pandemic), it was transmitted by the black rat. Thought to have originated in Central Asia before being carried to Egypt, it spread via the canal boats into Alexandria, then Constantinople and on to Rome where it killed a fifth of the population. Many resorted to home remedies, but medical physicians were on call as well. Alexandria had also been hit by one famine after another. First, when the Persians attacked other parts of Egypt and Palestine in the early sixth century, refugees fled to Alexandria, suddenly increasing the population and causing food shortages. A less sunny period also affected the harvests for months on end. Then, a crop failure in the early seventh century led to widespread starvation until a rich man donated grain and money to the city in exchange for becoming a deacon. In the mid-seventh century, a drought in Egypt led to another exodus to Alexandria that further burdened the struggling city.

The royal quarter had lost its grandeur, its tree-lined, perfumed roads now a sandy expanse. The two Jewish districts, previously brimming with busy tradesmen and crowds of women and children, were shabby and lifeless. The Serapeum and Caesareum, once adorning the harbour with their glistening façades, had become modest churches. The Library shelves were emptier than ever, the scrolls disorganised and damaged. The Museum was in ruins, the sound of lively conversation replaced by the echoes of the lone footsteps of those who bothered to enter it. The Neoplatonic academy – which had flourished again in the early sixth century under

Isidore of Alexandria and Damascius – was now permanently closed. Alexander's tomb, previously a site of pilgrimage, was nowhere to be seen. The population had fallen severely and having shifted from outright Roman rule to regional Eastern Roman rule under the Byzantines, it also lacked the military power it once had. Alexandria's Koine Greek was still the administrative language, but day-to-day, it had been replaced by Coptic, a late form of Egyptian.

Coptic was the language of the Church, which had also seen changes. Since the mid-fourth century, it had been split into two: there was the traditional Coptic pope, who had economic but not political power, and a newer Constantinople-appointed pope who doubled as Egypt's prefect (the emperor's governor) but whom Alexandrian Christians tended to oppose.

Nonetheless, the Church was now key to the economic and political setup of the city. During its early days, the Church was by no means wealthy. By the sixth century, Alexandrian winemaking had flourished and the Church was producing, storing and selling barrels. The Church also started to play an active role in land ownership and maritime trade, with its own fleet of ships and boats and hundreds of staff on its payroll. As usual, Alexandria's main export was grain. An intriguing story recorded in the early 600s and hidden deep in the multi-volume Latin *Acta Sanctorum* (*Acts of the Saints*) tells of an incident involving Pope John V, who held the papacy for a decade beginning in 606. When a sailor is stranded on the coast of Alexandria and appeals for help, the pope allows him to travel in a Church-owned ship delivering corn. After twenty stormy days at sea, he gets off 'on the islands of Britain' where the crew, coming from what turned out to be a comparatively prosperous Alexandria, is surprised to discover 'a great famine'. The British officials are delighted: 'God has brought you', they exclaim, before offering either coins or tin in return for the grain. The crew takes half of each back to Alexandria, where they sell the tin for a good profit.[1] The details of this story suggest that at this time ships may have sailed from Alexandria to the south of Britain (probably Cornwall or Devon) to export grain and import tin, which would be mixed with copper to create bronze. They are also a reminder of a more certain fact, that by the sixth century the pope was making decisions about what came in or out of the harbour, had the power to tax imports and was running a money-lending operation.

Neither the officials nor the wider population in early seventh-century Alexandria would have predicted that a new imperial force was making its way across the region. This was a united group of Arabs who were getting stronger by the day. They called themselves *al-muslimūn*, 'the ones who submit', or the Muslims.

For at least three centuries, Alexandria had been home to a small population of Arab heritage thanks to two tribes. The Lakhmids originated from Yemen and, as their numbers increased, spread over the region. The Judhams had spread from the deserts of southern Levant and recently joined the Byzantine army. These tribes would have been aware of an Arabian pilgrimage site in a town called Mecca.

It is in Mecca that Muhammad ibn Abdullah was born and lived, and where he developed such a fine reputation that he was nick-named 'the truthful and trustworthy'. A spiritual man who left the bustle of town each day to worship alone in a mountainous cave, one evening in 610 the forty-year-old made his way home quivering. He had received a divine revelation. Its first order, soon to be the first word of a new holy book, was 'read'. As the revelations increased, the new faith clearly aligned with many Jewish and Christian teachings, with a self-admission that it was continuing the message of Moses and Jesus. But the new faith's severe criticism of the Arabian communities' practices, not least its disparaging percep-tion of polytheistic idolatry, resulted in a predictable backlash. To escape the physical persecution of the Meccan tribal leaders, Prophet Muhammad's followers fled to Axum (modern-day Ethiopia and Eritrea), where they were protected by its Christian king Ashamah, commonly known as Najashi. The first group of refugees consisted of twelve men and four women; the second, a couple of years later, comprised more than one hundred people.

Attracted to his ideas of equality, many of Muhammad's initial followers were from the lower classes, including slaves. They were challenged by the tribal elites, who didn't want to see their tradi-tions and lifestyles affected. Amr ibn al-As was one of a handful of influential men whose primary aim was to quash the new faith. He made no secret of his spite for Muhammad to such an extent that the Quran refers to him as one of 'the mockers'.[2] A wealthy Meccan in his thirties, Amr had inherited a significant estate that included several successful vineyards. His contemporaries described him as having exemplary 'acumen, guile, and firmness'.[3] It is not well known that Amr visited Alexandria, probably no later than 615, after meeting an Alexandrian deacon on pilgrimage while trading. By introducing Amr to Alexandria, a city he would invade for the Muslims some three decades later, this deacon might have changed the religious makeup of the world as we know it.

The ninth-century Arab historian Ibn Abd al-Hakam, who wrote the earliest detailed history of the Islamic conquest of Egypt, has described this unlikely encounter. While Amr was feeding his horses outside the holy site of Jerusalem, an Alexandrian deacon came out of the church wheezing from thirst. Amr gave him water, and the deacon fell asleep nearby. As the man snoozed, Amr spotted a snake out of the corner of his eye and instinctively fired an arrow at it. When the deacon awoke, he saw the dead snake beside him, and, after learning what Amr had done, invited him to his home. 'Where is your country?' Amr asked. 'Egypt, in a city they call Alexandria.' Amr's reply indicates that the Meccans remained in something of a bubble: 'I don't know it and I have never been to it.' The deacon exclaimed: 'If you go to it, you will know that you've never been anywhere like it!' After a ten-day camel journey, they arrived at its gates. Ibn Abd al-Hakam describes how Amr stepped into another world: he 'looked at Alexandria and its tall buildings, the quality of its construction, the abundance of its people, and what money it has, so his amazement increased'. Amr even attended a 'great fête' dressed in a silky brocade presented to him by the deacon, and played a ball game with the Alexandrians, amusing them when he caught it inside his sleeve. The deacon even gathered money for him as a reward for saving his life.[4] Amr was clearly infatuated with Alexandria: a lavish, built-up city so much more advanced in its architecture, entertainment and civic life than tribal Mecca, and one in which the wealth must have appeared abundant.

As a merchant, Amr also went to Axum regularly via the Red Sea. In fact, he was acquainted with its king and would bring him aromatic spices and smooth silks from Arabia. When the Muslims sought refuge with Najashi, Amr was perfectly placed to stir up trouble and even capture them back as slaves for the Meccan leaders. But the monarch refused to hand over the Muslims, protecting his refugee community.

Meanwhile, Heraclius – who became emperor of the Eastern Roman Empire the same year as Muhammad's revelation – was hardly aware of the threat coming from Arabia. The fourteenth-century Muslim historian ibn-Kathir writes that one day Heraclius was in a foul mood because he saw in the stars a warning about a 'king of the circumcised' rising to power. Another Arabic source, the landmark *History of the Patriarchs* by tenth-century bishop Severus ibn al-Muqaffa, records that Heraclius had a dream about 'a circumcised people that will beat you and take your land'. In both histories, Heraclius and his advisers, unaware that Muslims also practise circumcision, naturally assume that Jews are about to gain power. In ibn-Kathir's version, Heraclius orders all Jews across the empire to be killed, and in Severus' he forcefully baptises them. While there is no further evidence of this story, it would be no surprise if the Jews of seventh-century Alexandria faced further persecution before the Muslim arrival.[5] As for the other faith groups in the city, the polytheists had already become a minority, and the Christians disliked the emperor, who'd placed a puppet bishop in charge with different beliefs from them.

Alexandria was a place living on reputation, hardly Heraclius' most important city. But its strategic location, coupled with a weak army, kept it on many a radar. The Persians decided to attack the city in 616, occupying it briefly before it was swiftly recovered. But Heraclius, at the helm of a long-standing empire, was still underestimating the power of the new and unknown group from the desert.

In Arabia, the Muslims, now more numerous, migrated with Muhammad to the town of Yathrib in 622. The town, which they renamed al-Medina al-Munawwarah (the Enlightened City), or Medina (City) for short, had witnessed decades of civil conflict between its tribes, which included polytheistic Arabs and several Jewish groups. Muhammad was welcomed by the tribal leaders as a neutral adjudicator and quickly drew up a constitution which specified that Jews 'shall not be oppressed or championed against' and that both they and the Muslims had a right to practise separate faiths: 'the Jews have their religion; and the Muslims have their religion.' As for Christianity, the Quran was positive:

> And you shall assuredly find that the nearest of them in genuine love to those who believe are those who say: We are, indeed, Christians. That is because there are among them priests and monks – and they do not grow arrogant (5.82).

Muhammad's initially healthy relationship with the Jews and Christians would have made Alexandria an interesting place to him. So much so that around 628 he wrote to Egypt's Alexandria-based prefect. Muhammad's companion, Hatib ibn-Abi Balta'ah, who was thought to have Egyptian ancestry, was tasked with travelling to the city. When the good-looking, lightly bearded messenger arrived, he found the prefect – usually assumed to be Pope Cyrus of Alexandria, but more likely to have been Pope George I of Alexandria – in a splendid ocean dwelling that required Hatib to take a short boat ride. He handed the pope the letter:

> In the name of God, the Most Gracious, the Most Merciful. From Muhammad, servant of God and his Messenger, to the Prefect, the Grand Copt. Peace be upon whoever follows the righteous path. As for what follows, I invite you to the call of Islam, submit, be safe, God will give you your reward twice. But if you turn away, then you bear the sin of the Copts. And 'O People of the Scripture! Come to an equitable word between us and you: That we shall not worship other than God. And we shall not associate anything at all in [our worship of] Him. And we shall not take one another as lords apart from God. Yet if they turn away, then say: Bear witness that we, indeed, are *muslims*, in willing submission to God'.[6]

It is a sign of respect that the pope ordered that this letter be placed in an ivory casket and stored in a monastery. Had he not done so, we may never have known about it. The letter – which includes a fine example of Muhammad's signet ring seal – remained in Egypt until the nineteenth century and is now on display in Istanbul. The pope's reply is respectful, too, indicating that he has extended a warm welcome to Hatib, who stayed in Alexandria for five days and was gifted money and five luxurious outfits. The pope begins his letter to Muhammad with the same phrase, 'In the name of God, the Most Gracious, the Most Merciful', before adding:

> I have read your letter, and I have understood what you mention in it and what you call towards . . . I have treated your messenger generously, and have sent to you two concubines who have a great regard in Coptic Egypt, and clothes, and gifted you a female mule to ride. Peace be upon you.

The pope's gifts went down well. Muhammad especially liked some Egyptian honey not mentioned in this letter. A donkey was included, too, which he rode, but not as much as the mule, that was named Duldul (thought to mean porcupine). No doubt, the most significant Alexandrian gifts were the sisters Maria and Sirin, said to be of noble blood and thought to have Roman ancestry. Once they arrived in Medina, Maria the Copt – described by historians as being of exceptional beauty owing to a fair complexion and curly hair – was chosen by Muhammad, much to the chagrin of his existing wives. Muhammad had four daughters live into adulthood, but until Maria gave birth to a boy, named Ibrahim, he had no sons. Tragically, though, Ibrahim became sick and died on his mother's lap shortly before his second birthday, with Muhammad falling to his knees in despair.

The same year that these letters were exchanged, Amr ibn al-As' work had taken him back to east Africa, where he once again met with Axum's king. Many of the early Muslims who'd taken refuge there had remained, building Africa's first ever mosque, and Najashi's admiration for Islam had grown. According to Islamic tradition, it is this gathering with the monarch that convinced Amr to embrace Islam. Amr's change of heart, which came two decades after Muhammad's revelation, was a huge coup for the Muslims. Not only had Amr been a sworn enemy, but he was an influential man and an experienced fighter from whom they could benefit. With military power becoming a requirement for the Muslims to maintain the peace in Medina and plot a return to Mecca, Amr was immediately utilised as a commander.

Egypt was already something of a holy land: it was a place in which the Quran set the stories of several prophets, most famously Joseph and Moses, one who deputised for a pharaoh and another who challenged a pharaoh. Egypt was fast becoming an even more important place for Muhammad and his followers. Not only did Muhammad have an Egyptian partner, but with the exponential increase in their numbers the Muslims were now thinking more economically. Before too long, Muhammad sent another messenger to Alexandria's pope. And as the Islamic Empire began to expand around the Arabian peninsula, Muhammad made a clear statement about Egypt's future, prophesying to his companions: 'You will conquer Egypt after me, so be advised to do good to its Copts, for they have with us close ties and kinship.'[7] Pope George I and Muhammad died within months of one another. Five years later, when Maria the Copt died in 637, she was buried near Muhammad in Medina.

Pope Cyrus became prefect just months before Muhammad's closest friend, Abu Bakr, became caliph. Abu Bakr sent two separate messengers to Cyrus, one of whom was Hatib again. Cyrus was an unpopular choice for most Alexandrians, who instead supported the long-serving non-Byzantine Coptic pope, Benjamin I. The tenth-century *History of the Patriarchs* records that Cyrus forced Alexandrians to embrace his version of Christianity, arresting, exiling and killing the priests who didn't agree with him. Pope Benjamin was forced into hiding, and his brother was tortured and thrown into a fire 'until his fat . . . dripped on the floor beside him'.[8] In response, there were attempts to assassinate Cyrus, but conspirators were caught and executed.

In Medina, Abu Bakr ordered Amr ibn al-As, who was already familiar with the relevant trade route, to head the Muslim conquest of the Levant. Amr managed to lead his army successfully, capturing Byzantine Palestine's capital, Caesaera, a city which Herod the Great had named in honour of Octavian after he defeated Cleopatra. Abu Bakr died two years into his caliphate; his successor, Omar ibn al-Khattab, also made sure to send a messenger with a letter to Pope Cyrus. In the meantime, Amr was continuing his advances in the Levant by capturing Damascus. In response, the emperor Heraclius sent a sizeable army to confront the Muslims, who despite being outnumbered, managed to defeat the Byzantines to take Syria then Gaza. As governor of Palestine, Amr still had his eye on a bigger prize. His travels had taught him that Egypt was bursting with natural resources and that Alexandria, in particular, was one of the world's great cities. In 639, the Muslims came for Egypt.

Eighth-century Arab historians suggest that in the meantime, Cyrus' daughter Armenosa was preparing to marry the Byzantine emperor's son, Constantine III. As her procession made its way to Constantinople for the wedding, she realised that the Muslim army was entering Egypt. Armenosa sent word to her father and kept her own regiment at the ready. It's for this reason that a Roman army was waiting for Amr at Pelusium, near Port Said. But the Muslims defeated their poorly reinforced counterpart within a month, sending Armenosa back to Cyrus unharmed.[9] They moved towards the Nile Delta for a further two months of fighting against the Romans, whose army included some Arab tribes of Egypt. Amr's next aim was to capture the Babylon Fortress on the Delta, some 130 miles south of Alexandria. This would be a strategic location from which to plan an attack on Egypt's most fortified city. So he made a request to the caliph, who sent him a total of 8,000 men, taking the army to 12,000 horse- and camel-back soldiers. It is at this stage that Pope Cyrus received three options from Amr's messenger: converting to Islam, paying an annual poll tax, or war. Cyrus felt that only one option, paying the tax, would maintain the peace – and it wouldn't make too much difference since Alexandrians were already taxed heavily by the Byzantines. But the emperor chose to fight. When the Babylon Fortress was captured, Cyrus wrote to Amr explaining that the Romans now realised that they should have listened to him, and asking to meet.

Amr and Cyrus met, each anchored by several trusted advisers, to agree a deal. Every Egyptian, excluding women, children and the elderly, was to be taxed two dinars per year, roughly £55 today, double what the non-Muslims of Arabia were paying. They also agreed that Christians would provide a three-day welcome for Muslim visitors to Egypt, and that the Muslims would not claim any land or homes not their own. But Cyrus was acting alone: news arrived that the emperor was not ready to make a deal with the

Muslims. Cyrus informed Amr that imperial backing wasn't necessary, so he would conclude the deal himself and ensure that taxes
were paid, under the condition that he could live out the rest of his
life and be buried in Alexandria. In December 640, the deal was
signed and although Alexandria was not physically occupied, Egypt
was under Muslim rule.

Cyrus, now removed from power, was being called out for betraying his imperial masters. With Amr still eyeing Alexandria, however,
a change of prefect would have unsettled the defence. So Cyrus was
swiftly reinstated. For Amr, the obvious next step was to advance
northwards from the Nile Delta straight to Alexandria. But Amr
planned a longer route, moving westwards into the desert, a terrain
he knew better than the shrubby, marshy Delta, and advanced
towards Alexandria from there. The attack would take months of
preparation.

In February 641, after a long day of planning, Amr returned to his
stately tent to find something he wasn't expecting: a dove sitting on
a newly laid egg. To Amr, this was some sort of divine sign. He left
for Alexandria and ordered those who stayed behind to make sure
the dove remained untouched. Despite encountering Byzantine
troops throughout the journey, the Muslim army arrived at
Alexandria's outskirts within a month. They were shocked at the size
of the city, the magnitude of its buildings and the extent of its gates
and fortifications. They found towering pillars and imposing obelisks,
and admired St Mark's Cathedral and the Pharos Lighthouse, which
they described as being surrounded by water from every direction as
though it were floating. The city was guarded by 50,000 soldiers and
had a navy in its harbour. The Muslims didn't have a single ship and
Amr himself had been described as a land-man. Before Amr's men
knew it, the Alexandrians mounted catapults on the city walls and
fired giant boulders, forcing the Muslims into an immediate retreat.
The odds were firmly stacked in the Roman corner.

But two serendipitous deaths complicated matters. First, in
Constantinople, the emperor Heraclius died in February 641 as he
was readying an army to protect the Egyptian capital. His son took
over for just three months before himself dying suddenly and
Heraclius' grandson was crowned aged just eleven. Second, Cyrus
died in March 642, and though he had chosen to work alongside the

Muslims, he was a divisive figure whose death caused more factional differences among Alexandrians, whose soldiers and citizens began fighting among themselves. At the same time, Amr promoted a seven-and-a-half-foot general named Ubadah ibn al-Samit, who ordered the digging of trenches on the city's outskirts, from which the Muslims could attack unexpectedly. The histories give only one further detail about this strategy: that it worked. Amr took Alexandria and the Arabs ended seven centuries of Roman rule in the city. On 29 August 642, 973 years after its founding, Alexandria was now part of the Islamic caliphate.

In the immediate aftermath, not much changed in Alexandria. Papyri from the time indicate the continuation of normal administrative life, with documents written in the same pre-Islamic style. Arabic did begin to replace Koine Greek as the official language, which the Christians saw as an opportunity to stop using Greek altogether in favour of Coptic. Alexandria also maintained its Christian and Jewish leaders. A new governor was appointed, as were civil and religious judges, a harbour captain and a customs chief. Further deals were made with city leaders in the Treaty of Alexandria: Muslims were to have nothing to do with the churches, the Jews would be allowed to remain and live in peace and Roman civilians could stay but their soldiers had eleven months to depart.

The claim that Amr may have destroyed the Library of Alexandria and set alight its books at the request of Caliph Omar is now accepted as a myth. There are no references to this in the following six centuries of Arabic, Coptic, or Byzantine histories. The first to mention the possibility are Abdullatif al-Baghdadi and Bar Hebraeus, all of 600 years after the alleged event, and both had reasons to spread such an idea. The former was a Shia Muslim who opposed the first three caliphs because he regarded Ali as the righteous heir to Muhammad. The latter was a Syriac bishop writing in the context of the Crusades, when anti-Muslim propaganda was rife, but when some Muslims might also have naïvely repeated these claims as the recollection of a time of unapologetic religious fervour. In addition to the fact there are no eyewitness accounts, it's also worth noting that, as mentioned in the previous chapter, when the Roman historian Orosius visited Alexandria in the early 400s, he reported empty shelves, so books may already have been destroyed or moved outside the city. Furthermore, within a couple of centuries, the Arabs became huge admirers of Alexandrian knowledge, not least that of Aristotle, one of the particular authors whose works could be found in Alexandria's Library; one of the reasons we have access to Aristotle's works is because Arab scholars translated and edited them extensively. Finally, there is evidence of Muslims destroying idols in their early conquests, but never libraries. It's safe to conclude that the Library of Alexandria underwent a slow and drawn-out decline, beginning from Julius Caesar and subsequently affected by the misfortunes that plagued the city.

If anything, Amr was in awe of Alexandria. He wrote to the Caliph Omar about the startling magnificence of the city they had just captured:

> I have conquered a city I cannot describe except by the fact I have in it 4,000 villas with 4,000 baths, and 40,000 Jews who will pay tax, and 400 places of entertainment for royalty.

These places of entertainment were surely theatres. The Muslims also found twelve public baths that housed at least 1,000 people each, and a staggering 12,000 shops. Amr is said to have reported a population of 600,000 on arrival, including the 40,000 Jews mentioned and 200,000 Romans. After the invasion, however, 30,000 Romans supposedly hurried away by sea.

In Medina, when he received news of the successful invasion, Omar prostrated himself in celebration and called a public gathering at the mosque to announce the victory. Though Amr admired the luxurious houses of Alexandria and decided to settle there, the caliph ordered him to establish rule of Egypt elsewhere. The caliph indicated, not irrationally, that there should be no water, in this case the Nile, between the Egyptian capital and the caliphate capital. Besides, the new Arab arrivals were perplexed by Alexandria: a multicultural megalopolis that looked as if it was from the future. Its location on the sea, seen as an asset by previous occupiers, was now a vulnerability, and its unpredictably riotous and exceptionally multicultural population a threat to stability.

Indeed, moving from the desert to the city came with practical challenges. One of the early Arab Muslims in Alexandria warned how the glaring 'whiteness of the marble . . . floors and walls' will hurt your eyes if you go out after dark. In fact, 'by night, the moonlight's reflection on the white marble lets a tailor get his thread into the needle' without needing a lamp.[10]

On the caliph's orders, Amr left Alexandria begrudgingly, assigning as governor Abdullah ibn-Hudhafa, a reputedly light-hearted companion of Muhammad's, who a couple of years earlier, had been tortured by Heraclius in Constantinople. Back at his base near the Nile Delta, Amr rushed to his tent to check that the dove he'd left behind six months earlier was still there. It had long flown away, but Amr proceeded to lay the foundations for his new city at the very spot he had first seen its egg. At this location, construction began on Egypt's first mosque (and Africa's second after the one in Axum). The Mosque of Amr would be the centre of the new city, whose name, Fustat, translates roughly as the City of Tents: a further hint of the cultural and experiential vacuum that separated Arabia from the extensively built-up metropolis of Alexandria.

Almost a millennium after its founding, Alexandria had been demoted from capital city, a title it would never again reclaim. Fustat (now in Old Cairo), with its more familiar and less populated desert terrain, would become Egypt's capital for the next 500 years.

Umayyads and Abbasids

The moment the Muslims arrived they discovered Alexander the Great's perpetual importance to the city. When Awf ibn-Malik – a loyal companion of Prophet Muhammad who'd contributed to the conquest – stepped into Alexandria, he was in awe: 'How beautiful is your land?' The Alexandrians replied: 'When Alexander built it, he said, "I will build a city poor to God, rich to people", so her delight remained'.[1]

As time went on, the Muslims of Alexandria felt an affinity with the city's history. They believed that Alexander had claim to a heroic mention in the Quran, a view that still exists today. Alexander had long been associated with Zeus Ammon, a deity who was titled and depicted as 'the two-horned'. So portraits of Alexander on coins, even long after his death, placed ram's horns on his head. The Quran, in turn, reports the story of a powerful, believing king, he 'Of Two Horns', for whom God 'established ascendancy . . . in the land' and 'endowed him with a way to all things'. This momentous leader 'Of Two Horns' travels from the western edge of the world – where he finds the sun 'setting in [the midst of] a black, turbid spring' – to its eastern edge. He then heads to the mountains where the tribes of Gog and Magog are causing havoc, and builds a colossal iron wall to trap the two tribes, who in Islamic eschatology, will only make their way out near the end of time (Quran 18.93–98).

So important was Alexander to the city that for the Muslims to feel at home he had to be transformed into a pious believer. Alexandria's Jews had been doing this through legends that had found their way into the Talmudic tradition, from his visits to Jerusalem and Judea to the conviction that he granted them full citizenship. The Arabs were keen poets and before the rise of technology and printing, oral history was often transmitted through verse. At the time of the Muslim conquest, tribes were expected to update one another on their latest news using grand poetry at the annual Ukaz Market gathering along the spice route. So it didn't take long for the newest Alexandrians to include their own ideas in poems that boasted a relationship with the city's founder:

> My grandfather, 'Of Two Horns', was a Muslim,
> A king whom kings owed and envied.
> He reached the easts and the wests seeking
> Occasions for knowledge from a guiding sage.
> So he saw the dusking of the sun as it set
> At a spring that was turbid with dark sludge.[2]

Almost two and a half millennia after he established the city – and one and a half millennia after the Muslims arrived – I still witness such feelings of intimate admiration for Alexander surfacing intermittently as Alexandrians continue to relate themselves to the founder. One afternoon, I walked onto the balcony to take my uncle's phone call in the Alexandria breeze. He asked if I would be visiting that evening. 'No, I'm meeting someone whose late father claimed to have located Alexander's tomb—'. I had barely managed to get out the name Alexander when my uncle responded with an unexpected, casual excitement, as if he'd just recalled a sweet memory: 'Alexander. You know, we were in Alexander's heart. And Alexander is in our hearts.'

Some of Muhammad's companions stayed in Egypt, including Maslama ibn-Mukhallad, who died in Alexandria, and Abu al-Darda, one of Muhammad's closest companions in the conquest. Originally a tradesman from Medina, Abu al-Darda had superior knowledge about the Quran and Islamic creed, so began to teach the people of Alexandria about the faith. Today, on a frantic street full of tool shops that bears Abu al-Darda's name, minibuses race perilously around the corner of his splendid white and green mausoleum. Abu al-Darda's story is steeped in local legend. First, that he died in Alexandria, which is untrue; he died in Damascus. Second, that the mausoleum was built because Alexandrians had a dream ordering them to do so. It's likely that the mausoleum was built closer to the thirteenth century to commemorate Abu al-Darda's previous dwelling in the city, possibly at the location in which he taught. The third and most elaborate legend relates to the council's expansion of the tramline in the 1940s, when the mausoleum was under threat of demolition. One version is that the engineers and builders were punished by losing all movement in their hands, another that the governor dreamed he should spare the mausoleum. City records tell a different story: that the planners simply found the road to be wide enough, so the mausoleum could stay where it was. That is why, uniquely, the tramline bends around both sides of the mausoleum today. Alexandria's expanse of tombs for celebrated Muslim figures, some of whom died in the city – such as Abdulrahman ibn-Harmaz, an authority on prophetic sayings – but most of whom died far away, has certainly presented challenges to urban planners. In the twentieth century, the Alexandria Mosque Complex was founded in order to move most of the city's mausoleums to one big piazza.

As Amr and Abu al-Darda arrived in 642, some Alexandrians, despite initially joining the Byzantine effort to defend the city, were now welcoming their new Muslim rulers. They hoped for a fresh start after so many years of Roman rule. For one, the Muslims were promising freedom of worship, something the Jews and Christians struggled to do for centuries. In the years following Muhammad's death, vigorous expansion meant that the caliphate now ruled over a multicultural population that also included significant non-Muslim populations. With these citizens from every walk of life having to pay a poll tax, Alexandria was a useful money bank for Muslims to control. And the Treaty of Alexandria meant that non-Muslims fared much better here than in some Levantine cities. A couple of centuries earlier, St Cyril had expelled Jews from Alexandria. Now, they were invited back in their thousands. These included the Karaite Jews, a group that trusted only written scripture, not oral tradition. Arabic sources indicate that the Karaites soon complained to Amr that the Egyptian Jews, by this time known as Rabbinic Jews, were undermining them, and that Amr wrote to the rabbis about not interfering with the Karaites. As for the Christians, the tenth-century bishop Severus writes that after the Muslims took Alexandria, Pope Benjamin, exiled for years by the Byzantines, returned from the desert to the city to cheering crowds. Amr met Pope Benjamin and offered him a 'fitting welcome and tribute', reinstating his authority.[3]

That being said, the locals and Muslims both remained mutually suspicious of one another. In fact, Amr had ordered the southern gate of Alexandria to be dismantled so that the city could be accessed with ease from the new capital; the gate's existence could allow a revolting populace to create a problematic defence line on the outskirts. Moreover, having agreed to leave the churches untouched, the Muslims established a new mosque on the western quarter of St Mary's Cathedral, which by this time was in ruins. The Mosque of a Thousand Columns, owing to its big green pillars, was also known as the Mosque of Seventy because it is said to have been located on the site where the 70 rabbis translated the Hebrew Bible into Greek during Ptolemy II's reign. Soon, a second smaller mosque would be established, this time directly in place of a church dedicated to St Athanasius, on a site that until 370 housed the Bendideion, a temple dedicated to Bendis, daughter of Zeus.

Two years after the conquest of 642, with the Roman soldiers gone and the citizens not causing trouble, the new caliph, Uthman, removed the Muslim troops from outside the city walls in order to keep the peace with its citizens. The Byzantines had not given up on Alexandria that easily and this was a chance to recapture it. Their advances were initially successful and some citizens now welcomed them in the hope that taxes would be lowered. They were quickly disappointed as the Byzantines seemed more interested in seizing the farmland around the city. Within months, the reoccupation was countered by none other than Amr ibn al-As, who returned to Alexandria to reassert Arab rule. From the minaret of the new mosque, he is said to have called on the residents not to harm the defeated Roman soldiers.

Despite this success, Amr's reign as governor of Egypt was short-lived due to alleged economic mismanagement, and he was affronted when his long-time second-in-command, Abdullah ibn-Said, who happened to be Caliph Uthman's foster-brother, was immediately given the role instead. The new governor arrived with a multitude of Arabs and the demographics of Alexandria continued to change. Since Muhammad's death, his cousin Ali had been tipped for leadership and Ali's supporters were becoming more vocal. They encouraged Egyptians to protest against Caliph Uthman, and an angry Amr may well have encouraged them. When the new governor returned from a visit to the caliph in Medina, he was stopped from re-entering Egypt. Four battalions set off from Egypt to Medina to topple Caliph Uthman, who was ultimately assassinated in his home. A struggle for power was sure to follow. Within 25 years of Muhammad's death, his followers were already clashing.

Ali did indeed become the next caliph, but within months he was engaged in a full-scale civil war with rival Muawiya, one of Muhammad's former scribes and governor of Syria, who wanted to avenge the previous caliph's assassination. Noticing the Muslim infighting, the Byzantines, led by the emperor Constans II himself, made one last effort to regain Alexandria in 654. This time, the attack came from the Mediterranean. For the first time, the land-loving Muslims of Arabia were forced to fight a significant battle at sea. They had already used the 200 warships left behind to invade Cyprus, but this was now a serious clash against at least 500 Byzantine ships. The Battle of the Masts, as it came to be known, was unexpectedly won by the Muslims. The victory meant that they were able to establish a significant navy that could be used to defend Alexandria in future and to expand their empire by sea, soon taking the whole of North Africa and moving towards Iberia (Spain and Portugal), while simultaneously conquering Persia. There was no longer any doubt that power in Alexandria and the broader region had shifted. And any shifts in the foreseeable future would be from one Muslim caliphate to another.

Still looking to snatch Egypt, Syria's governor Muawiya decided to bring Amr on board despite the fact they had been on different sides during the previous caliph's reign. Muawiya knew that if he offered Amr the chance to become lifetime governor of Egypt, he would guarantee the support of a competent general who remained popular among the Muslim troops stationed there. In 658, Amr conquered Egypt again. Its governor was executed before being placed inside a dead donkey and burnt, even though his father was Abu Bakr, Muhammad's successor and closest friend. By 661, the caliph Ali had also been murdered, paving the way for Muawiya to take power. Muawiya moved the capital from Medina to Damascus, marking the birth of the Umayyad caliphate.

Egypt played a key role in the first civil conflict among Muhammad's followers. These events set in motion a denominational split that still exists today. Shia Muslims are an extension of those who supported Ali's right to rule from the time of his cousin Muhammad's death and into the civil war with Muawiya, while Sunni Muslims maintain that Muhammad's companions, rather than family, were rightful successors.

Amr was essentially Egypt's semi-independent governor. In 664, aged around ninety, he lay on his deathbed tearful about his previous enmity to the Muslims. After describing the sky and earth tightening on his chest, he died.

The Umayyads began to place loyalists in charge of Egypt, which would now be little more than an extension and servant to the more important Levant region. Utba ibn-abi-Sufyan became governor, and he immediately moved 12,000 troops to Alexandria and built a new palace, Dar al-Imara (House of Governance), so that Egypt's governor could have a firmer grip on the city. He would eventually die at the palace, making him Muhammad's only companion indisputably buried in Alexandria. Muawiya died just months after Amr, but had already done something that changed the course of Islamic rule – and was not part of Islamic teachings: he established hereditary succession. With that, the second Islamic caliphate became a dynasty. The majority of its rulers would be born in Damascus and maintain close ties with Medina, the two central cities. With the geographical expansions to the west and south of Egypt, the remit of the country's governor became even less significant. And with resources reserved for the new capital anyway, Alexandria was becoming the second city of a second-tier country. Essentially, as the Umayyad dynasty grew bigger, Alexandria's role grew smaller.

The Umayyads did maintain Alexandria's general grandeur by leaving the city's buildings intact, but it remained a confusing place to them. For instance, as citizens and visitors bought and sold essentials and luxuries in the bustling markets – now packed with fragrant, colourful spices, as well as popular items like dates and honey – the money changing hands was beyond anything the Arabs thought possible. Coins were desperately needed and were in increasingly low supply. Perplexed, the government decided that the easiest thing to do was to melt down a bronze statue, so they picked one seemingly at random and did just that. In seventh-century Alexandria, a single bronze coin was enough to buy a hot bean dinner, though an Alexandrian prostitute cost more than 70 bronze coins. Eventually, the Umayyads began minting gold coins in Alexandria, mining the metal from Egyptian land and introducing the gold dinar that weighed 4.25 grammes – each one worth around £200 in today's money – and the silver dirham weighing three grammes.

The majority of the caliphate's citizens, including those in Alexandria, remained non-Muslims. This began to change in the eighth century during the reign of the eighth Umayyad caliph, Umar ibn-Abdulaziz, or Umar II, whose policies included financial incentives. Not only would becoming a Muslim mean exemption from the poll tax, Umar II rewarded new Muslims with gold coins, especially Christian leaders, one of whom he's said to have given 1,000 gold dinars.

With their extreme wealth, the Umayyads began to build new, ostentatious mosques influenced by the unique, advanced architecture they'd found in Alexandria. When they arrived, the Muslims had recorded that 'one of the marvels of Alexandria' was a golden dome. This is likely to be the Tychaion, the only temple apart from the Serapeum for which we have a surviving description: its dome was made from gilded bronze to give a shimmering, golden layer, a technique long used in Alexandria. So, in late seventh-century Jerusalem, the Umayyads built the Dome of the Rock, complete with a golden dome, in addition to an octagonal design borrowed from the Alexandrian cathedral that replaced the Serapeum, the Church of St John the Baptist. They also filled the Dome of the Rock's interior walls with mosaics that may have been completed by Alexandrian artists. We know that the Umayyads transported experienced artisans and builders from Alexandria to the Holy Land to help construct the al-Aqsa Mosque a few years later, so it is likely that they did the same with the Dome of the Rock. Non-Muslim artisans received a tax waiver for their efforts. The Umayyads then sent the skilled Alexandrians to the capital to construct the Mosque of Damascus in the early eighth century. Now known as the Umayyad Mosque, it boasts astonishing Alexandria-inspired mosaics and wall paintings, proving Alexandria's influence on early Islamic architectural style and pictorial tradition. An anonymous note shortly after the construction describes the Great Mosque of Damascus as one of the 'four Wonders of the World'. One of the other three on the list is the 'Lighthouse of Alexandria', indicating that, despite all the recent changes on its shores, the Pharos Lighthouse was standing strong and maintaining its sense of wonder.

As the eighth century continued, the Umayyads were losing their grip on power with both Christians and Muslims turning against them. The period of Pope Alexander II, from 704 to 729, was unpredictable for Christians. Under one caliph, their poll tax was increased and their properties sporadically seized. Despite some respite under the reformist regime of Umar II, when the Christian population lived more peacefully, his successor ordered that all crosses in homes and churches be destroyed. The continued survival of many contemporary crosses in Alexandria suggests that the Christian stronghold in the city managed to evade this policy. More detrimental for the Umayyads than the persistence of Christianity was the fact that non-Arab Muslims now outnumbered Arab Muslims. Arabs were given the top governmental and military roles, and non-Arab Muslims were often made to pay the poll tax alongside the Christians and Jews. Intermarriage, a fabric of Alexandrian society, was also forbidden. Giving Arabs preferential treatment proved to be a major mistake.

Across different countries, under the organised instruction of the Abbasids (descendants of Muhammad's uncle Abbas), the Abbasid Revolution ousted the Umayyads in 750. Every member of the Umayyad family was tracked down and killed, and, with the exception of that of the still popular Umar II, the tombs of the Umayyad caliphs were desecrated. Knowing that Syria still housed Umayyad loyalists, the Abbasids moved their administration to Iraq, founding Baghdad, which would soon become the world's most populous city. This moved the empirical capital further east than it had ever been and focused Islamic expansion in that direction. But it also marked the start of an Islamic Golden Age when economic prosperity led to cultural and scientific advancements.

From 786, Harun al-Rashid, later popularised in the West through the *Arabian Nights* stories, led the dynasty for over two decades. Like the Ptolemies in Alexandria, he opened a grand library in Baghdad, the House of Wisdom, where scholars and translators are said to have received the weight of any book they wrote in gold. Having shifted from parchment to paper after learning the technique from the Chinese, the Abbasids were able to create and distribute books quickly (Europe would follow suit in the eleventh century). Scholars began to study and translate Alexandrian scholarship, especially related to astronomy, maths and medicine, embracing the knowledge created in Alexandria's Museum. They even revived the Alexandrian study of alchemy, translating into Arabic fragments of work by Maria the Jewess, whom they revered. Homer's epics and the Alexander romances, both so important to Alexandria's heritage, were also translated. By translating Greek works, Arab scholars saved many texts and ideas, works that would otherwise have been lost to the world and to the West, simultaneously turning Arabic into something of a lingua franca. Though they had Alexandria at their disposal, the Abbasid dynasty's keenness to make its own mark, and its aim to elevate the status of its religion and language, meant that the new global knowledge hub of the Islamic Golden Age had to be the new Arab capital, not the diverse, historically loaded Alexandria.

In Egypt, realising that the capital Fustat was too small for their army, the Abbasids founded a new city a little further north. Its name, al-Askar, literally meaning 'The Military', explained its main purpose. Egypt's strategic location meant the Baghdad-based dynasty could surround Syrian rebels from both east and west. But after Harun, his sons, the next two caliphs, introduced ad hoc taxes in Egypt that led to uprisings. With its heavily Christian population, Alexandria was less important to the Abbasids than their new cities. Alexandria was little more than a fort town, but this meant that a stronger naval base was also established. The Abbasid navy, headquartered and ready to move from Alexandria, was necessary as other dynasties garnered power around the Mediterranean.

During the Abbasid Revolution, one Umayyad prince had managed to escape to Iberia, where the Umayyads would resurrect themselves as the emirs of Andalusia, ruling from a newly founded kingdom called Córdoba. The next threat to Alexandria came from there.

In an impoverished area of Córdoba, thousands rebelled against their hard-nosed Umayyad ruler al-Hakam I, the third of the

Andalusian emirs and described as the most bloodthirsty of them all. True to his reputation, al-Hakam suppressed the revolt, crucifying 300 leading figures and exiling anyone remotely involved. On this occasion, thousands ended up in the Moroccan city of Fez, the first major re-immigration from Andalusia to North Africa. The rest of these Andalusian refugees ventured to sea. They were led by a loud, imposing man named Umar abu-Hafs al-Balluti, more commonly known as al-Ghaliz; literally 'the thick'. The group began to use their manpower and ever-increasing fleet to seize ships and boats unlucky enough to cross their path in the Mediterranean.

In the early ninth century, Alexandria, which had already lived through such a range of different leaders and authorities, fell to the pirates of the Mediterranean. Arabic and Byzantine sources differ on the extent to which this was a planned or opportunistic attack. It seems that what started as a simple trip to Alexandria turned into an occupation. The pirates stopped at Alexandria regularly: it was a perfect place to disembark and stroll through the markets, selling and swapping the goods plundered from the other ships. When the significant fleet of 40 ships docked in the harbour in the winter of 815, there were suddenly 5,000 to 12,000 new foreigners – known to be refugees – walking the streets of Alexandria, returning to their ships by night. They had done this in previous winters, but this time, with conflicts taking place in most other significant cities in the region, staying in the Alexandrian harbour became more appealing. Better yet, nothing was stopping them from staying in the city itself. By the summer, they were doing just that. The Alexandrians had already welcomed several hundred Andalusians a few years earlier, but they became hostile to the presence of thousands of pirates on land. It is perhaps that response which encouraged the new visitors to begin attacking the citizens. Without any prior warning, abu-Hafs and his militia took control of Alexandria. They ruled without public approval and with difficulty navigating the city's significant economic demands.

After refusing to prioritise Alexandria for a whole decade, the Abbasid caliph al-Ma'mun (son of Harun) decided that enough was enough and dispatched an army led by one of his most trusted generals to the city. Following a ferocious start to the battle, the Andalusians surrendered and their ships began to leave Alexandria, one after another. Typically, some of the pirates, including abu-Hafs, managed to flee. They went on to attack and seize the island of Crete, ending 900 years of Roman rule there and establishing an independent Muslim emirate with abu-Hafs as its leader. As their ships sailed into the horizon, what remained of their fleet was set on fire. As the flames rose, Alexandria began yet another journey towards recovery. But it was far from straightforward: with the return of high taxes, the Christians, who'd been protesting intermittently in other parts of Egypt, attempted a revolt in Alexandria, only for the Abbasids to quash it immediately.

How do you smuggle something out of a Muslim country? Well, according to ninth-century Venetians, you cover it in pork. Far from a distasteful joke, this was the very tactic utilised by Venetian merchants to steal St Mark's body from Alexandria.

At this stage, some churches had been turned into mosques and there was unease on the other side of the Mediterranean about Mark's remains resting in a Muslim country. Perhaps more significantly, as the Venetian ruling class of merchants became richer and expanded their city, it became clear that the Republic of Venice's capital needed an impressive patron saint to match its economic success and show up its rivals. Not only was Mark present in the Gospels, his spreading the faith in new parts of the world served to increase his veneration. And as there was constant commerce with Alexandria, Venetian traders knew their way around the Egyptian city.

Noted for his ability to navigate rough waves and starless skies, Buono da Malamocco had been in the navy before settling down as a sea captain, escorting Venetian merchants to Alexandria and Constantinople aboard the *San Nicola*. At sea, Buono befriended a merchant named Rustico da Torcello, who was also an experienced carpenter. Buono trusted Rustico so much that he made him first officer. In December 827, they set sail from Venice among a fleet of ten ships. A few weeks prior, the Byzantine emperor Leo V had temporarily banned trade with the Arabs, but Buono and Rustico had a secret mission in mind. They slipped away from the fleet and headed to Alexandria to carry out their great heist.

Since their ship was full of trade goods, they first hustled everything into the nearby Alexandrian markets. They then turned their attention to the main job at hand. Arriving at the Christian sanctuary in Alexandria, they were met by its custodians, the priest Theodore and the monk Staurazio. To start with, they tried the simplest tactic: politely asking for Mark's relics. Naturally, the custodians were having none of it. Whether they convinced them or tricked them is uncertain, but once the Venetians were inside the sanctuary, they began to dig for the body. The Renaissance artist Tintoretto depicts the ordeal in two canvases. The first, *Finding of the Body of Saint Mark* (1562), shows the merchants pulling several bodies out chaotically, only for a haloed Mark to appear on the other side and, rather ironically, plead with them to stop.

As the Venetians found and removed Mark's body, they realised that it needed to be replaced in order to avoid suspicion. In the panic of the moment, they picked up the nearest body they could find, which happened to be that of a woman, St Claudia, one of seven virgins martyred in the early fourth century during Roman persecution; before being killed, their breasts were cut off with knives. At this stage, with corpses being moved around, a smell began to emanate from the area near the church. Hearing the commotion and finding that locals had risen from their beds to find out what was going on, they quickly ensured St Claudia was in Mark's place. The locals were now afraid that something had happened to Mark, but the body had already been hidden inside a wicker basket. Next, Buono and Rustico carried out the most innovative part of the erratic operation: they surrounded and covered Mark's body with cabbage and (probably pickled) pork. This, they anticipated, would allow it to escape the attention of the Muslim border guards who were less likely to search a product they considered unclean. Their risky plan worked like a charm.

In January 828, at the Port of Olivolo in Venice, the bishop Doge Giustiniano awaited the body's arrival and, as the ship docked, the patron saint of Alexandria swiftly became the patron saint of Venice. While subsequent writing suggests crowds waiting in celebration, this was in all likelihood a quiet event. Since the body and relics were stolen, they were not displayed as proudly as might have been expected. Instead, the bishop kept them in his palace, though he did advise in his will that a dedicated church should house Mark's body.

But Buono and Rustico's plan wasn't finished yet. They described to the bishop and the locals how, as they departed Alexandria, a wild storm began. They had all but drowned, they explained, until all of a sudden, the ghost of Mark appeared to calm the storm and save the ship. This was an extremely useful account for the pair: they had now not only succeeded in bringing Mark to Venice but also claimed to have seen his saintly apparition and witnessed a miracle. They were swiftly rewarded with 100 pieces of silver each.

Their narrative surrounding the theft suggested that Mark needed saving from the Alexandrians. While the stolen body wasn't necessarily a big loss for the Muslim and Jewish citizens, it was certainly a relic that would have been cherished in Alexandria. As time went on, accounts of this event have neglected to mention just how important these relics were to the Christians of the city. The Venetian merchants were fully aware that this was nothing short of theft. But the narrative surrounding the miracle assured anyone who had doubts that this is what Mark would have wanted. Not only did this mean Mark had no issue with being dug out of the ground, squashed into a basket and covered in cabbage and pork, he was seemingly pleased to be taken to Venice.

Only after the bishop's death was a church built to house Mark's body. By order of Napoléon at the turn of the nineteenth century, that church was designated as the city's cathedral. The French commander, who would show interest in Alexandria, also showed interest in Mark. He even took statues of Mark back to Paris, though he did spare the body. Today, this site is the famous Basilica di San Marco, the city's premier attraction. Venice feels as though it is built in the shadow of this magnificent basilica, with its vast square, grand domes and gold mosaics. And Mark would become the symbol of the city more widely; for instance, he was depicted on the Venetian ducat, Europe's most dominant currency during the late Middle Ages. To think that a precarious heist by two friends could change the fortunes of Venice in such a way is astounding. Its new mascot coincided with its rise and it became a major power from the ninth century. It is no surprise that Buono and Rustico are two of the most honoured robbers in history.

One of the most important mosaics adorning the basilica depicts these very events. The colourful seventeenth-century illustration portrays the process in three stages. The right side of the arch pictures the Venetians breaking into the crypt and removing and replacing the body. The left side shows the body being placed in a basket, followed by olive leaves, and then the pork. In the central lunette, the Muslims at the port, dressed in robes and white turbans, turn away from the container rather dramatically, one holding his nose in disgust (pork aside, there was a dead body in there, after all). In his second canvas, Tintoretto also portrays the moment the body is stolen, presenting it in the middle of a strangely ominous storm amid thundering black and orange clouds. But given the fiery backdrop, as well as some legends about a storm stopping the mob from cremating Mark, this painting might be imagining the moment Mark's body was rescued by the Christians on the day he was killed.

The twist in this tale is that the Venetians actually forgot one thing . . . Mark's head. Alexandrians believe that the head remains in the city. Does this mean that, in their rush, the resourceful pair didn't notice that the head was missing? If there was a head, does it mean that they took a different person's body entirely? A recent theory even suggests that they may have taken Alexander's remains – especially as the Baucalis church was built over a temple – which would be an extraordinarily high-profile case of mistaken identity. Or is it not actually Mark's mummified head in Alexandria?

Some relics were recovered in 1968. And to this very day, Alexandria's Christians celebrate the fact that this head remains in St Mark's Cathedral.

Five years after St Mark's body was stolen, a third son of Harun al-Rashid's became caliph in Baghdad. Born to a Turkic woman, al-Mutasim removed Arab commanders and introduced an army of Turkic slave-soldiers into the mix in order to protect himself. As slaves, these were commonly known as Mamluks, literally meaning 'The Owned', and they began to be recruited across Caucasia, Eastern Europe, the Balkans and Nubia. Ahmad ibn-Tulun was the son of one of these initial Turkic slave-soldiers, but, unlike his father, he rose through the ranks from slave-soldier all the way to commander. When the Abbasids sent ibn-Tulun to Egypt as governor alongside his army, he took advantage of their instability; successive caliphs had been assassinated and there were serious splits in the military. Ibn-Tulun made his move in Egypt, swiftly removing everyone around him, including the heads of each city, until he was ruling the country alone. By establishing the Tulunid dynasty in 868, Egypt became an independent power again for the first time since the Ptolemies. In further defiance of the Abbasids, ibn-Tulun created yet another capital, al-Qata'i (The Quarters).

Alexandria had been getting weaker and weaker, with no visible advancement and a diminishing population looking for opportunities elsewhere. Around two-thirds of the city was uninhabited, and its buildings, the 4,000 villas and 400 theatres the Muslims found when they arrived, were badly maintained or in ruins. The new ruler realised that since Amr had removed the southern gate, the city was open to attack. To protect himself and Alexandria, he built new walls around the city, making it both safer and grander. He also split the city into two, one half housing the extensive Greek and Roman cemeteries, the other for people to live among newly bedded plants and trees. For the first time in centuries, Alexandria underwent renovation. The famed underground cisterns of the Hellenistic and Roman periods were updated with a brand-new cistern for storing drinking water. The ninth-century Cistern of Ibn el-Nabih (today the only accessible cistern in the city) has three floors, each with semi-circular arches that feature the creative reuse of 48 of the city's fallen white marble and rose granite columns. Ibn-Tulun also built upwards extensively: around 100 new towers re-established the city's status as a place keeping up with the times. His respect for Alexandria's history and his ambition to leave a mark became most clear when he ordered the renewal of the Pharos Lighthouse. The historian al-Masudi, who was in Alexandria in the mid-tenth century, writes that ibn-Tulun renovated the damaged western wall of the lighthouse. He also confirms what illustrations from the time indicate: that ibn-Tulun added a dome at its peak in place of Zeus' statue so that it looked recognisably Islamic. But turning this architectural appropriation on its head, when the Mosque of ibn-Tulun was built next to the palace in his new capital, his Christian architect used the three-stage design of the lighthouse for the minaret, which looks like a delightful mini-Pharos.

Ibn-Tulun's renovations of the Pharos Lighthouse, and more so the later reports by travellers, debunk another rumour that the Byzantine emperor Michael III (known as Michael the Drunkard) had spread. Envious of Alexandria and irritated that the Muslims had captured it, he claimed that an early eighth-century caliph had destroyed the lighthouse because gold treasure was apparently hidden under its foundations.

Within a decade, ibn-Tulun had expanded into Syria, but kept Egypt as his base. After his death, however, things started to fall apart. The Tulunid military, formed of Turks, former Nubian slaves and Greek mercenaries, was increasing in power and serious rifts began between the dynasty's rulers and their army, leading to major defections. This gave the Abbasids the opportunity to reconquer an unprotected Egypt in 905, which they did with the support of newly converted Muslims, the Byzantine Greeks of Cilicia (southern Turkey), who were now in charge of the Abbasid navy. As a show of power, the Abbasids demolished ibn-Tulun's capital – but they didn't touch its lighthouse-inspired mosque, today one of Africa's oldest surviving mosques.

Despite an unsuccessful dynasty that lasted only 37 years, ibn-Tulun himself was the first popular ruler in Alexandria for some time. It's reported that he often distributed cattle and sheep to citizens and that he paid his army well. As a former slave forced to fight without pay, such policies seemed to be borne of personal experience. His leadership represented an important moment for Egypt, which had returned to housing an empirical capital. Ibn-Tulun's reign also proved that the regional and racist biases of the earlier dynasties were unsustainable and that the ruling Islamic caliphate did not automatically hold universal legitimacy.

In fact, all this time, the factional divisions between the Sunnis and Shias had been bubbling. A Shia group that traced their ancestry to Muhammad's daughter Fatima – the Fatimids – had long considered both the Umayyads and Abbasids to be usurpers of the Islamic caliphate. They were now getting ready to establish their own – with Egypt at the centre of their plans.

Fatimids

As the tenth century got underway, a controversial Shia missionary who disguised himself as a merchant in order to avoid arrest had successfully transformed himself into a military and political leader. And he was setting his eyes on Alexandria, a city in which many Shias had already found a haven from the Sunni Abbasids.

For the early Shias, the Muslim leader had to descend from Prophet Muhammad's family. The Sunnis, despite swiftly turning their caliphates into dynasties, maintained that they had received no such instruction from Muhammad before his death. In fact, they argued that the premature death of Muhammad's son – from Maria the Copt, who moved from Alexandria to Medina – was a divine sign that blood succession wasn't a consideration. The Shias created their own leader, an imam, beginning with Ali himself. Influenced by Judeo-Christian ideas and encouraged to create an anticipative, opposing narrative to the Abbasids, the group also believed that a messiah-like figure descending from Ali, *al-mahdi* (the guided one), would appear to restore Islamic utopia.

By the time the sixth imam died, the Shias were split between two different successors, Ismail (his sect becoming the Ismaili Shias) and his brother Musa (the Twelver Shias). The Ismailis created a base in the ancient town of Salamieh in the Syrian desert. When they began to spread their word as far east as India, the Abbasids issued warrants for their arrest. One of their leading proselytisers, Ubayd-Allah, dressed and acted as a merchant, selling whatever he could get his hands on, as he travelled through Egypt towards the north-west of Africa, or the Maghreb region. Though his trick worked in Egypt, he was captured in the Maghreb and imprisoned in a dungeon for four years until a group of his followers managed to free him. Moving further west, he reached Kabylia (modern-day Algeria), where he converted a sizeable Berber tribe, and in turn managed to assemble a vast army. Knowing that the Maghreb wasn't an Abbasid stronghold, he began to attack key locations, ultimately capturing Kairouan (modern-day Tunisia) with his 200,000-strong army. In 909, Ubayd-Allah, now claiming to be the awaited messianic figure, restyled himself as al-Mahdi, leader of a new caliphate, the Fatimids.

Despite a diminishing population, Alexandria was still an attractive place to control. It had a significant non-Muslim population forking out the poll tax. An early tenth-century manual for civil servants, written by an Abbasid treasurer, records as one of its examples the annual tax income from each of the states. That year, 'Egypt and Alexandria', listed as a single location, brought into the treasury one of the highest incomes, 1.5 million gold dinars (around £300 million today). This was more than southern Iraq, the most prosperous rural land on which the Abbasids relied (130.2 million silver dirhams, around £200 million today, though silver's comparative value to gold was higher than it is today).[1] This record tells us that while the eastern states continued to use silver, Alexandria had an ample supply of gold. More importantly, despite the neglect it had been suffering, Alexandria's location and demographics worked in its favour as it continued to generate money from export levies and the non-Muslim poll tax.

In 914, a Fatimid general, a Berber named Habasa, led his army to Alexandria. They were met by some Abbasid resistance on the western outskirts, but continued with relative ease into the city itself. The Berbers began to loot the city until Ubayd-Allah sent his son al-Qaim to Alexandria. A new city governor, also a Berber, was appointed, in addition to a head judge, an Ismaili. In a symbolic act, the call to prayer that emanated from the minarets of Alexandria five times a day was altered to include 'witness that Ali is the guardian of Allah', a slogan that began to be engraved on mosque walls. The Abbasid imams, who had long worn black like the Christian monks before them, were barred. The new Fatimid imams, ordered to wear white, began to preach Shia doctrine to the Alexandrians.

As the Fatimids moved towards the Egyptian capital Fustat, the Abbasids responded by sending soldiers and money to defend it.

The Fatimids struggled to damage the Abbasid defences across the Nile and retreated to Alexandria. But when the general Habasa returned unexpectedly to the Maghreb with his Berber army, al-Qaim decided that it was unsafe to stay in Alexandria and hastily escaped, even leaving stacks of weapons behind. The Abbasids decided to place a Byzantine Greek governor in charge whose main claim to success was executing anyone who had conspired with the Fatimids. Alexandria was once more becoming a dangerous place to live.

Five years later, the Fatimids launched their second attack on Egypt, starting with Alexandria, whose governor and supporters decided to flee rather than fight. As the people panicked, the Fatimid army sacked the city and ransacked its homes. Alexandria was left to the Berber troops, who were ordered to construct catapults and place them on the harbour. Again, the Fatimids failed to capture Fustat from the Abbasids, and worse yet, as they focused on the rest of Egypt, the Abbasids were able to recapture Alexandria by land. For the Abbasids, constantly having to defend Alexandria on two fronts was becoming unsustainable. For the Fatimids, they had failed to take Egypt for a second time; it would take half a century for them to return in full force. For the Alexandrians, the years of instability were refusing to end. Many more decided to pack up and head either east or west.

The fourth Fatimid caliph – and fourteenth imam – was twenty-year-old al-Moez li-Din-Allah (the Glorifier of God's Religion). Known as al-Moez, he had spent his childhood in the Maghreb, specifically modern-day Tunisia and Sicily, so was multilingual. Fifteen years into his reign, al-Moez had successfully taken land from the Byzantines and Abbasids, controlling the Maghreb region and stabilising his empire. In 969, he decided that it was time for the Fatimids to return to Egypt, and this time, with their significant wealth and a well-trained army, there was only going to be one outcome. Alexandria had suffered two earthquakes in the 950s, the second causing the top of the Pharos Lighthouse to fall off. The city was now in a poor economic state, its harbour hardly operating as it had before and its defence lines non-existent. The Fatimids entered its gates with little resistance. This time, soldiers were under instructions not to sack the city. News reached Fustat that Alexandria had been captured and its leaders proposed a peaceful arrangement. The Fatimids agreed, promising to invest in rebuilding the country and to allow Egyptians to worship as they pleased.

After two tumultuous centuries of Abbasid rule, Egypt was now part of the Fatimid caliphate. Unsurprisingly, the capital was changed yet again. When the Muslims arrived in 641, around a millennium after Alexandria's founding, they established Fustat. In 750, the Abbasids then introduced al-Askar, which remained the capital until 868 when the Tulunids established al-Qata'i. In 905, the Abbasids returned to destroy al-Qata'i and restore Fustat. Now, in 972, another capital was being established: Qahirat al-Moez, meaning the 'Conqueror of al-Moez', soon shortened to Qahirah, or Cairo. It remains the capital city of Egypt today, though with its growth it now encompasses the areas of Fustat and Qata'i, too. Alexander's eponymous city, founded more than 1,300 years before al-Moez's Cairo, would continue its story as Egypt's second city.

When al-Moez went to Alexandria in May 973, he only stayed for a few days, moving swiftly onto his newly established capital. There, he found himself in a palace that had been speedily built in anticipation of his arrival. Cairo wouldn't just be Egypt's capital, but the capital of the Fatimid Empire. Two new cities had also been established on the eastern coast of Tunisia before the Fatimids took Egypt, Mahdia and Mansouria, both Fatimid capitals before Cairo. The majority of trade ships leaving Alexandria's harbour – carrying grain, olive oil and fresh fruit – were now heading to these cities on the far west of the Mediterranean as the Fatimids controlled sea trade from east to west. The ships would go round the Maghreb region and return to Alexandria reloaded with goods. They also returned with multitudes of Maghrebi migrants who began settling in Alexandria, from modern-day Tunisia, as well as Sicily, Algeria, Morocco and Libya. Cairo was accessible to Alexandria via the canals, so both these and some of the roads were expanded. Many of Alexandria's exports went to Cairo before being distributed eastwards to the new significant trade hub of Baghdad and beyond. The Fatimid operation put Alexandrian trade back into shape, confirming its prominent position in the expanding network of trade routes that connected Asia and Europe. The city was beginning to see the fruits of its labour returning.

Alexandrian society was also reverting to its old ways: Christians, Jews and Shia Muslims enjoyed relative freedom. The Christians adopted Arabic language and culture and their assimilation is evidenced by the important civic roles they held. Arabic had also begun replacing Coptic as the dominant language because from the early tenth century, bishops had to be approved by the authorities, who were more likely to favour Arabic speakers. One such example is the physician turned bishop Said ibn Batriq, commonly known as Eutychius of Alexandria. Knowing no Greek, someone like Eutychius wouldn't have dreamed of a senior Church appointment in the past, but now he became renowned as an early Christian champion of Arabic.

Many North African Jews migrated to Alexandria, where the Jewish authorities were financially independent and Talmudic schools were being established. Residents became bilingual in both Hebrew and Arabic, but their main language was now a mix known as Judeo-Arabic. Slightly different from what their Arab neighbours spoke, it came in two main dialects from Mosul (Iraq) and Alexandria. Given their population in the city, the Judeo-Arabic of Alexandria was the most common, so even the Jews of Cairo spoke the Alexandrian dialect. With the Muslim adoption of Alexander the Great, the city's founder became an even more pronounced part of Alexandrian Jewish identity, evidenced by a Hebrew version of the *Alexander Romance* adapted from an Arabic rendition.

Similar to the Cleopatras before them, the Fatimid princesses boasted enormous influence. When she died, al-Moez's daughter Rashida left behind 1.7 million gold dinars, higher than the annual tax income of Alexandria. Al-Moez's son, the new caliph al-Aziz, favoured a Byzantine concubine of Sicilian origin, Durrah, who appointed her two brothers to leading Church roles in Jerusalem and Alexandria, making one of them a de facto governor of the city. Having a Christian woman – in effect a queen – with such authority was good news for the Christian population.

Despite the fact that Alexandria's Muslims were still predominantly Sunni, Fatimid tolerance didn't extend to them. Inscriptions began to appear denouncing Muhammad's companions (those who'd beaten Ali to caliph); night prayers in Ramadan, which those companions had initiated, were banned; and one report even tells of the execution of a man found with a Sunni book. Instead, a new library called the House of Knowledge was built in Cairo that housed 200,000 books, in addition to an Islamic university, al-Azhar, today one of the oldest universities in the world. In Alexandria, the Fatimids fortified the city's gates reusing fragments of ancient buildings, and went on to build civic, military and religious buildings, including palaces, schools, mausoleums and mosques, all in spotless streets as road sweeping became an ongoing policy.

As the first millennium came to a close, tensions were beginning to rise again. Al-Moez's grandson, famed for his blue eyes, became caliph at just eleven. As he grew older, al-Hakim struggled to contain his opposition; with public executions becoming more common, Egyptians reviled in him in silence. Alexandria's already declining wine production completely ceased as alcohol was banned, meaning that it was no longer available for Christian rites or Jewish festivals. He also introduced a horrific Law of Differentiation that ordered non-Muslims to be identified by wearing black girdles (the colour of the Abbasids). Men were instructed to wear necklaces (iron cross for Christians, wooden for Jews), non-Muslim women to wear different coloured shoes and Muslim women to cover their faces. Eventually, al-Hakim began to close churches in Alexandria and beyond, destroying the Holy Sepulchre in Jerusalem.

Some of his alleged policies verged on the ridiculous. At the public baths, loins had to be covered at all times and officials were tasked with peeking into the baths to make sure this dictate was being observed; one group was found naked, and arrested and beaten in public. In 1004, al-Hakim went as far as outlawing the consumption of two popular edible leaves: molokhia and rocket. Both were thought to have aphrodisiacal qualities, but that wasn't the reason they were banned. Molokhia, also known as jute mallow, a dish enjoyed by Egyptians for thousands of years – boiled in stock to create a thick, slimy, but delectable broth – was the dish of choice of Muawiyah (the first Abbasid caliph). And rocket, beloved of the Romans, too, was a favourite of Aisha, daughter of Abu Bakr (who, for Shias, had usurped Ali's right to be Muhammad's heir). Further laws bellowed by the bell-waving crier affected Alexandria even more directly. For the fishermen and fishmongers on the harbour: 'No fish shall be sold without skin.'² Al-Hakim, it seems, wasn't a fan of fish fillet.

Unconventional groups were developing within the Muslim population, some preaching about the imminent end of time, others about the divinity of the presiding imam, in this case al-Hakim. Two mystics, Hamza ibn-Ahmad and Muhammad al-Darazi, arrived in Egypt to propagate a sect in which devotion to God meant devotion to the imam as divine incarnation. Though they seem to have been welcomed initially by al-Hakim – after all, they were saying that he was deific – their ideas became more eccentric. Al-Darazi announced that absolute monotheism meant that God didn't have any attributes, but that divinity existed in humans through their pursuit of oneness with God. As such, there was no need for religious rituals and laws to be followed. Al-Darazi was now a heretic and had to be executed; ibn-Ahmed continued to lead the followers of the new faith, now called the Druze.

By his thirties, the eccentric al-Hakim had become an ascetic, swapping the palace for the hills where he would meditate every evening. One night, he didn't come back. It's widely thought that he was assassinated. Given his unpredictable personality, it could even have been pseudocide. The Druze believed that he had gone into occultation and would return at the end of time.

With his mysterious disappearance, his half-sister, daughter of the Byzantine concubine Durrah, took control. The famed Princess Sit al-Mulk (literally Lady of Kingship) had been given her own military unit when she was a child and her power was palpable. She arrested and probably ordered the killing of the heir apparent, her cousin, appointing her fourteen-year-old nephew in his place. Until he turned sixteen, she was the de facto ruler, and even after that continued to pull the strings.

Their first action in Alexandria was to hunt the Druze down. The Druze had developed a significant community in the city, hoping that its reputation for freethinking and philosophy would serve them well. But the authorities were trying to eradicate them once and for all. In the Levant, they managed to survive underground, but the Druze in Alexandria, likely to have numbered in the thousands, were all captured or killed.

After quashing a new religious movement, the Fatimids were left to deal with a huge famine that spread across Egypt and is said to have taken 10,000 lives a day. People resorted to eating dogs and cats. We get a better sense of the famine from the Cairo Genizah, a collection consisting of 400,000 Jewish manuscript fragments, including Fatimid administrative documents, that were locked away in the *genizah*, or storeroom, of a Fustat synagogue for centuries. Discovered in 1896, the Jewish treasure is the largest collection of medieval manuscripts in the world. Some letters, written by Alexandrians in Judeo-Arabic – Arabic using Hebrew letters – evidence the instability of this period. In 1030, one anonymous woman complains that 'the day when we were beaten by the soldiers, was the most terrible for us'.

As for the famine, letters by an Alexandrian called Ismail ibn-Farah to a Joseph ibn-eli-Cohen in Fustat confirm its extent. In a letter dated 29 October 1056, Ismail writes: 'there is famine in the city . . . the swamp of swamps.' A week later, on 6 November, he writes, 'there is nothing more in demand in this city than anything which can be eaten'. The documents reveal that Egypt, including Alexandria, suffered a shortage of wheat and bread, coupled with extreme inflation. Still in November 1056, Ismail writes to his son Farah with news of a family that has left Alexandria, 'but we do not know where they went to, nor where we should go', with the rest of this letter revealing a truly horrific detail: 'as whoever goes out of his house's door dies and is eaten, and if he stays home he will die of hunger.'[3] Alexandria, for so long the bread basket of the world's most powerful cities, was now resorting to cannibalism.

As the famine and its horrendous ramifications spread, plague was sure to follow. Homes were filled with the hungry and the dead. The eerie inactivity, in stark contrast to its usual urban bustle, signalled a city on the verge of becoming a lurid ghost-town. The Arabs in Egypt labelled the 1050s and 1060s the Great Adversity.

The government was forced into an economic overhaul. When it became possible, they purchased grain directly from the merchants and handed it over to the bakeries, which were obliged to sell it at a fixed rate, around a third of the market price.[4] Despite again slipping into famine over the next couple of decades, by the end of the 1070s Egypt began to return to its usual prosperity. When merchants

arrived at the harbour, they paid a 20 per cent lump sum on the
value of the products they brought with them. The Venetians were
exempt from this and enjoyed revenue-based tax rates. Alexandria
also saw an influx of traders from Amalfi in southern Italy, who
purchased regular supplies of silk that they could resell further
north. The wealthy also hired Alexandrian artisans to return with
them to complete mosaics in their Amalfi homes. And realising the
city's abiding position as an international trade centre, Amalfitani
entrepreneurs saw an opportunity for their most innovative business venture: opening several hotels in Alexandria.

But the famine had left its mark and Alexandria was beginning to
run independently, especially among the Arab residents. Caliph
al-Mustansir's vizier, a title given to the key civil and military officer,
was a man of Armenian origin called Badr al-Jamali, who in 1085
took an army to Alexandria to ensure the city was centrally
controlled. Alexandria's governor was the vizier's son, Awhad,
who'd betrayed his father by leading a rebellion against the government. The vizier placed the city under siege for a month before
storming it. After executing his son, he raised taxes in Alexandria as
punishment. To balance the population's high number of Arabs,
al-Jamali encouraged Armenian emigration to Egypt, with tens of
thousands, both Muslim and Christian, moving to Alexandria. They
brought with them the Armenian Church and began to take key
roles in the city.

The Muslims only had one major place of worship in Alexandria,
the Mosque of a Thousand Columns that Amr had founded on the
ruins of the western quarter of St Mary's Cathedral. So some of the
tax revenue was used to expand the smaller mosque that had been
built where the Church of St Athanasius, and before that, the
Temple of the Bendideion had once stood. This area was known as
the spice market, with Jewish and Christian merchants there long
selling products that had arrived from traders sailing across the
Indian Ocean. New, fragrant goods were on sale now, including
amber, musk and rose water. The mosque was therefore named
after them: Masjid al-Attarine literally means the Mosque of the
Spice Dealers.

Today, the first Alexandrian mosque no longer exists. To the west
of the city, near the harbour, a narrow neighbourhood called the

Green Door owes its name to a shabby looking green door at the bottom of an undistinguished high-rise; but the area and door owe their name and colour to the Mosque of a Thousand Columns, which centuries ago stood at this very location with distinctive green columns. The Attarine Mosque, on the other hand, still stands: its splendid marble and granite mosaics blend into the odd mix of old and new in downtown Alexandria, where some spice markets remain. The heartening but confusing blend of Alexandrian identity and history is exemplified by the fact that it's sometimes referred to as the Mosque of St Athanasius.

Returning to the eleventh century, the disorders of famine and rebellion were followed by splits over succession, with Alexandria at the heart of events in 1094. As the eldest son, Nizar perceived himself to be the rightful successor, but his younger brother, Ahmad, had married the powerful vizier's daughter and was being manoeuvred into power. Nizar had developed a group with an innovative purpose: to carry out covert murders of select enemies. A letter from the period gives the group the derogatory title *al-Hashashin*, meaning hashish users, and which Europeans pronounced as 'assassin'. While there is no evidence that they used the drug, the letter confirms that hashish had arrived in the region by this time, though it was eaten not smoked.

With his Order of Assassins, Nizar left Cairo for Alexandria, where the local governor and population's support was enough for him to declare himself caliph. When his brother's army arrived in Alexandria, they were unable to enter. The vizier bribed the various Arab tribes in the region, who joined him in placing Alexandria under siege until Nizar surrendered and Ahmed took power as al-Mustali. These events placed Alexandria under the spotlight as a rebellious city and consolidated the increasing power of the vizier, a role that became akin to a prime minister today; they would soon be rebranded as sultans and have their heads minted on coins. In Alexandria, the vizier was being viewed as the key authority, as confirmed by an early twelfth-century report of an Alexandrian Jew being arrested, then pardoned, for excessively cursing the visiting vizier. The events of this period also caused a division among the Ismailis: the view that Nizar's leadership was usurped, especially among the Persians, developed into the Nizari faction. Today,

Ismailis remain split into two groups: the majority Nizaris and the Mustalis.

Such splits gave the Sunnis a bigger chance of revival in Egypt. In 1096, the first *madrasa* (Islamic school) was founded in Alexandria by an Andalusian political theorist, Abu Bakr al-Turtushi. Named al-Hafiziyya, this was the first school of Islamic law in the world. Its founder had arrived in Alexandria in his mid-thirties after studying in Zaragoza, and he didn't hide his intention of saving Alexandrians from their erroneous ways or his disdain that the city's Christians still yielded any power. He was welcomed by the city's Sunnis, and ended up marrying a wealthy Alexandrian who owned a large two-storey house, which he converted into the *madrasa* with a big reception hall downstairs and living quarters upstairs. Students came from across the region and hundreds of them followed him on his perambulations. His pupils report a love for Alexandria's outdoors, and he tutored them in nearby orchards during picnics. Scholars who visited him were also attracted by Alexandria's Aristotelian and Neoplatonic history: the Persian polymath al-Ghazali, who ventured to Alexandria and spent some time with al-Turtushi before writing hugely influential works that revived philosophical and spiritual aspects of the faith. Before long, two more Sunni schools were founded in Alexandria, one by a local judge, another by a migrant from Jerusalem. Al-Turtushi also affected policy by questioning the inheritance rules until Alexandria became a city where two different Islamic laws could be applied depending on whether the deceased was a Shia or a Sunni. Such a change meant that Alexandria had become a new Sunni stronghold in a region where anti-Fatimid sentiment was already simmering. Today, the al-Tartushi Mosque, which includes its founder's mausoleum, is surrounded by noisy workshops and rushing cars.

As the turbulent eleventh century drew to a close, a new alliance of European Christians was already making its way across the region. For them, their actions represented a pilgrimage, but not to worship. The objective of this journey was to recover the Holy Land from the Muslims. In Latin, each of these men was referred to as a *crucesignatus* – a person signed by the cross – or in other words, a Crusader.

The Crusaders and Saladin's Ayyubids

Alexandria was now about to serve one primary purpose: it was a defence fort against the Crusaders. With around two-thirds of the ancient Christian world now ruled by Muslims, the crusades were labelled as a Christian holy war from the outset. In 1096, efforts were underway to end Muslim rule of the Holy Land in particular. The first attempt, later known as the People's Crusade, was initiated by the Catholic pope, who informed his followers that they had a duty to go on an armed pilgrimage to Jerusalem. After they were easily defeated, a more institutional attempt was planned, with Western Europe, led by the Catholic Church and French noblemen, mobilised and ready. But there was a schism between this Western Church and the Eastern churches, including Alexandria's, who perceived the Catholic pope as merely one of five popes, not the primary one, and hardly representative of their congregation's political views. Despite not supporting the Catholic pope, the Eastern Christians of Jerusalem were expelled by the Fatimid governor for fear that they might take sides with the approaching Crusaders. Some of these exiles are likely to have travelled to Alexandria. As the Crusaders advanced towards the Levant, many Syrians also fled to Alexandria, causing yet more food shortages in the city.

The Crusader army sieged and pillaged Jerusalem in 1099, slaughtering every Muslim they could find and setting a synagogue on fire knowing that Jews were hiding inside. One of the Genizah letters reveals that the Jewish elders in Ascalon, just west of Jerusalem, wrote to their Alexandrian counterparts describing how the Jewish community had amassed enough money to ransom some of their captives and holy books being held in Jerusalem with the intention of sending them to Alexandria, where they would be safer. They go on to describe the difficulties faced by those who had already escaped to Alexandria: some died en route from the weather or at sea, others made it after arranging pricey camel transportation. By the time they reached Alexandria, with refugees from all three of the monotheistic faith groups having recently arrived, they found severe food shortages akin to another famine. As the twelfth century began, the westernmost mouth of the Nile Delta, the Canopic branch, began to silt up, so the water was no longer reaching Lake Mariout, which began to shrink. Not only did this reduce freshwater, it also meant that Alexandria was no longer as connected to the rest of the country.

Meanwhile, the Crusaders had founded their first state, the Kingdom of Jerusalem, with a population consisting mainly of European settlers, predominantly French, who were referred to as Franks. There was very little response from the Muslims, who, far from creating a pan-Islamic alliance, were divided among themselves. The Fatimids had already split into two factions and as they rebuffed Crusader assaults around the region were becoming so weak that Alexandria was constantly susceptible to attack. In 1123, Berbers from North Africa managed to take brief control of Egypt until they reached Alexandria, where they were defeated.

When the Fatimids appointed Bahram al-Armani as vizier in 1135, the Christian was given the title Saif al-Islam (Sword of Islam). Encouraged by his heritage, Armenian migration to Egypt shot up. As Armenians built several new churches to accommodate the 30,000 who'd arrived, the Muslims blamed the visible changes on the appointment of a Christian vizier. The indignation materialised in the emergence of the Fatimid military commander, Ridwan ibn-Walakshi, a Sunni Muslim serving as governor of Ascalon and the western Nile Delta, as the leader of a new opposition. With Ridwan's 30,000-strong army arriving in Cairo in 1137, the Christian vizier was forced to resign and was given refuge by the caliph. Ridwan, now giving himself the controversial label of king, wished to depose the Shia Fatimids in favour of a new Sunni caliphate. The changes he initiated were most obvious in Alexandria, where Christian officials were replaced with Muslims, Christians and Jews were required to wear differentiating clothing, and Armenian troops had the option of working as peasants or leaving. Most significantly, he began the process of shifting Egypt from a Shia to a Sunni state. Since Fatimid Shia rule, Cairo had remained a Shia centre but Alexandria had attracted more illicit Sunnis than any other place in Egypt and had three Sunni *madrasas*, so it was only natural that the city was used as a base to revive Sunnism. It's likely in this context that mausoleums like Abu al-Darda's were built: since Shias favoured Muhammad's family over his companions, erecting shrines for Muhammad's friends was a Sunni power move. More importantly, Ridwan opened a new, bigger theological school in Alexandria that would become Egypt's foremost *madrasa*, confirming the city's religious and therefore political allegiance.

Ridwan's attempt to overthrow the Fatimids was ultimately unsuccessful and he was imprisoned for a decade before being assassinated. But he'd already affected Alexandria's religious future. The governor of Alexandria appointed in 1148, a Kurdish Jerusalemite called ibn al-Salar, publicly announced his denominational switch from Shia to Sunni. Scholars of Sunnism began to arrive in Alexandria and more Sunni schools were opened, with seven of Egypt's eight *madrasas* finding a home in the city. Ibn-Salar was soon assassinated, but his role in Alexandria's Sunni resurgence, which might be the reason he was killed, was already complete.

The Fatimid Empire was already starting to crumble when Caliph al-Hafiz, by this stage a puppet to the vizier, died in 1149 without a clear successor. In Alexandria, a man claiming to be a Fatimid nobleman used Berbers to attack the city, but their chiefs were bribed to retreat. Elsewhere, fighting began between the Turkish and Nubian regiments of the Fatimid army, and between different governors trying to become vizier. There was also a new military Turkic Empire, the Seljuks, gaining power across the region and the Fatimids had shrunk to the extent that they controlled little beyond Egypt. As the Crusaders came back for Damascus, a Turkish nobleman called Nur al-Din led the Seljuks in a successful defence.

The rising force of both Nur al-Din's Seljuks and the Kingdom of Jerusalem indicated the beginning of the end for the Fatimids. It wasn't so much a question of whether Alexandria was going to change hands, but, rather, of who was going to get to it first.

*   *   *

Najm al-Din Ayyub was a Kurdish soldier who had become governor of the Mesopotamian city of Tikrit in the 1130s. When his
brother, Shirkuh, killed a man in a quarrel – variously reported as a
Christian of Greek heritage who'd sexually assaulted a woman – the
family was banished from the city. According to the twelfth-century
historian ibn-Shaddad, that very same day in 1137, Ayyub's wife
gave birth to baby Yusuf. Carrying the newborn with them, they
eventually ended up in Damascus, where Ayyub was given the role
of governor. Yusuf, who knew Arabic, Kurdish, Persian and Turkish,
studied the Quran alongside the mathematical works of Euclid of
Alexandria and the astronomical writing of Ptolemy of Alexandria,
and he took great interest in horses.[1]

By his teenage years, Yusuf had begun a military career alongside
his uncle. By his mid-twenties, he accompanied his uncle to Egypt
to help the local-born Arab vizier, Shawar, whose position was being
usurped. They completed their task successfully, but when Shawar
was ordered to pay tax to the Seljuks or risk losing Egypt, the vizier
allied with the Crusaders in order to keep his position. That year,
1163, the Crusaders led by King Amalric of Jerusalem had made an
unsuccessful attack on Egypt, reaching the city of Belbes, just over
one hundred miles south-east of Alexandria, where Egyptians
opened up the Nile's dams to stop the advance. Now, the Fatimid-
Crusader – or more accurately Egyptian-Crusader – alliance
returned to Belbes to attack Shirkuh's Seljuks, and after a couple of
months of stalemate the Crusaders and Seljuks both retreated.
Shirkuh, however, had seen the precarious state of Egypt and began
to prepare his return. As 1166 came to a close, he was back in Egypt
with his nephew Yusuf now the highest-ranking officer in the army.
Yusuf's feats in battle had earned him a new name meaning 'right-
eousness of the religion'. He was to be known as Saladin.

Their return prompted the Crusaders to do the same. With a
strong navy, the Crusaders arrived at Alexandria, preferring a coastal
route while the Seljuks fought their way through sandstorms. They
clashed in a ferocious battle in which the Crusader knights struggled in the steep, sandy terrain. Despite winning, the Seljuks lost
many of their men, who now numbered no more than 2,000, and
weren't in a position to continue through the rest of Egypt. Knowing
that the Crusaders had left a fleet in Alexandria, the Seljuks decided

Raphael's early sixteenth-century *School of Athens*, the Vatican Palace. The large fresco gathers the greatest scholars of antiquity under one roof.

Detail, Hypatia of Alexandria

Mohamed Nagy's *School of Alexandria* is an Alexandrian take on Raphael's *School of Athens* some four centuries earlier. With the Alexandrian coast and an equestrian statue of Alexander the Great, the figures represent Alexandria's historic achievements, moving from right to left across the ages. The pictured version, from 1949, is a quarter of the size of the one lost when the governorate building was torched in 2011.

Contemporary Alexandrian art has tended to focus on scenes of everyday life, like *Fish Market in Alexandria*, by Khaled Hanno, 2019. Hanno is one of the most prominent artists chronicling Alexandria today.

One of Egypt's most iconic painters, Mahmoud Said, depicted many scenes of early twentieth-century Alexandrian life from across the social strata, including *At the Ball Room*, 1949.

Muhammad Ali Square at the turn of the twentieth century.

Cleopatra's Needle in London, with the plaque commemorating its arrival from Alexandria.

THIS OBELISK
PROSTRATE FOR CENTURIES
ON THE SANDS OF ALEXANDRIA
WAS PRESENTED TO THE
BRITISH NATION A.D. 1819 BY
MAHOMMED ALI VICEROY OF EGYPT
A WORTHY MEMORIAL OF
OUR DISTINGUISHED COUNTRYMEN
NELSON AND ABERCROMBY

A diver discovers an ancient sphinx sitting comfortably on the Alexandrian seabed in 1995. Only 1 per cent of the underwater artefacts of Ptolemaic and Roman Alexandria have yet been found.

Transporting the statue of an early Ptolemy through the busy streets of Alexandria, surrounded by the iconic yellow-and-black taxis. This statue once stood near the foot of the Pharos Lighthouse.

Muhammad Ali's portrait, painted by my late nan, Qadria, in 1993. As a child, I would sit opposite this portrait every weekend.

The erroneously named Pompey's Pillar still stands tall, surrounded by residential high rises. Today's Alexandrians refer to it in Arabic as the Pillar of Masts.

The Canopic Way, once sketched by Alexander the Great on the sand, remains the oldest planned street still in use today. It was renamed Rue Fuad and then Freedom Way, and includes one of Alexandria's oldest florists.

The abu-al-Abbas al-Mursi Mosque was originally built in 1307, shortly after the death of the city's beloved Sufi saint. It was redesigned in the twentieth century by the Italian architect Mario Rossi.

The waterfront promenade known as the Corniche is testament to the city's original design, with wide roads angled for an optimum breeze.

Protesters filling the Corniche in 2011.

Contemporary Alexandria. The Qaitbay Citadel stands where the Pharos Lighthouse once welcomed visitors. The extended Heptastadion that connected Pharos island to the mainland is clear. And the thirteen-mile Corniche facing northwest into the Mediterranean connects the entire city.

Alexander the Great, on his trusted horse Bucephalus, sculpted by Constantinos Balic
Loghos in 2002. In Alexandria, it's hard to forget the city's founder.

to head to the coastal city to stop those ships from attacking. Alexandria had maintained a distance from the other battles and had limited access to day-to-day essentials, let alone weapons. When the Seljuks arrived, they were welcomed by Alexandria's predominantly Sunni population, who disliked the vizier and hoped that Shirkuh might reprioritise the city. But Shirkuh departed Alexandria with most of the army, leaving the rest under the leadership of his nephew, Saladin. Now Alexandria's new governor, Saladin had the tough job of protecting a city that, thanks to his uncle's decision, was asking to be attacked.

Before long, the Egyptian and Crusader armies arrived at Alexandria by land; so, coupled with the Crusader navy in the harbour, the city was surrounded. Shirkuh took his army south hoping the Crusaders would follow, but they remained at Alexandria. According to the medieval Crusader chronicler William of Tyre:

> Surrounding the city like a leafy forest were fertile gardens of most delightful aspect, full of fruit trees and medicinal plants. The very sight of this charming retreat invited the passer-by to enter and, having entered, to rest there.

The Crusaders began to cut down these orchards, initially to build a tall watchtower and make weapons, but within a short time 'the aromatic trees' were being cut for 'the sole desire of causing injury and loss . . . Before long, the orchards were levelled to the ground, and no trace of their former condition remained'. The people of Alexandria were understandably upset, not least because Islamic teachings prohibit harming trees during war. This event tipped the balance for anyone unsure about who to support, and some 20,000 Alexandrians joined Saladin's forces. When the Crusaders also began to limit food supplies to the population, the Seljuks realised that they lacked the resources to fight back and agreed to depart from Egypt if the Crusaders stopped their offensive. William of Tyre claims that the Crusader flag was raised above the Pharos Lighthouse. But he also notes the heartening relief of both the besieging army and the Alexandrians, who'd been forced to fight, starve and live in fear. The Alexandrians went out into the streets, celebrated, ate abundantly and returned to their daily work. For their part, the Crusader troops couldn't wait to enjoy 'this splendid city', and 'wandering freely about the streets, they gazed at the ports and the ramparts', taking souvenirs with them.[2] Politically, the Crusaders now placed garrisons and advisers in Alexandria and received payments from Egypt's vizier, making the country a protectorate of the Crusaders. Saladin had garnered the support of the local Sunni population but had failed to do his job of defending Alexandria, his first major independent military assignment. The Jerusalem-based Crusaders were edging closer to taking full control of Alexandria.

When Alexandria's vizier failed to pay the taxes in time, King Amalric of Jerusalem, backed by the Catholic military orders of the Knights Templars and Knights Hospitaller, used the opportunity to cement their control over Egypt. The Venetian fleet refused to join the Crusaders in order to keep business relations with Alexandria intact. The Crusaders entered Belbes and, according to William of Tyre, killed every last person there. The result was that the Egyptian population, including its Coptic Christians, turned against the Crusaders. Ironically, the vizier Shawar, who'd previously switched sides, pleaded with the Seljuks to return and help him. He also ordered the city of Fustat to be evacuated before deciding it was better for it to be set alight than for the Crusaders to capture it. The fire lasted almost two months, during which time Shawar attempted to negotiate with the Crusaders. As the Seljuk army, led by Shirkuh and Saladin, arrived in Egypt in January 1169, the Crusaders retreated. Shawar had proved that he couldn't be trusted, so Saladin was given the task of executing the vizier. Shirkuh took control of Egypt, but died just two months later after enjoying an excessive feast, so in March 1169, Saladin became vizier of Egypt and commander of its army.

In May 1169, Saladin, now in his early thirties, arrived in Alexandria. Contemporary Arabic sources note that Saladin, ready to take on this new and important role, made the decision to stop frequenting taverns and brothels: 'he repented from wine, turned away from the causes of frivolity, and dressed himself in the clothes of seriousness and diligence'.[3] In Alexandria, he gave immediate orders for the fortifications to be strengthened and began to construct a navy. Hundreds of the city's columns were broken in half and thrown on the shore to offer protection from enemy ships and the waves; today, some of these broken columns can be seen on the site of the Serapeum where Pompey's Pillar survives. Despite having to answer to the Fatimids, he sacked their loyalists from the army, replaced Shia judges with Sunni ones, and Alexandria's mosques reverted to the Sunni call to prayer. Saladin also eliminated various taxes and announced that Jews and Christians could keep any political and economic positions. One of the most respected Jews was the court physician, whom Saladin kept until the doctor's eyesight weakened, at which stage he was given a handsome pension. When Saladin arrived, a Jewish philosopher named Maimonides, who had escaped persecution in Andalusia, was also in the city, where he began writing his *Mishnenh Torah*, the only medieval work to compile every aspect of Jewish observance. Both Jews and Christians were now talking Arabic and just as Alexandria's Jews had shifted from Hebrew to Greek in the past, in the twelfth century, the Church officially adopted Arabic as its liturgical language because its worshippers no longer understood Coptic.

Saladin was not safe from revolts within the army and government, but was able to quash them all. His popularity among Alexandrians was growing, in large part because he was protecting them from suffering the same fate as the cities of Belbes and Fustat. By 1171, the Fatimid caliph al-Adid died. Whether Saladin played a part in his death is a matter of speculation, but what we do know is that Saladin saw this as an opportunity to declare the end of the Fatimid dynasty. That week, in the mosques of Alexandria, the Friday sermons of 17 September 1171 declared the return of an Abbasid, Sunni caliphate. The Fatimid rule of Alexandria, which lasted for over two centuries, was over. It was a period of ups and downs, but one in which the Fatimids had recovered the city's position as a prosperous trade centre and spread its artistic and architectural character across the region. Saladin was in reality ruling independently of the Abbasid caliphate and his conquest was most notable as the turning point from a Shia Egypt to a Sunni one. In the process, Saladin's own expanding empire – named after his father Ayyub – was beginning to develop. Alexandria had become part of the Ayyubid dynasty.

*   *   *

Saladin began to expand his empire east and west, sending family members to conquer parts of North Africa and the Arabian peninsula. His manoeuvres didn't impress Nur al-Din, the Seljuk leader, who realised that Saladin was becoming an independent ruler and not paying the agreed taxes. Nur al-Din began to prepare an army that would head to Egypt. But the threat that came to Alexandria was from elsewhere. In 1174, less than three years after the Ayyubid Empire was founded, King William II of Sicily, keen to become a successful Crusader, decided to attack Alexandria with a substantial navy, hoping that Saladin was too busy expanding elsewhere. According to ibn al-Athir's early thirteenth-century *Complete History*, the Sicilians arrived at Alexandria with 200 warships, 36 ships carrying horses and 46 ships laden with supplies including siege towers and catapults, with a total of 50,000 infantry and 1,500 cavalry. The Alexandrians took key positions with their catapults on the walls of the city. The Sicilians managed to anchor by 'the lighthouse' and fighting began on land. For two days, fighting continued between the Sicilians and the Alexandrians, who'd already sent word to Saladin. By the third day, Saladin had posted one of his men ahead on horseback, and when he arrived to spread the news that Saladin and his army were on their way, the Alexandrians left their homes and camps to fight, 'each of them thinking that Saladin is with him'. That night, they surprised the Sicilians by opening the city gates and attacking them, setting fires and looting their belongings. Some Sicilians escaped by sea, others were killed or ended up drowning, and 300 sought refuge on the nearby hill.[4] By morning, every Crusader had either died, been captured, or escaped. The victory didn't end up involving Saladin physically, but news of his arrival had encouraged the Alexandrian army. As the victory was celebrated, Saladin received news that the Seljuk leader, Nur al-Din, had died, so he returned to Damascus where he took over as Sultan of Egypt and Syria and married Nur al-Din's widow.

Saladin, now controlling multiple armies with hundreds of thousands of fighters at his disposal, was also surrounding the Kingdom of Jerusalem. It was only a matter of time before he would launch an attack to retrieve the holy city for the Muslims. Saladin conquered most of the Crusader states in the Levant, culminating in his most famous siege of Jerusalem in 1187.

In the immediate aftermath of Saladin taking Jerusalem, Crusader ships were turned towards Alexandria. Divers on Alexandria's shore today find many fragments from sculptures and buildings: random blocks that residents threw on the shoreline to prevent the Crusaders from getting too close to the harbour.

When Saladin arrived in Jerusalem, around half of its population were Christian refugees who'd fled the towns he'd previously attacked. Saladin now ordered guards to protect these refugees until they arrived at their place of asylum. Ironically, at the Crusader city of Tripoli, they were not allowed to enter and were instead attacked and had their possessions stolen. According to the eyewitness account of Ernoul, squire of Jerusalem's defence minister during the siege, Alexandria was more heroic. Surviving in Old French, the manuscript notes that those who fled to Alexandria tried to do so by sea. As the refugees attempted to board, the captains from Genoa, Pisa and Venice refused to accept them because they had no money. In response, the governor of Alexandria refused to issue the Italians with sailing permits until they agreed not only to take the fleeing Christians but to treat them well during the journey. When they arrived in Alexandria, they were greeted with bread and money.[5]

The lesser-known result of Saladin's triumph in Jerusalem is that the Crusades that followed would turn their attention to Egypt. Any chance of the Crusaders recovering Jerusalem meant capturing Egypt first because of its geographical location and more so because it was the main supply house for the Ayyubids, providing grain to troops during long expeditions. In 1192, King Richard I of England (known as the Lionheart) was intent on attacking Egypt, though his plans didn't materialise. The year after that, in Damascus, Saladin was struck with a two-week fever that resulted in his death at the age of fifty-six.

The following year saw numerous attempts to capture Egypt. The Fourth Crusade (1202–4) all but ended the Byzantine Empire. The Fifth Crusade (1217–21) was initially successful before a decisive battle won by the Egyptians on the east bank of the flooding Nile saw the Crusaders surrender. The Seventh Crusade (1248–54) saw King Louis IX of France, supported by English and Scottish nobles, capture the coastal city of Damietta, around one hundred miles east of Alexandria. They had two options in order to reach Cairo: attacking Alexandria or moving to the Nile Delta. After heated debate, they opted for the latter, ending up at a town the Ayyubids founded in 1219 called Flower Island, because it had water around it on three sides and the biggest flower park in the country. Battles ensued in 1250, and in France reports spread that Cairo had been seized and Alexandria was defenceless. In reality, the Crusaders ended up suffering a humiliating defeat, killed and captured in great numbers, including Louis, with Flower Island renamed Mansoura (The Victorious).

The heroes of these victories were the Mamluks, slave-soldiers who had risen up the ranks over the last 300 years to become a knightly military class upon which the Ayyubids relied. Originally Turkic, they included non-Arab nomads from Caucasia, Eastern Europe and the Balkans. Having successfully fought off the Crusaders from Egypt, they were now preparing to consolidate their own power.

Mamluks and the Plagued Century

During the French-led Crusader attack on Egypt, Saladin's great nephew, the Sultan al-Saleh, had fallen ill and died. His wife, Shajarat al-Durr (meaning Tree of Pearls), was a slave of Turkic or Armenian descent whom he'd purchased and married after she bore him a son. When her husband died, fearing their disruption and demoralisation, Shajarat al-Durr hid the news from the army troops. The Mamluk generals, the Turkish-speaking warrior class who'd effected the victory, particularly a man of Turkic origin named Aybak, saw an opportunity. The generals felt that the Ayyubid heir looked down on them, so they decided to kill him and place Shajarat al-Durr, herself a freed slave, at the helm. Coins minted in Alexandria in 1250 confirm that she held the same title as her predecessors, 'Sultan', but also fashioned a new one, 'Queen of the Muslims'.

The Abbasids in Iraq, where the caliph had for decades accepted Egypt's de facto independence, rejected the decision on the grounds of gender, writing that if Egypt had run out of men, they were to let him know so that he could send them some. The Ayyubids in Syria rejected the decision and vowed to fight it. This outright rejection meant the Mamluks had to take a riskier approach. They arrested Ayyubid loyalists in Egypt. Then, Shajarat al-Durr resigned and married the commander-in-chief, Aybak, in the hope that the Mamluks could finally govern. Despite ruling alone for only 80 days, Shajarat al-Durr's reign indicates wisdom and diplomacy, permitting the captured King Louis IX to leave for a huge ransom. The Mamluks were able to cement their position in power, leaving the Ayyubids with little more than Syria and southern Palestine.

The Mamluks had both military might and numbers, but political and personal issues remained unresolved. Both Aybak and Shajarat al-Durr regarded themselves as the true ruler, and they kept information from one another in order to achieve political superiority. But Aybak's downfall came from a more personal rift: he married another woman, and as he was bathing one day in 1257, servants hired by Shajarat al-Durr stabbed him to death. In response, his teenage son arranged for maids to strip and beat Shajarat al-Durr to death. The naked body of the slave who had risen to become ruler, the first Muslim queen, the first woman to rule Egypt since Cleopatra and Zenobia a millennium earlier, was dragged by the feet and thrown into the Cairo Citadel's moat where it remained for days before eventually being buried.

Within a couple of years, Sultan Kutuz – a man who'd been sold into slavery in Egypt when he was younger, fought heroically in the Seventh Crusade and risen to become a trusted vice-sultan for two decades – was taking the Mamluk Sultanate from strength to strength. By 1260, the Mamluks had captured the Ayyubid lands, marking the collapse of the dynasty that Saladin had founded less than a century earlier.

The military prowess of the Mamluks was good news for Alexandria. The Mongol Empire, founded by Genghis Khan in Central Asia a few decades earlier, was expanding rapidly: his grandson Hulagu successfully invaded Baghdad and Damascus between 1258 and 1260. The Abbasid caliphate was finished, and Alexandria – now populated with more Mesopotamian and Levantine refugees – was in real danger. The Mongols sent messengers to Cairo demanding surrender; in a bold act of defiance, the heads of these envoys were hung on the city's walls. So the Mongols approached via Galilee. But Egypt had military rulers and an army accustomed to Central Asian war tactics. Kutuz's Mamluk army didn't wait for the Mongols to get any further. Confronting them at the Battle of Ayn Jalut, the experienced Mamluks predicted the feigned retreat tactic on which the Mongols relied, flanked the opposition from an unexpected direction and used hand cannons for the very first time. The Mamluk victory saved Alexandria from what seemed like an inevitable Mongol invasion. With the fall of Iraq and Syria, the Islamic world was refocused on Egypt.

A decade later, in 1271, Edward, Duke of Gascony, embarked on the Ninth Crusade along the North African coast, but avoided

Alexandria because of its strong fleet and garrison. Despite the limited success of his crusade, he was crowned King Edward I on his return to England. By 1291, the last of the Holy Land's Crusader cities, Acre, was captured by the Mamluks, and by the start of the fourteenth century all the lands won in the Crusades were lost to this new Egypt-based Sultanate. After two centuries of uncertainty, Alexandria finally appeared to be safe from attacks.

Under the Mamluks, Alexandria became central to the region's trade again, connecting the East and West as it had so often done before, and with the canals re-dug in the early 1300s, the trade route between Alexandria and Cairo became even easier. There was a sorting office begun by the Ayyubids that continued to receive international post twice a week. Despite intermittent papal bans on trading with Muslims, the Italians were particularly keen to make use of Alexandria. The Italian slave trade, monopolised first by the Genoese then the Venetians, saw thousands of Turkish and Tartar slaves transported from the Black Sea ports to Alexandria where they would be sorted before distribution: an ironic source of income given that former slaves were controlling the city. A new pidgin language, Sabir, began to develop and reached the harbour area of Alexandria. Also referred to as the Mediterranean lingua franca, Sabir was a simplified language in which the vast merchant class communicated, borrowing terms from their routes and backgrounds in a mix of Spanish, Italian, French, Greek, Arabic and Persian.

The rise and fall of the Mongol Empire also renewed Alexandria's importance as traders avoided areas of conflict to the east, preferring to get to and from the Indian Ocean via the Mediterranean and Egypt. Alexandria produced and sold, among other things, large quantities of silk, cotton and wool. It sold coral, marble, pearls and mercury. Spices were abundant and Venice alone bought 700,000 kilograms of pepper every year. Alexandria also became the region's oil and soap capital, with its olive- and almond-based products in demand in Europe, North Africa and the Levant. A new candle-making district was also formed, with Alexandrian candles spreading across the region. Alexandria also grew the carob, a plant which became popular for food and drink across North Africa and Andalusia. Even today, carob is one of the city's most cherished drinks, sold by street vendors who crush and boil its pods, caramelising them into a cool, chocolatey drink enjoyed in the summer.

Alexandria, then, continued to develop as taxation and port duties provided reliable sources of revenue. With the Jews actively involved as merchants and middlemen, great synagogues began to be built in the fourteenth century, including the impressive Eliyahu Hanavi Synagogue dedicated to the biblical Elijah, in 1354. The mingling of faiths and cultures returned and led to new traditions, spices and clothing, as well as innovative ideas. A smaller group known as the Franks now lived in Alexandria: these were the Western European Christians from Italy and France who'd remained in the city after the Crusades. Alexandria also became part of the Islamic Hajj pilgrimage route to Mecca so people of the Maghreb, both Moroccans and Andalusians, who were the furthest away from Arabia, were encouraged to settle in Alexandria on their way home.

Anyone who took the pilgrimage caravan from the west passed through Alexandria. It was a good chance to meet non-Maghrebi tradesmen and scholars, too, as people gathered from Damascus and Baghdad especially during pilgrimage and trading seasons. Al-Idrisi, a respected Moroccan geographer, went there in the mid-1100s before creating the magnificent *Tabula Rogerian*, one of the most advanced maps of the world, which he worked on for fifteen years. Alexandria is clearly labelled on the map with a little illustration of a lighthouse popping off its shore. Around that time, an Andalusian named Yusuf ibn al-Shaikh left Malaga for Mecca in 1165. His journal, discovered 700 years later in Cairo, gives another detailed description of the Pharos Lighthouse.

During Saladin's time, in the early 1180s, a Valencia-born writer in his late twenties named ibn-Jubayr headed for Mecca and ended up chronicling his travels with a wider variety of details than his contemporaries. On arrival, officials boarded the ship he was travelling on to check it, taking every Muslim's name and city of origin, and asking everyone to declare customs and pay tax. Ibn-Jubayr describes a chaotic and crowded city, but praises its public spending on free schools, hostels for foreign students and an abundance of baths, hospitals and, he estimates, 8,000 to 12,000 mosques. He is particularly intrigued by the network of cisterns, adding that the city underground is no less advanced than the city overground. 'We had never seen a town with broader streets or higher buildings or one more lofty and beautiful', he continues, describing marble columns 'beyond imagination' and a wondrous lighthouse: 'the eyes fail to comprehend it, relating it [in words] is inadequate, and the spectacle is vast.' He also finds it 'remarkable' that Alexandria's 'people are as active in their affairs at night as they are by day'.[1] Ibn-Jubayr went home to Grenada after completing the pilgrimage to Mecca but was so captivated by Alexandria that when his wife passed away, he returned to spend the rest of his life there, teaching the Islamic faith until he died in his seventies.

Those who remained in Alexandria on their way back from Mecca played a role in the esoteric development of the city, with Sufi Islam becoming more prominent. Sufism had developed during the Umayyad period in response to the lavishness of the caliphate. Sufis – literally meaning wool-wearers in reference to their simple clothing – focused on spirituality and asceticism, attempting to summon divine presence through recitation and meditation.

Mystics who made the city their home include Bishr al-Gohary, whose family moved from the Maghreb to Alexandria in the twelfth century, and who used to meditate in isolation on the seashore. After his death, this area off the Corniche was named after him, Sidi Bishr (*sidi* means saint in Moroccan Arabic). The mosque bearing his name is on a hilly corner, and the area is also home to the Two Saints Church dedicated to St Mark and Pope Peter of Alexandria, a lavish chain hotel, and a traditional café that validates ibn-Jubayr's observation about the city's nocturnal nature. Another neighbourhood, Sidi Gaber, is named after Gaber al-Ansari, an Andalusian mystic who moved to Alexandria in the thirteenth century. And the area of Shatby, where the new Alexandria Library is situated, is named after Abdullah al-Shatby, who came from Shatiba (today called Xàtiva), near Valencia, and settled close to Pompey's Pillar. Al-Shatby was a Sufi scholar whom the Mamluk Sultan of Egypt, Baybars the Great, would meet in Alexandria in order to receive counsel.

But no Maghrebi is as iconic to the city as Shehab abu-al-Abbas, an Andalusian from Murcia, known as abu-al-Abbas al-Mursi (the

Murcian). When he was a youngster, his family, headed by a wealthy businessman father, left Murcia either to visit Mecca or to relocate to North Africa. On the shore of Tunis they were met with a severe storm and he lost his parents at sea. Having made it to Tunis with his brother, al-Mursi found solace with the founder of a key Sufi movement, the Moroccan Abu-al-Hassan al-Shadhili, who became their spiritual leader. One day in 1244, al-Shadhili dreamed that the Prophet Muhammad ordered him to move to Egypt, so he travelled to Alexandria, taking his loyal student with him. Al-Shadhili's disciple, al-Mursi, couldn't have predicted that he would become even more popular and important in Alexandria than his mentor. On their trip to Alexandria, al-Mursi writes, he felt severe anxiety. They arrived at Pompey's Pillar, poor and hungry, but a local immediately offered them food. That they didn't eat until al-Shadhili saw another vision telling him it was permissible to do so suggests the food may have been gifted by a non-Muslim. Al-Shadhili's new house in Alexandria had a mosque on one floor, a convent with meditation rooms on another and his family residence on the top storey. His teachings became popular, with leading figures taking interest and the officials presenting him one of the city's towers. It's said that despite losing his sight, al-Shadhili still participated in battles against Louis IX's Crusaders. After his teacher's death, al-Mursi became the most prominent Sufi in the city. He taught that humans have four conditions: grace and calamity, obedience and disobedience. All four are good: grace leads to gratitude, calamity to patience, obedience to bounty and disobedience to repentance. Al-Mursi spent over forty years preaching his spiritual ideas in Alexandria, dying on New Year's Day 1288. Within twenty years, a small mosque had been built around his tomb, which was expanded in the 1770s and 1940s.

Through the likes of al-Shadhili and al-Mursi, Sufism continued to develop in the thirteenth century despite Sunni Islam being the state-sponsored denomination. Wary of a developing clerical class, the Mamluks decided to endorse rather than suppress Sufism, eventually noticing that, if it took centre stage, their Sultanate could lay claim to having its own, identifiable state religion. Alexandria became a safe haven for Sufis where they could worship and meet travellers. With the state's support, prominent Sufi scholars were invited to move and reside there and state-funded Sufi ceremonies became commonplace. Egypt's leading Jew, Abraham Maimonides, openly praised Sufism as Alexandria's Jews began to adopt practices that merged their law with Sufi mysticism, such as solitary meditation.

Although Egypt has never been considered part of the Maghreb, Alexandria's connection was tangible. The Maghrebi influence on the city still exists in certain Moroccan expressions that have made their way into the Alexandrian dialect. And the merchants and mystics who settled in the city didn't just bring their mysticism with them, but variations of their national dish, too – there's a saying that 'the Maghreb ends where couscous ends, and couscous ends in Alexandria'. Near Sidi Bishr, I stop to try sweet couscous, a popular, sugary dessert that comes with a cup of milk to pour over it. I don't fancy the milk, so I offer it to a cat lingering nearby: she doesn't hesitate and slurps it down. Having held the cup for long enough, I put it on the ground and a couple of her mates arrive. The three cats enjoy the milk as I enjoy the sea breeze. I ponder the transnational influences on the city's life and how this place has seen so many short-lived dynasties. I smile at the thought that, apart from the distant waves, the only constant in Alexandrian history might be the cats.

Al-Mursi is even more important than the couscous here: he is Alexandria's patron saint. Some Alexandrians still swear by his name if they want to convince you they're not lying. Visitors flock to the most famous mosque in the city, just off the harbour, where his tomb lies in the back corner of the octagonal, marbled prayer hall. Built in 1307, it was redesigned in the twentieth century by the Italian architect Mario Rossi. The abu-al-Abbas al-Mursi Mosque is a masterpiece, an oriental dream. In 1945, the year of the first prayer after its reopening, Rossi thrilled the locals by announcing his conversion from Catholicism to Islam; he went on to become one of the most influential modern Islamic architects and designed two more mosques in Alexandria. On the outside, the al-Mursi Mosque has four huge domes decorated with flower motifs. On the inside, elaborate geometric designs, including stars and flowers, gleam in gold and blue.[2] Today, women with fertility problems travel across the country so that al-Mursi can comfort them with a pregnancy. On a recent visit, two women, one in dark clothes and another wearing a colourful bandanna, competed melancholically to offer me food and water so that their visit might be blessed. 'By the Murcian abu-al-Abbas', I swore to them, 'I've just eaten couscous.'

When the Maghrebi mystics arrived in Alexandria, it had already experienced an unusual share of ups and downs. If that tsunami a millennium earlier had been the Day of Horror, the fourteenth century might be known as the century of horror. It would witness yet more natural disasters, the spread of history's deadliest pandemic and the obliteration of the city's most wondrous building.

The Pharos Lighthouse had already been damaged by earthquakes in the eighth and tenth centuries, when the first structural collapses probably took place. A thirteenth-century Italian mosaic depicting St Mark approaching the lighthouse cannot be relied upon to tell us its state at that time, since it erroneously has a dome at its summit, which wouldn't have been there when Mark arrived. This might be an indication of the inaccurate conflations of the time in which the mosaic was produced, though it may also be a comment on the thirteenth-century Muslims of Alexandria needing to be saved as the polytheists were before them. We have a better idea about the lighthouse in this period from eyewitness accounts. Iraqi historian Abdullatif al-Baghdadi saw it in the 1190s and praised it with delight and awe. Then, by the 1220s, travellers from Aleppo describe an anticlimactic and rather ordinary watchtower, not the marvel they had read about. By the 1270s, the lighthouse was in such a state that, according to contemporary sources, Sultan Baybars ordered the restoration of its tiers from top to bottom and its northern façade. The wretched fourteenth century was now finishing the lighthouse off. In 1303, an earthquake struck Alexandria, resulting in the collapse of some of the building's key structures. It's for this reason that a French monastery manuscript gives the date of destruction as August of that year. Then, another earthquake in 1323 all but confirmed its demise.

The following year, one man on his route to Mecca caused a commotion across the city. This individual came with an entourage of 60,000 soldiers, slaves and supporters, every one of them dressed in brocades of fine Persian silk. With hundreds of horses and camels, they travelled with more than 25,000 kilograms of gold (today worth over £1 billion) and possibly more: the slaves carrying bars, the camels carrying gold dust. This man was Mansa Musa, the emperor of a relatively unknown kingdom called Mali that made its fortune from its abundance of gold, salt and ivory. Every Friday, when he needed to pray, he would build a mosque along the route. Whenever he encountered anyone selling something, he'd buy it. And he handed out gold to anyone and everyone. All this was possible because Musa was probably one of the richest people in the world. He made a point of stopping in both Cairo and Alexandria for a few months during his 3,000-mile trip from west Africa.

In Alexandria he met the Mamluk Sultan al-Nasir, who was insulted that Musa refused to prostrate himself, but who eventually presented his visitor with fine Alexandrian cloth. Musa distributed so much gold to the residents of Alexandria that it precipitated an economic crisis: gold became so abundant that its value decreased by 12 per cent and in an attempt to adjust to everyone's newfound wealth inflation rocketed. It would take a decade for Egypt's economy to recover. Ironically, even Musa's gold ran out and he had to borrow from a leading Alexandrian merchant in order to get home. That merchant, Siraj al-Din ibn-al-Kuwayk, had hosted Musa in his garden villa and would end up returning with Musa to Mali and dying there. When Musa got home, he expanded his main mosque into the Sankoré University and library, gathering scholars there and stocking it with hundreds of thousands of manuscripts, the largest collection of books since the Library of Alexandria. Musa's trip put him on the radar of the Mediterranean and European powers. Alexandria's Venetian traders returned to Venice with stories of Musa's vast wealth, placing him in the European imagination and adding Mali to the maps created in that period. His dynasty would come to an end in 1591 when the Moroccan Sultan Ahmad al-Mansur used firearms and specialist military provided by Queen Elizabeth I to sack Mali, take its gold and enslave its residents, including the scholars.

Just months after Alexandria welcomed one of the world's wealthiest men, a less prosperous pilgrim turned explorer recorded much of what we now know about fourteenth-century Alexandria, and indeed Africa, Asia and Europe. As the spring of 1325 drew to a close, twenty-one-year-old Shams al-Din al-Tangi ibn-Battuta prepared to travel for the Hajj pilgrimage. As his name suggests, he was a Berber 'of Tangier' in northern Morocco, just across the water from Gibraltar. Ibn-Battuta means the 'son of Duckling'; the Arabic for 'duck' was and remains a popular nickname for Fatimah, which was his mother's name. Ibn-Battuta was well educated in Islamic jurisprudence, which he knew would come in handy during his travels. Like many who ventured to Mecca and Medina, he travelled through Alexandria and its surrounding regions. Seeing the diversity of Alexandria and speaking to its locals thrilled ibn-Battuta, and his interactions in the city led to an exciting new plan.

Ibn-Battuta arrived in Alexandria in April 1326, staying there for several weeks that would change his life. Of course, one of the first things he saw was the Pharos Lighthouse. He was struck by its height and its elevated entrance accessible via a wooden bridge. But he also saw that it had considerably disintegrated: 'one of its sides was run down.' In contrast to the lighthouse, Pompey's Pillar was still standing strong, 'an oddity . . . a gigantic marble column . . . in the middle of a forest of palm trees, distinguishably loftier and higher than the trees'. By the time he returned to Alexandria in 1349, the once iconic lighthouse had become a disappointing wreck. He records how he 'found it completely ruined, so that it wasn't possible to enter it or to climb its doorway'. Now rudimentary rather than innovative, ships were observed from a man-made hill called Kom el-Nadura, or 'hill of the watch'. According to ibn-Battuta's contemporary, the Syrian historian al-Umari, the hill was on cemetery grounds and, despite having unstable foundations, a small tower was built at its twenty-five-metre peak. Finally, there is a record to suggest that in 1365 a new, smaller watchtower had to be built, which was referred to as Pharillon, or Little Pharos. All these contemporary accounts allow us to identify two periods of severe decline for the Pharos Lighthouse: the early thirteenth century and the early fourteenth century, when it finally stopped being used. The structure is unlikely to have survived much beyond the late fourteenth century. The Mausoleum at Halicarnassus may have endured a little longer but the only Ancient Wonder still standing today is the Great Pyramid of Giza.

A city so different from anything young ibn-Battuta had ever seen, Alexandria also piqued his curiosity to explore the many other varied and unfamiliar places around the world. His awe, when he first arrived in Alexandria, sounds as heartfelt as anything else he says:

> She is a well-guarded citadel, a friendly region, wondrous in its nature, solid in its construction, it has whatever you wish for in the way of embellishment and embattlement, and feats both worldly and religious . . . its architecture combining enormity and succinctness.

Ibn-Battuta also provides one of the finest summaries of Alexandria: it is a 'unique' city that is capable of 'uniting the excellences shared out (by other places) through her mediation between the East and the West, for every fresh marvel is unveiled here, every novelty ends up here'.

Alexandria's influence on ibn-Battuta is clearest when he spends time with some of the locals, whom he describes as friendly and hospitable. The most notable of these is Burhan al-Din the Lame, with whom he lodges for three nights. 'I see that you like tourism and travelling,' he said to ibn-Battuta, who recollects that 'at that time, it hadn't crossed my mind to venture to the far lands'. The Alexandrian host then told ibn-Battuta that he must visit his brothers in India, Sindh (Pakistan) and China, 'and it cast in my mind to head to these lands'. Did this Alexandrian have relatives that far east? It's entirely possible, due to the trade links that connected Alexandria with those nations. Merchants who arrived from these lands to Alexandria or Alexandrians who travelled to sell their goods may have married. Or, these could be Sufi brothers with whom there was a spiritual rather than biological link, showing that Alexandria's Muslim mystics were connected the world over. These connections were vital to travel: with no telecommunications, explorers had to rely on word of mouth, on recommendations about places to go and people to seek; where better to do this than the global hub of Alexandria? By his own admission, without this stop in Alexandria, there might never have been an eminent explorer called ibn-Battuta.

Ibn-Battuta ended up travelling as far as the east coast of Africa, the desert mountains of the Arabian peninsula, Shiraz in the Persian east, the Sultanate of Delhi in India (where he was appointed the religious judge), the Sumatra mountains and China's Fujian province, to name but a few. His now cherished narrative is filled with details about the cultures and sites he encountered, and the people he met, not least the women. In the Maldives, he writes, the coconut and fish diet serves as an aphrodisiac and he alternates every night between four wives and several concubines. In Mahratta, the Indian women 'have in intercourse a deliciousness and a knowledge of erotic movements beyond that of other women'. But what most differentiates ibn-Battuta from other travellers is that his adventures were actually recorded. In the spring of 1350, in a garden near Grenada, he began to tell the notable company about his travels and one of the attendants was soon transcribing everything he said. Ibn-Battuta travelled more than twice as many miles as the Chinese explorer Zheng He and five times as many as Venetian merchant Marco Polo. And by recording everything before he died in the substantial *Rihla* (*Travels*), the man whose inspiration originated in Alexandria became one of the most important explorers in history.[3]

But ibn-Battuta went to Alexandria during its most difficult century. Given its proximity to three continents and being at the centre of many trade routes, Alexandria consistently suffered the undesirable, destructive consequences of its position as a central hub, most notably plagues. The city had already experienced epidemics in the third and sixth centuries. The new bubonic plague, the Black Death, was causing even more far-reaching damage. It began to ravage Europe in the summer of 1347 when apocalyptic ships reached Constantinople from Crimea with the plague on board and every member of the Genoese crew infected. It didn't take long for the disease to reach the ports of Alexandria. In particular, one Sicilian merchant ship, its cargo including slaves, had made its way from Constantinople to Alexandria that autumn. When it arrived, everyone on board was either dead or dying. Ships were still in the harbour, everyone on board dead. As the ships were looted, more and more people became infected. From Alexandria, the plague spread eastwards and southwards, reaching the Levant and

Mecca. In Egypt, hundreds of thousands died and corpses filled the Nile. Around a third of the population may have perished. On his second trip to Egypt, ibn-Battuta reports 1,080 daily deaths in Alexandria: a high toll, but much lower than the 21,000 daily deaths in Cairo. The desperate situation led to the city's inhabitants fleeing into the countryside, while those in the countryside thought things would be safer in the big city. The Black Death continued to affect Alexandria intermittently for more than 150 years, though not as badly as it ultimately affected the countryside, where the demise of agriculture had a detrimental impact on people's lifestyles and livelihoods.

As though two earthquakes, the destruction of the Pharos Lighthouse and the Black Death weren't bad enough, in 1365 a new crusade also made its way to Alexandria. Known as the Alexandrian Crusade, or, more accurately, the Sacking of Alexandria, King Peter I of Cyprus instigated an attack on the city that was far more economic and self-promoting than religious. After spending three years travelling around Europe to gather financial and military support, including that of the Catholic military Order of Knights of Saint John, he finally gathered his army on the island of Rhodes in August 1365. One manuscript provides us with a detailed eyewitness account; al-Nuwayri al-Iskandarani was a manuscript copyist whose services were sought by the rich merchants of the city. He tells us that on 7 October, 70 trade-ships appeared at Alexandria, with Venetian, Genoese, Rhodian, Cypriot and French crews. But they didn't dock at the harbour, instead hovering around its vicinity. Alexandrians knew something was amiss and started to panic.

The next day, a new fleet arrived on the western harbour, but arrows were immediately fired at them, forcing a retreat. The following morning, 9 October, Peter's ships were back. After overcoming the first line of defence, they landed onshore. As some of Peter's troops disembarked, Alexandria's army continued to guard the city. But their attempts to cover all angles were jeopardised when they found the customs gate – their only route to the water's edge of the eastern harbour – locked to protect stored merchandise while the governor was on pilgrimage. With the Alexandrians forced to assemble on other parts of the coast, some of Peter's ships disembarked on the unmanned harbour and climbed the wall into the city. According to al-Nuwayri, the officer in charge of the gate was later tried for treason.

Citizens began to flee as Peter's army of 30,000 – about the same size as the entire population of London at the time, and probably close to a third of Alexandria's – started to loot the city, killing, raping and enslaving thousands of civilians, and destroying the libraries and mosques. The Crusaders returned at night to their ships, but continued to ransack the city for three devastating days. As the Mamluks sent the commander of the Egyptian army to fight the Crusaders on land, Peter was advised that he did not have the resources to battle or run the city, so on 15 October he retreated with the proceeds of his looting, including 5,000 prisoners. It was even purported, in his own propaganda, that the king was the last man to board the final departing ship. As they left for Cyprus, the loot was so heavy that some of it was dumped into the sea to prevent the ships from sinking. For the Alexandrians, that the city was freed so soon after an invasion was something of a miracle.

In an unprovoked attack, Peter I had ravaged Alexandria and killed at least 4,000 of its citizens. There would be consequences. It might have seemed like a victory in the short-term, but in the longer term its costs would be felt. Christians in the Mamluk lands were bound to suffer. Across the Sultanate, some were imprisoned, taxes were raised especially for Christians and, closer to home, they were ostracised by their neighbours. Christians who wanted to go on pilgrimage to the Holy Land were no longer welcome to do so or to travel via cities like Alexandria. More significantly, the Mamluks suspended trade with the Christian West in light of these events. European investors with outposts in Alexandria could no longer access their warehouses or businesses, most of which were ransacked or torched.

Al-Nuwayri's account labels Peter I as 'the cursed, the scornful dog' and is full of prayers that he may live out a terrible life and suffer eternally in hell. It also criticises the Cypriots for their odd habits, such as eating alone rather than communally.[4] While eyewitness accounts of Alexandrian historians lambasted this event, particularly the 72 hours of terror, Peter I was venerated around Europe for daring to attack the momentous city, even if he couldn't capture it. In 1369, Peter was assassinated by his own knights while in his palace bed, but before then two of the period's most promi-nent poets were inclined to praise his sacking of Alexandria. A letter sent by contemporary Italian sonneteer Petrarch to the humanist Giovanni Boccaccio lauds this crusade but laments the soldiers, whose greed was greater than their piety, for not holding onto Alexandria. The French poet and composer Machaut's *Prise d'Alexandrie* presents the Cypriot king as a chivalric hero. And twenty years later, Geoffrey Chaucer confirmed how important this attempt on Alexandria remained to the Christian populations of Europe. In *The Canterbury Tales*, the Monk lists 'worthy' Peter I as one of his heroes because he took 'Alisaundre . . . by heigh maistrye' (2392), great mastery or force. More strikingly, the opening lines of *The Canterbury Tales* introduce readers to Chaucer's first protago-nist: 'A KNIGHT ther was, and that a worthy man . . . At Alisaundre he was whan it was wonne' (43, 51).[5]

In Alexandria, this frantic fourteenth century – its recurring earthquakes, ravaging pandemic and destructive crusade – resulted in a sharp population drop that would severely impact the agricul-tural and trade activities of a city well on the road to decline.

Ottomans

The plagued fourteenth century was followed by the three quietest centuries in Alexandria's history, with drastic changes to the trade routes, immigration patterns and power dynamics that had long placed the city at the centre of the world. For the first time, the vast city was beginning its decline into a mere town.

By 1400, Egypt's population was two-thirds the size it had been before the Black Death. Public records indicate that there were 12,000 weavers in Alexandria in 1295; with the majority of the city working either on the port or in handicraft, we can estimate a population of up to 100,000 for much of the fourteenth century. By 1434, however, there were only 800 weavers, suggesting a decline in work opportunities coupled with a sharp drop in the overall population. An Italian-Jewish businessman, Meshullam of Volterra, records that he found only 60 Jewish families in Alexandria in 1481, and that the older Alexandrian Jews told him that they remembered there being 4,000 Jews. This was a similar story to Rome's, whose population had also declined into the tens of thousands, with Cairo and Milan now housing hundreds of thousands instead.

The fifteenth century didn't begin well either, as the Mamluk Sultan Barsbay ordered Alexandria's tax revenues to go straight to his personal rather than the imperial treasury. In 1429, he went on to send imported and exported spices through Cairo before Alexandria, ending the direct transportation of spices between Alexandria and the Red Sea and cutting their profit. But one of the Sultan's decisions would make a most unexpected impact on Alexandria: his purchase of a slave called Qaitbay.

Qaitbay was born in Circassia, today around southern Russia, just east of the Black Sea. The teenage Qaitbay displayed skills in cavalry and archery that caught the unwanted attention of a slave dealer. Before he knew it, Qaitbay was in Egypt, sold to none other than the Sultan – for 50 dinars (roughly £10,000). Qaitbay began a new life as a palace guard, but within months the Sultan was dead and his slaves became state property. The successor freed Qaitbay, who swiftly began his ascent from commander of ten Mamluk knights to commander of a thousand. Qaitbay became popular with the Mamluk hierarchy, taking on various roles that included bringing the Sultan's medicines to him, a highly trusted position. At around the age of fifty, three decades after he had been enslaved, Qaitbay was announced as the commander-in-chief of the entire Mamluk army. The slave who had been purchased for 50 dinars had also amassed a huge personal fortune.

Unhappy with how quickly Mamluk sultans were changing and the increasing power of their advisers, the new army chief decided to surround the palace with his troops and take control. Qaitbay, it's said, argued that he did not want to be Sultan himself, but was convinced to take the role in early 1468. Once ordained, he didn't let go, ruling for almost three decades.

Qaitbay was faced with two immediate dangers. First, the pirates of Catalonia were terrorising the Mediterranean, attacking ships heading to and from Alexandria. Second, the Turkish Empire, which started in 1299 as a small municipality under a man named Osman Ghazi, had conquered Anatolia, the Balkans and Greece. Now known as the Ottomans, they were fast becoming the strongest force in the world. In 1453, their young sultan Mehmed the Conqueror captured the Byzantine capital of Constantinople (soon Istanbul), a key moment that alongside the arrival of Europeans in the Americas a few decades later signalled an end to the Middle Ages. The demise of the Eastern Roman Empire also confirmed the rising dominance of Islam. Alexandria remained a curious place: it was diverse and had a complicated history to which different groups laid claim. Nonetheless, yet another empire was now looking to Egypt and it was only a matter of time before the Ottomans would come for Alexandria.

Needing to control the pirates and wary of an attack from the Turks, in 1477 Sultan Qaitbay built a fort on the narrow peninsula of the Pharos island. He also placed a long metal chain around the perimeter of the eastern harbour to prevent ships from entering without permission; that area is now called al-Silsila (the Chain). Today, the Citadel of Qaitbay is the most recognisable feature of Alexandria's skyline, visible from every angle of the Corniche. Its many rooms housed thousands of soldiers. Its outer walls, which provide wonderful views of the harbours and city, include semi-circular towers. The main square tower has three floors: a mosque on the lowest, with passages and rooms on the top two. At the citadel, some of the remains of the Pharos Lighthouse can be seen. By building his citadel on the foundations of the great lighthouse, Qaitbay may have agonisingly removed the final remains of the Ancient Wonder. But he remains popular for his architectural accomplishments in the three holy cities of Islam: Jerusalem (the Fountain of Qaitbay in the Temple Mount), Mecca (the Gate of Qaitbay at the grand mosque) and Medina (restoring the Tomb of Prophet Muhammad after fire). In fact, Alexandria's infrastructure, including its economic apparatus and architectural design, was so unimaginably far ahead of cities towards the Arabian peninsula that when Qaitbay went on pilgrimage, he was dumbfounded by the austerity and poverty in Mecca and Medina, which led him to such acts of patronage.

Meshullam of Volterra provides one of the earliest accounts of the citadel in 1481: 'When you enter Alexandria, you find a fort beautiful with twenty-two turrets and a wall ten cubits thick between turret and turret and surrounding them like a crown on one side of the city.' He adds that Alexandria 'is well built and the city walls are high and fine, but all the city is very dry and it has more ruins than buildings'. He continues: 'The houses are beautiful, and in each house you will find a courtyard paved with white stones and with a tree and in the middle a cistern. Each house has two cisterns, one for new water and one for old water.'[1] Meshullam was delighted to see a handsome manuscript of the Hebrew Bible in Alexandria, but was disappointed to find few fellow Jews in the city. This would change later in Sultan Qaitbay's reign. After recapturing the Iberian peninsula, the Catholic monarchs of Spain were unhappy with the number of Jews there; the Muslims had previously given these Jews protected status. In 1492, the Alhambra Decree, also known as the Edict of Expulsion, ordered the eviction of all practising Jews from Spanish lands. As a result, thousands of Jews crossed the water to Alexandria, recovering their population.

Qaitbay's most profound impact remained architectural; he even created a governmental Head of Edifices role. Many more mosques appeared: most of those built in Alexandria before the fifteenth century reused columns and capitals from Roman buildings, with some of the capitals used in Cairo's mosques, too. Qaitbay also led effective economic policies. The sons of the Mamluks had long received salaries for their service to the army, but like any aristocracy they abused it, not serving in the army but still receiving hefty salaries. Qaitbay tested each of them in archery and those who failed saw their salary cut off and were forced to fund the salary of a new soldier. Qaitbay also subsidised food and ordered public punishments for bakers and grocers who charged too much.

Qaitbay was ultimately too popular, stable and powerful to be attacked. But when he died in 1496, a five-year battle for succession signalled the downhill trajectory of the Mamluks. Only two more Mamluks would autonomously rule Egypt. The Ottomans, knowing better than to attack by sea, instead crossed Sinai, seizing Cairo in 1517 to bring an end to the Mamluk Sultanate, before moving northwards to Alexandria via land.

As the sixteenth century progressed, the known world was expanding. European travellers were making their way to distant lands.

Claudius Ptolemy's *Geography* was translated into Latin in 1409, its first edition distributed in 1472 as the printing press took off. After more than a millennium, Europeans finally had access to maps that detailed the earth as they'd never seen it and outlandishly claimed that the earth was round. It became a bestseller, and among its readers was a young Christopher Columbus. Around a decade later, in his early thirties, Columbus was pitching his proposed voyage to the monarchs of Europe. Claudius Ptolemy's work in second-century Alexandria fired Columbus' imagination and inspired him to explore the world. In the 1490s, Columbus reached the Americas – though he insisted he was in Asia.

At that time, another explorer, the Portuguese Vasco da Gama, actually did arrive in Asia, the first to reach India by sea in the longest ocean voyage that had ever been recorded. In third-century BCE Alexandria, Eratosthenes realised that it was possible to sail all the way around Africa. Da Gama survived this dangerous southern sea route to India, known as the Cape Route, going around Africa and back up the Indian Ocean. In doing so, Alexandria's unique claim to linking East and West began to diminish. Europeans could finally avoid the Mediterranean and the Arabian peninsula, bringing an end to the trade routes controlled by the Ottomans since the capture of Constantinople and allowing the Europeans to trade independently of the Muslims. Egypt swiftly lost its monopoly on the spice trade and Alexandria's importance as a connecting port city immediately started to shrink, its trade beginning an irreparable decline.

The Ottomans were forced to retain the Mamluks as Egypt's ruling class, but Egypt's leader, to whom they pledged allegiance, was now an Ottoman governor. In reality, the Mamluks still had arguably as much influence over Egypt as the Ottomans and at certain points in the seventeenth century even became de facto rulers. Alexandria certainly maintained some Mamluk culture and their soldiers continued to operate.

The city was not a priority for the Ottomans. It became an isolated place, with Rosetta, that little bit closer to Turkey, Cyprus and Cairo, replacing it as the key port in Egypt. As soon as they took control of Egypt, the Ottomans silted up the canal connecting Alexandria and Rosetta. The Heptastadion with which Alexander connected the city and Pharos island was surrounded by silt and soil, so the Ottomans began to build on this isthmus, which gradually widened. During the construction process, many artefacts were lost. By expanding and constructing on the Heptastadion, the Ottomans relocated the town centre to this neck of land. The Alexandrians who chose to stay began to gravitate to this pristine, breezy area (today the Ras el-Tin quarter). The older, larger part of the city started to empty until it became dangerous, crime-ridden Bedouin ground. The famines that followed, most notably in 1619, desolated these outskirts further, though Alexandria fared better than the countryside and even Cairo thanks to its fishing culture. As usual, the famine was followed by a plague which led to thousands more deaths.

When English travellers visited Alexandria in the late 1500s, they were far from impressed. In 1577, John Foxe saw convicts employed as galley slaves, rowing boats into Alexandria's harbour during strong winds, 'every prisoner being most grievously laden with irons on their legs, to their great pain'.[2] John Evesham, who was in Alexandria in 1586, wrote: 'The said city of Alexandria is an old thing decayed or ruinated, having been a fair and great city.' He adds that fresh 'water cometh thither but once every year', whereas 'in a town called Rossetto, it doth come ... with such abundance'. Evesham spots 'Turks, Moors, and Jews' in Alexandria, suggesting that the Ottoman, Maghrebi and Jewish populations were distinctly visible. He adds that 'the town' – not city – exists 'along the water-side pleasantly'.[3]

In the 1590s Richard Hakluyt, a priest who promoted English colonialism in North America, published his *Principal Navigations, Voyages, Traffics and Discoveries of the English Nation*, and introduced Alexandria as 'a haven town', one that welcomes foreigners.[4] We also know from the English merchant Sir Lewes Roberts' book a few decades later, *The Merchant's Mappe of Commerce*, that despite the challenges, the 'principal' port on the 'Mediterranean Sea is Alexandria', which he describes in his 1638 publication as 'a free port for friend or enemy; the harbour commanded by a Castle, and the entrance guided by an eminent watch-tower to give light to sail-ors'. The description of Alexandria as a 'free port' is intriguing: it does not indicate a tax-free zone, but, rather, that anyone and every-one is welcome to trade in Alexandria. 'Alexandria, built by Alexander the Great ... the most eminent Seaport of all Egypt ... before the discovery of the Indies was the Scale [i.e. centre of trade] of all those commodities', Roberts adds. He also indicates that it was 'most frequented by the Venetians, who had almost the sole trade of the commodities of India and Egypt in their own hands, and from them dispersed and transported through Europe, and who to this day yet keep a Consul there for the protection of their Merchants'.[5] England followed suit in 1583: in the name of Queen Elizabeth I, a 'Consul for the English nation in Alexandria, Cairo, and other places of Egypt' was appointed.[6]

Answering to Istanbul and only on duty for short periods, the Ottoman governors struggled to maintain Alexandria. As the oldest inhabitants, Alexandria's Jews saw an opportunity to operate as middle-men with the Venetians, selling the goods on to the merchants in Cairo for further profit. The Ottomans responded to this inflation by allow-ing Venetians access all the way to Cairo. Jews nonetheless remained in charge of tax collection at the port. When, towards the end of the sixteenth century, the Ottoman governor ordered foreign merchants to pay a lump-sum tax or leave Cairo, all the European consuls made a collective decision to go to Alexandria, signalling that it was not under absolute Ottoman control and remained a safe haven for diverse groups. From this point on, Europeans preferred to stay in Alexandria rather than Cairo. The Venetian consul became an influential figure in Alexandria, just as important as the Ottoman governor. Venetians had long enjoyed revenue-based tax rates in Alexandria, so when the Ottomans changed this to a value-based tax of 20 per cent on arrival, trade plummeted further. Roberts tells us that there were two taxes of around 10 per cent, one for the Sultan and one for the city, and a 1.5 per cent tax on cash:

> the customs of which place is formed by Jews . . . all goods entering here pays the custom in species [i.e. in kind], or compounded for at 10 in the hundred, only moneys entering pay but one and half per cent: but outward all commodities pays 11 per cent. but this is to be accounted the Sultan's custom, and called the great custom: the other customs raised here is as much[.]⁷

As for the Christian population, while they weren't thrilled about Ottoman rule, they had more of an issue with Catholicism. With Catholics increasingly powerful and proselytising their ideas to Orthodox Christians around the region, the Alexandrian Church was severely weakened and under threat. In the early seventeenth century, Alexandria's Pope Cyril III was particularly active in its defence, communicating and publishing anti-Catholic polemics and even attempting to introduce Protestant ideas that were ultimately rejected. More than a thousand years earlier, as we have seen, Alexandria's Christian scholars had combined the Old Testament and New Testament into a single, authoritative manuscript, the Codex Alexandrinus. After feuding with both the Catholics and

Ottomans, Cyril III escaped Alexandria in the 1620s, taking this manuscript with him. He went on to give it to the most anti-Catholic and Bible-obsessed monarch, King James I.

With neighbouring cities getting more business, in 1628 Alexandria was for the first time declared an actual free port void of customs for traders no matter where they came from. The Egyptian population had more goods to choose from and the competition caused prices to plummet. But this wasn't as successful an economic policy as expected. The comparatively more expensive Venetian exports were priced out of the Egyptian market, so the state of Venice decided to protect only the convoys heading for Syria, meaning that Alexandria had lost its most important trade partner. The free port appears to have lasted only a few years. By the seventeenth century, even Venetian commerce had died down because the Portuguese and Dutch were dominating the spice trade via the sea. As a result, Alexandrian and Venetian trade became much more basic: staple foods, salted fish, linen and art. And many Venetian merchants living in Venice and Greece decided that if trade was to be predominantly local, it was a better idea to move to Alexandria instead. They were followed by some French and English merchants, too.

On the bright side, Alexandria was a hub for two new and exciting trends. The magical coffee bean arrived in the early sixteenth century, half a decade before Italy and more than a century before England and the Americas received it. It was shortly followed by the tobacco plant.

The coffee bean was found in the Abyssinian Highlands and began to be exported to the Yemeni town of Mocha. There, it helped Sufis make their mystical worship more focused and intense; thanks to coffee, they could chant God's name long into the night. With its strong Sufi tradition and connections, coffee quickly found its way into Alexandria. Coffee houses began to open, especially around the religious sites and monasteries.

The new craze didn't go unnoticed. In 1511, the Mamluks tried to ban coffee and, after they were ousted by the Ottomans, Meccan scholars prohibited the bean because of its intoxicating effect, even issuing a ruling that ships carrying it should be sunk. But Egypt was under the Sultan's jurisdiction and he swiftly overturned the Meccan rulings. As the debate about coffee's legality went on, Alexandrians continued to drink it. Coffee, coffee, everywhere. By the end of the sixteenth century, the debate was pointless. The coffee trade was in full swing, arriving from Yemen to Alexandria before being transported into Europe, and recovering some of the losses caused by the reduced spice trade. By the mid-eighteenth century, coffee became one of Alexandria's key trading commodities, sold especially by Maghrebi merchants who'd developed their own quarter that included the Maghrebi bazaar.

With the Spanish arriving in the Americas, particularly the Caribbean, tobacco was making its way to the Mediterranean, too. Tobacco quickly became popular in the region, an echo of the initial coffee boom and a popular complement to the drink. As one popular verse whose rhyme works as well in English as it does in Arabic contends: 'a coffee without a cigarette, is like a mosque without a minaret.'

In Alexandria, tobacco was initially interesting to physicians; Arabic medical manuals from the end of the sixteenth century discuss its medicinal qualities when applied to bites and burns. But it didn't take long for people to start smoking tobacco in the streets and markets. Within a century, the Ottoman Empire was producing its own tobacco, Alexandria perfectly positioned to welcome shipments from the Ottoman lands of Macedonia and Anatolia, as well as higher quality Persian tobacco.

Smoking was more affordable than drinking coffee. People smoked tobacco – or 'drank smoke' as the verb phrase remains in Arabic – in a small hookah or a pipe. The hookah, known as the nargileh, meaning coconut, was originally made from the plant before glass was introduced. The pipes were made of wood or clay and sold very cheaply. In Alexandria, artisans would have begun to add new styles and colours onto the nargilehs and pipes. Everyone was smoking. Tobacco, tobacco, everywhere. Men, women, even children. Tobacco and coffee consumption weren't solitary activities: they marked a social occasion and became hugely popular among women, who would gather outdoors in numbers to sip and smoke. An early seventeenth-century book by the Egyptian scholar Ibrahim al-Laqqani reports that women should avoid smoking because it is having an adverse effect on their 'plumpness'.[8]

Naturally, tobacco lent itself to even more debates about religious permissibility. Eating hashish, a pastime that arrived as early as the eleventh century, had already been prohibited by religious scholars to no avail and was by the sixteenth century common among the working classes. Some scholars in Egypt now warned that tobacco was a Christian evil, while others argued that it had positive effects on the body. With no precise scriptural evidence, it was difficult to make a clear-cut ruling. From 1611 to 1617, the Ottomans banned tobacco, which seemed to have a positive effect on Egypt's economy. In the 1630s, Sultan Murad IV made smoking tobacco – and in fact drinking coffee – a capital offence in Istanbul, though these laws didn't extend to Alexandria. Seventeenth-century Egypt's unapologetic smoking culture was exemplified by the experience of Abdulghani al-Nabulsi, one of the most respected Muslim theologians of that period: when he travelled from Syria to Egypt in his fifties, he tried smoking and never looked back, even penning a treatise in praise of tobacco.

Whatever the debate around coffee or tobacco, it is clear that Alexandrians were able to enjoy these and other pastimes before many others. Chess, for instance, had arrived after the Islamic conquest of Persia in the seventh century, spreading to Europe in the tenth century. So the people of Alexandria, even if reduced in number, drank coffee and smoked tobacco socially in street gatherings and on their rooftops. The new coffee houses, brimming with the earthy aroma of roasting and brewing beans, became the talk of the town. People conversed and played chess as they sipped the bitter drink, and musicians and dancers began to gravitate to these streets. The ports also played a part in spreading coffee and tobacco around the Western world, where the Catholic Church joined the furore, dubbing coffee 'the devil's cup' before Pope Clement VIII purportedly took a taste and announced that 'it would be a pity to let the infidels have exclusive use of it'. At least three ships continued to berth at Alexandria's harbour daily. But maintaining its position as a place of new marvels seemed always to come at a price. Western Europe was expanding at a startling pace. The new sea routes that seemed initially to reduce Alexandria's importance had initiated a surge of European colonial projects whose leaders began to turn their eyes towards the city.

Napoleon

When in 331 BCE Alexander the Great arrived at the spot that would become Alexandria, it was a mere fishing village opposite an uninhabited little island. Within a century, the city he founded here was one of the biggest on earth, boasting a population in the hundreds of thousands for the next millennium, only beginning its steady decline after the Muslim annexation moved the capital in the seventh century. By the late eighteenth century, it was closer to where it had started: its population, once the highest in the world, was no more than 15,000. Despite the pleasing remnants of grandeur – wide roads in a street grid, city walls, stone buildings, old villas, a towering fort, numerous columns, cisterns, cemeteries – Alexandria was little more than an unimposing fishing town whose only bustle centred around the ports serving the Ottoman trade centres of Istanbul and Izmir. Like everyone else in the empire, Alexandria's residents were involuntarily regarded as Ottoman subjects.

Alexandria had pushed the world into the future, constantly pioneering ideas, inventions and ways of life. This was no longer the case, but events at the turn of the eighteenth century were about to dictate the city's resurgence into a new but externally defined realm of modernity. In Europe, an industrial revolution was creating huge leaps in mechanisation, many of which were based on the ancient findings of Alexandria's Museum, such as Heron of Alexandria's steam engine. As machines took over and manufacturing increased in speed and quantity, so, too, did the urban life of Europe, its population doubling to 200 million in the eighteenth century, and again to 400 million by 1900. Alexandria was Egypt's fifth city by this time, already fading in comparison to Damietta and Rosetta. But even Egypt's capital Cairo couldn't compete with the imperial seat of

Istanbul, let alone Europe's newest powerhouses of Paris and London, or the crowded cities in China, India and Japan further east. Predominantly concerned with making their industrialisation even more effective, the French and British turned their sights on Alexandria. They were about to rekindle its position as a geographical crossroad and commercial hub, though not without drastic consequences for its residents, architecture and economy.

The Industrial Revolution was rapidly changing Western Europe. Much of Europe had split from the Catholic Church during the sixteenth-century Reformation. In the seventeenth century, the English toyed with republicanism, beheaded their monarch, engaged in bitter civil wars and founded a unified Kingdom of Great Britain in 1707. Jealous of the Iberian exploration and expansion of the sixteenth century, both Britain and France also fostered uncompromising imperial goals, and by the seventeenth century they were the two biggest colonial powers. France had already colonised much of the Americas and was expanding into west Africa and India. Britain followed suit, and by capturing Menorca and Gibraltar in the early eighteenth century was able to develop a strong naval and trade base that could also dictate the Mediterranean passage into the Atlantic, helping it expand its territories in the Americas. France and Britain had each founded an East India Company, but in the 1750s Britain consolidated its control over the Indian subcontinent. And in France, a series of revolutions led to the public guillotining of King Louis XVI in 1793 to chants of *liberté, égalité, fraternité*. The French Revolution caused uproar across the European monarchies, who engaged in a decades-long conflict against the newly founded République.

During the first set of battles between 1792 and 1797, the War of the First Coalition, a Corsican in his twenties rose up the ranks of the French army from gunner to commander, masterminding several of the republican campaigns and becoming the most powerful person in France. His name was Napoleon Bonaparte. Short, and with an accent alien to his peers, Napoleon was intrigued by the warriors of antiquity, Alexander the Great and Julius Caesar, and fantasised about finding antiques, owning treasures and creating a legend of his own. As he developed questionable habits, such as looting valuable items from the countries he entered, French royalists warned that this man would soon become a dictator. Napoleon overran much of continental Europe. Among the royal coalition, only Britain avoided collapse, and Napoleon's next target was to invade it. To do so he had to overcome its strong navy. A naval port on the Mediterranean would allow him to prepare and position, as well as limit Britain's access to India. Napoleon kept the destination of his next expedition secret from his troops until the morning of the departure, when he renamed his flagship *L'Orient* and his military *L'Armée d'Orient*. Inspired by the Enlightenment, he brought together a group of 167 *savants*: scientists, engineers and artists whose tasks were to assist the campaign and research the region, in turn helping Napoleon to create a legacy. In 1798, alongside the army and scholars, he began the voyage to Egypt.

The oldest of Napoleon's generals was Jacques Menou, an unpopular, sloppy nobleman of almost fifty whom Napoleon complained didn't know how to put his uniform on properly. Even scruffier than Menou, the general Jean-Baptiste Kléber was of peasant stock and had been an architect before joining the military. And the key admiral, François-Paul Brueys, was one of many in the army who'd fought against the British in the American War of Independence, when the American patriots were joined by the French and Spanish to secure independence from Britain.

Napoleon's plans were sure to hurt Britain so he knew that they would be in hot pursuit. The man tasked with hunting the French fleet down was thirty-nine-year-old Admiral Horatio Nelson. Having joined the navy shortly before becoming a teenager, Nelson was held in high regard both by his superiors and subordinates. The physical scars of his service were clear: he had lost both an eye and an arm. Nelson missed Napoleon at Toulon, giving the French a nine-day head start. Where was Napoleon heading? British intelligence had spotted the French near Sicily and Nelson wrote home to his superiors with a theory about Napoleon's Alexander-like plan for world domination. Napoleon, he deduced, wanted to capture Alexandria but would also send another fleet on the Cape Route towards India. What Nelson did not anticipate was that Napoleon wanted to emulate Alexander more literally. He wanted to get to India the much harder way: by land, via Alexandria.

On 22 June 1798, Nelson was informed by Genoese merchants that Napoleon had invaded Malta a week earlier and left the following day. Nelson's conviction that the French were heading for Alexandria was confirmed. But the inaccuracy (or mistranslation) of the news these merchants shared had a much greater impact on Alexandria's history than they would ever know. Napoleon had only left Malta three days earlier. Nelson, thinking he had reduced Napoleon's head start to six days, set sail for Alexandria at high speed. In the misty distance, Nelson's fleet spotted three ships, confirmed to be French. Nelson made another decision that would again affect Alexandria for ever: he decided not to pursue them. Surely, he thought, the actual French fleet, not merely three ships, was closer to Alexandria. In reality, the entire French fleet was there, but the foggy conditions made them invisible. As the British navy fired guns at regular intervals to keep in close contact with each other in the gloom, Napoleon's fleet must have known they were nearby and continued in silence. The British unknowingly passed the French and arrived at Crete on 25 June, where Nelson decided not to rest in order to continue on to Alexandria. Ironically, Napoleon's next stop wasn't Alexandria, but also Crete; had Nelson stayed there overnight, he would have found the French arriving the next morning.

The British fleet made it to Alexandria's coast on 28 June. To Nelson's confusion, the French were nowhere to be seen. Alexandria was serene, just one warship and some commercial vessels on the bay. When Nelson sent one Captain Hardy into the city to investigate, nobody knew a thing about a French fleet. Alexandria's popular governor, Muhammad Karim, a former shopkeeper born and bred in the city, became suspicious of the British, refusing to allow them to disembark. Nelson headed for Crete the next day to continue what was turning into a wild goose chase across the Mediterranean. In Britain, politicians and press lambasted him for his failure.

The very same day, the French fleet could see the North African coast in the distance. And the next day, 30 June, six weeks after he'd left Toulon, Napoleon finally set his eyes on the erroneously named Pompey's Pillar in the distance. The Alexandrians going about their everyday lives could scarcely believe their eyes as a fleet of 280 ships

approached on the horizon. On 1 July 1798, the French sailed into
Alexandria unopposed. Like Alexander two millennia earlier,
Napoleon had arrived at Pharos.

'The time I spent in Egypt was the most delightful of my life',
Napoleon would go on to write. After all, 'Europe is a molehill . . .
Everything here is worn', he reflected separately, 'tiny Europe has
not enough to offer'. Like many before him, the mixed ambitions
and delusions of General Bonaparte were inspired by none other
than Alexander. A few decades before Napoleon landed in
Alexandria, the French philosophers Montesquieu and Voltaire had
written in praise of Alexander's ventures eastwards, his expansion
of the navy and his ability to found cities like Alexandria. But
Napoleon's assessment of the ancient hero was different. He saw
Alexander as someone who excelled on land, not by sea. He also
learnt from Alexander that it was important to understand the
native people to win their support. 'When Alexander arrived in
Egypt, they ran to him, greeting this great man as a liberator', he
noted. So, every night in his cabin aboard *L'Orient*, Napoleon read
the Quran before shelving it under books about 'Politics'. Napoleon's
outspoken respect for Prophet Muhammad was in stark contrast to
the common French view, typified by Voltaire's disparaging play
Mahomet. All these ideas combined to form Napoleon's 'oriental'
fantasy. The ambition of venturing as far as India, of creating an
empire, founding a new religious cult, adapting to and renovating
the existing culture, absorbing rather than crushing the people – all
this he learnt from Alexander. So it was only fitting that his plan to
conquer the Eastern world, to change the global landscape, would
commence in Alexandria.

'Soldiers,' Napoleon began: 'You are about to undertake a
conquest the effects of which, on civilization and commerce, are
incalculable. The blow you are about to give to England will be the
best aimed, the most sensibly felt, she can receive until the time
arrives when you can give her her death-blow.' He urged his troops
not to 'contradict' the Muslim population's religious customs, but
to 'respect' and 'extend . . . toleration' to them and their mosques as
they do to Jews and their synagogues. Wary of the infamously

shallow and windy Alexandrian harbour, Napoleon's fleet moored some miles away at a nearby fishing village, where the soldiers had to swim to shore before advancing on foot to Alexandria. Napoleon told his troops that they were about to enter a place of historic importance: 'The first town we are about to encounter to was built by Alexander: at every step we shall find great recollections, worthy of exciting the emulation of the French.'[1]

The contemporary Egyptian historian Abdulrahman al-Jabarti's account indicates that the local governor, Karim, immediately sent to Cairo for help. Napoleon's official line was that French merchants were being harassed in Egypt. Karim received a letter from the French telling him not to fear anything, but also threatening retribution if the Alexandrians repelled the incoming troops. He ignored the letter and began what, given his small army and the Ottoman indifference to Alexandria, would only be a futile resistance. With twenty of his Mamluk soldiers, Karim captured French soldiers scouting around the outskirts of the city. Before long, their captain's decapitated head was being paraded around Alexandria. It was a message to the local population that they needed to join the resistance.[2]

By now, the French army was tired, having swum to shore, slept on the sand and marched on Alexandria in the hot sun. They were agonisingly thirsty, longing to enter the city and claim its freshwater. Napoleon split his troops so they could attack Alexandria from different angles behind the city walls, sending General Menou in one direction and General Kléber in another. The French artillery, 170 cannon, began its attack. As they proceeded past the gates, Alexandrians responded with musket fire and hurled stones. Menou was the first to enter but was wounded in the process. Kléber was shot in the head by a musket ball but survived. And as Napoleon himself entered Alexandria around midnight, a bullet shaved his left leg. Soldiers ran in the direction of the firing to find a solitary Alexandrian inside his house, with six muskets pointing out of his window. That man was one of at least 700 Alexandrians killed that day, as the terrified screams of men, women and children echoed across Alexandria.

The French immediately began building several new fortresses. Among these was the Kom el-Dikka fort, fifty metres high to protect them from attacks from the south, named the Fort Crétin after its designer. At the Kom el-Nadura, the hill which replaced the Pharos Lighthouse, the French added another fort, still standing today, named after Napoleon's trusted friend Caffarelli (whose wooden leg led locals to rename it 'Abu-Khashabah', father of wood, or more colloquially, wood man). The French also called the obelisks that had been transferred from a Heliopolis temple to Alexandria in 13 CE Cleopatra's Needles. And the fort built adjacently to the obelisks was named Fort Cleopatra, a reminder that their fascination with Alexandria didn't stop at Alexander, but included the Ptolemaic queen.

Before even setting foot in the city his hero founded, Napoleon had already destroyed and damaged many of its buildings and homes, and killed and terrified its residents. Napoleon had told his troops to respect places of worship, but in reality one the most devastating blows in his siege of Alexandria was the blowing up of the Eliyahu Hanavi Synagogue in order to erect a firing barrier in its place between Fort Crétin and the sea. Alexandria's main synagogue, which had stood strong for almost half a millennium, was reduced to rubble.

More positively, the scientists on the expedition ended up writing and etching a detailed multi-volume *Description de l'Égypte*, the illustrations in which show a desolate Alexandria with crumbling buildings and bare trees. They also estimated its population to be between 8,000 and 15,000, suggesting that much of the civilian population joined the initial resistance to Napoleon's 50,000 troops and many lost their lives.

As they walked through the streets, surrounded by packs of barking stray dogs, Napoleon's army realised that Alexandria wasn't quite what he'd billed it to be. The diary of a French captain notes: 'Alexandria, which from far away looked a superb city was now little more than a heap of ruins.' He goes on to describe an 'unhappy city', whose residents look ill and impoverished, a high proportion of them with diseased eyes and some blind.[3] Another Frenchman describes the surprise of going to the market, where he found 'sheep, pigeons, smoking tobacco, and above all many barbers, who put the customer's head between their knees' and look more like they're about to chop off the head than shave it. He 'saw many women' wearing 'long clothes that completely hide their shapes, and which leave only their eyes uncovered'.[4] The troops also found venues at which women, wearing much less, danced enchantingly into the night. They were introduced to hashish, which had been used for at least seven hundred years in Alexandria, and which they took back to France with them. Soon, the drug would take Paris by storm, embraced in the literary salons of Paris by the likes of Victor Hugo, Théophile Gautier and Charles Baudelaire.

Alexandria's leaders escaped to the Qaitbay Citadel, but with their ammunition exhausted, Napoleon had won. After being captured, Karim was surprised to learn that he would in fact continue to govern Alexandria. This fitted Napoleon's grand plan of restoring the peace and pulling the strings. He began remapping the city: excavating the canal, opening offices, hospitals and barracks, and knowing that his troops couldn't live without drinking, ordered the production of wine. Napoleon also made the ridiculous promise that any Frenchman who died working in Alexandria would have his name engraved on the millennia-old Pompey's Pillar. As for Alexandrians, they were now to pay money into the French exchequer to raise local currency. They were ordered to hand in their weapons, with judges and imams excepted. Even their clothes were altered: the French tricolour had to be included, either as a rosette on one's headgear or for the judges and imams as a sash across the body. The judges were also assured that the judicial system would not change.

From one of the French ships, a device was transported that would introduce printing to Egypt. Alexandria had previously pioneered the production and distribution of books, but had fallen behind China and Europe. A printing press, Imprimerie Nationale, was established in Alexandria, and its first task was to mass-produce Napoleon's address to the nation that began, like Prophet Muhammad's letter to Alexandria in the past, 'In the name of God, the Most Gracious, the Most Merciful':

People of Egypt: they may say to you that I have only come here to destroy your religion. This is an outright lie, so believe it not. Tell the slanderers that I have come to restore your rights, punish your usurpers, and that I venerate, more than do the Mamluks, God, his prophet and the Quran. Tell them that all people are equal before God and that wisdom, talents and virtues alone make the difference between them. And what are the virtues that distinguish the Mamluks, that entitle them exclusively to the best and most pleasant of life? If Egypt is their farm, let them show their lease that God has given them. But the God of all is merciful and just, and He has ordained that the Empire of the Mamluks shall come to an end . . . Thrice happy will be those who side with us! They shall prosper in their fortune and their rank. Happy are those who will be neutral! They shall have time to get to know us, and will side with us. But woe, thrice woe, to those who will arm for the Mamluks and fight against us! For them there shall be no hope; they shall perish.[5]

Across Alexandria, Napoleon's proclamation – in French, the local and liturgical language of Arabic, and the now official language of Turkish – was pinned to doors and trees, and shouted by street criers. Napoleon made a point of living up to his word. According to an eyewitness, when 'a soldier was brought [to Napoleon] who had raised a dagger to a peaceful Arab; the fact was verified in an instant, the soldier was shot on the spot'.[6] As Napoleon looked towards his next destination, Cairo, the governor Karim was informed that General Kléber would become Alexandria's co-leader. On 7 July 1798, about a week after he'd arrived, Napoleon left Alexandria.

Napoleon continued to build his image as a heroic fighter, tactician and philosopher. In France, his Egyptian expedition was making him more popular. His deeds were now being recorded in writings and paintings. It is rumoured that in an attempt to emulate what he heard about Alexander, Napoleon had his only homosexual encounter in Egypt, though this has never been confirmed.[7] Napoleon had wanted to bring his wife Josephine to Alexandria, but it's said that she wept all the way from Paris to Toulon. The real reason she didn't want to travel is because she wanted to stay close to her lover and enjoy the affair even more in her husband's absence. Napoleon had assumed Josephine's infidelities were over. Arriving in Alexandria, he was told that the woman he had waved off from *L'Orient* was still being unfaithful. He was livid, and as he wrestled with his campaign, Napoleon was also thinking about what he'd do about this when he returned to France.

The French soldiers weren't allowed to bring their partners with them. But many defied this rule, dressing their wives and mistresses as men in order to board the ships. Perhaps it was an unwritten rule that the women should be allowed onboard since it's hard to imagine them not being spotted on a voyage that took almost two months. The most notable stowaway was a twenty-year-old named Pauline Bellisle, who'd recently adopted her husband's surname Fourès. Pauline's honeymoon had been cut short when her husband, a cavalryman, was called up. Refusing to part from one another, Pauline's skill as a hatmaker came in handy as she disguised herself as a member of the light cavalry and boarded a transport ship. Alongside dozens of other women, Pauline ended up walking the streets of Alexandria – not in disguise but in one of the wavy dresses she had packed. Described as petite in height but a little plump, Pauline had a delightful smile and a perfectly centred brunette fringe that mesmerised the French troops. Her husband could hardly believe the power of her charm: it was getting him invited to high-ranking parties. When Napoleon noticed her, he asked for a dance. He complimented the hat she was wearing and her hair. Pauline refused Napoleon's initial advances. He persisted, ordering his henchmen to court her on his behalf and flattering her with gifts. Finally, Napoleon ordered that her husband be sent as a courier to Paris. That very night, Napoleon dined with Pauline, and when water spilled onto her dress it was the perfect opportunity for Napoleon to offer to help her in his quarters. The pair disappeared into his bedroom.

Her husband's ship had, meanwhile, been intercepted by the British, who were confused as to why he was delivering such old and useless letters to Paris. Surely, he was carrying a verbal report, which they tried to get out of him. When the British gave up, they set him ashore near Alexandria. His wife was now Napoleon's mistress. The young woman who during her honeymoon had disguised herself as a man and headed for Alexandria became known as 'Napoleon's Cleopatra'.

Napoleon's scientific delegation was exploring Alexandria – and taking whatever antiques they pleased. The most famous of these was a stone bilingually carved with Ptolemaic decrees from the time of Ptolemy V. The slab had been reused as part of the masonry for a fort near Rosetta, just east of Alexandria, so it was named after the area where the French had stumbled upon it. The Rosetta Stone's content was in both Egyptian and Greek, so it would soon provide a ground-breaking development in the deciphering of the ancient Egyptian language.

The French also heard a local legend about the tomb of Alexander the Great, which was thought to be in the courtyard of the Attarine Mosque. So geologist Déodat de Dolomieu went there and, sure enough, he found the basin of a large sarcophagus covered in hiero-glyphics. With twelve plug-holes drilled around its base, it had obvi-ously taken on the more practical purpose of storing water for use during pre-prayer ablutions in the yard. Dolomieu had found Alexander; Napoleon had done it. *Vive la France!* Locating Alexander's sarcophagus really appeared to be as simple as following up on a single local legend. It wouldn't take long to disprove any sure link between the sarcophagus and Alexander's resting place, but for now the French expedition delighted in finding one of the world's most important and elusive tombs, storing the casket with the other arte-facts that would be shipped to France.

Alexandria was full of French soldiers, now filling the public baths; not bathing, but doing their laundry. New arrivals also began causing trouble, with locals complaining that the Frenchmen were not respecting their mosques, were drinking alcohol and were engaging inappropriately with local women. The sailors, for their part, felt that they didn't need to obey Napoleon because they weren't in the army proper. But their bad behaviour became so pronounced that Kléber ended their shore leave privileges so they were no longer allowed to spend time off duty in the city.

Although the Bedouin chiefs around Alexandria agreed to help Napoleon, news from Cairo's chief imam arrived confirming that the French were an enemy against whom Muslims should fight. Despite the challenge, Napoleon was able to march towards Cairo, where the Mamluk leaders Ibrahim Bey and Murad Bey – two Georgians who had been sold as slaves earlier in their lives – put up an unsuccessful fight. But Napoleon's soldiers struggled with diarrhoea and fly stings and many developed ophthalmia, blaming Alexandria, where they'd noticed residents with similar symptoms of itchy or red eyes.

On the Mediterranean, Nelson had spent the whole month trying to find the French fleets that had somehow evaded him. As he sailed towards Cyprus, he decided to give Alexandria one more try. As the British approached Alexandria, they stumbled upon a ship flying the French flag. It was a merchant vessel, but its crew were able to confirm that Napoleon had indeed gone to Alexandria. Nelson hurried to Alexandria's harbour, but for a second time there wasn't a single French ship to be seen. Nelson left again, reportedly suffering a nervous breakdown from this seemingly endless search. Then, on 1 August 1798, just a dozen or so miles east along the coast, he happened upon the unmistakable French fleet.

Knowing that the British would be in close pursuit, before Napoleon departed he had ordered the fleet to shift to the less shallow coast of Abu-Qir Bay (named in honour of the fourth-century local physician turned saint, Father Cyrus). They moved to the bay, around ten miles north-east of Alexandria, where the ancient towns of Canopus, Heracleion and Menouthis lay submerged beneath the waters. There, a major sea battle ensued between Nelson's British Royal Navy and Brueys' French Republic Navy. Refusing to waste any more time, Nelson decided to attack the French, who'd anchored in a defensive position. The British ships split into two groups. One approached the French from the seaward side, the other passed between the anchored French ships and the shore and turned to face the sea. The French ships were thus trapped from both sides and, caught in the crossfire, thousands were killed and most of the ships destroyed including *L'Orient*, which exploded after engaging with HMS *Alexander*, the British ship named after Alexander the Great. Fire rose from the French ships. Debris from masts and boats littered the bay, but most of all, hundreds of bodies quickly began to decompose in the heat of the sun.

Nelson's decisive attack and subsequent victory proved that Napoleon's forces were far from invincible. In the city of Mansoura, an angry local populace chased the French army out of a place they thought they'd secured. In Cairo, a local uprising saw Egyptians attacking any Frenchman they encountered; Napoleon responded by placing cannons in the citadels and firing them. Nelson remained at Abu-Qir and occupied Abu-Qir Island, a couple of miles from the coast and around ten miles from Alexandria. In Alexander's time, a narrow piece of land connected it to the coast, but it had now become a tiny island. It was Nelson, not Napoleon, who ended up emulating Alexander: he renamed the place Nelson's Island – or so he thought, Alexandrians today call it Greisha Island, after the durum wheat that grows on it. The ancient Egyptians had called this the Town of the Dead because it had no access to freshwater, so it was used as a cemetery. But excavators looking for Egyptian or Ptolemaic traces in 2000 instead stumbled on the remains of officers and sailors from the Battle of Abu-Qir Bay. The bodies included three infants in wooden coffins, two stillborn and one who died a few months after birth. Next to one of them, in a box marked with the letter G, is the body of a woman dressed in white, possibly but not necessarily the mother. As soon as the coffin was opened, trapped gases escaped to ominously transform her dress from white to black. There are records of at least three British women dying at Abu-Qir, and four women being aboard HMS *Goliath*, a ship whose name begins with the letter G. One of Nelson's sailors writes that on that ship, a woman from Edinburgh 'bore a son in the heat of the action'. Another woman, from Leith, was injured while operating the guns, dying of her wounds before being 'buried on a small island in the bay'.[8] The corpse, probably that of a Scottish woman and found just east of Alexandria two centuries after the battle, proves that women played a part in Nelson's Royal Navy.

Napoleon continued to the Levant, and after some initial success, events culminated in Acre, where the British, led by Admiral Sidney Smith, helped the Ottomans to secure their city. Napoleon's plague-stricken army retreated during the night, reportedly euthanising the suffering soldiers. After four months away, as the spring of 1799 drew to a close, Napoleon was back in Egypt, putting on a victory parade as he marched into Cairo, soldiers waving palm branches around him. But news quickly arrived that an Ottoman army of at least 9,000 was hovering around Alexandria in a fleet of 100 ships, both Ottoman and British. Its leader, Mustafa Pasha, was an experienced, white-bearded Ottoman commander born in Edirne (today the far north-west of Turkey). When they arrived at Abu-Qir, they killed the French troops that were there and replaced the tricolour on the fort with the Ottoman flag (red and green with three yellow crescent moons). Napoleon sprang into action, ordering 1,200 soldiers to protect Alexandria and taking 10,000 towards Abu-Qir. The British helplessly failed to navigate the shallow waters to get closer to the shore, and when the French attacked by land, the Ottomans had only one direction to go: towards the sea. Thousands of Ottomans died, the majority drowning as they tried to escape. The Battle of Abu-Qir was a decisive French victory.

Napoleon returned to Cairo having reconsolidated his power in Egypt. But France was having its own more direct troubles with Britain and the political unrest in Paris meant that there might be an opening in government for Napoleon, or that he could fall out of favour. Besides, venturing eastwards wasn't as straightforward as Napoleon had hoped. In August 1799, leaving Kléber in charge of Egypt, Napoleon travelled to Alexandria on horseback before departing from its harbour towards France.

One of Kléber's first actions was to found Egypt's first Masonic lodge, which he called 'Isis'; the freemasons of Egypt would soon centre around Alexandria. Kléber had never believed in this campaign and attempted to negotiate the departure of the battered French troops as Egyptians rose against his rule. In June 1800, Suleiman al-Halabi, a twenty-three-year-old student from Aleppo, disguised himself as a beggar and stabbed Kléber to death outside his residence. As punishment, the arm al-Halabi used was burnt to the bone and he was executed by horrific anal impalement. In Egypt, al-Halabi was celebrated by many as a nationalist hero. His skull ended up in a French medical school, where it was used to demonstrate a theory (now quashed) about how the details on the skull can indicate mental traits, such as al-Halabi's savagery. Kléber was succeeded by Menou as chief of Egypt. Menou chose a different trajectory, announcing that he was a Muslim, changing his name to Abdullah and marrying a local Egyptian woman, with whom he had a son that, according to contemporary historian al-Jabarti, he called Suleiman, the same name as his predecessor's assassin.

Backed by the Ottomans and British, the Egyptians remobilised against the French, culminating in the Battle of Alexandria in March 1801 (1,831 years after the first Battle of Alexandria, which led to Roman rule and ended the Ptolemaic reign). A British army of 15,000, led by Scotsman Sir Ralph Abercromby, clashed with Menou's army of 12,000 halfway between Alexandria and Abu-Qir. During their siege, the British did something that changed Alexandria's landscape for ever: they ruined the ancient Lake Mariout, the freshwater lake that had attracted Alexander to build a city on this very spot. In the eighteenth century, a storm caused seawater to flood into Abu-Qir a few miles east of Alexandria, creating a new saltwater lake. So when the British army decided to cut the canal, seawater from Lake Abu-Qir rushed into the canals and found its way to Lake Mariout. As a result, Lake Abu-Qir dried up and Lake Mariout would never again supply freshwater. What's more, Alexandria's connection to the Nile was severed.

The British stormed to victory, and Menou retreated with his weakened army to Alexandria to hold out for support from France. Abercromby died in the battle and was replaced by his second-in-command, John Hely-Hutchinson, who in August 1801 marched to Alexandria and forced the French to formally surrender, signing the Capitulation of Alexandria. This document gave the Ottomans and British the French spoils, including the ships on the harbour. By 2 September, the British Siege of Alexandria was complete and the French troops who had survived began making their way home.

The Capitulation of Alexandria signed by both European parties included an article that gave the British control of the Egyptian antiquities collected by the French scholars over the last years. One of these was the Rosetta Stone, though that slab was nowhere near as important as the sarcophagus of Alexander the Great that the French had taken from the Attarine Mosque. The sarcophagus was swiftly shipped to the British Museum, where the Rosetta Stone came in useful as it helped the archaeologists to make sense of the hieroglyphics on the sarcophagus. Disappointingly, it turned out that this tomb was made for the last pharaoh of the 30th Dynasty, Nectanebo II, Egypt's ruler when Alexander was born and attending school under Aristotle. Nectanebo's reign came to an end when the Persians invaded Egypt, with the pharaoh escaping to Nubia in 340 BCE. The fact that Nectanebo went into exile – where little is known of his fate – means that the sarcophagus was never used for its original purpose. Nine years later, Alexandria was founded by Alexander, who'd been welcomed by Egyptians as a liberator from the Persians. When Ptolemy I snatched Alexander's corpse and brought it to Egypt, he needed to place it somewhere suitable, and maybe even hide it. One particular story in the *Alexander Romance*, advocated by the early Ptolemies, suggests why the unused sarcophagus might have been particularly appropriate: when the Persians arrived in Egypt, Nectanebo disguised himself as Amun-Re before sleeping with Olympias, which could have made him Alexander's real father. Reusing sarcophaguses for different people (or in this case as a water vessel) was common – so did Nectanebo's coffin really remain empty, or could Alexander have been placed in it at some stage, thus leading to the local legend? Today, both of these Alexandrian artefacts continue to astonish visitors to the British Museum: the Rosetta Stone is the museum's most visited item but many overlook the fascinating saga of Nectanebo's sarcophagus turned ablution tank. Napoleon's expedition – including the Rosetta Stone and the *Description de l'Égypte* he commissioned – ignited European interest in ancient Egypt, founding the field of European Egyptology and propelling Egypt into the Western imagination. The rise of Egyptomania saw the usage and appropriation of Egyptian ideas and symbols – like hieroglyphics, obelisks and the figure of Cleopatra – in popular culture and architecture.

As the search for Alexander went on, the man who had tried to emulate him had to settle for the title Napoleon I Emperor of the French. In Paris, he showed off the items he had looted in a recently opened museum called the Louvre, which he renamed Musée Napoléon, appointing as director one of the scholars who'd accompanied him to Alexandria. Napoleon continued to attempt geographic expansion but was ultimately defeated by rival Europeans. Towards the end of his life, detained in exile on the Atlantic island of St Helena, he still couldn't let go of the Alexandrian

Dream: 'I should have done better to remain in Egypt; by now I should be emperor of all the East.' In one letter, he reflected: 'After ten years of French administration, the fortification of Alexandria would have been complete; this city would be one of the best fortified spots; its population would be very considerable.' The population, he adds, would have quadrupled as Africans, Arabs and Europeans relocated. The old harbour, canals, Mariout and Nile, would have connected so that there is an 'open' link between the Red Sea and the Mediterranean. This would have uplifted the trade of 'sugar, cotton, rice, indigo' and 'spread civilisation', so that within fifty years everyone could 'enjoy the benefits of the arts, sciences, and the religion of the true God'. To him, Alexandria was central to the European and world narrative, and no matter how much its size had diminished, it remained the gateway to Eastern and African 'enlightenment and happiness'.

Napoleon went as far as stating that 'Alexandria, more so than Rome, Constantinople, Paris, London, Amsterdam; would have been, and was meant to be, the head of the universe'.[9]

But despite Napoleon's grand ambitions to change the world, it was the British – who by virtue of fighting the French – found themselves edging ever closer to Alexandria.

The Father of Egypt

When the French won the Battle of Abu-Qir in 1799, thousands of Ottoman soldiers drowned in the sea, but hundreds managed to swim to safety towards either the neighbouring fort or the British ships nearby. One of these soldiers was a thirty-year-old officer of Albanian descent called Muhammad Ali. He was born to a respected family in Kavala, a small town in the Ottomans' Macedonian province (today in Greece), where his father exported tobacco, the town's most valuable commodity. Ali – an intelligent man, of short stature and with light hazel eyes – rose to become the town's tax collector before joining the volunteer army that went to recover Egypt from Napoleon. Within six years of swimming to safety, Ali would go on to achieve what Napoleon failed to do: become the city's second Alexander.

The French attempts on Alexandria ended in 1801, but 4,500 British troops remained in place. In February 1803, two Britons decided to explore Pompey's Pillar. Using a kite, naval commander John Shortland managed to get ropes over the Pillar before fixing a temporary rope ladder to it. With his friend John White, they climbed to the top, the locals watching with interest below. When they reached the top, the two Johns seem to have thought of the three most British things they could do in celebration: they displayed the Union Jack, drank a toast to King George III and gave three cheers. Exhilarated by the experience, four days later, they did it again, this time better prepared to enjoy the summit, fixing a staff and a weathervane to show their authority, before toasting the king, enjoying a bizarre beefsteak dinner, and if illustrations are anything to go by, exploring Alexandria through a telescope. For the locals, they'd trivialised a historical landmark. But when the men returned home to Portsmouth, the Pillar's erroneous name followed them: they were nicknamed the Pompey Boys and their naval base became known as Pompey, a nickname that the city's football club would also adopt when it was founded in 1898.

The British departed Alexandria in March 1803, leaving the Ottoman general Khurshid Pasha, the Muslim son of a Christian monk, as its governor. But they also left Egypt in a power vacuum. With Napoleon's continued rise in France, a Franco-Ottoman alliance was certainly on the cards. In fact, in May that year, Napoleon sent an official as consul to Alexandria: Bernardino Drovetti arrived by sea and entered the city without anyone really noticing. Meanwhile, the British offered their support for the Mamluks, who still governed the country despite its presence in the Ottoman Empire. The Ottoman forces, including the Albanian mercenaries, were also present. This led to a three-way civil war between the Mamluks, Ottomans and Albanians. When the Ottoman governor of Egypt only paid his Turkish soldiers, ignoring the Albanians, the furious soldiers surrounded the treasury, which the Ottomans quickly fired at with missiles from the rooftops. Under the command of Tahir Pasha, Albanian forces managed to squeeze into Cairo's citadel – built by Saladin some six centuries earlier – through its narrow slitted windows. From there, they attacked the Ottoman forces before seizing the governor's palace. But Tahir's inability to pay the Turkish soldiers meant that within a few weeks he was assassinated. With Cairo's buildings in flames, the Turks and the Albanians were now engaged in serious conflict, with the Mamluks unsure who to support. It is in this context that the regimental commander Muhammad Ali was chosen, in the spring of 1803, to replace Tahir Pasha as commander-in-chief of the Albanians. Ali immediately made a pact with the Mamluks against the Ottomans. In the process, he managed to turn the Mamluks and Ottomans, who had essentially been co-ruling Egypt since the sixteenth century, against each other.

The Mamluks, led by Osman Bey al-Bardisi, and the Albanians, led by Ali, were controlling Cairo. They now started towards Alexandria. After capturing Rosetta, the Ottomans stopped their advance by destroying the walls around Lake Mariout, effectively swamping Alexandria's surroundings like a moat. This also meant it was difficult to leave Alexandria, which was now becoming a danger-ous place, especially its European quarter, where indiscriminate shots were often fired on anyone walking through it. The Corniche area of that quarter was also witnessing regular public executions, and Ottoman soldiers, perhaps of their own accord, were targeting Europeans, with shots fired at the Russian, Spanish and Swedish consulates, their staff escaping to the Ottoman ships on the harbour.

During this time, the British were keeping a close eye on events. The British ambassador, the Scottish Earl of Elgin, negotiated a deal for the Mamluks so they could live in peace and receive generous salaries. So when Ottoman troops mustered near Cairo, Ali was now without Mamluk support and forced to act alone. Ali's army still managed to surround the Ottomans, capturing the soldiers and their supplies.

Meanwhile, the most powerful Mamluk, Muhammad Bey al-Alfi, was Britain's guest in London. He returned to Egypt in 1804 to find that most of the country had turned against him: al-Bardisi, an ally of Ali's, was now the strongest of the Mamluks. With the Mamluks split, Ali made his move, attacking both of their residences as Cairo descended into chaos. Ali decided to bring Alexandria's governor Khurshid Pasha to Cairo as the new governor of Egypt. Why Ali did so is unclear, though he may have been testing the waters with Britain. Khurshid Pasha had initially been appointed by Britain, so maintained ties with the British ambassador, who joined him in a plan to weaken Ali by bringing the Ottoman army branch known as the *deli* – literally meaning 'the lunatics' – into Egypt. This was a big mistake: the former criminals soon began pursuing their own agenda and Ali convinced them to take his side instead. As supplies dwindled and crime increased, the Albanians could make an easy case for change.

To add to the complexities, events on the Arabian peninsula were threatening Ottoman supremacy over the Islamic world. In the mid-eighteenth century, a tribal leader named Muhammad bin Saud made a historic pact with a religious leader named Muhammad ibn Abdul-Wahhab, who preached a puritanical version of Islam. In 1765, Abdulaziz bin Saud took over from his father and with Abdul-Wahhab's support began to expand, capturing the city of Riyadh. The preacher died in 1792 but left behind an army of religious followers ready to support the politics of the Saud family. Shortly after the French departed Alexandria, Abdulaziz led 10,000 followers of Abdul-Wahhab to sack the Ottoman city of Karbala in Iraq. By 1804, the Saud family had captured the two holy cities of Mecca and Medina from the Ottomans. These aggressions and expansions raised alarm bells for the Ottomans. Abdul-Wahhab had justified Saudi politics through religion so it was easy to denounce the decadent nobility running Egypt and to mobilise support against them. In Egypt, Ali was expanding and modernising his disciplined army and the Ottomans realised that having him onside could be the answer to the threat from the peninsula. On 28 May 1805, a ship docked in Alexandria carrying an official correspondence from the Ottoman Sultan in Istanbul. Against the odds, the Ottomans were now supporting Muhammad Ali.

Ali had come out on top – but he still needed to remove the Mamluks and their military regime that had influenced Egypt for centuries. An invitation was sent to the leading Mamluks. On 17 August 1805 the ceremony for the cutting of the dam was to take place. Or so they thought. As the Mamluks entered the citadel, Ali's forces were waiting in ambush and fired from the surrounding rooftops. Ali's rise to power was complete. He had successfully taken over from the Mamluks to become the most powerful person in Egypt.

The Mamluks were weakened but by no means gone. Many of them had fled to the north of Egypt, including Alexandria, where they were safer than in Cairo. They were also given a lifeline by the British, who were now hoping to rule Egypt through the Mamluks and to weaken the Ottomans. This became especially important as Napoleon, now France's emperor, created a formal alliance with the Ottoman Sultan Selim III. So much so, that it triggered another of the Napoleonic Wars, the Anglo-Turkish War, in which the Ottomans, supported by France, squared up against Britain. The events of the last few years had centred around Cairo, but in 1807 the British decided to attack the Ottomans by invading Egypt, starting with Alexandria.

The Aberdonian general Alexander Mackenzie Fraser, who'd previously fought in the American War of Independence, commanded the

Alexandria Expedition. On 13 March 1807, an English ship surprised Alexandria's Albanian garrisons when it arrived at the shore. Another larger gunship came two days later, announcing war against the Ottomans and offering Egypt terms of surrender. Then, on 17 March, 6,000 troops arrived just west of Alexandria.

Supported by the French consul Drovetti, the Albanians began to plan their defence as 700 soldiers sailed through stormy waters, disembarking on 18 March. As they approached the gate at Pompey's Pillar, they were met with barricades and an armed defence line, forcing them to flee. The British decided that their only chance of winning was if they entered the city before the Ottomans managed to send any substantial reinforcements, which were likely to come by sea. So they set out to take the two key citadels of Qaitbay in Alexandria and Abu-Qir further east. The plan seemed to work: as the British ships appeared around the harbour, they received a message that the Alexandrians were not going to fight. The British entered Alexandria unopposed. And any French plans to return faded.

Britain's closest Mamluk ally, al-Alfi, had recently been welcomed in London where he had agreed a deal to support Britain's control of Egypt in exchange for governorship. On arrival, the British were surprised to learn that he was now dead. Meanwhile, Muhammad Ali offered the Mamluks power and money in return for their support. The British had no political backing in Alexandria, let alone Egypt.

Thousands of troops had arrived in Alexandria, but the Royal Navy hadn't sent a full fleet, so supplies were limited. The British army moved towards the nearby town of Rosetta in an attempt to bring supplies to their troops in Alexandria. They entered Rosetta as easily as they had Alexandria. But the silence with which they had been met was a trick: as they walked through its streets, a loud call came from the mosque before gunfire opened up at them from every direction. The local garrison was hiding behind windows and on roofs, and their tactic worked. Leaving hundreds of dead behind, the British hurried back to Alexandria. Determined to capture Rosetta, they returned with 2,500 men and bombarded a stubborn resistance that was refusing to give up. The British advance guard a few miles away warned of an imminent and sizeable reinforcement on its way. The reinforcements sent by Ali, both infantry and cavalry, surrounded and captured the advance guard, forcing the British to withdraw from Rosetta, sailing back to Alexandria. There, influential Mamluks had returned and were also making a claim to power.

For his part, Muhammad Ali, described by contemporaries as Machiavellian, was now trying to find a way of ruling independently of the Ottomans. If he had negotiated with the British, he may have been able to secure that independence. Ali defied Ottoman decrees prohibiting wheat export, giving the British the steady grain supply that their widespread armies required. He also gave Britain safe access to India via Alexandria and released their prisoners of war. Britain was even less sincere than Ali, refusing to recognise his independence officially, but paying him with arms: correspondences show that in one month alone, Ali received a delivery of 8,000 bombs from Britain. With such a deal, Britain's physical presence in Alexandria was not required. With the heads of British soldiers still displayed on stakes around the country, the Mamluks still split about whether to support Britain and with supplies running dangerously low, the British expedition proved unsustainable. On 14 September 1807, Britain signed an agreement to leave. For Ali, he was a hero who had evicted the foreign occupiers. For the British, the Alexandria Expedition was nothing short of a fiasco.

Ali was now ruling Egypt with Ottoman support. He had two key jobs. The first, to remove the Mamluk influence once and for all. So Ali adopted a plan that had worked for him before. He issued the Mamluks with another invitation. On 1 March 1811: a grand ceremony in the citadel. After a warm welcome, coffee, sweets and small talk, the ceremonial procession led the 600 or so Mamluks down a narrow citadel passageway. The gates were slammed shut and from the top of the walls the soldiers fired their muskets without mercy. The Mamluk leaders had been dealt with – all but one, who leapt over the gate to his horse to make a famous escape. And any remaining Mamluks, including families, were killed throughout Egypt. The Mamluks were finished.

Next, Ali could focus on the Saudis: the Ottoman–Saudi War saw Ali's son, Tusun Pasha, recapture Medina, Jeddah and Mecca by January 1813 using his Egyptian army. In 1817, Ali's other son, Ibrahim Pasha, led troops to siege the Saudi capital, Diriyah, arresting their preachers and the ruler Abdullah bin Saud. Ridiculing the Saudi belief that music was evil, the preachers, including Abdul-Wahhab's grandson, and Abdullah bin Saud himself, were forced to listen to guitars and lutes playing before being executed by firing squad. Britain and France both welcomed Ali's decisive victory. Ali was now being recognised by the Sultan as His Highness the Viceroy Muhammad Ali Pasha, the ruler of Egypt. Finally, he could turn his attention to Alexandria.

The Alexandria inherited by Muhammad Ali was no glorious city. The French writer René de Chateaubriand describes his disappointment when he visited in 1806:

> If I may have been enchanted with Egypt, Alexandria seemed to me the saddest and most desolate place on earth. From the top of the terrace of the Consul's house, I saw only the naked sea, which broke on a low shoreline that was even more naked, harbours almost empty . . . Everywhere the new Alexandria mixing its ruins with the ruins of the ancient city; an Arab galloping on a donkey amid the debris; a few skinny dogs devouring carcasses of camels on the beach; the flags of the European consuls floating above their residences, displaying enemy colours amid the tombs: such was the spectacle.[1]

Within a few years, Ali's defiance of the Ottomans meant beginning to export grain again. The decision revitalised Alexandria's harbour. Despite another major challenge, the Ottoman Plague, breaking out in Istanbul in 1812 and reaching Alexandria by sea as early as January 1813, things were better than they might have been. By 1817, Alexandria's newly established Egyptian Board of Health had introduced a quarantine system, a whole two decades before any other city. With the quarantine in place, that year the bustling atmosphere lost for decades finally returned, hammers echoing as new ships were being built, men shouting as they loaded the vessels and sacks of wheat, rice and vegetables lining the shore ready for export. Some 1,092 ships are recorded as having berthed in Alexandria in 1830 – three ships a day as 94 per cent of Egypt's exports left from the city. Some ships also sent young Egyptians to France and Italy, with Ali pioneering a new scheme that sponsored their education abroad. Not everyone welcomed this: some sent their porters' sons instead and Ali responded by ordering those who were rejecting the offer to clean the streets as punishment.

Ali spent four months in Alexandria in 1818, during which time he realised the potential of the city compared to Cairo. By 1822, he was living in Alexandria and had moved the European consulates to the city and re-established it as the unofficial capital of Egypt. To do so, Ali maintained good relations with European countries, including Britain, to whom he gave one of the misleadingly named Cleopatra's Needles for their part in protecting Alexandria from France in 1801. Transporting the obelisk to London was going to cost a huge amount, so the monument remained in Alexandria. Despite arriving in Egypt to fight Napoleon, Ali began to admire him and brought French specialists to rebuild both the city and its military. The British had contaminated Lake Mariout's water, so Ali hired the French engineer Pascal Coste to clear the channels of the ancient canal and create a new, extended canal, forty-five miles long and almost ten feet deep, that started at the Nile in the newly founded town of Mahmudia (named after the Sultan Mahmud II) east of Alexandria, and extended to the city and into the Mediterranean Sea. Building the Mahmudia Canal in just three years and during a plague came at great cost, with many of the 200,000 forced labourers dying. To fund it, Ali took his first major monetary loan from Europe, something he would do again to build his grand residence in the 1830s. The Ras el-Tin Palace was designed by Pietro Avoscani, an Italian in his twenties who'd recently escaped to Alexandria after attempting a nationalist revolt in Italy. The new palace was constructed on the western edge of the peninsula where the island of Pharos once stood. Overlooking the harbour, the palace had a divan for receptions and a harem, where uncounted numbers of concubines lodged.

Thanks to the new canal, Alexandria now had access to fresh river water and ample supplies of food were arriving via steamships. The vineyards surrounding Alexandria recovered and new exotic fruits were introduced, including mangoes, bananas, pineapples and figs. Most importantly, though, the cotton industry sprung to life.

When a French-Swiss engineer saw cotton growing decoratively in palace gardens, he took the idea to Ali, who began cultivating the crop. Cotton became such a priority to Ali that he sent soldiers to work in the plantations during harvest, increasing production from 50,000 kilograms to a staggering eleven million kilograms per year. By 1865, with the American Civil War affecting US production and the Alexandria Cotton Exchange founded, production reached ten times that amount. The long fibres on the cotton created smooth yarns that made Egyptian cotton as famous as Italian olive oil and French wine, and Alexandria's economy was now going to be built around this valuable commodity. As the powerhouse of the country's cotton trade, foreign traders and Egyptian workers began arriving in numbers. And in 1826, the city founded its first chamber of commerce.

By the end of the 1820s, Ali had also overseen the levelling of the surrounding hills and the removal of the outer walls to expand the city, in addition to the construction of a new, larger dockyard. Looking to further develop his army, Ali opened a naval school by the western harbour, starting the first Egyptian fleet, and closer to the city an arsenal to manufacture and store weapons. Both were supervised by French officers, signalling Ali's reliance on the French and how he was modelling his court on theirs, Alexandria on Paris. He was also welcoming visitors to his residence, a long list that included a young Benjamin Disraeli and the French orientalist painter Horace Vernet. The French had taken their printing press back with them, but a new one was established in 1820, as was an elite book club, newspapers in both French and Arabic, a new local postal service (with Italian inscriptions on the stamps) and international postal services (*Poste Francaise* printed stamps in Alexandria for the next century).

Ali's lack of interest in past monuments, as demonstrated by his gift of one of Cleopatra's Needles to Britain, was in stark contrast to his eagerness to build anew. Ali may have imagined that an Egyptian antiquity would inspire people thousands of miles away in London, an ironic thought today, given the expansive and often controversially obtained Egyptian holdings of the British Museum. It has been rumoured that Ali even suggested using already quarried stones from the pyramids to build a dam across the Nile, and that the French engineer Linant de Bellefonds supposedly convinced him otherwise. Materials from ancient constructions had long been used to build new ones, but this event is only ever reported by one person, Linant himself. It is ludicrous to suggest that Ali considered demolishing the pyramids. The engineer, along with British and Italian archaeologists, framed Egyptians as savages unable to care for their heritage while simultaneously setting out to take ancient objects to their home countries. Tomb raider Giovanni Belzoni wrote that his 'purpose . . . was to rob the Egyptians'.[2] The orientalist Jean-François Champollion boasted that he tore an inscription from the wall of a temple before taking it to the Louvre. And British travellers John Gardner Wilkinson and Edward Lane used an ancient tomb to furnish the decor of their own homes, and had no qualms about using ancient mummy cases as cooking fuel. In fact, these new 'Egyptologists' were acting in such a way that Ali introduced a ground-breaking decree in 1835, prohibiting the removal, export and trade of Egyptian antiquities. That the Europeans felt they were entitled to Egyptian antiquities is best exemplified by the London *Morning Post*'s response to the decree: '*A propos* of monopolies: Mehemet Ali, not satisfied with those he has established on the living has lately introduced one also in the kingdom of the dead.'[3]

Ali was making important additions to Alexandria, including the first city square in the modern Middle East, between the new Ottoman town on the peninsula (which now housed a third of the population) and the original town. Designed by Francesco Mancini, the Italian architect charged with heading the city's urban planning, the square was lined with wide roads and trees and surrounded by tall buildings containing shops and apartments. At the cafés, the cotton kings met over coffee to cut their deals. These mall-like buildings boasted European products and the consulates began to move into some apartments, flying their flags in the square that would become known as the Place des Consuls. Around the square, dozens of black horse-drawn carriages waited in line. Lavish hotels appeared, including one that would welcome King Edward VII, then Prince of Wales, in 1868.

A new episcopal church, the Coptic Cathedral of Evangelismos, was built between 1847 and 1856, and signified the diversity of Alexandria's architecture under Ali. The interior was created by an architect from Istanbul, the doors and windows by a Greek designer, the icons made in Alexandria, the windows in Paris, chandeliers from Russia and the clock from London's Frederick Dent, who had recently completed Big Ben. During the very same years, the Catholic St Catherine's Cathedral was also built nearby, but its neo-Baroque façade indicated an Italian influence compared to the Coptic cathedral's mix of neo-Byzantine and neo-Gothic. Ali reserved some land in the prestigious square for the first Anglican church in Egypt, and when St Mark's Anglican Church opened in 1854 it signalled the arrival of a new Christian denomination and a freedom of worship unavailable elsewhere in the region, where Anglicans usually prayed in consular chapels. It also showed architectural assimilation: the British architect James Wild was even criticised in England for betraying the Gothic style, seen as more Christian, in favour of a rounded Byzantine structure with Islamic features. Ali also lifted a ban on the ringing of church bells as Christians and Jews began to return to Alexandria. In 1850, the Eliyahu Hanavi Synagogue, which Napoleon had destroyed, was rebuilt for the Jews of the city, who had also recovered their economic and social prosperity. Much as Apion had spread the rumour that Jews were sacrificing Greeks hundreds of years earlier, Jews across Europe were now being accused of blood libel: killing gentiles and using their blood to bake matzo. Such accusations did occur in Alexandria – one was recorded in 1844 – but thanks to the counsel of high-profile Jewish visitors to Alexandria, Ali dropped these charges. In 1860, construction of another synagogue began, this time funded not by the Ali dynasty but by one of the city's richest families: the Menasces of Alexandria, who'd emigrated to Egypt from Morocco and Palestine and become formidable bankers. Thousands attended the opening of the Menasce Synagogue, including Ottoman officials. The Jewish ambition for the city was evident in the opening of several schools and hospitals, and the establishment of the first Hebrew press in 1862 – one of three to be established in that decade – around the same time as the first private Arabic press, founded in Alexandria in 1873.

With the changing landscape of the city, day-to-day dress began to change, too. In 1829, a mandate from Sultan Mahmud II decreed that all civil, religious and military officials had to adopt the fez, whose colour came from a crimson berry dye. Over the next century, the fez was adopted by everyone from the lower middle to the upper classes. With pocket watches and round-lensed pince-nez spectacles that they held to their faces when reading, men dressed meticulously as they walked the glistening cobbled streets, whether in dark suits or in immaculately pressed traditional *galabeyas*. As visible members of their society, middle-class women began to opt for straight-cut shin-length black dresses, and sometimes wore longer, wavy dresses of lighter colours, with their hair reaching their shoulders. The lower classes covered their hair but not their faces, since they needed to work. But the elite classes wore face veils regardless of their religion.

Those arriving from anywhere in the region, even from Cairo, wondered whether they'd been transported to Europe. Alexandria was something of a Francophone city: at the *fin de siècle*, road names, shop signs and even people's greetings had become French. The look and feel of the place and its people had been transformed. Alexandria was now attracting thousands of emigrants: more than half of residents were from elsewhere in Egypt. Non-Egyptians formed over a tenth of the city, with significant Turkish, Greek, Armenian, Syrian and Italian populations, as well as French, Austro-Hungarian, British and German residents. In fact, non-Arabs and non-Muslims filled the city and palace to such an extent that some sermons began to criticise Ali's leadership, though in a city of thirty mosques, these imams were in the minority and were swiftly exiled. In reality, Alexandria was regaining its tolerant character.

How did metropolitanism dominate an Ottoman city? Alexandria was a special case in which Ottoman and non-Ottoman subjects could enter, well before strict immigration laws, and affiliate themselves to a foreign consulate. A fascinating account, written in 1949 by Alexandrian Eugenie Sinano Horwitz, gives a flavour of this extreme cosmopolitanism: 'My grandfather, of Syrian origin, living in Egypt, with an Italian passport, was consul of Portugal. His brother was consul of Denmark. I never knew what motivated the choice of these countries and led them into the family circles.'[4] These Europeans were born and bred in Alexandria; some had never even seen their countries of origin. Though they could associate with different groups in the city and continue their own cultures, they still did so in their hometown of Alexandria as citizens of Alexandria. In the 1840s, the Greeks were the first to develop their own communities, with the Jews and Italians following suit. These locales included schools, hospitals, theatres and places of worship. Like the Jerusalem Jews in the past, mainland Greeks regarded Alexandrian Greeks, especially the women, as overly liberal. Some communities began to associate themselves with the Greeks and Italians by providing them with services in the hope of avoiding tax. In particular, with Jews from Livorno moving to Alexandria, many of Alexandria's original Jews, especially the higher classes, became adopted Italians. In fact, when in the 1850s news arrived of a fire destroying identification documents at the Livorno city archive, Alexandria's Italians were asked to renew their citizenships in the consulate. Hundreds of Jews went to the Italian consulate claiming to be from Livorno and were granted Italian citizenship.

This did, however, come at the price of polarisation. Alexandria now had two different worlds, one which centred on the European district, known as the Frank quarter (a name for Europeans that had persisted since the Crusades). This quarter, just south of the new Ottoman city, housed around one in eight of Alexandria's residents. Its wider roads were silent in comparison to the bustle elsewhere, with spacious villas and apartments. Here lived around two-thirds of the entire country's non-Egyptians. Like those who came to the Museum in the past, they were exempt from tax and customs. Many had diplomatic immunity, the rest resorted to the consulates for protection. They also had the right to be tried in mixed tribunals, thus avoiding the Egyptian judicial system, especially problematic when they didn't pay rent to a local landlord.

Alexandria also developed a reputation as the place to be for fancy restaurants, casinos, theatres and brothels. There were extravagant soirées and enthralling masquerade balls, complete with seafood and drinks on ice imported from the mountains of Turkey. The Europeans and the local elites mingled into the night, with a constant stream of love affairs providing the most guaranteed point of conversation. The brothels were plentiful and packed. The sensual *sha'bi* (folk) dancers were called *ghawazi*, meaning conquerors, presumably of one's heart. Ali found the folk dancers distasteful so banned them, but he allowed the courtesan dancers, the *awalim*,

meaning the learned, to continue working. The *awalim* were traditionally well versed in poetry and conversation, but could also sing
and dance. Before long, all Alexandria's dancers claimed to be the
legal *awalim*; some danced artfully, others erotically, and many went
further by offering sexual services, too. It was around this time, in
the mid-nineteenth century, that the French developed a new orientalist term for the Egyptian folk dance, *danse du ventre*, or 'belly
dancing'. The city was fast becoming a capital of indulgent sensuality. Rooms could be hired by the hour, and on certain narrow side
streets, men and women were lined up waiting for their clients.

And there was another world in which the locals worked tirelessly as blacksmiths, artisans and merchants. They navigated the
stray dogs hovering around the narrow streets of the Ottoman
quarter – three times as densely populated as the European quarter
– walking through the bazaars and around the coffeehouses with
their camels, mules and donkeys. Europeans dared not enter this
part of town.

Many Egyptians also built small mud huts on the outskirts of the
city, where they lived in extreme poverty and lacked basic amenities in
a city that was modernising exponentially. Foreigners and wealthy
locals owned slaves, both men and women. Contemporary accounts
indicate 'the multitude of negro slaves',[5] the selection of women that
the elites kept in their homes for sex and the constant wail of mourning females in the streets. Alexandrian society was guilty of racist
inequalities, gender violence and high mortality rates among the
lower classes. The working class also suffered most from several chol-
era epidemics, especially in 1831 and 1865. At the peak of the disease,
in the 1830s, 11,000 Alexandrians died over a four-year period.
Thought to have been brought by returning pilgrims from Mecca,
ships sailing from Alexandria were responsible for introducing the
disease to such port towns as Marseilles, Valencia and Southampton.

As he grew older, Ali's health deteriorated, and a few months
after his eightieth birthday in 1849 he died in the Ras el-Tin Palace.
His successors, especially son Said Pasha and grandson Ismail Pasha,
continued the work he had started. Engineering projects carried on
renovating, among other things, the harbour, water supplies and
transport links that had propelled Alexandria back to its former
glory. The trade routes, which included steam trains, were better

than almost anything in Europe. Ali had already made plans for a railway, and in 1854, despite the Ottoman Sultan's objection, the first railway in Africa, the Middle East and the Ottoman Empire connected Alexandria to Rosetta. Where water was encountered, as between Alexandria and Cairo, a rail barge with tracks on it carried the train carriages. That year, 4,000 passengers were transferred across Egypt, in addition to over £6 million of currency. The British, having played a significant part in its construction, were keen to use it for their own trade routes, too. The Royal Navy even sent two warships to Alexandria to assure the Ali dynasty that they had made the right decision despite the Sultanate's opposition.

When Egypt's heir, Muhammad Ali's grandson Ahmad, fell into the river and drowned, a swing bridge was built instead of the rail barge. By 1858, a ground-breaking railway line was connecting Alexandria to Cairo to Suez so that, for the first time in history, there was now a transport link between the Mediterranean and the Indian Ocean. Discussions that Ali had initiated about building a major canal to connect two oceans were also advancing, and the French diplomat Ferdinand de Lesseps received permission to create a company to construct such a canal, with work starting in 1859 and the inauguration of the Suez Canal taking place a decade later. With the railway and canal, Alexander's vision of connecting East and West was being mapped out.

In 1863, getting around Alexandria was transformed as the city's streets were connected by bright orange horse-drawn trams: the first in Africa and the Middle East. Their drivers were mostly Italians, and the ticket inspectors Maltese. Some trams included a black carriage at the very back that served as a hearse, transporting coffins regardless of religion. In 1897, large crowds appeared as the first electric tram whizzed through the city. Today, the trams remain an iconic feature of the city. Women especially enjoyed the increased mobility and a third carriage, reserved solely for them, was soon added to the trams. This symbolised their relative freedom and access to opportunities in Alexandria. By the end of the nineteenth century, the female literacy rate in Alexandria was double that of Cairo, with women's publications also appearing for the first time.

Garden spaces were extended across the city, but at the same time many of the public spaces became private. The Ptolemaic Garden of Eleusis occupied the exact spot on which the Roman ambassador had drawn a circle in the sand around Antiochus in 168 BCE, stopping him from advancing into Alexandria. This garden was enlarged to fifty acres and planted with trees of different varieties. Ismail Pasha, who was given the title Khedive (Persian for Lord), had stayed at Versailles in France, and created a miniature version of the perfectly proportioned Parisian garden in the heart of Alexandria. In 1860, Sir John Antoniadis, a Greek community leader who had co-founded the Bank of Alexandria a few years earlier, purchased the garden and added a mini-Versailles palace designed by a French architect. The Palais d'Antoniadis, which he built as an extension of the originally Ptolemaic Nouzha Park, became the most famous garden estate in the city and a key location for elite parties. It was one of many fanciful palaces and villas to appear around the city in the next half-century.

Architects, predominantly Italian, also reshaped the promenade and the city's squares. The city embraced its wonderful architectural mixture of art deco, beaux arts, neoclassical, neo-Byzantine, neo-pharaonic, neo-Renaissance and even fascist buildings. In 1873, the Place des Consuls became the Place Muhammad Ali as his equestrian statue stood gracefully in the middle, the very first public statue to be erected in a Muslim country. Public unease about the idolatrous nature of statues was put to rest when the Islamic moderniser Muhammad Abduh was asked to issue a ruling that such a sculpture was permissible.

All of these innovations started with the son of an Albanian tobacco merchant who'd left a small Macedonian town to volunteer in the war against Napoleon. Muhammad Ali Pasha was a vivid part of my childhood and for years I sat opposite a huge portrait of him at my Nan Qadria's maisonette every weekend. In the picture, he sits in a gold chair, wearing a traditional black cloak that contrasts markedly with his big white beard, and a red fez to match his red shoes. Nan Qadria was closer to me than all my blood-grandparents put together and visiting her was a highlight of my week. I would have regular, long chats with her about all manner of things into my adult life, right up until her death. Her influence on me was profound. She was constantly reminding me to be a 'gentleman', and, in a way, I couldn't have learnt this from anyone better: she was the great-granddaughter of Muhammad Ali Pasha (her great-grand-mother was one of his nine wives). An aristocrat born and raised in Egypt, Nan Qadria became estranged from her family, living the second half of her life alone and cherishing visits from her adopted family. She always introduced me proudly as her grandson, and on more than one occasion, usually as we sipped tea, she would smile heartily as she explained that blood relations aren't everything, that we shared a special bond that transcended such limitations. In spite of her estrangement, the huge gold-framed oil painting in her living room – which she'd expertly copied from the portrait that Scottish painter Sir David Wilkie was commissioned to paint – was certainly an homage to her bloodline. Besides oil painting, she possessed many fine talents and etiquettes such as elaborate settings for the dinner table, gourmet cooking (I've yet to taste finer homemade food; she would memorably include a single, small piece of coal in the gas oven for flavour), and horse-riding. Her decency and intui-tiveness are exemplified by the fact than when she came to bless my first apartment, she arrived clutching my favourite painting of hers. A parting gift, in some ways, since she never visited again. It hangs in my hallway and is my most cherished possession.

When her great-grandfather died in his beloved Alexandria palace, he was the father of 95 children. Before long, Ali was dubbed the father of modern Egypt. Also called the Lion of Alexandria, he is credited with the renaissance of a city that, under his rule, under-went major modernisation. The increased trade, best exemplified by the surprising cotton rush, confirmed that Ali had created a boom in Alexandria, which was resurrected as a court city and a commercial hub. Beyond doubt, it was a city once again. Its popula-tion increased to 16,000 by 1825, shooting up to 40,000 by 1833, 60,000 by 1840, and in the census of 1848 there were 104,189 resi-dents. The caveat, however, was that only 22.6 per cent of these were original Alexandrians.

British Invasion

The railway line built in 1858 connected the Mediterranean Sea and Indian Ocean for the first time. As Ismail Pasha and his French dignitaries watched the fireworks from his $1 million yacht party in 1869, the inauguration of the Suez Canal, around 250 miles east of Alexandria, marked a significant transformation of how the world connected. The 120-mile canal created a new and direct link between Europe and Asia. It paved the way for more efficient European colonisation of Africa and Asia, enabling easier shipping and storage of goods, which included slaves. The canal's connection of East and West meant that Alexandria's role became less important. Ships could go straight to the canal's opening near Port Said. The British vehemently opposed the new canal. As far as they were concerned, not only had the French beaten them to the building contract, but the very premise gave European countries on the Mediterranean a huge advantage over Britain.

Ismail and his predecessors had also been taking significant amounts from creditors – including Britain, France, the US and two wealthy banking families, the Greek Sursocks and the Jewish Cattauis – to foot the colossal construction bill. Before that, the dynasty had made costly renovations to Egypt, not to mention enjoying a highly extravagant lifestyle. The spending was exorbitant and the borrowing unsustainable. With limited liquidity, gifts could be used as a form of debt repayment.

At this time, Britain finally decided to bring the Cleopatra's Needle that had been gifted to them from Alexandria to London. A surgeon, Sir Erasmus Wilson, agreed to cover the transportation costs, between £10,000 and £15,000 (today £1–1.5 million). Moving a sixty-nine-foot, 200-tonne obelisk across the seas wasn't a straightforward task. So, at the Thames Iron Works in London a flat pontoon boat was designed, essentially a ninety-three-foot iron cylinder into which the obelisk would be slipped. It was sent to Alexandria in sections so that it could be fitted together. There, the cylindrical vessel, which looked like a big cigar on land and a submarine in the water, was named *Cleopatra*. On 21 September 1877, it left Alexandria, towed by the steamship *Olga*. Some three weeks into the journey, a storm in the Bay of Biscay swamped *Cleopatra* and she began rolling uncontrollably. Six of *Olga*'s crew were sent out on a rescue boat, but as they tried to save *Cleopatra* their boat capsized. The *Olga*'s crew managed to navigate closer to *Cleopatra* and in an attempt to rescue their colleagues they cut the towrope, leaving Cleopatra's Needle to drift into the distance. The six men still lost their lives, and the rest of the crew sailed on, certain that they'd never see the obelisk again. Five days after they'd reported its sinking, however, *Cleopatra* was spotted by fishermen off the northern coast of Spain, where it was towed to the port of Ferrol by a Glasgow steamship. After being repaired, and after £2,000 was paid to the demanding Glaswegians, *Cleopatra* was towed to the British Isles. On 16 January 1878, school-children in Gravesend, Kent, were given the day off to witness the obelisk's arrival, before it travelled upriver to Westminster. One of the bronze plaques around its base commemorates the six men who died at sea; another notes that 'this obelisk prostrate for centuries on the sands of Alexandria', gifted by Ali, serves as a memorial to Nelson and Abercromby. As it was being erected, within its pedestal was deposited a time capsule that contained a bizarre range of items: photographs of the twelve most beautiful English women of the time, cigars and pipes, a set of imperial weights, a portrait of Queen Victoria, a bible and a foundational Christian verse from John's Gospel in 215 different languages. On 12 September 1878, a year after it had left Alexandria, and having almost been lost to the stormy waters, Cleopatra's Needle was erected on Victoria Embankment, where today it has managed to blend into the unconscious background of commuters' lives and is much appreciated by pigeons.

Egyptomania was still on the rise, and in the American imagination it served a more important role than in Europe. Alexandria's indistinct ethnic identity and hybridity, as represented by the city being part of both East and West, as well as standing at the intersection of three continents, gave Americans a point of reference about the creation of their country's new diverse identity as well as a history that they could all enjoy. When news spread in 1877 that London was preparing to transport the obelisk, the US realised that it, too, would be legitimised as a world power if it could boast one (France got one, as well, but from Luxor). So the US go-getters simply asked for one, explaining to Ismail Pasha that 'our nation was so young and all its works of so recent a date that one of the ancient monuments of Egypt would be much more highly prized in the United States than in England or France'. In his memoir, the US ambassador who requested the obelisk, Elbert E. Farman, notes that the Khedive was 'surprised' by the idea, adding that he 'did not think it best even to mention it, since the people of that city would be opposed to its removal'. The next time they met, however, the Khedive agreed to Farman's request: 'I do not see why we could not give them one. It would not injure us much and it would be a very valuable acquisition for them.' With debts racking up at 7 per cent interest, it made sense to ease relations with lenders. Such a gift could also encourage trade and keep the US onside as a neutral power, unlike France and Britain who continued to quarrel over Egypt. Everyone involved in trying to bring this antiquity to the US was a prominent Freemason, and since Ismail was also Egypt's Grand Mason, it's likely that he felt a camaraderie with his US counterparts. Records show that at least twelve new Masonic lodges were initiated in Alexandria between 1830 and 1871. There, Alexandria's elites of all faiths and nationalities rubbed shoulders, and members visiting from abroad were welcomed (such as Victorian explorer Sir Richard Burton, on his way to Mecca masquerading as a pilgrim).

Despite opposition from all classes of society delaying the finalisation of the gift, by 1880 the US had begun preparations to take the other obelisk. As they dug under the obelisk so that it could be laid on the ground, it fell suddenly and narrowly avoided being broken up. An American flag fluttered over the scaffolded obelisk. Alexandrians had already seen one of their landmarks disappear and were now concerned that this would continue to happen. With the lavish lifestyle of the Ali dynasty and the relative poverty of the lower middle classes, it made no sense to be giving ancient and valuable antiquities away. Although the US stopped their operation until things calmed down, Alexandrian protests were essentially fruitless.

Transportation was funded by the richest American alive, William Henry Vanderbilt, son of railroad magnate Cornelius Vanderbilt. With his $100,000 (today $2.5 million) donation, the US could now boast a piece of ancient Egyptian history. The second Cleopatra's Needle was transported onto a steamship that had been modified with a large hole into which the obelisk could slip. It set sail for the US on 12 June 1880, arriving in New York just three weeks later in a contrastingly smooth voyage. There, it was rolled out before spending more than 100 days on internal transport, pulled uphill by 32 horses then carried by steam engine on an especially built railway to its final destination in Central Park. On 2 October 1880 the foundation was laid in a Masonic ceremony, with 9,000 members present. As in London, the obelisk's 50-tonne Egyptian pedestal also contained a time capsule, this time including Masonic emblems, a facsimile of the American Declaration of Independence, the Bible, a copy of *Webster's Dictionary* and the *Complete Works of Shakespeare*. A small metal box was also placed in the pedestal, the contents of which remain unknown to the public today.

Both obelisks had made epic journeys from Heliopolis, where they were constructed in the fifteenth century BCE, to Alexandria's Caesareum in 12 BCE where they remained for almost two millennia before arriving in London and New York.

The loss of Cleopatra's Needles symbolised the ever-increasing foreign influence on Egypt and especially Alexandria. It was also a reminder of the misgovernment and corruption of an out-of-touch family ruling from its pristine palaces. The Ali dynasty certainly modernised Alexandria, but they'd spent money as if there was no tomorrow.

In around fifteen years, Ismail Pasha had put in place astonishing reforms. He constructed 5,000 miles of electric telegraph lines, 900 miles of railways and 400 bridges. He established hundreds of schools (which were open to all, including girls and peasant families), hospitals and publishers, as well as theatres and opera houses. Taking inspiration from ancient Alexandria, he commissioned a national library in Cairo and fifteen lighthouses at sea. He continued to grow cotton into an international industry (Alexandria would dictate the prices of the Liverpool Cotton Exchange), and coupled this with sugar production. He also tried an unsuccessful and costly invasion of Ethiopia. All this came at a price: since taking power, Ismail had been borrowing at increased interest, multiplying Egypt's debt thirtyfold to £100 million (over £10 billion today), more than ten times the country's annual revenue. No more loans were available: even his closest confidant, the influential Jewish banker Yacoub Cattaui, refused to lend him money, and instead assisted him in selling the Egyptian shares of his most costly project, the Suez Canal. After seeking permission from Queen Victoria and Parliament, Prime Minister Benjamin Disraeli borrowed £4 million to purchase 44 per cent of the Suez Company.

Realising that the debts still weren't going to be repaid, the British and French were able to repursue their long-term goal of taking over Egypt. In 1876, an Anglo-French alliance took control of Egypt's government and finances and by 1879 the British and French had successfully convinced the Ottoman Sultan Abdulhamid II to depose Ismail and replace him with his twenty-six-year-old son Tewfik Pasha, who for his part punched the messenger who brought him the news. As Ismail Pasha made his way by sea from Alexandria to Naples, British and French vessels drew into the harbour. Alexandria's reform had come at the costly price of independence.

The Ottomans hadn't been in control of Egypt for some time, but the European powers wanted to give the impression that the decision had come from Istanbul. Egyptians, however, knew that the British and French were behind the change. Non-Egyptians already made up a fifth of Alexandria's some quarter of a million population, which included over 20,000 Greeks, around 10,000 Italians and 10,000 French residents. They had their own legal systems, while British and French consortiums were running Egypt's economy. The upper ranks of the civil service were dominated by Europeans and by simply comparing lifestyles alone, the pay gap was evident, with European residents exempted from tax despite earning more. Even in the army a dangerous hierarchy was developing, best exemplified by an Egyptian artilleryman being killed in a street in Alexandria with no repercussions. In fact, when his comrades took his body to the palace to protest, they were given long prison sentences for defying the orders of the palace officers at the entrance.

It couldn't be clearer that Egypt was at the forefront of British and French colonial ambitions. And it didn't take long for anger to be fuelled among the local population, including the army. The popular orator General Ahmed Urabi – who came from a simple peasant background and had established the Egyptian National Party to demand equal rights for Egyptians in the army – became the symbol of a new national uprising. In early 1882, members of the army began a revolt that demanded equal treatment of Egyptians before the law. There was a nationalist surge, with the middle classes joining to demand equal rights, and before long the peasant class was onboard. Having picked up momentum, the Urabi Revolt, as it came to be known, was trying to default Egypt's debt and retake the Suez Canal.

Anti-European protests surged: the sizeable Muhammad Ali Square, notable for its trees, gaslights and outdoor coffee shops, became the centre of this revolution. The elites and the peasants both joined in, as did Muslims and Copts. Britain and France could not risk this spreading further, so in May 1882 six ships arrived at the city's harbour, the rest of the fleet awaiting orders near Crete. By June, more gunships were arriving, some hovering on the coast. Rather than putting Egyptians off, the tension reached breaking point on 11 June, when thousands of Egyptians took to the streets in protest. Before long, the angry crowd were targeting any Europeans they could find, attacking them with wooden sticks and hurling stones at their homes. Chaotic quarrels broke out on street corners, one particularly large fight between Egyptian and Maltese residents the result of a Maltese man stabbing an Egyptian donkey boy who'd hit him with a stick. The Egyptian police and army arrived, but to the horror of the Europeans they were there to help their own citizens. Some even pretended to aid the Europeans but actually led them to the mob. By the time the unrest reached the main square, gunfire was being exchanged, with Europeans shooting down from their balconies and soldiers responding from the ground. Closer to the sea, the injured and dead were being hurled into the water. Two days of rioting were only halted when Urabi was begged to intervene. Around fifty Europeans were killed and 125 Egyptians. Many Europeans had taken refuge in their consulates and police stations, and dozens of ships were now arriving to evacuate them, with escorts protecting them on the way to the harbour. By 6 July, there wasn't a single European left in Alexandria.

With only Egyptians in the city, Britain made a decision to attack Alexandria – something they were apparently waiting for an opportunity to do. As the British prepared to strike, the French – whose ambassador had already written to Paris stating that Egypt's rulers were loyal and needed support – decided to retreat. On the harbour, 'Rule, Britannia!' and 'See, the Conquering Hero Comes!' were blasted loudly from the decks as the Egyptians armed themselves on the forts.

At 7 a.m. on 11 July, British warships began shelling Alexandria heavily. They targeted each of the Alexandrian forts, including the Qaitbay Citadel, whose minaret was demolished. They also shelled the Ras el-Tin Palace and the European quarter. The latter was turned to rubble – including hundreds of civilian apartments and European consulates, most ironically the empty British Consulate. St Mark's Anglican Church, though struck by one shell, is the only building in the European quarter to have survived the bombardment. The statue of Muhammad Ali stood firm in the middle of the wreckage.

After ten hours of shelling, hundreds of Alexandrian civilians and soldiers were dead, anonymous in their multitude. As soon as the shelling stopped, thousands of families made their way out of the city on foot, walking on the railway line and beside the canal. Fire and panic ravaged the city for two whole days as a large proportion of its buildings, old and new, fell to the ground. That night, darkness and silence reigned. Alexandria was the emptiest it had been for decades.

With Egyptian soldiers still patrolling the empty city, it still wasn't clear whether the British attack had been a success. In fact, it appears that they missed most of their targets. Fearing for his life, the Khedive Tewfik Pasha had already been in hiding in Alexandria and he ended up escaping to a British ship, from which he declared Urabi a rebel, allowing Britain to enter by land. Meanwhile, Urabi was still declaring war: he cut the dam separating the canal from Lake Mariout so the water entering Alexandria became salty, though distillation apparatus soon arrived. Urabi also secured a decree from the religious authorities that proclaimed the Khedive a traitor to Egypt and Islam, paving the way for military conscription. The

British forces advanced to Cairo, but were halted by Urabi's await-ing army less than twenty miles from Alexandria at the town of Kafr el-Dawwar. Though they retreated, British troops continued to arrive at Alexandria by sea.

With an expeditionary force of 40,000 on land, Britain now held both Alexandria and the Suez Canal, and by 7 August dozens of ships were bringing the Europeans back to Alexandria. Near Cairo, on 13 September the Anglo-Irish Viscount Wolseley attacked Urabi's army unexpectedly during the night and the British cavalry managed to enter Cairo. As news of Britain's success reached Alexandria, the returning Europeans closed their businesses and paraded in the streets, bands playing 'God Save the Queen'. The British swiftly set up military tribunals for those who'd supported the revolt. Muhammad Ali Square became the site of brutal public executions by hanging. Corpses piled up in the once coveted square.

For their part, the US remained relatively neutral. The US ambas-sador at the time even named his memoir *Egypt and its Betrayal: . . . how England Acquired a new Empire*, arguing that Britain had long had its eye on Egypt. Urabi's trial by the restored but nominal Khedivate garnered much international attention. Urabi was defended in court by two of Britain's leading Freemasons. Suleiman Sami, Alexandria's military commander, who told the court that Urabi had ordered him to ravage the city and kill the Khedive, was contradicted in court by other prisoners. Naturally, both Sami and Urabi were sentenced to death. Sami was hanged in Alexandria, but killing Urabi would have caused serious uproar. 'Banishment for life' was adjudged more sensible. Britain controlled a number of islands suit-able for such exiles. Urabi was sent to the far-distant island of Ceylon (Sri Lanka), as Egypt and Alexandria entered a new phase under a British occupation that had no legal basis.

The buildings that were damaged by the shelling were now finished off by British troops, around 7,000 of whom patrolled the streets. By April 1883, fearing reprisals from the Egyptians, 2,600 Europeans had signed a petition calling for the British occupation to be made perma-nent. They presented it to the recently appointed British commissioner Lord Dufferin, who'd been sent by the newly elected Liberal govern-ment whose manifesto rejected colonisation of Egypt. Dufferin's report concluded that Egypt should be led by both the British and native Egyptians and though Egyptian ministers could hold office, they could also be removed instantly if they failed to obey British orders. By the end of October 1883, more than half of the British soldiers had departed, leaving 3,000 in Alexandria. Locals discouraged one another from engaging with them, and off-duty, the soldiers confined themselves to the European bars and brothels.

The Liverpool-born William Earle was stationed in Alexandria as General Officer and brought confidence to the European community, who are said to have erected a statue of him in the city. E. M. Forster described it as 'a funny little bust' just outside the Anglican Church and since the mid-twentieth century all that remained of it was this description. When historian Michael Haag enquired about it at the church in 1987, the second-generation gardener, named Mustafa, recalled how, when he was a child, his father had buried a sculpture in the garden to protect it during riots in the 1950s. Mustafa pinpointed the exact location, and, sure enough, General Earle's bust appeared from the under the ground, moustache intact but with the front of the hat damaged.[2]

The following years saw the urban population increasing again. One in five Egyptians in Alexandria worked in transport, with many also being employed in construction, food preparation and as merchants. Taxes became payable only by cash, not in kind, so locals began to trade more adamantly. With the establishment of the Municipality of Alexandria in 1890, whose power was mostly concentrated in the hands of European merchants, numerous reno-vation projects got underway. The land on the seafront was flat-tened, a public library opened, in addition to the landmark Greco-Roman Museum. Several palaces appeared, as well as four new synagogues. Europeans once again formed a fifth of the population, which at 350,000 was second only to Cairo in Egypt. Alexandria was home to Muslims and Jews, as well as Christians of many denomi-nations including Coptic Orthodox, Greek Orthodox, Greek Catholic, Roman Catholic and Protestant. As the twentieth century commenced, there were 25,000 Greeks, 18,000 Italians and 9,000 French residents in Alexandria. The British, numbering 11,000, remained the city's leading power. But the events of the 1880s were still a recent memory. There was little doubt that Egyptian national-ism was still brewing.

The First World War and Revolution

Alexandria-born Abbas, great-great-grandson of Muhammad Ali, hadn't yet turned eighteen when he received news of his father Tewfik Pasha's passing in early 1892. In the style of Hamlet, Abbas hurriedly returned from college in Geneva. As Abbas II, he was a new and idealistic ruler who immediately opposed British occupation, facing off to its consul, Lord Cromer. He finalised construction of the Montazah Palace, a summer hunting residence that mixed Turkish and Florentine architecture, as well as the Salamlek Palace (now a stylish hotel and casino) where he could safely entertain his Italian mistress. As time went on, though his relationship with the British improved, he was secretly supporting the new nationalist movement led by the lawyer Mustafa Kamil. In March 1896, Kamil had delivered his first popular speech to a mesmerised, cheering Alexandrian crowd – and the support base for his freedom movement began to grow in the city. When France agreed with Britain to withdraw its support for Egyptian independence, Kamil warned that Egypt would be absorbed into the British Empire unless Egyptians fought for independence. Alexandria was at the centre of a growing independence movement.

When the First World War broke out in 1914, the stakes suddenly became higher for both Egypt and Britain. As the Ottomans sided with the Germans, becoming an enemy of the Allies, Britain took decisive action to oust the Khedives, still nominally Ottoman. Abbas II was replaced by his pro-British uncle, Hussein Kamel, who became Sultan of Egypt, independent of the Ottomans. Britain's de facto occupation of Egypt now became a formal one.

Britain swiftly poured troops into Egypt. In what is a largely unacknowledged sacrifice today, over a million and a half Egyptians were forcefully conscripted to the war effort. In addition to more than a million soldiers, half a million peasants became labourers in the Egyptian Expeditionary Force. Around 55,000 of these were placed in the Egyptian Labour Corps, where they spent long days constructing railways and roads, or loading and unloading trains and ships. With 75,000 camels, 170,000 men joined the Egyptian Camel Transport Corps to carry heavy supplies and equipment for the British soldiers, and to patrol the desert. Horror stories soon reached Alexandria about injured Egyptian soldiers left to die in the wilderness with resources put in place to rescue and rehabilitate British soldiers instead.

Egypt became an important camp for Commonwealth troops, particularly from Britain but also from Australia, New Zealand, South Africa and India. Britain set up fortifications in and around Alexandria that included a sturdy cannon inside the city. With soldiers camping on the outskirts, all residents faced a night-time curfew. Egypt also made a monetary and material contribution that set its economy back and led to poverty even among its middle classes, while Britain was purchasing cotton and livestock at well below market price. A levy was imposed on Alexandria forcing its residents to contribute to the war or face the wrath of martial law.

In March 1915, Alexandria became the base for the Mediterranean Expeditionary Force as the city became a military station and hospital centre for British, French and Commonwealth troops. An internment camp opened in the Sidi Bishr area (and the popular Maltese revolutionary, Manwel Dimech, was imprisoned there, accused of spying for the Germans). Even as the Allies advanced eastwards that year, Alexandria's camps remained in place for breaks, and local hotels and schools filled up with hospital beds. Ships at Alexandria's harbour brought new troops and reinforcements into the theatres of war and took wounded soldiers away. By 1916, so many soldiers had died that Alexandria's main cemetery was full. A new Commonwealth Cemetery was created in the centre of town that holds the graves of 1,674 war casualties, all but seventy-three of them British.

The wider implications of the war included the weakening of the Ottoman Empire and the creation of a Zionist state in Palestine. Both of these affected Alexandria and shed light on the city's unique position at this time.

When the First World War began, thousands of Jews, who were not Ottoman citizens, moved to Alexandria, especially from Palestine. An Alexandrian Zionist association had been founded in 1898 in an attempt to unite the city's Jewish population. They were now joined by early Zionist icons like Vladimir Jabotinsky and Joseph Trumpeldor, who convinced Alexandria's Jewish leaders to form Jewish battalions to fight with the Allies in order to snatch Palestine from the Ottomans. From Alexandria, they gathered a Jewish Legion formed largely of Russians who'd moved to the city to escape persecution. But the British refused to enlist them: the official line was that they were foreign nationals, but it was most likely because there was a risk associated with Jews fighting in Palestine. Britain instead suggested the creation of a volunteer transport group. Jabotinsky didn't agree, leaving for Europe to try to find support for the legion. Trumpeldor remained, recruiting hundreds of Alexandrian Jews to the newly established Zion Mule Corps, whose 562 members were soon serving in Gallipoli.

When it came to weakening the Ottomans, Hussein bin Ali, the King of Hejaz (centred around Mecca and Medina), began negotiating in secret with the Allies in order to execute an Arab Revolt against the Turkish-centric Ottomans. The Ottomans were attacked in Mecca in a battle that lasted over a month, with Egyptian troops sent to support. For the next couple of years, with the help of British planning by such officers as T. E. Lawrence, soon to become known as Lawrence of Arabia, Arab armies and tribes continued to attack Ottoman transport links and important sites, severely weakening the Ottoman Empire. By the end of the war in 1918, the Allies had taken over Palestine, Lebanon, Syria and parts of the Arabian peninsula, distributing the Arab territories among themselves.

Palestine remained a special case, and the one-sentence Balfour Declaration of 1917 read: 'His Majesty's Government view with favour the establishment in Palestine of a national home for the Jewish people, and will use their best endeavours to facilitate the achievement of this object.' Some of Alexandria's Jews, especially those who'd arrived a few years earlier, decided to leave for Palestine. It might come as a surprise to learn that Alexandrians welcomed the Balfour Declaration, with reports of parties hosted by Muslims and Christians for their Jewish neighbours. Alexandria's governor,

Ahmad Ziwar (soon to become prime minister), sent a telegram of gratitude to Lord Balfour, the British foreign secretary. But as problems between newly arrived Jews and Palestinians escalated in Jerusalem, and as pan-Arab and pan-Islamic messages became paired, the longer-term consequences of the Balfour Declaration became clearer and Arab–Jewish rivalry started to spread to Egypt.

By the time the war came to an end in 1918, Alexandria's demographic had undergone yet more changes. Thousands of Jews had left, replaced by Armenians escaping an Ottoman-backed genocide. But the city's economy was ravaged by inflation and unemployment, with working-class areas seeing increased crime and poverty. At this time, at least seventeen women, most of whom were sex workers, were murdered for their gold in a spree led by two sisters called Raya and Sakina. Their trial garnered significant national attention, and their names appeared in local songs even before they became the first females to be executed in modern Egypt. For many, they proved that public morality was at an all-time low and that addressing it would be central to building a new Egyptian nation. Outside Alexandria, people assumed that being around so many Europeans had corrupted the sisters, further justifying the independence movement. Alexandria's streets were certainly full of prostitutes, Egyptian women peering through their shiny, bead veils with kohl-lined eyes, wearing long, black satin dresses that hugged their figures and covered their dancing costumes, the gold coins that dangled from their headbands ringing as they walked. Even among the prostitutes, those who took on British clients were ostracised both by their peers and their regular Egyptian customers. The feeling was that Egyptians had given far too much to Britain for no justifiable reason. Egypt was set to demand its independence.

A new and varied coalition, known as *al-Wafd* – or the Delegation – sought to make a case for Egypt's independence at the post-war Paris Peace Conference of 1919. The idea had been floated by Prince Omar Toussoun, a popular great-grandson of Muhammad Ali, who'd met former minister Saad Zaghlul at a ball in an Alexandria hotel. Zaghlul ended up heading the delegation to France. For their part, Britain refused the request for independence and instead detained Zaghlul. Like Urabi before him, he was exiled to an island, this time Malta.

Protests erupted across the country. In Alexandria, despite laws banning large gatherings, school and college pupils began demonstrating on 12 March, skipping lessons and gathering at the al-Mursi Mosque's square. The military's threats didn't work and the pupils continued to Muhammad Ali Square, where they were attacked and 50 of them arrested. Two days later, with news of British martial law spreading, thousands joined protests after Friday prayers and the numbers kept increasing. Then, on 17 March, as another protest set out, young men were confronted by British soldiers who began shooting, killing sixteen demonstrators, one of whom was only thirteen, and injuring many more. This would become a key date in the modern history of the city: the attack sparked outrage and for months life in Alexandria stopped for everyone, no matter their age, gender, class, or faith, as protests became the norm. The Egyptian Revolution of 1919 was in full swing and included significant involvement from the women who would go on to become Egypt's trailblazing suffragettes. The uprising that began with young men was now being led by women of all ages. Regardless of class or faith, Egyptian women now became visible as they covered their faces with white veils, not for religious reasons but in order to disassociate themselves from the occupiers. Protesters held green flags with a crescent moon and cross on them to signify unity. They chanted for independence. British sites and railways were attacked, and their black cars toppled to cheers from the crowds. On occasion, Britain's Egyptian Expeditionary Force, led by Lord Allenby, attempted to repress the protests violently, with hundreds of civilians losing their lives in the unrest. A recently discovered diary belonging to an Alexandrian Christian man named William records protests taking place daily and residents following the news eagerly on the radio.

Independence began to feel possible in Egypt. Zaghlul returned to Alexandria from exile to a hero's welcome from thousands of cheering supporters, and was soon in Paris attempting independence negotiations. In Britain, Egypt was a huge topic of discussion in Parliament. The newly appointed Secretary of State for the Colonies, Winston Churchill, went to Egypt for a secret set of meetings in 1921, later called the Cairo Conference, where he received counsel from Lawrence, now Special Adviser to the Colonial Office.

Britain had its own plans to keep the Suez Canal, and Churchill took the overnight train to Palestine where he confirmed his support for a Jewish state. Talks with Zaghlul, however, constantly broke down, and Alexandria was fast becoming the epicentre of anti-British sentiment, as protests were coupled with intolerance towards anyone opposing independence.

On 21 May 1921, fighting broke out between Egyptian protesters and European residents that ended with buildings being set alight and gunfire being exchanged. A concerned Parliament in London received an update that 'Alexandria is practically in a state of insurrection, the police forces are not functioning and the foreign inhabitants have sent an urgent telegram to Lord Allenby asking for the despatch of further British troops'.[1] To Churchill, the Alexandria riots justified his conviction about remaining in Egypt. Egyptians decided to boycott Britain at every level of society: for most, this meant refusing to talk or sell to anyone British, while the independence leaders rejected any negotiation with British representatives. As a result, in December 1921 martial law was reimposed and Zaghlul was again deported, first to the Seychelles then Gibraltar. Protests and strikes restarted until the influential politician Viscount Milner was sent to Egypt and recommended to Prime Minister David Lloyd George and King George V that they soften their grip. In February 1922, the British government finally declared Egyptian independence, shifting the country from Protectorate to Kingdom, with Sultan Fuad I becoming King Fuad I. The country's flag changed from red to the green held aloft by protesters. In reality, Britain remained in control of most of the country's affairs – not least the Suez Canal, the army and the economy. They continued to station naval troops in Alexandria, which would come in useful as a base in the Second World War.

Since the nineteenth century, Alexandria had been known for its active sex industry. With a rise in sexually transmitted diseases, the city founded the Bureau des Filles Publiques (Public Girls' Office) to try to manage the issue. Egyptian sex workers, both women and men, were predominantly from poorer backgrounds or had been kidnapped, with several slave dealers operating in the city. The youngest Egyptian women were being disproportionately infected; the Bureau put this down to European women already having 'all sorts of infections' that provided 'resistance'.[2] But the Europeans of the city were specifically concerned about the white woman. In 1905, they founded the Société Pour la Suppression de la Traite des Blanches (Society for the Suppression of the White Slave Trade), which discouraged the sale of white women specifically and ended up repatriating over 2,000 white 'children' from the brothels. Although the Egyptian government had been taking steps to ban slavery since the 1850s, the abolition ruling of 1877 only banned slave trading from Sudan, where the majority of male slaves were coming from. Then, in 1884, a ban was placed on the import of white women, who were preferred by Egyptian rather than European elites. The brothels and hourly-rented apartment rooms continued to fill with European men buying the services of young Egyptian women and men. And Egyptian domestic workers continued to try, often unsuccessfully, to divert the sexual attentions and harassments of their European superiors, with one account describing how maids were allowed to sleep under their mistress's bed to hide from the men in the house.

Women's increased freedom also put them in the spotlight. They were certainly objectified, and in different ways, no matter their ethnicity or class. An upper-class or European woman was a prize to be sought. A lower-class or Egyptian woman was a conquerable, orientalist fantasy. In the 1940s, Europeans were going on winter holidays to Alexandria, both for the weather and the women, as a Frenchman confirmed to his company: 'What do you expect, my friends, we are in the East?' But in Alexandria this orientalism met a significantly liberal society. With 'their delicate little feet with painted toe nails, Alexandrians have a furious desire to break with all prejudices, to taste every sensation', writes a French teaching inspector in the 1930s. 'They are free beings, the living ornament of the city', he adds. A Belgian judge in the exclusively European courts of Alexandria writes that Alexandrian women are 'pretty little beasts of prey', explaining that 'their beauty, charm and frenetic joie de vivre let them permit themselves everything'. The British police chief Charles Coles, known as Coles Pasha, wrote in his 1918 memoir that he was constantly 'surrounded by some of the prettiest and best dressed women in the world', and British author Lawrence Durrell wrote to a friend about 'the women of Alexandria, certainly the loveliest and most world-weary women in the world'.[3] Even for the Egyptians, the tune of an old Turkish folk song that had arrived with the Ottomans was altered by the late nineteenth-century to the city's very own 'Ya Banat Iskindiriyyah (O Girls of Alexandria)', its opening verse: 'O Girls of Alexandria, your love is forbidden.'

Nonetheless, independence movements signalled a significant shift in the public role of Alexandrian women. Since the British invasion, women's activism included signing petitions and boycotting businesses. But in 1919, their street demonstrations were a vital indication that it wasn't a loud minority but an entire nation that sought independence. These women came from all strands of society, including the middle and lower classes – and those who didn't protest were providing food and care for those who did. Women from the aristocratic class who were arrested were made to stand under the hot sun for hours as punishment. But the middle- and lower-class women are remembered in Egypt as martyrs of the revolution: their arrests led to humiliation, harassment and, for hundreds, death.

Some elite women living in the palaces of Alexandria quietly denounced the independence movement because they had benefitted immensely from the status quo and class divide through business or inheritance. They were a minority, and understandably, the most visible activists came from the upper classes, who were unexpectedly active in the late 1800s. Huda Sharawi, the most famous of them, frequented Alexandria around that time. Here, she could enjoy freedoms that may sound normal today, but were unattainable in most of Egypt, including Cairo. She met friends, went on seaside walks and sunbathed. In her memoir, Sharawi explains how 'in Alexandria, that very summer, I had the first experience of its kind . . . I decided to buy my clothes myself from the huge stores.'[4] Keen to see such liberties normalised for women around the country, Sharawi became a pioneer whose early feminism was concerned with the societal restrictions imposed on women. She delivered public lectures about everyday freedoms that brought many women out of the private and into the public sphere for the first time. She began a women's charity, collecting money from wealthier attendees and distributing it to struggling families. And she founded a women's school that taught vocational subjects like midwifery.

Sharawi was not the first or by any means the only female liberationist. In the late nineteenth century, several Alexandrians were already bringing gender issues to the fore in order to mobilise fellow educated women. They did so primarily in the form of writing. The first feminist paper in the Arab region, *al-Fatah*, was established in 1892 in Alexandria by Hind Nawfal, whose Lebanese-Christian parents had moved to the city when she was of school age. Hind's mother, Maryam al-Nahhas, wrote a biographical dictionary of women around that time.

Such activists also played a part in the creative culture of the period. Zaynab Fawwaz wrote the first modern Arabic novel by a woman, *The Happy Ending* (1899), and the first Arabic play by a woman, *Passion and Fidelity* (1893). After her divorce in Lebanon, Fawwaz moved to Alexandria with her father to receive tuition from three leading writers. Before long, she was married to an Egyptian soldier and embarking on her own creative work at a time when such writing was reserved for men. She earned fame in a city that allowed her to explore her potential and she continued to advocate for women's rights, writing a detailed biographical dictionary of over 450 women and their achievements, as well as her own tracts in which she noted:

As long as man and woman are equal in mental status and members of the social body, and each is indispensable to the other, then what prevents the woman from participating in the work of the man, or to engage in the work of political circles and such, when she is competent at performing that to which she aspires?

She goes on to explain that 'women in history worked in politics and participated in wars', giving the example of two queens who ruled Alexandria, Cleopatra and Zenobia.[5]

By the *fin de siècle*, then, Alexandrian women had already been expressing themselves through writing. They had already begun to make a point of going out alone, travelling on the women-only tram carriage and shopping independently in the trendy department stores, all previously unimaginable and symbolic precursors to the more formal activism that would follow. By the time of the 1919 revolution, Alexandrian women already had a louder voice and more mobility than their counterparts in the rest of Egypt.

During the independence movement, Sharawi was influenced by Safiya Fahmi, wife of the revolutionary Saad Zaghlul. When he returned to Alexandria after his exile, Safiya surprised the public by removing her veil at the port – a shocking step – before slowly beginning to appear without it in public. This was as much a comment on colonialism as it was on equality. The presence of Britain was further restricting Egyptian women's mobility and position in the workplace. Dress served as powerful symbol of this reality: Egyptian women were purposely dressing in a uniform manner, differentiating themselves from the colonisers and sending a message to British soldiers and officials to keep their distance. Safiya's gesture had a clear message that women's liberation in twentieth-century Egypt was contingent upon independence.

With the success of the revolution, upper-class women led by Sharawi marked independence from Britain by forming a women's philanthropic organisation, a political organisation and the pioneering Egyptian Feminist Union. Her partners included Nabawiyya Musa, who was raised and lived in Alexandria, and became the first Egyptian woman to achieve a bachelor's degree. She also became the first headmistress and founded several girls' schools and newspapers, alongside writing about girls' education and women's work. And Saiza Nabarawi, who received her school education in Alexandria, went on to became editor of the union's feminist magazine. Together, these three women travelled to Rome for the 1923 Conference of the International Women Suffrage Alliance, and upon returning, Sharawi and Nabarawi removed their veils to the waiting crowd. The veil had served its purpose as a symbol of nationalism during the independence movement, but now Egyptian dress was changing as women enjoyed more freedom to make decisions.

Cultural Hub

Before independence, the nineteenth century saw flocks of Europeans exploring Alexandria. As a city on the front line of modernity, orientalist travellers expecting exotic stereotypes were bitterly disappointed. European art from this period featured Cairo, not Alexandria, for that very reason. But many Europeans also made Alexandria their home. Its cosmopolitan nature hugely influenced local arts with each group adding something to the Alexandrian mix. And as nationalist sentiment grew into the twentieth century, the city's arts would change yet further and serve a new purpose.

Alexandria's love for theatre had dwindled with the Islamic annexation, but it was an Islamic scholar who rekindled it. When Napoleon arrived, the French found puppet shows, pantomimes and jesters performing in the public squares, but no theatres. Then, when Muhammad Ali sent young Egyptians to study in France and Italy, they were accompanied by an imam. In 1826, twenty-four-year-old Rifa'a al-Tahtawi headed to Paris as the students' religious counsellor, leaving Egypt for the very first time. In Paris, he refused to be an idle spectator. Instead, al-Tahtawi plunged himself into the language and culture, devouring the writings of the Enlightenment philosophers and attending famous theatres and opera houses. When he returned five years later and wrote about his experiences, Ali invited him to design a drama curriculum for schools. With the arrival of Levantine troupes soon after this, Alexandria was set for a theatrical revival. Writers and performers had struggled in Syria and Lebanon due to Ottoman censorship, so Alexandria's relative freedom provided them with explorative opportunities. By the 1840s, farces and operettas were being performed at small theatres, attracting the upper classes who could understand French and Italian.

Within a decade of arriving from Italy as a political refugee in his early twenties, Pietro Avoscani had designed the Ras el-Tin Palace and become a very wealthy man. So he sponsored the production of three Italian operas in 1841, including Gaetano Donizetti's melodramatic *L'elisir d'amore* (*The Elexir of Love*), the first opera to be performed in Alexandria. By the 1850s, the elites were enjoying plays and ballet, too, and Avoscani organised a three-day palace celebration that included all these shows. Though he received permission to build an Italian theatre, it never came about. Instead, the Greek consul for Belgium, Count Etienne Zizinia, who'd made a fortune in Alexandria from cotton, commissioned Avoscani to design the city's first major theatre, its terracotta façade based on La Scala, Milan's opera house. With a capacity of 2,000, the Zizinia Theatre was inaugurated in 1863 and became one of Alexandria's most important cultural centres, though locals complained that only cotton traders could afford its tickets. The theatre initially welcomed Italian sopranos and French comedy troupes, not to mention celebrities like French actress Sarah Bernhardt, before Levantines and Egyptians finally began to perform there, too.

Before long, this hub representing wealthy, colonial Alexandria was being used for populist, nationalistic gatherings. In 1907, the activist Mustafa Kamil made a captivating speech from the stage of the Zizinia Theatre as he founded Egypt's National Party.

> The ignorant and the poor say that I am reckless in my love for her – but is it possible for an Egyptian to be reckless in loving Egypt? For however much I love her, it does not reach the degree demanded by her beauty and majesty and history and greatness, of which she is worthy . . . Ask the entire world, it will answer you in a single voice that Egypt is the heaven of earth and that the most generous of people do inherit her, living – and cherishing. The biggest of crimes towards her and towards themselves? If they are lenient about her rights and surrender her crises to the stranger. If I were not born an Egyptian, I would have wished to be an Egyptian.[1]

This final phrase is as famous to Egyptians as Martin Luther King's dream is elsewhere.

Fire hit the theatre in 1916, after which its remains were torn down to make way for the Théâtre Mohamed Aly, opened in 1921 as Alexandria's opera house, designed classically with scroll-like Ionic columns and four grotesque faces carved into the façade. The opera house went on to host renowned sopranos such as the American-Greek singer Maria Callas in the 1950s. By then, Alexandria was home to around fifty theatres of differing sizes, with both European and Arabic companies performing anything from serious tragedy to suggestive slapstick. The city's arts scene included theatre, opera and dance, with an array of establishments, both well-known and underground, dotted around its quarters.

The rise of theatre led to another phenomenon: the moving picture. In 1896, the renowned Lumière brothers chose to visit Alexandria less than a year after their very first short film screened in Paris. In November 1896, Alexandria's elites donned their best hats at the stock exchange's Café Zawani to watch several short films, each less than a minute long, of everyday life in France: the first moving pictures ever played in Egypt. The brothers became the talk of the town, especially when they began to film locally. They captured a train arriving in the central station and showed the footage to delighted crowds later that evening.

Alexandria became the cinematic capital of the region as Egypt's first cinema opened there in January 1897, its name, Cinématographe Lumière, commemorating their visit just a couple of months earlier. And within weeks, the brothers had sent a cameraman to Alexandria to shoot their film, *Place des Consuls, à Alexandrie*. As cinemas began to appear around the city, Italian investors founded a dedicated local production company in 1917. Even today, there are two types of cinema in Alexandria. There are the new ones inside malls that you can find anywhere. And there are the grand cinemas, art deco buildings that transport you to a different era. These still screen a single film every evening and it runs for several weeks. As the gates clunk open shortly before the show, people rush in chaotically to take their seats, vendors walking around screaming 'Popcorn! Popcorn!'. The huge red curtains at the front of the hall are pulled apart to reveal the stage, on top of which a giant screen begins playing trailers.

*   *   *

When the local production company was established in 1917, British soldiers were still in Alexandria. One spring morning that year, a British soldier in his late thirties set eyes on a young, clean-shaven tram conductor and was captivated. The soldier worked alongside the Red Cross, touring the city's hospitals to check for missing soldiers or to get information from their comrades. Every morning, he began to wait at the Mustafa Pasha stop for the tram to arrive. He knew the conductor's badge number, 86, but not his name. Finally, he exchanged words with seventeen-year-old Mohammed el-Adl, and before long, they met on the beach during the night and made their feelings known.

This soldier was Edward Morgan Forster, or E. M. Forster, who before the war was one of England's most acclaimed novelists. His letters to a confidante while in Alexandria describe the development of his relationship with the tram conductor. The spring they met, Forster describes himself as having 'plunged into an anxious but very beautiful affair', three months later describing one night in el-Adl's room in the Bacos neighbourhood as 'perhaps the happiest of my life'. El-Adl married in October 1918, a few months before the war concluded, and Forster departed. They had continued their unlikely but passionate relationship through those months, and taken daytrips to the Catacombs and Pompey's Pillar. They also exchanged many letters in English and had photographs taken. They met twice more in the years that followed as Forster travelled to and from India via Egypt, though by then el-Adl's tuberculosis was getting worse after he was imprisoned briefly under British martial law. When he left jail, el-Adl wrote to Forster that the 'English are revengable' (sic), wishing that Forster had been American instead. El-Adl died in his early twenties.

For many British and French soldiers, Egypt was a place of oriental fantasy where they could enjoy belly dancing at bawdy cafés, instigate casual flings with well-meaning locals and engage prostitutes. Forster's private papers indicate what he called 'losing R [respectability]' with an injured soldier on the beach of Alexandria. He even reflected on the effect of losing his virginity that night: 'I should have been a more famous writer if I had written or rather published more, but sex prevented the latter.' But his response to el-Adl's death indicates serious intimacy. Forster continued to send letters to his dead lover: 'I still write once a week on the chance. It will be painful stopping, for then I shall realise for ever that he is not there.' Forster went on to write a history of Alexandria which he published in the city, and an invocation to Alexandria titled *Pharos & Pharillon*, which he dedicated to el-Adl: 'O Hermes, the conductor of the Souls'. Forster's diary continues to mention el-Adl for another decade, writing in 1929 that 'I am close on 51 and can never love any one so much', and even in his eighties he confided to a friend that he had kept all of el-Adl's letters and was transcribing them. In fact, Forster wrote an elegy titled 'Mohammed El Adl's Book', which he began following el-Adl's death, and a ten-page memoir, 'Incidents of War Memoir', which he wrote during two years in Alexandria, strongly condemning British colonialism in Egypt. Forster felt both of these pieces were unpublishable. His experiences in Alexandria may have seriously stifled his writing, but they were key to his understanding and assertion of sexuality. They also encouraged him to continue to India, inspiring fiction about those travels. Back in Egypt, el-Adl had done something before he died: he had named his first son Morgan.[2]

In Alexandria, Forster happened upon 'a Greek gentleman in a straw hat, standing absolutely motionless at a slight angle to the universe'.[3] This man was Konstantinos Petrou Kavafis, soon to become known in the English-speaking world as C. P. Cavafy, one of Alexandria's most famous poets. Cavafy was born in Alexandria in 1863 to a wealthy family who worked in import and export. When his father died, seven-year-old Cavafy moved with his family to Liverpool, but the Long Depression, a financial crisis that hit Europe and North America in 1873, caused them to move back to Alexandria a few years later. Following the 1882 bombardment of the city, the family fled to Istanbul as their apartment was burnt to the ground by the British. By 1885, Cavafy was back in Alexandria where he would stay for the rest of his life, spending most of it as a civil servant in the Egyptian Ministry of Public Works.

In Alexandria, Cavafy lived with his beloved cat and wrote poetry. His verses were never intended to be read beyond the city. Some he would print and hand out to acquaintances, not just friends but also strangers with whom he struck up conversations as they sat on wooden chairs lining the pavements outside cafés. Some he agreed to print in local magazines and newspapers, and some were never published. His verse was unconventional: poems were consistently short, richly metaphorical and, barring cases of irony, purposely unrhymed. The topics link his Alexandria with history and myth, the likes of Homer, Alexander the Great and the Ptolemies making regular appearances. By making Alexandria rather than himself the subject of the poetry, Cavafy explored the inescapable relationship of Alexandrians to their home, best summarised when he acknowledges that 'The city will follow you'.[4] Cavafy reminds us that comprehending a place so infused with history and myth is not a matter of either perception or conception – it is both.

To Cavafy, past and present Alexandria are strikingly similar. He imagines the city through the eyes of Greek Byzantines who've migrated from Constantinople, halfway in time between Alexandria's founding and his own life: 'Always, Alexandria remains herself', he wrote, 'For all the harm it's suffered in its wars, / for all that it's diminished, still a marvelous place'.[5]

The act of imagining Alexandria's past inspired Cavafy to understand its present. In 'Alexandrian Kings', he visualises Cleopatra and Antony's festival in which the queen crowned her children, insinuating that the whole population has always been able to see through the political façades:

and the Alexandrians rushed to the festival
filled with excitement, and shouted acclaim
in Greek, and in Egyptian, and some in Hebrew,
enchanted by the lovely spectacle –
though they knew what they were worth,
what empty words these kingdoms were.[6]

In his homoerotic poems especially, the young men might have come straight out of this ancient world. While living with his mother, Cavafy would sneak out by night, paying the servant to muss up his bedsheets and instead staying over at the bawdy upstairs brothels near the spice markets, where women and men could be hired for next to nothing. The young sex worker there, 'he'd sell his body for a half-crown or two', writes Cavafy, for whom the boy is even more beautiful than those carved into sculptures in the ancient city:

> I ask myself if the great Alexandria
> of ancient times could boast a boy
> more exquisite, more perfect.[7]

But in the modern city, the boy will remain anonymous, will never be memorialised and will continue to be exploited by wealthy men; ironically, Cavafy isn't innocent of this exploitation. Moreover, Cavafy was able to write about sexuality in this way precisely because he was in Alexandria: as the historian Philip Mansel reminds us, 'in all other cities except Paris, Cavafy's poems would have provoked horror or imprisonment. There was no English or German Cavafy.'[8]

In his later life, Cavafy became ill with cancer, dying in April 1933 on his seventieth birthday. It was only after his death that his first book of poems was published, his writing translated, and his fame increased. Despite his local focus, he has ended up as one of the most esteemed Greek language poets of the twentieth century. It has long been assumed that Forster is the man behind Cavafy's international fame, but it was primarily two Alexandrians who introduced him to England. The Menasce family arrived in Egypt from Morocco and Palestine in the eighteenth century, their banking, cotton and sugar businesses placing them at the top of Alexandria's high society. From the late nineteenth century, members of the family became the long-term presidents of Alexandria's Jewish Community and were close friends with Chaim Weizmann, who would become Israel's first president. Jean de Menasce, born in 1902, who spoke fifteen languages, studied at Oxford and the Sorbonne, where he promoted the poetry of his friend Cavafy. He helped publish three poems, translated into English by George Valassopoulo, a fellow Alexandrian studying at Cambridge, in February 1924's *The Oxford Outlook*. De Menasce became friends with T. S. Eliot, who called him 'my best translator' after he rendered *The Waste Land* in French in 1926, the same year that he shocked his family by converting to Catholicism. It is thanks to these Alexandrians, de Menasce and Valassopoulo, that Cavafy became popular among the English literati with such influential fans as Eliot. Ninety years after his death, Cavafy inspired the singer Leonard Cohen, who adapted one of his poems to create the song 'Alexandra Leaving'.

As historian Michael Haag splendidly summarises, Alexandria had such an influence on Cavafy that it was beyond doubt 'the capital of [his] imagination [and] art'.[9] Since the glory days of its Museum, Alexandria had a long-proven ability to inspire its residents to aspire, imagine and invent – and it played this role for Cavafy, too. Today, his apartment is a sombre museum on a road that has now been renamed Cavafy Street. In the Greek Orthodox Cemetery of Alexandria, near the surviving foundations of the ancient city's east gate, Cavafy's tombstone includes a one-word epitaph: 'Poet'.

As part of his modernisation programme in the 1860s, Ismail Pasha invited an Italian lawyer to Alexandria to act as legal adviser for its companies. A decade or so later, the lawyer had a son, Filippo Marinetti, who soon enrolled in the city's French Jesuit school, where his enthusiasm for an Émile Zola novel detailing the psychology of a woman's extramarital affair almost got him expelled. Marinetti loved poetry and painting, advocating cubism, then a new avant-garde movement that abstracted artistic subjects. In 1909, after studying at the Sorbonne, Marinetti published his *Manifesto of Futurism*, on the front page of the French newspaper *Le Figaro*. In his manifesto, Marinetti rejects history, nostalgia and tradition, instead emphasising youth, modernisation and speed. 'We will destroy the museums, libraries, academies', it states, and 'fight against morality, feminism and all opportunist and utilitarian cowardice'.[10] And in his literature, Marinetti envisaged a future driven by technology, with one play including robots before the term was even invented. Futurism became the subject of debate around Europe. Though Marinetti returned to Alexandria, the founder of futurism ultimately became concerned with Italian politics, joining its Fascist Party.

Many influential European artists were raised in Alexandria. They include Giuseppe Ungaretti, for whom futurism was an inspiration to write obscure, symbolic poetry that defined Italian modernist literature, and French artist Jean Cortot, known for the inclusion of poetic lines in his bright, popping art. Those born elsewhere who travelled to Alexandria include Lawrence Durrell, whose time there inspired his most famous work, *The Alexandria Quartet*, published between 1957 and 1960. In his twenties, Durrell moved to Corfu, but after Greece was attacked in the Second World War he escaped to Alexandria. During the war, he served as a press attaché for the British consulate in Alexandria, where he met his second wife, a Jewish woman called Eve Cohen on whom he based the titular character in his first Alexandria novel, *Justine*. The novels, which refer to Cavafy often, are driven as much by setting as they are by character. The city of Alexandria is a complex protagonist in its own right, its cultural diversity an influential force in the complicated relationships of love and loss. There are countless other creative works that use Alexandria as their setting, like Nobel laureate Anatole France's 1890 novel *Thaïs*, about St Thaïs, the beautiful courtesan who sinned in fourth-century Alexandria before repenting. In 1894, the novel was adapted as an Alexandria-based opera by Romantic composer Jules Massenet.

Today, writings by Forster and Durrell are renowned for their engagement with Alexandria. But pedestalling their works as the most important Alexandrian literature offers a skewed, inward-looking and hierarchical view of the city's culture. Forster and Durrell were profoundly affected by Alexandria, but they only lived there for a few years; while they developed a relationship with it and wrote about it, they did not venture far beyond their own circles, didn't speak the local language and didn't see the place outside of wartime. It is indeed fascinating to think of the influence of the city on these writers, but they were the ones who were enhanced by Alexandria, not the other way around. The same cannot be said of Cavafy: a poet who not only understood and enhanced the city, but continues to embody it.

Cultural Renaissance

Outside the Eurocentric bubble, modern Alexandria saw a democratisation of the arts for all classes and created its own masterpieces in the local language. Egypt's cultural *nahdah* – its renaissance – from the late nineteenth century until the Second World War, was strongly anti-colonial. Throughout this period, in a bid to strengthen and protect national identity, Egyptian cultural heritage was promoted alongside an attempt to ratify Arabic as the official language. Rather than leading to staid traditionalism and inwardness, the arts were reinvigorated, adapting Western ideas and experimenting with new notions and styles. During this renaissance, literary and musical outputs were unapologetically experimental. Western modes of artistic creation and reception had been imposed by the Napoleonic and British invasions, and by the Ali dynasty's obsessive admiration of Western Europe. Rather than sticking to these, Egyptian artists tried to understand and embrace Western ideas then adjust them into local culture and language. The biggest practical achievement of the renaissance was that the arts became more inclusive for the masses. As a city where the European influence was so weighty and obvious, this was especially significant for Alexandria. Given its diverse history, the concept of national identity was also a newer phenomenon to Alexandria than elsewhere. This meant that artists dabbled with the idea differently – and that it was more pronounced when it came to the fore.

Sayed Darwish is today known as the father of Egyptian music. During his own time, he was dubbed the Artist of the People. One of the most adored Egyptian singers and composers, in 1892 Darwish was born in Kom el-Dikka, an area where locals believed Alexander might be buried and where an ancient archaeological site was later uncovered. After Islamic school, Darwish trained as a religious singer, but provided for his family as a bricklayer, singing in cafés during evenings without much success. He always sang on the construction site, too, and one day two Syrian theatre managers happened to be sipping coffee nearby. The Attallah brothers approached Darwish, and though he had to continue working in a furniture shop to make ends meet, it was only a matter of years before he was composing and singing for Egypt's leading theatres.

Darwish's contribution was as political as it was musical, with his works helping to incite the 1919 Revolution. That year was by far his most productive as the twenty-seven-year-old composed no fewer than 75 nationalist songs. The most famous of these, 'Aho Dali Sar', translates as 'Well That's What Happened', or 'This is Where We're At'. Egypt has to face up to its reality, the song declares, in a subtle call for national action from the masses. When the songwriter was asked by a minister why the formal robe he was wearing wasn't made in Egypt, his reply eventually became the chorus: 'How can you blame me, Sir, when the good of our country isn't in our hands?'

At that time, the revolutionary Saad Zaghlul was exiled from Alexandria for his part in instigating the uprising. Across the streets of the city, protesters chanted 'long live Zaghlul' to the extent that it became a national motto. In response, praising Zaghlul publicly became an imprisonable offence. So Darwish composed a song in praise of zaghlul dates, the name given to red dates in Egypt, claiming it was an ode to the fruit not the man. Meanwhile, those who were exiled wrote patriotic poetry about missing home: on one level, they increased interest in foreign cultures, but on another they evoked a deeper sense of national pride.

When Darwish watched the most orientalist of art pieces, Giuseppe Verdi's opera Aïda, which had earlier been commissioned to open Cairo's opera house, it appears to have both inspired and angered him. He began a transformation of Egyptian music, giving it a unique identity. The usual ensemble, called the takht, which involved just a few musicians, one on each instrument (usually an oud, qanun, ney and drum), was replaced with bigger orchestras and multiple musicians on each instrument. Unconstrained by British occupation and with his own company, Darwish speeded up

Western opera to create popular Arabic operettas that could be enjoyed by a wider range of people. In these operettas, he introduced polyphonic singing to Egypt's music for the first time, so more than one melody was sung simultaneously.

Egyptian musical theatre had gained popularity in the late nineteenth century thanks to one of Darwish's Alexandrian mentors, Salama Hegazi, whose plays tended to be adaptations of European classics. Now, however, the works boasted an Egyptian disposition from start to end. For instance, the romantic hero of Darwish's landmark operetta *The Good Ten* (1920) is from the peasant class. His sensual attraction to his love object is reciprocated by the unconventional hot-blooded peasant woman whom he woos as the sun rises – like Romeo, but at her rustic hut. In a complete overhaul of the genre, not only is this a story about the lower classes, but the Turkish aristocrats are ridiculed on stage, too.

Sending a clear message about the autonomy and ownership of Cleopatra, he also composed the *Cleopatra and Mark Antony* operetta, inverting the order of the names and presenting the Alexandrian queen as a hero. Darwish received the invitation to compose it from singer Mounira el-Mahdia, who as an orphaned child moved to live with her sister in Alexandria. In 1915, shortly after she turned twenty, el-Mahdia became the first female actor to take the stage professionally, in a play about Saladin. Strikingly, when *Cleopatra and Mark Antony* was performed in the 1920s, el-Mahdia began by taking the role of Cleopatra before switching to Antony. She also became one of the earliest women in the world to play a male Shakespearean protagonist when she was cast as Romeo in 1927. By joining a developing cultural renaissance that was important to national identity, women also coupled the country's independence with their own.

These operettas became so popular that Alexandria's opera house was established in 1921. Its first show, in a grand hall of golden walls and tiered red seating, was *Scheherazade*. Not the orientalised Russian symphony of the same name based on *One Thousand and One Nights*, but an Egyptian operetta created by two Alexandrians, composed by Sayed Darwish and written by Bayram al-Tunisi. A strong critic of both Britain and the Egyptian monarchy, al-Tunisi was exiled in 1920, but had already presented the playscript to Darwish who made sure it saw the light of stage. 'The British have always argued before the world, to justify our enslavement, that we are a weak people incapable of governing themselves and that we need continuous protection', al-Tunisi said in a later interview. 'That's why I see that the operetta from its beginning to its end must contain glorification of the Egyptian human being.'[1] In the operetta, the Princess Scheherazade asks the protagonist his name. 'I am the Egyptian,' he replies, in a patriotic melody that introduces the allegory. He explains that he has left behind his love, Huriya, which sounds similar to *hurriyya* (freedom) but means Mermaid (Alexandria is often called the Mermaid of the Mediterranean). But this doesn't stop Princess Scheherazade from falling in love with him and luring him closer by granting him authority over her lands. At the end, he has remained loyal to Mermaid and Egypt, finally telling the princess: 'I wish at this hour to find myself in my country', before ending:

> If I ask my tears or the flames in my ribs,
> They all demand my return to the original shore.
> For so long as the Nile is running,
> I shall be humiliated no more.

Darwish became one of the most loved celebrities in Egypt. His legacy lives on through his composition of Egypt's current national anthem just before he died, its words – 'My homeland, my homeland, my homeland, / You have my love and my heart' – inspired by the nationalist Mustafa Kamil's speech at Alexandria's Zizinia Theatre in 1907. Darwish taught it to the students at his institute so that it could be played at the harbour when Zaghlul returned from his second exile. But Darwish would pay the price for his politically motivated works, dying shortly before Zaghlul's return in 1923. Darwish claimed to be the subject of an assassination attempt by the British, and after his sudden death at just thirty-one, news spread that the British had poisoned him using arsenic oil. That a state autopsy was not permitted continues to raise eyebrows in Alexandria, where Darwish is buried in one of the city's oldest seafront parks, today named the Garden of Immortals.

*   *   *

The Arab renaissance responded indirectly to British occupation by responding directly to British culture. For one, English literature signified the culture of the occupier so translation was actively discouraged. The renaissance's relationship with English literature is exemplified by a 1927 verse tragedy by Egypt's poet laureate Ahmad Shawqi. *The Death of Cleopatra* responds directly to plays that sexualised and orientalised the final Ptolemaic queen – by Shakespeare, John Dryden and George Bernard Shaw. Cleopatra was fittingly played by an Alexandrian star, Fatima Rushdi, known as 'Sarah Bernhardt of the East', whom Sayed Darwish had spotted singing in a café a few years earlier. Shawqi presents Cleopatra as a confident orator and poet, a spiritually grounded family woman who prioritises her nation. Like Darwish's operettas, this was an elevation of Arabic art that both renewed the artistic landscape and highlighted Egypt's autonomous nature. Not only could Egyptians understand and engage with foreign art, they could also correct and surpass it. In the play's anonymous preface, probably written by Shawqi himself, Cleopatra's reputation is defended, the Roman mistreatment of the queen and their subsequent 'suspect history' placed parallel to the European attacks on Alexandria:

> The ones who rose to this serious task . . . were either Romans or the culturally Romanised, so they recorded . . . a history of this political shift in a fictive style, in which the Caesars of Rome won all the laurel wreaths . . . This while the maltreated Egyptian queen, Cleopatra, the final representative of the glory of the Ptolemies and their progeny, who was used to settle this dangerous case at the expense of her reputation, dignity and fading stardom, got nothing but a heap of accusations, sins and curses . . . Should not the Egyptian author remove the screaming oppression off of this Egyptian queen, given the three centuries that her great ancestors spent on the banks of the Nile . . .?[2]

Sometimes, the indignation was more apparent. The description of the coloniser, by Hafez Ibrahim, a working-class poet who advocated political Islamic identity, must have resonated with the Egyptians of Alexandria, where the flags of the lofty consulates waved in the seaside breeze: 'He kills us without retribution, or compensation, or fear. / And he walks towards his flag, and it protects him from harm.' But Ibrahim also translated the first volume of Victor Hugo's *Les Misérables* in 1903, further indication that Egyptians were specifically avoiding British literature.

Building on such works, by the 1930s the Alexandria-born Tawfiq al-Hakim was pioneering the Arabic novel and drama forms. In particular, his prose dramas introduced Arabic theatre as an independent and worthy literary genre, neither lewd like previous prose farces nor neoclassical like Shawqi's verse tragedies. Al-Hakim's writings took on daring topics, used religious themes and mixed grand language with colloquialism, serving as social commentaries about everyday life and insights into the human condition. For instance, in his most absurd play, *The Fate of the Cockroach*, the protagonist is the cockroach vizier whose son has been killed by the ants. The allegory imagines the complicated politics of the two groups of insects, shedding light on the absurdities of absolute authority and blind faith, and raising questions about freedom and individualism. That is, until an unwitting human suddenly brings an end to the cockroach's life.

With the Arabic language reinvigorated, the European communities of Alexandria had little choice but to learn it. Greeks in twentieth-century Alexandria did what their ancestors hadn't always done in previous decades, speaking the very same Arabic as an Egyptian would in the city. Alexandria also became the hub of Arabic calligraphy learning. Since the nineteenth century, calligraphy was being used on book bindings and paintings, as well as some buildings.

There were periods in Alexandria's ancient history when there were statues on every corner. Muhammad Ali's statue from the 1870s was the work of a French sculptor, Alfred Jacquemart, and was exhibited on the Champs-Élysées before being shipped to Alexandria. Ismail Pasha's statue was by an Italian sculptor, Pietro Canonica. These contrasted with the statue of freedom fighter Saad Zaghlul, made in the 1930s by an Egyptian, Mahmoud Mokhtar. Just off the Corniche, the Saad Zaghlul Square is surrounded by grass and balconied buildings in white, yellow and pink. The sculpted figure stands tall at the top of a long column. He wears a long coat and a fez and sternly faces the historic eastern harbour. The column is adorned with bronze reliefs of Zaghlul defiantly pointing at a British official, and being carried heroically by crowds. At the stepped base of the column are two seated figures: on one side a Ptolemaic woman and on the other an ancient Egyptian. Together, the three statues unite three of the most important identities of the city. This sculptor also expressed his desire to create statues of Alexander the Great and Cleopatra, but died in his early forties before he could do so.

Visual artists who trained in Europe, such as Mohamed Nagy and Mahmoud Said, returned to the city, painting in a new, rich style full of Alexandrian life and colour. Nagy and Said represent the first wave of modern Egyptian artists. Painting during the cultural renaissance against a backdrop of foreign occupation and independence movements, they became pioneers by embedding Egyptian and Alexandrian identity directly into their art. They illustrated scenes from the city's history and its everyday life, and in the process became the founders of modern Egyptian art.

Nagy, born in 1888, was the first Egyptian to train at the Academy of Fine Arts in Florence, from 1910 to 1914. In early 1919, he ventured to Paris, where he was taught European impressionism by a seventy-eight-year-old Claude Monet, then a successful painter but not yet among the most famous in the world. Nagy's trip was cut short when the revolution kicked off and he hurried back to Alexandria to take part in the protests. In 1934, Nagy opened his studio and began work on his first commission, murals depicting the history of medicine for the Alexandria Hospital. His aptly named mural, *Renaissance of Egypt*, adorns the Parliament building in Cairo and won him the Salon du Paris award. His most Alexandrian paintings include the fishing boats resting peacefully near the Qaitbay Citadel, and a fisherman proudly carrying his catch.

Begun in 1939, his *School of Alexandria* painting, seven by three metres, is an Alexandrian take on Raphael's *School of Athens* 400 years earlier. With the Alexandrian coast and the sea in the background, an equestrian statue of Alexander the Great stands in the centre in front of the city's ancient buildings. On the mosaiced floor, an array of figures represent Alexandria's historic achievements and its cultural amalgamations.

A white-bearded man, Archimedes or Euclid, is in deep conversation with another bearded man who looks like the Andalusian polymath ibn-Rushd, indicating the influence of ancient Alexandria's Museum on the scholars who followed. St Catherine of Alexandria's saintly presence is paralleled with a common Jewish woman reading the Alexandria-translated Torah in her own Greek language. On the right, with the bottom of Pompey's Pillar as a backdrop, the figures include a woman holding a harp-like instrument, no doubt Hypatia of Alexandria, looking at the modern-day suffragette Huda Sharawi. The third-century Pope Dionysius of Alexandria stands alongside modernising Islamic scholars including Muhammad Abduh. On the left, more pioneers stand in front of the Qaitbay Citadel: the poets Constantine Cavafy and Ahmed Shawqi, and the founder of futurism Filippo Marinetti. The sculptor Mahmoud Mokhtar is also included. Aristotle's absence is explained by the presence of the nationalist intellectual Ahmed Lutfi, whose most Alexandrian contribution was translating the ancient philosopher's works into Arabic. For decades, the painting was placed in the governorate building. But the tolerance of the piece is in stark contrast with the fact that it disappeared during the anti-government protests of 2011 when the building was set alight. Two smaller versions survive.

In the *School of Alexandria*, Nagy also placed two artists in the scene: himself and Mahmoud Said. Born in 1897, as a child Said saw his father, Muhammad Said, become prime minister. Despite being part of the old guard, his father's stances against the British saw him appointed as minister of education under the revolutionary government. After reading law and being appointed assistant to the public prosecutor, Said followed his passions by travelling to Paris for a summer, where he took free drawing classes at the Académie Julian. When he returned, although he shot up the legal ranks until he became judge, he continued to create art, becoming arguably the most important Egyptian painter of the twentieth century. Said's unique style is rooted in Egyptian character. Two of his paintings depict naked Egyptian women on the night-time coast of Alexandria. In one, a plump woman stands in the ocean, the water reaching her shin as life goes on in the background. His most captivating piece, *The Mermaid of Alexandria*, shows a brunette whose bare, olive skin emphasises the green Egyptian emerald of her ring, earrings and bracelets. Seated in the stern of a boat, she looks serene in the middle of the stormy Alexandria sea. She covers her genitals and legs with her hands and a transparent cloth, but her naked breasts take centre stage. Twisting her neck, she looks to the side: no matter what angle you view her from, she avoids your gaze. Said predominantly used two lower-class women as his muses. But the muse for his Alexandrian mermaid is unknown, and he certainly imagined more erotic details here compared to the other women he painted. To Said, the mermaid of his painting personifies Alexandria: an Egyptian woman calm amid the storm, attractive, sexual, perfect.

The influence of Nagy and Said meant that Alexandria became the capital of Egyptian painting. But not everyone agreed with what they were doing. Marinetti returned to Egypt to preach his theory of futurism and the result was the foundation of the Art and Liberty Group in 1937. Its members, Egyptians of European origin who were based not in Alexandria but in Cairo, attempted to show that not everyone was keen on independence or its serious realist art. Their manifesto, *Long Live Degenerate Art!*, brought surrealist art into Egypt so that it could transcend geographic location and national identity to emphasise cosmopolitanism and universalism.

Their efforts only created a clear differentiation between the surrealism of Cairo's art and the social realism of Alexandria's. Alexandrian art, inspired by Nagy and Said, recentred itself on the working and peasant classes, on folk symbolism and tradition, and on the collective unconscious of the nation. The *School of Alexandria* was no longer just an art piece; the city's second generation of artists now belonged to an artistic School of Alexandria.

Margaret Nakhla, born in 1908, studied at the École du Louvre and in 1932 her first major exhibition hit Alexandria. Her spiritual but realistic works often depict crowds or people in different locations: a church, a Turkish bath, an outdoor market, or, in her most Alexandrian piece, enjoying a day on the beach. The brothers Seif Wanly and Adham Wanly, born in 1906 and 1908, pioneered a magnificently modernist style of art. After training in Italy, they returned to create avant-garde paintings. Adham's paintings varied between the movement of dancing women and the stillness of naked muses. He also painted the more serious moments of daily life, like a peasant man and woman kissing with their eyes closed, and two women with their daughter and goat standing at Lake Mariout. His brother Seif's bright colours depict the celebratory scenes of street life, duller colours for the commoner's daily strife, and included some cubist elements that hadn't previously existed in Egyptian art. In 1973, Seif Wanly was awarded the honorary key to the city.

During the Second World War, a third generation of Alexandrian artists, born in the 1910s and 1920s, founded their own Contemporary Art Group, again anti-surrealism, pro-social-realism. Hussein Bicar painted scenes of Alexandrian life that mixed the ancient with his present in a minimalist style. Hamed Ewais moved to Alexandria to join the group and expressed anti-imperialism by emphasising the everyday: one painting shows a man and woman carrying their fishing net, another a barber shop from the mirror-view as a man gets a shave. Hamed Nada took ancient Egypt as a source of inspiration with paintings that included the sacred bull deity Apis. Abdelhady el-Gazzar, the son of an Alexandrian imam, reflected desolate and dark scenes of hopelessness and anguish. The Contemporary Art Group's manifesto confirms that well into the twentieth-century the city's artists were expressly continuing what those before them had started: attempting to locate and express 'the Egyptian soul'.

In the twentieth century, cinema was dubbed the seventh art, following architecture, sculpture, painting, music, poetry and dance – all of which had a fascinating history in Alexandria. The city that once boasted the seventh Ancient Wonder was especially ahead of its time with the seventh art. Since the Lumière visit in 1896, film had become incredibly popular in the city. Cafés invested in projectors and began to put films on, making huge profits. Soon, many of the countless theatres in the city began to project movies, some even reinventing themselves exclusively as cinemas in the early twentieth century. By 1925, there were at least thirty projection halls, some on rooftops. At first, tickets came at a high price and the upper classes dressed up to attend: men in suits and women in even more revealing gowns than those they wore to the theatre. By 1912, tickets became affordable and locals were packing the cinemas every night, especially those that had three classes of seating. Tea and snack vendors walked through the audiences during the shows. For movies that needed translation, a live interpreter stood at the front. For the silent movies, like Charlie Chaplin's, a live musician was present. The cinema was an interactive experience: people demanded parts to be replayed, they cheered and booed, and they even had a well-known chant for electricity cuts: 'fraudulent cinema, give us our money'. Around Alexandria, films were advertised on banners in the roads, and lucky smokers could win cinema tickets in their cigarette packs. The subsequent cinemas of the 1940s gave Alexandria a taste of art deco architecture. Under their pillars and marble exterior, crowds would wait for the doors to be opened before everyone flocked in excitedly.

In the 1930s, Egypt's pioneering film director, Mohammed Bayumi, emerged in Alexandria. Born in 1894, he refused to fight for the British in the First World War and after the revolution, began an acting troupe in Alexandria and worked as a cameraman for an Italian director. Bayumi made a point of filming independence figures like Zaghlul, before creating the first movie to be written, filmed and directed by an Egyptian. *Barsoum Looks for Employment* (1923) purposely displayed Egyptian unity by telling the story of a Muslim–Christian friendship, with a Muslim actor cast as a Christian and a Christian actor as a Muslim. Bayumi went on to found the Egyptian Cinematographic Institute in Alexandria, paving the way for further films. Alexandria's most influential director is Youssef Chahine, born in 1926, who cemented Egypt as the Hollywood of the Arab region. Chahine's magnum opus, the *Alexandria Quartet* (1978, 1982, 1989, 2004), introduced Egyptian cinema to the world. Its Hamlet-obsessed autobiographical protagonist is called Yehia al-Iskandarani. His first name is used by both Christians and Muslims, and his surname is 'the Alexandrian'; together, the full name sounds like 'Long live the Alexandrian'. This character represents how the city and its people attempt to navigate the curiosities and contradictions of cosmopolitanism during times of war and globalisation. Chahine also introduced another Alexandrian to Hollywood, Omar Sharif, who shot to fame in David Lean's *Lawrence of Arabia*. Both Chahine and Sharif worked with the Alexandrian actress Hind Rostom, who became so influential that she was dubbed the 'Marilyn Monroe of the East'.

Alexandria was able to become a cinema city quickly because of its expanse of coffee shops, theatres and social clubs. Many of these clubs were established in the nineteenth century by the European elites to provide private spaces for conversation, reading, smoking, billiards and card games. Gambling sometimes led to unpleasant arguments. The first of these clubs, founded by the Menasce family, only admitted royalty, ministers, diplomats and British officers. Regular Egyptians were not welcome here, though Egyptian officers were eventually allowed to ballot for temporary membership or pay entrance fees. The Sporting Club in Cairo was founded in 1882 for British troops, later opening to European members but not allowing Egyptian membership until 1918, while the Sporting Club in Alexandria was founded in 1890 by the British police chief Coles Pasha and allowed selected members of Egypt's aristocratic class. In 1904, British High Commissioner Lord Cromer founded a club in Alexandria that only allowed Britons to join. In addition, the city's numerous Masonic lodges continued to be exclusive; in fact, local press reports in 1925 record how women in Alexandria were demanding entrance into the secretive society.

The exclusive clubs began to play sports including football. Although the ancient Egyptians played a similar sport, when it was introduced into school curricula at the turn of the century it was seen as part of Cromer's imperialist agenda. Soon, however, it would become Egypt's national sport. In 1903 Cairo, Egypt's first football club, the Railway, was founded by British and Italian engineers. In response, in 1905, Alexandrians working in customs created the first Egyptian football club, Red Star, later renamed Olympic.

The following year, workers' unions got together to create a club called *al-Ittihad* (The Union). This club attracted people from different classes, including employees from around the city who'd begun unionising and protesting for independence. As four pro-independence groups merged to form a bigger club in '1914, the club announced its goal bluntly: 'al-Ittihad al-Sakandari [The Alexandrian Union] for sporting *and* nationalist events.' By 1921, al-Ittihad had played a key role in founding the Egyptian Football Association. Its members came from across society and it remains the only major club in the country never to have had a non-Egyptian president. Today, al-Ittihad continues to play in its all-green kit, the colour of the Egyptian flag used during and after independence, and the club's nickname is *Sid al-Balad* (Master, or Forefather, of the Country). 'Alexandria is my life, and al-Ittihad is in my blood', a big banner recently read in the stands. Though al-Ittihad haven't won a trophy for half a century, they remain a symbol of the city's nationalistic, cultural renaissance through sport. On the club's social media pages, a bust of Alexander the Great can often be seen adorned with the club's jersey.

In 1929, Alexandria Stadium became the first football stadium in the continent of Africa. It remains a subtle work of art. Its gate – on a square near the equestrian statue of Alexander the Great – is a surprising Roman-style neoclassical arc with Greek-style pillars. Entering it gives the feeling of an ancient Greek theatre, not a modern football stadium. One of the stands behind the goalposts has a gap so that the arc is always visible. The turnstiles are hidden behind large mahogany doors, and the main stand, built on the remains of an ancient city wall, extends from a series of Ottoman-style latticeworks.

The cultural renaissance of Alexandria – in music, poetry, theatre, sculpture, visual art, film and sport – essentially advocated autonomy and independence. These would lead the city to its newest chapter, one in which Arab and Islamic fervour would change its landscape and people yet again.

The Second World War

Mohammed had had several jobs during his life: fishing, farming, transporting large quantities of mud from the riverbank to maintain the city's demand for bricks. He was about to start a business importing fruit from Turkey, especially apples, one of the only fruits difficult to grow in Egypt.

One ordinary morning in 1918, Mohammed congratulated the local postman abdel-Nasser on the birth of his baby boy Gamal. A year later, in 1919, the congratulations would be reversed when Mohammed celebrated the birth of his own son Ibrahim. Baby Gamal (abdel-Nasser) would go on to become one of the most iconic leaders in modern history. And baby Ibrahim (Issa) is my granddad.

They lived in the Bacos area – a reminder of ancient Alexandria's much-loved deity, Bacchus. The neighbourhood was home to many Jews, in addition to Armenians and Greeks. Its main street included a theatre, cinema, church, mosque and synagogue, as well as the bustling fruit and vegetable market. In 1920, as baby Ibrahim began to crawl, King Fuad I had a child of his own: the crown prince Farouk.

One day, a young Gamal abdel-Nasser was walking past Muhammad Ali's statue in the elegantly rebuilt square when he witnessed police attacking a large group of demonstrators. He decided to join in the rally, unaware of the cause. The nationalist Young Egypt Society was calling for the end of colonialism. The police proceeded to arrest the protesters and, before he knew it, Nasser found himself squashed into a police pick-up van and spending the night in a crowded cell. The next morning, as his father waited in the lobby carrying his postbag, the guard informed him that he'd been bailed and warned him not to cause more trouble. The event affected Nasser deeply and he became more rather than less vocal, while his father became more protective. At school aged sixteen, he was cast to play Caesar in an anti-British performance of Shakespeare's *Julius Caesar*. During the climactic assassination scene, biographers claim that 'the honest postman' his father, 'seeing his eldest son fall under the dagger of Brutus, nearly rushed to the rescue'.[1]

As the teenage years of Ibrahim Issa and Gamal abdel-Nasser drew to an end, Egypt was experiencing tumultuous times. King Fuad I died in 1936 and his sixteen-year-old son returned from the department stores, football stadiums and brothels of London to be crowned King Farouk I. Independence remained on everyone's mind. In 1937, the king was in Alexandria to be briefed by the prime minister about the Conference of Montreux, which resulted in the abolition of the mixed tribunals system so that foreigners were finally subject to the same judicial system as everyone else – big news for Alexandrians. And nationalism was in full flow around the world, not just in Egypt. The First World War had propelled some nations to pursue independence. But the Treaty of Versailles which followed that war hadn't left everyone satisfised, not least the Germans who'd been forced to pay severe reparations and lose significant home and overseas territories.

Extreme nationalism saw the Nazi Party come to power in Germany, led by Adolf Hitler and his Alexandria-born deputy Rudolf Hess, who'd helped him write *Mein Kampf*. Hess's grandparents had moved to Alexandria a couple of decades before his birth, and he lived there until he was fourteen. In September 1939, Germany attacked Poland, and Britain and France declared war on the Axis powers that would include the German Third Reich, Fascist Italy and Imperial Japan. It became clear why the British had never really left Alexandria, why so many warships had remained at the western port all these years. Overnight, the city became the British navy's largest base in the Mediterranean. Troops and ammunition began arriving at the harbour, from where they'd be transported westwards and southwards via the rail and road links. Despite Britain's imposition of martial law, the draining of resources and the economic turmoil, Alexandria had survived the First World War relatively unscathed. The Second World War was going to be different.

Within less than a year of the outbreak of war, the conflict reached Egypt. On the Mediterranean coast the British crossed over to Libya to attack the Italians, and the Italians retaliated by crossing over to Egypt. Fighting continued on the border, with the German field marshal Erwin Rommel ultimately intending to fight his way to Alexandria.

Alexandria's diverse population meant that it was home to residents from both sides of the conflict. Italians had been in Alexandria for centuries; unlike the Greeks, they lived in modest neighbourhoods, with many Italian workers joining the Egyptian unions. For the last fifty years, Alexandria had also been home to Salesians, Catholic missionaries from Turin who perceived Alexandria's Italian community as being overly assimilated in the city and came to encourage them to take their religious rites more seriously. As Italy prepared to enter the war on 10 June 1940, its consulates sought to protect the country's key institutions. These included Italy's international cultural organisation, the Dante Alighieri Society, and the Italian Chamber of Commerce, both of which had branches in Alexandria. The night Italy joined the war, Egyptian police, under orders from the British, arrested 150 of Alexandria's Italian men, including priests, before surrounding the consulate and freezing Italian banks. This didn't go down well with the Egyptian population, who'd grown closer to their Italian neighbours. Many Egyptian children also went to Italian schools, so when this happened, Italian women were quickly hired as teachers in the hope that they were less likely to be arrested.

In spring 1941, Hess attempted to make peace with the Allies by venturing to Britain behind Hitler's back. During his childhood in Alexandria, the Deputy Führer had admired British rule – claiming that it civilised the natives – which may have influenced his decision to make the solo flight across the North Sea. As he read the letter Hess had left him, Hitler was furious, abolishing the Office of the Deputy Führer and ordering that his former confidante be shot instantly if seen. Low on fuel and with British jets in pursuit, Hess parachuted into Scottish farmland and was swiftly arrested. At the Nuremburg trials after the war, Hess received a life sentence.

Meanwhile, Italy was fighting the Greeks, and that same spring Hitler assisted Benito Mussolini by invading Greece. For Alexandria, this meant a new wave of refugees as Greeks scrambled onto anything leaving their shores: traditional fishing boats, small steam-boats and tugs usually used to tow larger boats into the ports. On 21 April 1941, the first of these vessels arrived in Alexandria, and more than a thousand refugees – hungry, weary and without identification papers – sat on the beach waiting to find out what to do next. Within a few days, more than 5,000 refugees had arrived from Greece, including politicians from the Free Greek Movement and members of the British consulate. The last steamer to arrive had previously been used to transport Italian prisoners of war and was in a terrible condition. It was carrying Georgios Seferiades, a diplomat who was by his own admission obsessed with the recently deceased Alexandrian poet Cavafy, and who would go on to write Nobel Prize-winning poetry. It also brought British Council lecturers to Alexandria. R. D. Smith soon taught English at the city's newly founded Fuad University, and his wife Olivia Manning went on to become a renowned novelist. Robert Liddell also joined the university and wrote several novels, as well as a biography of Cavafy. Despite the conflict edging closer to Alexandria, the founding of the university gave Alexandrians confidence that things would work out. Lawrence Durrell also arrived at this time, and though these Britons were taken to Cairo, they found it unwelcoming, noisy and grimy, returning swiftly to cosmopolitan Alexandria, where Smith, Manning and Liddell shared an apartment.

On the night of 24 May, Greece's royal family left Crete for Alexandria, where King George II of Greece and his cabinet formed a government-in-exile. That both refugees and royalty affiliated to the Allies were flocking to Alexandria thrust the city onto the Axis radar. In June 1941, panic spread across Alexandria as it suffered an unexpected and heavy bombing raid. Tens of thousands of residents began to flee, including dock workers on whom the British relied. The city faced constant German bombardment for months, with blackouts becoming a nightly routine that sent residents into a state of dejection and dread. Bombs dropping on them from the sky were a step too far for Alexandrians, who hadn't much faith in the British anyway – and many Egyptians, let alone Alexandria's Italians, Austro-Hungarians and Germans, must secretly have been hoping for the Allies to be defeated.

There are countless local legends about this period. One involves a Greek man awoken by shelling, who ran into the street where his attention was caught by a white dove escaping from the mausoleum of Prophet Muhammad's companion Abu al-Darda. The man then saw someone dressed in white walk out of the mausoleum and protect the building with his bare hands, catching the falling missiles and throwing them clear. The war log in the city's archive does indeed record shelling at this location in 1941, specifically by parachute bomb. It also notes that a missile got stuck in a nearby tree and therefore didn't detonate – so perhaps a miracle did occur after all.

British troops were stationed in Alexandria but hardly seemed to be defending it. They enjoyed its beaches, cinemas and exclusive social clubs. Like the soldiers in the First World War, they frequented the brothels, especially the popular Mary's House. Here, women waited in the bar downstairs, others worked upstairs and each prostitute could be booked by 35 men a night. Mary's House was attacked one evening, though the bomb only damaged the area around the bar. The madam, Mary, had another brothel in Cairo, so she sent the terrified Alexandrian women there and brought the oblivious Cairo ones back to Alexandria in their place. In an autobiographical novel, Manning relates how the wounded British soldiers arrived at the hospital after the attack, saying, 'one after the other, "I got mine at Mary's House", and a little sweetie of a nurse said to the doctor, "Mary's house must've been giving a very big party"'.[2]

By the winter, Alexandria was also under threat from the sea as the Italians fired torpedoes from the harbour towards the British naval base, where they damaged battleships. And by land, more than 200,000 Axis troops had managed to invade Egypt and were pushing the Allies back from the Libyan border until they reached el-Alamein, less than sixty miles west of Alexandria. The Axis were now dangerously close to the key city, the loss of which would signal a defeat for the Allies on the Mediterranean and Middle East Theatre of the war.

As news reached Alexandria, residents received it with a mixture of apprehension and anticipation. On 28 June 1942, German radio boasted that its troops would be in Alexandria within a week. And a German radio announcement for the city delivered an anticipated victory message to the female population: 'Ladies of Alexandria get out your party frocks. We are on our way.'[3] Winston Churchill, now Britain's prime minister, gave orders to protect Egypt 'drastically as if it were Kent or Sussex, without any regard to any other consideration than destruction of the enemy'.[4] But that same day, British commanders deduced that Alexandria might also be attacked by air and that their resources should be split between the other important ports of Port Said, Haifa and Beirut. Alexandrians watched on as the British ships left the harbour, one after another. To the Alexandrians, the British had proved that they couldn't be trusted to protect the city.

As BBC radio bulletins spread propaganda about British troops in Alexandria fighting on against a more powerful German army, locals began to do one of two things: prepare a welcome for the oncoming army, or leave as quickly as possible. Cars blocked the road to Cairo and the trains were so packed that people were jumping in through the windows (some Alexandrians are recorded as having left for Palestine and even South Africa). Those on the outskirts picked up on the panic and began to pack up, too, as rumours spread that the British were planning to sack the place before leaving. Alexandria's 25,000 Jews were especially scared – not of their neighbours, but of the Nazis. Hitler's Final Solution was well-known to them and they'd heard radio reports about Polish Jews suffering at the hands of the Nazis in the last few years. Some joined the flight to Cairo, others attempted to move to Palestine and many stayed home in fear. The Greeks and Italians of Alexandria, however, began to hang up welcome banners and bunting for the approaching army, to bake victory cakes and to prepare celebration parties. Merchandise appeared around the city, including postcards of Hitler, one with his face on the Muhammad Ali statue. And anyone who'd rented a room to a British officer began to destroy incriminating evidence.[5] Any celebratory mood was cut short, however, as air raids began again on 29 June, two days before the Allies and Axis finally came face-to-face at nearby el-Alamein.

The First Battle of el-Alamein was a stalemate but the Allies vitally managed to stop the Axis from advancing further. Three months later, the Second Battle of el-Alamein, fifty miles from Alexandria, was a decisive victory for the Allies, who had almost 200,000 troops facing around 120,000 from the Axis. An Alexandrian legend claims that at midnight, St Mina, whose monastery isn't far from the battlefield, appeared to the Germans, charging at them with an army of camels. The apparition terrified the Germans and ultimately led to their defeat. Neither the Allies nor the Nazis reported this (for the former, it put into doubt their military might; for the latter, it implied divine condemnation), but the next morning, on 11 November 1942, St Mina's miracle made headlines in the *Egyptian Gazette*. For Churchill el-Alamein was a turning point in the war, the first significant land victory, ending the Axis threat in Egypt and ensuring that the Suez Canal (with its access to resources, including oil) would remain in the hands of the Allies.

Alexandria had survived yet another scare. Its residents made their way back. At the coffeehouses, they shared legends about how Alexandria's Muslim saints had protected the city from the air raids, and how the Christian saint had appeared to the Germans with his camel army to tip the scales of battle.

The remnants of the war remained, of course: signs of shelling, the schools that had closed to become hospital centres, the rest camps and hostels, the communications centres, the anti-aircraft base, and, most ominously of all, the Hadra cemetery which already held First World War graves and was now extended to house a further 1,305 victims of the Second World War. Alexandria's port had also welcomed many Jews during the conflict, offering them a safer haven at a time when they'd been turned away by other countries. In fact, some of the already resident Egyptian Jews were worried that this influx of new Ashkenazi Jews might affect them. Ashkenazim would go on to become the most educated Jewish group in Alexandria, where they joined the long-established Karaites (who spread across the social strata) and Sephardim (who were largely wealthy).

Though the global conflict continued on other fronts, the city was returning to normal – if such a thing existed here. Even the polarisation returned. English lecturer and poet Robin Fedden – who married an Alexandrian Greek-Italian – observed how the elite's 'parquet floors quake over an abyss of poverty; the black satin and pearls are complementary to rags and tatters'. Starkly, 'nothing but their labours link the peasant to the cotton kings. Even their diseases are different.'[6] There were also some positives: on 8 February 1943, King Farouk arrived to inaugurate the city's university, making it autonomous from Cairo's and changing its name from his father's to his own. He made sure to use the opportunity to do what many others had done before him: relate himself to the city's founder. The commemorative medal from the university's opening ceremony displays his picture on one side and Alexander's on the other. Its Arabic inscription reads: 'King Farouk University – Alexander the Great who established Alexandria – and King Farouk the First is the King.'

Egypt's ministers, meanwhile, were busy discussing plans that might enable the Arab countries to share a united stance in future. On 7 October 1944, representatives from Egypt met heads of state from Iraq, Jordan, Lebanon and Syria, and the Alexandria Protocol was signed, marking the birth of the Arab League.

With the US joining the Allies, the war was tipping in their favour, and following the invasion of Germany and its subsequent surrender, the conflict drew to an end in the spring of 1945.

Before long, more high-profile refugees were making their way to Alexandria, joining the exiled Ottoman and Greek royalty already there. The crown prince and princess of Greece had arrived in 1944. In Italy, the war had ended in disaster. A public referendum was announced and King Victor Emmanuel III decided to abdicate in favour of his son in the hope that this would repopularise the monarchy. But Italians voted for republicanism instead, bringing the Kingdom of Italy to an end. In an inadvertent exchange, the Italians of Alexandria left to try life in the new republic, and the ousted Italian king made his way to Alexandria. A Jewish-Iraqi friend named Joseph Smouha had created a little garden city on the east side of town, so Victor Emmanuel took a small villa there. When he died in 1948, he was buried behind the altar at St Catherine's Cathedral, though the Italian government decided to repatriate him some forty years later. Then came nine-year-old King Simeon II of Bulgaria, who'd taken the throne at six before the Communists abolished the monarchy in 1946. When in 1990 Communism fell in Bulgaria, Simeon returned and eventually became prime minister in his sixties. And there was King Zog of Albania, who'd proclaimed himself monarch after serving as prime minister and president. When the Communists took over, he escaped to Alexandria where he purchased a magnificent villa in what was fast becoming the royal capital.

Egypt's king was clearly enjoying the city's royal prestige. But one day in October 1950 he returned from a spending spree in Europe's exclusive stores to find an anonymous letter in his Alexandria palace. It warned the king of an imminent plan to remove him from power.

The Postman's Son

When sixteen-year-old King Farouk made his first public address in 1936, the nation – including my great grandad Mohammed and his postman abdel-Nasser – were glued hopefully to their radios. His Majesty was talking to them in Arabic; his Turkish-speaking predecessors didn't even learn the local language. A couple of years later, his popularity increased further when he married an Alexandrian, Safinaz Zulficar, renamed Farida since every member of the royal family's name had to start with the same letter. The king's mother had been a queen consort with a limited public role; Queen Farida was now the first Alexandrian monarch since Cleopatra. The daughter of a judge, the granddaughter of the former prime minister Muhammad Said and the niece of the painter Mahmoud Said, she came from a popular family that proved to the public how the elites could remain both nationalistic and pious.

The cultural renaissance of the last half-century had cemented a nationalist sentiment in the public consciousness. The influence of non-Muslim governments had clearly harmed Egypt, and nationalism began to be coupled with religious conviction. The common person's aspiration to improve their country was an act of worship. After all, the British were non-Muslims forcing Egyptians to fight for them, taking the country's resources and imposing cultural imperialism. The leading Wafd party had secular views and was constantly accused of corruption (including insider trading in the Alexandria Cotton Exchange). And the royal family were frivolous money wasters out of touch with the people. With Karl Marx's books being passed discreetly around Alexandria, the Egyptian Communist Party was founded in 1921 and declared the city its headquarters. A third of its nationwide membership was in

Alexandria. Communists were often arrested and the populace was told that this group was committing the worst offence of all, atheism. The Muslim Brotherhood was also established in 1928 near Suez and gained popularity in Alexandria through the 1930s. They established social services like hospitals and schools. But some of their messages were alarming, like a call in 1936 to boycott Jewish businesses, in line with Friday sermons that began to alert worshippers of plans to annex Palestine to a new Zionist state. The new and active student union at Farouk University developed and played a significant role in the regional rise of both the Communists and Muslim Brotherhood.

The newly wed royal couple couldn't take their popularity for granted. Politics aside, the young king was spending excessive amounts of money on shopping, food and women. He was buying out department stores in Europe, growing visibly fatter and keeping dozens of women at his disposal. Even during the Second World War, revelations about his hedonistic lifestyle were hitting the over-burdened Egyptian population hard. In his early twenties, as the Axis powers approached Alexandria, the king's Italian valet was gathering a different woman each evening from the city's brothels and dance halls, and driving them to his palace for the night. Farouk's birthday every February involved a big celebration, with fireworks and convoys that saw him driven in a red Rolls-Royce from the Montazah Palace in the far east of the city to the Ras el-Tin Palace in the far west. They sped across the main boulevard, the historic Canopic Way that Alexander had drawn out on the sand, and which had recently been renamed after Farouk's father to become Rue Fuad (Fuad Street). On his twenty-fifth birthday in 1945, the king arranged a relay race from his Alexandria palace to his Cairo palace, again in red cars, this time in long-hooded two-seater racing cars. The king enjoyed every fast, red car, and since that was his favourite colour car, no one else in Egypt was allowed to drive a red vehicle.

One of the royal family's palaces in Alexandria – with its stained glass, ceiling art and chandeliers – gives a taste of the monarchy's lifestyle. Now the Royal Jewellery Museum, a bronze sculpture stands casually under the stairs: the *Neapolitan Fisherboy* listening to a conch shell, presumably by French sculptor Jean-Baptiste Carpeaux since there is a matching marble version in the Louvre. There are candy and snuff boxes encrusted with diamonds and white rubies; desk stationary sets, toiletry sets and a chess board, all made of gold, silver and ivory. Even the shisha pipe's mouthpiece is overwhelming, an enamelled concoction of gold, silver, black marble, ebony, tortoise shell, coral and amber, inlaid with diamonds, sapphires, red rubies and emeralds! It's no wonder that as time went on, there were recurring rumours that the king was eating 600 oysters a week and that his breakfast was being delivered by air from Paris.

King Farouk was also committing political suicide. He was accused of playing a part in a rigged election that ousted the popular nationalist Wafd party in 1938. He sympathised with the Axis powers, especially the Italians, during the war, which turned the British against him, too. In 1942, the British ambassador went as far as presenting the king with an oven-ready abdication decree, but instead Farouk ceded to their demands, placing a Wafd government back in power. The Egyptian public and military watched closely: it didn't escape them that the Wafdists were now cooperating with Britain and that the monarchy wasn't half as powerful as it made itself out to be. Dissatisfaction with all three was becoming ever more pronounced.

In 1948, there were two further disasters for the king, both political and personal. The first was the Arab–Israeli War, instigated by the Arab League states and led by Egypt, the king's support seemingly an attempt to prove his loyalty to a pan-Arab cause. The Arabs entered Palestine as soon as the British Mandate was formally ended and the Israeli Declaration of Independence passed by the United Nations came into action. The war ended badly for Egypt as Israel kept the land mandated to it and added half of the area proposed for the Arab state. According to the United Nations, more than 700,000 Palestinians left their homes in an event so significant in the collective Arab consciousness that it is still referred to as the *nakba* – the catastrophe. Some of these refugees ended up in Egypt. As for the Jews of Alexandria, a 1947 census counts 21,128. The 1948 war no doubt resulted in a newfound mutual hostility. Between 1935 and 1940, one in every twenty-six of Egypt's Jews married a non-Jew, indicating the extent to which intermarriage had endured. The increased hostilities in the 1940s may be the reason why this changed by 1945, when only 1.4 per cent of Jewish marriages were to non-Jews. In Alexandria, divorce courts are said to have been busier in that year. And thousands of Jews ended up leaving Alexandria for the new Zionist state; some quarter of a million would move from across the Arab states over the next three years.

But it was another divorce in 1948 that added to the monarchy's troubles. Queen Farida had borne three daughters but no son for the king, and he suspected infidelity. Farouk opted for divorce. The popular Alexandrian queen was the chair of the Red Crescent Society and honorary president of the Egyptian Feminist Union. Parting ways with her was a PR disaster.

By the 1950s, Egyptian police were helping the resistance movements, covering their tracks and providing them with protection. When, on 25 January 1952, British troops discovered Egyptian fighters hiding in police barracks in the town of Ismailia, near Suez, trouble ensued. The British negotiator was killed and the troops responded by attacking the police station. They killed around 50 Egyptian policemen and injured almost 100 more. As news spread, violent uprisings began around the country. As a result of this occurrence, 25 January went on to become the National Police Day (and the first protests in Egypt's 2011 revolution purposely coincided with this date). In the immediate aftermath of this event, a group of mostly junior army officers who'd named themselves the Free Officers – no more than 100 men – began their defiant plan to seize power. Their leader was none other than the postman's son from Bacos, Gamal abdel-Nasser, by this time a lieutenant-colonel. He was joined by the higher ranked General Muhammad Naguib. They'd also sought the Muslim Brotherhood's support.

On 23 July, the officers arrested key royalists, filled Egyptian airspace with fighter jets and made a public broadcast about seizing government that sent people onto the streets in support. They now turned their attention to Alexandria, where, in the Montazah Palace, King Farouk was residing. The previous day, he'd announced a new cabinet from Alexandria. By 25 July, he'd sent for help. CIA reports from that date, labelled 'TOP SECRET' and only released in 2019, indicate that 'King Farouk has repeatedly advised Ambassador Caffery not to underestimate the seriousness of the situation in Egypt'. Yet he still hoped that Alexandria would not be lost: 'He stated that Cairo was "gone" and that he did not know what would happen in Alexandria. "If anything is to be done," the King warned, "it must be done at once."' But the CIA memo also adds that the British embassy had to 'inform Farouk that Britain can "not intervene with force in what appears to be an internal Egyptian problem."'¹ By the end of that day, the army had arrived in Alexandria and taken control of the streets. The king left the Montazah Palace for the Ras-el-Tin Palace nearer the harbour. Naguib sent orders for the king's luxurious yacht *Mahrousa* not to sail without permission.

On 26 July, with both Britain and the US now taking a backseat and letting the coup take shape, Alexandria became the centre of this anti-monarchy revolution. One of the officers, Anwar Sadat, who would later become president, met the prime minister to deliver a final ultimatum to the king. The prime minister took the abdication document from his office to the palace, where the king signed it, passing the throne to his six-month-old son. With a military presence around the city, the defeated king emerged, covering his face in the backseat of a car, this time black not red. His fate was unknown, but trial and execution were certainly on the cards. Alongside the US ambassador, he was whisked from the palace towards the port where he boarded *Mahrousa* for Italy. At 6 p.m., people gathered on their balconies and rooftops to witness the yacht slowly sailing away, with Egyptian navy ships behind it. Farouk had been spared a much starker fate than other toppled rulers in Alexandria's history. As he looked back at the city, and as the ship faded from view, it became clear that the dynasty Muhammad Ali had founded was finished. Within a year, the monarchy was completely abolished and Egypt was to be a republic.

The nationalist revolution of 1952 led to drastic changes across the country. Nasser and the Free Officers, now the Revolutionary Command Council, immediately launched reforms that limited land ownership to 200 *feddans* (208 acres) and set a minimum wage for agricultural workers. Any extra land was to be sold to the government in return for bonds, then redistributed and sold to peasants. Alexandria's wealthy landowners began to lose their power. Naguib was declared Egypt's first president in June 1953 and Nasser became prime minister. Realising their role in the popularisation of the revolution, Naguib continued to engage with the Muslim Brotherhood and even reopened communication with the Wafd party, all as the Communist movement grew. Nasser played a modern-day Brutus, placing Naguib under house arrest. Protests began, with the Muslim Brotherhood aware that Nasser wouldn't give them any role in government. The unrest led to Naguib being reinstated.

Nasser's pan-Arab nationalism was a threat to the new state of Israel. Since Israel's foundation, Arabs had questioned the loyalties of Egypt's Jews, a doubt that wasn't helped by the Lavon Scandal in 1954, when Israeli intelligence recruited thirteen Jews from Alexandria to carry out terrorist attacks on Western targets so they could pin the blame on Egyptian nationalists and force Britain to maintain its presence in the country. On a summer's day in Alexandria, several small packages detonated at a US-run post office and various postboxes around the city. A couple of weeks later, bombs went off simultaneously in Alexandria and Cairo's US Information Agency libraries. On the second anniversary of the revolution, 23 July, the cell targeted the Metro and Rio cinemas in Alexandria. Egyptian intelligence was nearby, and when an explosive ignited in a bomber's pocket in the street, he was taken to hospital. The detonation was a result of a chemical reaction, and after searching his home police began arresting members of the cell, finding a small explosives factory in the home of an optician. Both Churchill and US president Dwight Eisenhower attempted to mediate the group's release, but two members were executed in Alexandria. As they were buried alongside loyal residents in the Jewish cemetery, every blameless Jew in Alexandria must have known that this botched Israeli plan would put them under the spotlight. At the time, the affair was a scandal of the highest order for Israel internally and externally, with the US and Britain bewildered by its conception and the Israeli government continuing to deny its role for almost fifty years, until 2005.

The Free Officers were garnering more support from their anti-Israeli and anti-British stances than from anti-monarchical sentiment. British troops remained at the Suez Canal but were being attacked regularly, so on 19 October, under pressure from Eisenhower, Britain signed the Anglo-Egyptian Treaty of 1954, withdrawing their troops from the canal. On 26 October, Nasser delivered a speech in Alexandria's Mansheya Square, previously Muhammad Ali Square, to celebrate this news. Nasser spoke to a big crowd as the rest of the nation listened to the radios on their living-room shelves: 'And I celebrate with you, you the children of Alexandria, who struggled in the past, whose parents struggled, whose grandparents struggled, and whose brothers were martyred in the past, whose fathers were martyred in the past, I celebrate with you today.' As the crowd cheered, gunfire was heard, one loud, echoing shot, then another, and another, eight shots in total. From the balcony, Nasser screamed with the rhetorical power of an unlikely tragic hero: 'O men, let everyone stay in their place. My life is a sacrifice for Egypt, my blood is a sacrifice for Egypt . . . Gamal abdel-Nasser's life belongs to you.'

After this assassination attempt, a crackdown on any perceived opposition began immediately, especially on the Muslim Brotherhood, whose members were apprehended and eight of its leaders sentenced to death. Naguib was placed under house arrest again, too. The Muslim Brotherhood have maintained a number of outlandish theories about the attack being a hoax, including the fact that the assailant missed eight times despite being only seven metres away. That week Egypt's leading newspaper made its own outlandish claim that a builder found the gun near the square and decided that he should take it to Nasser himself, enduring a week-long trek, on foot, from Alexandria to Cairo. The day after the assassination attempt, Nasser was carried shoulder-high as he waved to thousands of Alexandrians cheering his name. The Mansheya Incident, as the assassination attempt came to be known, altered the political landscape as he became more popular than ever and solidified a lasting grip on power.

By 1956, after a series of high-profile rallies and speeches, Nasser's new constitution, which included the implementation of a single-party system, passed a referendum and he simultaneously took the seat of president. Opposition became impossible as Alexandria became filled with secret police and some residents took it on themselves to become informants. Nasser was a Muslim and a socialist, but any organised Islamic or Communist movement was quashed. Having noticed the power of political Islam, he changed the

authoritative position of Grand Imam from an institutionally
elected position to its current status of governmental selection.
Although Nasser censored more than his successors and was backed
by a strong propaganda machine, even his critics would find it hard
to deny the ground-breaking nature of his first constitution. It
included Egyptian women's right to vote. While the monarchy had
been close to Britain, France and the US, Nasser swiftly challenged
these ties by, for example, remaining neutral in the Cold War, trading arms with Czechoslovakia, recognising Communist China,
ensuring that the Suez Canal did not ship to Israel and banning
Israel from using the strait connecting Sinai and the Arabian peninsula. Nasser quickly developed an iconic status across the Arab
world due to his pan-Arab ideology and defiant stance on European
colonialism. He set out Six Principles, including 'the eradication of
all aspects of imperialism', and more local Principles that made him
popular among the significant working and farming classes: 'the
eradication of feudalism' and 'the eradication of monopolies'.

It is from Alexandria that Nasser would announce his biggest
policy. The revolution's date, 26 July, had quickly become an annual
celebration in the city. On its fourth anniversary in 1956, just weeks
after becoming president, Nasser stood in front of hundreds of
thousands in Mansheya Square. This location had become central
to his own life narrative, having been arrested here in his youth and
narrowly escaping assassination there two years earlier. Thousands
waited for him to appear, and at 9 p.m., he strolled onto the balcony
of the stock exchange high above the square. He spoke sternly
about Egypt's right to self-determination. He then gleefully
announced the most anti-colonial gesture possible: nationalisation
of the Suez Canal. Before he finished his sentence, a thunderous
cheer emanated from the large crowd, and the city came out into
the streets to celebrate.

Reports in the West noted that the stability of the free world was
being put to the test in Alexandria. 'A lifeline between the East and
West, the free world does not want it [the Suez Canal] dependent on
the Egyptian government', confirmed a newsreel in America. For
Britain, this unexpected announcement was an open act of defiance. In London, Parliament decided on a military response, with
the assistance of France and Israel. Operation Musketeer would

begin at Alexandria, which was to be captured by sea as the first step, before forces advanced southwards. As the operation was about to get underway, the plan was altered: given its naval strength, Alexandria might be too hard to capture, and the city's dense population could cause issues and lead to a higher death toll. Alexandria, which the CIA predicted was receiving missiles for its defence from the Soviet Union, remained safe as the coalition headed towards Port Said and began air offensives.[2] The Egyptians disabled ships and sank obstacles in the Suez Canal so that it couldn't be accessed. In the US, Eisenhower objected to the invasion and Britain was pressured to withdraw from Egypt, earning the US president public praise from his Egyptian counterpart.

The Suez Crisis, known in Egypt as the Tripartite Aggression, and the subsequent Egyptianisation and Nationalisation laws, were all changing the country. Land reform, socialist nationalisation, redistribution of assets and limits imposed on free trade: these significantly affected Alexandria, where the stock and cotton exchanges were also closed. Wealthy non-Egyptians were not free to trade or keep their belongings, and those who weren't wealthy knew that they were no longer welcome. The year 1956 marked the start of the mass exodus of the city's non-Egyptian population. When the Suez conflict began, British and French families were told to leave immediately; they packed their suitcases in haste and boarded ships to Marseilles. By the time the crisis was over, most of the city's European and Levantine population was also on its way out. The Italians and Armenians were among those to leave, and the large Greek community shrank significantly as its prosperous members departed.

The war of 1948, the Lavon Scandal, and now the Suez attacks, all indicated that Israel was an enemy of the new republic of Egypt. The Jews who had not already left for Israel in 1948 were expelled from Alexandria in their thousands, especially those who held non-Egyptian citizenships. They moved to Israel, the US, France and South America. The 1960 census lists fewer than 3,000 Jews in Alexandria, approximately one-eighth of the pre-1948 population.

There was also an unexpected rise in internal migration as Egyptians left their rural homes knowing that jobs would now be available to them in the newly nationalised factories. Thousands of rural families arrived in the big city, bringing with them their life-styles and a set of very different social values and cultural expecta-tions from the ones that had long existed in the metropolis.

The demographic of Alexandria was drastically changed, its multicultural identity coming to an end at the hands of nationalism and nationalisation. The roads and landmarks were changing, too, deconstructing the city's European and royalist histories. There was Saad Zaghlul Square in the centre of town. Nearby, a small square is dedicated to the nationalist leader Ahmed Urabi. And the Ismail Pasha statue, once surrounded by a grand arched memorial right on the Corniche, was moved to a less predominant street near the ancient Roman theatre, with the square left empty in memory of the Unknown Soldier. The main boulevard, Rue Fuad, once known as the Canopic Way, continued to serve as a symbol of changing times as it was renamed *Shari al-Hurriya*, Arabic for Freedom Way.

Further gestures of self-determination followed. For one, Nasser abolished the fez that had been introduced by Muhammad Ali. He created the first Egyptian automobile called Nasr, meaning Victory, which was also a nod to his name. Nasser, who was constantly seen with a cigarette in his mouth, realised that tobacco was a heavily imported product prevalent in everyday life. Greeks had monopo-lised the Egyptian tobacco market: Alexandria's first tobacco company, which had opened in 1882, was founded by the Greek Nestor Gianaclis, who also established the first Alexandrian wine company in centuries, the Cru des Ptolémées (Vineyard of the Ptolemies). The competing Coutarelli cigarette company, founded in 1890, displayed its two locations on its boxes – Paris' Champs-Élysées and Alexandria's Moharrem Bey. When Nasser nationalised such companies, they were given Egyptian identities. The vineyard and winery became the Pyramids Brewery, and the Egyptian-made cigarettes had to represent autonomy, so they were named after fellow Alexandria-born leader Cleopatra.

My granddad Ibrahim had been working at the Levantine-owned cotton factory, Sabahi, in his densely urban neighbourhood. He rose up the ranks to become a shift manager in the spinning section. Operating colossal machines with massive rollers, he turned cotton fibres into yarns before they were sent to the weaving section to be transformed into cloth. He alternated between three long shifts, including one from 11 p.m. to 7 a.m. When he wasn't in the factory, he had also managed to open a shop nearby. It sold staples to the neighbourhood: rice, flour, sugar, oil and tea.

It is at this shop that he developed a family recipe: *el-borg* (the tower). Among the sacks of supplies laid around the peripheries of the square shop, next to the little spirit burner that he used to brew his coffee, he also had a little steam-powered stove on the floor for making tea and for cooking. In a deep steel pan, he'd begin to lay the tower, each of its layers topped with generous quantities of black pepper and salt, both ground in his copper pestle and mortar. First, sliced rounds of onion were placed into the pan, then chunks of Egyptian water buffalo on top of them, then round, flat slices of potato. Then he'd repeat it: more onions, meat, potatoes, and the same a third time before topping it off with a layer of sliced tomatoes and a little water and oil. After it was covered, it was left to simmer: the longer and slower it cooked for, the tastier – and the more the divine aroma spread around the neighbourhood.

My grandfather loved his fez. He wore it with both his suit and his *galabeya* robe. He looked forward to every Eid when he would take it to the local ironer, who specialised in pressing the hats by spinning them around a fez-shaped metal instrument. By 1958, fezzes were outlawed. The 1952 revolution had also triggered changes in both of my grandad's lines of work. The factory was nationalised, renamed Nasr for Spinning and Weaving, and though the workers went on strike briefly, the sole major change was that the factory only employed Egyptians. In the past, Europeans arrived with the machines, but now Egyptian technicians were being trained in Czechoslovakia before the machines arrived. As for his business, it became a food ration and subsidy shop. Under his one-time neighbour, the government controlled the distribution and pricing of all staple products, only stocking them in specific stores and rationing quantities for sale and purchase. The shop survived, in large part because there was only one authorised seller in each neighbourhood, in his case a heavily populated central district, and since food stamps meant sales were steady. But given the limitations imposed, it was a less ambitious venture than the one he'd probably envisaged.

I do wonder what my grandad thought of his vastly changed city. It appears to me that, like most people, he must have respected and even celebrated Nasser's nationalism. The reforms also meant that, as a worker, his children, including my own father, would access education previously reserved for the middle classes. But living in a police state where trade was heavily regulated, my grandad was also one of many who felt some nostalgia for the relative freedoms and ideals that had existed under the monarchy.

My mother, growing up on the rural outskirts of Alexandria, recalls two notable events from this period. The first is when Nasser passed the main street near her home in an open-roofed car, when she was a little girl, and everyone lined up to cheer ecstatically. The second is when she returned from school to find her mother sitting on the staircase crying. As she was cleaning that morning, my grandmother – a matriarch who'd only completed primary education – had stumbled on a book which she opened and began to read. Before she knew it, she'd spent the entire day reading Victor Hugo's republican novel, *Les Misérables*. 'I'd read a little bit and cry. Then read another little bit and cry.' The translation and distribution of a French, rather than British text, and a republican one at that, is no coincidence. On my maternal side, my grandad was an only son who funded his three sisters' educations after his father's untimely death. Two became teachers who, under Nasser, emigrated to Algeria and Yemen respectively, one post-French-colonialism and one mid-pan-Arab-idealism. The third sister was a *hakīmah* – literally a sage – and anyone in her area who was about to give birth, or stubbed their toe, or was trying to fend off some evil demons, would pop over to her small apartment in the family compound. Before this, as a teenager in the 1930s, my granddad would gather unwanted scraps, put a mat down on the bridge and trade. He eventually made enough to buy a bicycle, which opened his market right up. He even bought one for my grandmother when they got married in the 1940s, by which time he was an apprentice to a bigger entrepreneur. When he was late back from work one day, she set out to check on him. With moonlight their guide, side by side and pedalling slowly, they made their leisurely way home.

*   *   *

The changes that occurred in Alexandria after Nasser's rise to power were tremendously palpable – and somewhat surreal. It's at this time that three Alexandrian artists – Said al-Adawy, Mahmoud Abdallah and Mostafa abdel-Moatei – embraced surrealism in their Alexandrian Experimentalists Society, painting distorted, caricatured images and combining them with Islamic calligraphy, to symbolise the new and changing nature of their city. It wasn't all doom and gloom, either. The city's artistic identity and cultural renaissance meant that it remained, despite these troubled decades, a place where culture and art lived on in the theatres and cinemas. But Alexandrians no longer greeted each other with 'bonsoir'; they'd say 'saida', Arabic for 'happy'.

In June 1967, with Egypt still barring Israel from accessing the strait and canal, Israel began a series of unexpected airstrikes. As home to the National Iron and Steel factory that provided material for artillery, Alexandria was under threat. Both of my parents, not yet adults, recall the air raid sirens ringing loudly every night of this six-day war. With no bunkers, families squeezed into whatever room they deemed safest on the ground floor. They took with them some rations and a radio, but made sure they remained in complete darkness, with the bottom-floor windows all painted in navy blue. On the radio, they heard Nasser announce Egypt's defeat; the nation wept collectively. He went on to tender his resignation but then reversed his decision following demonstrations calling for him to stay. The week of the war, during which cars drove at night without headlights, Alexandria was attacked twice by air on consecutive nights. Members of the Israeli navy also managed to infiltrate the harbour before being captured. During the war, 350 Alexandrian Jews were arrested, including the Chief Rabbi – and by the time it was over those who'd escaped imprisonment were ready to renounce their Egyptian citizenships so they'd be allowed to fly to France. This marked the end of any substantial Jewish community in Alexandria.

When Nasser died in 1970, millions mourned him in the streets. Members of the Muslim Brotherhood who'd sought refuge in Saudi Arabia began to return. A new wave of Islamic thought spread around the country: the sahwah (awakening) called on people to reassess their religious adherence, then help their families and neighbours do the same. Some of this was positive for local communities as people cleaned the streets and revived family values. But a rise in Islamic conservatism also led to new societal regulations on such issues as women's work and dress. Alexandria also became a university city again: its young population crowded the campuses. The ancient, surviving lecture theatre in Kom el-Dikka, with three levels of benches, used to accommodate around 30 students, with a single block of stone in the middle like a podium on which the teacher would stand and students would present. Now, though, more than a thousand pupils from all classes of society crammed into each lecture hall. After class, many went to mosques, joined by hundreds of men and women from around the country, to listen to the prominent preachers Ahmed el-Mehellawi and Mahmoud Eid. But the Muslim Brotherhood's popularity was being overtaken by the Salafi movement, a group who supported the literal interpretation of established tenets of the faith rather than the risks of reinterpretation. In Alexandria, they found a safe haven where they could establish a base and their own mosques. Even those who didn't adhere to either group felt pressure to adopt a more conservative interpretation of the faith.

Islamic and Arab identities were only intensified by the October War of 1973 on the Sinai peninsula, the last of Egypt's conflicts with Israel. Egypt's president was now Anwar Sadat, a member of the Free Officers from the 1952 revolution – though rumour had it that during the key moments of the coup he was at the cinema. During the war, Alexandria was central to talks between the Arab nations and was where Sadat met Syrian and Jordanian heads of state. It was also key to Egypt's supplies: a CIA report showing a night-time aerial photograph of the harbour notes that 'two large hatch Soviet cargo vessels, traditionally known to be arms carriers, were observed'.[3] The recently declassified documents explain why the American 'defence readiness condition' alarm level was raised, just as it was on 9/11: the US believed that the shipment included nuclear weapons. Egypt had been told by Soviet intelligence that Israel was arming three nuclear weapons. It makes complete sense for arms to arrive at Alexandria, but as they were never unloaded we will never know for sure whether that autumn nuclear weapons sat stationed and ready for use on the shore of Alexandria.

Both Egypt and Israel celebrated the costly war as a success. In Alexandria, Egyptians cheered the news that the eastern bank of the Suez Canal was secured. The war's most lasting effect was the peace treaty agreed in 1978 that would trigger the assassination of President Sadat a couple of years later. Closer to home, my family's lasting memory of the October War is the receipt of a telegram bearing news that one of their beloved members, my aunt's husband, father to two baby boys, would be returning to Alexandria in a flag-draped coffin. The tank he was operating detonated a landmine, making him one of the many thousands of victims of this conflict.

For the next three decades, the metropolis continued to grow. Alexandria, both the city and governorate, expanded in three directions. Prices near the coast were hiked and construction shot skywards so that low-rises became high-rises blocking the sea view. Further inland, as one forgets that they are in a seaside city, the roads feel tight, and further still, it's a labyrinth. The narrow streets somehow accommodate the market stalls, the cars, the playing children and the waves of pedestrians. In these noisy areas, everyone knows their neighbour's news and there's a community elder who settles disputes. Alexandria isn't a city of shanty slums. It is a city of *hārāt* – the alleys of Alexandria. Here, many millions built their concrete homes, also upwards, and three-generation families have lived on top of one another for decades.

In contrast to this growth, each generation felt more pressure than the one before. Years of inflation and a weakening currency raised the price of bread. Freedoms were suppressed, with a state of emergency continually in place since Sadat's assassination in 1981 and one-candidate presidential confirmation referendums that gave his successor, Hosni Mubarak, mandates of between 94 and 99 per cent. And a proportion of society saw that social justice was lacking as bribes became normal, unemployment rose, healthcare deteriorated and modernisation took a break.

On 6 June 2010, as twenty-eight-year-old Khaled Said sat at a computer in an internet café in downtown Alexandria, two men marched up the stairs to confront him. The pair, who were plainclothes officers, dragged him down to the street. Before long, he was lying in a pool of his own blood. He had been beaten to death, his head apparently bashed repeatedly against the building's walls. When a powerful photograph of his horrendously beaten corpse was leaked from the morgue, it went viral. The brutal event became the talk of the country, and especially Alexandria. That month, the creation of the 'we are all Khaled Said' social media page was followed by a small and rare public rally, headed by Nobel Peace laureate Mohamed ElBaradei.

As 2010 drew to a close, things turned even more sour. New Year's celebrations were dampened when suicide bombers attacked the Two Saints Church during the midnight service, killing 23 people. Eyewitnesses report that the first victim was a Muslim selling copies of the Quran outside the nearby mosque.

Just a couple of weeks earlier, the economic and political situation in Tunisia had led a young man to set himself on fire, and anti-government protests erupted. By 14 January 2011, Tunisians, in a country of eleven million with a small army, managed to topple their president of 23 years. The fever was spreading across the Mediterranean. Could a country as expansive as Egypt, with a population of 90 million and the world's tenth biggest army, do the same with its leader of 30 years? On 25 January 2011 – the National Police Day commemorating the Egyptian officers killed by the British army – protests began in Egypt.

It had been decades since Alexandrians had taken to the streets to protest. In recent memory, big gatherings saw them either grieve or celebrate. Only in Alexandria was the death of Princess Diana doubly mourned, because she died alongside an Alexandrian in Dody Fayed. And thousands had rejoiced in the successes of Egypt's national football team.

The use of social media (including the Khaled Said page) and instant messaging services had played an important role in mobilising people on 25 January. That day, as social media was shut down, thousands of Alexandrians flooded the streets of the city. They increased day after day until the Friday of Anger on 28 January; despite internet and mobile services being cut, huge numbers were expected after the weekly noon prayers. And while the cameras focused on Tahrir Square in Cairo, Alexandria was playing a pivotal role. Without a public square of Cairo's size and with so many small ones, Alexandria's protesters gathered in their neighbourhoods, where police knew better than to find a way in. The demonstrators were in several places at once.

Eventually, they dared to enter the main streets: a big risk that led to clashes with the authorities and government supporters. Some groups opposed the uprising, like the supposedly apolitical orthodox Salafi Muslims, who'd made Alexandria a base and developed a large following over the last half-century. Like so many times before, fires spread around the city as police stations and the governorate headquarters were set on fire. The protesters walked up and down the promenade, now occupying both the outskirts and the main road. They hurried back to their neighbourhoods at night, with armed vigilantes protecting the alleys. As the days passed, protests continued; on a day billed as the Friday of Departure, it's estimated that well over a million Alexandrians gathered on the promenade and neighbouring locations, including Saad Zaghlul Square, Sidi Gaber Square, Qaed Ibrahim Mosque Square and on the Stanley Bridge. At the top of their lungs, they called for 'bread, freedom, social justice'. Here, everyone was Egyptian. Christians held hands to create a human shield around Muslims as they prayed. And people began to camp into the night. On 11 February, with the army now on the side of the people, Mubarak announced his resignation to the sound of fireworks.

Now known as the Arab Spring, our conclusions about these popular revolutions remain incomplete. Alexandrians enjoyed aspects of the interim year. Hope and pride were renewed as citizens cleaned their streets and stencils of crescent moons and crosses spread on the walls and underpasses. But the unknown territory brought complications. Further protests have followed since and notions of unity have fluctuated.

In a sign of what was to come, the Salafis conveniently U-turned their political quietism and founded a party in their strong base of Alexandria, its headquarters close to where the Zizinia Theatre stood. The parliamentary elections in late 2011 saw them win a quarter of Alexandria's 24 seats, second only to the Muslim Brotherhood, who did almost twice as well in a result that reflected the nationwide outcome. In 2012, the Brotherhood candidate

Mohamed Morsi narrowly won a historic presidential election, but swiftly attempted to pass a controversial referendum in a year at the helm that was defined by challenges and shortages in everyday life. One year after his inauguration, on 30 June 2013, protests against the Brotherhood took place in the same locations as a couple of years earlier. Alexandria saw several clashes between pro- and anti-Brotherhood supporters. On 4 July, the defence minister Abdel Fattah el-Sisi led a decisive takeover, supported by the country's Grand Imam and pope. In Alexandria, large pictures of el-Sisi have punctuated the Corniche since he became president in 2014.

The uprisings proved the continued power of the Alexandrian population. They also served to show that the city's enigmatic modern history is still unfolding. Yet with all the convoluted pressures facing so many in the last several decades, Alexandrians still enjoyed a coffee and a smoke in their local café, the sound of the backgammon and dominoes echoing across the entire street as the music from the old cassette player competes with the buzz of the car horns. They said good morning to their neighbours as they opened the green shutters and walked onto their decorated balconies with a glass of tea in one hand and the laundry in another. Women and men fell in love as they gazed into each other's eyes from that height across the narrow streets, went on their first dates at the roadside juice bar where they stood next to each other holding big mugs of fresh sugarcane juice, before their wedding in a marquee on the street with every neighbour invited. Alexandria might get sick, as the Arabic idiom goes, but it never dies. That much is clear from its long and eventful history.

Epilogue

How did Alexandrian identity come to be what it is today?

With so many shifts of power and demographics over its history, Alexandrian identity is a complex concept. Most people born or raised in the city today, whether Muslim or Christian, will identify distinctly as both Alexandrian and Egyptian.

'I'm not from Egypt, me, I'm from Alexandriaaa.' When the country's most popular trap artist, Marwan Pablo, screams these lyrics in his seaside concerts, the Alexandrian crowd goes wild. Although colloquially, Cairo is referred to as 'Egypt', and Alexandrians make a point of disidentifying from the capital, national identity remains important. It's visible in the patriotic street names, the military presence, the slogans alongside posters of the president. It's visible in how often you'll see the country's flag on streets and boats and buildings, including one that flutters heroically atop the city's Citadel. Alexandrian and Egyptian aren't mutually exclusive identities. But unlike most of Egypt, metropolitan rather than national self-identification also remains prominent here.

No doubt, what it means to be Alexandrian has changed over time. But so, too, has what it means to be Egyptian. At this moment in time, Egyptians also tend to identify as Arabs. There was the pro-independence cultural renaissance at the turn of the twentieth century. Then the First World War, when Arabs fought against the Ottomans. Then came the 1948 Arab–Israeli War, in which Egypt led the Arab League states in an ethnically driven conflict. Then the anti-European, anti-monarchical revolution of 1952 and its subsequent politics. All these events didn't just couple the notions of independence and self-determination with nationalism, but the notion of nationalism with Arabism. Nasser took this further in the

1950s and 1960s when Arab nationalism became state policy. It was presented alongside Arab socialism and anti-Zionism, making the pan-Arabic dream attractive to the majority of Egyptians, from Communists to Islamists. Even the handful of Jews who stayed included anti-Zionists and socialists. Though some Christians weren't willing to identify as Arabs due to their Coptic ancestry, they were still patriotic Egyptians, which meant supporting pan-Arabism (in fact, the pan-Arab movement was led by Christians in Lebanon). Those years of Arab nationalism cemented Egypt's position as the heart of the Middle East, where, until now, a collective nostalgia has maintained that Egypt is the key to solving the issues of the region.

Events up until 1967 severely wounded, but didn't completely eradicate, Alexandria's multicultural makeup. Most European elites affected by the land redistribution and state ownership programme of the 1950s left Alexandria for financial reasons. But many of the middle and lower classes remained despite the nationalist sentiment because this was their home. My father fondly recalls the local pâtissier of his teenage years: a man of Greek heritage. When a customer ordered a custard bougátsa, the pâtissier responded in perfectly Alexandrian, Egyptian Arabic, and why wouldn't he? He came from a long line of Alexandrians – and just like my father, defined himself as Alexandrian.

As Egypt's 1967 war with Israel intensified, the nature of Alexandrian identity was changed again. Previously, you could be an Alexandrian anything – an Alexandrian Armenian, for instance, or an Alexandrian Jew. But with the country at war and under threat, an Alexandrian had to be Egyptian. And if you were Egyptian, then you had to be Arab.

That moment marked the death of Alexandria's multiculturalism. That's not to say that it's a place of monoculture: far from it. One just needs to walk around the city to hear this in the music and see it in the people. In a single space, there will be Muslims and Christians sitting together, a bearded man and a goth on adjacent tables, and in the queue, a woman wearing a colourful beach dress in front of another wearing a black face veil. In today's Alexandria, in this globalised city, you are free to adopt whatever cultural identity you want. The city blurs more lines than it connects; in the words of ibn-Battuta, it's a place of both 'embellishment and embattlement', not to mention East and West, religion and science, tradition and renovation, myth and reality, past and present. That being said, it is now a monoglot, Arab and majority Muslim city in which a dominant identity does reign supreme. Yet every other person in Alexandria has a story to tell about ancestors coming from a faraway land. Today's apparent hegemony is living in the shadow of a melting pot.

It's a multiculturalism that resurfaces at the most challenging times. When suicide bombers attacked the Two Saints Church in 2011 and St Mark's Cathedral in 2017, Alexandrians were united in outrage, strengthening themselves with their own versions of Alexandrian nostalgia. For some, this took them back to an ancient era. For others, it was as recent as the 1950s when my Muslim grandmother and her Christian neighbour were the best of friends and it didn't cross their minds that this would ever become something worth noting.

Perhaps every generation unconsciously perceives their own moment as the ultimate epoch, assuming that, for better or for worse, their present is how things will remain. Who'd have thought, to name but a few things, that native Egyptian rule would end, that Alexandria would be part of the Roman Empire, that it would become Muslim, that it would lose its status as a capital, that its Jewish population would dwindle, that one in six of its population today would be illiterate? Alexandria's long history teaches us that societies undergo change, that harmony is inconstant, that external influences can appear out of the blue, and that peaks and troughs are inescapable.

The present Alexandria, with all the emphases of its current personality, is about three-quarters of a century old. If Alexandria's history were a full day, this period would represent a mere 45 minutes.

Around two and a half millennia after the Pyramids of Giza were constructed, Alexander the Great founded this city. And around two and a half millennia after Alexander, here we are. So, who's to know what will happen two and a half millennia from now?

*　　*　　*

How did the physical city of Alexandria come to be what it is today?

It can be difficult to grasp that its millions of residents are living on a spot that was once nothing more than a small fishing village opposite an even smaller uninhabited island. At its heart, this has been a story about how the village and island became a regional capital, a global knowledge centre, an international trading hub and the central concern of the most power-grabbing empires.

Part of the answer lies in the fact that this is a space that was purposely, not organically, expanded. It was born not out of war or geographical divisions, but out of one man's opportunism and ego. Finding a space located at the intersection of the continents was one thing. The hypothesis that attracting people from far and wide to live in relative tolerance can bring about economic prosperity is another much more ambitious concept. All in all, despite swaying back and forth between tolerance and prejudice, the bigger plan worked. The idea of migrating for the Alexandrian Dream became a reality. The maritime city turned into a significant trading centre and transport hub, welcoming merchants and travellers from around the world and exporting its own goods in all directions. The intent by Alexander's successors to yield strength by gathering and generating knowledge, also worked wonders. Its philosophies, inventions and instruction gave Alexandria momentous soft power.

Within a single century, the two premises combined to make Alexandria the region's trade capital upon which whole empires relied and the world's knowledge capital that propagated philosophies and pioneered innovation.

Both of these early strategies advocated and put into practice a grand departure from traditional expectations, values and links associated with space, population, knowledge and authority, in turn making Alexandria the first modern city.

And Alexandria's very existence and overall design still point to its conception. The main road that Alexander scribbled on the sand, the Canopic Way, may have changed names over the ages – to Rue Fuad during the Kingdom, then Freedom Way since the Republic – but it remains the world's oldest planned street still in use today. The promenade has remained true to its original design, with its wide roads, perfectly angled breeze and curved harbour. Such aspects of Alexandria's design are far from coincidental. They serve as a reminder of human ambition and legacy.

Alexandria was built by the sea and for the first two thousand years this meant that everyone tried to live as close as possible to the shoreline. Attempting to keep this hope alive, since the second half of the twentieth century Alexandria has been constructing upwards. When first-century BCE geographer Strabo visited the city, the place was so built up he decided to let Homer's description of the mythical Odysseus Palace do the talking: 'to quote the words of the poet', he wrote, 'there is building upon building'.[1] What would Strabo say today? Hundreds of lanky tower blocks line the promenade, separated every now and then by a small side road. These towers continue inwards, further away from the sea, for miles on end. A city like Alexandria, with its oceanic beauty and breeze, simply shouldn't have been built upwards in this way. Unless you are walking on the promenade or able to squint down the length of one of the adjacent side roads, you might be forgiven for forgetting you're in a coastal city.

There's building skywards, and then there's the sheer density of the roads, residences and businesses in the promenade and downtown areas that once formed the ancient town. Both of these mean that we have very little hope of finding the Alexandria of antiquity. How can a chaotic urban metropolis with an official population of six million (and 40 per cent of Egypt's industrial capacity) possibly be disrupted for an archaeological dig? Life in Alexandria has always moved fast: so fast that there's rarely been time to look back. Even in the nineteenth century, when stratified excavations began, those areas of interest were simultaneously under development and the search for clues about the ancient city came to a halt.

Alexandria's population has overwhelmed its space. The latest solution is to construct a new city near the Second World War site of el-Alamein, inaugurated in 2018, and housing developments beyond the peripheries of Alexandria, stretching its scope to reduce its density. Theoretically, even the Alexandria of the past wasn't confined only to the urban quarters, but included the rural areas that were harvested by peasants to keep the city alive. So when it comes to excavation, archaeologists can still look further south, beyond Lake Mariout, and further west, into the desert. It is just west of Alexandria that a temple dedicated to Osiris in Taposiris, the ancient town built by Ptolemy II, is being excavated as a possible burial site for Cleopatra and Antony. And as the desert west of Alexandria gets built up, archaeologists are regularly discovering artefacts. In 2017, for instance, as a residential complex was being planned, a ruined building was found, its black granite floors and limestone walls surrounded by ancient pots and lamps. More centrally, around the less built-up cemeteries, an ancient settlement was discovered in 2021. Dating back as early as the second century BCE, its adjacent streets are connected by sewage systems and cistern tunnels. Archaeologists found fishing nets and weaving weights, not to mention an alabaster bust of Alexander the Great. Diving expeditions continue to search for the sunken city, not only discovering artefacts but protecting it from being looted. It's estimated that, to date, only 1 per cent of the underwater artefacts of Ptolemaic and Roman Alexandria have been found.

Artefacts from the past are bubbling beneath the surface, trying to re-emerge, asking to be found. They could be from any period: pharaonic, Ptolemaic, Roman, Byzantine, Ottoman. One of Alexandria's recently retired police chiefs told me that during his tenure a bride in her full white gown fell into a ditch on what used to be the Canopic Way, revealing the entrance to a section of the ancient city. 'If you put your hand in the ground, you might find something', he jokes, in reference to the number of residents who reported discovering ancient objects when they weren't looking, usually coins from the Roman period. One day in 2008, he rushed to the main railway station after employees reported that they'd stumbled on a cellar they never knew existed. As he ventured down with a torch, the possibilities were endless. He discovered British army uniforms stored inside it.

Twenty-first-century Alexandria is something of a street theatre, but in contrast with Athens or Jerusalem or Rome the physical manifestations of Alexandria's past do not stare us in the face. To get a glimpse of how an ancient Alexandrian garden and sacred space looked, for instance, your best bet is the early second-century Hadrian's Villa in central Italy. Alexandria's sites have endured a different fate. They have been torn down and reconstructed. They have found themselves far under the ground. They have fallen into the dark depths of the oceanic abyss. All the earthquakes, tsunamis, tidal waves, fires and conflicts were bound to take their toll.

Excavation uncovers the past, but preservation protects for the future. Alexandria complicates preservation, too, because it's only possible when something still exists.

'My city destroys itself and annihilates itself from instant to instant,' reflected the Alexandrian-Italian modernist poet Ungaretti, 'nothing at all survives – even of what happened a moment ago.'[2] Some landmarks, like the Great Library and the Pharos Lighthouse, disintegrated and perished. Others, like Alexander the Great's Mausoleum, seemingly vanished. Buildings also suffered during civil wars and foreign invasion. Sometimes, there was purposeful erasure. During religious persecution, like the Christian destruction of the Serapeum in the fourth century. During political aggression, like the British bombardment of Alexandria's main square in the nineteenth century. Or during civil unrest, like the Bread Riots of 1977 when the stock exchange building from which Nasser delivered his Suez speech was burnt. And some lost sites weren't destroyed per se, but signal shifts in power or the imposition of change. The Attarine Mosque is a mosque that replaced a church that replaced a temple. Alexandria is proof that few things are for always.

Erasure of the past is, ironically, an inevitable part of history. But the form of such erasures continues to change. Since the twentieth century, objects have been altered, like road signs; removed, like monarchical statues; or simply overlooked, like the ancient city's treasures waiting underground. In recent memory, it's ceased to be about stamping the authority of a dynasty, empire, or religion on the physical city. It's been about modernisation and capitalism – our contemporary overlords – embodied in the construction of bridges, housing and shopping malls.

The palaces and villas built in the late nineteenth and early twentieth centuries raise contentious questions. Any building under a century old can be demolished. In 1982, the government surveyed the city and the result wasn't just a long list of heritage buildings, but entire streets and neighbourhoods that needed to be listed. This makes sense: even Fuad Street is slowly being changed. In 1997, when conservation laws were cancelled by the local leadership in favour of business development, 102 villas and palaces were demolished in a single district in just three months.[3] In 2006, when the most comprehensive conservation laws were passed, a building would be listed because of its unique architecture, representation of a historical period, relation to a historical figure or event, or touristic value. Some owners appealed. They didn't want to be stuck with a building that needed repair or preservation, that couldn't be altered, and without tax relief. Some distorted the façades and features of their buildings before the inspectors arrived, and a few even set fire to them.[4] To those owners, there is more value in using the old villa's land to build a mall or selling it to one of the clamouring international hotel chains. Some made use of the disorder in the immediate aftermath of the 2011 uprising, when several demolitions took place, and people from across society started building without planning permission, whole towers or at least an extra floor or two, impeding the sea and archaeological excavation yet more.

The law, let alone popular culture, can be interpreted selectively with regard to what constitutes heritage worthy of preservation. It is known, for instance, that ancient Egyptian heritage is generally favoured: anything that isn't pharaonic in southern Egypt, especially, risks being removed to build wider streets so that international tourists can save time on their way to see artefacts from dynasties that may have been comparatively inconsequential. For example, the little-discussed pharaoh Tutankhamun shot to fame when his tomb was found in immaculate condition by a Briton and the news of the discovery was licensed exclusively by a London newspaper. But Egyptians know that there are many more inspiring figures and epochs in the country's long history.

Preservation isn't only economic, it's political, too. In 2017, it was reported that there remained only twelve elderly Jews in the whole of Alexandria. The previous year, when wind and rain battered through the roof of the Eliyahu Hanavi Synagogue, the largest and most historic of Alexandria's seven remaining synagogues, rumours that Israel had offered to renovate it were quickly quashed. The law makes no distinction between different types of heritage, from pharaonic to Islamic to Jewish, so the Egyptian government committed to fixing it. Three years and $4 million later, the synagogue had been completely restored from its foundational supports to the most delicate decoration. It was reopened, with two women in attendance: Cairo's youngest Jew, sixty-seven, and Yolande, in her eighties, one of the last few Alexandrian Jews.

There is no clear answer when it comes to preservation, only lots of questions. Mustn't every place of heritage simply be maintained? Can it be right to demolish something because it's 90-something rather than 100 years old? Shouldn't the government try to take control of places that aren't being maintained? Then again, in a place of restricted space, isn't it inevitable that some beautiful or historic places should fall victim to development? What's the other option in a place that's overpopulated, in which land is running out and where investors are queuing up? What is the benefit to Alexandrians of having these reminiscences of the past around them?

There are also questions about the value of building and rebuilding from scratch. There exist three fountains depicting mermaids, for instance, all of which have been vandalised or covered at some stage since 2011 because of their exposed bodies. The trilingual library opened in 2002 as an ode to the ancient one. It attempts to gather all knowledge, not in scrolls, or even in its 1.5 million books in three languages, but via its Internet Archive that records every webpage in existence since the internet went public. But if this is revivalism, then that can be controversial, too. Plans to rebuild the Pharos Lighthouse were reportedly approved in 2015, a megaproject that faced an immediate backlash because it would cost billions of pounds, destabilise the historic harbour area and its current citadel and be open to political exploitation.

That's not to mention the politics of naming. Walk through the city and look at the names of the neighbourhoods – they are not the typical Arabic names found in the rest of Egypt. There are historically informed names, like Camb Shezar (a distortion of Camp Caesar) and el-Bab el-Sharqi (Eastern Gate). There are areas named after old Muslim figures, like Sidi Bishr, Sidi Gaber and Shatby. There are Greek names, old and new, including Bacos, Blokly (possibly ancient Bacaulis), Gianaclis, Glymonopolou and Soter. There are Coptic, French and Italian names: Karmoz, Lazarita, Louran,

San Stefano, Zizinia. And there are British ones, like Fleming (the inventor of penicillin, Alexander Fleming), Stanley (colonial administrator Henry Morton Stanley), Wingate (Britain's High Commissioner in Egypt, Reginald Wingate) and Victoria. On the one hand, these are a celebration of the city's diverse past. On the other, they are a reminder of its power struggles and potentially incongruent identity.

We can try all we want. It is nigh on impossible to decode heritage and to decide value. But we might reflect on the potential short-sightedness of fast-paced growth dictating decisions related to preservation and development. Considering our position in the longer narrative, is it our right, at this specific moment, to decide which parts of history hold importance or worth, and which do not?

In a dramatic speech at the global climate summit in 2021, Britain's then prime minister Boris Johnson addressed the world about rising temperatures: 'Four degrees', he warned, 'and we say goodbye to whole cities – Miami, Alexandria, Shanghai – all lost beneath the waves'.[5]

Alexandria is listed by UNESCO as a World Heritage site at risk of coastal flooding and erosion. But it is no stranger to this: after all, some of the ancient city was swallowed by the sea during the seventh to tenth centuries, and since Alexandria's founding the sea has risen at least a metre, the land sinking at least five. In modern times, some erosion has occurred on the shoreline. The Egyptian government notes that the sea level has been rising at an average of 3.2 millimetres per year since 2013. The good news is that only the lowest sites would be at risk of flooding, not the whole city, as Alexandria is not as low-lying as previously assumed. It also has several coastal defences against rising waters, both natural and manufactured. The city was founded on ridges of limestone. The coastline is predominantly hard rock. The sandy beaches are protected by the vertical wall of the Corniche highway. Several breakwaters, concrete barriers built out into the sea to protect from the waves, are already in place.[6]

Like Alexandria, oceans have their own origin myths. Aristotle spoke of their birth, and in antiquity it was assumed that the

Mediterranean was once a desert flooded by the Atlantic Ocean. In the first century BCE, Pliny records that Hercules 'dug through' the mountains with his sword to create the Strait of Gibraltar, 'upon which the sea, which was before excluded, gained admission, and so changed the face of nature'.[7] With the rise of gradualism in nineteenth-century science – the idea that nature developed over time – the importance of this story resurfaced. Twentieth-century geological and botanical research confirmed that Pliny's story has some truth: the strait was blocked until five million years ago when it opened and the Mediterranean was flooded. As the only link between the two oceans, and a mere eight miles wide, any changes to the water's minerals and temperature could theoretically put the strait at risk of blockage. That would render the Mediterranean dry within a few thousand years.[8]

For the first time, the Egyptian government seems serious about its green agenda. It is setting that agenda from the latest seat of government in the country's long history: the New Administrative Capital just east of Cairo. The first statue commissioned there came as a surprise to everyone: a woman whose fame had dwindled in recent centuries – Hypatia of Alexandria.

I am now arriving at Alexandria, not by air or road as I normally would, but towards the harbour by sea. I am excited, as always, to see my grandad. I put away the pocket version of Homer's poetry that I was reading en route.

In the distance, I can see a giant metropolis: tall tower blocks glued to one another and extending deep into the land. The approach to Alexandria really emphasises its design: a long road all the way down the coast, with a strip of land popping out, a citadel on its edge and harbours either side of it.

The whole coastal road, from one side to another, is just thirteen miles. Two millennia ago, it was thirty furlongs, or around four miles. All of that history, with all its ups and downs and love and hate, took place in such a tight space! All of that knowledge, the inventions, the developments.

We're docking, and I glimpse a cobbler sitting nearby. I imagine him to be St Anianius and that St Mark is about to get off the boat with me, ready to transform the global reach of Christianity. I am standing under the Citadel of Qaitbay, the sky is bright, the sea even brighter. In the courtyard, some narrow stairs lead to a Byzantine bath. These are 'the remainings [sic] of the old lighthouse', the sign reads, in casual reference to one of the Ancient Wonders of the World. I've been around this citadel so often before, but I'm now feeling the magnitude of standing on the exact spot of Pharos. This was a small island when Alexander the Great arrived and it is from here that he founded the vast city. On the eastern harbour, empty fishing boats of white and yellow and blue are rocking softly. The calmer waves and clearer colour of the water have made this one of my favourite spots. The fresh catch is on display in neatly arranged piles nearby: red mullet, bluefish, seabream, seabass, stone-bass, sole, catfish, eel, lobster, crab, shrimp, squid.

As I step onto the Corniche promenade, the car horns begin their endless symphony. There are battered old Lada taxis, black and yellow, that have been driving up and down the promenade all day and turning the road to start again. There's a shop sign that says 'Troy' on it, and I look back at Pharos, where I imagine Helen of Troy, the most beautiful woman in the world, arriving at the island even before Alexander. There's a Starbucks with a roof terrace over-looking the sea. There's a big mermaid mosaic on its wall: I smile as I remember that Alexandria is the Mermaid of the Mediterranean. I look back at the water and remember that Eidotheë – the sea-goddess whose father Proteus ruled Pharos in ancient mythology – might be swimming gracefully at this spot.

For many travellers, Pompey's Pillar was the first thing they saw. The Pillar is backgrounded by one apartment block after another. Its steadfast motionlessness emphasises the fluttering laundry on the balconies behind it. Back at the promenade, as I get ready to cross the wide and energetic highway, a welcome breeze hits my face. I imagine Deinocrates of Rhodes hard at work designing the city with wind directions in mind. There's a set of traffic lights here that wasn't around a few years ago: it seems to take for ever to count down from 270. A motorbike skids into a side road that suddenly reveals the perfectly proportioned al-Mursi Mosque. There's a couple enjoying lime sorbet under a palm tree, and a small car drives past with eight people squeezed inside it. I pass the memorial of the unknown soldier, where a huge Egyptian flag is waving. I walk in towards Mansheya Square, formerly Place de Consuls and Place Muhammad Ali. The father of Egypt's equestrian statue stands in front of a panoramic set of elegant, Parisian-style buildings. It was from a balcony here that Gamal abdel-Nasser announced the Suez Canal's nationalisation, two years after escaping assassination at the same spot. Cars whizz around the rectangular piazza. A woman sits near the statue selling red and green berries out of a bucket. Another hoists a basket filled with fresh mint and tomatoes up to her balcony.

I'm further inland now and the sounds of the waves are fading. The streets around me are named after twentieth-century independence heroes: el-Nasr Street, Ahmed Urabi Street. In the Attarine (Spice Dealers) neighbourhood, I enter the labyrinthine outdoor bazaar. I can find anything here, from right-angled wooden furniture to polished, vintage tableware; from old-fashioned radios and telephones to decorated shisha pipes; from chiming belly-dancing costumes to antique nick-nacks of every age, many of which belonged to the European Alexandrians who left the city. I pass a couple of art deco cinemas on the way to the Attarine Mosque on the corner, walking distance from St Catherine's Cathedral in one direction and my favourite coffee roastery in the other. I pass the cathedral, with its dome and columns, and find myself at a row of chic houses and shops. The sign says Freedom Way but locals still call this Fuad Street. An even older name jumps to mind: the Canopic Way. Almost two and a half millennia ago, Alexander scribbled this main road on the sand. Entering the street is like emerging from a time machine: this is Alexandria at its most quintessentially European. The houses, four or five storeys, have lovely balconets and grand wooden doors. There's a scent coming from the city's oldest flower shop, with its battered yellow façade and tall roses on display outside. At the intersection, the block in which Cavafy lived looks unassuming. In the second-floor apartment, I imagine him sitting with his beloved cat at the carved wooden desk, dabbing his fountain pen into the ink.

I need a coffee. The café has two dozen backgammon boards piled up by its entrance. On the wall is a picture of Alexander the Great's famous bust – only the city's founder is blowing a big, pink bubble with his gum. A smiling man emerges and from a height pours my slowly prepared, aromatic coffee from the copper *kanaka* (a tiny long-handled pot) into the small cup on his tray. As I look at its crema, or the *wesh* (the coffee's face), I think about how important this drink has been to Alexandrians over the centuries. In the background, Sayed Darwish's music is creating a melancholy ambience as I look back towards the hypnotic sea.

I continue to Prophet Daniel Street, where, after the mosque of the same name, I see the Cathedral of St Mark and the recently restored Eliyahu Hanavi Synagogue behind a security cordon. The changes to the Canopic Way's name indicate shifting powers and agendas, but Prophet Daniel Street's three places of worship seem to retain at least some ideal of Alexandria as a multicultural city. As I arrive at the iconic sculpture of Saad Zaghlul, a man is taking a nap in the middle of the square surrounded by the white, yellow and pink buildings. Two young boys are kicking a ball to each other under the statue, and a man is sitting on the steps of its pedestal with his son, tearing a falafel sandwich in half for them to enjoy.

Another Starbucks. Another mosque. It's the Qaed (Commander) Ibrahim Mosque, built in 1948 to commemorate the centenary of the death of Ibrahim Pasha, Muhammad Ali's son. The square outside it was an epicentre of the 2011 protests when Alexandrians from all walks of life came together, eventually filling the streets of the promenade. Ironically, it's the quietest place I've visited today. There are dogs napping under a car and their puppies are rolling around in the mosque yard.

There's an ancient Roman theatre nearby with a horseshoe auditorium. Standing in the middle of the stage area, the tight but glorious intimacy of the space gives me goosebumps. I wander past the city's football club, the Union, where there's a green banner that explains its goal: 'for sporting and nationalist events'. I pass the new city library and think of Ptolemy I asking about the number of books, of the first librarians Zenodotus and Callimachus. I imagine hordes of great scholars walking in and out, congregating at its doors as they clutch scrolls of Homeric poetry and Aristotelian thinking. There's Euclid and there's Claudius Ptolemy. There's Eratosthenes talking about how the earth is spherical and Heron explaining his steam engine. Theocritus and Callimachus are debating their poetry, Aristyllus and Aristarchus are gazing at the sky. This was the world knowledge capital, the leading crucible of intellectualism and debate. I'm interrupted by a street vendor selling face masks. This is just the latest plague to hit an increasingly mobile world. Someone's buying a box of Cleopatra Cigarettes. But my nose is leading me elsewhere. I pause to munch a famous Alexandrian liver sandwich, contemplating its international variety of spices and how they all arrived here. In the middle of the busy roundabout, there's a statue of Alexander the Great on his trusted horse Bucephalus. I notice something for the first time: Alexander is holding up a dove – he comes in peace. I have only just left the world's oldest planned street, and now I see Nouzha Park, where a couple are trying to enjoy a picnic as children chase each other in the oldest surviving garden on the globe.

There are so many cemeteries here. No wonder Strabo coined a term especially to describe Alexandria: *Necropolis*, the city of the dead. The big Greek cemetery has a white gate and statues inside. There's a graveyard nearby that dates to the Ptolemaic period. Here rest Muslims and Jews, Anglicans, Copts, Catholics and Protestants. My ancestors, grandparents and aunties. Cavafy captured something of this when he reminisced about the deceased we continue to love: 'Sometimes in our dreams they speak to us; / sometimes in its thought the mind will hear them'.[9] I remember that there are many more ancient, undiscovered cemeteries under the ground.

But life goes on at the Stanley Bridge, the first in Egypt to be built over the sea, and I hear a horse galloping across it. I recall the chariots that filled the place in ancient times and the black carriages that carried couples to the theatre not so long ago. I imagine those who came from far away, riding through the city on horseback: Amr ibn al-As, Saladin, Napoleon. An elaborate but dilapidated villa catches my attention. Sabahi lived here, the owner of the cotton factory at which my grandad worked. There's commotion by the enormous mall where the highbrow San Stefano Hotel and Casino once stood. As I rush frantically across the tramline, I remember Muhammad Ali's innovation. The tram goes past and two teenagers have jumped onto one end of it, facing away from the direction of travel. This tram stops at Mustafa Pasha station where E. M. Forster stood every morning for months on end. Part of the canal reaches here, and I visualise Cleopatra sitting majestically in her golden barge. The abundant image contrasts with the desolate, unkempt grass across the road, where the cotton factory used to be.

The full setting sun is getting lower. As the street lights come on, the call to prayer resonates from multiple locations around the brightly lit gold stores. I'm getting closer to Bacos now. It's crowded. I imagine the carnivals of the ancient times, when they celebrated Bacchus, who wasn't just the god of wine and theatre, but also of festivity. As the roads narrow, I visualise Hypatia holding an astro-labe one moment, but being dragged brutally through the street the next. The local postman hurries past and I wonder whether his baby will become the next president.

Like living ghosts, the men and women of the past appear to be lingering on every corner of this magical city – as are myriad empires, histories and events. Though of course I never lived through these times or met any of these figures, I cannot help but feel their formidable presence.

The door creaks open and I light the old gas lamp. I gravitate to the portrait of my late granddad, Ibrahim, whom I also never met. He looks on with vitality in a freshly pressed fez. I am finally home.

Bibliography

The following is a selective list of the main writing consulted. The author also utilised numerous archival items such as newspapers, maps and public records.

Primary Sources*

Aciman, André, *Out of Egypt: A Memoir* (Picador, 2007).

Adler, Elkan, ed., *Jewish Travellers* (Routledge, 1930).

Aelian, *Historical Miscellany*, trans. N. G. Wilson (Harvard University Press, 1997).

Al-Dhahabi, Shams al-Din, *Sir I'lam al-Nubala'* (*The Lives of Noble Figures*), vol. 3, ed. Shuaib al-Arna'ut. (Risalah, 1982).

Al-Jabarti, Abdulrahman, *'Aja'ib al-Athar fi al-Tarajim wal-Akhbar* (*The Marvellous Compositions of Biographies and Events*), 3 vols (Al-Jil, 1997).

Al-Laqqani, Ibrahim, *Nasihat al-Ikhwan bi-ijtinab al-Dukhan* (*Advising Brothers to Avoid Smoke*), ed. Ahmed Mahmud (n.p., 1993).

Al-Maqdisi, Abu-Shama, *Al-Rawdatayn fi Akhbar al-Dawlatayn al-Nuriyyah wa-l-Salihiyyah* (*The Book of the Two Gardens, Concerning Affairs of the Reigns of Nur al-Din and Salah al-Din*), 2 vols, ed. Ahmed al-Baysumi (Syrian Ministry of Culture, 1991–1992).

Al-Maqdisi, Abu-Shama, *Al-Rawdatayn fi Akhbar al-Dawlatayn al-Nuriyyah wa-l-Salihiyyah* (*The Book of the Two Gardens, Concerning Affairs of the Reigns of Nur al-Din and Salah al-Din*), vol. 2, ed. Ibrahim al-Zaybaq (al-Risalah, 1997).

Al-Maqrizi, *Itti'az al-Hunafa' bi-Akhbar al-A'immah al-Fatimiyin al-Khulafa'* (*Lessons for Truth-Seekers from the History of the Fatimid Imams and Caliphs*), ed. Mohamed Ahmed (Ahram, 1970).

Al-Maqrizi, *Itti'az al-Mawa'iz wal-I'tibar bi-Dhikr al-Khitat wal-Athar* (*Sermons and Considerations from Plans and Effects*), ed. Salim Mohamed (Al-Kutub al-Ilmiyyah, 1997).

Al-Masudi, Abu al-Hassan, *Muruj al-Dhahab* (*Gold Meadows*), vol. 1, ed. Kamal Miriy (al-Maktaba al-'Asriyyah, 2005).

---

* Listing the year the edition was published, not the original year of publication.

Al-Nuwayri al-Iskandarani. *al-Ilmam . . . fi Waq'at al-Iskandariyyah* (*Familiarity . . . with the Incident of Alexandria*), vol. 1, ed. Aziz Atiya (al-Ma'arif al-Hindiya, 1968).

Al-Sayuti, Jalal al-Din, *Husn al-Muhadarah li-Tarikh Misr wal-Qahirah* (*An Agreeable Discussion of the History of Egypt and Cairo*), vol. 1, ed. Muhammad Ibrahim (Ihya' al-Kitab, 1967).

Ammianus Marcellinus, *The Late Roman Empire*, trans. Walter Hamilton (Penguin, 1986).

Aristotle, *Oeconomica*, trans. E. S. Forster (Clarendon Press, 1920).

Aristotle, *The 'Art' of Rhetoric*, trans. John Henry Freese (William Heinemann, 1926).

Arrian, *Alexander the Great: The Anabasis and the Indica*, trans. Martin Hammond (Oxford University Press, 2013).

Athenaeus, *The Deipnosophists, or, Banquet of the Learned of Athenaeus*, vol. 3, trans. C. D. Yonge (Bohn, 1854).

Baha-al-Din ibn-Shaddad, *Sirat Salah-al-Din al-Ayyubi, al-Musamma al-Nawadir al-Sultaniyya wal-Mahasin al-Yusufiyya* (*The Biography of Saladin the Ayyubid, called the Sultanic Anecdotes and Josephly Virtues*) (Hindawi, 2015).

Baronio, Cæsare, *Annales Ecclesiastici*, vol. 3 (Typis Leonardi Venturini, 1776).

Belzoni, Giovanni Battista, *Narrative of the Operations and Recent Discoveries Within the Pyramids, Temples, Tombs, and Excavations, in Egypt and Nubia* (John Murray, 1821).

Bollandus, Joannes, *Acta Sanctorum*, vol. 3 (Paris, 1863).

Bonaparte, Napoleon, *Oeuvres de Napoléon Bonaparte* (*Napoleon Bonaparte's Works*), vol. 2, ed. C. L. F. Panckoucke (Paris, 1881).

Budge, E. A. Wallis, *The Decrees of Memphis and Canopus*, 3 vols (Routledge, 1904).

Caesar, Julius, *Commentaries on the Civil War*, trans. W. A. McDevitte and W. S. Bohn (Harpers, 1859).

Callimachus and Lycophron, trans. G. R. Mair (William Heinemann, 1921).

Callimachus, *Aetia, Iambi, Lyric Poems, Hecale, Minor Epic and Elegiac Poems, and Other Fragments*, trans. Cedric Whitman (Harvard University Press, 1975).

Cavafy, C. P., *Complete Poems*, trans. Daniel Mendelsohn (Harper, 2013).

Cavafy, C. P., *The Collected Poems*, trans. Evangelos Sachperoglou (Oxford University Press, 2007).

Central Intelligence Agency, 'Top Secret Security Information: 25th July 1952', *Central Intelligence Agency Current Intelligence Bulletin*. CIA Archive.

Central Intelligence Agency, 'Top Secret Ruff: 17th May 1968', *Central Intelligence Agency*. CIA Archive.

Central Intelligence Agency, 'Secret: Soviet Merchant Ship Activity: Alexandria Port Facilities, Egypt, 27th October 1973', *Central Intelligence Agency*. CIA Archive.

Central Intelligence Agency, 'Soviet Merchant Ship Activity, Alexandria Port Facilities, Egypt'. *Freedom of Information Act Electronic Reading Room. CIA-RDP83-0107R000300250028-1*. Approved for Release 2009/01/23. CIA archive.

Central Intelligence Agency, 'Mission 1103, Probable Cruise Missile (Samlet) Site Alexandria, Egypt', *Freedom of Information Act Electronic Reading Room*.

CIA-RDP78T05929A003100030001-3. Approved for Release 2009/07/15. CIA archive.

Chaucer, Geoffrey, *The Canterbury Tales*, ed. Jill Mann (Penguin, 2005).

Chronique d'Ernoul et de Bernard le Trésorier (Chronicle of Ernoul and Bernard the Treasurer) (French History Society, 1871).

Chrystostom, 'Homilies on the Epistles of Paul to the Corinthians', in *Nicene and Post-Nicene* Fathers, vol. 12, ed. Philip Schaff (Cosimo, 2007).

Cicero, *Letters to Atticus*, trans. L. P. Wilkinson (Bristol Classical Press, 1966).

Clement of Alexandria, *The Writings of Clement of Alexandria*, 2 vols, trans. The Rev. William Wilson M. A. (T. & T. Clark, 1867).

Clement of Alexandria, *The Exhortation to the Greeks: The Rich Man's Salvation to the Newly Baptized*, trans. George Butterworth (William Heinemann, 1919).

Cyril of Alexandria, 'Against Julian', vol. 5, trans. Norman Russell, in *Cyril of Alexandria* (Routledge, 2000).

Damascius, *Life of Isidore*, reproduced in *The Suda*, trans. Jeremiah Reedy (Phanes, 1993).

De Chateaubriand, René, 'L'Itinéraire de Paris à Jérusalem (1811)', in *Œuvres completes*, vol. 5 (Garnier, 1861).

Debelius, Harry, 'Escape from Egypt.' *ABC News Backgrounders. Freedom of Information Act Electronic Reading Room. CIA-RDP69B00369R00200290033-7*. Approved for Release 2001/11/01. CIA Archive.

Diels, Hermann, ed. *Poetarum Philosophorum Fragmenta (Fragments of Poets and Philosophers)*, vol. 3 (Weidmann, 1901).

Diodorus of Sicily, *The Library*, Books 16–20, trans. Robin Waterfield (Oxford University Press, 2019).

Diogenes Laertius, *The Lives and Opinions of Eminent Philosophers*, trans. C. D. Yonge (Bohn, 1853).

Durrell, Lawrence, *The Durrell–Miller Letters, 1935–80*, ed. Ian MacNiven (New Directions, 2007).

Édouard-Thomas, Simon, *Correspondance de L'armée Française en Égypte* (Garnery, 1799).

Epigrams from the Greek Anthology, trans. Gideon Nisbet (Oxford University Press, 2020).

Epiphanius, *Treatise on Weights and Measures*, trans. James Dean (University of Chicago Press, 1935).

Eunapius, *Lives of the Philosophers and Sophists*, trans. Wilmer Cave Wright (Harvard University Press, 1921).

Eusebius, *Eusebius Bishop of Cæarea: The Ecclesiastical History and the Martyrs of Palestine,* vol. 1, trans. Hugh Jackson Lawlor and John Ernest Leonard Oulton (Society for Promoting Christian Knowledge, 1927).

Evetts, B., *History of the Patriarchs of the Coptic Church of Alexandria I: Saint Mark to Theonas (300) and II: Peter I to Benjamin I (661)* (n.p., 1904).

Fawwaz, Zaynab, *al-Rasa'il al-Zaynabbiyah (Zainab's Messages)* (Hindawi, 2014).

Flavius Josephus, *Antiquities of the Jews*, in The *Complete Works of Flavius-Josephus: Comprising the Antiquities of the Jews, a History of Jewish Wars, and life of Flavius Josephus, Written by Himself,* trans. William Whiston (S. S. Scranton Co., 1905).

Forster, E. M., *Pharos & Pharillon: An Evocation of Alexandria* (Michael Haag, 1983).

Forster, E. M., *Selected Letters of E. M. Forster,* vol. 1, ed. Mary Lago and P. N. Furbank (Collins, 1983).

Forster, E. M., *Alexandria: A History and a Guide and Pharos and Pharillon,* ed. Miriam Allott (André Deutsch, 2004).

Forster, E. M., *The Journals and Diaries of E. M. Forster,* vol. 3, ed. Philip Gardner (Pickering & Chatto, 2011).

Graffin, R., and F. Nau, 'History of the Patriarchs of the Coptic Church of Alexandria', vol. 1, trans. B. Evetts (Firmin Didot, 1907).

Habermann, Charles George, *The Catholic Encyclopedia: an international work of reference on the constitution, doctrine, discipline, and history of the Catholic Church,* 4 vols (Encyclopedia Press, 1907–1912).

Hakluyt, Richard, *The Principal Navigations, Voyages, Traffiques, and Discoveries of the English Nation,* vol. 11, ed. Edmund Goldsmid (Goldsmid, 1889).

Hammad, Ahmed Zaki, trans. *The Gracious Quran* (Lucent, 2008).

Herodian of Antioch's History of the Roman Empire, trans. Edward Echols (University of California Press, 1961).

Herodotus, *The Histories,* ed. Carolyn Dewald, trans. Robin Waterfield (Oxford University Press, 2008).

Herophilus, *The Art of Medicine in Early Alexandria,* trans. Heinrich von Staden (Cambridge University Press, 1989).

Homer, *The Iliad,* trans. Anthony Verity (Oxford University Press, 2012).

Homer, *The Odyssey,* trans. Anthony Verity (Oxford University Press, 2016).

Ibn Abd al-Hakam, *Futuh Misr wa Akhbariha (The Conquest of Egypt and its News),* ed. Henri Massé (al-Ma'arif al-Firinsiyyah, 1913).

Ibn al-Athir, *al-Kamil fi-l-Tarikh (The Complete History),* ed. Omar Tadmari (Al-Kutub al-Arabiyyah, 1997).

Ibn-Battuta, *Rihlat ibn-Battuta (The Travels of ibn-Battuta),* vol. 1, ed. Muhammad al-Iryan (Ihya' al-Ulum, 1987).

Ibn Jubayr, *Rihlat ibn-Jubayr (The Travels of ibn-Jubayr),* vol. 1 (Hilal, n.y.).

Ibn-Kathir, *al-Bidaya wal-Nihaya (The Beginning and the End),* 15 vols, ed. Ahmed Gad (Al-Hadith 2006).

Ibn-Kathir, *Tafsir (Exegesis)* vol. 4, ed. Sami al-Salamah (Tayba, 1999).

Johnson, Boris, 'Speech delivered by Prime Minister Boris Johnson at the COP26 World Leaders Summit Opening Ceremony'. Prime Minister's Office, 10 Downing Street and the Rt Hon Boris Johnson MP. Published 1 November 2021. Gov.uk.

Josephus, *Antiquities of the Jews,* in *The Complete Works of Flavius-Josephus: Comprising the Antiquities of the Jews, a History of Jewish Wars, and life of Flavius Josephus, Written by Himself,* trans. William Whiston (S. S. Scranton Co., 1905).

Josephus, *Jewish Antiquities,* vol. 6, trans. Ralph Marcus (Harvard University Press, 1943).

Justinus, Marcus Junianus, *Epitome of the Philippic History of Pompeius Trogus,* trans. John Selby Watson (Bohn, 1853).

Lucan, *The Civil War*, Books I–X *(Pharsalia)*, trans. James Duff (Heinemann, 1928).

Lucian of Samosata, *Lucian: With an English Translation*, 8 vols, trans. K. Kilburn (Harvard University Press, 1947–1959).

Marinetti, Filippo, *The Manifesto of Futurism* (Passerino, 2016).

Muslim Ibn Al-Hajjaj, *Sahih Muslim* (*The Correct Traditions of Muslim*) (Beirut: Dar Al-Kotob Al-'Ilmiyah, 2008).

Néret, Gilles, ed., *Description de l'Egypte* (Taschen, 2007).

Nicol, John, *The Life and Adventures of John Nicol, Mariner*, ed. Tim Flannery (Canongate, 2000).

'Official: Prime Minister: Printed personal telegrams exchanged between WSC and General Claude Auchinleck [Commander in Chief Middle East]', *The Churchill Papers* (CHAR 20/89). Churchill Archives Centre, Cambridge.

Orosius, *The Seven Books of History against the Pagans*, trans. I. W. Raymond (1936) and revised by A. T. Fear (Liverpool, 2010).

Palladius of Galatia, *The Lausiac History of Palladius,* trans. W. K. Lowther Clarke (Macmillan, 1918).

Pasha, Coles, *Recollections and Reflections* (Saint Catherine, 1918).

Philo, *Philo,* 9 vols, trans. F. H. Colson (Harvard University Press, 1939).

Philo, *The Embassy of Gaius*, trans. F. H. Colson (Harvard University Press, 1991).

Pliny the Elder, *The Natural History*, trans. John Bostock (Taylor & Francis, 1855).

Pliny the Elder, *Natural History*, trans. John Healey (Penguin, 2004).

Plutarch, *On Education: Embracing the Three Treatises: The Education of Boys*, trans. Charles Super (Bardeen, 1910).

Plutarch's Lives, vol. 2, *The Dryden Translation*, ed. Arthur Hugh Clough (Modern Library, 2001).

Plutarch's Morals, trans. Arthur Shilleto (George Bell, 1898).

Polybius, *World History*, trans. Evelyn Shuckburgh (Indiana University Press, 1962).

Porphyry on the Life of Plotinus and the Arrangement of His Work, trans. Stephen MacKenna (Alexandrian Press, 1984).

Proclus, *A Commentary on the First Book of Euclid's 'Elements'*, trans. Glenn Morrow (Princeton University Press, 1970).

Quasten, Johannes, and Joseph C. Plumpe, eds, *The Works of the Fathers in Translation*, trans. Robert T. Meyer (Newman, 1950).

Qudamah ibn-Jaafar. *Kitab al-Kharaj wa Sana'at al-Kutabah* (*The Book of Land Tax and the Art of the Secretary*), ed. Muhammad al-Zubaydi (Al-Rashid, 1981).

Quintus Curtius Rufus, *The History of Alexander*, trans. John Yardley (Penguin, 1984).

Quintus Curtius Rufus, *The Life & Death of Alexander the Great, King of Macedon* (Samuel Speed, 1673).

Roberts, Alexander Rev., and James Donaldson, eds, *Ante-Nicene Christian Library: Translations of the Writings of the Fathers down to A.D. 325: The Writings of Cyprian*, vol. 8 (T. & T. Clark, 1868).

Roberts, Lewes, *The Merchant's Mappe of Commerce wherein, the Universall Manner and Matter of Trade* (Eliot's Court, 1638).

Satrap Stela: recorded decree issued in autumn 311 BCE, Egyptian Museum, CG.22182.

Select Epigrams from the Greek Anthology, ed. J. W. Mackail (Longmans, 1911).

Seneca, *Moral Essays*, vol. 2, trans. John W. Basore (Heinemann, 1932).

Severus ibn al-Muqaffa, *Tarikh Batariqat al-Kanisah al-Misriyyah* (*The History of the Patriarchs of the Egyptian Church*), ed. Aziz Attiah, 4 vols (Athar al-Qibti-yyah, 1948).

Severus ibn al-Muqaffa, *Tarikh al-Batariqah* (*The History of the Patriarchs*) ed. Anba Samuel, 4 vols (Niam, 1999).

Severus ibn al-Muqaffa, *Makhtutat Tarikh al-Batariqah* (*The Manuscript of the History of the Patriarchs*), ed. Abdelaziz Gamal-el-Din, 4 vols (General Organisation of Cultural Palaces, 2012).

Sharawi, Huda, *Mudhakirat Huda Sharawi* (*The Memoirs of Huda Sharawi*) (Hindawi, 2017).

Socrates Scholasticus, *The Ecclesiastical History* (Bohn, 1853).

Strabo, *The Geography of Strabo*, vol. 8, trans. Horace Jones (Loeb Classical Library, 1932).

Suetonius, *Divine Julius*, trans. R. Graves (Penguin, 2007).

The Apocryphal New Testament: Apocryphal Gospels, Acts, Epistles, and Apocalypses, trans. Montague Rhodes James (Clarendon Press, 1924).

The Book of the Thousand Nights and a Night, vol. 10, trans. Richard F. Burton (Burton Club, 1886).

The Chronicle of John, Bishop of Nikiu, trans. R. H. Charles (Evolution, 2007).

The Grand Procession of Ptolemy Philadelphus, trans. E. E. Rice (Oxford University Press, 1983).

The Greek Alexander Romance, trans. Richard Stoneman (Penguin, 1991).

The Greek Anthology and Other Ancient Greek Epigrams, ed. Peter Jay (Allen Lane, 1973).

The Greek Anthology, vol. 3, trans. W. R. Paton (William Heinemann, 1916).

The Greek Anthology, vol. 5, trans. W. R. Paton (William Heinemann, 1927).

The Holy Bible: Quatercentenary Edition: King James Version, ed. Gordon Campbell (Oxford, 2011).

The Letter of Aristeas: 'Aristeas to Philocrates' or 'On the Translation of the Law of the Jews', trans. Benjamin Wright (De Gruyter, 2015).

The New Posidippus: A Hellenistic Poetry Book, ed. Kathryn Gutzwiller (Oxford University Press, 2005).

The Theodosian Code and Novels and the Sirmondian Constitutions, trans. Clyde Pharr (Lawbook Exchange, 2001).

The William Davidson Talmud (Koren, 2017–2022).

Tyrannius Rufinus, *The church history of Rufinus of Aquileia, books 10 and 11*, trans. Philip R. Amidon (Oxford University Press, 1997).

Tzetzes, John, *Book of Histories*, trans. Konstantinos Ramiotis (Mitolgia, 2018).

UK Parliament, 'HC Deb 26 May 1921 vol 142 cc304-6', in *Commons and Lords Hansard, the Official Report of debates in Parliament*.

Vertray, M. *L'armée française en Égypte, 1798–1801: journal d'un officier de l'armée d'Égypte* (*The French Army in Egypt, 1798–1801: Diary of an Army Officer in Egypt*) (H. Galli, 1883).

Vitruvius, *The Ten Books on Architecture*, trans. Morris Morgan (Harvard University Press, 1914).

Von Minutoli, Baroness, *Recollections of Egypt*, trans. Susette Harriet Lloyd (Carey, Lea and Carey, 1827).

William of Tyre. *A History of Deeds Done Beyond the Sea*, trans. Emily Atwater Babcock and A. C. Krey (Columbia University Press, 1943).

Secondary Sources

Ager, Sheila L., 'The Power of Excess: Royal Incest and the Ptolemaic Dynasty', *Anthropologica* 48.2 (2006).

Ágoston, Gábor, and Bruce Masters, eds, *Encyclopaedia of the Ottoman Empire* (Infobase, 2009).

Al-Awa, Mohammad Salim, *Muhadarat fi al-Fath al-Islamiy* (*Lectures on the Islamic Annexation*) (Shuruq, 2012).

Al-Jahni, ed., *Al-Mawsu'a al-Muyassarah fi al-Adyan wal-Madhahib wal-Ahzab al-Mu'asirah* (*The Simplified Encyclopaedia of Contemporary Religions, Sects and Parties*), 2 vols (Al-Nadwa, 1999).

Al-Rafii, abdul-Rahman, *Mustafa Kamil* (al-Ma'arif, 1984).

Alic, Margaret, 'Women and technology in Ancient Alexandria: Maria and Hypatia', *Women's Studies International Quarterly* 4.3 (1981).

Amr Abdo, *Alexandria Antiqua: A Topographical Catalogue and Reconstruction* (Archaeopress, 2022).

Ashton, Sally-Ann, *The Last Queens of Egypt* (Pearson, 2003).

Atta, Zubeida, *Yahud Misr: al-Tarikh al-Ijtima'iy wal-Iqtisadiy* (*The Jews of Egypt: A Social and Economic History*) (Ein, 2011).

Báez, Fernando, *A Universal History of the Destruction of Books* (Atlas, 2008).

Bagnall, Roger S., 'Alexandria: Library of Dreams', *Proceedings of the American Philosophical Society* 146.4 (2002).

Baring, Evelyn, *Modern Egypt* (Macmillan, 1916).

Bartlett, John, *Jews in the Hellenistic and Roman Cities* (Routledge, 2002).

Bauschatz, John, *Law and Enforcement in Ptolemaic Egypt* (Cambridge University Press, 2013).

Behrens-Abouseif, Doris, 'The Islamic History of the Lighthouse of Alexandria' *Muqarnas* 23 (2006).

Bell, H. Idris, and W. E. Crum, eds, *Jews and Christians in Egypt: The Jewish Troubles in Alexandria and the Athanasian Controversy; Illustrated by Texts from Greek Papyri in the British Museum* (Oxford University Press, 1924).

Bellemore, Jane, 'Who was Cicero's Regina?' *Ciceroniana* 3.1 (2019).

Berg, Beverly, 'An Early Source of the Alexander Romance', *Greek, Roman, and Byzantine Studies* 14.4 (1973).

Bing, Peter, 'Between Literature and the Monuments', in *Genre in Hellenistic Poetry*, ed. M. A. Harder (Brill, 1998).

Black, Ian, and Benny Morris, *Israel's Secret Wars: A History of Israel's Intelligence Services* (Grove Weidenfeld, 1991).

Bonnici, W., 'Inspector of Hospitals and the Plague in Malta of 1813', *J E Army Med Corps* 44 (1998).

Borges, Jorge Luis, *The Total Library: Non-Fiction 1922–1986*, trans. Esther Allen and Suzanne Levine (Penguin, 2001).

Bowden, Hugh, *Alexander the Great: A Very Short Introduction* (Oxford University Press, 2014).

Bowman, Alan, *Egypt after the Pharaohs: 332BC–AD642* (British Museum Press, 1986).

Bright, Benjamin, 'The Exodus revisited', *Jerusalem Post* (18 April 2006).

Budge, E. A. Wallis, *A History of Egypt from the End of the Neolithic Period to the Death of Cleopatra VII BC 30*, vol. 8 (Routledge, 1902).

Budge, E. A. Wallis, *An Egyptian Hieroglyphic Dictionary*, 2 vols (John Murray, 1920).

Byrne, Joseph P., *Encyclopedia of the Black Death* (ABC-CLIO, 2012).

Canfora, Luciano, *The Vanished Library: A Wonder of the Ancient World* (Hutchinson Radius, 1987).

Carney, Elizabeth Donnelly, *Arsinoë of Egypt and Macedon: A Royal Life* (Oxford University Press, 2003).

Carney, Elizabeth. *Olympias: Mother of Alexander the Great* (Routledge, 2006)

Cassar, Paul, 'The Correspondence of a Senglea Merchant during the Plague of 1813', *Hyphen* 2.4 (1980).

Casson, Lionel, *Libraries in the Ancient World* (Yale University Press, 2002).

Cavendish, Richard, 'The Abdication of King Farouk: July 26th, 1952', *History Today* 52.7 (2002).

Cavendish, Richard, 'King Farouk's Succession in Egypt: Anniversaries', *History Today* 61.4 (2011).

Chauveau, Michel, *Egypt in the Age of Cleopatra: History and Society under the Ptolemies* (Cornell University Press, 2000).

Clayton, Peter, and Martin Price, eds, *The Seven Wonders of the Ancient World* (Routledge, 1988).

Colvin, Auckland, *The Making of Modern Egypt* (Seeley & Co., 1906).

Cooper, Artemis, *Cairo in the War: 1939–1945* (John Murray, 2013).

Cormack, Raphael, *Midnight in Cairo: The Female Stars of Egypt's Roaring '20s* (Saqi, 2022).

Cummings, Lewis, *Alexander the Great* (Grove, 1968).

D'Alton, Martina, *The New York Obelisk, or, How Cleopatra's Needle Came to New York and What Happened When It Got Here* (Metropolitan Museum of Art, 1993).

Dauphin, Claudin, 'Brothels, Baths and Babes Prostitution in the Byzantine Holy Land', *Classics Ireland* 3 (1996).

Deeb, Muhammad, 'Alexandria as E. M. Forster's Rainbow Bridge to the Middle East & India: A Comparative Inquiry', *Canadian Review of Comparative Literature* 37 (2010).

Delia, Diana, 'From Romance to Rhetoric: The Alexandrian Library in Classical and Islamic Traditions', *American Historical Review* 97.5 (1992).

Djurslev, Christian Thrue, 'Did Alexander Read Cratinus' Eunidae on his Deathbed?' *Greek, Roman, and Byzantine Studies* 58.4 (2018).

Drach, S. M., 'Tablet of Alexander IV Aegus', in *Records of the Past*, vol. 10, ed. S. Birch (London, 1878)

El-Akkad, Farah, 'Alexandria's maritime heritage', *Ahram Online* (30 January 2021).

El-Daly, Okasha, *Egyptology: The Missing Millennium: Ancient Egypt in Arabic Writings* (Routledge, 2016).

El Sayed Frihy, Omran et al., 'Alexandria-Nile Delta Coast, Egypt: Update and Future Projection of Relative Sea-level Rise', *Environ Earth Sci* 61 (2010).

Ellis, Walter, *Ptolemy of Egypt* (Routledge, 1994)

Elshinnawy, Ibrahim, and Abdulrazak J. Almaliki, 'Vulnerability Assessment for Sea Level Rise Impacts on Coastal Systems of Gamasa Ras El Bar Area, Nile Delta, Egypt', *Sustainability* 13.7 (2021).

Elsorady, Dalia, 'Heritage Conservation in Alexandria, Egypt; Managing Tensions Between Ownership and Legislation', *International Journal of Heritage Studies* 17.5 (2011).

Empereur, Jean-Yves, *Alexandria: Past, Present and Future* (Thames & Hudson, 2002).

Encyclopaedia Britannica: A Dictionary of Arts, Sciences, Literature and General Information, vol. 9 (Cambridge University Press, 1910).

Erskine, Andrew, 'Culture and Power in Ptolemaic Egypt: The Museum and Library of Alexandria', *Greece & Rome* 42.1 (1995).

Farman, Elbert Eli, *Egypt and Its Betrayal: An Account of the Country during the Periods of Ismail and Tewfik Pashas, and of How England Acquired a New Empire* (Grafton, 1908).

Fathi, Tamer, 'The Once Golden Cotton Road', *correspondents. org.* 22 February 2016.

Fedden, Robin, ed., *Personal Landscape: An Anthology of Exile* (Poetry Limited, 1945).

Finneran, Niall, *Alexandria: A City & Myth* (Tempus, 2005).

Finney, Paul Corby, ed., *The Eerdmans Encyclopedia of Early Christian Art and Archaeology*, vol. 1 (Eerdmans, 2017).

Fouad, Ameera, 'The Demise of Alexandria's Historic Cicurel Villa', *Ahramonline* (6 May 2012).

Franz Manni et al., 'Y-Chromosome Analysis in Egypt Suggests a Genetic Regional Continuity in Northeastern Africa', *Human Biology* 74.5 (2002).

Fraser, Peter M., 'A Syriac "Notitia Urbis Alexandrinae"', *Journal of Egyptian Archaeology* 37 (1951).

Fraser, Peter M., *Ptolemaic Alexandria*, 3 vols (Clarendon Press, 1972).

Gibbon, Edward, *The History of the Decline and Fall of the Roman Empire* (1782), vol. 5. (Bohn, 1845).

Gil, Moshe, *Palestine in the First Muslim Period* (Tel Aviv, 1983).

Gil, Moshe, 'Institutions and Events of the Eleventh Century Mirrored in Geniza Letters (Part I)', *Bulletin of the School of Oriental and African Studies* 67.2 (2004).

Gower, Jim, 'A Sea Surface Height Control Dam at the Strait of Gibraltar', *Nat Hazards* 78 (2015).

Granatstein, J. L., and Norman Hillmer, 'Peacekeeping was Pearson's Legacy [Canada's century]', *Maclean's* 112.26 (1999).

Green, Peter, *Alexander to Actium: The Historical Evolution of the Hellenistic Age* (University of California Press, 1990).

Grehan, James, 'Smoking and "Early Modern" Sociability: The Great Tobacco Debate in the Ottoman Middle East (Seventeenth to Eighteenth Centuries)', *American Historical Review* 111.5 (2006).

Guimier-Sorbets, Anne-Marie et al., *The Mosaics of Alexandria* (AUC, 2021).

Haag, Michael, 'The Funny Little Bust of General Earle', *Michael Haag's Blog* (2014).

Haag, Michael, *Alexandria: City of Memory* (AUC, 2004).

Hadid, Diaa, 'Remembering My Mother's Alexandria', *New York Times*, 29 November 2016.

Hamdan, Jamal, *Shakhsiyyat Misr: Dirasah fi 'Abqariyyat al-Makan* (*The Character of Egypt: A Study on the Genius of the Place*), 4 vols (Al-Hilal, 1967–1984).

Hamilton, Nigel, *Monty: The Making of a General 1887–1942* (McGraw Hill, 1981).

Hamouda, Sahar, *Omar Toussoun: Prince of Alexandria* (Bibliotheca Alexandrina, 2005).

Harper, Kyle, 'Pandemics and Passages to Late Antiquity: Rethinking the Plague of c. 249–70 Described by Cyprian', *Journal of Roman Archaeology* 28 (2015).

Harper, Kyle, 'Another Eyewitness to the Plague Described by Cyprian, with Notes on the "Persecution of Decius"', *Journal of Roman Archaeology* 29 (2016).

Harper, Kyle, 'People, Plagues, and Prices in the Roman World: the Evidence from Egypt', *Journal of Economic History* 76.3 (2016).

Harper, Kyle, 'Solving the Mystery of an Ancient Roman Plague', *The Atlantic*, 1 November 2017.

Hassan, Hassan Ibrahim, *Tarikh al-Islam* (*The History of Islam*), 4 vols (Al-Jil, 2001).

Hawass, Zahi, and Franck Goddio, *Cleopatra: The Search for the Last Queen of Egypt* (National Geographic, 2010).

Heba, K., 'Preserving Architectural Heritage in Historical Cities: Study of the Architectural Heritage with the End of the Nineteenth Century and the Beginning of the Twentieth Century in Alexandria, Egypt', *Transactions on the Built Environment* 118 (2011).

Heikal, Mohamed, *Cutting the Lion's Tail: Suez Through Egyptian Eyes* (Corgi, 1988).

Hemeda, Sayed, 'Geotechnical Modelling of the Climate Change Impact on World Heritage Properties in Alexandria, Egypt', *Heritage Science* 9.73 (2021).

Henderson, William, 'Palladas of Alexandria on Women', *Acta Classica* 52 (2009).

Hirsch, August, *Handbook of Geographical and Historical Pathology*, trans. Charles Creighton, 3 vols (New Sydenham Society, 1883).

Hölbl, Günther, *A History of the Ptolemaic Empire*, trans. Tina Saaverda (Routledge, 2001).

Hollerich, Michael, 'The Alexandrian Bishops and the Grain Trade: Ecclesiastical Commerce in Late Roman Egypt', *Journal of the Economic and Social History of the Orient* 25.2 (1982).

Huebner, Sabine R., 'The "Plague of Cyprian": A Revised View of the Origin and Spread of a 3rd–c. CE Pandemic', *Journal of Roman Archaeology* 34.1 (2021).

Hughes-Hallett, Lucy, *Cleopatra: Histories, Dreams and Distortions* (Vintage, 1991).

Ibrahim, Mahmood, 'The 727/1327 Silk Weavers' Rebellion in Alexandria: Religious Xenophobia, Homophobia, or Economic Grievances', *Mamluk Studies Review* 16 (2012).

Jordan, Paul, *The Seven Wonders of the Ancient World* (Longman, 2002).

Kamal, Ahmed Adil, *Al-Fath al-Islamiy li-Misr* (*The Muslim Annexation of Egypt*) (Al-Dawliyyah, 2003).

Kato, Hiroshi, and Erina Iwasaki, 'Cairo and Alexandria at the Beginning of the 20th Century: An Analysis based on Population and Education Censuses for 1907/8', *Mediterranean World* 18 (2006).

Keeley, Edmund, *Cavafy's Alexandria* (Princeton University Press, 1995).

Kells, Stuart, *The Library: A Catalogue of Wonders* (Text, 2017).

Koestner, Elena, 'The linouphoi of P. Giss. 40 II Revisited: Applying the Sociological Concept of Ethnic Colonies to Alexandria's Linen-Weavers', in *The Impact of Mobility and Migration in the Roman Empire*, eds Elio Lo Cascio et al. (Brill, 2017).

Lacouture, Jean, *Nasser* (Editions du Seuil, 1971).

Lane Fox, Robin, *Alexander the Great* (Penguin, 2004).

de Lannoy, Guillebert, *Oeuvres de Ghillebert de Lannoy, Voyageur, Diplomate et Moraliste* (*Works of Guillebert de Lannoy, Traveller, Diplomat and Moralist*) (Toronto, 1878).

Lascaratos, John, and Spyros Marketos, 'Didymus the blind: an unknown precursor of Louis Braille and Helen Keller', *Documenta Opthalmologica* 86 (1994).

Lewis, Celia, 'History, Mission, and Crusade in the *Canterbury Tales*', *The Chaucer Review* 42.4 (2008).

Lo Cascio, Elio, Laurens E. Tacoma, Miriam J. Groen-Vallinga, eds, *The Impact of Mobility and Migration in the Roman Empire: Proceedings of the Twelfth Workshop of the International Network Impact of Empire* (Brill, 2016).

Loewenfeld, Erwin, 'The Mixed Courts in Egypt as Part of the System of Capitulations after the Treaty of Montreux', *Transactions Grotius Society* 26 (1940).

Luttrell, Anthony, 'Intrigue, Schism, and Violence among the Hospitallers of Rhodes: 1377−1384', *Speculum* 41.1 (1966).

Lyons, Malcolm Cameron, and D. E. P. Jackson, *Saladin: The Politics of the Holy War* (Cambridge University Press, 2008).

Mackesy, Piers, *British Victory in Egypt: The End of Napoleon's Conquest* (TPP, 2010).

Macleod, Roy, ed., *The Library of Alexandria: Centre of Learning in the Ancient World* (I. B. Tauris, 2004).

Malek, Jaromir, *The Cat in Ancient Egypt* (British Museum Press, 1993).

Manni, Franz et al., 'Y-Chromosome Analysis in Egypt Suggests a Genetic Regional Continuity in Northeastern Africa', *Human Biology* 74.5 (2002).

Manning, Olivia, *The Danger Tree* (Atheneum, 1977).

Mansel, Philip, *Levant: Splendor and Catastrophe on the Mediterranean* (Yale University Press, 2011).

Mansel, Philip, 'The Rise and Fall of Royal Alexandria: from Mohammed Ali to Farouk', *The Court Historian* 17.2 (2012).

Marlowe, John, *The Golden Age of Alexandria* (Victor Gollancz, 1971).

Marr, John S., and Charles H. Calisher, 'Alexander the Great and West Nile Virus Encephalitis', *Historical Review* 9.12 (2003).

Martin, Thomas, and Christopher Blackwell, *Alexander the Great: The Story of an Ancient Life* (Cambridge University Press, 2012).

McKenzie, Judith S. et al., 'Reconstructing the Serapeum in Alexandria from the Archaeological Evidence', *Journal of Roman Studies* 94 (2004).

McKenzie, Judith, *The Architecture of Alexandria and Egypt: 300 BC–AD 700* (Yale University Press, 2010).

Mearns, David L., David Parham and Bruno Frohlich. 'A Portuguese East Indiaman from the 1502–1503 Fleet of Vasco da Gama', *International Journal of Nautical Archaeology* 45.2 (2016).

Merrilat, Herbert Christian, *The Gnostic Apostle Thomas: 'Twin' of Jesus* (Xlibris, 1997).

Mikhail, Maged, *The Legacy of Demetrius of Alexandria 189–232* (Routledge, 2019).

Milner, Alfred, *England in Egypt* (Edward Arnold, 1894).

Montefiore, Simon Sebag, *Jerusalem: The Biography* (Phoenix, 2011).

Mulder, Stephennie, 'The Mausoleum of Imam Al-Shafi'i', *Muqarnas* 23 (2006).

Nader, Aya, 'The Decimation of Alexandria's Architectural Heritage', *Egyptian Streets* (20 July 2016).

Nilsson, Maria, *The Crown of Arsinoë II: The Creation and Development of an Imagery of Authority* (Gothenburg, 2010).

Nixey, Catherine, *The Darkening Age: The Christian Destruction of the Classical World* (Macmillan, 2017).

Northrup, Cynthia Clark et al., *Encyclopedia of World Trade: From Ancient Times to the Present* (Routledge, 2004).

Nouvelle Revue Encyclopedique (*New Encyclopedic Journal*), vol. 5 (Firmin Didot Frères, 1847).

O'Hara, Vincent P., and Enrico Cernuschi, 'Frogmen against a Fleet: The Italian Attack on Alexandria 18/19 December 1941', *Naval War College Review* 68.3 (2015).

O'Nolan, K., 'The Proteus Legend', *Hermes* 88.2 (1960).

Osman, Tarek, *Egypt on the Brink: From Nasser to Mubarak* (Yale University Press, 2010).

Parca, Maryline, 'Children in Ptolemaic Egypt: What the Papyri Say', *The Oxford Handbook of Childhood and Education in the Classical World* (Oxford, 2013).

Paris, Michael, 'El Alamein: The People's Battle', *History Today* 52.10 (2002).

Pearce, Sarah, 'The Cleopatras and the Jews', *Transactions of the Royal Historical Society* 27 (2017).

Pearson, Lionel, 'The Alexander Romance', review of Reinhold Merkelbach's *Die Quellen des griechischen Alexanderromans*, *Classical Review* 6 (1956).

Pedani, Maria Pia, 'Venetian Consuls in Egypt and Syria in the Ottoman Age', *Mediterranean World* 18 (2006).

Pollard, Justin, and Howard Reid, *The Rise and Fall of Alexandria* (Penguin, 2007).

Pomeroy, Sarah B., *Women in Hellenistic Egypt: From Alexander to Cleopatra* (Wayne State University Press, 1990).

Porter, Roy, *The Greatest Benefit to Mankind: A History of Humanity from Antiquity to the Present* (Fontana, 1999).

Raafat, Samir, 'The Rise and Fall of Alexandria's Cotton Exchange', *Egyptian Mail* (1 November 1997).

Rabinovich, Abraham, *The Yom Kippur War: The Epic Encounter That Transformed the Middle East. Revised and Updated Edition* (Schocken, 2017).

Redon, Bérangère, 'An Egyptian Grand Cru: Wine Production at Plinthine', *Egyptian Archaeology* 55 (2019).

Reime, Michael, *Colonial Bridgehead: Government and Society in Alexandria, 1807–1882* (Routledge, 1977).

Retief, François, and Louise Cilliers, 'The Death of Alexander the Great', *Acta Theologica* 26.2 (2006).

Ridley, Ronald, *Napoleon's Consul in Egypt: The Life and Times of Bernardino Drovetti* (Rubicon, 2001).

Ritner, Robert, 'Khahabash and the Satrap Stela-A Grammatical Rejoinder', *Zeitschrift für ägyptische Sprache und Altertumskunde* 107.1 (1980).

Rodenbeck, John, 'Literary Alexandria', *Massachusetts Review* 42.4 (2001–2).

Rowson, Alex, *The Young Alexander: The Making of Alexander the Great* (William Collins, 2022).

Royle, Charles, *The Egyptian Campaigns, 1882–1885* (Hurst and Blackett, 1900).

Rubenstein, Jeffrey, *The Land of Truth: Talmud Tales, Timeless Teachings* (Jewish Publication Society, 2018).

Russell, Norman, *Cyril of Alexandria* (Routledge, 2000).

Russell, Norman, *Theophilus of Alexandria* (Routledge, 2007).

Saad, Kamal, *Bayram al-Tunisi: 'Asifa min al-Hara al-Misriyyah (Bayram al-Tunisi: Storm from the Egyptian Neighbourhood)* (Cairo, 1993).

Saunders, Nicholas, *Alexander's Tomb: The Two Thousand Year Obsession to Find the Lost Conqueror* (Basic, 2016).

Schäfer, Peter, *The History of the Jews in the Greco-Roman World* (Routledge, 2003).

Schuemann, Verena J. et al., 'Ancient Egyptian Mummy Genomes Suggest an Increase of Sub-Saharan Ancestry in Post-Roman Periods', *Nature Communications* 8.1 (2017).

Shoshan, Boaz, 'Fatimid Grain Policy and the Post of the Muhtasib', *International Journal of Middle East Studies* 13.2 (1981).

Sinano Horwitz, Eugenie, 'La Première Génération', in *Des Femmes Écrivent l'Afrique: L'Afrique du Nord*, ed. Fatima Sadiqi et al. (Karthala, 2013).

Sly, Dorothy, *Philo's Alexandria* (Routledge, 1996).

Smith, William Sier, ed., *A Dictionary of Greek and Roman Biography and Mythology*, 3 vols (Little, Brown and Co., 1867).

Stadiem, William, *Too Rich: The High Life and Tragic Death of King Farouk* (Carroll & Graf, 1991).

Stephens, Susan, *The Poets of Alexandria* (I.B. Tauris, 2018).

Stoneman, Richard, *Alexander the Great: A Life in Legend* (Yale University Press, 2010).

Strathern, Paul, *Napoleon in Egypt* (Vintage, 2008).

Thornhill, Michael T., 'Informal Empire, Independent Egypt and the Accession of King Farouk', *Journal of Imperial and Commonwealth History* 38.2 (2010).

Tomlinson, Richard, *From Mycenae to Constantinople: The Evolution of the Ancient City* (Routledge, 1992).

Turiano, Annalura, and Joseph John Viscomi, 'From Immigrants to Emigrants: Salesian Education and the Failed Integration of Italians in Egypt, 1937–1960', *Modern Italy* 23.1 (2018).

Tyldesley, Joyce, *Cleopatra: The Last Queen of Egypt* (Profile, 2009).

Van Steenbergen, Jo, 'The Alexandrian crusade (1365) and the Mamluk sources: reassessment of the "Kitab al-Ilmam" of an-Nuwayri al-Iskandarani (d. AD 1372)', *East and West in the Crusader States* 3 (2003).

Verena Schuenemann et al., 'Ancient Egyptian mummy genomes suggest an increase of Sub-Saharan African ancestry in post-Roman periods', *Nature Communications* 8 (2017).

Von Staden, Heinrich, 'The Discovery of the Body: Human Dissection and its Cultural Contexts in Ancient Greece', *Yale Journal of Biology and Medicine* 65.3 (1992).

Vrettos, Theodore, *Alexandria: City of the Western Mind* (Free Press, 2001).

Wasserstein, David, 'The Ptolemy and the Hare: Dating an Old Story about the Translation of the Septuagint', *Scripta Classica Israelica* 17 (1998).

Watt, Donald, 'Mohammed el Adl and "A Passage to India"', *Journal of Modern Literature* 10.2 (1983).

Watts, Edward, *Hypatia: The Life and Legend of an Ancient Philosopher* (Oxford University Press, 2017).

Wessel, Susan, *Cyril of Alexandria and the Nestorian Controversy: The Making of a Saint and of a Heretic* (Oxford University Press, 2004).

Whieldon, Esther, 'Scientists more than triple estimate of people at risk from sea-level rise', *SNL Asia-Pacific Financials Daily* (New York, 1 November 2019).

White, Rachel Evelyn, 'Women in Ptolemaic Egypt', *Journal of Hellenic Studies* 18 (1898).

Whitehorne, John, *Cleopatras* (Routledge, 1994).

Wilkins, Ernest H., 'Petrarch and Giacomo de' Rossi', *Speculum* 25.3 (1950).

Wissa, Karim, 'Freemasonry in Egypt 1798–1921: a study in cultural and political encounters', *British Journal of Middle Eastern Studies* 16.2 (1989).

Withycombe, E. G., *The Concise Dictionary of English Christian Names* (Omega, 1976).

Zeitlin, Solomon, '"The Tobias Family and the Hasmoneans": A Historical Study in the Political and Economic Life of the Jews of the Hellenistic Period', *Proceedings of the American Academy for Jewish Research, 1932–1933* 4 (1932–1933).

Zohry, Ayman, 'Ethnic Minorities in Alexandria, Egypt: Findings from the 1947 and 1960 Population Censuses.' Paper presented at the AISU Conference 2018: Multi-Ethnic Cities in the Mediterranean World. 5 June 2018.

Notes

Preface

1 Ibn-Battuta, *Rihlat ibn-Battuta (The Travels of ibn-Battuta)*, vol. 1, ed. Muhammad al-Iryan (Dar Ihya' al-Ulum, 1987), 38. To make for easier reading, I do not use Arabic diacritics when transliterating the names of authors or their books.

Chapter 1. The Ancient Era

1 Herodotus, *The Histories*, ed. Carolyn Dewald, trans. Robin Waterfield (Oxford University Press, 2008), 114.
2 Homer, *The Odyssey*, trans. Anthony Verity (Oxford University Press, 2016).

Chapter 2. Alexander's Dream

1 The description of Aristotle is from Diogenes Laertius, *The Lives and Opinions of Eminent Philosophers*, trans. C. D. Yonge (H. Bohn, 1853), 181.
2 *The Greek Alexander Romance*, trans. Richard Stoneman (Penguin, 1991).
3 *Plutarch's Lives*, vol. 2, *The Dryden Translation*, ed. Arthur Hugh Clough (Modern Library, 2001).
4 Aristotle, *The 'Art' of Rhetoric*, trans. John Henry Freese (William Heinemann, 1926), 247–9.
5 *Plutarch's Morals*, trans. Arthur Shilleto (George Bell, 1898), 181.

Chapter 3. Alexander's Dream City

1 Arrian, *Alexander the Great: The Anabasis and the Indica*, trans. Martin Hammond (Oxford University Press, 2013), 3.2.
2 The Gregorian date has been subject to debate: Tobi falls in January or February, but the city very soon started to celebrate its anniversary on the equivalent of 7 April.
3 Lucian of Samosata, 'How to Write History', in *Lucian*, vol. 6, trans. K. Kilburn (Harvard University Press, 1959), 19.

4 Vitruvius, *The Ten Books on Architecture*, trans. Morris Morgan (Harvard University Press, 1914), 2.2–2.3.

5 Diodorus of Sicily, *The Library*, Books 16–20, trans. Robin Waterfield (Oxford University Press, 2019).

6 Guillebert de Lannoy, *Oeuvres de Ghillebert de Lannoy, Voyageur, Diplomate et Moraliste* (*Works of Guillebert de Lannoy, Traveller, Diplomat and Moralist*) (University of Toronto Press, 1878), 106.

7 Aristotle, *Oeconomica*, trans. E. S. Forster (Clarendon Press, 1920), 1352.

8 Athenaeus, *The Deipnosophists, or, Banquet of the Learned of Athenaeus*, vol. 3, trans. C. D. Yonge (Bohn, 1854), 860.

Chapter 4. Ptolemy the Saviour

1 The historian Aelian a few centuries later makes the unlikely claim that Ptolemy had prepared a decoy corpse dressed in the same clothes that Perdiccas' men took away before realising, hundreds of miles later, that they had been duped. Aelian, *Historical Miscellany*, trans. N. G. Wilson (Harvard University Press, 1997), 12.64.

2 Quintus Curtius Rufus, *The History of Alexander*, trans. John Yardley (Penguin, 1984), 9.8.

3 *Satrap Stela: recorded decree issued in autumn 311 BCE*, Egyptian Museum, CG.22182. Amun is the god whose oracle Alexander visited in Siwa. 'Re' is the sun-god fused to become Amun-Re. 'Alexandros is Alexander the Great. Aegeans: 'Hau-Nebu' means 'behind the islands' so was used to refer to the people of the Aegean Sea, in other words, the Mediterranean. Rhakotis is referred to as Râ-Kedet. I have benefitted from the translations of Amr Abdo in *Alexandria Antiqua: A Topographical Catalogue and Reconstruction* (Archaeopress, 2022) and S. M. Drach, 'Tablet of Alexander IV Aegus', in *Records of the Past*, vol. 10, ed. S. Birch (London, 1878).

4 Strabo, *The Geography of Strabo*, vol. 8, trans. Horace Jones (Loeb Classical Library, 1932), book 17.

Chapter 5. The Ptolemies

1 Ptolemy I's successors now became pharaohs by virtue of ruling Egypt. They also remained kings and queens since they headed the Ptolemaic kingdom.

2 This poem is recorded by Athenaeus in *The Deipnosophists*, trans. C. D. Yonge.

3 Plutarch, *On Education: Embracing the Three Treatises: The Education of Boys*, trans. Charles Super (Bardeen, 1910), 74–5.

4 Polybius, *World History*, trans. Evelyn Shuckburgh (Bloomington, 1962), 1.63.

5 *The Grand Procession of Ptolemy Philadelphus*, trans. E. E. Rice (Oxford University Press, 1983).

Chapter 6. Wonder of the World

1 The Seven Wonders are themselves an Alexandrian concept; the first reference to them appears on a papyrus fragment thought to have been written in second-century BCE Alexandria, the *Laterculi Alexandrini*, which contains several lists in sevens. Only the Great Pyramid of Khufu may have been taller than the lighthouse.

2 Ibn Jubayr, *Rihlat ibn-Jubayr (The Travels of ibn-Jubayr)*, vol. 1 (Dar Hilal, n.y.), 14–15.

3 John Tzetzes, *Book of Histories*, trans. Konstantinos Ramiotis (Mitolgia, 2018).

4 *The New Posidippus: A Hellenistic Poetry Book*, ed. Kathryn Gutzwiller (Oxford University Press, 2005). Posidippus' poem begins by invoking Proteus, the water-god, who was still regarded as the owner of the island. It explains that a lighthouse is necessary 'for Egypt has no cliffs or mountains', praises the lighthouse's practical nature, its magnificent height and its distant visibility by both day and night. It adds that sailors arrive at 'the Bull's Horn', in reference to the shape of the harbour, and that Zeus stands atop the lighthouse as the ships arrive. The first ever edition of Posidippus' poetry was published in 2001.

5 Pliny the Elder, *Natural History*, trans. John Healey (Penguin, 2004), 83.

6 Lucian of Samosata, 'How to Write History', 73. Lucian uses this claim as a case study: 'History then should be written in that spirit, with truthfulness and an eye to future expectations rather than with adulation and a view to the pleasure of present praise.' Lucian's is the only surviving work from antiquity on the theory of history.

7 Peter Bing, 'Between Literature and the Monuments', in *Genre in Hellenistic Poetry*, ed. M. A. Harder (Brill, 1998), 21–43.

Chapter 7. All the Books in the World

1 *The Letter of Aristeas: 'Aristeas to Philocrates' or 'On the Translation of the Law of the Jews'*, trans. Benjamin Wright (De Gruyter, 2015), 9.

2 The Letter of Aristeas offers the cover letter of one such report: 'To the Great King from Demetrius. As you commanded, O King, concerning the books that are wanting for the completion of the library, how they are to be collected, and those that have by chance fallen away from proper repair, paying more than incidental attention to these matters, I submit a report to you here.'

3 Epiphanius, *Treatise on Weights and Measures*, trans. James Dean (University of Chicago Press, 1935), 25.

4 Josephus, *Antiquities of the Jews*, in The *Complete Works of Flavius-Josephus: Comprising the Antiquities of the Jews, a History of Jewish Wars, and life of Flavius Josephus, Written by Himself,* trans. William Whiston (S. S. Scranton Co., 1905), 358.

5 Jorge Luis Borges, *The Total Library: Non-Fiction 1922–1986*, trans. Esther Allen and Suzanne Levine (Penguin, 2001).

Chapter 8. Shrine of Knowledge

1 Timon of Phlius, 'Fragment 12', in *Poetarum Philosophorum Fragmenta* (*Fragments of Poets and Philosophers*), vol. 3, ed. Hermann Diels (Weidmann, 1901); the bases for my translation are those by Luciano Canfora in *The Vanished Library: A Wonder of the Ancient World* (Hutchinson Radius, 1987) and by Andrew Erskine in 'Culture and Power in Ptolemaic Egypt: The Museum and Library of Alexandria', *Greece & Rome* 42.1 (1995); Timon is comparing the scholars to chickens.

2 Euclid's reply to Ptolemy is described in Proclus, *A Commentary on the First Book of Euclid's 'Elements'*, trans. Glenn Morrow (Princeton University Press, 1970), 57.

3 Other important mathematicians include Hypsicles (second century BCE), Menelaus of Alexandria (first century), Diophantus of Alexandria (third century), and Pappos of Alexandria and Theon of Alexandria (fourth century).

4 'Epigram 32', *Select Epigrams from the Greek Anthology*, ed. J. W. Mackail (Longmans, 1911), 188.

5 The Julian calendar was used until the sixteenth century, when minor modifications made it known as the Gregorian calendar. The modification is changing each year from 365.2425 days to 365.2422 days, which meant that the Julian calendar was overestimating one day per century. The Gregorian calendar solved this by removing leap year status from any year that is divisible by 100 (e.g. 1900, 2100), unless it's dividable by 400 (e.g. 2000, 2400 remain as leap years).

6 John Bauschatz, *Law and Enforcement in Ptolemaic Egypt* (Cambridge University Press, 2013).

7 Quoted in Herophilus, *The Art of Medicine in Early Alexandria*, trans. Heinrich von Staden (Cambridge University Press, 1989), 187.

8 Callimachus, *Aetia, Iambi, lyric poems, Hecale, minor epic and elegiac poems, and other fragments*, trans. Cedric Whitman (Harvard University Press, 1975), 7.

9 *The Greek Anthology*, vol. 5, trans. W. R. Paton (William Heinemann, 1927), 13.10, 5.85. I use 'protect' rather than Paton's more literal 'grudge' (i.e. 'won't grant'). Hades is the Greek god of the underworld; Serapis was often linked to Hades.

10 'Epigram 30', in *Callimachus and Lycophron*, trans. G. R. Mair (William Heinemann, 1921), 157. I use 'epic' in place of 'cyclic'.

Chapter 9. Cleopatras

1 The Rosetta Stone, or the Decree of Memphis from 196 BCE, is the most recent of the four discovered Ptolemaic decrees carved in both Egyptian and Greek. The oldest is the Decree of Alexandria from 243 BCE, which proclaims the divinity of Ptolemy III and Berenice II, followed by the Decree of Canopus (Ptolemy III, 238 BCE), and the Decree of Memphis (Ptolemy IV, 218 BCE).

2 Philo, *Philo*, vol. 7, trans. F. H. Colson (Harvard University Press, 1939), 585.

3 Marcus Junianus Justinus, *Epitome of the Philippic History of Pompeius Trogus*, trans. John Selby Watson (Henry G. Bohn, 1853), 38.8.

Chapter 10. Ageless Cleopatra

1 Lucan, *The Civil War*, Books I–X *(Pharsalia)*, trans. James Duff (Heinemann, 1928), 623.

2 Suetonius, *Divine Julius*, trans. R. Graves (Penguin, 2007), 45.

3 Julius Caesar, *Commentaries on the Civil War*, trans. W. A. McDevitte and W. S. Bohn (Harpers, 1859), 3.111.

4 Seneca, *Moral Essays on Tranquility of Mind*, 9.5; Ammianus Marcellinus, *The Late Roman Empire*, trans. Walter Hamilton (Penguin, 1986), 22.16.

5 Orosius, *Histories Against the Pagans* trans. I. W. Raymond (1936), 6.19.

6 Cicero, *Letters to Atticus*, trans. L. P. Wilkinson (Bristol Classical Press, 1966), 15.15.2; 14.20.2.

7 Philo, *The Embassy to Gaius*, trans. F. H. Colson (Harvard Univeristy Press, 1991), 149–51.

8 Abu al-Hassan al-Masudi, *Gold Meadows*, vol. 1 (al-Maktaba al-'Asriyyah, 2005), 229.

9 Verena Schuenemann et al., 'Ancient Egyptian mummy genomes suggest an increase of Sub-Saharan African ancestry in post-Roman periods', *Nat Commun* (2017); Franz Manni et al., 'Y-Chromosome Analysis in Egypt Suggests a Genetic Regional Continuity in Northeastern Africa', *Human Biology*, 74.5 (2002). The percentages in Alexandria, one of the furthest Egyptian cities from sub-Saharan Africa, are likely to be even lower. It is also worth noting that some genes are dominant, such as curly hair.

Chapter 11. Jewish Hub

1 Translation quoted in Josephus, *Jewish Antiquities*, vol. 6, trans. Ralph Marcus (Harvard University Press, 1943), 515.

2 Josephus, *Antiquities of the Jews*, in The *Complete Works of Flavius-Josephus: Comprising the Antiquities of the Jews, a History of Jewish Wars, and life of Flavius Josephus, Written by Himself,* trans. William Whiston (S.S. Scranton Co., 1905), 352.

3 Josephus, *Antiquities of the Jews*, 352, 717.

4 *Philo*, vol. 7, trans. F. H. Colson (Harvard University Press, 1939), 547.

5 Quoted in the Sukkah 51b:6–7, a tractate of the Talmud; *The William Davidson Talmud* (Koren, 2017–2022).

6 Josephus, *Antiquities of the Jews*, 475.

7 Philo, *The Embassy of Gaius*, trans. F. H. Colson (Harvard University Press, 1991), 338

8 Josephus, *Antiquities of the Jews*, 593.

9 H. Idris Bell and W. E. Crum, eds, *Jews and Christians in Egypt : The Jewish Troubles in Alexandria and the Athanasian Controversy ; Illustrated by Texts from Greek Papyri in the British Museum* (Oxford University Press, 1924).

Chapter 12. St Mark the Evangelist

1 Matthew 2.13, in *The Holy Bible: Quatercentenary Edition: King James Version*, ed. Gordon Campbell (Oxford, 2011).

2 *The Apocryphal New Testament*, trans. Montague Rhodes James (Clarendon Press, 1924), 75, 58–9.

Chapter 13. Horror

1 Quoted in Elena Koestner, 'The linouphoi of P. Giss. 40 II Revisited: Applying the Sociological Concept of Ethnic Colonies to Alexandria's Linen-Weavers', in *The Impact of Mobility and Migration in the Roman Empire*, eds Elio Lo Cascio et al. (Brill, 2017), 193.

2 *Herodian of Antioch's History of the Roman Empire*, trans. Edward Echols (University of California Press, 1961), 4.9.

3 Quoted in P. M. Fraser, 'A Syriac "Notitia Urbis Alexandrinae"', *Journal of Egyptian Archaeology*, 37 (1951), 104. Fraser's study concludes the notitia's 'fundamental reliability' and dates it 'not later than the end of the fourth century' (104–7).

4 Ammianus Marcellinus, *The Late Roman Empire*, trans. Walter Hamilton (Penguin, 1986), 26.10.

5 *The Greek Anthology*, vol. 3, trans. W. R. Paton (Leob Classical Library, 1916), 9.501.

Chapter 14. Early Christianity

1 Philo, *Philo*, vol. 9, trans. F. H. Colson (Harvard University Press, 1939), 475. The name of the Therapeutae may derive from the Greek word for healing (*therapeuo*), perhaps of the soul. But Philo himself does not know why they are called the Therapeutae, and it has been suggested that he may have been referring to the Theravada, the oldest school of Buddhism.

2 Clement of Alexandria, *The Exhortation to the Greeks: The Rich Man's Salvation to the Newly Baptized*, trans. George Butterworth (William Heinemann, 1919), 123, 211.

3 *Porphyry on the Life of Plotinus and the Arrangement of His Work*, trans. Stephen MacKenna (Alexandrian Press, 1984). Although Porphyry mentions two Origens, Origen of Alexandria's views interested non-Christians and he met Plotinus; some scholars believe that aspects of the two Origens' biographies have overlapped.

4 *Eusebius Bishop of Cæarea: The Ecclesiastical History and the Martyrs of Palestine*, vol. 1, trans. Hugh Jackson Lawlor and John Ernest Leonard Oulton (London: Society for Promoting Christian Knowledge), 181–2.

5 *Eusebius*, 233.

6 *Eusebius*, 7.21. For the precise calculations, see 'Pandemics and Passages to Late Antiquity: Rethinking the Plague of c. 249–70 Described by Cyprian', *Journal of Roman Archaeology*, 28 (2015), 223–60.

7 Palladius of Galatia, *The Lausiac History of Palladius*, trans. W. K. Lowther Clarke (Macmillan, 1918), 107.

8 *The Catholic Encyclopedia: an international work of reference on the constitution, doctrine, discipline, and history of the Catholic Church*, vol. 3 (1907), 445.

9 *Eusebius*, 273.

10 St Anthony was born in the town of Fayum, a home to Greeks, Jews and Romans, who intermarried with Egyptians. In Fayum, hundreds of realistic painted portraits were attached to mummies, probably around the third century, and they show that people of mixed heritage were common. In 2013, the *National Catholic Reporter* included Anthony in its Black Saints series; although it was common practice for European artists to lighten skin tones and straighten hair, there is however no extant history specifying that Anthony was black.

11 Catherine, or the 'Christian lady', died around 305, while St Anthony travelled to Alexandria around 311 to offer himself for martyrdom. Anthony didn't succeed in becoming a martyr, but the connection to martyrdom has endured. Although he didn't meet that 'Christian lady' of Alexandria, he may have met many 'Catherines' during his time in the city.

Chapter 15. Destruction

1 I avoid the term 'pagan' due to its connotations of supremacy and because in Alexandria's case it is inaccurate. The word derives from the Latin *paganus*, meaning 'country dweller', since Christians in the Roman cities perceived those living rurally as being less rational in comparison to the city-dwelling *urbānus*. Since Alexandria was an urban city that for centuries maintained its polytheistic Greek and Egyptian beliefs, the term pagan is especially unsuitable.

2 Chrystostom, 'Homilies on the Epistles of Paul to the Corinthians', in *Nicene and Post-Nicene Fathers*, vol. 12, ed. Philip Schaff (Cosimo, 2007), 26.5.

3 Marcellinus, *The Late Roman Empire*, 22.16.

4 Tyrannius Rufinus. *The church history of Rufinus of Aquileia, books 10 and 11*, trans. Philip R. Amidon (Oxford University Press, 1997), 11.22–29.

5 Eunapius, *Lives of the Philosophers and Sophists*, trans. Wilmer Cave Wright (Harvard University Press, 1921), 472.

6 *The Theodosian Code and Novels and the Sirmondian Constitutions*, trans. Clyde Pharr (Lawbook Exchange, 2001), 16.8.9.

7 'Against Julian', vol. 5, trans. Norman Russell, in *Cyril of Alexandria* (Routledge, 2000), 203.

8 Socrates, *The Ecclesiastical History* (Bohn, 1853), 7.13.

Chapter 16. Hypatia

1 Damascius, *Life of Isidore*, reproduced in *The Suda*, trans. Jeremiah Reedy (Phanes, 1993).

2 On Hypatia's relation to the different schools of Neoplatonism, see

Edward J. Watts, *Hypatia: The Life and Legend of an Ancient Philosopher* (Oxford University Press, 2017), 37−62.

3 Socrates Scholasticus, *The Ecclesiastical History* (Bohn, 1853), 7.15.

4 *The Chronicle of John, Bishop of* Nikiu, trans. R. H. Charles (Evolution, 2007), 84.79.

5 *The Theodosian Code and Novels and the Sirmondian Constitutions*, trans. Clyde Pharr (Lawbook Exchange, 2001), 16.2.42.

6 *Epigrams from the Greek Anthology*, trans. Gideon Nisbet (Oxford University Press, 2020), 9.400.

7 Gideon Nisbet, ed., *Epigrams from the Greek Anthology*, 220.

Chapter 17. Islamic Conquest

1 Joannes Bollandus, *Acta Sanctorum*, vol. 3, 'XXIII Januarii, Caput III' (Paris, 1863), 114−15.

2 Quran 15.95; Ibn-Kathir, *Tafsir (Exegesis)*, vol. 4, ed. Sami al-Salamah (Tayba, 1999), 551−2.

3 Al-Dhahabi, *Sir I'lam al-Nubala' (The Lives of Noble Figures)*, vol. 3, ed. Shuaib al-Arna'ut (Risalah, 1982), 55.

4 Ibn Abd al-Hakam, *Futuh Misr wa Akhbariha (The Conquest of Egypt and its News)*, ed. Henri Massé (al-Ma'arif al-Firinsiyyah, 1913), 49−50.

5 Ibn-Kathir, *al-Bidaya wal-Nihaya (The Beginning and the End)*, vol. 4, 303; Severus ibn al-Muqaffa, *Makhtutat Tarikh al-Batariqah (The Manuscript of the History of the Patriarchs)*, ed. Abdelaziz Gamal-el-Din, vol. 2 (General Organisation of Cultural Palaces, 2012), 28.

6 Quoted by Ibn Abd al-Hakam, *Futuh Misr*, 41−48. The quoted text within the letter is a verse of the Quran; the basis for my Quranic translation is Ahmed Zaki Hammad's 2008 translation.

7 Hadith in Muslim, 2543. In another version, Copts are described as 'your instrument and help'.

8 Severus, *Tarikh al-Batariqah*, 17−18.

9 Al-Maqrizi, *Itti'az al-Mawa'iz wal-I'tibar bi-Dhikr al-Khitat wal-Athar (Sermons and Considerations from Plans and Effects)*, ed. Salim Mohamed (Dar al-Kutub al-Ilmiyyah, 1997), 39−40.

10 Ibn Abd al-Hakam, *Futuh Misr*, 42.

Chapter 18. Umayyads and Abbasids

1 Ibn-Kathir, *al-Bidaya wal-Nihaya (The Beginning and the End)*, vol. 7, ed. Ahmed Gad (Dar al-Hadith 2006), 97.

2 Quoted variously in ninth-century manuscripts including Ibn Abd al-Hakam, *Futuh Misr*, 33.

3 Severus, *Tarikh al-Batariqah*, 102.

Chapter 19. Fatimids

1 Qudamah ibn-Jaafar, *Kitab al-Kharaj wa Sana'at al-Kutabah* (*The Book of Land Tax and the Art of the Secretary*), ed. Muhammad al-Zubaydi (Al-Rashid, 1981), 182–4.

2 Al-Maqrizi, *Itti'az al-Hunafa' bi-Akhbar al-A'immah al-Fatimiyin al-Khulafa'* (*Lessons for Truth-Seekers from the History of the Fatimid Imams and Caliphs*), ed. Mohamed Ahmed (Ahram, 1970), 53–4.

3 Letters T-S 8J20.2, 13J16.19, 10J20.12, trans. Moshe Gil, *Palestine in the First Muslim Period* (Tel Aviv University Press, 1983), docs 199, 493–5.

4 Al-Maqrizi, *Lessons for Truth-Seekers*, 226.

Chapter 20. The Crusaders and Saladin's Ayyubids

1 Baha-al-Din ibn-Shaddad, *Sirat Salah-al-Din al-Ayyubi, al-Musamma al-Nawadir al-Sultaniyya wal-Mahasin al-Yusufiyya* (*The Biography of Saladin the Ayyubid, called the Sultanic Anecdotes and Josephly Virtues*) (Hindawi, 2015). The earliest manuscript of this work is from 1228 CE.

2 William of Tyre, *A History of Deeds Beyond the Sea*, trans. Emily Atwater Babcock and A. C. Krey (Columbia University Press, 1943), 337–42.

3 Abu-Shama al-Maqdisi, *Al-Rawdatayn fi Akhbar al-Dawlatayn al-Nuriyyah wa-l-Salihiyyah* (*The Book of the Two Gardens, Concerning Affairs of the Reigns of Nur al-Din and Salah al-Din*), vol. 2, ed. Ibrahim al-Zaybaq (al-Risalah, 1997), 69.

4 Ibn al-Athir, *al-Kamil fi-l-Tarikh* (*The Complete History*), ed. Omar Tadmari (Dar al-Kutub al-Arabiyyah, 1997), 402–3.

5 *Chronique d'Ernoul et de Bernard le Trésorier* (*Chronicle of Ernoul and Bernard the Treasurer*) (French History Society, 1871), 232–3.

Chapter 21. Mamluks and the Plagued Century

1 Ibn Jubayr, *Rihlat ibn-Jubayr* (*The Travels of ibn-Jubayr*), vol. 1 (Dar Hilal), n.y., 12–15.

2 In 2007, Abu Dhabi unveiled its $545 million grand mosque, which takes clear inspiration from Alexandria's al-Mursi Mosque.

3 Ibn-Battuta, *Rihlat ibn-Battuta* (*The Travels of ibn-Battuta*), 38–40.

4 al-Nuwayri al-Iskandarani, *al-Ilmam . . . fi Waq'at al-Iskandariyyah* (*Familiarity . . . with the Incident of Alexandria*), vol. 1, ed. Aziz Atiya (al-Ma'arif al-Hindiya, 1968).

5 Geoffrey Chaucer, *The Canterbury Tales*, ed. Jill Mann (Penguin, 2005). 'Alisaundre' is Alexandria in Middle English.

Chapter 22. Ottomans

1 Rabbi Meshullam ben R Menahem of Volterra, in *Jewish Travellers*, ed. Elkan Adler (Routledge, 1930), 156–60.

2 Richard Hakluyt, *The Principal Navigations, Voyages, Traffiques, and Discoveries of the English Nation*, vol. 11, ed. Edmund Goldsmid (Goldsmid, 1889), 12.

3 Hakluyt, *The Principal Navigations*, 44–5.

4 Hakluyt, *The Principal Navigations*, 11.

5 Lewes Roberts, *The Merchant's Mappe of Commerce wherein, the Universall Manner and Matter of Trade* (Eliot's Court, 1638), 92.

6 Hakluyt, *The Principal Navigations*, 53.

7 Roberts, *The Merchant's Mappe*, 100.

8 Ibrahim al-Laqqani, *Nasihat al-Ikhwan bi-ijtinab al-Dukhan* (*Advising Brothers to Avoid Smoke*), ed. Ahmed Mahmud (n.p., 1993), 72.

Chapter 23. Napoleon

1 Napoleon Bonaparte, *Oeuvres de Napoléon Bonaparte* (*Napoléon Bonaparte's Works*), vol. 2, ed. C. L. F. Panckoucke (Paris, 1881).

2 Abdulrahman al-Jabarti, *'Aja'ib al-Athar fi al-Tarajim wal-Akhbar.* (*The Marvellous Compositions of Biographies and Events*), 3 vols (Dar al-Jil, 1997).

3 M. Vertray, *L'armée française en Égypte, 1798–1801: journal d'un officier de l'armée d'Égypte* (*The French Army in Egypt, 1798–1801: Diary of an Army Officer in Egypt*) (H. Galli, 1883), 28–32.

4 *Correspondance de L'armée Française en Égypte* (Garnery, 1799), 25–26.

5 Translated from a combination of the original Arabic and French declarations. Note that Napoleon's expedition also printed its own newspaper, *Courier de l'Égypte*.

6 *Correspondance de L'armée Française en Égypte*, 29.

7 Several of Napoleon's biographers have added this detail. Their main source appears to be a note by Richard Burton in his nineteenth-century translation of *Arabian Nights*: 'A friend learned in these matters supplies me with the following list of famous pederasts . . . Alexander of Macedon, Julius Caesar and Napoleon Buonaparte held themselves high above the moral law.' *The Book of the Thousand Nights and a Night*, vol. 10, trans. Richard F. Burton (Burton Club, 1886), 701.

8 *The Life and Adventures of John Nicol, Mariner* (Canongate, 2000), 85.

9 *Nouvelle Revue Encyclopédique* (*New Encyclopédic Journal*), vol. 5 (Firmin Didot Frères, 1847), 255.

Chapter 24. The Father of Egypt

1 René de Chateaubriand, 'L'Itinéraire de Paris à Jérusalem (1811)', in *Œuvres completes*, vol. 5 (Garnier, 1861), 414–15.

2 Giovanni Battista Belzoni, *Narrative of the Operations and Recent Discoveries Within the Pyramids, Temples, Tombs, and Excavations, in Egypt and Nubia* (John Murray, 1821), 157.

3 *The Morning Post* (London: 26 November 1835), 3.

4 Eugenie Sinano Horwitz, 'La Première Génération', in *Des Femmes*

Écrivent l'Afrique: L'Afrique du Nord, ed. Fatima Sadiqi et al. (Karthala, 2013), 271.

5 Baroness von Minutoli, *Recollections of Egypt*, trans. S. H. L (Lea and Carey, 1827), 17–18.

Chapter 25. British Invasion

1 Elbert Eli Farman, *Egypt and Its Betrayal: An Account of the Country during the Periods of Ismail and Tewfik Pashas, and of How England Acquired a New Empire* (Grafton Press, 1908), 149–52.

2 Michael Haag, 'The Funny Little Bust of General Earle', *Michael Haag's Blog* (2014).

Chapter 26. The First World War and Revolution

1 'HC Deb 26 May 1921 vol 142 cc304-6', in *Commons and Lords Hansard, the Official Report of debates in Parliament*.

2 Philip Mansel, *Levant: Splendor and Catastrophe on the Mediterranean* (Yale University Press, 2011), 144.

3 Fernand Leprette and Firmin Van den Bosch, cited in Mansel, *Levant: Splendor and Catastrophe*, 248. Coles Pasha, *Recollections and Reflections* (Saint Catherine Press, 1918), 41; *The Durrell–Miller Letters, 1935–80*, ed. Ian MacNiven (New Directions, 2007), 279.

4 Huda Sharawi, *Mudhakirat Huda Sharawi* (*The Memoirs of Huda Sharawi*) (Hindawi, 2017), 59.

5 Zaynab Fawwaz, *al-Rasa'il al-Zaynabbiyah* (*Zainab's Messages*) (Hindawi, 2014), 29–33.

Chapter 27. Cultural Hub

1 My translation was commissioned for BBC Radio 3's *Words and Music* episode, 'Encountering Egypt', which aired on 6 November 2022.

2 In a 16 October 1916 letter that helps us date the incident on the Alexandria beach, Forster writes to a friend: 'Yesterday, for the first time in my life I parted with respectability'; '"Incidents of War" Memoir, Alexandria (1915–1917)', *The Journals and Diaries of E. M. Forster*, vol. 3, ed. Philip Gardner (Pickering & Chatto, 2011); *Selected Letters of E. M. Forster*, vol. 1, ed. Mary Lago and P. N. Furbank (Collins, 1983); 'Mohammed El Adl's Book', in *Alexandria: A History and a Guide and Pharos and Pharillon*, E. M. Forster, ed. Miriam Allott (André Deutsch, 2004).

3 E. M. Forster, *Alexandria: A History and a Guide and Pharos and Pharillon*, 245.

4 C. P. Cavafy, 'The City', (1894, 1910), 5. Unless otherwise stated, Cavafy's poetry is from *C. P. Cavafy: Complete Poems*, trans. Daniel Mendelsohn (Harper, 2013).

5 C. P. Cavafy, 'Fugitives' (unpublished, 1914), 325.

6 C. P. Cavafy, 'Alexandrian Kings', 26.

7 C. P. Cavafy, 'Days of 1909, '10, and '11'. I here choose a different

translation: *C. P. Cavafy: The Collected Poems*, trans. Evangelos Sachperoglou (Oxford University Press, 2007), 187.

8 Philip Mansel, *Levant: Splendor and Catastrophe,* 144.

9 Michael Haag, *Alexandria: City of Memory* (AUC Press, 2004), 47, 69.

10 Filippo Marinetti, *The Manifesto of Futurism* (Passerino, 2016).

Chapter 28. Cultural Renaissance

1 Kamal Saad, *Bayram al-Tunisi: 'Asifa min al-Hara al-Misriyyah* (*Bayram al-Tunisi: Storm from the Egyptian Neighbourhood*) (Cairo, 1993).

2 My translation was commissioned for BBC Radio 3's *Words and Music* episode, 'Encountering Egypt', which aired on 6 November 2022.

Chapter 29. The Second World War

1 Jean Lacouture, *Nasser* (Editions du Seuil, 1971), 34.

2 Olivia Manning, *The Danger Tree* (Atheneum, 1977), 103; Artemis Cooper, *Cairo in the War: 1939–1945* (John Murray, 2013).

3 Nigel Hamilton, *Monty: The Making of a General 1887–1942* (McGraw Hill, 1981), 608–9.

4 'Official: Prime Minister: Printed personal telegrams exchanged between WSC and General Claude Auchinleck [Commander in Chief Middle East]', *The Churchill Papers* (CHAR 20/89). Churchill Archives Centre, Cambridge (accessed 2022).

5 Philip Mansel, *Levant: Splendor and Catastrophe,* 257–8.

6 Robin Fedden, ed., *Personal Landscape: An Anthology of Exile* (Poetry Limited, 1945), 11.

Chapter 30. The Postman's Son

1 'Top Secret Security Information: 25th July 1952', *Central Intelligence Agency Current Intelligence Bulletin* (CIA Archive), 8.

2 'Top Secret Ruff: 17th May 1968', *Central Intelligence Agency* (CIA Archive).

3 'Secret: Soviet Merchant Ship Activity: Alexandria Port Facilities, Egypt, 27th October 1973', *Central Intelligence Agency* (CIA Archive).

Epilogue

1 Strabo, *The Geography of Strabo*, vol. 8, trans. Horace Jones (Loeb Classical Library, 1932), book 17, and he quotes *The Odyssey*, book 17.

2 Quoted in John Rodenbeck, 'Literary Alexandri'', *Massachusetts Review* 42.4 (2001–2), 551.

3 K. Heba, 'Preserving architectural heritage in historical cities: study of the architectural heritage with the end of the nineteenth century and the beginning of the twentieth century in Alexandria, Egypt', *Transactions on the Built Environment* 118 (2011). 233–45

4 Dalia Elsorady, 'Heritage conservation in Alexandria, Egypt: managing tensions between ownership and legislation', *International Journal of Heritage Studies* 17.5 (2011).

5 'Prime Minister Boris Johnson spoke at the COP26 World Leaders Summit Opening Ceremony'. From: Prime Minister's Office, 10 Downing Street and the Rt Hon Boris Johnson MP (1 November 2021).

6 Sayed Hemeda, 'Geotechnical modelling of the climate change impact on world heritage properties in Alexandria, Egypt', *Herit Sci* 9.73 (2021); Omran El Sayed Frihy et al., 'Alexandria-Nile Delta coast, Egypt: update and future projection of relative sea-level rise', *Environ Earth Sci* 61 (2010), 253−73.

7 Pliny the Elder, *The Natural History*, trans. John Bostock (Taylor and Francis, 1855), 3.0.

8 Jim Gower, 'A sea surface height control dam at the Strait of Gibraltar', *Nat Hazards* 78 (2015).

9 C. P. Cavafy, 'Voices', 180.

Acknowledgements

Writing this book really has taken me on a journey of discovery. It has been enhanced by the many people I've met along the way – in Alexandria and beyond. I spent day after day immersed in the past, walking the city's streets and getting to know different characters. I was often disappointed to return to the present. I tried but ultimately failed to meet someone: let's call them Ancestor the Great – that first grandparent of mine, who, like Alexander the Great, ventured to the part of the world we now call Alexandria. I hope that remembering my predecessors – and positioning their progeny within the city's lofty history – returns any debt. Naturally, then, I thank my parents – for their loving support. My father, Ahmed, told me tales and imbued me with a passion for our city; he's paid the price by having to listen to my ramblings. I will never forget that my auntie Ahlam passed on – in Alexandria – the same day that I submitted the first draft of this book.

I am obliged to the hundreds of scholars, old and new, whose research was essential to building this picture of Alexandria's history. In Egypt, I am grateful to Wael Issa and always thankful for the generosity of Ahmed Abbas. I also thank the locals – too many to name – who took the time to talk to me, from renowned experts at research centres to friendly folk in cafés. In the UK, my (dream) agent Adam Gauntlett realised how much Alexandria has to offer. His enthusiasm was matched by my wonderful editor at Sceptre, Juliet Brooke, whose every thought carried immense value. I was lucky enough to end up with two editors; Charlotte Humphery managed to combine insight, skill and patience. The diligence of copyeditor Richard Collins and assistant editor Nico Parfitt continued to enhance the book. I appreciate the support of Andrew Kehoe and David Roberts at Birmingham City University, where Izabela Hopkins provided stimulating research assistance. I also thank Omneya Abdelsalam and B. L. for their support, and for their friendship during this project, Zainab Latif, Thomas Knowles and Peter Herman.

This book is about the place closest to my heart, so I dedicate it to the person closest to my heart. Alaa has been an astute sounding board, but more importantly, my best friend and unfailing companion. I look forward to sharing many more happy moments with her in Alexandria.

Index